More Praise for *Inside AutoCAD*

This is a complete reference to AutoCAD that any office using AutoCAD for 2D work should own.

—architectstore.com, Editor's Choice

If you need a thorough guide to AutoCAD... this is the one to buy.

—Computer Graphics Editor's Recommended Book, Amazon.com

Inside AutoCAD is a comprehensive tutorial and reference that takes you a long way toward becoming an AutoCAD expert.

—CADALYST Bookshelf

The *Inside AutoCAD* series has proven to be the most valuable resource to my collection of AutoCAD references, and I have recommended this series to beginners and advanced users alike.

—Carol L. Polack
CAD Drafter
Toys "R" Us National Headquarters

"This is THE book to buy if you plan to use Autocad. I am a very experienced AutoCAD user and I was amazed at the amount of timesaving information I was able to extract from this book. The writing is very well done with a good amount of "How & Why" information. New Riders has been my preferred choice for learning various software programs since the late 70's and early 80's and this book reflects the depth of their knowledge."

— Zachary Richardson
Senior Design Engineer/Network Administrator Power Engineers, Inc
Atlanta Georgia

"As an AutoCAD user since Version 2.6, I found that the New Riders books could help get me up to speed FAST."

—Bud Schroeder, Autodesk

"The "Inside" series by New Riders is by far the best learning tool for Autodesk products."

—Tom Brown
AUGI #14840
President, EFnet Autodesk User Group

"I have used the Inside AutoCAD series since Release 12. They are by far **the best references on AutoCAD available today.** I purchase them for myself and make them available to my staff. I find them to be better teaching tools than the manuals put out by Autodesk."

—Gail Pruszkowski
Philadelphia Water Department
AUGI member W2216

INSIDE

AUTOCAD® 2000

LIMITED EDITION

BILL BURCHARD AND DAVID PITZER

WITH SAMIR BAJAJ, DAVID HARRINGTON, AND MICHAEL TODD PETERSON

New
Riders

New Riders Publishing, Indianapolis, Indiana

Inside AutoCAD® 2000 Limited Edition

International Standard Book Number: 0-7357-0947-5

Library of Congress Catalog Card Number: 99-067442

Printed in the United States of America

First Printing: February 2000

03 02 01 00   7 6 5 4 3 2 1

Interpretation of the printing code: The rightmost double-digit number is the year of the book's printing; the right most single-digit number is the number of the book's printing.

Trademarks

Warning and Disclaimer

Executive Editor
Steve Weiss

Acquisitions Editor
Laura Frey

Development Editor
Michael Beall

Managing Editor
Sarah Kearns

Project Editor
Jennifer Chisholm

Copy Editors
Daryl Kessler
Audra McFarland

Proofreaders
Debra Neel
John Rahm

Indexer
Angie Bess

Technical Editor
David Harrington

Software Development Specialist
Craig Atkins

About the Authors

Bill Burchard is an information systems consultant with Psomas, in Riverside, CA. He has been in the AEC business for over 20 years. He has extensive experience in computer modeling and applications development for AEC projects, including plan preparation, technical publications, and engineering design, as well as Web Development, GIS, 3D modeling, 3D photo-realistic renderings, and 3D animations. Additionally, Mr. Burchard is a registered Autodesk author/publisher, and is a consulting author and technical editor with New Riders Publishing. In these capacities, he has worked on numerous book projects regarding the use of AutoCAD, including *Inside AutoCAD 14 Limited Edition*, *Inside AutoCAD 14*, *Inside AutoCAD 13c4*, and *AutoCAD Performance Tuning Toolkit*. Mr. Burchard is also a contributor to *Inside AutoCAD*, a monthly newsletter published by ZD Journals, and regularly writes articles and product reviews for *CADalyst Magazine*. Mr. Burchard can be contacted by email at **bburchard@psomas.com**.

David Pitzer has been an AutoCAD user for over 10 years. He currently teaches AutoCAD and AutoLISP at the college level. David is also a contributing editor for *CADalyst Magazine* and his articles have also appeared in *CADENCE Magazine* as well as in the *AutoCAD Technical Journal*. He has been a speaker at AutoCAD conferences including Autodesk University. This is David's third *Inside AutoCAD* book for New Riders. David resides in the San Francisco area.

Samir Bajaj has been working at Autodesk, Inc., for four years as a software development engineer in the AutoCAD team. He was a key contributor to the design, implementation, and integration of the Internet features in AutoCAD 2000. Samir graduated from the University of California at Riverside with an MS degree in computer science as well as an MBA. His interests include distributed systems, computer networking, computational finance, and his wife, Shelly.

David Harrington is the office computer manager at Walter P. Moore, where he specializes in commercial structural CAD work. Although he currently specializes in commercial structural CAD work using AutoCAD 2000, his experience ranges from commercial landscape irrigation design to system services for NASA at Cape Canaveral. He has been active in the local user group community for over 10 years, holding offices in the Tampa Bay AutoCAD User Group as newsletter editor, treasurer, and president. Since 1994, Harrington has been an active member of the board of directors of the Autodesk User Group International. He has served as the local user group representative, AEC Industry Group chair, president-elect, and currently serves as president. Harrington has been devoted to Autodesk and AutoCAD since 1987, when he began working with AutoCAD Release 2.6. He has written hundreds of AutoLISP routines and has been published in trade magazines. An avid writer, Harrington has authored many articles for the user community in trade magazines as well as the *PaperSpace* and *WorldView* newsletters, published by AUGI. He has been certified as an Autodesk Certified Expert for Release 14 Level II. Additionally, Harrington won the 1997 CADENCE Top Gun contest and the 1998 CADalyst Challenge contest. He also is a member of the faculty for Autodesk University, teaching at both 1997 and 1998 conferences.

Michael Todd Peterson is the owner of MTP Graphics (www.mtpgrafx.com), a full-service 3D animation shop that specializes in architectural rendering, multimedia development, Render Farm, and Special FX. In the past, Todd has taught at universities and community colleges. In addition to this book, Todd has also authored or co-authored a variety of other books for New Riders Publishing, including *Inside AutoCAD 14* and *Inside 3D Studio MAX 2*, Volumes II and III.

Dedications:

Bill Burchard:

I dedicate this book to the women in my life: Lynn, Katie, and Kim.

David Pitzer:

I would like to dedicate this book to my AutoCAD students—past and present. Their excitement over this software program is a constant source of inspiration for me; through their eyes, I see AutoCAD afresh every new semester.

Acknowledgments

Bill Burchard:

I wish to thank my friends and family for their support while writing this book, and I especially wish to thank my wife and daughters for their support, and their tolerance, while I spent six months of our lives dedicated to this book project. I also wish to thank my friends and associates at Psomas for their help, guidance, and support with my endeavors, with special thanks to Craig Gooch, Wayne Kauffman, Jerry Wagner, Blake Murillo, and Sherri Bayer. I wish to thank Autodesk for its support, with special thanks to Mike Phillips, Shawn Gilmour, and Cynde Hargrave. Finally, I wish to express my gratitude and thanks to this book's project team—Dave Pitzer, David Harrington, and Laura Frey—without whom this book would not have been possible.

David Pitzer:

I would like to acknowledge the contributions and assistance of the following people: Ron LaFon for helping me keep my computer running virus-free and for keeping all the software necessary to write a large-scale book about AutoCAD up to date; Tony Peach of Autodesk for being there when questions needed answering; Nancy Moss and Cynde Hargrave of Autodesk for helping to get the information from dozens of people; Michael Beall and David Harrington for developing and technical editing the book; Laura Frey of New Riders Publishing for pulling it all together and keeping Bill and me on track; and lastly to Sylvester Katz for first showing me AutoCAD eleven years ago.

A Message from New Riders

As the reader of this book, you are our most important critic and commentator. We value your opinion and want to know what we're doing right, what we could do better, in what areas you'd like to see us publish, and any other words of wisdom you're willing to pass our way.

As the Executive Editor for the Graphics team at New Riders, I welcome your comments. You can fax, email, or write me directly to let me know what you did or didn't like about this book[md] as well as what we can do to make our books better. When you write, please be sure to include this book's title, ISBN, and author, as well as your name and phone or fax number. I will carefully review your comments and share them with the authors and editors who worked on the book. For any issues directly related to this or other titles:

Email: steve.weiss@newriders.com
Mail: Steve Weiss
        Executive Editor
        Professional Graphics &
        Design Publishing
        New Riders Publishing
        201 West 103rd Street
        Indianapolis, IN 46290 USA

Visit Our Website: www.newriders.com

On our website you'll find information about our other books, the authors we partner with, book updates and file downloads, promotions, discussion boards for online interaction with other users and with technology experts, and a calendar of trade shows and other professional events with which we'll be involved. We hope to see you around.

Email Us from Our Website

Go to www.newriders.com and click on the Contact link if you

- Have comments or questions about this book

- Want to report errors that you have found in this book

- Have a book proposal or are otherwise interested in writing with New Riders

- Would like us to send you one of our author kits

- Are an expert in a computer topic or technology and are interested in being a reviewer or technical editor

- Want to find a distributor for our titles in your area

- Are an educator/instructor who wishes to preview New Riders books for classroom use. (Include your name, school, department, address, phone number, office days/hours, text currently in use, and enrollment in your department in the body/comments area, along with your request for desk/examination copies, or for additional information.

Call Us or Fax Us

You can reach us toll-free at (800) 571-5840 + 9+ 3567. Ask for New Riders. If outside the USA, please call 1-317-581-3500 and ask for New Riders.

If you prefer, you can fax us at 1-317-581-4663, Attention: New Riders.

Technical Support/ Customer Support Issues

Call 1-317-581-3833, from 10:00 a.m. to 3 p.m. US EST (CST from April through October of each year—unlike most of the rest of the United States, Indiana doesn't change to Daylight Savings Time each April).

You can also email our tech support team at: userservices@ macmillanusa.com, and you can access our tech support: website at http://www.mcp.com/product_support mail_support.cfm.

Contents at a Glance

Table of Contents

INTRODUCTION

AutoCAD is a software phenomenon; its users far outnumber those of any other CAD system. AutoCAD has grown from a micro-curiosity to a full-fledged CAD system by any set of standards. AutoCAD also has grown from a relatively simple program to a large and complex one, but you should not be intimidated by its size and complexity. More than one million designers and drafters have learned to use AutoCAD with the help of Inside AutoCAD, *the best-selling AutoCAD book for more than 12 years.*

How This Book Is Organized

This book is organized into parts to help you digest the many features of AutoCAD 2000.

Part I: Introducing AutoCAD 2000

Welcome to AutoCAD 2000, the fifteenth release of the world's most popular Computer Aided Design software package. Part I of this book is devoted to an extensive overview of the many new features of this release of AutoCAD, features that include new commands, new interface functionality, and a host of added capabilities that will increase your use of AutoCAD by making your work more efficient. The remaining sections of the book consist of groups of two or more chapters devoted to specific aspects of AutoCAD. They are designed both for easy reference and to present AutoCAD 2000 in a logical, easy-to-use, and easy-to-read manner.

Part II: Starting New Projects with AutoCAD 2000

In Part II, you learn how to set up and control the AutoCAD environment to work efficiently. You learn how to use AutoCAD's layers to organize your drawings, and your projects. You learn how to control an object's appearance using AutoCAD's Linetypes, and you also learn how to effectively use Lineweights, a new feature introduced with AutoCAD 2000.

Part III: Creating and Editing Drawings

Part III shows you how draw and edit both basic and complex objects in AutoCAD. You learn how to use AutoCAD's coordinate system and its Object Snaps to draw very accurately. You also learn how to properly create and use blocks, block attributes, and external references (xrefs) to harness the incredible power they offer toward true productivity in AutoCAD. You also learn about AutoCAD's DesignCenter, a brand-new and very powerful tool that allows you to search for objects in drawing files and automatically insert their data into the current drawing, all without opening the source drawings.

Part IV: Annotating, Dimensioning, and Plotting

In Part IV, you learn about some of AutoCAD's more complex features, such as creating text and hatch patterns. You learn how to use AutoCAD's dimensioning tools, a very powerful feature that is enhanced with AutoCAD 2000. You learn how to properly use model space and paper space, and how to take advantage of a new AutoCAD 2000 feature called Layouts, which is designed to make working in paper space easier. You also learn how to create plots of your drawings using AutoCAD's new plotting paradigm, which consists of plotter configuration files, plot style tables, and page setups.

Part V: Customizing and Advanced Concepts

Part V of this book covers several advanced topics, such as the customization of your AutoCAD 2000 interface to make it work more efficiently. You will also learn the basics of AutoCAD's customization programming language: AutoLISP. In addition you will learn about programming AutoCAD for use in the Windows OLE and SQL environments.

Part VI: CAD on the Internet

Part VI of the book is concerned with AutoCAD and its relationship to the latest vehicle of collaborative drafting and project sharing—the Internet. AutoCAD 2000 is fully "Internet aware," and there are many features that make working on and over the Internet both easy and efficient.

Part VII: AutoCAD in 3D

In Part VII of this book you are introduced to the world of 3D modeling in AutoCAD 2000. Several new features make working in true three dimensions to build your AutoCAD models even easier and more efficient. The last chapter in this section introduces you to rendering and making photo-realistic presentations of your models.

Part VIII: Advanced Topics

Part VIII gives you insight into some of the advanced features of AutoCAD 2000. You learn the ins and outs of Visual LISP, how to create Menu Macros and custom toolbars, and how to convert your system from a previous version of AutoCAD to AutoCAD 2000 using AutoCAD 2000 Migration Assistance. You also learn about DIESEL and its functions, how to plan network installations, and how to use the AutoCAD Batch Plot Utility and ePlot.

Part IX: Reference Materials

Inside AutoCAD 2000 is equipped with two appendixes. One gives you the basic information you need to better plan and organize your AutoCAD 2000 projects. In the second, you will get an overview of the Express Tools included with AutoCAD 2000. These tools provide powerful "extra" commands that can speed the work of the new and veteran AutoCAD user alike.

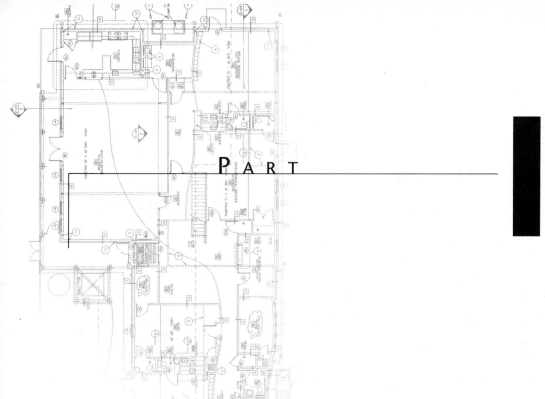

INTRODUCING AUTOCAD 2000

Chapter 1: What's New in AutoCAD 2000

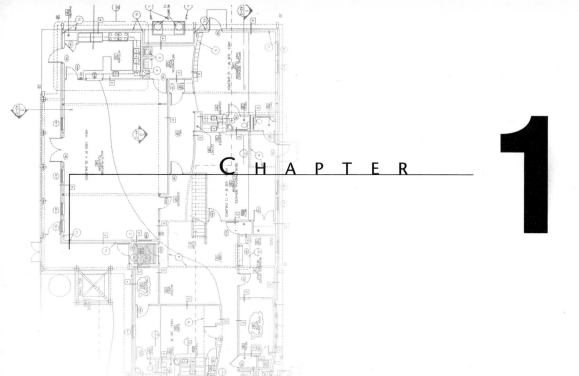

WHAT'S NEW IN AUTOCAD 2000

The Fifteenth Release of AutoCAD

It's not often that we begin both a new century and a new millennium. Autodesk (the company behind AutoCAD) and several other major software producers are taking the opportunity to name the newest versions or releases of their flagship products "Software 2000." Thus, the newest release of AutoCAD is not designated AutoCAD Release 15, but AutoCAD 2000. The excitement over the approach of the year 2000 aside, AutoCAD 2000 represents the 15th release of what has become the world's leading computer-aided-design software package. The designers of AutoCAD 2000 have taken a very popular AutoCAD Release 14 and expanded its capabilities in several significant ways.

The key features of AutoCAD 2000 can generally be divided into five major categories. It is the purpose of this first chapter to take a brief look at these categories and some of the specific tools and capabilities that they contribute to AutoCAD 2000. These categories encompass:

- **Improved productivity** with features that, taken together, Autodesk terms a Heads-Up™ Environment

- **Improved access** and usability of the software's features

- **Expanded reach** by easing connectivity to data and the work of others

- **Streamlined output** to enhance documentation

- **Greater customization** to allow the software to more closely meet the individual user's needs

This chapter presents a fairly large-scale overview of the new features in AutoCAD 2000. Such a survey should prove useful to veteran AutoCAD users as each feature or usability improvement is briefly described and, where appropriate, illustrated. Each feature is, of course, covered in more detail in later chapters and chapter references are included. Not all features are included here, but you are referred to the index for further help.

Improved Productivity

The general category of improved productivity includes a host of new features and capabilities that work together to speed up the everyday tasks of drafting. Autodesk claims that many of these features tend to lessen the use of the keyboard, and this is largely true of such AutoCAD 2000 features as Multiple Design Environment (MDE), the new AutoCAD Design Center, and the enhanced AutoSnap™ and AutoTrack™ features.

Multiple Design Environment (MDE)

Multiple Design Environment (MDE) is AutoCAD's implementation of the now-standard Windows capability that allows you to have more than a single document open within a single session of the parent software. With AutoCAD 2000's MDE, you can easily multitask among several open drawings, much as you would with multiple files in a word processing application. Figure 1.1 shows an MDE session in AutoCAD 2000.

Figure 1.1

*You can now open
multiple drawings
in a single session of
AutoCAD 2000.*

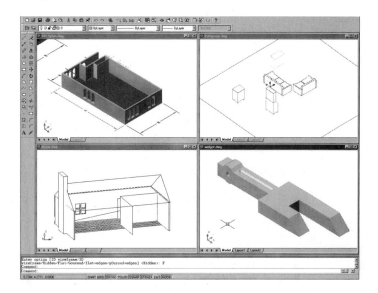

MDE capability offers several advantages to the AutoCAD user; some are obvious, but some are not so apparent.

- **Opening several drawings**. In AutoCAD 2000, you can open numerous drawings. Using the OPEN command, you can select any number of drawings from a standard File Open dialog box. Or, you can open one or more drawings by dragging them into AutoCAD from Windows Explorer.

- **Object Drag and Drop.** In the MDE environment, you can either move or copy objects between drawings with a drag and drop operation. By right-dragging an entire file into a drawing from Windows Explorer, you can open, insert, xref, copy as an OLE object, or create a hyperlink to the receiving drawing.

- **Cut/Copy/Paste.** You can now copy drawing objects from one drawing to another with only one session of AutoCAD 2000 running.

- **Property Painter support.** You can transfer properties such as layer, color, linetype, and linetype scale from one drawing to another.

- **Concurrent command execution.** You can switch between open drawings without canceling the current command.

The new MDE feature provides you with several ways to significantly increase your drawing efficiency by using the settings and objects from one drawing in other drawings. For more information about using the features of AutoCAD 2000's Multiple Drawing Environment, see Chapter 13, "Creating and Using Blocks."

AutoCAD DesignCenter

The AutoCAD 2000 DesignCenter (see Figure 1.2) resembles the Windows Explorer in both appearance and function. With the AutoCAD DesignCenter (ADC), you can "mine" your previous design effort and work. ADC allows you to view the content of any drawing available to you—whether locally or from a network or the Internet— and copy material into the current drawing. You don't even have to open the drawing you're copying from because ADC uses its Explorer-style display to present drawings and their categorized content in a tree-like fashion.

Figure 1.2

Find, view, and use
material from any drawing
with DesignCenter.

It would be difficult to overestimate the power and usefulness of DesignCenter as a tool for saving work. If, for example, you want to find a block you may have created some time ago and you don't recall the parent drawing, ADC allows you to search for it. As you can see in Figure 1.3, ADC uses a search facility to look for drawing content based on several criteria. In the example shown in Figure 1.3, the block LM was found in a drawing titled 1st floor.dwg.

Figure 1.3

Using DesignCenter
to find a block.

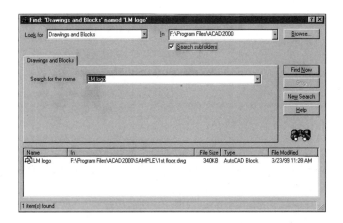

Once you find the content, you can easily move it into the current drawing with a simple dragging operation. ADC has other features that make working with current content in other drawings and locations quick and easy. You will learn more about the AutoCAD DesignCenter in Chapter 12, "Applications for the New AutoCAD DesignCenter."

AutoTrack

AutoTrack helps you draw objects at specific angles or in specific relationships to other objects. When you turn on AutoTrack, temporary alignment paths help you create objects at precise positions and angles. AutoTrack includes two tracking options: polar tracking and object snap tracking. You can toggle AutoTrack on and off with the Polar and Otrack buttons on the status bar. Object snap tracking works in conjunction with object snaps. You must set an object snap before you can track from an object's snap point; the AutoSnap aperture settings control how close you must be to the alignment path before the path is displayed. With AutoTrack, finding and using points relative to other points is quick, easy, and accurate. Figure 1.4 shows AutoTrack acquiring a point for the center of a circle. You'll find out more about AutoSnap and AutoTrack in Chapter 6, "Accuracy in Creating Drawings with AutoCAD 2000."

Figure 1.4

Using AutoTracking to acquire points.

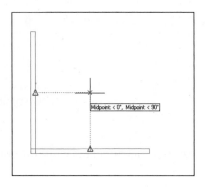

Figure 1.4

Using AutoTracking to acquire points.

Partial Open and Partial Load

Large drawings are unavoidable and can significantly slow down a drawing's loadtime and operations such as regens after loading. AutoCAD 2000 addresses this problem by providing Partial Open and Partial Load capabilities. With the Partial Open feature, for example, you can open only certain desired portions of a drawing and any external references based on saved views, user-specified layers, or the geometry shared by both. The Partial Open dialog box is shown in Figure 1.5.

Figure 1.5

Opening portions of a drawing based on views and layers.

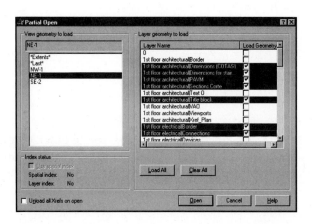

When the drawing is partially opened, the Partial Load feature allows you to load additional portions—views and layers—on an as-needed basis. These features not only speed load times but also reduce a drawing's memory requirements and often make your work easier by providing a less cluttered view. Partial Open and Partial Load are discussed in Chapter 14, "Working with Drawings and External References Productively."

Quick Dimensioning (QDIM)

Dimensioning is often a tedious, time-consuming task. With AutoCAD 2000's new QDIM command, many of the steps formerly required to dimension even a relatively simple geometric object can be reduced to a few screen picks. In Figure 1.6, for example, the dimensions were generated with two picks—one on the gasket outline and another on the circle. QDIM supports several standard dimension placement styles, such as baseline, staggered, and ordinate, among others. The QDIM shortcut menu (which you access by right-clicking while the command is in progress) allows you to quickly modify such dimensioning elements as dimension style and precision. The QDIM command is covered more fully in Chapter 17, "Productive Dimensioning."

Figure 1.6

QDIM: *dimensioning with minimal screen picks.*

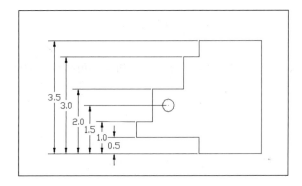

3DOrbit: Persistent Shading and 3D View Control

AutoCAD 2000 introduces a completely new 3D visualization mechanism: the 3DORBIT command. 3DORBIT enables you to quickly view your 3D model interactively with full real-time rotation of the viewpoint about any axis in 3D space. You can also set your model "in motion" with a Continuous Orbit option and view it from a continuously changing viewpoint.

In addition, not only is shading in AutoCAD 2000 more sophisticated and realistic, but it remains in effect until you change it to a conventional 2D wireframe or hidden line view. You can create and edit with shading active and even save your drawing in a shaded mode. Figure 1.7 shows both a 3DORBIT view and a standard 2D wireframe view.

A new 3D UCS icon is active in any shaded mode and offers a more informative, less ambiguous presentation of 3D space. This new UCS icon is shown in the right viewport of Figure 1.7.

Figure 1.7

3DORBIT *(right) with realistic Gouraud shading.*

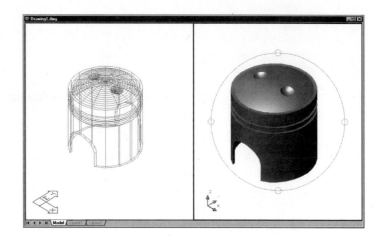

3DORBIT also supports adjustable front and back clipping planes to allow you an even more informative view into 3D models. The clipping planes are stationary, and during continuous orbit mode, they give a changing "slice" view. A clipped view is shown in Figure 1.8. You learn more about 3DORBIT in Chapter 31, "Rendering in 3D."

Figure 1.8

3DORBIT *allows you to establish clipping planes (left).*

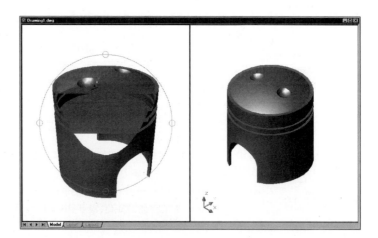

UCS per Viewport

For those working extensively in 3D, the new UCS per viewport feature will be welcome. Now each viewport can have a separate and independent UCS setting. A long-requested feature by both 2D and 3D users, this new ability allows you to switch between active viewports without resetting your UCS. This feature is clearly shown in Figure 1.9. Chapter 6 and Chapter 28, "Drawing in 3D AutoCAD," discuss the use of independent viewport UCS settings.

Figure 1.9

The UCS can now be set on a per viewport basis.

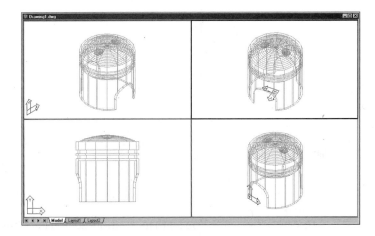

In-Place Reference and Block Editing

With AutoCAD 2000's new in-place reference editing, you can edit both the current drawing and any referenced drawings simultaneously or *in-place*. This method is both more intuitive and faster. Any changes you make to the referenced drawing can be either temporary or saved permanently to the reference drawing. As an added benefit, you can also edit blocks within the parent drawing without first exploding the block. Figure 1.10 shows the new Reference Edit dialog box. You can find out more about in-place reference editing in Chapter 13 and Chapter 14.

Figure 1.10

Editing an xref within the host drawing.

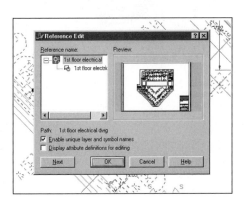

Improved Access

AutoCAD has traditionally been a command-line–driven application. Even after its integration into the Windows environment (which began with Release 13), most of the prompts required keyboard input. In AutoCAD 2000, several enhancements have been added or expanded to lessen the need for keyboard usage. Some of these features include the new Properties dialog box, improved selection filters, and right-click shortcut menus. And for the commands that still logically require a command-line interface, the presentation of prompts and options has been standardized.

Properties Dialog Box

The way you obtain and edit an object's properties has been streamlined in AutoCAD 2000. The Properties dialog box, shown in Figure 1.11, combines the functionality found in the older DDCHPROP and DDMODIFY commands and adds several other object-specific editing commands. The Properties dialog box enables you to set virtually all properties of any AutoCAD object from a single dialog box. You can learn more about the Object Properties tool in Chapter 11, "Advanced Geometry Editing."

Figure 1.11

The Properties dialog box.

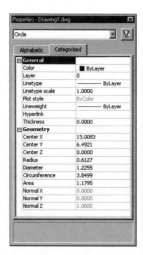

Find and Replace Text

A new Find feature is introduced in AutoCAD 2000 (see Figure 1.12). You can use the FIND command to find and replace standard text as well as block attributes, dimension text, and hyperlink/URL names. The FIND command is covered in Chapter 15, "Text Annotation."

Figure 1.12

The Find and Replace Text dialog box.

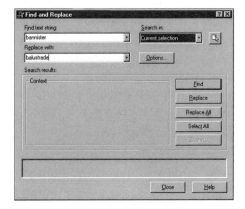

Quick Select

The FILTER command, first introduced in Release 12, is a powerful AutoLISP-based method of building selection sets based on object-specific and general criteria. The QSELECT (Quick Select) command takes up where FILTER falls short by providing a more intuitive, much easier to use means of filtering AutoCAD objects. With QSELECT, you can quickly build selection sets based on properties such as layer, color, and object type. Filters compiled by QSELECT can be applied to the entire drawing database or to a current selection. The QSELECT dialog box is shown in Figure 1.13, and its use is discussed in Chapter 11.

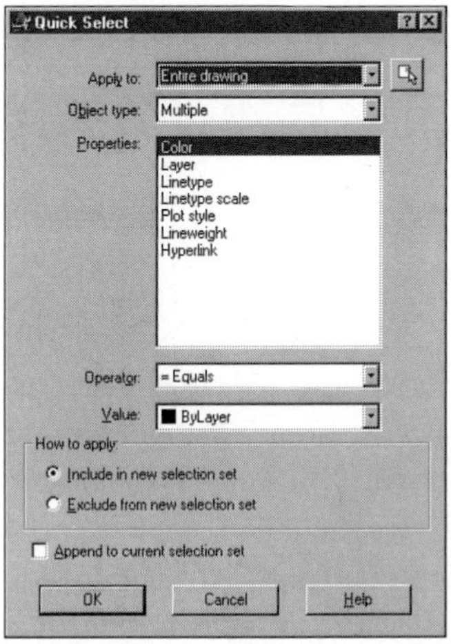

Figure 1.13

The Quick Select dialog box.

Shortcut Menus

If AutoCAD 2000 is truly moving toward a more keyboard-free Heads-Up™ Environment, the new right-click shortcut menus are largely responsible. These shortcut menus abound in AutoCAD 2000. They enable the user to perform many tasks, such as specifying options or panning and zooming, that formerly required keyboard input. For example, when you're performing a dimensioning task, the right-click shortcut menu displays a list of dimensioning options, such as changing the degree of displayed precision. As their name implies, these shortcut menus are tremendous timesavers. The difficult part will be remembering that they are available and using them when appropriate.

There are five basic types of shortcut menus, each of which is described in the following list. A right-click displays the menu that's appropriate to the task underway when the menu is activated.

■ **Default menu.** This menu, shown in Figure 1.14, appears any time you right-click in the drawing area but have no command in progress and no objects selected.

Figure 1.14

The Default shortcut menu.

■ **Edit-mode menu.** This menu, shown in Figure 1.15, appears any time you right-click when you have objects selected but no command in progress.

Figure 1.15

The Edit-mode shortcut menu.

■ **Command-mode menu.** This menu, shown in Figure 1.16, appears when you right-click with a command in progress.

Figure 1.16

The Command-mode shortcut menu.

■ **Dialog-mode menu.** This menu, shown in Figure 1.17, appears when you right-click in a dialog box or a dialog box tab.

Figure 1.17

The Dialog-mode shortcut menu.

■ **Other shortcut menus.** These menus (an example of which is shown in Figure 1.18) appear, for example, when you right-click over the command line. Right-clicking on any tool displays a list of available toolbars.

Figure 1.18

Another shortcut menu.

The Edit-mode, Command-mode, and Dialog-mode menus will, of course, display varying options and choices depending upon the context. For example, the Command-mode menu shown in Figure 1.16 appears when you right-click during the CIRCLE command. Shortcut menus are featured throughout this book.

Solids Editing Capabilities

Prior to AutoCAD 2000, AutoCAD has never supported true solids editing to any significant extent. AutoCAD 2000, however, offers a full set of powerful solids editing tools. Once they're created, solids can be easily modified using techniques for face, body, and edge editing. The Solids Editing toolbar is shown in Figure 1.19, and solids editing is discussed in Chapter 30, "Solid Modeling."

Figure 1.19

The Solids Editing toolbar.

Extended Symbol Names

In AutoCAD 2000, the allowable length for symbol names such as those for layers, blocks, dimstyles, views, and so on has been expanded from 31 to 255 characters. Spaces in symbol names are also allowed and names appear as you originally type them, including uppercase awareness. Figure 1.20 shows an example of extended layer naming. Extended symbol names are covered in several chapters, but especially in Chapter 4, "Organizing a Drawing with Layers."

Figure 1.20

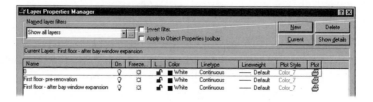

Extended (long) symbol names.

Command-Line Standardization

Even with the move away from the necessity for keyboard input in AutoCAD 2000, some input is still required for many command options. The presentation of command-line data has been standardized to allow for greater ease of use and consistency. When you become used to the new format, it becomes easier to read and interpret. A comparison between the older command-line format and the new AutoCAD 2000 format is shown here for the CIRCLE command:

R14 format:

```
Command: circle
3P/2P/TTR/<Center point>: [input]
Diameter/<Radius>: [input]
```

AutoCAD 2000 format:

```
Command: circle
Specify center point for circle or [3P/2P/Ttr (tan tan radius)]:
[input]
Specify radius of circle or [Diameter] <default>: [input]
```

You will see examples of the new command-line format throughout the exercises in this book.

Expanded Reach

In today's Internet/Facsimile high-speed data transmission environment, clients and customers are used to sharing project and design information quickly. AutoCAD 2000 extends the Internet capabilities of AutoCAD by adding features such as Web-aware file access, database connectivity, hyperlinks, plotting of Drawing Web Format (DWF) files, and DXF enhancements. Together or singly, these features enable you to connect and communicate your designs to anyone, anywhere.

Direct Browser Access

AutoCAD 2000 incorporates a number of new Internet-aware tools that simplify the process of retrieving and accessing data from the Internet. Files such as reference drawings, AutoLISP code, and script and menu files are now easily obtained over the Internet. Most of the dialog boxes in AutoCAD 2000 dealing with file operations provide a means for direct access to the Internet through three new buttons: Search the Web, Look in Favorites, and Add to Favorites. These buttons are shown in the Select File dialog box in Figure 1.21.

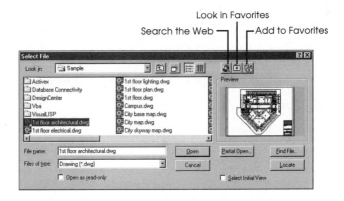

Figure 1.21

AutoCAD 2000's new Internet buttons.

AutoCAD 2000 is Universal Resource Locator (URL) aware during selected file input/output operations so that you can easily open or save drawing files to and from Internet sites using the same familiar file operation dialog boxes. This means that the following example address could be entered in the (drawing) File Open dialog box or recalled from the Look in Favorites feature:

```
http://www.project-drawings.com/project992/site.dwg
```

In addition, you can attach xref files from URL paths so that drawings residing on a remote Internet site can be utilized to keep local projects up-to-date. Using the Internet is discussed in Chapters 25 and 26 "Publishing on the Web" and "Project Collaboration over the Internet," respectively.

Object Hyperlinks

You can attach hyperlinks to AutoCAD objects with AutoCAD 2000's new hyperlink feature. You can then traverse the link to any drawing file, a Windows document file, or a URL. The Insert Hyperlinks dialog box is shown in Figure 1.22. See Chapter 25 for information about hyperlinks.

Figure 1.22

The Insert Hyperlinks dialog box.

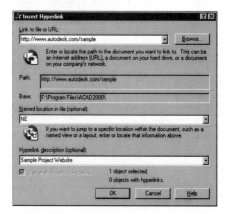

ePlot: Electronic Plotting of DWF Files

AutoCAD 2000 supports a new feature called electronic plotting (ePlot). With ePlot, you can plot to a secure, Internet-ready, vendor-neutral DMF file. ePlot provides you with the control, precision, and accuracy of a paper plot yet saves the time and cost associated with distributing hard copy output. The ePlot feature is discussed further in Chapters 25 and Chapter 26.

Database Connectivity: dbConnect

With AutoCAD 2000's new dbConnect functionality, you can tap the power and flexibility of a modern database. You can view database tables and queries using dbConnect's Data View dialog box, and you can otherwise utilize the features of a database. Figure 1.23 shows some of the dbConnect dialog boxes. See Chapter 24, "Using External Databases," for more details about the dbConnect feature.

Figure 1.23

The dbConnect Manager and Query Editor.

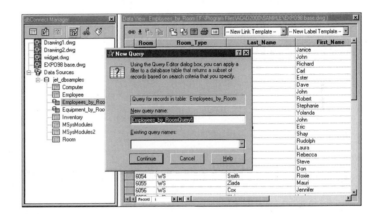

Streamlined Output

AutoCAD 2000 offers many new features and improvements to give you greater flexibility and control of your output. These features include the new multiple layout concept, the ability to create nonrectangular viewports, the addition of lineweights as an object property, and a more flexible plotting interface.

Layouts—Multiple Paper Spaces

You can now create multiple paper space layouts in a single drawing with AutoCAD 2000's Layouts feature. You can visually compose a drawing on a "virtual" sheet of paper aided by such visual cues as plotting area. Configure a layout for plot scale, paper size, plot area, or paper orientation, and the plotting device becomes a fast, straightforward task. Multiple drawing layouts allow you to consolidate multiple drawing sheets into a single drawing file. Figure 1.24 shows the new Model and Layout tabs. You will learn more about multiple layouts in Chapter 19, "Paper Space Layouts."

Figure 1.24

*AutoCAD 2000's new
Model and Layout tabs.*

Non-Rectangular Viewports

In AutoCAD 2000, viewports can be defined with any closed shape. As you can see in Figure 1.25, viewports are no longer confined to rectangular shapes. This not only allows more efficient use of your plotting sheet, it also allows you the freedom to design viewports that better suit the geometry of the drawing. You can read more about non-rectangular viewports in Chapter 19.

Figure 1.25

*AutoCAD 2000's new
non-rectangular viewports.*

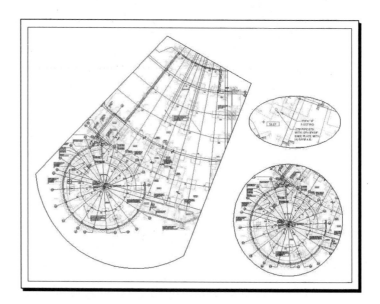

Lineweights

AutoCAD 2000 introduces a new object attribute—lineweight. Objects can now be displayed and plotted with variable lineweights. Like an object's color or linetype scale, its lineweight can be assigned on either a by-layer or a by-object basis. A new

Lineweight Control list, shown in Figure 1.26, is provided on the Object Properties toolbar. Using lineweights is covered in Chapter 5, "Using Linetypes and Lineweights Effectively."

Figure 1.26

AutoCAD 2000's new lineweight attribute.

Plotting Enhancements

Several plotting enhancements are incorporated into AutoCAD 2000. The stream-lined plotting in AutoCAD 2000 offers more flexibility in producing paper output and the ability to output the new DWF and ePlot formats.

The following list outlines some of the new AutoCAD 2000 features:

■ Plot settings can be saved with the drawing.

■ The new Plot dialog box (shown in Figure 1.27) closely emulates the Windows Print interface, making it easier to learn and use.

■ Plot Preview utilizes true WYSIWYG, in which color, lineweights, fill patterns, and so on are effectively portrayed.

■ Plotter configurations are portable and can be shared with project members.

■ Screening allows you to control the display intensity of plotted objects so that you can emphasize portions of the plotted output.

■ Plot styles enable you to move away from traditional color-based plotting by assigning a plot style to a layer or individual object.

You can read more about layouts in Chapter 19. Chapter 20, "Productive Plotting," discusses plotting in general.

Figure 1.27

The Plot dialog box's Settings tab.

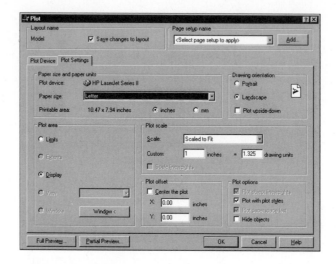

Greater Customization

One of the reasons for AutoCAD's wide acceptance and popularity over the last decade is its open architecture and ease of user customization.

Visual LISP

AutoCAD 2000 takes the most popular of AutoCAD's programming interfaces—AutoLISP—and extends its usability by incorporating Visual LISP. Visual LISP updates and modernizes the AutoLISP environment and provides a complete LISP development environment inside AutoCAD. The Visual LISP interface is shown in Figure 1.28, and you can read more about customization with AutoLISP in Chapter 22, "Introduction to AutoLISP Programming." Other customization topics are discussed in Chapter 21, "Customizing Without Programming."

Options Dialog Box

AutoCAD 2000's new Options dialog box, shown in Figure 1.29, provides a single-source access point to the many customizable features AutoCAD users have grown used to setting for themselves. Many of the system variables and other settings that tailor AutoCAD's operation to user preferences can be accessed easily from this dialog box. The Options dialog box settings are discussed in Chapter 3, "Controlling the AutoCAD 2000 Drawing Environment."

Figure 1.28

The Visual LISP interface provides a complete developmental environment.

Figure 1.29

The Options dialog box (User Preferences tab).

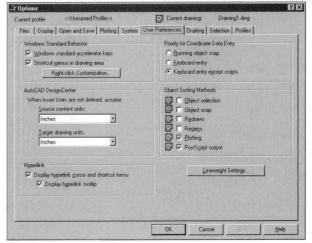

Summary

In many ways, the new features in AutoCAD 2000 reflect the changing software needs of AutoCAD users worldwide in a quickly evolving information age. On the other hand, many new features and capabilities are the result of user requests for an even easier to use drafting and design platform. No matter what your specific design needs are, AutoCAD 2000 stands as a worthy successor to the preceding fourteen releases of the world's most popular CAD software package.

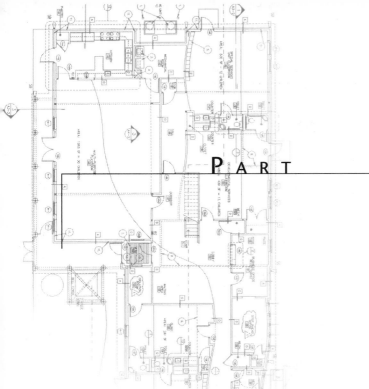

PART

II

STARTING NEW PROJECTS WITH AUTOCAD 2000

C H A P T E R

2

STARTING A DRAWING IN AutoCAD 2000

AutoCAD is a versatile drawing application that is used by many industries to draft and design a multitude of products. It is used by architects to create buildings, by civil engineers to design streets, highways, and utilities, and by cartographers to map the world. Mechanical engineers use AutoCAD to develop three-dimensional working models of a wide array of useful tools used in the day-to-day activities of working professionals. From heavy construction equipment to the most delicate medical instruments, AutoCAD provides state-of-the-art tools for turning dreams into reality.

Because of the diverse and wide range of industries using AutoCAD, the program is designed to allow users to easily customize AutoCAD's drafting settings to suit their unique needs. This chapter explains AutoCAD's drafting settings, and looks at how AutoCAD simplifies setting up your drawing environment with the Startup dialog box.

This chapter covers the following topics:

- Understanding AutoCAD's default values

- Using wizards to automate settings

- Using templates to start a drawing

- Revisiting the drawing limits

- Controlling drawing units

- Defining drafting settings

The Startup Dialog Box

AutoCAD 2000 provides users with a simple way to begin drawing with AutoCAD: the Startup dialog box. This dialog box provides several methods for starting your drawing session, which allow you to open an existing drawing, start a drawing from scratch, use a predefined drawing template, or use a wizard to walk you through the steps necessary to define your drawing's configuration.

The Open a Drawing button at the upper-left of the Startup dialog box allows you to select an existing drawing. When you click this button, the Startup dialog box displays a list of the most recently opened drawing files, as shown in Figure 2.1. You may select one of the files in the list, or click the Browse button to locate other files. The Browse button opens the Select File dialog box, which enables you to browse your system's folders for the drawing file you wish to open.

Figure 2.1

*The Open a Drawing
button displays the most
recently opened files in the
Startup dialog box.*

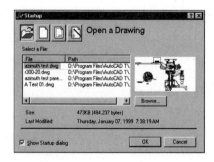

The other three buttons at the top of the Startup dialog box allow you to start new drawings, each of which presents a different approach. Depending on the button you choose, the Startup dialog box presents you with choices that automate the process of setting up your new drawing's default values.

The following sections describe in detail the various ways you can use the Startup dialog box to set your drawing's default values, and provide examples and exercises that demonstrate its ease of use.

Starting from Scratch: Understanding AutoCAD's Default Values

The Start from Scratch button (the second button at the top of the Startup dialog box) is the simplest to use when starting a new drawing. When you choose this option, it presents you with only two choices in the Default Settings area. You can choose English or Metric units of measurement, as shown in Figure 2.2. If you choose English units, AutoCAD creates a new drawing based on the Imperial measurement system, which uses the acad.dwt template file, and sets the drawing boundaries, called *limits*, to 12 × 9 inches. If you choose Metric units, AutoCAD creates a new drawing based on the metric measurement system, which uses the acadiso.dwt template file, and sets the drawing limits to 420 × 297 millimeters.

Figure 2.2

The Start from Scratch button displays only two options for default settings.

When you choose English or Metric units, you are actually setting two system variables: MEASUREMENT and MEASUREINIT. The MEASUREMENT system variable sets the drawing units as either English or Metric for the current drawing, whereas the MEASUREINIT system variable sets the drawing units as either English or Metric for new drawings when they are created.

Specifically, the two system variables control which hatch pattern and linetype files an existing or a new drawing uses when it is opened. When the system variables are set to 0, the English units are set, and AutoCAD uses the hatch pattern file and linetype file designated by the ANSIHatch and ANSILinetype Registry settings. When the system variables are set to 1, the Metric units are set and AutoCAD uses the hatch pattern file and linetype file designated by the ISOHatch and ISOLinetype Registry settings.

NOTE

Each time you launch AutoCAD and the Startup dialog box appears, you may choose the Cancel button. The Cancel button dismisses the Startup dialog box and creates a new drawing using the current values for MEASUREMENT and MEASUREINIT, including the associated drawing template and drawing limits. This occurs because AutoCAD stores these values in its system Registry AutoCAD.

It is important to determine which system of measurement you will use before starting your drawing because the system of units you select influences how objects appear in your drawing. For example, Figure 2.3 shows two rectangles that contain a hatch pattern. Both hatch patterns are the same (ANSI31), and their rotation and scale are identical: 0 and 1.0000, respectively. However, it is obvious the hatch pattern on the left displays lines much closer together than does the hatch pattern on the right.

Figure 2.3

The MEASUREMENT *system variable affects the appearance of hatch patterns when they are inserted in a drawing.*

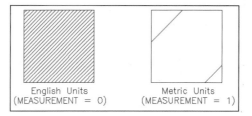

The difference in the two hatch patterns occurs because the hatch pattern on the left was drawn first with the MEASUREMENT system variable set to 0 (English units). Next, the MEASUREMENT system variable was set to 1 (Metric units). Then the same hatch pattern was drawn on the right. This example demonstrates that AutoCAD uses two different hatch pattern files based on the current value of MEASUREMENT. Therefore, to ensure that AutoCAD inserts the proper hatch patterns and linetypes into your drawing, be sure to choose the correct units of measurement.

INSIDER **T**IP

To correct a hatch pattern inserted with the wrong units of measurement, after changing the MEASUREMENT system variable, select the hatch pattern, click the right mouse button, then choose Hatch Edit. After AutoCAD displays the Hatch Edit dialog box, choose the same hatch pattern from the list, then click OK. AutoCAD updates the hatch pattern based on the current units of measurement.

Using Wizards to Automate Settings

AutoCAD provides *wizards* to help you set up a new drawing. As you complete setting one value, the wizard takes you to the next, using a standard Windows wizard interface that enables you to go to the next default setting, or back to edit previous settings. By using AutoCAD's wizards, you can quickly set certain default values and change them again if needed.

Understanding the Wizard Selections

When you click the Use a Wizard button (the fourth button at the top of the Startup dialog box), the Startup dialog box offers two wizard choices: The Advanced Setup Wizard and the Quick Setup Wizard, as shown in Figure 2.4. The Advanced Setup Wizard takes you through five dialog boxes, allowing you to set values for units, angle, angle measure, angle direction, and area. The Quick Setup Wizard offers a subset of these values, removing options for setting the various values related to angles. Specifically, the Quick Setup Wizard enables you to set values for units and area only.

Figure 2.4

The Use a Wizard feature offers two wizards to choose from.

The following describes the various values you can set with the Startup Wizard:

■ **Units.** The Units dialog box allows you set the way linear units are displayed in your drawing.

■ **Angle.** The Angle dialog box allows you set the way angles are displayed in your drawing.

■ **Angle Measure.** The Angle Measure dialog box allows you to set the base angle from which all angles are measured (it represents 0 degrees).

- **Angle Direction.** The Angle Direction dialog box allows you to set the direction all angles are measured from the base angle (clockwise or counter-clockwise).

- **Area.** The Area dialog box allows you to set the drawing's limits, which represent the area in which your model should be drawn and contained.

NOTE

In the Start from Scratch discussion, you learned how to select between English and metric measuring systems to control the hatch pattern and linetype files AutoCAD uses in a drawing. However, the Units dialog box discussed here controls how units in the selected measurement system are displayed.

The Units dialog box allows you to set how AutoCAD displays measured values, such as the length of a line, the radius of a circle, or the area of a polygon. It also controls how AutoCAD displays coordinate values. For example, if the units are set to Decimal, and you list the values of a circle object in a drawing, AutoCAD displays values as shown:

```
center point, X=   5.8796  Y=   4.2286  Z=   0.0000
         radius     1.1396
  circumference     7.1601
           area     4.0797
```

However, if the units are set to Fractional, and you list the values of the same circle, AutoCAD displays values as shown:

```
center point, X=   5 7/8  Y=   4 1/4  Z=        0
         radius     1 1/8
  circumference     7 3/16
           area     4 1/16
```

Notice the difference between the two formats. The Decimal format displays values less than one unit as decimals. In contrast, the Fractional format displays values less than one unit as fractions. This is true even though the values for the exact same objects are listed.

INSIDER **T**IP

> If you use the fractional-based unit settings, measurements will be rounded to the nearest fractional unit. This can lead to drafting inaccuracies if assumed to be exact values. Therefore, if you require precise values, use decimal-based units.

NOTE

> The selected units display mode does not affect AutoCAD's dimensions, which are controlled by their own system variables.

The Units dialog box also allows you to control the precision of the measured values. In Decimal mode, it represents the number of decimal places displayed for a value. In Fractional mode, it represents the smallest fractional increment displayed for a value (for example, 1/32 or 1/64).

When you select a Units value, you are actually setting the LUNITS system variable. The LUNITS system variable is based on integer values, with each integer value representing a units display mode, as shown in Table 2.1.

Table 2.1

Units Display Mode Examples for the LUNITS Variable

Integer	Display Mode	Example
1	Scientific	1.1356E+00
2	Decimal	1.1356
3	Engineering	0'–1.1356"
4	Architectural	0'–1 1/8"
5	Fractional	1 1/8

Additionally, another system variable, LUPREC, controls precision for units. Like the LUNITS system variable, LUPREC uses integer values to determine the number of decimal places displayed with a value. The range of acceptable values is 0 through 8. In the case of values displayed in Fractional mode, the integer value represents a fractional increment. Table 2.2 shows examples of the precision display for each value.

Table 2.2

Units Precision Display Examples for the LUPREC Variable

Integer	Decimal	Fractional
0	0	0
1	0.0	0–1/2
2	0.00	0–1/4
3	0.000	0–1/8
4	0.0000	0–1/16
5	0.00000	0–1/32
6	0.000000	0–1/64
7	0.0000000	0–1/128
8	0.00000000	0–1/256

INSIDER TIP

You can adjust the value of a system variable by typing its name at the Command prompt, then entering the desired value.

NOTE

The selected precision display mode does not affect the accuracy AutoCAD uses in its calculations. All calculations are double-precision and carried out to 16 decimal places.

The Angle dialog box allows you to set how AutoCAD displays angle values, such as the angle of an arc, or the angle between two lines. It also enables you to set the precision of displayed angles.

Like the Units dialog box, the Angle dialog box controls two system variables: AUNITS and AUPREC. When you select an angle value, you are setting the AUNITS system variable. The AUNITS system variable is based on integer values, with each integer value representing a units display mode, as shown in Table 2.3.

Table 2.3

Angular Display Mode Examples for the AUNITS Variable

Integer	Display Mode	Example
0	Decimal degrees	23.9493
1	Degrees/minutes/seconds	23d56'57"
2	Gradians	26.6103g
3	Radians	0.4180r
4	Surveyor's units	N 66d3'3" E

The AUPREC system variable controls the precision of displayed angles, and functions similarly to the LUPREC system variable, using integer values to determine the number of decimal places displayed with a value. The range of acceptable integer values is 0 through 8. In the case of values displayed in degrees/minutes/seconds or Surveyor's units, the integer values control the display of minutes and seconds. If the precision value defines the precision beyond minutes and seconds, the seconds are displayed in decimal format. Table 2.4 shows examples of the precision display for each value.

Table 2.4

Angle Precision Display Examples for the AUPREC Variable

Integer	Decimal	Surveyor's Units
0	8	N 82d E
1	8.2	N 81d46' E
2	8.23	N 81d46' E
3	8.235	N 81d45'55" E
4	8.2347	N 81d45'55" E
5	8.23469	N 81d45'55.1" E
6	8.234689	N 81d45'55.12" E
7	8.2346894	N 81d45'55.118" E
8	8.23468944	N 81d45'55.1180" E

Notice that the Surveyor's units for integer values 1 and 2, and values 3 and 4, respectively, display the same level of precision. This occurs because minutes and seconds must be displayed as full values. This is true because there are 60 minutes of angular arc in one degree, and 60 seconds of angular arc in one minute.

NO T E

When displaying angles in degrees/minutes/seconds or Surveyor's units, the ' symbol stands for minutes, not feet, and the " symbol stands for seconds, not inches.

The Angle Measure dialog box allows you to set the base angle from which all angles are measured. AutoCAD uses the default value of 0 degrees being due East. The Angle Measure dialog box allows you to choose from four preset base angles (East, North, West, or South), and allows you to enter your own user-defined base angle. The value for the base angle is stored in the ANGBASE system variable, and can represent any angle value.

NO T E

The base angle is associated with the X axis of the current UCS. If you rotate the UCS, the base angle also rotates.

The Angle Direction dialog box works in conjunction with the Angle Measure dialog box and allows you to set the direction all angles are measured from. The only possible directions are counterclockwise or clockwise. The current direction value is held in the ANGDIR system variable, with 0 indicating a counterclockwise direction, and 1 indicating a clockwise direction.

The Area dialog box allows you to set the drawing's *limits*, which generally represent the area in which your model is contained or the area within which you will be creating your drawing. The limits are intended to help you manage your drawing.

When you set the width and length of the limits, AutoCAD defines the limits as a rectangle, with its lower-left corner located at coordinates 0,0, and its upper-right corner based on the values you enter for Width and Length. The Width and Length values are stored in the LIMMIN and LIMMAX system variables, respectively.

You can instruct AutoCAD to not allow you to accidentally draw outside the drawing limits, thereby adding a level of error checking to your drawing session. This is called *limits checking*, and is controlled with the LIMCHECK system variable. By setting the variable to 0, you turn off limits checking, and by setting it to 1, you turn on limits checking. The LIMCHECK variable will only protect you against acquiring points outside the limits. You can copy objects outside limits and position other items as well.

The drawing area within the limits is also the area in which AutoCAD will display its grid. The *grid* is made up of a series of dots, and is used as a frame of reference when creating objects. The grid is useful for quickly drawing objects based on grid locations. The grid's visibility is controlled from the GRID button located on the status bar at the bottom of AutoCAD's screen. You may also press the function key F7 to toggle the grid on and off.

Finally, you can use the limits with the ZOOM command, and when plotting. When zooming, you can select the All option to immediately display the entire Limits area on AutoCAD's screen. When plotting from model space, you can select the Limits option to plot the entire area defined by the Limits setting.

You have learned how AutoCAD can make starting a drawing easy by using its wizards to walk you through the setup process. Next, you learn how to take advantage of previous drawing setups by using templates.

Using the Available Templates to Start a Drawing

A *template* is a drawing file that contains predefined drawing settings and/or geometry, such as a title block, and is used to begin your drawing. Templates are intended as a quick way to take advantage of an existing drawing that contains the proper drawing settings and base geometry you use in every drawing.

For example, suppose you are creating 10 drawings, and those drawings will use the same units and angle settings, and use the same title block. To minimize your work effort, you can create the drawing once, defining the proper units and angle settings, and inserting the desired title block, then save the drawing as a template. As you begin each new drawing, you select the template file you previously created, which contains the correct units, angle settings, and title block. The template acts as a base for your new drawing, and thereby eliminates a lot of repetitious preparation and setup work.

When you choose the Use a Template button (the third button at the top of the Startup dialog box), AutoCAD displays the list of available templates, as shown in Figure 2.5. AutoCAD 2000 comes with 26 predefined template files, and you can add your own. You create a template file by defining the proper units and angle settings, and inserting any desired geometry, and saving the drawing as a .DWT file.

Customizing and Saving a Template File

Although Autodesk has made a considerable effort to provide a broad array of templates, chances are you will want to customize your own templates. You can do so by modifying one of the template files provided with AutoCAD 2000, or by creating a drawing from scratch.

In the following exercise, you begin with an existing template file, modify a few of its drawing settings, then save the drawing as a new template file.

CREATING A TEMPLATE DRAWING

1. Launch AutoCAD, and in the Startup dialog box, click the Use a Template button.

2. From the Select a File list, choose the Ansi_b.dwt template file, then click OK.

3. At the Command prompt, type **LUPREC**, then press Enter.

4. Type **2**, then press Enter. This sets the display of units to two decimal places.

5. At the Command prompt, type **AUNITS**, then press Enter.

6. To set the angle display to surveyor's units, type **4**, then press Enter.

7. At the Command prompt, type **AUPREC**, then press Enter.

8. Type **2**, then press Enter. This sets the angle display to degrees and minutes.

9. From the File menu, choose Save As.

10. In the Save Drawing As dialog box, from the Save as Type drop-down list, choose AutoCAD Drawing Template File (*.dwt).

    When you choose the AutoCAD Drawing Template File (*.dwt) option, AutoCAD automatically switches to the Template folder, as shown in Figure 2.6. Although you don't have to save your template in this folder, it is the default folder the Startup dialog box looks in for template files. Therefore, it's a good place to store your custom template files unless the files are specific to a project.

Figure 2.6

To save the drawing as a template file, choose the AutoCAD Drawing Template File (*.dwt) option from the Save as Type drop-down list.

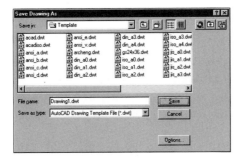

11. In the File Name edit box, type **ansi_b-survey units**, then click Save.

12. In the Template Description dialog box that appears, type **Angles are measured in Survey units**, as shown in Figure 2.7, then click OK to save the current drawing as a template file.

Figure 2.7

The Template Description dialog box allows you to enter a description for your template file.

13. To start a new drawing using the template you just created from the File menu, choose New.

14. In the Start Up dialog box, click the Use a Template button.

Your newly created template file should appear in the Select a Template list, as shown in Figure 2.8. Notice that the Template Description area displays your modified description.

Figure 2.8

The new template appears in the Select a Template list.

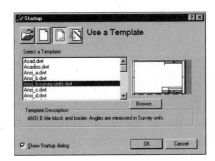

The ability to create your own custom templates is very powerful. By creating custom template files, you minimize repetitive tasks and reduce errors by using the same templates repeatedly.

NOTE

> The LUPREC, AUPREC, and AUNITS system variables can be set using the Drawing Units dialog box.

So far, you have seen how to control drawing settings using the Startup dialog box. Next, you will learn how to control drawing settings during the current drawing session.

Controlling Drawing Settings

AutoCAD provides the ability to modify drawing settings during the current drawing session. By changing these settings, you control how AutoCAD behaves. Therefore, you can modify the current session to optimize your productivity.

In the next few sections, you learn how to control drawing settings for the current drawing session. Some of the settings are similar to previous versions of AutoCAD, and some are brand new to AutoCAD 2000.

Revisiting the Drawing Limits

Previously, you learned about setting the limits for a drawing using a wizard. While this information is useful, it doesn't provide an easy method to modify the limits during the current drawing session.

So how do you easily change the limits during the current drawing session? The process is simple. To change the current drawing's limits, from the Format menu, choose Drawing Limits. When you choose Drawing Limits, AutoCAD starts the LIMITS command, which prompts you to enter new values for the lower-left and upper-right corners of the Limits rectangle. You can enter values by picking them on screen using your pointing device, or you can enter the coordinates explicitly using your keyboard. After you enter the new Limits values, AutoCAD resets the drawing limits to the new values.

Controlling Drawing Units

In the previous discussion about using AutoCAD's Advanced Setup Wizard, you learned how to set various Unit and Angle values, and how those values affect AutoCAD's display. You also learned how to set those values using the appropriate system variables. In this section, you learn how to control those settings using AutoCAD's Drawing Units dialog box.

The AutoCAD 2000 Drawing Units dialog box is very similar to its Release 14 predecessor. Although its interface has changed slightly, and a new sizing control option has been added, its overall functionality is the same.

One minor change includes the dialog box's name. In Release 14, it was called the Units Control dialog box. In AutoCAD 2000, it's now called the Drawing Units dialog box.

Another minor change is the location of the Counterclockwise/Clockwise direction control. In Release 14, the Counterclockwise/Clockwise direction control was accessed by clicking the Direction button, then choosing the desired direction from the Direction Control dialog box. In AutoCAD 2000, the Counterclockwise/Clockwise direction control is accessed from the Drawing Units dialog box, as shown in Figure 2.9. You will notice the Counterclockwise/Clockwise direction is controlled by toggling the Clockwise feature on or off.

Figure 2.9

The Counterclockwise/ Clockwise direction control appears in the Drawing Units dialog box.

In addition to the minor changes, the Drawing Units dialog box includes a new feature. The new feature works in conjunction with the new AutoCAD DesignCenter and controls the unit of measure used for block insertions. This new feature automatically adjusts the size of blocks as they are inserted. If a block created in different units is inserted into the drawing, it is automatically scaled and inserted in the specified units of the current drawing.

This is a powerful feature, making the insertion of blocks with predefined units very simple. You no longer need to worry about properly scaling a block when it is inserted. On the other hand, if you don't want to automatically adjust the block, select the Unitless mode to insert the drawing as a block and not scale the block to match the specified units. You will learn more about how to use this feature in Chapter 12, "Applications for the New AutoCAD DesignCenter."

Although most of the features and functions of the Drawing Units dialog box were covered in the discussion about AutoCAD's Advanced Setup Wizard, one handy feature was not discussed. The feature is accessed from the Direction Control dialog box, and allows you to define a new base angle by picking points onscreen. By choosing Other, then the Angle button, shown in Figure 2.10, you can select two points onscreen using your pointing device. AutoCAD calculates the angle, and uses it as the new base angle.

Figure 2.10

The Pick an Angle button allows you to set the base angle by picking two points onscreen.

Defining Drafting Settings

Drafting settings are tools you use as an aid when drawing in AutoCAD. These features can increase accuracy, ease object editing through onscreen visual enhancements, and automate object creation and editing by providing a mouse-only interface. By controlling AutoCAD's drafting settings, you make working with AutoCAD easier, quicker, and more accurate.

The Drafting Settings dialog box is accessed from the Tools menu by choosing Drafting Settings. When the dialog box appears, you see three tabs, as shown in Figure 2.11. These tabs control features such as Snap and Grid, and Object Snap. The Object Snap tab introduces the new Parallel snap, and a new feature called Object Snap Tracking. The third tab introduces a new feature called Polar Tracking, which allows you to automate certain command processes, such as drawing lines from one point to another, by making the process more intuitive.

Figure 2.11

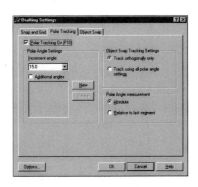

The new Drafting Settings dialog box controls settings for Snap and Grid, Object Snap, and the new Polar Tracking features.

for R2000

The Drafting Settings dialog box is new to AutoCAD 2000, and is a combination of the features of two dialog boxes from Release 14: the Drawing Aids dialog box and the Osnap Settings dialog box. In AutoCAD 2000, these features have been incorporated in the multiple tabs of the Drafting Settings dialog box. For detailed information on the functions and features of the Drafting Settings dialog box, including the new Polar Tracking feature, see Chapter 6, "Accuracy in Creating Drawings with AutoCAD 2000."

Summary

In this chapter, you have learned about controlling various AutoCAD settings when creating a drawing with the Startup dialog box, and during the current drawing session through different menu commands and dialog boxes. By controlling AutoCAD's drafting settings, you can develop an environment that's appropriate for your needs.

The insight you gained in this chapter is expanded upon in Chapter 3, "Controlling the AutoCAD 2000 Drawing Environment," where you learn about controlling AutoCAD's behavior with the core system control: the Options dialog box.

CONTROLLING THE AUTOCAD 2000 DRAWING ENVIRONMENT

In Chapter 2, "Starting a Drawing in AutoCAD 2000," you learned how to control drawing settings using the Startup dialog box, the Drawing Units dialog box, and Drafting Settings dialog box. In addition to the features controlled by these dialog boxes, AutoCAD also allows you to control many other features through its Options dialog box (formerly known as the Preferences dialog box in Release 14). Through the Options dialog box, you control where AutoCAD searches for and saves files, how its display appears, as well as certain drafting features including AutoSnap, AutoTracking, and object selection methods.

This chapter covers the following topics:

- *Defining support paths*

- *Controlling AutoCAD's display*

- *Configuring plotters*

- *Setting user preferences*

- *Defining profiles*

In this chapter, you review the Options dialog box in detail, and go through examples and work through exercises that help you master its many powerful features.

Specifying Search Paths and Filenames

When you start AutoCAD, it determines where certain files are that may be used during the drawing session. These items include support files and device drivers, which are located in various folders on your computer system. AutoCAD also determines where to store certain file information, like temporary and backup files. In the Files tab, you specify where to find all the files needed, and where to save temporary and backup files.

The Files tab is located in the Options dialog box, which is accessed from the Tools menu by choosing Options (see Figure 3.1). The Files tab identifies all necessary files and their locations in several folders. The folders are used to organize and display the information into a list of logical groups. As you select each folder in the list, a description is displayed in the description field under the list. The yellow folder icons in the list specify where AutoCAD searches for support, driver, menu, and other files. The white papers icons specify optional, user-defined settings such as which dictionary to use for checking spelling.

Figure 3.1

The Options dialog box controls many of AutoCAD's features.

By modifying the paths and files in the folders, and adding new information, you can control the files AutoCAD uses during its drawing session. In the following exercise, you add a new path to the Support File Search Path folder, which provides AutoCAD with another folder to look in for files it needs to use during a drawing session.

ADDING A NEW SEARCH PATH

1. With AutoCAD running, from the Tools menu, choose Options.

2. Choose the Files tab if it is not already displayed.

3. Double-click on the Support Files Search Path folder to display its contents. You can also expand a folder by selecting the plus (+) sign. If the sign is minus (-) then the folder is already expanded.

4. Click the Add button to add a new search path.

5. Click the Browse button to display the Browse for Folder dialog box.

6. In the Browse for Folder dialog box, scroll to the top of the list, and choose Desktop, then click OK.

   AutoCAD adds the new path to the Support File Search Path folder, as shown in Figure 3.2. With this new path added, AutoCAD will now search the desktop for any files it needs. However, because you probably don't keep AutoCAD's files on your desktop, let's remove the path from the folder.

Figure 3.2

A new path is added to the Support File Search Path folder.

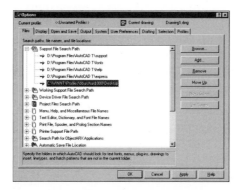

7. Choose the path you just created to highlight it.

8. Click the Remove button to remove the highlighted path from the folder.

WARNING

AutoCAD has default locations for all search paths. Although you can change these locations, caution should be used. If you modify a location, AutoCAD may not be able to find the files it needs to run properly.

NOTE

> Third-party products will frequently place their own menus and LISP routines in separate
> directories created during installation. If you find that your third-party software is not
> performing properly, make sure the Support File Search Path and Device Driver File Search
> Path in the Files tab contain the proper path references.

As you just learned, adding and removing paths is very simple. It's also very simple
to redefine the files AutoCAD uses during the editing session. To demonstrate this,
in the following exercise, you replace the current alternate font file setting, Simplex,
with Arial.

REPLACING THE DEFAULT ALTERNATE FONT FILE

1. Continuing from the previous exercise, click the plus sign (+) in front of the Text
   Editor, Dictionary, and Font File Names item to expand its list.

2. Click the plus sign (+) in front of the Alternate Font File item to display the current
   setting of simplex.shx. Then select the Simplex.shx listed.

3. Click the Browse button to display the Alternate Font dialog box.

4. In the Alternate Font dialog box, scroll to the top of the Font Name list, choose the
   Arial font, then click OK.

AutoCAD replaces the Simplex Alternate Font File with Arial, as shown in Figure 3.3.
If you are satisfied with the changes to the paths and files, you can click the Apply
button. However, if you do not want to apply the modified settings, click Cancel.

Figure 3.3

*The Alternate Font File is
changed to Arial.*

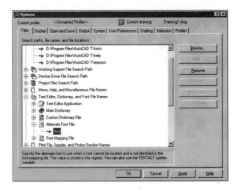

As you just learned, modifying the default paths and files AutoCAD uses is easy. Next, you learn about customizing AutoCAD's display.

Options for Display

AutoCAD's display represents the look of your drawing session. By editing the settings found in the Display tab, you can control how AutoCAD looks, how layouts appear, and even increase performance.

The Display tab is organized into six areas, as shown in Figure 3.4. The six areas are as follows:

- **Window Elements.** This area controls different display settings in the AutoCAD Window, including the number of lines in the command line window and the screen's background color.

- **Layout Elements.** This area controls the appearance of paper space layouts.

- **Crosshair Size.** This area controls the size of the cursor's crosshairs.

- **Display Resolution.** This area controls the appearance of objects on screen.

- **Display Performance.** This area controls the display settings that affect AutoCAD's performance.

- **Reference Editing Fading Intensity.** This area specifies how much background objects fade during in-place reference editing.

Figure 3.4

The Display tab in the Options dialog box controls AutoCAD's screen appearance.

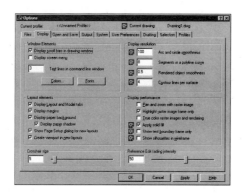

Window Elements

In the Window Elements area, you can turn the scrollbars that appear in each drawing window on or off. The scrollbars allow you to pan the current view by sliding the buttons along the scrollbar. You can also depress the arrow keys at either end of the scrollbars, or click in the bar itself to pan the view. A handy feature of the scrollbars is that you can pan to a new view during a command.

The Window Elements area also allows you to control the display of the screen menu, which is a leftover relic from much earlier AutoCAD versions. The screen menu was used before pull-down menus were available, and well before toolbars were developed. The screen menu appears on the right side of the screen, and it's still available for those who have been using AutoCAD for many years and prefer it as the main interface with AutoCAD commands. Although it is perfectly acceptable to execute commands in AutoCAD using the screen menu, if you're new to AutoCAD, you should avoid using it since it is not as intuitive as the pull-down menus, nor as easy to use as the toolbars.

In the Window Elements area, you can also control the number of lines that appear in the command line window at the bottom of AutoCAD's screen. The default number of lines is three, and you can enter a new value in the text box. A value of three will show the previous two prompts, plus, provide another line for the active command line prompt. You can also modify the number of lines on screen without using the Options dialog box by dragging the top of the command line window up or down.

The Window Elements area also enables you to control the font that appears in the command line window. By clicking the Font button, AutoCAD displays the Command Line Window Font dialog box, as shown in Figure 3.5. To change the font, choose the desired Font, Font Style, and Size, then click the Apply & Close button.

Figure 3.5

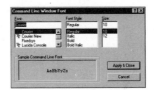

The Command Line Window Font dialog box controls the font that appears in the command line window.

Finally, you can control AutoCAD's screen colors by clicking the Color button, which displays the AutoCAD Color Options dialog box, as shown in Figure 3.6. From this dialog box, you independently control the background screen color of model space, paper space layouts, and the command line window. You can also change the color of the crosshairs, and AutoCAD's AutoTracking vectors.

By modifying the colors of the various elements, you can adjust the display of your drawings to make viewing more comfortable, and place less strain on your eyes, which is a real advantage if you spend eight hours a day or more working with AutoCAD.

Figure 3.6

The AutoCAD Color Options dialog box controls the color of AutoCAD's screen.

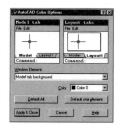

After you have modified the screen's colors, you can easily set them back to their original color scheme. By clicking the Default All button, you change all color settings back to their original mode. By clicking the Default One Element button, you change the currently selected item back to its original color.

Layout Elements

NEW
for R2000   In the Layout Elements area, you control options for existing and new layouts. A layout is an individual paper space environment in which you set up drawings for plotting. The various options toggle features off or on. Paper space layouts are discussed in detail in Chapter 19, "Paper Space Layouts."

Crosshair Size

The Crosshair Size area controls the size of AutoCAD's crosshairs. The crosshairs appear on the cursor when you move the cursor into AutoCAD's drawing area. The valid range is from 1% to 100% of the total screen. At 100 percent the ends of the crosshairs extend to the edges of the drawing window. When the size is decreased to 99% or below, the crosshairs have a finite size, and the ends of the crosshairs are visible when situated at the edge of the drawing area. The default size is 5%. Some users find it helpful to set the size to 100% when visually aligning points using the cursor display.

Display Resolution

The Display Resolution area controls the number of segments AutoCAD uses when displaying curved objects or curved areas. When AutoCAD draws curved objects, it actually simulates the shape of the curve by drawing short, straight line segments. By using a high number of line segments, AutoCAD enhances the appearance of the curved object. The smaller the number, the fewer line segments used by AutoCAD, and the poorer the simulation of the curve. The advantage of using smaller numbers for the values is that regen times are shorter, and AutoCAD displays objects quicker. For example, Figure 3.7 shows the effect of changing the Arc and Circle Smoothness value. The circle on the left simulates the effect of a value of 100; the circle on the right simulates the effect of a value of 4. By setting the value to 100, the onscreen appearance of the circle is smooth.

NOTE

Because of the high speed of today's processors, you may not experience much degradation in AutoCAD's performance when setting high smoothness values.

Figure 3.7

A Display Resolution setting of 100 generates the smoother circle on the left, while the one generated with a setting of 4 is on the right.

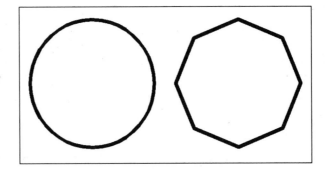

NOTE

The number of line segments used by AutoCAD to display objects on screen does not affect the accuracy AutoCAD uses when creating or plotting the objects. The values in the Display Resolution area only affect how objects appear on screen.

Display Performance

The Display Performance options control how AutoCAD deals with raster images (bitmaps) when panning or zooming, when editing them, and when displaying them in true color. By toggling these options off or on, you can dramatically affect your system's performance. For example, by toggling off the Pan and Zoom with Raster Image option, AutoCAD displays only an outline of the raster image when you pan or zoom, thereby improving display performance. Otherwise, when this option is toggled on, as you pan or zoom, AutoCAD continuously redraws the image.

Similarly, by toggling on the Highlight Raster Image Frame Only option, you increase your system's performance because it highlights only the image's frame when you select it for editing. Otherwise, when this option is off, AutoCAD highlights the image's frame and the entire area of the image.

You also affect display performance by toggling off the True Color Raster Images and Rendering option. When this option is off, you increase performance because AutoCAD does not use 16.7 million colors to display the image, but uses 256 colors instead. Although the number of colors is significantly reduced with this option toggled off, it is usually adequate for display purposes.

Other options include the Apply Solid Fill and Show Silhouettes in Wireframe options. The Apply Solid Fill option controls whether solid fills are displayed in objects like arrowheads on dimension lines, and in polylines in which a width greater than zero is assigned. By toggling off this feature, only a wireframe representation of the object is displayed. The Show Silhouettes in Wireframe option controls whether silhouette curves of 3D solid objects are displayed as wireframes. It also controls whether the wire mesh is drawn or suppressed when a 3D solid object is hidden. To increase performance, toggle off these two options. Silhouettes are discussed in Chapter 29, "Surfacing in 3D."

One final option is the Show Text Boundary Frame Only option, which displays a box representing the location of text objects instead of displaying the text. If you have a drawing with numerous text objects, and you notice your system is performing slowly, toggle on this option. AutoCAD will then replace all text objects with rectangular outlines representing the limits of the text objects. When this feature is toggled off, the rectangular outlines are removed, and the original text reappears.

Reference Edit Fading Intensity

NEW
for R2000

AutoCAD 2000 introduces a new feature called *In-Place Reference Editing*. This new feature allows you to edit blocks and external references from the drawing they're inserted in, and save the changes back to their original location. The fading intensity value controls the visibility of objects that are not being edited, and displays them at a lesser display intensity than objects being edited. This makes focusing on the object(s) being edited much easier. The valid range is 0% through 90%. The default setting is 50%. This feature is discussed in detail in Chapter 14, "Working with Drawings and External References Productively."

Open and Save Settings

The Open and Save tab controls a variety of features associated with opening and saving files. By editing the features, you can control the format AutoCAD saves files as, whether AutoCAD automatically saves files, and whether AutoCAD makes a backup copy when it saves a file. These, and other related features, are discussed in this section.

The Open and Save tab is organized into four areas, as shown in Figure 3.8. The four areas are as follows:

- **File Save.** Controls various features associated with saving files.

- **File Safety Precautions.** Controls elements dealing with automatically saving backup files.

- **External References (Xrefs).** Controls several features associated with external references.

- **ObjectARX Applications.** Controls several features associated with AutoCAD's Runtime Extension (ARX) files.

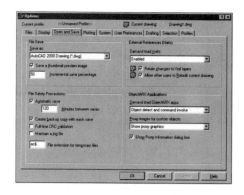

*The Open and Save tab in
the Options dialog box
controls how AutoCAD
handles files.*

File Save

In the File Save area, you control the type of file AutoCAD saves the current drawing as, whether a thumbnail image is saved with the drawing, and AutoCAD's incremental save percentage.

AutoCAD provides several different file types to save the current drawing as. These file types represent the default file types and can be overridden using the Save As command from the File menu. The file types include .DWG formats for Releases 2000, 14, and 13, AutoCAD's Drawing Template Format (.DWT), and .DXF formats for Releases 2000, 14, 13, and 12.

You also control whether AutoCAD saves a thumbnail image with the current drawing. By toggling on this option, AutoCAD snaps an image of the current drawing's display, and saves it with the drawing. When opening an existing drawing, the image appears in the Select File dialog box when you select the drawing's filename. This feature is useful for visually identifying a drawing without opening it. This thumbnail image is not saved in .DXF format files.

Finally, you can set the percent value for AutoCAD's Incremental Save Percentage feature. This feature controls the frequency at which AutoCAD performs a full save when saving a file. Performing a full save removes wasted space from the drawing's database, which reduces a drawing's file size. The percent value refers to the amount of wasted space that is allowed in the drawing's database. After the percentage of allowable wasted space is reached, AutoCAD performs a full save, removing the wasted space.

The advantage of this feature is that if you make small modifications to your drawing and frequently save the drawing, you do not spend a lot of time waiting for

AutoCAD to finish a full save. The disadvantage is that because AutoCAD does not perform a full save each time it saves a drawing, the drawing's file size is larger than necessary because the wasted space is not removed. Generally speaking, the default value of 50% is adequate for most users' needs. However, if your drawing's file size is too large and consuming too much disk space, reduce the number to 25% to make file sizes smaller. Reducing the number to below 20% optimizes drawing file sizes, but degrades performance when saving drawings because full saves are performed much more frequently.

Note

> The Incremental Save Percentage feature does not affect how much data is saved. AutoCAD always saves all data, including edits, during an incremental save. What AutoCAD does not do during an incremental save is remove wasted space, which makes the .DWG file as small as possible. Therefore, if AutoCAD crashes, even though your last save was an incremental save, all data is retained. The only data lost is the new edits performed since your last save.

File Safety Precautions

In the File Safety Precautions area, AutoCAD provides tools for helping you avoid data loss and for detecting errors in drawings. The following list gives you an overview of these features:

- **Automatic Save.** Controls whether AutoCAD saves the current drawing automatically, and how frequently it does so. Enter the Save Frequency value in minutes and AutoCAD will automatically save the current drawing when the time limit is reached, after which, it starts tracking the time from zero.

- **Create Backup Copy with Each Save.** When this feature is on, AutoCAD saves the current drawing, then makes a backup copy (.BAK). Generally, it's a good idea to let AutoCAD save a backup copy of your drawing. However, bear in mind that the backup file is just as large as the drawing file, which can consume a lot of disk space.

- **Full-Time CRC Validation.** This option specifies whether a *cyclic redundancy check (CRC)* should be performed each time an object is read into the drawing. CRC is an error-checking mechanism. If your drawings are being corrupted and you suspect a hardware problem or AutoCAD error, turn on this option.

- **Maintain a Log File.** Controls whether AutoCAD saves the contents of the text window to a log file. This feature is useful if you need to retrace the command performed during an editing session. This file can also get very large.

- **File Extension for Temporary Files.** This feature controls the file extension AutoCAD uses for the temporary files it creates during an editing session. The default extension is .ac$, and generally is adequate. When an AutoCAD editing session is ended improperly, AutoCAD does not have the opportunity to remove temporary files. Consequently, you must search your system for files ending with the designated extension, and remove them.

NOTE

> You define the location where AutoCAD stores temporary files in the Files tab, in the Temporary Drawing File Location folder.

External References (Xrefs)

In the External References (Xrefs) area, AutoCAD enables you to control demand loading, retain modifications to xref-dependent layers, and allow the current drawing to be edited from another drawing.

The Demand Load Xrefs feature allows you to disable demand loading, enable demand loading, or enable demand loading with copy. Demand loading is discussed in detail in Chapter 14.

The Retain Changes to Xref Layers option allows you to save the current state of xref-dependent layers in the current drawing. Layer states such as Freeze/Thaw and On/Off can be changed in the current drawing for xref-dependent layers. By toggling on this option, changes made to the layer states are saved, and reinstated when the drawing is opened again.

The Allow Other Users to Refedit Current Drawing option controls whether the current drawing can be edited when it is attached as an xref. This toggles off or on the new AutoCAD 2000 in-line reference editing feature, and is discussed in detail in Chapter 14.

ObjectARX Applications

The ObjectARX Applications area allows you to control settings that relate to AutoCAD Runtime Extension (ARX) applications and proxy graphics.

The Demand Load ARX Apps feature specifies if and when AutoCAD demand-loads a third-party application if a drawing contains custom objects created in that application. *Demand loading* means AutoCAD loads the application in the current drawing session in order to display the custom object(s). This feature has four options:

- **Disable Load on Demand.** Turns off demand loading.

- **Custom Object Detect.** Demand-loads the source application when you open a drawing that contains custom objects. This setting does not demand-load the application when you invoke one of the application's commands.

- **Command Invoke.** Demand-loads the source application when you invoke one of the application's commands. This setting does not demand-load the application when you open a drawing that contains custom objects.

- **Object Detect and Command Invoke.** Demand-loads the source application when you open a drawing that contains custom objects or when you invoke one of the application's commands.

The Proxy Images for Custom Objects feature controls the display of custom objects in drawings. Proxy images are created when you open a drawing that contains custom objects, but you do not have access to the application that created the objects. Because AutoCAD cannot properly display the objects with the application, it creates a place holder called a Proxy Object. This feature has three options:

- **Do Not Show Proxy Graphics.** Specifies to not display proxy objects in drawings.

- **Show Proxy Graphics.** Specifies to display proxy objects in drawings.

- **Show Proxy Bounding Box.** Specifies to show a box in place of custom objects in drawings.

The Show Proxy Information Dialog Box option specifies whether AutoCAD displays a warning when you open a drawing that contains custom objects. The dialog box provides the total number of proxy objects in the drawing (both graphical and non-graphical), the name of the missing application, and additional information about the proxy object type and display state.

Setting Output Options

The Output tab controls a variety of features associated with plotting. By editing the features, you can control default plotting settings, the general plotting environment, plot style behavior in all drawings, and options related to script files.

The Output tab is organized into four areas, as shown in Figure 3.9. The four areas are as follows:

- **Default Plot Settings (for new drawings).** Controls settings that relate to the default plotting settings.

- **General Plot Options.** Controls options that relate to the general plotting environment.

- **Default Plot Style Behavior (for new drawings).** Controls options related to plot style behavior in all drawings.

- **Scripts.** Controls options related to script files in AutoCAD drawings.

Figure 3.9

The Output tab in the Options dialog box controls how AutoCAD handles plotting features.

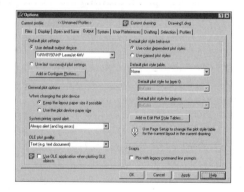

Default Plot Settings

The Default Plot Settings area allows you to control various settings that relate to the default plotting settings. These include settings such as the default output device used for new layouts and model space, the plotting settings based on the settings of the last successful plot, and the Autodesk Plotter Manager (a Windows system window). These features are discussed in detail in Chapter 20, "Productive Plotting."

General Plot Options

The General Plot Options area allows you to control options that relate to the general plotting environment, including paper size settings, system printer alert behavior, and OLE objects in an AutoCAD drawing. These features are discussed in detail in Chapter 20.

Default Plot Style Behavior

The Default Plot Style Behavior area controls options related to plot style behavior in all drawings. A *plot style* is a collection of property settings defined in a plot style table and applied when the drawing is plotted. These features are discussed in detail in Chapter 20.

Scripts

The Scripts area controls whether legacy plot scripts are enabled in AutoCAD drawings. *Legacy plot scripts* are those created for releases earlier than AutoCAD 2000. Script files are discussed in detail in Chapter 21, "Customizing Without Programming."

Configuring the System

The System tab controls AutoCAD's system settings. These settings control the current 3D graphics display, options relating to the current pointing device, options relating to database connectivity, and other general options.

The System tab is organized into four areas, as shown in Figure 3.10. The four areas are as follows:

- **Current 3D Graphics Display.** Controls settings that relate to system properties and configuration of the 3D graphics display system.

- **Current Pointing Device.** Controls options that relate to the pointing device.

- **General Options.** Controls general options that relate to system settings.

- **dbConnect Options.** Controls options that relate to database connectivity.

Figure 3.10

*The System tab in the
Options dialog box
controls AutoCAD's system
settings.*

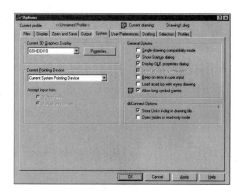

Current 3D Graphics Display

The Current 3D Graphics Display area has two features. The first allows you to select from the list of available 3D graphics display systems. The second displays the 3D Graphics System Configuration dialog box.

These two features work in conjunction with each other. For example, when you select a 3D graphics display system from the drop-down list, the Properties button displays the 3D Graphics System Configuration dialog box set for the current 3D graphics display system.

The default 3D graphics display system is the Heidi 3D graphics display system (GSHEIDI10). When this system is selected, the 3D Graphics System Configuration dialog box display appears as shown in Figure 3.11. If you are using a different graphics display system, the options on the 3D Graphics System Configuration dialog box will be different from the ones shown here. You will need to refer to AutoCAD's documentation for more information.

Figure 3.11

*The 3D Graphics System
Configuration dialog box.*

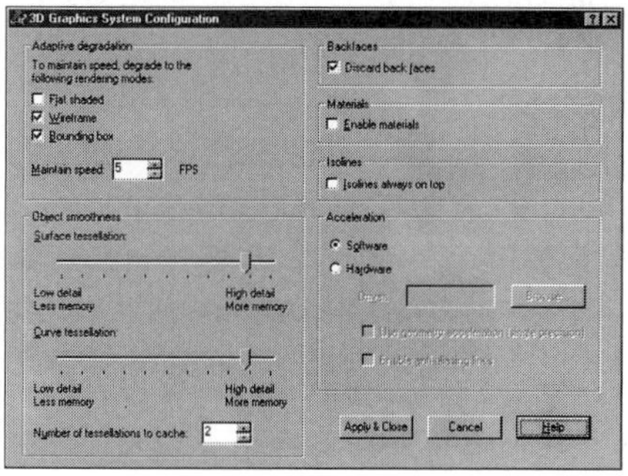

Current Pointing Device

The Current Pointing Device area controls options that relate to the pointing device. In this area, you can select the desired pointing device from a drop-down list, which displays the available pointing devices.

AutoCAD comes installed with two pointing device options. The first is the Current System Pointing Device option, which sets the current Windows pointing device (typically your mouse) as the AutoCAD pointing device. The second is the Wintab Compatible Digitizer option, which sets the Wintab Compatible Digitizer as current. (This option is only available if you have a Wintab compatible digitizer installed on your system.) If you choose the Digitizer option, you can specify whether AutoCAD accepts input from both a mouse and a digitizer, or ignores mouse input and accepts only digitizer input.

General Options

The General Options area allows you to control such features as whether you can open multiple drawings in a single AutoCAD session, whether the Startup dialog box displays when you launch AutoCAD, or whether you can use long symbol names. There are seven features you can control in this area, described as follows:

■ **Single-Drawing Compatibility Mode.** This toggle specifies whether a Single-Drawing Interface (SDI) or a Multi-Drawing Interface (MDI) is enabled in AutoCAD. If you select this option, AutoCAD opens only one drawing at a time. If you clear this option, AutoCAD can open multiple drawings. AutoCAD's Multiple Drawing Environment (MDE) feature is discussed in Chapter 1, "What's New in AutoCAD 2000."

■ **Show Startup Dialog Box.** This toggle controls whether the Startup dialog box appears when you start AutoCAD, or when you start a new drawing in the current AutoCAD session.

■ **Display OLE Properties Dialog Box.** This toggle controls the display of the OLE Properties dialog box when inserting OLE objects into AutoCAD drawings. OLE objects are discussed in detail in Chapter 23, "Effective Applications for OLE Objects in AutoCAD 2000."

- **Show All Warning Messages.** This toggle controls whether all dialog boxes that include a Don't Display This Warning Again option will appear. If you select this option, AutoCAD displays all dialog boxes with warning options, regardless of previous settings specific to each dialog box. If you clear this option, dialog boxes with the Don't Display This Warning Again option toggled on will not appear.

- **Beep on Error in User Input.** This toggle controls whether AutoCAD sounds an alarm beep when it detects an invalid entry.

- **Load acad.lsp with Every Drawing.** This toggle specifies whether AutoCAD loads your acad.lsp file into every drawing. If this option is cleared, only your acaddoc.lsp file is loaded into all drawing files. Clear this option if you do not want to run certain LISP routines in specific drawing files. The acad.lsp and acaddoc.lsp files are discussed in Chapter 22, "Introduction to AutoLISP Programming."

- **Allow Long Symbol Names.** Named objects can include up to 255 characters. Names can include letters, numbers, blank spaces, and any special characters not used by Windows and AutoCAD for other purposes. When this option is enabled, long names can be used for layers, dimension styles, blocks, linetypes, text styles, layouts, UCS names, views, and viewport configurations. This option is saved in the drawing.

dbConnect Options

The dbConnect Options area allows you to control two features that deal with connecting to external databases. The features are described as follows:

- **Store Links Index in Drawing File.** This feature stores the database index within the AutoCAD drawing file. Select this option to enhance performance during SQL queries. Clear this option to decrease drawing file size and to enhance the opening process for drawings with database information.

- **Open Tables in Read-Only Mode.** Specifies whether to open database tables in Read-only mode within the AutoCAD drawing file. Select this option to open tables in read-only mode, preventing unwanted edits. Clear this option to allow the table to be edited.

The dbConnect Options are discussed in detail in Chapter 24, "Using External Databases."

Setting User Preferences

The User Preferences tab controls various features within AutoCAD. These features include the behavior of your pointing device when you right-click, how AutoCAD responds to input of coordinate data, and how AutoCAD sorts objects during certain functions, as well as other features.

The User Preferences tab is organized into five areas, as shown in Figure 3.12. The five areas are as follows:

- **Windows Standard Behavior.** This area controls whether Windows behavior is applied when working in AutoCAD.

- **AutoCAD DesignCenter.** This area allows you to control settings that relate to the new AutoCAD DesignCenter (ADC).

- **Hyperlink.** You control settings that relate to the display properties of hyperlinks.

- **Priority for Coordinate Data Entry.** This area controls how AutoCAD responds to coordinate data input.

- **Object Sorting Methods.** This area provides options that determine the sort order of objects during specified AutoCAD functions.

Figure 3.12

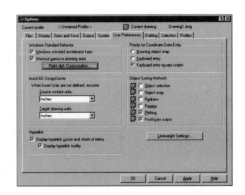

The User Preferences tab in the Options dialog box controls certain aspects of AutoCAD's behavior.

Windows Standard Behavior

The Windows Standard Behavior area allows you to control such features as whether AutoCAD accelerator keys adhere to Windows standards, and how your pointing device functions when right-clicking. There are three features you can control in this area, described as follows:

■ **Windows Standard Accelerator Keys.** This option controls whether AutoCAD follows Windows standards in interpreting keyboard accelerators (for example, CTRL+C equals COPYCLIP). If this option is cleared, AutoCAD interprets keyboard accelerators by using AutoCAD standards rather than Windows standards (for example, CTRL+C equals Cancel, and CTRL+V toggles among the viewports).

■ **Shortcut Menus in Drawing Area.** This option controls various things such as whether your pointing device displays a shortcut menu or responds as though you've pressed Enter when you right-click in the drawing area.

■ **Right-Click Customization.** This button displays the Right-Click Customization dialog box shown in Figure 3.13. This dialog box allows you to control how the right-click feature functions under certain conditions. You can determine whether the right-click repeats the last command, acts the same as though you'd pressed Enter, or displays the shortcut menu. You can also specify the behavior when you right-click under different circumstances, such as when no objects are selected, when one or more objects are selected, or when a command is in progress.

Figure 3.13

The Right-Click Customization dialog box controls how your pointing device behaves when you right-click.

AutoCAD DesignCenter

The AutoCAD DesignCenter area allows you to control how blocks are scaled when inserted in the current drawing. To scale blocks properly when they are inserted from another drawing, there are two units to consider. The first is the units used in the source drawing, and the second is the units used in the target (current) drawing. There are two features that allow you to control how AutoCAD deals with the units of the source drawing and the target drawing when no units are specified. They are described as follows:

- **Source Content Units.** Sets which units to automatically use for an object being inserted from another drawing into the current drawing when no insert units are specified with the INSUNITS system variable.

- **Target Drawing Units.** Sets which units to automatically use in the current drawing when no insert units are specified with the INSUNITS system variable.

The available unit settings for both options include Unspecified-Unitless, Inches, Feet, Miles, Millimeters, Centimeters, Meters, Kilometers, Microinches, Mils, Yards, Angstroms, Nanometers, Microns, Decimeters, Decameters, Hectometers, Gigameters, Astronomical Units, Light Years, and Parsecs. If Unspecified-Unitless is selected, the object is not scaled when inserted. AutoCAD DesignCenter (ADC) is discussed in detail in Chapter 12, "Applications for the New AutoCAD DesignCenter."

Hyperlink

The Hyperlink area allows you to control two options that deal with how your cursor reacts when it moves over a hyperlink in a drawing, and is described as follows:

- **Display Hyperlink Cursor and Shortcut Menu.** This option controls the display of the hyperlink cursor and shortcut menu. Select this option to have the hyperlink cursor appear whenever the pointing device moves over a hyperlink, and to make the shortcut menu available. The hyperlink shortcut menu provides additional options when you right-click over a hyperlink in a drawing. If this option is cleared, the hyperlink cursor never displays, and the shortcut menu is not available.

- **Display Hyperlink Tooltip.** This option controls the display of the Hyperlink tooltip. Select this option to have a hyperlink tooltip display when the pointing device moves over an object that contains a hyperlink.

Hyperlinks are discussed in Chapter 25, "Publishing on the Web."

Priority for Coordinate Data Entry

The Priority for Coordinate Data Entry area allows you to set one of three options that control whether running object snaps take precedence over coordinates entered from the keyboard, described as follows:

■ **Running Object Snap.** Select this option to have running object snaps override keyboard-entered coordinates at all times.

■ **Keyboard Entry.** Select this option to have keyboard-entered coordinates override running object snaps at all times.

■ **Keyboard Entry Except Scripts.** Select this option to have keyboard-entered coordinates override running object snaps at all times, except when running scripts.

Running object snaps are discussed in Chapter 6, "Accuracy in Creating Drawings with AutoCAD 2000."

Object Sorting Methods

When you create an object, AutoCAD adds it to the current drawing's database. As subsequent objects are created, they are added to the end of the database, in the order in which they are created. Therefore, objects are stored in the drawing's database in the order in which they are created.

When AutoCAD sorts through a drawing's database, it can do so by sorting in the order in which the objects are created, or by random selection of objects. The advantage of this sorting order is that you have predictability as to how an object is drawn or selected. For example, when plotting objects in the order in which they are created, you know objects created first will lie under objects created last. The disadvantage of this sorting order is it usually takes AutoCAD longer to sort through objects in the order in which they are created than to sort randomly.

The Object Sorting Methods area allows you to control how AutoCAD sorts through objects in certain situations. By toggling off or on options, you control the order in which AutoCAD deals with an object. If an option is selected (toggled on), AutoCAD sorts objects in the order of those created first to those created last. If an option is cleared (toggled off), AutoCAD sorts objects randomly. There are six options you can set to control object sort methods, described as follows:

- **Object Selection.** If this option is selected, the order in which AutoCAD selects objects is affected. For example, if two overlapping objects are chosen during object selection, AutoCAD recognizes the newest object as the selected object.

- **Object Snap.** If this option is selected, the order in which AutoCAD selects an object to snap to is affected. For example, if two overlapping objects are chosen when using object snap, AutoCAD recognizes the newest object as the object to snap to.

- **Redraws.** If this option is selected, when you use either the REDRAW or REDRAWALL command, AutoCAD redraws objects onscreen in the order in which they were created.

- **Regens.** If this option is selected, when you use either the REGEN or REGENALL command, AutoCAD regenerates objects onscreen in the order in which they were created.

- **Plotting.** If this option is selected, when you plot a drawing, AutoCAD plots objects in the order in which they were created.

- **PostScript Output.** If this option is selected, AutoCAD exports objects in the order in which they were created.

To demonstrate the effect of the options in the Object Sorting Methods area, review the two rectangles shown in Figure 3.14. The dashed rectangle on the right was drawn first, and the solid rectangle on the left was drawn second. When a regen is executed, with the Regens option in the Object Sorting Methods area toggled off, AutoCAD randomly selects objects. In this particular case, AutoCAD draws the solid rectangle on the left first, then draws the dashed rectangle on top of the solid rectangle. However, with the Regens option in the Object Sorting Methods area toggled on, AutoCAD is forced to sort objects in the order in which they were created. Consequently, AutoCAD draws the dashed rectangle first, and then draws the solid rectangle on top of the dashed rectangle, as shown in Figure 3.15.

Figure 3.14

Even though the dashed rectangle was created first, with Object Sorting turned off for regens, AutoCAD randomly selects objects and regenerates the dashed rectangle second and on top of the solid rectangle.

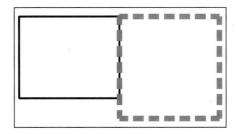

Figure 3.15

With Object Sorting turned on for regens, AutoCAD selects objects in the order in which they were created, and regenerates the solid rectangle second and on top of the dashed rectangle.

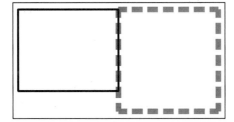

Lineweight Settings

The User Preferences tab also includes a Lineweight Settings button. This button displays the Lineweight Settings dialog box, which sets lineweight options, such as display properties and defaults, and also sets the current lineweight. You learn how to use lineweights in Chapter 5, "Using Linetypes and Lineweights Effectively."

Choosing Drafting Options

The Drafting tab controls settings that relate to object snaps, AutoTracking, and the AutoSnap marker. You can also control how AutoCAD displays alignment vectors, and the display size for the *aperture* (the square in the center of the crosshairs).

The Drafting tab is organized into five areas, as shown in Figure 3.16. The five areas are as follows:

- **AutoSnap Settings.** Controls settings that relate to object snaps.

- **AutoSnap Marker Size.** Sets the display size for the AutoSnap Marker. The *Marker* is a geometric symbol that displays the object snap location when the crosshairs move over a snap point on an object. By dragging the button left or right, you increase or decrease the size of the AutoSnap Marker.

- **AutoTracking Settings.** Controls the settings that relate to AutoTracking behavior.

- **Alignment Point Acquisition.** Controls the method of displaying alignment vectors in a drawing.

- **Aperture Size.** Sets the display size for the aperture. The aperture box is the box that appears inside the crosshairs when you select an object snap. By dragging the button left or right, you increase or decrease the size of the aperture.

Figure 3.16

The Drafting tab in the Options dialog box controls various snapping features.

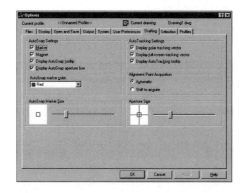

AutoSnap Settings

The AutoSnap Settings area allows you to control settings that affect the display and behavior of the crosshairs when using object snaps. There are five features you can control, described as follows:

- **Marker.** Controls the display of the AutoSnap Marker. When you move over an object, a geometric symbol appears, indicating the type of snap.

- **Magnet.** This option turns the AutoSnap magnet on or off. The *magnet* is an automatic movement of the crosshairs that locks the crosshairs onto the nearest snap point. The magnet is affected by the size of the AutoSnap Marker. With this option selected, when AutoCAD displays a marker, and the center of the crosshairs enters the marker symbol, AutoCAD snaps the crosshairs to the center of the Marker.

■ **Display AutoSnap Tooltip.** This option controls the display of the AutoSnap tooltip. A *tooltip* is a text flag that describes which object snap is active.

■ **Display AutoSnap Aperture Box.** This option controls the display of the AutoSnap aperture box. The *aperture box* is a box that appears inside the crosshairs when you select an object snap. When AutoSnap is activated, the AutoSnap markers appear only on objects that cross or lie within the aperture box.

■ **AutoSnap Marker Color.** This option allows you to specify the color of the AutoSnap marker to make viewing the AutoSnap Marker easier.

AutoSnaps and object snaps are discussed in detail in Chapter 6.

AutoTracking Settings

The AutoTracking Settings area allows you to control settings that affect the display and behavior of AutoCAD's new Polar Tracking feature. There are three features you can control from this area, described as follows:

■ **Display Polar Tracking Vector.** This option turns Polar Tracking on or off. When selected, this feature allows you to draw lines based on predefined angles. These predefined angles, known as *Tracking Vectors*, cause AutoCAD to snap to the Tracking Vector as you move the cursor during a drawing command.

■ **Display Full-Screen Tracking Vector.** This option controls the display of tracking vectors. By selecting this option, AutoCAD displays Tracking Vectors as infinite construction lines, extending through the snap point and the cursor and crossing the width of the screen. By clearing this option, the Tracking Vectors extend as rays from the snap point through the cursor to the edge of the screen.

■ **Display AutoTracking Tooltip.** This option controls the display of the AutoTracking tooltip. When selected, this option displays the AutoTracking tooltip.

Alignment Point Acquisition

The Alignment Point Acquisition area allows you to set the method used to display Polar Tracking alignment vectors in a drawing, either automatically or manually, and is described as follows:

- **Automatic.** If this option is selected, AutoCAD displays tracking vectors automatically when the aperture pauses over an object snap.

- **Shift to Acquire.** If this option is selected, AutoCAD displays tracking vectors only when you press the Shift key and move the crosshairs over an object snap.

When a Tracking Vector is set, a small *X* appears in the center of the object snap. The Polar Tracking feature is new to AutoCAD 2000. For detailed information about this new feature, see Chapter 7, "Creating Elementary Objects."

Controlling Selection Methods

The Selection tab controls settings that relate to object selection methods, display size for the pickbox, and AutoCAD's grips. The Selection tab is organized into four areas, as shown in Figure 3.17. The four areas are as follows:

- **Selection Modes.** Controls settings that relate to object selection methods.

- **Pickbox Size.** Controls the display size of the AutoCAD pickbox. The *pickbox* is the box that appears inside the crosshairs, and is used to select objects. By dragging the button left or right, you increase or decrease the size of the pickbox.

- **Grips.** Controls the settings that relate to grips. *Grips* are small squares displayed on an object after it has been selected.

- **Grip Size.** Controls the display size of AutoCAD grips. By dragging the button left or right, you increase or decrease the size of the grips.

Figure 3.17

The Selection tab in the Options dialog box controls object selection methods and various grip features.

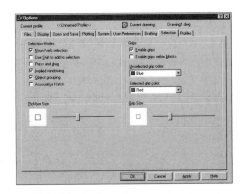

Selection Modes

The Selection Modes area allows you to control settings that affect AutoCAD's behavior when selecting objects. There are six features you can control, described as follows:

- **Noun/Verb Selection.** When selected, this option allows you to select an object to edit before invoking a command. You can also select multiple objects to edit before invoking the command. When cleared, you can still select multiple objects, but invoking a command clears the current selection set and prompts you to create a new selection set.

- **Use Shift to Add to Selection.** This option controls how multiple objects are added to a selection set during the selection process. When selected, you must press the Shift key to add selected objects to the selection set. When cleared, AutoCAD automatically adds multiple objects to the selection set as you select them.

- **Press and Drag.** When this feature is on, you can draw a selection window by clicking a start point and dragging the pointing device to the end point. If this option is cleared, the dragging feature is disabled, and you must draw a selection window by clicking a start point, and then clicking the end point.

- **Implied Windowing.** When this feature is on, a selection window is automatically initiated by avoiding objects when picking onscreen, and picking a blank area instead. After a blank area is picked, the selection window is invoked, and dragging the selection window from left to right initiates a window selection, which selects only those objects within the window's boundaries. Dragging from right to left initiates a crossing window selection, which selects objects within and crossing the window's boundaries. When cleared, you must invoke a selection window during a command by typing **w** to initiate a window selection, or by typing **c** to initiate a crossing window selection.

- ■ **Object Grouping.** When this feature is on, an entire object group is selected when you select one object in that group. When cleared, selecting an object that is in a group selects only that object. For detailed information about object grouping, see Chapter 11, "Advanced Geometry Editing."

- ■ **Associative Hatch.** When this feature is on, an associative hatch's boundary objects are selected along with the associative hatch. When cleared, selecting an associative hatch selects only the associative hatch, not its boundary elements. For detailed information about associative hatches, see Chapter 16, "Drawing Hatch Patterns."

Grips

The Grips area allows you to control settings that affect AutoCAD's grips. Grips are small squares displayed on an object after it has been selected. There are four features you can control, described as follows:

- ■ **Enable Grips.** When selected, this option controls whether grips are displayed on an object after you select it. You can edit an object with grips by selecting a grip to make it "hot." When the grip is hot, you may move the grip, or you can invoke the shortcut menu to select a command. When you clear this option, you disable grips.

- ■ **Enable Grips within Blocks.** This option controls how grips are displayed on a block after you select it. If this option is selected, AutoCAD displays all grips for each object in the block. You can edit an object with grips by selecting a grip to make it hot. When the grip is hot, you may move the object by the grip, or you can invoke the shortcut menu to select a command. If this option is cleared, AutoCAD displays one grip located at the insertion point of the block.

- **Unselected Grip Color.** You determine the color of an unselected grip from this drop-down list. AutoCAD displays an unselected grip as the outline of a small square.

- **Selected Grip Color.** You determine the color of a selected grip from this drop-down list. AutoCAD displays a selected grip as a small, filled square.

For detailed information about using grips, see Chapter 10, "Basic Object Editing," and Chapter 11, "Advanced Geometry Editing."

Saving the Options to a Profile

So far, you have dedicated quite a bit of time to reviewing the numerous features in the Options dialog box. As you may have noticed, there are well over one hundred different settings you can control. Although having over one hundred different settings provides you with the ability to set up your drawing environment exactly the way you want, it doesn't necessarily help if you must work on a different computer temporarily, one that doesn't have your custom setup. A worse situation occurs when someone else works on your computer while you're gone, and wipes out your custom settings with their own custom settings. Not only is it frustrating to be forced to redefine your custom settings, it may be impossible to completely restore them if you can't remember what your settings were.

Fortunately, the Options dialog box provides a simple method for saving and restoring your custom settings. By saving your custom settings in a Profile, not only can you restore settings if they are accidentally lost, but you can even copy your custom settings to another computer.

In the following exercise, you create two profiles and use them to restore default and custom settings in the Options dialog box.

CREATING PROFILES

1. Launch AutoCAD, and start a new drawing from scratch.

2. From the Tools menu, choose Options, then choose the Profiles tab.

   The Profiles tab appears in the Options dialog box, as shown in Figure 3.18. If no one has added any profiles, the only profile that displays in the Available profiles list is the <<Unnamed Profile>>, which is AutoCAD's default profile.

Figure 3.18

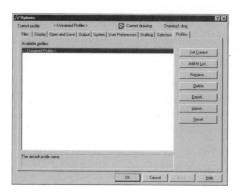

*AutoCAD's default profile,
the <<Unnamed Profile>>,
is the current profile.*

Notice that the current profile is listed at the top of the Options dialog box, and in Figure 3.18, the <<Unnamed Profile>> is the current profile. When you make changes in the Options dialog box, it is very important to note which profile is current because those changes are immediately saved to the current profile.

Next, you create two new profiles that contain the current default settings.

3. Click the Add to List button to display the Add Profile dialog box (see Figure 3.19).

4. In the Profile name text box, type **Default Profile**.

5. In the Description text box, type **This is AutoCAD's Default Profile**, as shown in Figure 3.19.

Figure 3.19

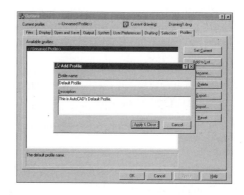

*The Add Profile dialog box
with the proper settings
for the Default Profile.*

6. Click the Apply & Close button.

7. Click the Add to List button again to create another profile.

8. In the Profile name text box, type **My Profile**.

9. In the Description text box, type **This is my custom Profile**, as shown in Figure 3.20.

10. Click the Apply & Close button.

Figure 3.20

The Add Profile dialog box with the proper settings for My Profile.

Two new profiles appear in the Available profiles list, as shown in Figure 3.21. The two new profiles you created currently have the same settings as the current profile. For this exercise, you will only modify settings in the newly created My Profile.

Figure 3.21

Two new profiles appear in the Available Profiles list.

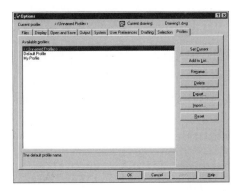

Modifying the settings in a profile is simple. To do so, make the profile you wish to modify the current profile. Then, make the desired changes to the settings.

11. In the Available Profiles list, select My Profile, then click the Set Current button. From this point on, any changes that you make to settings in the Options dialog box are saved to My Profile.

12. Choose the Display tab.

13. In the Window Elements area, set the Text Lines in Command Line Window value to 6.

14. In the Crosshair Size area, set the value to 25, as shown in Figure 3.22.

15. Click the Apply button, then click OK.

Figure 3.22

The new values are entered in the Display tab.

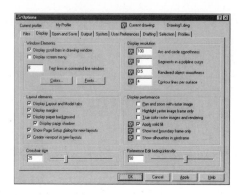

The new values are saved to the current profile, and AutoCAD resets the drawing environment based on the new values, as shown in Figure 3.23. Notice that the crosshairs are much larger than the default size (originally set to 5), and the command line window can now display six lines of text rather than the three lines displayed when you first launched AutoCAD.

Figure 3.23

The new values are saved to the current profile, and AutoCAD implements the changes.

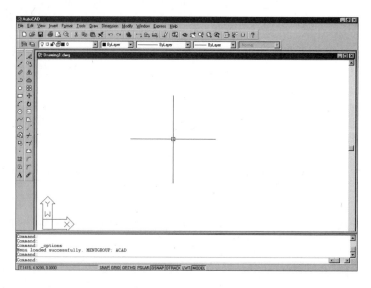

In addition to storing settings of the Options dialog box, Profiles can also save the display and position of toolbars. In the next exercise, you add a toolbar to My Profile.

ADDING TOOLBARS TO THE CURRENT PROFILE

1. Continuing from the previous exercise, move your pointer over any existing toolbar, and right-click.

2. From the shortcut menu, choose Customize to display the Toolbars dialog box (see Figure 3.24).

   If you select an empty box next to a toolbar name, AutoCAD adds the toolbar to the screen. For this exercise, be sure the ACAD menu is selected from the Menu Group drop-down list.

3. Scroll to the top of the Toolbars list, then choose the box next to Dimension to display the Dimension toolbar shown in Figure 3.24.

Figure 3.24

Toolbar settings can be saved with the current profile.

The profile named My Profile now contains the information necessary to display the Dimension toolbar, and to restore it to its current position on screen. To demonstrate this, continue with the exercise and change the current profile to Default Profile, which restores AutoCAD's original settings and removes the Dimension toolbar.

4. Click the Close button to dismiss the Toolbars dialog box.

5. From the Tools menu, choose Options, then choose the Profiles tab.

6. In the Available Profiles list, choose Default Profile, then click the Set Current button, then click OK.

When you set Default Profile as the current profile, AutoCAD restores its settings, removing the Dimension toolbar, and setting the crosshairs and the command line window back to their original sizes. To restore the Dimension toolbar, and increase the sizes of the crosshairs and the command line window, make My Profile the current profile.

The Profile tab has several commands that allow you to manage profiles. You can rename a profile by highlighting it in the Available Profiles list and clicking the Rename button. Similarly, you can delete unwanted profiles by highlighting them in the Available Profiles list and clicking the Delete button. (AutoCAD allows you to highlight only one profile at a time.)

You can also import and export profiles. To export a profile, highlight it in the Available Profiles list and click the Export button. When you export a profile, AutoCAD saves it as an .ARG file in the folder you select. After a profile is saved as an .ARG file, you can import it by clicking the Import button.

Finally, if you want to set a profile back to AutoCAD's original default settings, highlight the profile in the Available Profiles list and click the Reset button.

Summary

This chapter covered a great deal of information regarding AutoCAD's drawing environment. You learned about the Options dialog box and its more than 100 settings. In addition to the many features, you learned how to define support paths and how to control AutoCAD's display. You saw how to configure plotters and how to set your own user preferences. Most importantly, you practiced setting and saving those options as profiles.

By mastering the topics discussed in this chapter, you not only increased your knowledge on how to work with AutoCAD efficiently, but you gained a fundamental understanding of AutoCAD at a level few users possess.

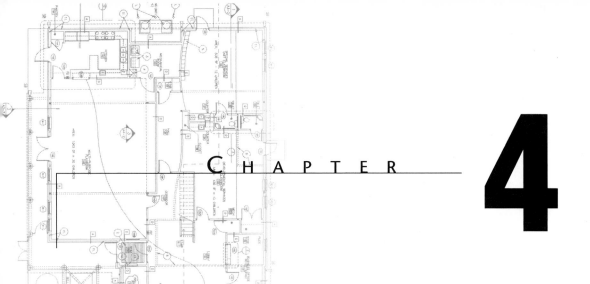

H A P T E R

4

ORGANIZING A DRAWING WITH LAYERS

Prior to the use of Computer Aided Design (CAD), projects consisted of dozens of mylar and vellum drawings that were ultimately printed as bluelines, and then taken into the field or the shop where they were used in the construction of buildings or the fabrication of parts. Although drawings are still necessary in the construction and fabrication process, today the person who initials the "Drawn by" box can more efficiently organize the information formerly drawn on those dozens of sheets by using AutoCAD's layers.

For those of us who have been in the business for a while, the pin-registered drafting days (where layers of mylar sheets were stacked one on top of the other to create a composite drawing) are just a faint memory. In those days, a single mylar sheet was dedicated to a particular item, such as the centerline and right-of-way lines for a street. Other mylars were dedicated to other specific items, such as curbs and gutters in the street, the street's underground gas lines, or sewer lines. Each mylar sheet contained a series of small holes along the top, and the holes on each sheet lined up, or registered, perfectly. When someone needed a composite drawing of, perhaps, the street's centerline, curb and gutter, and sewer line, those particular mylar sheets were stacked on top of one another on a special table with "register" pins along its top. Then, a blueline print was made of the stacked mylar sheets. By layering the desired mylars on top of one another, a composite sheet was created that contained the information needed for a specific purpose.

In AutoCAD, layers mimic individual pin-registered mylar sheets. By placing specific information on a layer, the former process of placing item-specific information on a mylar sheet is emulated. Because AutoCAD can contain an unlimited number of layers, you can expand upon the idea of composite sheets and include layers for the object geometry, dimensions, and notes, and so on. By using layers to organize your drawings, you can create a single model that serves many purposes and satisfies many needs.

This chapter discusses using layers to organize your drawings, and shows you how to use AutoCAD's Layer Properties Manager, improved for AutoCAD 2000. This chapter explores the following topics:

- Implementing layering standards
- Controlling the drawing's layer features
- Creating and assigning a color to new layers
- Locking layers
- Setting a layer filter

The New Layer Properties Manager

NEW
for R2000

In AutoCAD 2000, the Layer Properties Manager dialog box is new. Well, it's not really new, but it has been updated from its Release 14 predecessor. To begin with, in Release 14, it was called the Layer and Linetype Properties dialog box, and it contained two tabs: one for dealing with layers and the other for dealing with Linetypes. With AutoCAD 2000, the Linetype tab has been removed, and the Layer Properties Manager dialog box dedicates itself to dealing only with layers. (The Linetype tab now has its own dialog box, called the Linetype Manager, which is discussed in Chapter 5, "Using Linetypes and Lineweights Effectively.") In addition to its new name, the Layer Properties Manager also has several new features, including Lineweights, Plot Styles, and Plot/No Plot. Also, the layer listing display area is three times larger than before and adjustable, allowing you to view more layers and layer status information than before, as shown in Figure 4.1.

Figure 4.1

The Layer Properties Manager has several new features.

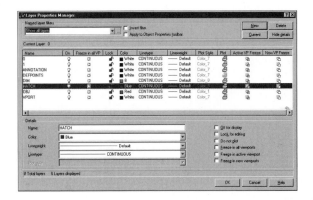

The Layer Properties Manager dialog box's new features, as well as those features found in previous versions, are explored in this chapter. But before you learn how to use the Layer Properties Manager to its fullest potential, in the next section you first learn about the importance of standardizing layer names.

Standardizing Layer Names

Whether you're the only person working with AutoCAD in your company, or one of several dozen, establishing standard layer names can increase your efficiency in layer management. By using layers to organize various elements in your drawing, you simplify the process of displaying the desired elements, which makes editing and plotting easier. For example, if your drawing has gas lines and sewer lines, but you only want to edit the gas lines, you can make your drawing visually easier to work with by turning off the layer on which the sewer lines were drawn.

Not only does organizing your drawing's elements by layers make editing and plotting easier, it also reflects on your level of skill as an AutoCAD technician. By following a preset layering standard and using it to organize objects in your drawing, you demonstrate your understanding of the importance of proper layer and object management. For example, the ability to quickly control which groups of objects are displayed by turning certain layers off or on can dramatically increase productivity, which demonstrates that you know what you're doing with AutoCAD.

Layer Name Considerations

The process of defining standard layer names can be daunting. Because the drawing you are creating represents only one portion of the project's life cycle, you must consider not only the number of layers and their names necessary to fulfill your needs, but also how many ways your drawing will be used by others. For example, will half-scale versions of your drawing be inserted into reports? If so, it may be necessary to place duplicate text on two different layers: one layer to hold text that is easy to read at full scale, and the other layer to hold duplicate text that is easily read at half scale. Will other departments or companies incorporate your drawing into theirs, creating a composite drawing? If so, you must establish layering standards that you both find acceptable. What different objects must you display on the set of hardcopy plots provided to the contractor for construction? Although a single model space drawing may contain both gas lines and sewer lines, your hardcopy plots must separate these two components, creating one set of plots showing only gas lines, and the other showing only sewer lines. Your understanding of the many ways your drawing will be used, and whether you properly develop and use layering standards, can make fulfilling all needs during a project's life cycle productively easy, or disastrously difficult.

Predefined Standards

Although there are many things you must consider when developing layer standards, the good news is that in reality, you probably don't have to do too much. Because AutoCAD has been around for nearly two decades, many companies have established their own internal layering standards. As a consequence, when you work for a company, you are typically issued a CAD Standards Manual, and are required to read it and use it in your day-to-day drafting activities. By using the company's layering standards, you ensure uniformity with all drawings.

NOTE

For information on CAD layering guidelines, browse E-Architect's Web site at www.e-architect.com, and search their site using the keyword "LAYER."

In addition to the layering standards, many companies have created drawing template files that already contain the proper layers. By using template files when starting a drawing, you are guaranteed that your drawing file has the layers you need, with each layer preset to the correct properties of color, linetype, and lineweight. You can learn more about creating your own drawing templates in

Chapter 2, "Starting a Drawing in AutoCAD 2000," in the section "Customizing and Saving a Template File."

Extended Layer Names

In prior releases of AutoCAD, when considering layering standards, the limitations imposed by AutoCAD were factored into the process. Previously, AutoCAD limited layer name lengths to 31 characters. Additionally, mixed casing of characters was ignored, and spaces were not allowed. These restrictions not only imposed limitations on creating descriptive layer names, but they often created problems when attaching xrefs because AutoCAD added the xrefs drawing name to the beginning of xref-dependent layers, which made it easy to exceed the 31-character limit. This in turn caused AutoCAD to abort opening the drawing.

With AutoCAD 2000, AutoCAD has extended the allowable length of layer names substantially. In AutoCAD 2000, layer names can now be 255 characters long. They can also include spaces, and AutoCAD preserves upper- or lowercasing of characters. With these enhancements, you can develop more meaningful, descriptive layer names.

NOTE

Although xref names are still appended to the beginning of xref-dependent layers, the xref's drawing name does not count toward the 255-character limit.

Although the extended features of layer names are good, you should use discretion when creating layering standards. For example, Figure 4.2 shows two different methods of using the new extended layer name features. The layer name on the bottom of the list reads, `This is the layer on which I placed all the existing sewer line text.`, and actually includes the period at the end. This layer name may be very descriptive, but it's not very practical in terms of layer name standards.

For example, if your drawing contains dozens, or even hundreds of layers, it is not easy to scroll down the list of layer names and locate the one for existing sewer line text because the layer name is so long. In contrast, the layer name in the middle of the list reads, `Existing Sewer Text.` This much shorter name relates the same information as its much longer counterpart, and allows users to easily peruse the layer list and find the correct layer. Because AutoCAD allows you to display names alphabetically, you can find the layer that holds existing sewer text by looking for it alphabetically. Additionally, this shorter version makes it easier to isolate the display of layer names using the Layer Properties Manager's layer filters, a feature described later in this chapter.

Figure 4.2

The new Layer Properties Manager allows for long layer names.

Controlling Object Properties

AutoCAD 2000 provides four object properties you can control through the Layer Properties Manager. The first two—color and linetype—are old-timers, having been included in previous versions of AutoCAD. The last two—lineweight and Plot Style— are new to AutoCAD 2000. The color, linetype, and lineweight properties affect object appearance when displayed on screen, and all four properties control the appearance of objects when plotted on paper.

Through the Layer Properties Manager, you can control the values of object properties. More importantly, the Layer Properties Manager provides a method of globally controlling properties. For example, by using the Layer Properties Manager to change a layer's color to red, you automatically change the color of all objects on that layer to red. This global method of changing the color of all objects by only changing one value in the Layer Properties Manager is a tremendous time-saver, especially if there are dozens, or even hundreds of objects on a layer. By using the Layer Properties Manager, you can simultaneously edit the color, linetype, lineweight, and Plot Style properties of numerous objects very quickly.

Although this global ability to edit objects is very powerful, it does have one catch: It only works when the properties for each object are set to ByLayer. Fortunately, AutoCAD provides a simple method for setting object properties to ByLayer. By understanding and controlling how AutoCAD assigns properties to objects, you can create objects whose property values are globally controlled through AutoCAD's Layer Properties Manager.

This section discusses how AutoCAD assigns properties to an object when it is created, and how to use the Layer Properties Manager to control the object's property values when they are set to ByLayer.

Assigning Properties to New Objects: The Object Properties Toolbar

When you create an object, AutoCAD automatically assigns the object to the current layer. Additionally, AutoCAD also assigns values of color, linetype, lineweight, and Plot Style. These four properties that AutoCAD assigns to an object are determined by the values displayed in the Object Properties toolbar. For example, to assign new objects the layer value of 0, and the color red, you select the desired values from the appropriate drop-down list in the Object Properties toolbar, as shown in Figure 4.3. After these values are set, when a new object is created, it is assigned to layer 0, and assigned the color red. To assign new objects to a different layer, simply choose the desired layer from the layer pull-down list.

Figure 4.3

The Object Properties toolbar sets the layer, color, linetype, lineweight, and Plot Style properties for new objects.

NOTE

AutoCAD's default layer is 0. Geometry created on layer 0 has unique properties with respect to blocks. Consequently, when creating new geometry for your project, you should typically create a new layer for the geometry, reserving layer 0 to create blocks with special properties. For more information on the relationship of layers and blocks, refer to Chapter 13, "Creating and Using Blocks."

The ByLayer Property Value

Notice that in Figure 4.3 the last three drop-down lists in the Object Properties toolbar all display the current property value as ByLayer. These last three lists are the object property values for linetype, lineweight, and Plot Style, respectively. When an object's property is set to ByLayer, it means those particular property values are controlled by the settings in the Layer Properties Manager. Therefore, with the property assignments shown in Figure 4.3, if you created a new object, its linetype, lineweight, and Plot Style values are controlled by the linetype, lineweight, and Plot Style values in the Layer Properties Manager. Consequently, to view the values for linetype, lineweight, and Plot Style, you must view the values for layer 0 in the Layer Properties Manager, as shown in Figure 4.4.

Figure 4.4

The Layer Properties Manager controls the color, linetype, lineweight, and Plot Style values for all objects whose different property values are set to ByLayer.

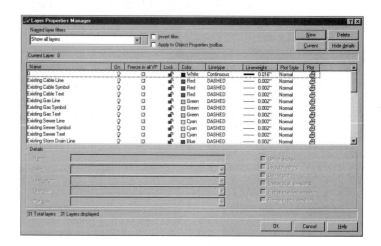

Remember that because the Object Properties toolbar is set to layer 0, all new objects are created on layer 0. This means that any properties set to ByLayer when an object is created are controlled by the property values for layer 0. As shown in Figure 4.4, the property values for layer 0 are as follows:

- Color = White

- Linetype = Continuous

- Lineweight = 0.016 inches

- Plot Style = Normal

NOTE

If the lineweights in your drawing display in millimeters (mm), you can switch to an inches format by choosing Lineweight from the Format menu. Then, from the Lineweight Settings dialog box, select the Inches option in the Units for Listing area. For more information, refer to Chapter 5.

AutoCAD uses these first three property values when drawing an object on screen, and AutoCAD uses all four property values when plotting an object on paper. Once again, AutoCAD looks to the property values in the Layer Properties Manager only when an object's properties are assigned as ByLayer.

It is important to note that although Figure 4.4 shows the ByLayer color value for layer 0 as white, newly created objects will be drawn in the color red. This is true because the Object Property toolbar shown in Figure 4.3 is set to the color red, and therefore explicitly assigns the color red to newly created objects. So although an object may reside on layer 0, and the ByLayer color value for layer 0 may be white, AutoCAD will display the object's color as red if the object's color is set explicitly in the Object Properties toolbar.

INSIDER TIP

> Always assign an object's property values as ByLayer. This provides you the ability to globally change color, linetype, lineweight, and Plot Style.

The Color Property

One of the simplest properties to understand is the color property. AutoCAD provides 256 colors to choose from, but your color choice should be influenced by two factors:

- How objects appear onscreen
- How objects appear on paper

For screen appearance, you should typically use various colors to help you differentiate between objects. By using an assortment of colors, you make viewing easier for objects that are drawn close together. However, when it comes to plotting objects on paper, there is more involved to an object's appearance than just color.

When plotting objects, AutoCAD allows you to assign lineweights by color. For example, when an object that is red is plotted, its lineweight may be 0.002 inches, whereas an object that is green may be plotted with a lineweight of 0.008 inches. The user determines these values at plot time by setting lineweight values in the Plot dialog box. For more detailed information on controlling lineweights when plotting, see Chapter 20, "Productive Plotting."

NOTE

> Quite often, the colors you assign to objects are determined by layering standards. If your company or your client has defined color assignments in their layering standards, you should use their color assignments instead of assigning your own.

The Linetype and Lineweight Properties

The *Linetype* property allows you to set the style of a linetype. A linetype style defines whether AutoCAD draws an object with a continuous, unbroken line, or with dashed or dotted lines. You can choose from a wide variety of non-continuous linetypes, and you can also select linetypes that have text in them. AutoCAD includes an assortment of linetypes, or you can create your own custom linetype styles.

The new *Lineweight* property, on the other hand, controls how heavy a line AutoCAD draws. In fact, the new Lineweight property performs the same function as the Plot dialog box described previously. Instead of assigning lineweights by color, however, it assigns the lineweight as a property. Consequently, you can display the lineweight on screen, as opposed to observing how wide a line is by plotting the objects. Therefore, you can set one object's lineweight very thin to make it appear subtle, and set another's lineweight much wider to make it appear bold, and then view the results on screen and without plotting.

NOTE

> Linetypes and lineweights are described in detail in Chapter 5.

In the following exercise, you use the Object Properties toolbar and the Layer Properties Manager to control the color, linetype, and lineweight of objects.

CONTROLLING AN OBJECT'S COLOR, LINETYPE, AND LINEWEIGHT

1. Open the drawing 04DWG01. The drawing displays a single horizontal red line.

2. From the Objects Properties toolbar, choose the Existing Gas Line layer from the drop-down list. (It's the fifth layer from the top.)

NOTE

If the entire layer name is too long to display in the layer drop-down list, hold your cursor over a layer name. After a few moments, AutoCAD displays the entire layer name in a text tip, as shown in Figure 4.5.

Figure 4.5

When viewing layer names from the Object Properties toolbar's layer drop-down list, hold the cursor over a shortened layer name to display its full name in the text tip.

3. Draw a circle with its center on the left end of the red line, and with a radius of 1 inch. Notice the circle is drawn with a thin, dashed, green line.

4. From the Object Properties toolbar, from the Color control drop-down list (the second list from the left), choose the color magenta.

5. From the Object Properties toolbar, from the Linetype control drop-down list (the third list from the left), choose the Continuous linetype.

6. From the Object Properties toolbar, from the Lineweight control drop-down list (the fourth list from the left), choose the 0.016"" line weight.

7. Draw a circle with its center on the right end of the red line, and with a radius of 1 inch. Notice that the circle is drawn with a heavy, continuous, magenta line, as shown in Figure 4.6.

Figure 4.6

The color, linetype, and lineweight properties can be set to ByLayer or set explicitly.

8. Notice how dramatically different the two circles are in Figure 4.6. Although both circles are drawn on the same layer, the circle on the right is assigned its color, linetype, and lineweight explicitly by the values in the Object Properties toolbar. The circle on the left, on the other hand, has its color, linetype, and lineweight values set to ByLayer. Therefore, AutoCAD draws the circle on the left based on the values of color, linetype, and lineweight set for the Existing Gas Line layer in the Layer Properties Manager, as shown in Figure 4.7.

Figure 4.7

The color, linetype, and lineweight values are highlighted for the Existing Gas Line layer in the Layer Properties Manager.

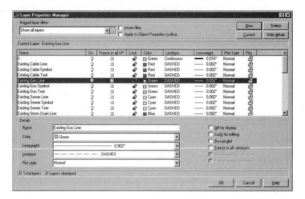

Next, you use the Layer Properties Manager to modify the color, linetype, and lineweight values.

9. From the Objects Properties toolbar, click the Layers button (the second button from the left). The Layer Properties Manager dialog box appears.

10. From the Existing Gas Line layer, under the Color column, choose the green box marked Green. The Select Color dialog box appears as shown in Figure 4.8.

Figure 4.8

The Select Color dialog box allows you to choose any one of 256 colors.

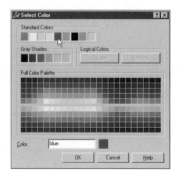

11. From the Select Color dialog box, choose the Blue color, then click OK. AutoCAD sets the Existing Gas Line layer color to blue.

12. From the Existing Gas Line layer, under the Linetype column, choose the DASHED linetype. The Select Linetype dialog box appears as shown in Figure 4.9.

Figure 4.9

The Select Linetype dialog box allows you to choose a layer's linetype.

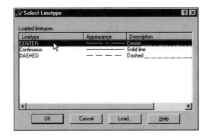

13. From the Select Linetype dialog box, choose the CENTER linetype, then click OK. AutoCAD sets the Existing Gas Line layer linetype to CENTER.

14. From the Existing Gas Line layer, under the Lineweight column, choose the 0.002"" lineweight. The Lineweight dialog box appears as shown in Figure 4.10.

Figure 4.10

The Lineweight dialog box allows you to choose a layer's lineweight.

15. From the Lineweight dialog box, choose the 0.016" lineweight, then click OK. AutoCAD sets the Existing Gas Line layer lineweight to 0.016", as shown in Figure 4.11.

16. From the Layer Properties Manager, click OK. AutoCAD updates the circle on the left to reflect the property changes made in the Layer Properties Manager, as shown in Figure 4.12.

Figure 4.11

The Existing Gas Line layer's new color, linetype, and lineweight are modified in the Layer Properties Manager.

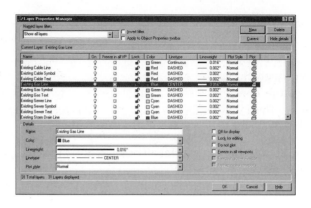

Figure 4.12

The circle on the left displays the new property values set in the Layer Properties Manager.

17. Notice that the appearance of the circle on the right did not change. This is true because the circle on the right had its properties set explicitly from the values you set in the Object Properties toolbar. Next, you complete this exercise by reassigning the properties of the circle on the right to ByLayer.

18. Choose the magenta circle on the right. AutoCAD highlights the object, indicating that it is selected.

19. From the Object Properties toolbar, from the Color control drop-down list, choose ByLayer.

20. From the Object Properties toolbar, from the Linetype control drop-down list, choose ByLayer.

21. From the Object Properties toolbar, from the Lineweight control drop-down list, choose ByLayer. AutoCAD redraws the circle on the right, as shown in Figure 4.13.

Figure 4.13

Choosing ByLayer from the Color, Linetype, and Lineweight control drop-down lists resets the selected circle's properties.

Notice that although the circle on the right remains selected, the Color, Linetype, and Lineweight controls display ByLayer as the current type. However, if you deselect the circle by pressing the Esc key twice, the values you originally set for color, linetype, and lineweight are redisplayed. This occurs because AutoCAD shows the currently selected object's property values in the Object Properties toolbar. This includes the selected object's layer and Plot Style assignments.

You can close the drawing without saving your changes. However, before exiting AutoCAD, be sure to deselect all objects, and then change the color, linetype, and lineweight values back to ByLayer in the Object Properties toolbar.

The Plot Style Property

NEW
for R2000

AutoCAD 2000 provides a new object property called *Plot Style*. This new property affects how objects appear when plotted by allowing you to assign a Plot Style to an object and override its color, linetype, and lineweight values. Additionally, Plot Styles allow you to specify end, join, and fill styles, as well as control output effects such as dithering, gray scale, pen assignment, and screening.

Plot Styles are intended to allow you to plot the same drawing in many different ways without making elaborate changes to the original color, linetype, and lineweight properties. By creating multiple Plot Style tables, you can create one plot of a drawing that displays objects with bold, heavy lines, and then plot the same drawing as a grayscale, all without making any changes to object color, linetype, or lineweight properties.

NOTE

For more detailed information on Plot Styles, see Chapter 20.

Controlling Object Behavior

In the previous sections, you learned how to control object properties that determine how an object looks when AutoCAD draws it onscreen, or plots it on paper. In this section, you learn how to control object behavior using the Layer Properties Manager. Specifically, you learn how to control object visibility, and to protect objects from accidentally being edited.

Layer Visibility

One handy feature of using layers to organize objects into logical groups is that you can use the Layer Properties Manager to manipulate groups of objects by modifying layer settings. In addition to controlling object colors and linetypes as previously discussed, you can control object visibility. With a simple click of your pointing device, entire groups of objects become invisible on screen, and non-plottable.

AutoCAD allows you to control object display on screen with two features in the Layer Properties Manager. You can turn layers off and on, and you can freeze and thaw layers. In any case, objects that reside on the layer that's turned off or frozen become invisible and non-plottable. Additionally, a new feature called Plot/Don't Plot is introduced with AutoCAD 2000, and it allows you to control whether objects appear on a layer plot. This is true even though the objects are visible on screen.

In the next few sections, you learn about the important differences of turning layers off and on, as opposed freezing and thawing, and you are introduced to the new Plot/ Don't Plot feature.

Turning Layers Off Versus Freezing Layers

When you place objects on a layer, you can control their visibility by turning the layer on and off or by freezing and thawing the layer. When you turn a layer off or freeze the layer, objects that are on the layer become invisible. They do not display on screen, and they do not plot.

Although the end result of making objects invisible by either turning layers off or by freezing layers may seem the same, there is a very important reason why AutoCAD makes both methods available. When a layer is *turned off*, even though the objects on the layer become invisible, AutoCAD still performs certain zoom and regeneration calculations on the invisible objects. In contrast, when a layer is *frozen*, AutoCAD does not include the objects on the frozen layer in zoom or regeneration calculations.

By freezing objects, you can dramatically reduce zoom and regeneration times, which improves your productivity. For example, suppose you have a drawing with thousands of objects. If you only need to edit objects that reside on one layer, then you can increase your productivity by freezing the layers on which all other unneeded objects reside. By freezing the layers that have unneeded objects, you eliminate those objects from AutoCAD's calculations, reducing the time AutoCAD takes for certain zoom and regeneration functions.

So, if freezing layers improves productivity, why not just always freeze layers instead of turning them off? Every time you thaw a layer that had been frozen, it causes AutoCAD to perform a regeneration, also called a *regen*. (For those who are new to AutoCAD, a regen is often the most frustrating thing a user can experience because the user must sit idly by, unable to do anything, waiting for AutoCAD to complete its regen calculations.) In contrast, turning layers off (or on) does not cause a regen. Therefore, turning layers off makes sense when you typically need to view the objects in your drawing during an editing session, and only want to temporarily make them invisible. In contrast, freezing layers is the proper choice when there are objects you don't need to view during a lengthy editing session. By freezing them, AutoCAD visually removes the objects from the screen, but no longer includes the objects on the frozen layers in future regens, which can dramatically reduce overall regen times.

In the following exercise, you experience the difference turning layers off versus freezing layers has on the ZOOM EXTENTS command.

TURNING LAYERS OFF VERSUS FREEZING LAYERS

1. Open the drawing 04DWG02. The drawing displays a circle and a square, side-by-side.

2. From the Object Properties toolbar, from the Layer control drop-down list, choose the light bulb symbol for the Circle layer, as shown in Figure 4.14, then pick any spot in the drawing. AutoCAD turns the Circle layer off, and removes the circle from the screen.

Figure 4.14

Choosing the light bulb symbol from the Layer drop-down list in the Object Properties toolbar turns off the Circle layer.

3. At the Command prompt, type **Z**, then type **E**. AutoCAD starts the ZOOM command, then executes the Extents option, resulting in the display shown in Figure 4.15.

Figure 4.15

With the Circle layer turned off, AutoCAD calculates the position of the invisible circle when a ZOOM EXTENTS is executed.

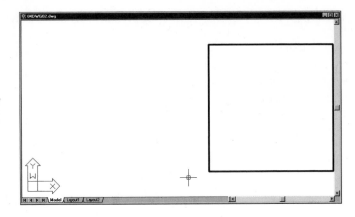

4. From the Object Properties toolbar, from the Layer control drop-down list, choose the sun symbol for the Circle layer, as shown in Figure 4.16, then pick any spot in the drawing. AutoCAD freezes the Circle layer off.

Figure 4.16

Choosing the sun symbol from the Layer drop-down list in the Object Properties toolbar freezes the Circle layer.

5. At the Command prompt, type **Z**, then **E**. AutoCAD starts the ZOOM command, then executes a ZOOM EXTENTS.

Notice now that after AutoCAD performs a ZOOM EXTENTS, the rectangle displays in the center of the screen, as shown in Figure 4.17. By comparing Figures 4.15 and 4.17, you can see the different effect turning a layer off versus freezing the same layer has when performing a ZOOM EXTENTS. When the layer is turned off, AutoCAD still takes the time to calculate the position of the circle. When the layer is frozen, AutoCAD ignores the circle, and only calculates the position of the square.

Although the difference in regen time initiated by the ZOOM EXTENTS was probably imperceptible, the time difference becomes much more obvious when the frozen layer contains thousands of objects.

When finished, you may close the drawing without saving your changes.

Figure 4.17

*With the Circle layer
frozen, AutoCAD does not
calculate the position of
the invisible circle when a
ZOOM EXTENTS is executed.*

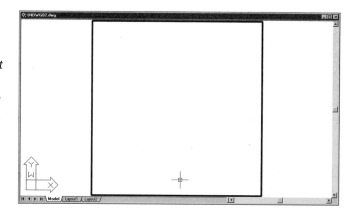

Freezing Globally Versus Freezing in the Active Viewport

In the previous section, you learned about the differences between turning off layers and freezing layers. Though the exercise didn't discuss it, the methods used to turn off and freeze layers were global. In other words, they affect all objects in all viewports. Although turning off or freezing layers in all viewports is generally acceptable, there are circumstances when it is not. Specifically, when you are working with paper space layouts that have multiple viewports, you may want objects on a layer to be visible in one viewport, but invisible in another. This effect is accomplished by freezing layers in the active viewport. For detailed information on freezing layers in the active viewport, see Chapter 19, "Paper Space Layouts."

The New Plot/Don't Plot Feature

AutoCAD 2000 introduces a new and very useful feature in the Layer Properties Manager: The *Plot/Don't Plot* toggle. This feature controls whether objects on a layer are plotted by toggling the feature on or off. What makes this feature useful is that objects that are visible on screen are prevented from plotting if the Plot/Don't Plot feature is toggled off. Therefore, you can display and use objects such as construction lines on screen, but prevent them from plotting on paper.

I N S I D E R   T I P

> You can use AutoCAD's Plot Preview feature to view the results of layers set to not plot. For more information, see Chapter 20.

NOTE

In previous releases, you could simulate the Plot/Don't Plot feature by creating a layer called DEFPOINTS, and placing objects on it that you wanted to view and edit on screen, but did not want to plot. The problem with this technique was that you could only have one DEFPOINTS layer, and therefore the layer could become cluttered with an array of objects that you needed to use on screen, but did not want to plot.

The Plot/Don't Plot feature affects blocks and external references (xrefs) in unique ways. For example, you can control which objects in a block won't plot by setting their layers to not plot. Also, you can prevent an entire block from plotting by setting the layer on which the block is inserted to not plot. This is true for xrefs, as well. Therefore, you can control whether entire blocks and xrefs plot, or you can control whether specific objects in blocks and xrefs plot. For more information, refer to Chapter 20.

Locking Layers

When editing a drawing with multiple layers, you probably will mistakenly select objects that you don't want to edit. Although this is frustrating, the good news is that you can control which objects are editable by locking and unlocking the layers on which they reside. The ability to *lock* layers enables you to display the objects on a layer without selecting any objects on that layer. More importantly, although objects on a locked layer are not selectable for edit commands, they can be snapped to using object snaps.

Therefore, the layer locking feature is most useful when working on drawings in which you simply need to see the objects on a layer for reference and object snapping purposes, and you want to ensure that you don't accidentally alter the objects. By locking a layer, you ensure that the objects on that layer are safe from unintended edits.

NOTE

You can place blocks on a layer that is locked and even though they may contain data from other layers, you will not be able to erase the blocks.

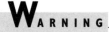

> You can create data on a locked layer and then be unable to modify the same object just created. This can often be a trap during lisp routines creating data but on locked layers.

Using Layer Filters

As discussed previously, organizing objects into groups using layer names is very useful. But although it's good to use layer names to organize your drawing, if the layers become too numerous, their usefulness degrades. The usefulness of layers degrades because too many layers makes it cumbersome to use the Layer Properties Manager to locate the specific layer whose properties you need to edit, or whose behavior you need to change. The more layers a drawing has, the more their usefulness degrades.

More than likely, you will work on drawings that contain dozens, hundreds, or even thousands of layers. This is especially true when you attach xrefs to the current drawing, adding to its list of layers the layer lists of each xref. Therefore, the likelihood that you will be presented with the challenge of working with too many layers is very high.

Fortunately, AutoCAD's Layer Properties Manager provides a feature called *Layer Filters* that allows you to control which layer names display by defining certain parameters. By using Layer Filters, you can realize the benefit of organizing your drawing with layers, and not be overwhelmed by viewing too many layer names in the Layer Properties Manager.

In this section, you explore how to create and apply Layer Filters to make working with layers easier.

Applying Layer Filters

Applying a Layer Filter is pretty simple. By opening the Layer Properties Manager dialog box, and then selecting a saved filter from the Named Layer Filters drop-down list, AutoCAD instantly adjusts the display of layers in the Layer Properties Manager's layer list.

Each AutoCAD drawings automatically includes three standard Layer Filters:

- Show All Layers
- Show All Used Layers
- Show All Xref-Dependent Layers

With these three layer filters, you can make viewing layer lists much easier. Additionally, the Layer Properties Manager includes two options that allow you to perform the following actions:

- Invert the current layer filter.
- Apply the current layer filter to the Layer control in the Object Properties toolbar.

In the next exercise, you learn how to use these standard layer filter features.

APPLYING THE LAYER PROPERTIES MANAGER'S STANDARD FILTER FEATURES

1. Open the drawing 04DWG03. The drawing displays a column of lines, symbols (block inserts), and text.

2. From the Object Properties toolbar, click the Layers button. AutoCAD displays the Layer Properties Manager dialog box.

3. From the Named Layer Filters drop-down list, choose the Show All Used Layers filter. AutoCAD invokes the selected layer filter.

   The Show All Used Layers filter displays only layer names on which objects reside. If a layer does not have any objects drawn on it, then it is not displayed in the Layer Properties Manager's layer list. This filter is useful in determining which layers are no longer used by objects, and can therefore be deleted.

   Next, you apply the Invert Filter feature.

4. From the Named Layer Filters area, select the Invert Filter check box. AutoCAD inverts the current layer filter, displaying only those layers that do not have objects on them, as shown in Figure 4.18.

Figure 4.18

The current layer filter is inverted, and therefore only displays layer names with no objects on them.

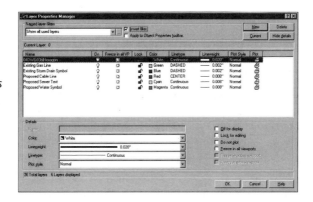

Notice in the lower-left corner of the Layer Properties Manager that AutoCAD indicates 36 total layers, but only six layers are displayed. Once again, the currently displayed layers have no objects on them. Consequently, you could delete these layers to reduce the number of layer names cluttering the layer list.

Next, you apply the Apply to Object Properties Toolbar feature.

5. From the Named Layer Filters area, select the Apply to Object Properties Toolbar check box, then click OK.

6. From the Object Properties toolbar, choose the down arrow to open the Layer control, as shown in Figure 4.19. This drawing is used in the next exercise. If you wish to continue the next exercise at a later time, be sure to save the changes you made during this exercise.

Figure 4.19

The current inverted layer filter is applied to the Layer control list in the Object Properties toolbar.

Notice that the current inverted layer filter is applied to the Layer control list in the Object Properties toolbar. This feature is very useful when you need to frequently switch between a few layers in a drawing that contains many layers.

The other layer filer that AutoCAD provides is the Show All Xref-Dependent Layers filter. This filter displays only the names of layers that reside in xrefs. By selecting this filter, you can easily view only the layers of attached xrefs. By inverting this filter, you can display all layers that do not reside in attached xrefs. This provides you the ability to remove unwanted xref layer names from the layer list and the Layer control list on the Object Properties toolbar.

Next, you learn how to create your own layer filters.

Creating Named Layer Filters

In the previous section, you learned how to use the standard layer filters provided with AutoCAD. Although these filters are useful, they probably will not fulfill all your filtering needs. To satisfy all your needs, the Layer Properties Manager allows you to create your own layer filters.

In the next exercise, you learn how to create custom layer filters.

CREATING CUSTOM LAYER FILTERS

1. Continue using the drawing from the previous exercise.

   From the Object Properties toolbar, click the Layers button. AutoCAD displays the Layer Properties Manager dialog box.

2. From the Named Layer Filters area, click the ellipses (...) button. (The ellipses button is next to the Named Layer Filters list down arrow.) AutoCAD displays the Named Layer Filters dialog box.

3. In the Filter Name list box, type **Symbols Only**.

4. In the Layer Name text box, type ***symbol**. The asterisk (*) is a *wild card* character that tells AutoCAD to accept any characters in front of the word "symbol." The Named Layer Filters dialog box appears as shown in Figure 4.20.

5. Click the Add button. AutoCAD adds the new filter to the list of available filters, then sets the filter fields back to their default value.

6. Click the Close button. AutoCAD displays the Named Layer Filters dialog box.

7. From the Named Layer Filters drop-down list, choose the Symbols Only filter. AutoCAD invokes the selected layer filter.

8. From the Named Layer Filters area, click the Invert Filter check box to turn it off. AutoCAD displays only those layer names that end with the word "Symbol," as shown in Figure 4.21. This drawing is used in the next exercise. If you wish to continue the next exercise at a later time, be sure to save the changes you made during this exercise.

Figure 4.20

The Named Layer Filters dialog box allows you to create custom layer filters.

Figure 4.21

The custom layer filter Symbols Only displays layer names that end with the word "Symbol."

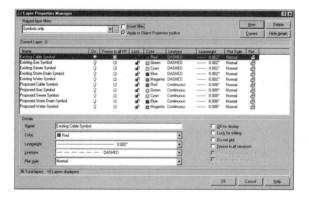

By using the numerous fields available in the Named Layer Filters dialog box, you can precisely identify the layers you want to display. Additionally, by inserting asterisks in the layer name, you can filter for layers whose differing names have only certain words in common.

Next, you learn how to more precisely identify layers.

CREATING PRECISE CUSTOM LAYER FILTERS

1. Continue using the drawing from the previous exercise.

2. From the Named Layer Filters area, click the ellipses (...) button. AutoCAD displays the Named Layer Filters dialog box.

3. In the Filter Name list box, type **Symbols and Text not Red**.

4. In the Layer Name text box, type ***symbol,*text**. (Be sure to include the asterisks, and do not insert a space after the comma.) You can enter multiple layer names by separating each name with a comma.

5. In the Color text box, type **~red**. The tilde (~) instructs AutoCAD to exclude layers whose color is red. The Named Layer Filters dialog box appears as shown in Figure 4.22.

Custom layer filters can include multiple layer names, and can exclude certain properties by placing a tilde symbol in front of the property value.

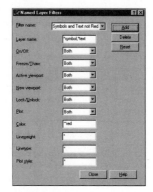

6. Click the Add button. AutoCAD adds the new filter to the list of available filters, then sets the filter fields back to their default value.

7. Click the Close button. AutoCAD displays the Named Layer Filters dialog box.

8. From the Named Layer Filters drop-down list, choose the Symbols and Text not Red filter. AutoCAD invokes the selected layer filter. AutoCAD displays only those layer names that end with the word "Symbol" or "Text," and excludes layers whose color is red, as shown in Figure 4.23.

When finished, you may close the drawing without saving your changes.

The custom layer filter Symbols and Text not Red displays only those layer names that end with the word "Symbol" or "Text," and excludes layers whose color is red.

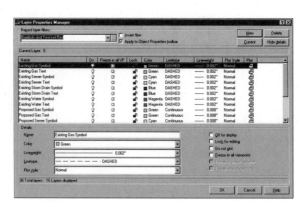

Using Wild Card Characters in Layer Filters

As you just learned, you can use wild card characters such as the asterisk (*), comma, and tilde (~) to control which layers display in the Layer Properties Manager's layer list. There are, in fact, 10 different wild card characters you can use with layer filters, and these wild card characters can be used in combination with each other. The following table lists the available wild card characters and their purposes.

Table 4.1

Wild Card Characters

Character	Description
# (Pound)	The # symbol matches any single numeric character. Suppose you have layer names that are labeled with numbers 1 through 400. You can filter for layer names 200 through 299 by typing **2##** as the layer name filter.
@ (At)	The @ symbol matches any single alpha character. Suppose you have two layers, named NORTH and SOUTH. You can filter for both these layer names by typing **@O@TH** as the layer name filter.
. (Period)	The . symbol matches any single non-alphanumeric character. Suppose you have layers named GAS-TXT, GAS TXT, and GAS_TXT. Notice that the alpha characters are separated by a hyphen, a space, and an underscore character, respectively. You can filter for these three layer names by typing **GAS.TXT** as the layer name filter.
* (Asterisk)	The * symbol matches any character sequence, and can be used at the beginning, middle, or end of the filter. Suppose you have layers whose names include the word LINE. You can filter for these layer names by typing ***LINE*** as the layer name filter.
? (Question Mark)	The ? symbol matches any single character. Suppose you have layers named GAS-TXT, GAS2TXT, and GASeTXT. You can filter for these three layer names by typing **GAS?TXT** as the layer name filter.

continues

Table 4.1, continued

Wild Card Characters

Character	Description
~ (Tilde)	If the ~ symbol is the first character in the filter, then it excludes the filter value. Suppose you have layers that include the name LINE. You can filter for layers that do not include the name LINE by typing ~*LINE* as the layer name filter.
[ ] (Brackets)	The [ ] symbol matches any one of the characters enclosed in the brackets. Suppose you have four layers whose names are 1LINE, 2LINE, 3LINE, and 4LINE. You can filter for the layers whose names begin with 1, 2, or 4 by typing [124]* as the layer name filter.
[~] (Tilde Brackets)	The [~] symbol excludes each of the characters enclosed in the brackets that follow the tilde. Suppose you have four layers whose names are 1LINE, 2LINE, 3LINE, and 4LINE. You can exclude the layers whose names begin with 1, 2, or 4 by typing [~124]* as the layer name filter.
- (Hyphen)	The – symbol used inside brackets allows you to specify a single-character range of values. Suppose you have four layers whose names are 1LINE, 2LINE, 3LINE, and 4LINE. You can filter for the layers whose names begin with 1, 2, or 3 by typing [1-3]* as the layer name filter.
, (Comma)	The , symbol separates multiple filters, allowing you to enter more than one filter in a text box. Suppose you have four layers whose names are 1LINE, 2LINE, 3LINE, and 4LINE. You can filter for the layers whose names begin with 1 or 3 by typing 1*,3* as the layer name filter.

The wild card characters listed in Table 4.1 can be used for several of the filters in the Named Layer Filter dialog box, including the following:

■ Layer name

■ Color

■ Lineweight

■ Linetype

■ Plot style

By using the wild card characters, you can develop powerful layer filters that display only the precise layers you want to view in the Layer Properties Manager or the Object Properties toolbar.

Summary

Managing objects through the new Layer Properties Manager improves your ability to organize your drawing. By using Layer Properties Manager's features, you can control object properties such as color, linetype, and lineweight, and you can control object behavior, such as object visibility.

In this chapter, you learned about the importance of layer standards. You also learned about the difference between turning off layers versus freezing them. Finally, you worked with layer filters, and discovered how you can use wild card characters to create sophisticated layer filters.

CHAPTER 5

USING LINETYPES AND LINEWEIGHTS EFFECTIVELY

Linetypes and lineweights provide a method for you to create objects that differentiate themselves from other objects. By applying different linetypes and lineweights to different objects in your drawing, you make objects distinguishable among themselves. By using linetypes and lineweights properly, you create a drawing that visually transfers its meaning to the viewer.

But using linetypes and lineweights effectively requires more than just making a drawing look good. It requires an understanding of the features AutoCAD 2000 provides for controlling the appearance of linetypes and lineweights. These features include setting defaults, controlling scale globally and individually, and customization. By learning about the range of features offered by AutoCAD, you can exploit the usefulness of linetypes and lineweights to their fullest. By understanding their features, you have the foundation needed to use linetypes and lineweights effectively.

This chapter discusses linetypes, which were available in previous versions of AutoCAD, and explores lineweights, which are new to AutoCAD 2000. This chapter covers the following subjects:

- Assigning linetypes
- The linetype scale factor
- Creating simple and complex linetypes
- Assigning lineweights
- Understanding lineweight display behavior

Working with Existing Linetypes

For many years AutoCAD has provided linetypes, which allow you to create drawings whose objects are more easily discernable. A *linetype* is a series of dashes and/or dots that have a specified spacing that is then applied to the object. By assigning different linetypes, you make identical objects such as lines and polylines stand out as unique entities in your drawing. Linetypes are one of the most useful tools in AutoCAD for getting your drawing's meaning across to viewers.

In this section, you learn about several features of linetypes that range from the simple, such as assigning linetypes to objects, to the advanced, such as creating your own custom complex linetypes.

Assigning Linetypes

Assigning a linetype to an object is a straightforward process, and can be accomplished by one of two methods. You can assign linetypes globally, through AutoCAD's Layer Properties Manager, or you can assign linetypes individually, from the Object Properties toolbar. Both methods are easy to use, and accomplish the same thing: assigning a new linetype to an object.

However, although both methods accomplish the same thing, one method definitely has an advantage over the other. By applying a linetype to a layer in the Layer Properties Manager dialog box, you control the appearance of all objects on that layer. This means you can instantly reapply a new linetype to hundreds of objects with a few simple clicks of your pointing device and change the linetype setting for a given layer.

In contrast, although assigning linetypes to objects individually does allow you to control their individual appearances, the process of individually changing the linetypes for dozens, or even hundreds, of objects can require tremendous amounts of editing time. Therefore, it is often best to avoid setting linetypes individually, and use the Layer Properties Manager to control a layer's linetype assignment.

Insider Tip

Always set the object linetype creation mode to ByLayer in the Objects Properties toolbar. This ensures all new object linetypes are controlled through the Layer Properties Manager, which provides a single point of control for modifying object linetypes.

For more information on controlling linetypes globally through the Layer Properties Manager, and individually through the Object Properties toolbar, refer to Chapter 4, "Organizing a Drawing with Layers," in the section "The Linetype and Lineweight Properties."

Loading Linetypes

In Chapter 4, in the section "The Linetype and Lineweight Properties," you work though an exercise that shows how easy it is to assign linetypes to objects. In one of the exercise's steps, you assign a linetype globally using the Layer Properties Manager. You select the desired linetype from the Select Linetype dialog box, shown in Figure 5.1.

Figure 5.1

The Select Linetype dialog box allows you to choose a layer's linetype.

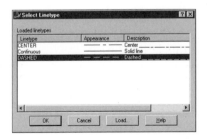

You will notice that there are not a lot of linetypes to choose from in the Select Linetype dialog box. However, AutoCAD 2000 is installed with dozens of predefined linetypes that you can use. You simply need to load them into your drawing.

In the following exercise, you learn how to load linetypes into the current drawing.

LOADING LINETYPES INTO THE CURRENT DRAWING

1. Open the drawing 05DWG01. The drawing displays a single dashed blue line.

2. From the Objects Properties toolbar, choose the Layers button (the second button from the left). The Layer Properties Manager dialog box displays.

3. From the Existing Gas Line layer, under the Linetype column, choose the DASHED linetype. The Select Linetype dialog box appears, as shown in Figure 5.1.

4. From the Select Linetype dialog box, click the Load button. The Load or Reload Linetypes dialog box appears.

5. From the Load or Reload Linetypes dialog box, scroll down the list of available linetypes, and choose the GAS_LINE linetype, as shown in Figure 5.2.

Figure 5.2

You can choose from a variety of predefined linetypes in the Load or Reload Linetypes dialog box.

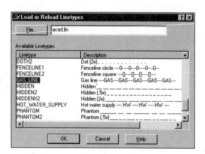

6. Click OK. The Select Linetype dialog box appears, and the GAS_LINE linetype appears in the Loaded Linetypes list, as shown in Figure 5.3.

Figure 5.3

The newly loaded GAS_LINE linetype appears in the Loaded linetypes list and can now be assigned to a layer.

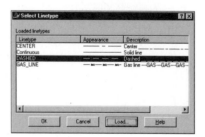

Notice in the Loaded Linetypes list that the DASHED linetype is still highlighted. When you click OK, the currently highlighted linetype is assigned to the Existing Gas Line layer. Therefore, to assign the newly loaded GAS_LINE linetype to the Existing Gas Line layer, the GAS_LINE linetype must highlighted.

7. Select the GAS_LINE linetype, then click OK. AutoCAD assigns the newly loaded GAS_LINE linetype to the Existing Gas Line layer, as shown in Figure 5.4.

Figure 5.4

The newly loaded GAS_LINE linetype is assigned to the Existing Gas Line layer.

8. Click OK. AutoCAD redraws the line using the GAS_LINE linetype, as shown in Figure 5.5.

9. You may close the drawing without saving the changes.

Figure 5.5

AutoCAD redraws the line using the GAS_LINE linetype.

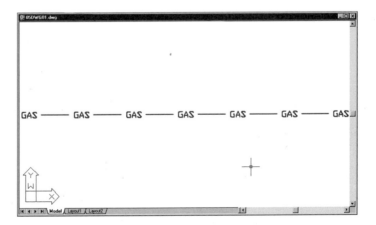

By using the Load or Reload Linetypes dialog box, you can assign a wide range of linetypes to layers or to objects. But assigning a linetype is only half the solution to displaying objects with linetypes. The other half is to apply the proper linetype scale. In the next section you learn about the Linetype Scale Factor.

Working with the Linetype Scale Factor

The ability to assign a linetype to an object is very useful for representing different things in your drawing. By assigning a linetype, you help viewers more clearly understand the meaning of different objects. But assigning a linetype to an object, either globally or individually, is only half of the necessary solution to making your drawings easier to understand with linetypes. The other half of the solution is assigning the linetype a scale factor.

For the most part, a linetype is simply a series of repeated dashes and spaces. The lengths of the dashes and spaces are initially defined by the linetype's description. However, the definition only specifies how many units long a dash or a space is. Depending on the scale of your drawing, the linetype may not be visible because the dashes and spaces appear too close together or too far apart. To compensate, AutoCAD allows you to assign a *linetype scale factor* to your drawing.

The linetype scale factor multiplies the current linetype style by the desired factor. As with linetypes, linetype scale factors can be assigned globally or individually. Unlike linetypes, however, you cannot assign a global linetype scale factor ByLayer using the Layer Properties Manager. When you set the linetype scale factor, it immediately affects all linetypes, no matter which layer they are on.

You change the linetype scale factor globally using the Linetype Manager dialog box, accessed by choosing Linetype from the Format menu. By clicking the Show Details button, you display the linetype details shown in Figure 5.6.

To change the global linetype scale, enter a new value in the Global Scale Factor text box. After this value is entered, and you click OK, AutoCAD immediately assigns the global scale factor to the display of all linetypes.

To assign a linetype individually to new objects, enter the desired linetype scale in the Current Object Scale text box. Don't be confused by the title of this particular text box. When you use this text box to define a linetype scale, you are actually applying it to all *new* objects, not the currently selected object.

Figure 5.6

The Linetype Manager dialog box allows you to change the linetype scale factor.

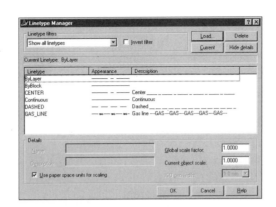

Although it may be useful to assign an individual linetype scale to new objects, it's also possible to edit the linetype scale of existing objects. To do so, click the Properties button on the Standard Toolbar, shown in Figure 5.7. Next, select the object(s) whose linetype scale factor you wish to change. Finally, enter the new linetype scale factor to apply to the objects in the Object Properties Manager dialog box as shown in Figure 5.8, then press Enter. AutoCAD assigns the new linetype scale factor individually to the selected objects. For more information about using the Object Properties Manager dialog box to assign new values to selected objects, see Chapter 11, "Advanced Geometry Editing."

Figure 5.7

The Properties dialog box is accessed from the Properties button on the Standard Toolbar.

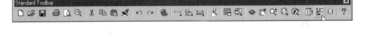

Figure 5.8

The Properties dialog box allows you to change many values for selected objects, including their individual linetype scale factor.

The final tool for controlling the linetype scale factor controls how linetypes appear in Layout viewports. This tool is necessary because AutoCAD allows you to create as many viewports in your Layout tab as you need to display your drawing. More importantly, you can apply a different zoom factor to each viewport. As a result, if one viewport is zoomed in close to an object, and another is zoomed out, the linetype will display differently in each viewport. Figure 5.9 illustrates two viewports that show the same object; each viewport is zoomed at a different scale. Notice the object's dashed lines in the left viewport appear much smaller than in the viewport on the right. This is the effect when the Use Paper Space Units for Scaling feature is cleared (when there's no check in the box). With this feature cleared, the dashed lines display proportionally to their zoom factor.

Figure 5.9

The dashed lines of the same object appear different in each paper space viewport with the Use Paper Space Units for Scaling feature cleared.

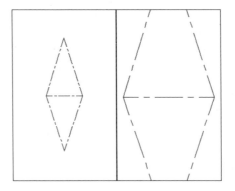

In contrast, review the same drawing with the Use Paper Space Units for Scaling feature selected, shown in Figure 5.10. Notice that the length of the dashes and the spaces are the same in both viewports. This is the effect the Use Paper Space Units for Scaling feature has on linetypes. Either method for scaling linetypes is acceptable. Whether the feature is selected or cleared depends on your needs.

There is one other property you should be aware of when dealing with linetypes and polylines, called *linetype generation*. Polylines are made up of a series of lines and arcs, connected at their endpoints by vertexes. When a linetype is assigned to a polyline, AutoCAD will either generate the linetype as one continuous line, or will generate the linetype anew at each vertex. In Figure 5.11, the polyline at the top has its linetype generated at each vertex, whereas the polyline at the bottom has its linetype generated as one continuous line. Once again, either method is acceptable, and the method you use depends on your needs.

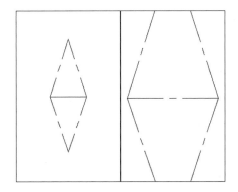

Figure 5.10

The dashed lines of the same object appear identical in each paper space viewport with the Use Paper Space Units for Scaling feature selected.

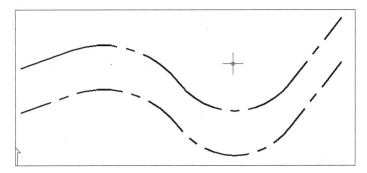

Figure 5.11

The Linetype Generation property affects how linetypes appear when assigned to polylines. The property is disabled on the polyline at the top.

INSIDER TIP

The Linetype Generation property can be enabled or disabled using the Properties dialog box.

Creating and Using Custom Linetypes

In a previous section in this chapter, you learned about loading linetypes into the current drawing. By loading linetypes, you present yourself with a fairly large and diverse selection of linetypes to use in your drawing. By loading the desired linetypes into the current drawing, you can create a drawing that more easily transfers the meaning of your drawing to the viewer.

Unfortunately, even though AutoCAD 2000 ships with a fairly large number of ready-to-use linetypes, you will probably come across situations in which the ready-made linetypes don't fit your needs. Whether your discipline is architecture, mechanical, electrical, civil, or surveying, your diverse needs will almost certainly exceed the variety of linetypes shipped with AutoCAD.

To compensate for the insufficient number and variety of linetypes provided, AutoCAD allows you to create your own linetypes. Additionally, there is no limit to the number of linetypes you can create to meet your needs. No matter what your discipline, you can use AutoCAD to create the linetypes you need to use in your drawings.

This section discusses the two types of linetypes you can create in AutoCAD. Most of your needs can be met by creating the first type, called simple linetypes. For situations in which an annotated linetype is required, you can create the second type, called complex linetypes. By creating your own simple and complex linetypes, you can produce a drawing that easily transfers its meaning to the viewer.

The Simple Linetype Definition

As its name implies, *simple linetypes* are relatively simple to create. In fact, you can create a simple linetype during your current session of AutoCAD by starting the command-line version for the LINETYPE command, and typing in just a few values. More importantly, you can instantly use the new linetype, and apply it to objects in your current drawing.

NOTE

> Both simple and complex linetypes are stored in ASCII text files that are appended with .LIN. It is possible to create and edit linetypes directly in this file, as discussed later in this chapter, in "The Complex Linetype Definition."

In the following exercise, you learn how to create simple linetypes during the current AutoCAD session.

CREATING SIMPLE LINETYPES

1. Open the drawing 05DWG02. The drawing displays a single horizontal line.

2. At the command line, type **-LINETYPE** (be sure to include the hyphen at the beginning). AutoCAD starts the command-line version of the LINETYPE command, and prompts you to create, load, or set a linetype.

NOTE

Only the command-line version of the LINETYPE command provides the ability to create simple linetypes within AutoCAD. The Linetype Manager dialog box does not offer this capability.

3. At the command line, type **C** to create a new linetype. AutoCAD prompts you to enter a name for the new linetype.

4. At the command line, type **Short Dash** for the new linetype name. AutoCAD displays the Create or Append Linetype File dialog box.

    As mentioned previously, AutoCAD saves linetype definitions in ASCII text files appended with .LIN. By default, AutoCAD lists its own standard linetype definition file, ACAD.LIN, as the file in which to save your new linetype definition. For this exercise, you will create a new linetype definition file.

INSIDER **T**IP

In practice, it is best to leave AutoCAD's standard files, such as ACAD.LIN, in their original condition. Customizations you make to AutoCAD should be stored in your own custom files.

5. In the Create or Append Linetype File dialog box, enter **MYLINES** in the File Name text box, as shown in Figure 5.12.

Figure 5.12

The new linetype file is named MYLINES.

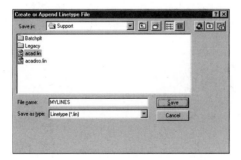

6. Click Save. AutoCAD creates the new linetype definition file, then dismisses the dialog box and prompts you to enter a descriptive name for the new linetype.

7. At the command prompt, type **This is a short dash** then press Enter. AutoCAD prompts for the linetype definition code, and begins the line of code for you.

The linetype definition code always starts with the letter "A" followed by a comma (**A,**). Because this is how all lines of code begin when defining linetypes, AutoCAD automatically specifies it for you. What AutoCAD expects you to enter now are the series of dashes and spaces you want to have to represent the linetype. All values are entered as real numbers, with positive values defining dash lengths, and negative numbers defining the length of spaces. A zero value represents a dot (a dash of zero length). A comma separates each number.

8. At the command prompt, type **0.25,-0.125** then press Enter. AutoCAD creates the new linetype definition, adding it to the new MYLINES.LIN linetype definition file. Then, it repeats the prompts to create, load, or set a linetype additional linetypes.

9. Press Enter to exit the LINETYPE command.

I N S I D E R   T I P

Upon completing a new linetype creation sequence, if you save the linetype to the ACAD.LIN file, AutoCAD will automatically load the linetype for immediate use.

The series of command-line prompts and the appropriate responses are shown in Figure 5.13. Now that the new linetype is defined, the next step is to assign it to the line in the drawing and see what it looks like.

Figure 5.13

The series of command-line prompts and the appropriate responses to create a new linetype.

```
AutoCAD Text Window - 05DWG03.dwg
Edit

Command: -linetype

Current line type:  "ByLayer"
Enter an option [?/Create/Load/Set]: c

Enter name of linetype to create: Short Dash

Creating new file

Descriptive text: This is a short dash
Enter linetype pattern (on next line):
    A,0.25,-0.125

New linetype definition saved to file.

Enter an option [?/Create/Load/Set]:

Command:
```

10. Click the Layers button in the Object Properties toolbar. AutoCAD displays the Layer Properties Manager.

11. Choose the Continuous linetype in the Linetype column. AutoCAD displays the Select Linetype dialog box.

12. Click the Load button. AutoCAD displays the Load or Reload Linetypes dialog box.

13.   Click the File button. AutoCAD displays the Select Linetype File dialog box.

14.   Choose the MYLINES.LIN file, as shown in Figure 5.14, then click Open. AutoCAD displays the Short Dash linetype in the Load or Reload Linetypes dialog box, as shown in Figure 5.15.

Figure 5.14

Choose the MYLINES.LIN file to display the newly created linetype.

Figure 5.15

The newly created Short Dash linetype appears.

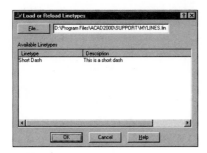

15.   Choose the Short Dash linetype, then click OK. AutoCAD loads the new linetype into the current drawing, and displays it in the Select Linetype dialog box, as shown in Figure 5.16.

Figure 5.16

The newly created Short Dash linetype is loaded into the current drawing.

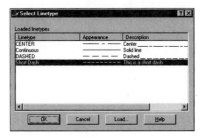

16. Choose the Short Dash linetype, then click OK. AutoCAD assigns the new linetype to layer 0.

17. Click OK to dismiss the Layer Properties Manager dialog box. AutoCAD redraws the line with the new linetype, as shown in Figure 5.17.

18. This drawing is used in the next exercise.

Figure 5.17

The newly created Short Dash linetype is assigned to the horizontal line.

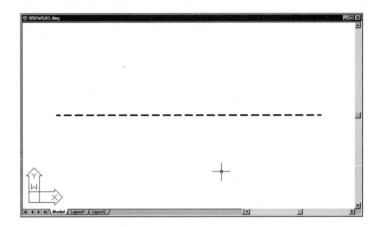

As you just learned, creating a simple linetype during an AutoCAD session truly is simple. Keep in mind that you can create as many simple linetypes as you need, and if you desire, you can save new linetype definitions in the MYLINES.LIN file. You can also create new linetype definition files to help you organize your linetypes. For example, you can create a UTILITY.LIN linetype definition file to store all utility-related linetypes.

Now that you know how to create simple linetypes, it's time to move on to the next level. Next, you learn how to create complex linetypes.

The Complex Linetype Definition

As its name implies, creating complex linetypes is a little bit more difficult than creating simple linetypes. But don't let its name intimidate you. The fact is that creating complex linetypes is almost as easy as creating simple linetypes. The main difference is that complex linetypes can't be created within AutoCAD using the

-LINETYPE command. Instead, you create them by entering linetype parameter values directly into a linetype definition file.

In the next exercise, you learn how to create complex linetypes using an ASCII text editor.

CREATING COMPLEX LINETYPES

1. Continue using the drawing from the previous exercise, or open the drawing 05DWG03. The first step in creating a complex linetype is to open the MYLINES.LIN file in an ASCII text editor.

2. From the command line, type **Notepad** to open this text editor.

3. Type **MYLINES.LIN** at the request for file to edit, then press Enter. Notepad opens the linetype definition file.

NOTE

If Notepad cannot find the MYLINES.LIN file, use Notepad to browse to the ACAD2000/ SUPPORT folder where the MYLINES.LIN file is located, then open the file.

For this exercise, you will modify the Short Dash simple linetype you already created. Complex linetypes contain two main elements. The first element is the same definition as a simple linetype, which describes the dashes and spaces in the linetype. The second is the text or shape that also displays in the linetype.

4. Change the first real number to **1.25**, and the second one to **-0.5**. This increases the length of the dashes, and the length (or gap) of the spaces.

5. Add the following text to the end of the Short Dash linetype values: **,["OIL",STANDARD,S=0.2,R=0.0,X=-0.1,Y=-0.1],-0.5**.

The Short Dash linetype values should now read as follows:

`A,1.25,-0.5,["OIL",STANDARD,S=0.2,R=0.0,X=-0.1,Y=-0.1],-0.5`

Recall that the first two real numbers define the length of the dash and the length of the space, respectively. Next is the code within the brackets, which defines the various parameters of the text to display within the complex linetype. After the closing bracket, another space is added, in this case, its value is set to –0.5. Notice that commas separate all values. For a detailed description of the values within the brackets, see Table 5.1.

6. In Notepad, choose File, Save. Notepad saves the modified linetype definition file.

7. In AutoCAD, click the Layers button in the Object Properties toolbar. AutoCAD displays the Layer Properties Manager.

8. Choose the Short Dash linetype in the Linetype column. AutoCAD displays the Select Linetype dialog box.

9. Click the Load button. AutoCAD displays the Load or Reload Linetypes dialog box.

10. Click the File button. AutoCAD displays the Select Linetype File dialog box.

11. Find and choose the MYLINES.LIN file, then click Open. AutoCAD displays the Load or Reload Linetypes dialog box.

12. Choose Short Dash then click OK. AutoCAD displays the Reload Linetype dialog box, asking if you want to reload the linetype.

    Because the previous exercise used this same linetype, you will have to reload the linetype in order to use it.

13. Click Yes. AutoCAD reloads the linetype into the current drawing.

14. Choose the Short Dash linetype, then click OK. AutoCAD assigns the modified linetype to layer 0.

15. Click OK to dismiss the Layer Properties Manager dialog box, then type **REGEN** and press Enter. AutoCAD redraws the line with the new complex linetype, as shown in Figure 5.18.

16. You may close the drawing without saving your changes.

Figure 5.18

The newly modified Short Dash linetype is assigned to the horizontal line.

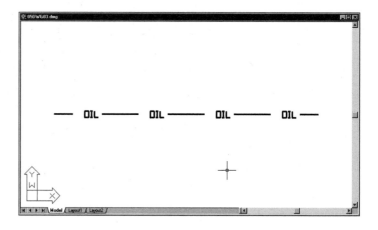

Table 5.1

Complex Linetype Text Values

Value	Description
OIL	The first value is the text string that is displayed in the linetype, in this case, OIL. Notice that the text value is enclosed in quotes.
STANDARD	The next value is the text style. You may enter any text style. Just be sure the one you use is loaded in the current drawing. For this exercise, AutoCAD's default STANDARD text style is used.
S=0.2	The next value is the text's scale. This value is multiplied by the selected text's height value. Because the height value of the STANDARD text style is set to zero, AutoCAD interprets the S value as the height literally, in this case, 0.2.
R=0.0	Next is the rotation value: the amount that the text is rotated relative to the line, in this case, 0. By setting the value to 0, as the line changes direction, including through curves, the text aligns itself parallel to the line. If the value is set to any other angle, the text is rotated at each point along the line where it occurs by the specified angle.
	Although R= indicates rotation *relative* to the line, you can define a rotation value with A=, which signifies *absolute* rotation of the text with respect to the origin. In other words, all text occurences along the line point in the same direction, regardless of their position to the line. Additionally, the value can be appended with a d for degrees (if omitted, degree is the default), r for radians, or g for grads. If rotation is omitted, 0 relative rotation is used.
X=-0.1,Y=-0.1	The X and Y values represent the offset of the text relative to the line. Typically, you will set both these values as negative real numbers, and at half the complex text's scale.

In the previous exercise, you actually accomplished two things. First, you edited an existing simple linetype. Second, you created a complex linetype. When creating both simple and complex linetypes, a little trial and error is usually necessary to achieve the desired results. Notice that after you saved the edited ASCII text file, you left Notepad running with the linetype definition file still open. Even so, you were able to reload the Short Dash linetype in AutoCAD to view it. The ability to leave a file open in Notepad while loading it in AutoCAD to view the results is very useful.

Using Shape Files in Complex Linetype Definitions

In the previous exercise, you learned how to create a complex linetype with text. You can also create complex linetypes with shape files. A *shape file* contains code that defines shapes that you can use over and over. For example, many of AutoCAD's text fonts are actually shape files. (They're the files that end with .SHX.) In addition to the text fonts, AutoCAD also ships with a shape file called LTYPESHP.SHP, which you can review and edit in an ASCII text editor. You can also create your own shape files, and use them to store your custom shape definitions.

NOTE

Shapes files are saved as ASCII text files with a .SHP ending, and can be viewed and edited in an ASCII text editor. However, for AutoCAD to use the shape definitions in the shape file, you must compile the shape file. Compiled shape files end with .SHX, and cannot be read by an ASCII text editor.

You define a complex linetype that uses shape files in much the same way as you did with text in the last exercise. You begin the definition with any dash and space code you may desire, then add the complex linetype code. The code for the shape is almost exactly the same as the code for text.

The following text string defines a complex linetype using a shape named CIRC1 from the LTYPESHP.SHX file:

```
A,1.25,-0.5,[CIRC1,LTYPESHP.SHX,S=0.2,R=0.0,X=-0.2,Y=0.0],-0.5
```

Notice that the preceding complex linetype definition is almost identical to the one in the last exercise. The major differences are that the text name and the text style are replaced. Table 5.2 defines the two major differences:

Table 5.2

Complex Linetype Shape Values

Value	Description
CIRC1	The first value that is displayed is the shape definition's name, in this case, CIRC1. The shape definition resides in a shape definition file. A single shape definition file can contain many shape definitions. Notice that in the case of shapes, their names are not enclosed in quotes.
LTYPESHP.SHX	The next value is the compiled shape definition file name. The file must be in AutoCAD's search path. A good location to save this file is in AutoCAD's Support folder.

The previous complex linetype definition creates a linetype as shown in Figure 5.19.

Figure 5.19

The CIRC1 shape definition is used to create a new complex linetype.

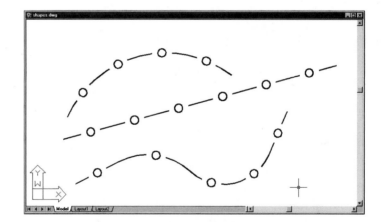

INSIDER TIP

Shape files involve the creation of complex, cryptic code, and are beyond the scope of this book. You can read about creating shape files in AutoCAD's Customization Manual (Chapter 3, "Shapes, Fonts, and PostScript Support," in the section "Creating Shape Definition Files").

In the first portion of this chapter, you learned about working with linetypes. Next, you learn about a new feature introduced with AutoCAD 2000, called lineweights.

Working with Lineweights

NEW for R2000

AutoCAD 2000 introduces a new feature called *lineweights*, which allows you to affect the appearance of objects. Just as linetypes make similar objects, such as lines and polylines, stand apart from each other, so, too, lineweights can make individual objects more easily identifiable.

In previous releases of AutoCAD, you could assign widths to polylines, which perform a function similar function to that of lineweights. The problem was that you could assign widths only to polylines—not lines, not circles, and certainly not text. Another problem with assigning widths to polylines was its unfriendliness. If a polyline was already created with the wrong width, you had to edit it to change the width. More importantly, unless you had access to specialized AutoLISP routines, you could edit the width of polylines only one at a time. In contrast, lineweights allow you to assign widths to a wide range of objects, including text, and assign the widths individually, globally, and even by layer using AutoCAD's Layer Properties Manager.

In this section, you learn about assigning lineweights to objects. More importantly, you learn how the appearance of lineweights is affected under different circumstances.

Assigning Lineweights

The topic of assigning lineweights is much the same as discussed for assigning linetypes: You can do it either globally through the Layer Properties Manager, or individually through the Object Properties toolbar. And, as in the argument presented in the "Assigning Linetypes" section, it is strongly suggested that you avoid assigning lineweights individually because doing so makes editing the lineweights of many objects a daunting, unproductive task.

If you are new to AutoCAD, you will probably find yourself tempted to pick just a single object and reassign its lineweight individually. After all, it is a very easy thing to do. You just pick the object, choose the desired lineweight from the pull-down list on the Object Properties toolbar, and you're done. But chances are, you will regret setting the lineweight individually as your drawing grows more and more complex, containing hundreds, or perhaps thousands, of objects. It is much better in the long run to consistently assign a lineweight globally using the Layer Properties Manager, even if it means creating a new layer for just that one object and assigning that layer the desired lineweight. By doing so, you create an understanding not only with yourself, but with anyone else who may work on your drawing, that lineweights are always edited using the Layer Properties Manager. This understanding provides a consistent pattern for everyone to use when editing objects.

For more information on controlling lineweights globally through the Layer Properties Manager, and individually through the Object Properties toolbar, refer to Chapter 4 in the section "The Linetype and Lineweight Properties."

Understanding Lineweight Behavior

Lineweights display differently under different circumstances. For example, while working in model space, lineweights are displayed by a certain number of pixels. Consequently, as you zoom in closer to a line, the number of pixels displaying the lineweight does not change. If a lineweight in model space is displayed as four pixels, it's always displayed as four pixels, no matter how far you zoom out or how close you zoom in. Therefore, the lineweight always appears as the same width. In contrast, while working in paper space (now referred to as a *layout* in AutoCAD 2000), lineweights are displayed at their true width. If a lineweight of 0.25 mm is assigned, then AutoCAD displays the line as 0.25 mm wide in the layout. Therefore, as you zoom in closer, the line appears wider. In other words, the lineweights of objects drawn in a layout display in real-world units. There is another feature of lineweights that you can control. When in model space, if you assign lineweights to objects, you can alter their apparent scale so they appear thinner or wider visually. This apparent scale does not affect lineweight widths when viewed in a layout or when plotted. Therefore, you can dynamically alter lineweights in model space to make viewing objects easier, without adversely affecting how they plot.

In the next exercise, you learn how lineweights act in model space and in a layout, and how to alter their apparent scale in model space.

UNDERSTANDING LINEWEIGHT BEHAVIOR

1. Open the drawing 05DWG04. The drawing opens a layout that displays objects drawn in both model space and paper space, as shown in Figure 5.20. The circle, triangle, line, and the text Model Space are drawn in model space. The text Paper Space is drawn in paper space in the Layout tab. The solid rectangle is the edge of the floating viewport, and the dashed rectangle represents the plotting limits.

Figure 5.20

The drawing in a layout view has several objects drawn in model space, including the text Model Space. The text Paper Space is drawn in paper space.

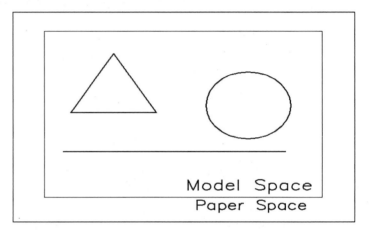

2. From the View menu, choose Zoom, Window, then pick a zoom window that surrounds the two text objects, as shown in Figure 5.21. Notice that the lineweights of both text strings appear equal in width. More importantly, they also appear wider. This occurs because you are viewing the layout in paper space mode. Therefore, AutoCAD displays the lineweights at their real-world size. As you zoom in closer, the lines appear wider.

Figure 5.21

In paper space, the lineweights of the two text objects appear wider as you zoom in closer.

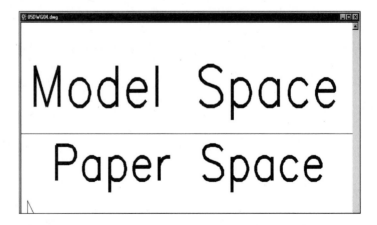

3. From the View menu, choose Zoom, Previous. The view again appears as shown in Figure 5.20.

4. Choose the Model tab (located near the bottom-left of the screen). AutoCAD switches to model space, and the model space objects display, as shown in Figure 5.22. (Although the objects in the figure appear with a heavy lineweight, your drawing may look different.)

Figure 5.22

The model space view of the objects.

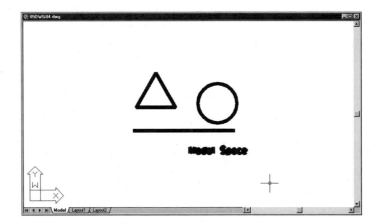

5. From the View menu, choose Zoom, Extents. AutoCAD zooms in closer to the objects, a shown in Figure 5.23. Notice that the lineweights of the objects did not get wider as you zoomed in. This occurs because in model space, the number of pixels that are used to display a lineweight does not change as you zoom in closer.

Figure 5.23

The lineweights of the model space objects do not get wider as you zoom in closer.

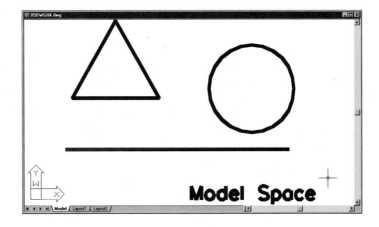

6. From the Format menu, choose Lineweight. The Lineweight Settings dialog box appears, as shown in Figure 5.24.

The Lineweights Settings dialog box allows you to control various features of lineweights.

7. Pick and drag the Adjust Display Scale button along its slide bar all the way to the right, then click OK. The lineweights will update to appear wider on screen, as shown in Figure 5.25.

The Adjust Display Scale feature affects how wide lineweights appear on screen in model space.

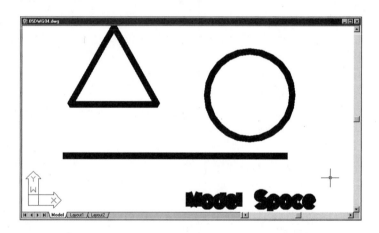

8. Choose the Layout 1 tab. AutoCAD switches to Layout 1, and displays objects in paper space, as shown in Figure 5.26. Notice that the lineweights are not as wide as they were in model space. Once again, this occurs because objects in the layout appear at their real-world scale. AutoCAD therefore ignores the Adjust Display Scale setting while in paper space and when plotting.

Figure 5.26

The Adjust Display Scale feature does not affect how wide lineweights appear on screen in paper space layouts.

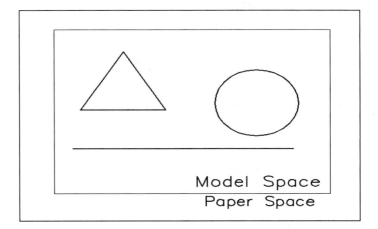

One last feature you should be aware of is how to control whether lineweights display onscreen. You can turn off lineweight display by clicking the LWT button in the AutoCAD 2000 status bar. By clicking this button, you toggle lineweights off and on. However, this button does not affect how lineweights plot.

Summary

In this chapter, you learned about working with linetypes and lineweights effectively. You reviewed assigning linetypes to objects, and you worked through an exercise on how to load linetypes. You reviewed how to control the linetype scale factor, both globally and individually. You also worked with custom linetypes, creating both simple and complex linetypes.

In the section discussing lineweights, you learned how to control the width of lines AutoCAD uses to draw objects. You learned you can assign lineweights by layer or individually. You learned that lineweights behave differently in model space and paper space. You also worked with controlling how lineweights appear onscreen in model space, by adjusting their apparent scale without affecting their width in paper space or when plotted.

Linetypes and lineweights provide tools that allow you to easily differentiate one object from another, even when the objects are of similar types, such as lines and polylines. By using linetypes and lineweights effectively, you make your drawing easier to understand, and transfer the meaning of your drawing to the viewer.

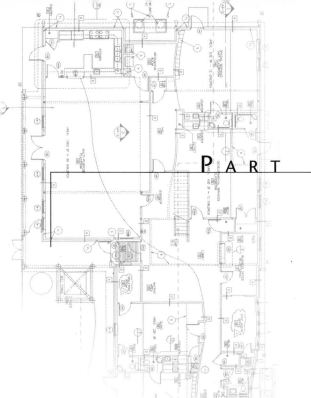

PART III

CREATING AND EDITING DRAWINGS

6

ACCURACY IN CREATING DRAWINGS WITH AUTOCAD 2000

To create accurate drawings with AutoCAD, you must understand how to specify and enter coordinates, and understand the points that compose them. This in turn, requires knowledge of AutoCAD's basic coordinate display systems: the World Coordinate Systems (WCS) and User Coordinate Systems (UCS). AutoCAD is an extremely accurate design and drafting package with the capability of 16 decimal places of precision stored in its database. To actualize this amount of accuracy, AutoCAD supports several drawing aids that enable you to draw, place, and edit objects in your drawings. This chapter discusses AutoCAD's coordinate systems and the methods you can use to make drawing with accuracy and precision easier.

This chapter covers the following topics:

■ *Coordinate systems*

■ *Coordinate point entry methods*

■ *Changing coordinate systems*

- Setting up drawing aids
- Object snapping
- Construction lines and rays

Coordinate Systems

No matter what kind of drawing you do in AutoCAD, you need a systematic method of specifying points. Points define the beginnings and endpoints of lines, the centers of circles and arcs, the axis points of ellipses, and so on. The capability to place points accurately is important. When an AutoCAD command prompts you for a point, you can either specify a point on the screen with the mouse or pointing device, or enter coordinates at the command line. When entering points, AutoCAD uses a three-dimensional *Cartesian*, or *rectangular*, coordinate system. Using this standard system, you locate a point in 3D space by specifying its distance and direction from an established origin measured along three mutually perpendicular axes: the X, Y, and Z axes. The origin is considered to be at 0,0,0. Figure 6.1 illustrates such a coordinate system. Only two dimensions are depicted with the Z axis projecting up, perpendicular to the page. If you are concerned only with two-dimensional drawings, this is the presentation of AutoCAD's coordinate system that will be seen.

Figure 6.1

The X and Y axes in a 2D coordinate system.

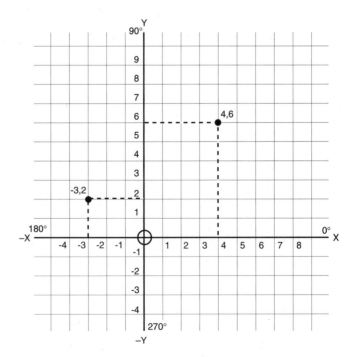

In Figure 6.1, the 4,6 coordinate indicates a point 4 units in the positive X direction and 6 units in the positive Y direction. Points to the left or below the origin have negative X and Y coordinate components, respectively. Figure 6.2 illustrates the same coordinate system, only now the third dimension and the Z axis are shown. To specify 3D points, you add a third element to the coordinate designation. The point 4,6,6 in Figure 6.2 is located 4 units in the positive X direction, 6 units in the positive Y direction, and 6 units in the positive Z direction. The system of reckoning coordinates is independent of the units used so that distances can be in any measurement; for example, the X direction could be English feet or inches, or metric centimeters or kilometers.

Figure 6.2

The 3D rectangular coordinate system.

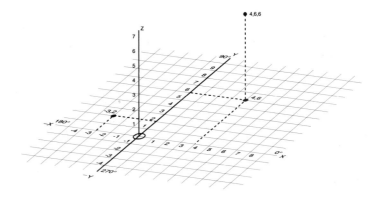

Later in this chapter, you will learn about the various ways that you can change the origin as well as the orientation of the three axes of AutoCAD's rectangular coordinate system. No matter how the coordinate system is oriented, you must know how to enter points.

Coordinate Point Entry Methods

Many of the drawings you make in AutoCAD—regardless of their eventual complexity—consist of a few relatively basic AutoCAD objects such as lines, circles, and text elements. These objects require that you enter points that specify their location, size, and direction. Additionally, many editing operations also require that you specify points. There are four ways to enter points or coordinates in AutoCAD

■ Using absolute coordinates

■ Using relative coordinates

■ Using direct distance entry

■ Using coordinate display

Using Absolute Coordinates

Absolute rectangular coordinates are always measured from the origin point: 0,0,0. In AutoCAD, you specify an absolute coordinate from the keyboard by typing in the X, Y, and Z axis values separated by a comma: *X,Y* for 2D points, or *X,Y,Z* for 3D points.

You don't need to use a plus sign (+) if the displacement from the origin is positive. You must, however, place a minus sign (–) in front of displacements in the negative direction: –2,3 or 4,–6,3.

Absolute polar coordinates also treat a 2D coordinate entry as a displacement from the origin, or 0,0, but you specify the displacement as a distance and an angle. The distance and angle are separated by a left-angle bracket (<) with no spaces: *distance<angle* (for example, 25<135).

Positive angles are measured counterclockwise from an assumed 0 degree that lies, by default, along the positive X axis as shown in Figure 6.3.

Figure 6.3

Default angle directions.

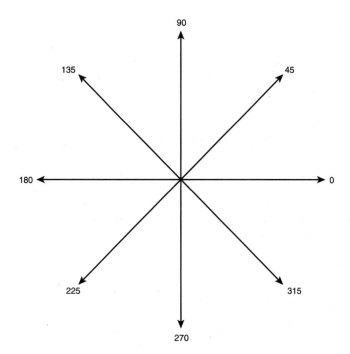

Insider **T**ip

When entering the angle portion of polar coordinates, you can specify the angle as either positive (counterclockwise) or negative (clockwise). Thus, 37<90 is equivalent to 37<–270.

This applies to both absolute and relative coordinate entries.

Note

You can reverse the positive and negative directions of angles, so that positive values measure clockwise and negative values measure counterclockwise. This is accomplished by selecting the Clockwise option from the Drawing Units dialog box. Additionally, you can control the direction of the 0-degree baseline from which all angles are measured. For more information, refer to Chapter 3, "Controlling the AutoCAD 2000 Drawing Environment."

In the following exercise, you use both absolute rectangular and absolute polar coordinates to draw the outline of a fastener.

Using Absolute Rectangular and Absolute Polar Coordinate Entry

1. If necessary, start AutoCAD and begin a drawing using the Start from Scratch option.

2. Start the LINE command by either typing **L** or clicking on the Line tool on the Draw toolbar. Enter the following coordinates at the prompts:

   ```
   From point: 4.5,5↵
   To point: 6.5,5 ↵
   To point: 9<38.34 ↵
   To point: 7.8<25.36 ↵
   To point: 6.5,4
   To point: 4.5,4↵
   To point: C ↵
   ```

3. Your drawing should look like Figure 6.4.

Figure 6.4

Outline drawn using absolute coordinates.

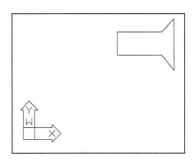

This exercise demonstrates the limitations of absolute coordinates. Although absolute coordinates are adequate for designating the beginning of a line, measuring subsequent points in relation to the drawing's origin is cumbersome and often inaccurate. When the lines outlining an object (such as the fastener in the preceding exercise) are not orthogonal, absolute coordinates are inadequate if any degree of accuracy and efficiency is desired. The use of relative coordinates solves this problem.

Using Relative Coordinates

In almost any kind of drawing, after you have established the beginning of a line, you usually know the X and Y displacement or the distance and angle to the next point. Relative coordinates do not reference the origin point but are determined relative to the last point. You can use this more straightforward method with either relative rectangular or relative polar coordinates. To distinguish relative coordinate entry from absolute entry, you precede relative coordinates with the @ symbol (for example, @1.5,3 for relative rectangular entry or @2.6<45 for relative polar entry).

In the preceding relative rectangular entry, the point specified lies at a displacement of 1.5 units in the X axis direction and 3 units in the Y axis direction from the previous point. In the relative polar entry, the point lies 2.6 units at an angle of 45 degrees from the previous point.

In the following exercise, the usefulness of relative coordinates is shown in drawing a fastener similar to the one in the previous exercise.

USING RELATIVE COORDINATES

Continue from the previous exercise.

1. Start the LINE command by typing **L** or clicking on the Line tool on the Draw toolbar. Enter the following coordinates at the prompts:

    ```
    From point: 9,5 ⏎ (Note this is an absolute coordinate.)
    To point: @2<0 ⏎ (Note this is a relative polar coordinate.)
    To point: @.8<46 ⏎
    To point: @0,-2.2 ⏎ (Note this is a relative rectangular coordi-
    nate.)
    To point: @.8<134 ⏎
    To point: @2<180 ⏎
    To point: C
    ```

2. Your drawing should now resemble Figure 6.5.

Figure 6.5

Outline drawn using relative coordinates.

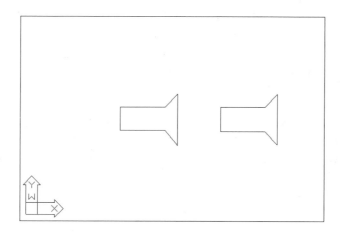

NOTE

The angles involved or the availability of distance information will usually determine whether it is easier to enter the next point using relative polar or relative rectangular coordinates.

As you can see, relative coordinate point entry is much easier to use and permits more accuracy than relative rectangular entry. Even when your drawing involves purely orthogonal displacements, relative coordinate entry is the superior and usually the only accurate method.

Direct Distance Entry

A variation of relative coordinate entry, called *direct distance entry*, is supported in AutoCAD 2000. In direct distance entry, rather than entering coordinate values, you can specify a point by moving the cursor to indicate a direction and then entering the distance from the first point. This is a good way to quickly specify a line length. This method is used primarily when the displacements involved are orthogonal and you can have the ORTHO drawing aid turned on. The following exercise demonstrates the use of direct distance coordinate entry.

USING DIRECT DISTANCE COORDINATE ENTRY

1. Continue from the previous exercise by starting the LINE command. Respond to the first prompt as follows:

   From point: **7.5,7.5** ↵

2. Ensure that ORTHO mode is active by observing the ORTHO button in the status bar at the bottom of the AutoCAD drawing window. If the button is depressed, ORTHO mode is on. If ORTHO mode is off, click the ORTHO button.

3. With ORTHO mode on, move the crosshairs cursor any distance to the right of the point entered in step 1. Answer the current prompt as follows:

   To point: **2.3** ↵

4. Note that the first polyline segment is drawn 2.3 units orthogonally to the right of point 7.5,7.5. Also note that your coordinate entry, although "relative" to the preceding point, did not require the @ prefix.

5. Now respond to the current prompt with a standard relative polar coordinate:

   To point: **@.8<46** ↵

6. Enter the next polyline segment using direct distance entry by moving the crosshairs cursor any distance below the last point and entering the following at the current prompt:

   To point: **2.2** ↵

7. Note again that the preceding entry did not require the leading @ symbol and that the line segment was drawn 2.2 units in the direction of the crosshairs cursor.

8. Again use standard relative polar coordinate entry for the next polyline segment:

   To point: **@.8<134** ↵

9. Respond to the current prompt by placing the crosshairs cursor to the left of the last point and entering the following:

   To point: **2.3** ↵
   To point: **C** ↵

10. Now complete the outline by typing **C** and pressing Enter. The outline should be similar to that completed in the previous exercises.

Direct distance entry provides a more direct and easier method of entering relative coordinates when the point lies in an orthogonal relationship to the previous point—a common situation in most drawings. Of course, if the point you want to designate lies on a snap point, whether orthogonal to the previous point or not, you can bypass keyboard entry by simply snapping the cursor to and clicking on the point. (The concept of *snapping* is covered later in this chapter.)

N o t e

AutoCAD 2000 introduces a new feature called *AutoTracking*, which allows you to simulate the effect of ORTHO mode—constricting the cursor's angular movement—but allows you to apply it in increments other than ORTHO mode's 90-degree increments. AutoTracking is discussed later in this chapter.

Coordinate Display

The coordinate display window located at the bottom-left of the status bar is useful when entering coordinates, whether you type them at the command prompt or pick points on the screen with the screen cursor. Figure 6.6 shows this display with two variations of the format.

Figure 6.6

9.50, 3.50 ,0.00
1'-6", 1'-3"   ,0'-0"

The coordinate display window shows coordinates in the current drawing units.

The upper display shows decimal units while the lower display shows architectural units. The are three types of coordinate display, which can display either absolute or relative coordinates, depending on the one selected and the command in progress. You can cycle through the various display types in four ways: by pressing either F6 or Ctrl+D, or by clicking or right-clicking in the display area itself. The three coordinate display types are as follows:

- **Static Display.** Displays the absolute coordinates of the last picked point. The display is updated whenever a new point is picked.

- **Dynamic Display.** Displays the absolute coordinates of the screen cursor and updates continuously as the cursor is moved. This is the default mode.

- **Distance and Angle.** Displays the distance and angle relative to the last point whenever a command prompt requesting either a distance or angle is active.

When Static Display is selected, the coordinate display appears grayed-out, although the coordinates of the last selected point are still visible. At an empty command prompt (one with no command in progress) or at an active prompt that does not accept either a distance or angle as input, you can only toggle between Static Display and Dynamic Display. At a prompt that does accept or require either a distance or angle as input, you can cycle among all three display types. Pay particular attention to the coordinate display window during the following exercise.

CYCLING THROUGH COORDINATE DISPLAY TYPES

1. Continue from the previous exercise or open a new drawing. (Use Start from Scratch. You will not need to save this drawing.)

2. Ensure that SNAP mode is off by observing the SNAP button in the status bar at the bottom of AutoCAD's application. If the button is raised, SNAP mode is off; if the button is depressed, SNAP mode is on. If necessary, click the button to turn SNAP mode off.

3. Ensure that the current mode setting of the coordinate display is off by pressing F6 until the display appears grayed-out.

4. Ensure that ORTHO mode is off by clicking the ORTHO button on the status bar if it is depressed.

5. Now move the screen cursor within the drawing area. Note that the coordinate display remains static.

6. Click in the coordinate display area. Note that the display is no longer grayed-out.

7. Now move the screen cursor and notice that the coordinate display is continuously updated. The coordinate display type is now Distance and Angle.

8. Start the `LINE` command by typing **L** and pressing Enter.

9. Respond to the `Specify first point:` prompt by typing **4,7** and pressing Enter.

10. Notice that after a point has been specified, the coordinate display changes to show relative polar coordinates as you move the cursor. Type in the following absolute rectangular point:

    To point: **6,7** ⏎

11. The line is drawn between the two points. Now press Ctrl+D. The display type changes to Dynamic Display, and the display is again in absolute rectangular format as you move the cursor.

12. Press F6. The display type is now Static Display. The display is grayed-out and static as you move the cursor.

13. Type the following at the prompt:

    To point: **2,3**

14. The next line is drawn. Now click in the coordinate display window. The display type is now back to Distance and Angle, with the read-out once again in relative polar format.

15. Right-click in the coordinate display window. The shortcut menu appears, and shows the three display types as Off (Static Display), Absolute (Dynamic Display), and Relative (Distance and Angle). Notice that the Relative option is grayed-out. This occurs because Relative display is the current mode.

16. Choose the Absolute option. The display type changes to Dynamic Display, and the display is again in absolute rectangular format as you move the cursor.

17. Right-click in the coordinate display window again, and choose the Relative option. The display type returns to Distance and Angle, with the read-out once again in relative polar format.

18. Press the Esc key to end the `LINE` command. Then press the U key and press Enter to undo the line. Note that the display reverts to absolute rectangular because no command that accepts distance or angle input is active.

In this exercise, you saw the three types of coordinate display and how they can aid you in selecting points. You also manually used the four methods available to you for cycling through the three display types. Although the absolute rectangular read-out type is of limited usefulness, it can, for example, be used to specify the starting point of an object such as a wall or to specify a set of known points in a surveying data context.

If you have the Static Display active and click a grip to make it hot, the system will display the coordinate of the grip location. This is an alternative to using the ID command.

Changing Coordinate Systems

The beginning of this chapter looked at AutoCAD's rectangular or Cartesian coordinates system from the standpoint of entering coordinates representing points in your drawing (refer to Figure 6.1). You learned about absolute and relative coordinate entry in both rectangular and polar formats. By using the Cartesian coordinates system, and entering either absolute or relative coordinates, you can create highly accurate, detailed drawings of anything.

When you begin a new AutoCAD drawing you are, by default, using a rectangular coordinate system that is called the *World Coordinate System*, or *WCS*. In addition to the WCS, you can create other coordinate systems called *User Coordinate Systems*, or *UCSs*. They are called UCSs because you, the user, define them to aid you in creating your drawings.

AutoCAD enables you to create your own UCS because this ability often makes defining points for your model easier. For example, suppose you are creating a model of a 3D pyramid, and you need to define points along the surface of one of the pyramid's faces. This is easily accomplished by aligning a UCS with the face. By doing so, you define an XY plane coincident with the face. After the UCS is properly aligned, it's just a matter of using the Cartesian coordinate system to create the points along the pyramid's face, a shown in Figure 6.7. Chapter 27, "Introduction to 3D," presents additional UCS concepts for use when creating 3D geometry.

In the next section, you learn about various UCS commands and features you can use to make creating detailed drawings of complex models easier.

Figure 6.7

By properly aligning a User Coordinate System (UCS), developing complex 2D and 3D models becomes easier.

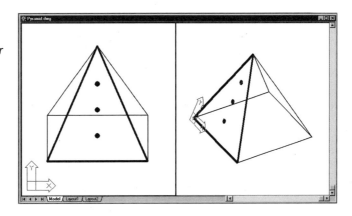

World Coordinate System

The World Coordinate System is nothing more than a standard rectangular coordinate system with the origin in the lower-left corner of the screen, a horizontal X axis running left to right and a Y axis extending vertically from the bottom to the top of the screen. The Z-axis is perpendicular to both the X and Y axes and is considered to extend out towards you in a direction perpendicular to the screen. To identify the WCS and establish its orientation, AutoCAD, by default, places the WCS icon at or near the origin. The WCS icon is shown in Figure 6.8. Its defining characteristic is the "W" appearing on the icon; this tells you that you are in the World Coordinate System.

Figure 6.8

The World Coordinate System (WCS) icon.

Indicates World Coordinate System

Origin Marker

User Coordinate Systems

You can create your own coordinate systems called *User Coordinate Systems*, or *UCSs*. In a UCS, the origin as well as the direction of the X, Y, and Z axes can be made to move, rotate, and even align with drawing objects. Although the three axes in a UCS remain mutually perpendicular, as they are in the WCS, a great deal of flexibility can be achieved in placing and orientating your UCS. The UCS command enables you to place a UCS origin anywhere in 3D space so that you can work relative to any point you want. You can also rotate the X, Y, and Z axes in 2D or 3D space. Figure 6.9 shows two UCS icons representing two different coordinate systems; one is the WCS, indicated by the "W" on the UCS icon; the other is a UCS defining a User Coordinate System. User Coordinate Systems are indispensable for working in 3D space.

Figure 6.9

The World Coordinate System and a User Coordinate System.

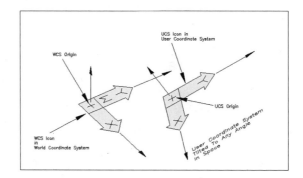

The following exercise demonstrates how to create a User Coordinate System by aligning the UCS with two 2D points.

ALIGNING A UCS WITH A 2D OBJECT

1. Start a new drawing, using 06DWG01.DWT from the accompanying CD as a template. (See Chapter 2 for information on using template drawings.)

2. Your drawing should resemble Figure 6.10. Note that the "W" in the UCS icon indicates the World Coordinate System is current.

3. Select Tools, New UCS, 3 Point. The following prompt appears:

   `Specify new origin point <0,0,0>:`

4. Shift+right-click to display the Cursor menu and select Endpoint. Then pick ① shown in Figure 6.10. The following prompt appears (the points given as a default may differ in your drawing):

   `Specify point on positive portion of the X-axis <6.58,2.04,0.00>:`

Figure 6.10

Pick a point to change the UCS.

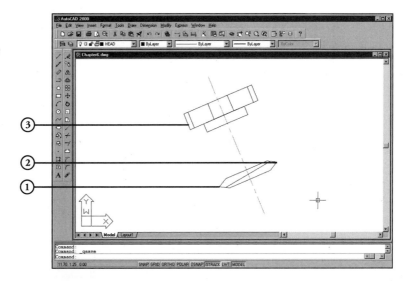

5. Shift+right-click to display the Cursor menu, choose Endpoint, and pick ②. The following prompt appears:

   ```
   Specify point on positive-Y portion of the UCS XY plane
   <5.19,2.96,0.00>:
   ```

6. Pick anywhere near ③. Note that the UCS icon changes orientation to align with the new UCS and that the "W" disappears, indicating that you are no longer in the WCS (see Figure 6.11).

Figure 6.11

The new UCS appears.

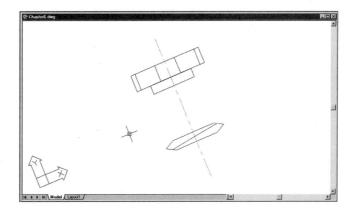

7. Select Modify, Array. The following prompt appears:

    ```
    Select objects:
    ```

8. Pick anywhere on the object near ① shown in Figure 6.11, and end the selection process by pressing Enter.

9. Answer the following prompts as shown:

    ```
    Enter the type of array [Rectangular/Polar] <R>: R ↵
    Enter the number of rows (---) <1>: 6 ↵
    Enter the number of columns (|||) <1>: ↵
    ```

10. The following prompt appears:

    ```
    Enter the distance between rows or specify unit cell (---):
    ```

11. Activate the Cursor menu (Shift+right-click) and select Intersection. Click at ②. Again activate the Cursor menu, select Intersection, and click at ③.

12. The array is carried out in a direction perpendicular to the X axis of the new UCS.

13. Return the UCS to the WCS with the UCS command. Type **UCS** and press Enter at the command prompt. When the following prompt appears, accept the default <World>:.

    ```
    Enter an option [New/Move/orthoGraphic/Prev/Restore/Save/Del/Apply/
    ?/World]
    <World>: ↵
    ```

    Your drawing should resemble Figure 6.12.

14. Save this drawing and name it **CHAPTER6.DWG**.

Figure 6.12

The completed array.

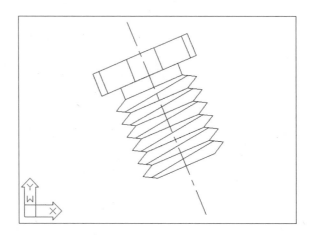

INSIDER **T**IP

It is possible to change the UCS to the position and orientation you want in more than one way. In the preceding exercise, for example, you could have rotated the UCS about its Z axis rather than using the 3 Point option. I generally prefer to use the 3 Point option because it's more intuitive and easier to use.

Although defining new UCSs is most frequently used in 3D drafting, the preceding exercise demonstrated that the capability to change the UCS is helpful in 2D work as well. By aligning the UCS with the horizontal axis of the thread object in the drawing, a simple 6-row array could be quickly carried out with the "axis" of the array perpendicular to the horizontal axis of the object. The following exercise demonstrates two more options of the UCS command, re-establishing the most previous UCS and controlling the display of the UCS icon.

DISPLAYING THE PREVIOUS UCS AND CONTROLLING THE POSITION OF THE UCS ICON

1. Continue using the CHAPTER6.DWG drawing from the previous exercise. The drawing will resemble Figure 6.12.

2. At the command prompt, type **UCS**, then press Enter. The following prompt appears:

   ```
   Enter an option [New/Move/orthoGraphic/Prev/Restore/Save/Del/Apply/
   ?/World]
   ```

3. Type **P** (for Previous), then press Enter. Note that the UCS reverts to the UCS defined in the previous exercise.

4. Now, select View, Display, UCS Icon, Origin. Note that the UCS icon moves to the origin point of the currently defined UCS as shown in Figure 6.13. This is the origin point you defined in step 4 of the previous exercise.

5. Again, select View, Display, UCS Icon, and notice that a check mark appears beside the Origin selection. Click on Origin to toggle off the feature, which moves the icon back to its former position at the lower-left corner of the screen.

6. Once again, select View, Display, UCS Icon, and notice that a check mark appears beside the On selection. Click On to remove the check mark. Note that the UCS icon is no longer visible.

7. Close and Save this drawing.

Figure 6.13

Placing the UCS Icon at the current origin.

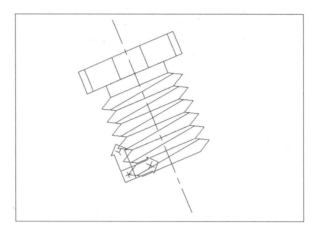

INSIDER TIP

Although the preceding exercise uses shortcuts from the main menu bar, I prefer to turn the UCS icon on and off by typing **UCSICON** at the command prompt, and then typing either **On** or **Off**. This method seems faster. You can also move the UCS icon to and from the current origin with the UCSICON command and typing either **OR** for origin, or **N** for no origin. This seems faster than traversing across three levels of cascading pull-down menus.

The UCS Command

The UCS command is the key to placing, moving, rotating, and displaying User Coordinate Systems. This command allows you to appropriately position UCSs to draw the elements necessary to properly define your 2D or 3D model. By understanding the various options available through the UCS command, you ease the task of defining your model.

Most of your 2D work can be accomplished with the following subset of UCS options:

■ **Origin.** Specifies a new X, Y, or Z origin point relative to the current origin.

■ **3point.** Enables you to set the X and Y axes by specifying the origin and a point on both the X and Y axes.

■ **OBject.** Defines a new coordinate system based on a selected object.

- **Z.** Rotates the X and Y axes about the Z axis.

- **Prev.** Reverts to the previous UCS. You can recall as many as the last 10 UCSs.

- **Restore.** Sets the UCS to a previously named UCS.

- **Save.** Enables you to store the current UCS with a name you specify.

- **Del.** Removes a stored UCS.

- **?/Named UCSs.** Lists saved UCSs by name.

- **World.** Displays the WCS.

The Restore, Save, Del, and ?/Named UCSs options are tools that allow you to manage UCS configurations. By using these tools, you can save defined UCS configurations, then restore them for later use. One feature that makes these options very useful is that named UCSs are saved with the current drawing. Therefore, as you develop a series of different UCS configurations, you can save the configurations with the drawing, knowing that you can recall them later during another editing session.

INSIDER TIP

You can use the new AutoCAD DesignCenter (ADC) to import saved UCS configurations from other drawings into the current drawing. For more information, see Chapter 12, "Applications for the New AutoCAD DesignCenter."

UCS Command Features New to AutoCAD 2000

AutoCAD 2000 presents several new features to the UCS command. These new features enhance the usefulness of UCSs by making them easier to manipulate. By using these new features, you make defining and controlling UCSs simpler.

The new features are described as follows:

- **Multiple UCSs.** This feature allows you to set a different UCS for each viewport you have open.

- **UCS Face Align.** This option allows you to quickly configure a new UCS by aligning it to the selected Face object. Face objects are discussed in Chapter 29, "Surfacing in 3D."

- **UCS Apply.** This option allows you to apply the UCS configuration of one viewport to another by simply selecting the viewport.

- **UCS Move.** This option allows you to move the origin of a UCS without the need to redefine or rename the UCS. For example, if you move the origin point of a named UCS, AutoCAD simply applies the new origin point to the named UCS.

- **UCS Manager.** Displays the new UCS dialog box.

The following exercise demonstrates the new features and options.

AUTOCAD'S NEW UCS FEATURES AND OPTIONS

1. Open the drawing 06DWG02. The drawing appears, showing four different viewports, all viewing the same cube object, and all having identical UCSs, as shown in Figure 6.14.

Figure 6.14

The UCS is identical in each viewport.

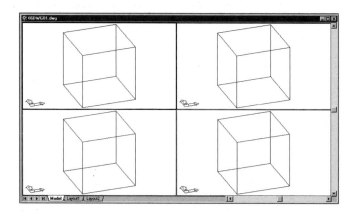

2. Pick anywhere inside the lower-left viewport. The lower-left viewport becomes active.

3. From the Tools menu, select New UCS, Face. AutoCAD prompts you to select the face of a solid object.

4. In the lower-left viewport, pick the line AB, picking near A. AutoCAD highlights the front face of the cube. (If AutoCAD highlights the top face of the cube, choose N to switch to the adjoining face, then press Enter to select to the front face.)

5. Press Enter to accept the front face selection. Notice that AutoCAD rotates the lower-left viewport's UCS, as shown in Figure 6.15. Also notice that no other UCS rotated in any of the other viewports.

Figure 6.15

The UCS Face option aligns the lower-left viewport's UCS with the selected front face of the cube. Notice that all other UCSs remained unchanged.

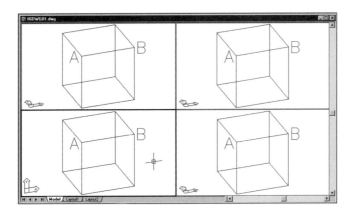

6. From the Tools menu, select New UCS, Apply. AutoCAD prompts you to pick a viewport to apply the current UCS.

7. Choose the upper-right viewport, then press Enter. AutoCAD updates the upper-right viewport's UCS to match the lower-left viewport's UCS.

8. From the Tools menu, select Move UCS. AutoCAD prompts you to specify the new origin point for the current UCS.

9. In the upper-right viewport, pick a point in the approximate center of the front face. AutoCAD redefines the UCS's origin point, and moves the UCS icon to the new origin point.

10. From the Tools menu, select Named UCS. AutoCAD displays the UCS dialog box, with the Named UCSs tab displayed. Notice that the current UCS is Unnamed.

11. Right-click the highlighted Unnamed UCS. AutoCAD displays the shortcut menu.

12. Select Rename, type **Front UCS**, and press Enter. AutoCAD renames the UCS, as shown in Figure 6.16.

13. Click OK. AutoCAD dismisses the UCS dialog box.

14. Select the lower-right viewport, then select Tools, Named UCS. AutoCAD displays the UCS dialog box.

15. Select **Front UCS**, click Set Current, and click OK. AutoCAD redefines the UCS's origin point, and moves the UCS icon to the new origin point in the current viewport.

16. Select Tools, Named UCS. AutoCAD displays the UCS dialog box.

17. Select the Orthographic UCSs tab. AutoCAD displays six predefined UCSs, as shown in Figure 6.17.

18. Select the orthographic UCS named Left, then Set Current, then click OK. AutoCAD aligns the lower-right viewport's UCS with the left face of the cube, as shown in Figure 6.18.

19. You can close the drawing without saving changes.

Figure 6.18

AutoCAD applies the orthographic UCS named Left to the lower-right viewport.

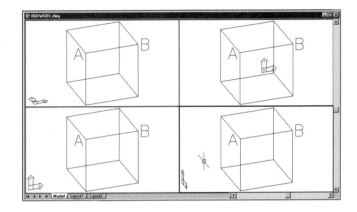

AutoCAD's new UCS features and options make using UCSs easier than before. By applying these new tools, you can simplify object editing, and increase your productivity.

The UCSICON Command

In an earlier exercise, you saw how the UCSICON command can be used to control the placement and visibility of the UCS icon. To round out the discussion of User Coordinate Systems, here is an explanation of the options for the UCSICON command. The UCSICON command displays the following prompt:

```
Enter an option [ON/OFF/All/Noorigin/ORigin] <ON>
```

- **ON.** Turns on the UCS icon.

- **OFF.** Turns off the UCS icon.

- **All.** Applies changes to the UCS icon in all displayed viewports; otherwise, changes affect only the current viewport.

- **Noorigin.** Displays the UCS icon at the lower-left corner of viewports.

- **Origin.** Displays the UCS icon at the 0,0,0 origin of the current UCS if possible. Otherwise, it displays the UCS icon at the lower-left corner of viewports.

INSIDER TIP

Another capability of the UCS icon that you should know about is the system variable UCSFOLLOW. This variable controls whether or not a plan view will be automatically generated whenever you change the UCS. Setting this variable to 0 will not affect the view; setting it to 1, however, will cause the plan view to be generated. For 2D drafting, I find the automatic plan view setting to be helpful.

The UCSICON options just described can be set from the command prompt, or from the new UCS dialog box. By selecting Tools, Named UCS, then selecting the Settings tab, AutoCAD displays the UCSICON options shown in Figure 6.19. By selecting or clearing the options, you toggle on or off the options, described as follows:

- **ON.** When selected, turns on the UCS icon. When cleared, turns off the UCS icon.

- **Display at UCS Origin Point.** When selected, displays the UCS icon at the 0,0,0 origin of the current UCS if possible. When cleared, it displays the UCS icon at the lower-left corner of the viewport.

- **Apply to All Active Viewports.** When selected, applies changes to the UCS icon in all displayed viewports. When cleared, changes to the UCS icon only affect the current viewport.

Figure 6.19

The new UCS Manager allows you to set options for the UCS icon.

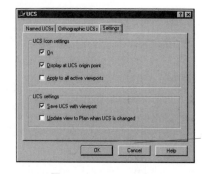

In addition to the UCS Icon settings, you can also control two UCS settings, described as follows:

- **Save UCS with Viewport.** When selected, this option allows you to set and retain a different UCS for each viewport. When cleared, the viewport reflects the current UCS each time the UCS is changed, even if the viewport is not the current viewport.

- **Update View to Plan when UCS is Changed.** When selected, the plan view is automatically applied when the UCS is changed. When cleared, the plan view is not invoked when the UCS changes. (This is the same as setting the UCSFOLLOW system variable, described in the previous tip.)

The *plan view* described here refers to rotating the view of the model in the current viewport so that the X axis of the UCS appears normal (horizontal) to the screen. For example, in Figure 6.20, the image on the left has its view rotated normal to the screen, whereas the image on the right does not. You can invoke a plan view by using the PLAN command.

Figure 6.20

The view of the image on the left is automatically rotated by using the PLAN command.

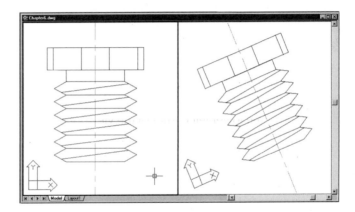

Setting Up Drafting Settings

AutoCAD allows you to control a number of drafting settings that help you work efficiently, and make your drawings more accurate. These settings consist of a series of system variables that you can set at the command prompt. Additionally, you can easily access them through the Drafting Settings dialog box (formerly the Drawing Aids dialog box.) The Drafting Settings dialog box is shown in Figure 6.21, and is accessed through the Tools menu by selecting Drafting Settings. This dialog box is also available from the command prompt by typing **DDRMODES**.

Figure 6.21

The new Drafting Settings dialog box.

The Drafting Settings dialog box consists of three tabs. The Snap and Grid tab controls snap and grid settings, including the X and Y increment spacing, the X axis angle, and the X and Y base point. The Polar Tracking tab controls polar tracking settings, and is new to AutoCAD 2000. It controls features that function similar to AutoCAD's ORTHO mode, but allows you to apply the features to angles in any increment. The Object Snap tab (formerly the Osnap Settings dialog box) controls running object snaps, which are object snaps that are always turned on.

This section reviews the system variables accessed through the Drafting Settings dialog box, and their related commands.

Understanding Snap and Grid Options

The Snap and Grid tab on the Drafting Settings dialog box is made up of four major sections. These sections control how AutoCAD's snap feature functions, and how its grid displays. By understanding how these features function, you make drawing objects with AutoCAD easier and intuitive.

Snap

Options in Drawing Aids dialog box control the Snap grid (refer to Figure 6.21). When the Snap grid is enabled (when a check mark, or X, appears in the Snap On check box), the movement of the crosshairs cursor is restricted to incremental displacements across a grid of invisible "snap" points. This enables you to snap to and select points on this grid with a high degree of precision. You can enter both Snap X and Snap Y spacing for your snap grid by typing in the input boxes in this section. The other options—Snap Angle, X Base, and Y Base—control the angle at which the grid is oriented with respect to the current UCS and the origin's coordinates of the snap's grid.

The Snap grid settings can also be controlled at the command prompt with the SNAP command. You can toggle on and off the Snap feature by pressing the F9 key, by pressing Ctrl+B, or by clicking the SNAP button on the status bar.

By carefully selecting the spacing of the Snap grid, you can usually make the picking of points much easier because you bypass the need to enter points at the keyboard.

INSIDER TIP

> When entering values in X and Y spacing text edit boxes in both the Grid and Snap sections of the Drawing Aids dialog box, typing a value in the X Spacing box and pressing Enter will automatically transfer the value to the Y Spacing box. Because I usually want the X and Y values of both of these settings equal, this shortcut eliminates the need to type anything in the Y boxes.

Grid

In addition to a grid of invisible snap points, you can apply a grid of visible points to the drawing area. This visible drawing aid is simply called Grid. The controls found in the Grid area determine the location of the grid's visible points.

When the Grid On option is selected, grid points are made visible with the spacing specified by the values (in drawing units) that you type into the Grid X Spacing and Grid Y Spacing edit boxes (refer to Figure 6.21).

It is common to link the spacing of the grid of visible points (the Grid) to the grid of invisible snap points. To establish this link, the X and Y spacing of the Grid points is set to 0. AutoCAD will then use the X and Y spacing of the Snap points and automatically apply these to the visible Grid. You can, of course, override this 1:1 relationship by explicitly entering values other than 0 for the Grid spacing. Keep in mind that regardless of the setting(s) of the Grid points, the origin and angle of the Grid is always kept the same as the origin and angle of the Snap points.

You can also control the visible Grid with the GRID command, and toggle on and off the Grid by pressing the F7 key, by pressing Ctrl+G, or by clicking the GRID button on the mode status bar.

INSIDER TIP

The Grid control section of the Drafting Settings dialog box largely duplicates functions available through the basic GRID command. Using the GRID command at the command prompt, however, offers an option: Grid spacing (X). Specifying a value followed by an "X" sets the Grid spacing to the specified value times the Snap interval. I often like to set my Snap spacing at a fraction—perhaps 1/4 —of my Grid value. By using the "X" feature of the spacing setting available with the GRID command, this relationship between Grid and Snap remains in effect no matter how often I change the Grid setting.

Snap Type & Style

The Snap Type & Style area controls whether rectangular, isometric, or polar snaps and grids are used. By selecting the Grid Snap option button, you can choose between the Rectangular or Isometric snap and grid modes. The *Rectangular* mode is AutoCAD's standard snap and grid mode. The *Isometric* mode allows you to easily draw isometric views of objects, such as the cube shown in Figure 6.22. Notice the alignment and skew of the cursor when Isometric mode is selected.

Figure 6.22

The Isometric snap mode is used to draw isometric views of objects.

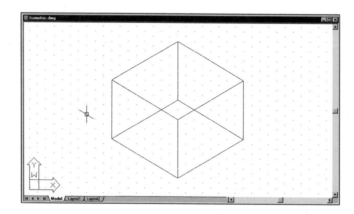

INSIDER TIP

The isometric view shown in Figure 6.22 is displayed in Isoplane Left mode. You can cycle through three modes—Isoplane Left, Isoplane Top, and Isoplane Right—by pressing F5 or Ctrl+E. As you cycle through each mode, AutoCAD realigns the cursor to match the selected mode.

The Polar Snap option causes the cursor to snap along polar alignment angles set on the Polar Tracking tab relative to the starting polar tracking point. The snap increment is determined by Polar Distance setting in the Polar Spacing area, discussed in the next section.

The New Polar Tracking Feature

The new AutoCAD 2000 Polar Tracking feature provides the ability to constrain cursor movement into predefined polar alignment angles. This feature functions similar to ORTHO mode, but instead of constraining cursor movement horizontally and vertically in 90 degree increments, you can set the polar alignment increments to any angle.

In the Polar Angle Settings area, you can select the desired polar alignment angle from a predefined list containing commonly used angles. The angles are selected from the Increment Angle drop-down list, which contains angles measured in the following degrees: 90, 45, 30, 22 1/2, 18, 15, 10, and 5. Additionally, you can set up to 10 user-defined angles. By selecting the Additional Angles option, then clicking the New button, AutoCAD allows you to add your own polar alignment angles in the Additional Angles list as shown in Figure 6.23. To remove user-defined angles, select the angle from the list, then click the Delete button.

Figure 6.23

The Polar Tracking tab allows you to define your own polar alignment angles, as displayed in the list box.

NOTE

When you select an angle from the Increment Angle drop-down list, AutoCAD constrains cursor movement every time the cursor crosses an angle increment (the cursor "snaps" to the angle increment). In contrast, a user-defined angle entered in the Additional Angles list only constrains cursor movement when the cursor crosses the listed angle(s). Therefore, using the Increment Angle and Additional Angles options shown in Figure 6.23, the cursor constrains its movement every 30 degrees (30, 60, 90, 120, and so on). Using these options also constrains cursor movement at 0 degrees, 00 minutes, 42 seconds; at 12 degrees, 32 minutes, 00 seconds; and at 78 degrees, 37 minutes, 01 seconds.

INSIDER **T**IP

You can temporarily constrain cursor movement to any angle not listed in the Polar Tracking tab by using angle overrides. For example, to constrain cursor movement to 33 degrees during a command, when prompted to specify the next point, type **<33**, and AutoCAD will temporarily constrain the cursor for the next point to 33 degrees.

The Polar Angle measurement area determines whether polar tracking alignment angles are measured absolutely or relatively. Angles measured *absolutely* are determined relative to the current UCS. Angles measured *relatively* are determined relative to the last point selected. For example, in Figure 6.24, with the Polar Angle measurement option set to Absolute, the image on the left displays the cursor's polar position at 45 degrees, as measured from the current UCS. In contrast, with the Polar Angle measurement option set to Relative to last segment, the image on the right displays the cursor's relative polar position at 90 degrees, as measured from the last line segment.

Figure 6.24

You can track polar alignments absolutely, based on the current UCS, or relatively, based on the last point selected.

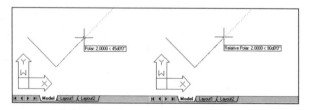

The Object Snap Tracking Settings area allows you to set tracking to orthogonal, or to all the polar settings displayed in the Polar Angle Settings area. The Track

Orthogonally Only option is the original option first introduced with tracking in Release 14. The Track Using All Polar Angle Settings option is new to AutoCAD 2000, and constrains cursor movement to the predefined polar alignment angles. These options are discussed in detail later in this chapter.

Object Snapping

No matter how carefully you set your Snap interval or how often you change that interval, it is highly unlikely that all the points in your drawings will conveniently fall on these predefined snap points. This becomes increasingly true as your drawing becomes populated with various objects that themselves have important geometric features, such as endpoints, centers, and tangent points, to which you will want to relate other drawing objects.

Most modern CAD applications, including AutoCAD, therefore, provide some means of identifying these geometric points. These tools simplify the construction of new geometry, and enable you to draw created objects more accurately, and to consistently maintain the results with far more precision than is possible in traditional manual drafting. In AutoCAD, this capability is called *object snapping*, and is also referred to as *Object Snap*, or *Osnap*. In AutoCAD, these modes consist of a set of tools that permit accurate geometric construction.

Osnaps are used to directly and easily identify key points either on or in relation to your drawing objects. Figure 6.25 shows the Object Snap toolbar and the pop-up Cursor menu.

Figure 6.25

The Object Snap toolbar and the pop-up cursor menu.

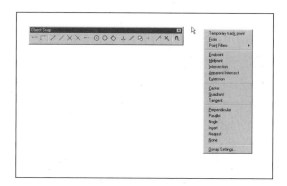

The Osnap toolbar and the Cursor menu contain the same Osnap modes presented in essentially the same order. You can display or activate the pop-up Cursor menu by pressing Shift and right-clicking, commonly called Shift+right-click, or simply pressing Shift+Enter because the right mouse button serves as an Enter button. If you use a three-button mouse, the middle button can usually be configured to "pop up" the Cursor menu.

The Osnap modes are also represented on the Standard toolbar by a "fly-out" toolbar. Figure 6.26 displays both the Osnap toolbar and the Osnap fly-out. As shown, the Osnap toolbar can be displayed in a vertical format and placed or moved to a convenient position in your drawing area. Figure 6.25 shows the same toolbar displayed horizontally.

Figure 6.26

The Object Snap toolbar and fly-out.

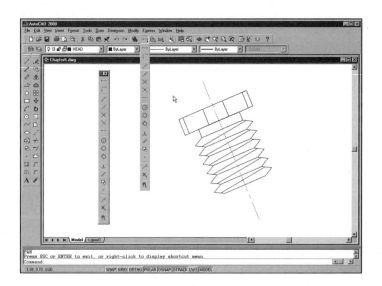

NOTE

To resize any toolbar, move your cursor to an edge of the toolbar. When the cursor is in the proper position to resize the toolbar, it turns into a double-headed arrow. Then just click and drag to resize the toolbar as desired.

INSIDER TIP

Depending on personal preference and the type of drafting you are involved with, you can use the Osnap toolbar (in either a horizontal or vertical format, or even a more compact rectangular arrangement), the Osnap fly-out from the Standard toolbar, or the pop-up Cursor menu. The fly-out has the advantage of being present only during Osnap selections, whereas the Osnap toolbar can be moved around and resized; the Cursor pop-up menu, on the other hand, requires very little cursor movement. I almost always use the cursor menu because it is the quickest for me.

NOTE

The position and size of a toolbar can be saved to a Profile, which can be recalled later to restore preferred toolbar layouts. For detailed information, refer to Chapter 3, "Controlling the AutoCAD 2000 Drawing Environment," in the section "Saving the Options to a Profile."

Osnap Modes

AutoCAD 2000 has 16 Object Snap modes, including the two new modes. Table 6.1 gives a description of each mode.

Table 6.1

AutoCAD 2000 Object Snap Modes

Mode	Description
Apparent Intersect	Finds a point that represents the apparent intersection of two objects, such as two non-parallel lines that do not actually cross in 3D space.
Center	Finds the center of a circle or an arc.
Endpoint	Finds the endpoint of all objects except a circle.
From	Establishes a temporary reference point as a basis for specifying subsequent points.
Insert	Finds the insertion point of text objects and block or external references.
Intersection	Locates the intersection of objects in the same plane.

continues

Table 6.1, continued

AutoCAD 2000 Object Snap Modes

Mode	Description
Midpoint	Finds the midpoint of a line, a pline, or an arc.
Nearest	Locates a point on an object that is nearest to the point you pick.
Node	Finds the location of a Point object.
None	Instructs AutoCAD not to use any Running Osnap modes.
Perpendicular	Returns a point at the intersection of the object selected and an angle perpendicular to that object from either the last or the next point picked.
Quadrant	Finds the closest 0-, 90-, 180-, or 270-degree point relative to the current UCS on a circle or an arc.
Tangent	Locates a point that is tangent to the selected circle or arc from either the last or the next point picked.
Tracking	Specifies a point that is relative to other points, using orthogonal or polar displacements.
NEW for R2000 Extension	Locates a point by extending a temporary, dashed construction line from an existing arc or line. This object snap is new to AutoCAD 2000.
NEW for R2000 Parallel	Allows you to select an angle by creating a temporary, dashed construction line that is parallel to an existing object whose vector is acquired. This object snap is new to AutoCAD 2000.

Running Osnap Toggle and Osnap Override

Running Osnap Toggle and Osnap Override are two useful AutoCAD features first introduced in Release 14. They are important adjuncts to the overall operation of object snaps and are therefore discussed here.

Running Object Snap Toggle

Running toggle is an Osnap enhancement that enables you to toggle off any running (continuing) Osnap prior to selecting a point without losing the running Osnap settings. This feature is accessed by clicking the OSNAP button on the mode status bar at the bottom of AutoCAD's screen. If this button is selected when no running Osnaps are set, the Object Snap tab on the Drafting Settings dialog box is displayed, giving you the opportunity to set a running Osnap.

Object Snap Override

AutoCAD 2000 provides an option that enables you to explicitly enter coordinate data that has priority over any running Osnaps that may be in effect. This enhances direct coordinate entry and you can be certain that such entries have precedence over any other settings. To temporarily override a running Osnap, simply choose an Object Snap using any method described previously in the Object Snapping section. AutoCAD uses the selected Snap override for the next pick only, then reverts back to running Osnaps.

AutoSnap

AutoSnap is an important feature in AutoCAD that was first introduced with Release 14. With AutoSnap, you can visually preview snap point candidates before picking a point. Depending on how you have AutoSnap features set, AutoSnap will display a *Snap Tip* placard similar to the toolbar's Tool Tip feature. Also, a marker distinctive to each Osnap mode can be displayed in the color of your choice, making for easy identification of the snap location and snap type. You can also enable a "magnet" feature that snaps the marker into place much like the action of AutoCAD's Grips feature.

In the following exercise, you use some of AutoCAD's Osnap modes and the three methods of invoking them. In addition, you will see how the AutoSnap feature makes looking for and confirming Osnap points an unambiguous, efficient means of picking Osnap points.

BISECTING AN ANGLE USING OBJECT SNAPS WITH AUTOSNAP

1. Open the drawing 06DWG03. The drawing appears, showing two line segments whose end points touch, creating an angle.

    If the Object Snap toolbar is not visible, proceed with steps 2 and 3.

2. Right-click any toolbar button. The available toolbars appear on the pop-up Cursor menu, as shown in Figure 6.27.

3. Select Object Snap from the cursor menu. Note that the Object Snap toolbar appears.

Figure 6.27

The available toolbars appear on the cursor menu.

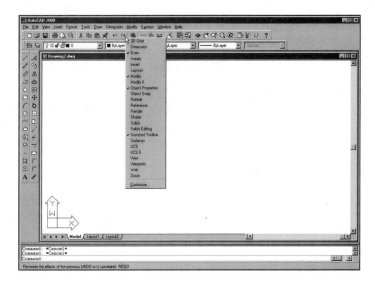

4. From the Tools menu, select Options to display the Options dialog box, then select the Drafting tab. Ensure that the Marker, Magnet, and Display AutoSnap tooltip features are all selected, and that the Display AutoSnap Aperture Box is cleared, as shown in Figure 6.28. Click OK to close the dialog box.

Figure 6.28

The Drafting tab on the Options dialog box controls AutoSnap settings.

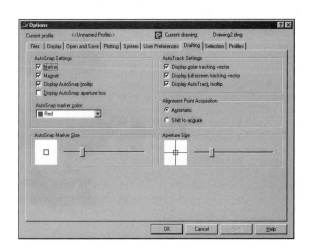

5. From the Draw menu, select Arc, Center, Start, End. You see the following prompt:

    ```
    Specify start point of arc or [CEnter]: _c Specify center point
    of arc:
    ```

6. Click the Snap to Endpoint tool from the displayed Osnap toolbar. Then move and rest the screen cursor to a point near ④ in Figure 6.29. Notice the AutoSnap marker that appears at ② and that the Snap Tip also appears, identifying the snap point as the line's endpoint.

Figure 6.29

The AutoSnap feature identifies the line's endpoint.

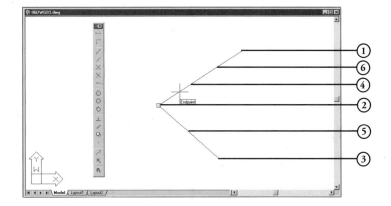

7. With the Endpoint Snap marker still displayed, pick a point near ④. AutoCAD then prompts for the arc's start point.

8. At the `Specify start point of arc:` prompt, click and hold the Osnap fly-out on the Standard toolbar (refer to Figure 6.26), select the Snap to Nearest Tool, and release the pick button. Move the cursor near the lower line at ⑤. Note the appearance of the nearest AutoSnap marker as you approach ⑤.

9. Pick near ⑤. At the `Specify end point of arc or [Angle/chord Length]:` prompt, Shift+right-click to display the Screen pop-up menu. Then select Endpoint and move the cursor toward ⑥. Note the appearance of the Endpoint marker.

10. Pick the upper line near ⑥. AutoCAD draws the arc as shown in Figure 6.30.

Figure 6.30

Bisecting an angle using Osnaps.

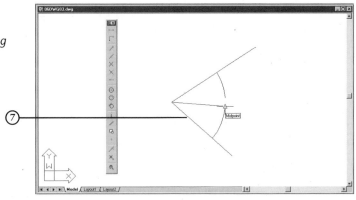

11. Type **L** and press Enter at the command prompt. At the `Specify first point:` prompt, type **endp** and press Enter. Note the appearance of the Endpoint AutoSnap marker as you approach ⑦ as shown in Figure 6.30.

12. Click at ⑦. Then at the `Specify next point or [Undo]:` prompt, click on the Midpoint tool on the Osnap toolbar and move the cursor to any point on the arc. Note the appearance of the Midpoint marker on the arc, as shown in Figure 6.30. With the marker showing, pick any point on the arc.

13. At the next `Specify next point or [Undo]:` prompt, press Enter to end the `LINE` command. The bisector line is drawn, as shown in Figure 6.30.

As seen in the preceding exercise, the use of Osnaps and the AutoSnap feature gives a definite, unambiguous indication of the geometry to which you are snapping. Even in crowded areas of a drawing, such as shown in Figure 6.31, positive identification of which point is the current snap target is possible.

AutoSnap also supports a feature that enables stepping through the object snap points of objects lying within the target aperture when it is enabled. The Tab key is used to cycle from the closest to the furthest Osnap point from the center of the aperture box. The target geometry is highlighted to further aid in identification. This highlighting feature is shown in Figure 6.32, where the midpoints of two objects lie very close together and both fall within the Osnap aperture box. Repeated pressing of the Tab key cycles among the objects, highlighting the target geometry so that you can snap to the correct object's midpoint.

Figure 6.31

AutoSnap provides positive identification of target geometry.

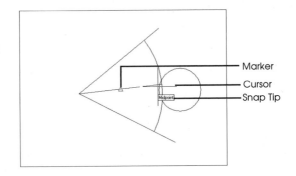

Figure 6.32

In crowded areas, AutoSnap's cycling feature highlights target geometry.

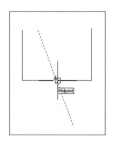

Using AutoTrack

NEW for R2000

AutoTrack is a new feature introduced with AutoCAD 2000. It's actually made up of two features. The first, *Object Snap Tracking*, was originally introduced with Release 14, and is enhanced in this new release. The other, *Polar Tracking*, is new to AutoCAD 2000. Together, these two tracking features are collectively called AutoTrack.

AutoTrack creates temporary alignment paths: dashed construction lines that appear on screen to help you identify pick points. When your cursor properly aligns with the preset Polar or Object Snap Tracking angle, the dashed line appears, and your cursor is constrained to it. This simplifies the identification of potential pick points.

The difference between Polar Tracking and Object Snap Tracking is this: Polar Tracking creates alignment paths for points you have already set, whereas Object Snap Tracking creates alignment paths based on acquired Osnaps. In other words, Polar Tracking displays alignment paths for the last point selected, and functions independently of Osnaps. In contrast, Object Snap Tracking displays alignment paths only if you use Osnaps, and move the cursor over an Osnap marker to acquire it.

This section describes both Object Snap tracking and Polar Tracking, and provides a simple exercise that shows you how to use these two powerful features.

Object Snap Tracking

Object Snap Tracking was introduced in AutoCAD Release 14, and was originally called Tracking. As with many new AutoCAD features, this feature was first introduced in AutoCAD LT where it has been very popular. Although not an object snap in the strict sense, Object Snap Tracking is used with standard Osnaps to enhance your ability to find points relative to another object's geometry.

You can use Object Snap Tracking whenever AutoCAD prompts for a point. If you try to use Object Snap Tracking when no command is currently running, AutoCAD displays an error message.

When you start Object Snap Tracking by acquiring an Osnap point, AutoCAD displays either orthogonal alignments, or preset polar angle alignments. You control whether Object Snap Tracking uses orthogonal or polar alignments from the Polar Tracking tab on the Drafting Settings dialog box (refer to Figure 6.23). By choosing Track Orthogonally Only option in the Object Snap Tracking Settings area, Object Snap Tracking displays only orthogonal alignment paths. If the Track Using All Polar Angle Settings option is selected, alignment paths are displayed for all angles listed in the Polar Angle Settings area, also found on the Polar Tracking tab.

You acquire an Osnap by moving the cursor over an Osnap marker. When prompted to select a point during a command, if Object Snap Tracking is enabled and you move your cursor over an Osnap marker, a small cross appears in the marker, indicating that the point is acquired. Then, as you move the cursor away from the point, the orthogonal or polar alignment paths appear, and your cursor is constrained to them as you move along the paths. To clear an acquired point, move the cursor back over the Osnap marker.

N O T E

It is important to understand that you acquire an Autotrack point by simply moving your cursor over the Osnap marker. Do *not* pick the point. Just move the cursor over the marker; AutoCAD will acquire the point automatically and display a small plus (+) sign in the center of the Osnap marker.

To remove the small symbol from an acquired point, move the cursor back over the small plus (+) sign. AutoCAD removes the symbol, and the point is "un-acquired."

I N S I D E R   T I P

You can set a temporary tracking point without using Osnap markers. By typing **TT** at any point prompt, AutoCAD prompts for a temporary OTRACK point. After a point is selected, AutoCAD places a small + at the point, indicating that the tracking point is set. To remove the temporary tracking point, move the cursor over the small +.

Polar Tracking

Polar Tracking is the perfect compliment to Object Snap Tracking. When enabled, Polar Tracking alignment paths appear on screen as you move away from the point you have already set. However, unlike Object Snap Tracking, you do not need to acquire a point to display the polar angle alignment paths. If Polar Tracking is enabled, the alignment paths automatically appear as you move away from the last point, and prepare to pick the next.

Polar Tracking is discussed in detail in this chapter in the section "The New Polar Tracking Feature."

In the following exercise, you use the AutoTrack features.

USING AUTOTRACK'S OBJECT SNAP TRACKING AND POLAR TRACKING FEATURES

1. Open the drawing 06DWG04. The drawing appears, showing two parallel line segments, three units apart.

2. From the Tools menu, select Drafting Settings. The Drafting Settings dialog box appears.

3. Select the Object Snap tab. Be sure the Endpoint and Midpoint Object Snap modes are selected, and that all other options are cleared, including the Object Snap On and Object Snap Tracking On, as shown in Figure 6.33.

4. From the Drafting Settings dialog box, select the Polar Tracking tab. Be sure the Polar Tracking On option is cleared, and that the Track Using All Polar Angle Settings and Absolute options are selected.

5. In the Polar Angle Settings area, from the Increment Angle drop-down list, select 30.0, as shown in Figure 6.34.

Figure 6.33

*The proper Object Snap
settings for this exercise.*

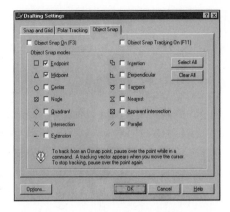

Figure 6.34

*The proper Polar Tracking
settings for this exercise.*

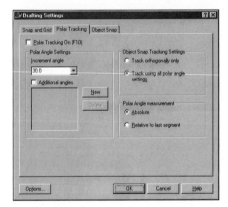

6. From the Drafting Settings dialog box, select the Snap and Grid tab. Be sure the Snap On and Grid On options are cleared.

7. In the Snap Type & Style area, select Polar Snap. The Polar Spacing area activates, and the Snap area grays.

8. In the Polar Spacing area, set the polar distance to 0.5, as shown in Figure 6.35, and click OK.

Figure 6.35

The proper Snap and Grid settings for this exercise.

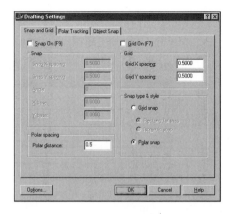

9. From the status bar at the bottom of the screen, click the SNAP, POLAR, and OSNAP buttons to activate the Snap grid, Polar Tracking, and Object Snap features.

10. From the Draw menu, select Line, then pick the endpoint of the line at location D.

11. Move your cursor away from the endpoint. Notice as you move your cursor around that dashed alignment paths appear at 30-degree increments. This occurs because you set the increment angle to 30.0, and select the Track Using All Polar Angle Settings option (refer to Figure 6.34).

12. Move your cursor up and to the right of the endpoint, until the 60-degree alignment path appears. Drag your cursor along the 60-degree alignment path. Notice that the cursor is constrained to the path, and that it snaps at 0.5 unit increments. This occurs because you set the polar distance to 0.5, and chose the Polar Snap option (refer to Figure 6.35).

13. Pick the line's endpoint when the AutoTrack tooltip reads `Polar: 1.0000<60`, as shown in Figure 6.36, then press Enter to end the `LINE` command.

Figure 6.36

The Polar Tracking feature displays alignment paths in the designated angle increments.

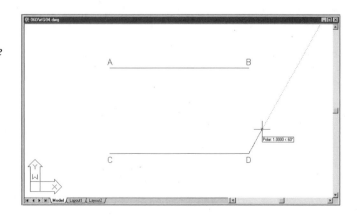

14. From the status bar at the bottom of the screen, click the OTRACK button to activate the Object Snap Tracking feature. Then click the SNAP and POLAR buttons to turn off the Snap grid and Polar Tracking features.

15. From the Draw menu, click Line, then pick the endpoint of the line at C. Move your cursor over the endpoint at C, and when the Endpoint Osnap marker appears, move cursor into the marker until a small cross (or plus sign) appears. When the small + appears, Object Snap Tracking is activated for this marker. (Do *not* pick the endpoint.)

16. Next, move your cursor to the endpoint of the first line you created. When the Endpoint Osnap marker appears, move the cursor into the marker until a small + appears. When the small + appears, Object Snap Tracking is activated for this marker. (Do *not* pick the endpoint.)

17. Move your cursor to the left along the Object Snap Tracking alignment path, toward the endpoint at C. As you near the endpoint at C, Object Snap Tracking alignment paths appear for its marker.

18. Continue moving your cursor toward the left until the AutoTrack tooltip reads `Endpoint:<120, Endpoint:<180`. Pick the point, as shown in Figure 6.37, then press Enter to end the `LINE` command. You will continue in this drawing in the next exercise.

Figure 6.37

The Object Snap Tracking feature displays alignment paths for acquired Osnap markers.

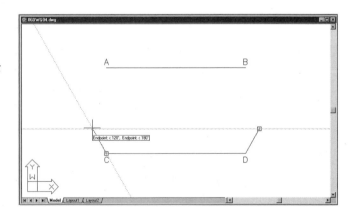

As you just experienced, AutoTrack's Object Snap Tracking and Polar Tracking features can help you pick points by displaying temporary alignment paths. Remember that Object Snap Tracking relies on Osnaps, and sets alignment paths only when an Osnap marker is acquired. In contrast, Polar Tracking functions independently of Osnaps, and displays alignment paths during a command as you move your cursor away from the last point set.

From and Apparent Intersection Osnaps

Much like the Object Snap Tracking feature, the "auxiliary" Osnaps From and Apparent Intersection supply data points that stand in some relationship to points on drawing objects. The *From* object snap establishes a temporary reference point as a basis for specifying subsequent points. The From object snap is normally used in combination with other object snaps and relative coordinates. For example, at a prompt for the center point of an arc, you could type **From Endp**, select a line, and then type **@4,5** to locate a point four units to the right and five units up from the endpoint of the selected line. The center of the arc would then be located at this point.

Apparent Intersection snaps to the apparent intersection of two objects that might or might not actually intersect in 3D space. In 2D drafting, Apparent Intersection is usually involved with the projected intersection of two line elements.

The following exercise demonstrates both the From and Apparent Intersection Osnaps as you center a circle at a distance from the apparent intersection of two lines.

DRAWING A LINE USING THE FROM AND APPARENT INTERSECTION OSNAPS

1.   Continue from the previous exercise, or open the drawing 06DWG05.

2.   From the status bar at the bottom of the screen, click the OTRACK and OSNAP buttons to turn off the Object Snap Tracking and Object Snap features.

3.   From the Draw menu, select Line. AutoCAD starts the **LINE** command.

4.   At the **Specify first point:** prompt, Shift+right-click to display the Cursor menu, then select From.

5.   At the **Base point:** prompt, Shift+right-click to display the Cursor menu, then select Midpoint.

6.   Pick the midpoint of line CD.

7.   At the **Offset:** prompt, type the relative coordinate **@1.5,1**, then press Enter. This establishes the starting point of the line.

8.   At the **Specify next point or [Undo]:** prompt, Shift+right-click to display the Cursor menu, then choose Apparent Intersection. The Apparent Intersection snap requires selecting two different objects. After these objects are selected, AutoCAD determines the "apparent" intersection point of the two objects.

9. At the **Of:** prompt, move your cursor to the line AB, near the endpoint at B. Notice the appearance of the Apparent Intersection AutoSnap marker, as shown in Figure 6.38. This line represents the first object.

Figure 6.38

The Apparent Intersection Osnap marker displays.

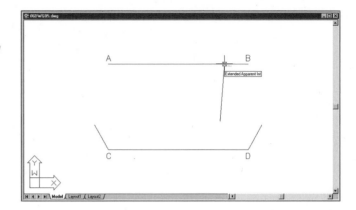

10. Pick the line near B. AutoCAD now prompts for the other object.

11. Move your cursor to the angled line extending up from point D. When you move your cursor over the line, AutoCAD displays the Intersection marker at the point the two objects "apparently" intersect, as shown in Figure 6.39.

Figure 6.39

AutoCAD displays the Intersection marker at the point the two objects "apparently" intersect.

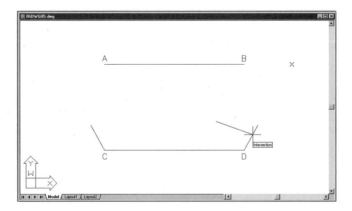

12. Pick the line. AutoCAD places the end of the line segment at the apparent intersection.

13. Press Enter to end the **LINE** command.

The From and Apparent Intersection snap features provide tools that allow you to snap to points where no objects exist. With these tools, you set the first point of a line by offsetting it from the midpoint of an existing line, and snap the other end of the line to the apparent intersection of the two objects.

Extension and Parallel Osnaps

The final set of object snaps discussed in this chapter are new to AutoCAD 2000. The *Extension* Osnap extends an existing object's vector, simulating the extension with a dashed construction line. Similarly, the *Parallel* Osnap displays a dashed line that is parallel and offset from an existing object.

In the next exercise, you use the Extension and Parallel Osnaps to draw a line parallel to an existing object.

DRAWING A LINE USING THE EXTENSION AND PARALLEL OSNAPS

1. Continue from the previous exercise, or open the drawing 06DWG06.

2. From the Draw menu, select Line. AutoCAD starts the LINE command.

3. At the Specify first point: prompt, Shift+right-click to display the Cursor menu, then select Extension.

4. Move your cursor to the angled line extending up from point C. Move your cursor up along the line to its endpoint. AutoCAD displays a small cross at the end of the line, indicating that it is acquired. (Do *not* pick the endpoint.)

5. Continue moving the cursor up along the imaginary extension of the line. AutoCAD extends the existing line, as shown in Figure 6.40.

Figure 6.40

AutoCAD displays the extension of the acquired line.

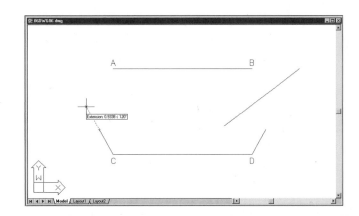

6. At the `Of:` prompt, type **1.5**, then press Enter. This establishes the starting point of the line.

7. At the `Specify next point or [Undo]:` prompt, Shift+right-click to display the Cursor menu, then select Parallel.

8. At the `To:` prompt, move your cursor to the line AB. When your cursor moves over the line, the Parallel Snap marker appears on the line, as shown in Figure 6.41. Then AutoCAD places a small + in the center of the Parallel Snap marker, indicating that it is acquired. (Do *not* pick the line.)

Figure 6.41

AutoCAD displays the Parallel Snap marker.

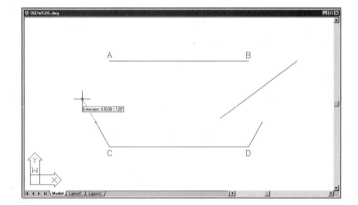

9. With the Parallel snap acquired, move your cursor downward, below line AB, until a dashed construction line appears, as shown in Figure 6.42. Notice the dashed line is parallel to line AB.

Figure 6.42

The Parallel snap creates an imaginary alignment line, parallel to the acquired object.

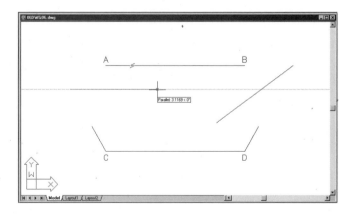

10. At the To: prompt, type **4.5**, then press Enter. AutoCAD sets the endpoint of the line.

11. Press Enter to end the LINE command.

Like the Osnaps discussed in the two previous exercises, the new Extension and Parallel snap features provide tools that allow you to snap to points where no objects exist. With these tools, and the tools described in the two previous exercises, you can snap to just about any point in your drawing, real or imaginary.

Construction Lines and Rays

With the existence of Apparent Intersection and From Osnaps, and the new AutoTrack, Extension, and Parallel snap features, little need exists for the "construction lines" used in traditional "pencil" drafting. After you become competent with these drawing aids, the time and effort required to draw and subsequently erase traditional construction lines will seem inefficient.

There may be occasions, however, when the inclusion of construction lines may be necessary to assist in visually presenting the relationship among the elements of a drawing. AutoCAD has two special line objects—xlines and rays—that function as traditional construction lines.

The XLINE command creates infinite lines, which are commonly used as construction lines. *Xlines* can be placed vertically, horizontally, at a specified angle, offset a specified distance, or as an angle bisector. Although xlines extend infinitely in both directions, they are ignored for the purpose of calculating the drawing's extents.

The RAY command creates "point to infinite" lines commonly used as construction lines. A *ray* has a finite starting point and extends to infinity. As with the xline, the infinite length of a ray is ignored for the purpose of determining a drawing's extents.

In conjunction with their use as a largely visual element, both xlines and rays are often placed on separate layers with a distinctive linetype and color assigned. Figure 6.43 shows a typical application of xlines.

Figure 6.43

Xlines and Rays serve as construction lines.

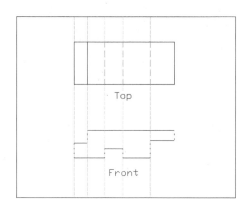

Summary

In this chapter, you learned about AutoCAD's coordinate system and the methods you can use to enter coordinate points in your drawings. Absolute coordinate entry enables you to specify points relative to the drawing's current coordinate system's 0,0 point, or origin. Relative coordinate entry, on the other hand, enables you to specify points relative to the previous point you entered. Relative coordinates are expressed either as an X and Y distance or a distance and angle from the last point. You also learned how to change the orientation of AutoCAD's coordinate system by creating User Coordinate Systems (UCSs). You also learned how to configure drafting settings for Snap and Grid, Polar Tracking, and Object Snap.

This chapter also covered the important concept of snapping to specific geometry in your drawings using various Osnaps. You also learned that AutoCAD 2000 has several powerful Osnap tools, including the new AutoTrack feature, and the new Extension and Parallel snaps, which make snapping to "apparent" points both easier and less ambiguous than in previous releases.

CREATING ELEMENTARY OBJECTS

No matter how complicated a drawing is, no matter how many layers and linetypes it contains, almost all AutoCAD drawings are composed of a few relatively basic shapes and forms. Circles, arcs, lines, rectangles, polygons, and ellipses are the basic elements from which both simple and complicated drawings are made. This chapter shows you the tools you will need to construct and control AutoCAD's basic drawing objects.

This chapter covers the following topics:

- *Using the LINE command*

- *Using the ARC command*

- *Using the CIRCLE command*

- *Using the POLYGON command*

- *Drawing ellipses*

Using the LINE Command

Perhaps the most common object in a typical AutoCAD drawing is the line. In addition to representing the shortest distance between two points, lines serve a myriad of other useful purposes. Centerlines locate other geometry; border lines indicate an area's constraints; and dashed lines represent objects or boundaries that are not visible from a given point of view. All these lines are usually further identified functionally by their *linetype*—the periodic pattern of interruptions in the line's continuity. Normal continuous lines are representative of things such as walls or the sides of objects. Lines are very versatile, and drawing a line is one of the most basic operations in AutoCAD.

In the following exercise, you will learn the basics of using the LINE command as you begin drawing a fixture base.

NOTE

The exercises in this chapter use the templates Elementary.dwt and Ellipse.dwt files found on the accompanying CD-ROM. These drawings have most settings, linetypes, and layers already set or defined for you. In the first part of the chapter, you learn about lines, circles, arcs, and polygons. When you finish this first section, your drawing will resemble Figure 7.1. Later in the chapter, you will begin a new drawing in which you will practice constructing and accurately placing ellipses. The use of template drawings is discussed in Chapter 2, "Starting a Drawing in AutoCAD 2000."

Figure 7.1

This chapter's completed fixture base.

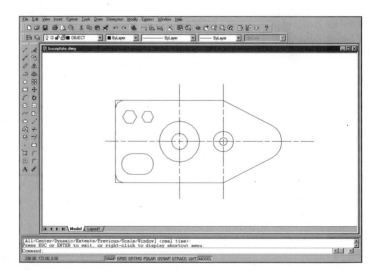

USING THE LINE COMMAND TO DRAW A FIXTURE BASE

1. Begin a new drawing called chap701.dwg using the file Elementary.dwt as a template. Using template drawings is discussed in Chapter 2. Make sure the current layer is Center.

2. Begin the LINE command by choosing Draw, Line. At the Specify first point: prompt, type **38,88** and press Enter.

3. At the Specify next point or [Undo]: prompt, use a relative polar coordinate entry by typing **@208<0** and pressing Enter. Note that the line segment is drawn with a linetype of Hidden. Close the LINE command by pressing Enter.

4. Restart the LINE command by pressing the spacebar. Respond to the Specify first point: prompt by typing **112,32** and pressing Enter. Make sure that the ORTHO mode is turned on by clicking the ORTHO button on the status bar or by pressing F8.

5. Use direct distance entry by moving the cursor above the last point. Then respond to the Specify next point or [Undo]: prompt by typing **112** and pressing Enter. End the LINE command by pressing Enter. Note that the line segment is drawn 112 units at 90 degrees to the first point.

6. Make sure that SNAP mode is on (press F9), and restart the LINE command by typing **L** and pressing Enter. Respond to the Specify first point: prompt by pressing F6 until the Coordinate display on the status bar displays absolute coordinates. Then find and pick point 156,144.

NOTE

> If you miss the point in the preceding step, type **U** to undo the last point placement. Restart the LINE command by pressing either Enter or the spacebar, then pick the point again.

7. At the Specify next point or [Undo]: prompt, type the relative coordinate **@0,-112** and press Enter. End the LINE command by pressing Enter again. Your drawing should now resemble Figure 7.2.

8. Leave this drawing open for the next exercise.

Figure 7.2

Setting up the center lines for the fixture base.

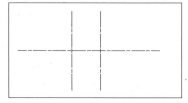

In the preceding exercise, you used several different methods to specify coordinate point entry while using the LINE command. You also saw how the coordinate display, which is located on the status bar at the bottom of AutoCAD's display, can be helpful in locating both absolute and relative coordinate points. Keep in mind that, depending on how your increment snap is set up and the value of the actual points, the snap feature can make finding many points much easier. For points that do not lie on your current snap pattern, direct coordinate entry through the keyboard is the only practical method of having line segments begin and end exactly where you want.

INSIDER TIP

In many situations, you will find yourself frequently changing the coordinate display mode as well as turning ORTHO and SNAP on and off. It can be more convenient to use the function key shortcuts to control these functions. F6 controls the coordinate display, F8 toggles the ORTHO mode on and off, and F9 toggles the SNAP function.

In the following exercise, you will continue to use the LINE command as you outline the fixture base. After establishing the first corner of the base, you will use the efficient direct distance method for entering points that are orthogonal to the previous point.

USING THE LINE COMMAND TO DRAW THE FIXTURE BASE OUTLINE

1. Continuing from the previous exercise, change the current layer to OBJECT. See Figure 7.3 to identify the following points.

Figure 7.3

Points used to draw the fixture base.

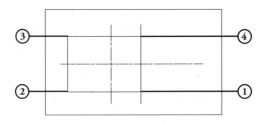

2. First, you will deliberately enter the wrong point to see how easy it is to recover from such a mistake. Begin the LINE command, type the coordinates **150,48**, and press Enter. Note that the point falls short of the right centerline. The X coordinate is incorrect.

3. To recover from your mistake, use the LINE command's Undo option by typing **U** and pressing Enter. Then re-enter the point at ① by typing **156,48** and pressing Enter.

4. Now with ORTHO on and the cursor placed to the left of the previous point, use direct distance entry to specify the point at ② by typing **108** and pressing Enter.

Note

From now on in this chapter's exercises, the instruction to "enter **80**," for example, will mean that you are to type **80** and press Enter. The instruction "enter **80**" or "enter **Line**" (without the double quotation marks) means the same as "type **80** and press Enter" or "type **Line** and press ENTER."

5. Move the cursor above the preceding point and enter **80** to draw a line segment to ③.

6. Move the cursor to the right of ③ and enter **108**. The line segment is drawn between ③ and ④.

7. Now close the outline by using the Close option of the LINE command (type **C** and press Enter). This closes to the start point and ends the LINE command.

8. The line segment from ④ to ① was drawn by mistake; it is not wanted. At the command prompt, issue the U command by typing **U** and pressing Enter. Note that, because the LINE command is no longer in progress, all four line segments completed during the LINE command are erased. At the command prompt, issue the REDO command by entering **REDO**. All four segments are redrawn.

INSIDER **T**IP

You can use the REDO command to recreate the sequences undone by an UNDO.

9. To erase the last line segment, issue the ERASE command by entering **E**. At the Select objects: prompt, type **L** and press Enter. Note that the last completed line segment is highlighted. Now, with the Select objects: prompt still current, press Enter. The line is erased. Your drawing should now resemble Figure 7.4.

10. Save your drawing at this point using the name Chap7.dwg. If you are continuing with the next section, leave this drawing open.

Figure 7.4

*Setting up the center lines
for the fixture base.*

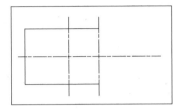

The LINE Command Options

The LINE command is straightforward and easy to use. It offers the following features:

- **Specify first point.** At this prompt, your input places the first point of the first line segment. If you press Enter at the Specify first point prompt, the line segment will start from the last specified endpoint of the last drawn line segment or arc.

- **Specify next point.** At this prompt, your input places the point to which the current line segment is drawn.

- **[Close/].** After two successive line segments have been drawn, you can type c (Close) to close the series. A line is drawn from the last endpoint to the first point of the series.

- **[Undo].** At any *Specify next point:* prompt, you can type u (undo) to undo the last line segment drawn. Repeating the U option will step back through multiple line segments.

Keep in mind that the LINE command draws individual lines or line *segments* whose only relationship to one another is that the endpoint of one segment shares the same coordinate as the start point of the next segment.

INSIDER TIP

If you are constructing a long series of line segments using the LINE command, break the continuity of the chain and restart it occasionally by pressing Enter three times. This has the effect of ending the series, restarting the command, and beginning a new series from the end of the last. Then if you perform a U option at a command prompt, it will undo only the last LINE command's series of line segments, instead of all the segments since the very first start point.

You can end or exit the LINE command at any time by pressing Esc or by pressing Enter at any Specify next point prompt.

Using the ARC Command

The ARC command is used to draw portions of circles known as arcs. Its several options make constructing an arc with a variety of known parameters such as center, start point, chord length, radius, and so on much easier than with traditional manual drafting methods.

In the following exercise, you will draw an arc by specifying three points on its circumference. After completing the arc, you will erase it and then draw two small arcs to round the corners of the fixture base. Use the coordinate display on the status bar and the Snap feature to identify points.

USING ARC TO DRAW CIRCULAR ARCS

1. Continue with the Chap6 drawing from the preceding exercise. If necessary, turn on the SNAP mode by pressing the F9 key. Begin the ARC command by selecting the Arc tool from the Draw toolbar. Respond to the Specify start point of arc or [Center]: prompt and specify the point at ① in Figure 7.5 by entering its coordinate: **156,48**.

2. At the Specify second point of arc or [Center/End]: prompt, specify the point at ② by typing **196,88** and pressing Enter. Note that the arc passes through ② as you move the cursor.

3. At the Specify end point of arc: prompt, specify the point at ③ by entering **156,128**. The ARC command draws the arc and terminates. Your drawing should resemble Figure 7.5.

Figure 7.5

Drawing an arc using the 3-Points method.

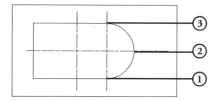

4. At the command prompt, issue the U command by typing **U** and pressing Enter. The arc is deleted.

   Before starting the next step, you may want to zoom in to enlarge the view. To do this type **Z** and press Enter. Then type **W** and press Enter. Click and drag a window around the left side of the baseplate, and then click to zoom.

5. Start the ARC command again by entering **A**. At the `Specify start point of arc or [Center]:` prompt, enter the coordinate **56,128** (see ④ in Figure 7.6).

6. Respond to the next prompt by typing **CE** and pressing Enter to select the Center option. Then, at the `Specify center point of arc:` prompt, specify the point at ⑤ by entering **56,120**.

7. Make sure that ORTHO is on (press F8 if necessary) and note that as you move the cursor, the arc snaps in 90-degree increments. Move the cursor to the left of ④ and pick. The ARC command draws the arc; ORTHO forces it to 90 degrees

Figure 7.6

Creating rounded corners with the ARC command.

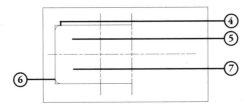

8. Restart the ARC command by pressing Enter. At the `Specify start point of arc or [Center]:` prompt, enter the coordinate **48,56** to start the arc at ⑥.

9. At the `Specify second point of arc or [Center/End]:` prompt, type **CE** and press Enter. This indicates that the next point you supply will be the center of the arc.

10. At the `Specify center point of arc:` prompt, enter the relative rectangular coordinate **@8,0**. This places the center of the arc at ⑦. With ORTHO on, the arc jumps to 90-degree increments as you move the cursor around.

11. Disable ORTHO mode by pressing F8 and notice that the arc now drags with the cursor. Answer the `Specify end point of arc or [Angle/chord Length]:` prompt by entering **A**. This indicates that you will next supply the included angle for the arc.

12. Turn ORTHO back on and move the cursor anywhere above the center point. Note that the arc now snaps to 90-degree points again. Pick any point directly above the center point near ⑤ to complete the arc and end the ARC command.

13. Save the changes you've made by pressing Ctrl+S. Leave the drawing open for a following exercise.

Whenever you draw an arc, you know either its center or its start point and can supply the other necessary information from existing geometry in the drawing. Figure 7.7 shows the Arc submenu from AutoCAD's Draw menu. This submenu conveniently lists the various choices you can make, depending on the information supplied. Starting the ARC command by using this submenu provides a shortcut for bypassing the longer prompt choices provided at the command prompt.

Figure 7.7

The Arc submenu offers 11 methods of drawing an arc.

The ARC Command Options

The ARC command requires three pieces of information to complete an arc, one of which must be either the center of the arc or its start point. The other required parameters can be supplied in various combinations. The following list explains these combinations:

- **3-Points.** This method creates an arc that passes through three points you supply. The first point is considered the start point, the second point is the endpoint, and the third point is any other point between those two. This is the default method of constructing arcs.

- **Start, Center.** This method requires the arc's starting and center points. The third piece of data can be the endpoint, an included angle, or the length of the chord. Counterclockwise arcs are drawn if the included angle is supplied as a positive angle; clockwise arcs are drawn if the angle is supplied as a negative angle. A positive chord length draws a minor arc (less than 180 degrees), and a negative chord length creates a major arc (greater than 180 degrees).

■ **Start, End.** This method enables you to supply the start point and endpoint of the arc and then to specify how to draw the arc. You define the arc with an angle, direction, radius, or center point. When you supply a positive angle, AutoCAD draws a counterclockwise arc; when you supply a negative angle, it draws a clockwise arc. If you choose the radius option, AutoCAD always draws the arc counterclockwise. A negative radius forces a major arc, and a positive radius forces a minor arc.

■ **Center, Start.** This method enables you to first identify the center of the arc and then the start point. Supplying either the angle, length of chord, or endpoint completes the arc. When you supply the length of chord, a negative length creates a major arc, and a positive length creates a minor arc. If you supply an angle, a negative angle draws the arc clockwise; a positive angle draws the arc counterclockwise.

■ **Continue.** This method is the built-in default. You invoke this option by pressing Enter at the first arc prompt. It begins a new arc tangent to the last line or arc that was drawn.

INSIDER TIP

Probably no other AutoCAD command seems at times to be as uncontrollable as the ARC command. The trick to drawing arcs with other than the basic and simple 3-Points or Start-Center-End options is knowing how to force the arc in the direction you desire. Understanding that AutoCAD, by default, thinks of arcs as developing *counterclockwise* from the start point is the key to controlling arcs. To force an arc to proceed clockwise, for example, you must supply a negative angle or a negative distance for a length of chord parameter. The same type of entries control whether an arc is drawn as a minor or a major arc. If you're armed with this knowledge and a little practice, your arcs can come out correctly—usually on the first try.

The ARC command's Continue option is often convenient for use when arcs are associated with line segments. The following exercise demonstrates this feature of the ARC command.

PUTTING LINES AND ARCS TOGETHER

1. Continue from the drawing in the preceding exercise. Make sure ORTHO mode is turned on, and then take a look at Figure 7.8. It will be helpful to zoom in to provide a larger view of the baseplate features you have drawn so far.

Figure 7.8

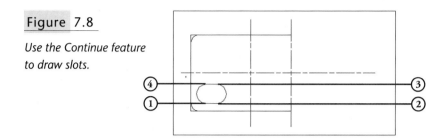

*Use the Continue feature
to draw slots.*

2. Start the LINE command by entering **L**. At the Specify first point: prompt, specify the point at ① by typing **64,56** and pressing Enter. Then at the Specify next point or [Undo]: prompt, enter the relative coordinate **@12,0**. See ② for reference.

3. Choose the Arc tool from the Draw toolbar to cancel the LINE command and start the ARC command.

4. At the Specify start point of arc: prompt, press Enter. This activates the Continue option of the ARC command and starts an arc tangent to the endpoint of the line you just drew. Then specify the point at ③ by entering **76,76**.

5. Restart the LINE command by selecting the Line tool from the Draw toolbar. At the Specify first point: prompt, press Enter. This activates the Continue option of the LINE command and starts the line tangent to the arc.

6. At the Length of line: prompt, enter **12**. This draws a line to ④.

7. Again, start the ARC command and press Enter. This again cancels the LINE command and starts an arc at the endpoint of the line.

8. At the Specify endpoint of arc: prompt, enter the relative polar coordinate **@20,270**. This completes the arc at ①.

9. Your drawing should now resemble Figure 7.8. Press Ctrl+S to save the drawing in its present form. If you are not continuing immediately with the next section, you can close this drawing and re-open it later.

The drawing shows the fixture base with rounded corners on the left side. After the preceding exercise, you should be familiar with the continuing features of both the LINE and ARC commands. The "trick" is to disregard the first Specify first (or start) point of these two commands and press Enter instead. When you're drawing an alternating series of line segments and arcs, this method can save you a significant amount of time selecting start points.

> Chapter 11, "Advanced Geometry Editing," explains the use of the FILLET command, which provides an easy alternate method of creating arcs tangent to lines.

Using the CIRCLE Command

Another basic AutoCAD shape is the circle. Circles are used to represent holes, wheels, shafts, columns, trees, and so on. Several methods exist for drawing circles, and unlike in manual drafting, constructing circles in AutoCAD is quick and accurate. Circles have centers, diameters, radii, and tangent and quadrant points. By providing a combination of these parameters, you can draw any circle and place it anywhere you want.

In the following exercise, you construct a few basic circles as you add holes and sleeves to the fixture base.

ADDING HOLES SLEEVES BY DRAWING CIRCLES

1. Continue working with the drawing from the previous exercise. Refer to Figure 7.9 throughout this exercise.

Figure 7.9

Drawing and placing circles.

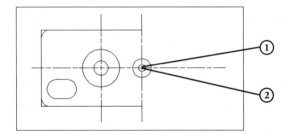

2. Start the CIRCLE command by typing **C** and pressing Enter or by selecting the Circle tool from the Draw toolbar.

3. At the `Specify center point for circle or [3P/2P/Ttr (tan tan radius)]:` prompt, specify the point at ① by entering **156,88**. Move the cursor and watch the radius and circle follow as you drag. The coordinate display in the lower-left of the AutoCAD window should show changing X,Y coordinates. If it doesn't, click on the display pane until it does. Then click twice in the coordinate display to change to a polar coordinate display. While you're watching the polar coordinate display, slowly move the cursor and pick when the display reads **4.00@,0.00**. AutoCAD draws a circle passing through ②.

4. Press Enter or the spacebar to restart the `CIRCLE` command. At the circle prompt, type **@** and press Enter. When entered at any AutoCAD "point" prompt, the @ symbol automatically enters the last point entered—in this case the center point of the circle you just drew.

5. At the `Specify radius of circle or [Diameter]:` prompt, enter **D** to specify a diameter and then enter **20**. This specifies the diameter and draws the circle.

6. Next, from the Draw menu, choose Circle and then 3-Points. At the `Specify first point on circle:` prompt, enter the point **104,88**.

7. At the `Specify second point on circle:` prompt, enter the point **112,96**. At the `Specify third point on circle:` prompt, enter the point **120,88**. AutoCAD draws the circle using the three points on the circumference that you picked.

8. Now press Enter to restart the `CIRCLE` command with the `Specify center point for circle or [3P/2P/Ttr (tan tan radius)]:` default prompt. Enter **112,88** for the center point.

9. To experiment with the effects of ORTHO mode, turn off ORTHO mode by pressing F8. Then move the cursor around while watching the polar coordinate display. Pick when a radius of 20 displays. AutoCAD draws the circle with a radius of 20 units.

    The baseplate should now resemble Figure 7.9. You will continue with this drawing in the next section.

CIRCLE Command Options

The `CIRCLE` command provides you with several options for controlling the sequence in which you create circles. In addition to the default center point/radius mode, you can create a circle by specifying three points on the circumference or by selecting two objects (lines, circles, or arcs) to which the circle is to be tangent and then specifying a radius.

When working with the CIRCLE command, you can use any of the following options:

■ **Center point.** Type or pick the center point, and you are prompted for a radius or diameter. Radius is the default option. You override the radius default by entering **D**. When using either the radius or diameter option, you can enter a value or pick two points to show the distance.

■ **3P (3 Points).** Use this option to specify the circumference by entering or picking three points that will lie on the circumference.

■ **2P (2 Points).** Use this option to specify two diameter points on the circumference.

■ **TTR (Tangent-Tangent-Radius).** Use this option to select two lines, arcs, or circles (any combination) that form tangents to the circle. Then specify the circle's radius.

Note

> Note the difference between Center point/Diameter and the 2P option. Both options enable you to specify a diameter, but if you pick the second point with Center point/ Diameter, it merely indicates the diameter's distance, and the circle does not pass through the second point. If you pick two points with 2P, a circle appears between those two points, and the distance is the diameter. The 2P option enables you to draw a diameter circle the way most of us intuitively think about the term diameter.

In the following exercise, you practice using the TTR option of the CIRCLE command.

PRACTICING CIRCLES WITH THE TTR OPTION

1. Continuing in the drawing from the preceding exercise, make sure object snap is on (press F3 if necessary and check the command line to see the Osnap status).

2. Start the CIRCLE command by selecting the Circle tool from the Draw toolbar. Respond to the `Specify center point for circle or [3P/2P/Ttr (tan tan radius)]:` prompt by entering **T** to indicate the tangent:, tangent, radius option.

3. Respond to the `Specify point on object for first tangent of circle:` prompt by resting the cursor anywhere on the circumference of the circle at ② (see Figure 7.10). Note the appearance of the tangent osnap symbol and the label Deferred Tangent on the circle's circumference. Pick to establish the tangent object.

Figure 7.10

Placing circles using the tangent-tangent-radius method.

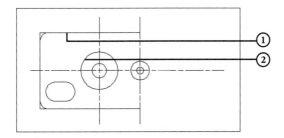

4. At the `Specify point on object for second tangent of circle:` prompt, rest the cursor anywhere on the line ①. Note the appearance of the tangent osnap symbol and the label Deferred Tangent on the line. Pick to establish the second tangent object.

5. At the `Specify radius of circle:` prompt, enter **20**.

6. AutoCAD draws the only circle that meets the requirements of being tangent to both the circle at ② and the line at ① and having a radius of 20 units (see Figure 7.11). Type **U** and press Enter to delete the circle.

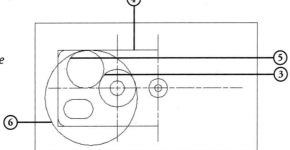

Figure 7.11

Drawing circles with the TTR option.

7. Repeat steps 2 through 5, but at step 5 type **50** and press Enter. Once again, AutoCAD draws the only possible circle ⑥ that is tangent to both the circle at ③ and the line at ④ and has a radius of 50 units (see Figure 7.11).

8. Issue the `Undo` command again to delete the last circle you drew. (It is not needed to complete the fixture.)

9. Save the changes you have made by pressing Ctrl+S.

NOTE

When you use the TTR option, you may encounter the message Circle does not exist. This indicates that a circle with the radius you specified or that was tangent to the two points you chose (or both) does not exist. Most often, the radius specified is too small.

Using the POLYGON Command

In AutoCAD, you use the POLYGON command to create regular polygons with sides of equal length. You can draw a polygon composed of from 3 to 1,024 sides. After you specify the number of sides, several options are available for completing the polygon:

- **Enter number of sides:** At the Enter number of sides: prompt, enter the number of sides (3 to 1,024).

- **Specify center of polygon or [Edge]:** At this prompt, choose whether you want to define the polygon by specifying its center or the endpoints of an edge.

- **Enter an option [Inscribed in circle/Circumscribed about circle]:** This prompt appears if you choose the center option. If you choose Inscribe in Circle, all vertices of the polygon fall on the circle; if you choose Circumscribed about Circle, the radius equals the distance from the center of the polygon to the midpoints of the edges. If you use the pointing device to specify the radius, you dynamically determine the rotation and size of the polygon. If you specify the radius of the circle by typing a specific entry, the angle at the bottom edge of the polygon equals the current snap rotation angle (usually zero degrees).

- **Specify first endpoint of edge, Specify second endpoint of edge:** If you place the polygon by specifying its edge, these prompts enable you to specify the endpoint of one edge.

In the following exercise, you practice drawing a polygon representing a mounting hole on the fixture base.

ADDING A MOUNTING HOLE WITH THE POLYGON COMMAND

1. Continuing in the drawing from the preceding exercise, start the POLYGON command by choosing Polygon from the Draw menu.

2. At the Enter number of sides: prompt, enter **6**.

3. At the Specify center of polygon or [Edge]: prompt, enter **62,112** to specify the center of the polygon.

4. At the Enter an option [Inscribed in circle/Circumscribed about circle]: prompt, enter **C**.

5. At the Specify radius of circle: prompt, enter **6**. AutoCAD draws the hexagon.

6. Press Enter to restart the POLYGON command. Repeat steps 3 through 6, but specify a center coordinate of **80,112** and enter **I** to choose the Inscribed option. Specify a radius of **6**.

7. AutoCAD draws the second hexagon. Note the difference in size between the two hexagons. Your drawing should now resemble Figure 7.12.

8. Save the changes you made in this exercise.

Figure 7.12

Adding mounting holes with the POLYGON command.

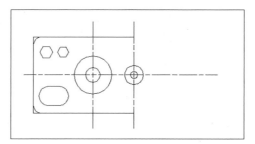

INSIDER TIP

> AutoCAD's POLYGON command produces polygons that are composed of *polylines*. Polylines are useful because they can be exploded into individual line segments for editing. You can also change their width by using the PEDIT command. In addition, you can fillet and chamfer all edges with one command sequence. You'll learn about those techniques later in this book.

AutoCAD's POLYGON command provides a convenient way to draw regular (equilateral) multi-sided polygons, including triangles. Several options make sizing and placing of the final polygon relatively easy.

The fixture base drawing that has gradually grown during this chapter is almost complete. In the following exercise, you will use the line/arc continue method of "rounding corners" that you learned earlier in this chapter to complete the drawing.

COMPLETING THE FIXTURE BASE WITH A ROUNDED CORNER

1. Continuing with the drawing from the preceding exercise, make sure coordinate readout is active. (If necessary, press F6 to make it active.) Also turn off ORTHO and turn on Snap.

2. Start the LINE command by typing **L** and pressing Enter. At the Specify start point: prompt, use the coordinate readout to find and pick the point 156,128 ①.

3. At the Specify next point: prompt, enter the relative coordinate **@48,_24**. AutoCAD draws a line to ②.

4. End the LINE command by pressing Enter. Then start the ARC command by typing **A** and pressing Enter. Press Enter again to take advantage of the Continue feature. At the Specify endpoint of arc: prompt, type the relative polar coordinate **@32,270** and press Enter. AutoCAD draws the arc to ③.

5. Now start the LINE command again and press Enter to activate the Continue feature. At the Length of line: prompt, use the coordinate readout to find and pick point 156,48 ④. (If necessary, press F6 until the coordinate display shows absolute coordinates.) Press Enter to end the LINE command.

   This completes the fixture base. Your drawing should look like Figure 7.13 (and Figure 7.1 at the beginning of this chapter). You are now finished with this drawing.

Figure 7.13

Finishing the fixture base.

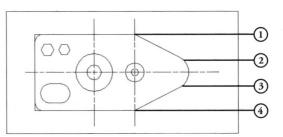

So far in this chapter, you have learned about the basic AutoCAD drawing elements of lines, circles, arcs, and polygons. You will use these elements over and over again in most of your drawings. You have also learned how AutoCAD gives you a large amount of flexibility in constructing and placing these basic elements. Next you will learn how to draw ellipses.

Drawing Ellipses

In AutoCAD 2000, you can draw true ellipses and elliptical arcs, both of which are exact mathematical representations of ellipses. The default method of drawing an ellipse is to specify the endpoints of the first axis along with the distance, which is half the length of the second axis. The longer axis of an ellipse is called the major axis, and the shorter one is the minor axis. The order in which you define the axes does not matter.

NOTE

AutoCAD is also capable of constructing elliptical representations of ellipses using polylines. The system variable PELLIPSE determines the type of ellipse that's drawn. A value of I creates a polyline representation; a value of 0 creates a true ellipse.

INSIDER TIP

In Release 14, the default method of drawing ellipses is to draw true ellipses. Unless you have a specific reason to use the less-accurate polygon approximation, leave the system variable PELLIPSE set to 0 and draw true ellipses. Polygon ellipses offer few, if any, advantages.

Ellipses are somewhat complicated geometric figures, but if you have a basic understanding of the geometry of an ellipse, AutoCAD enables you to draw them easily. An ellipse has both a major axis and a minor axis, as shown in Figure 7.14. Although from a mathematical point of view an ellipse has two "centers" or foci, AutoCAD considers the geometric center to be the intersection of the two axes. The quadrants of an ellipse are the points of intersection between the axes and the ellipse. In AutoCAD, you can use both the quadrants and center of an ellipse as object snap points.

Figure 7.14

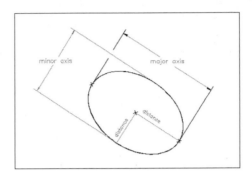

The geometry of an ellipse.

AutoCAD offers you several ways to specify the various parameters of an ellipse. Those methods are covered in the following section.

ELLIPSE Command Options

When you issue the ELLIPSE command, the following prompt appears:

```
Specify axis endpoint of ellipse or [Arc/Center]:
```

To respond to this prompt, you can use one of the following methods:

- **Axis endpoint.** You specify an axis (major or minor) endpoint. The Specify other endpoint of axis: prompt will appear, at which you specify the second axis endpoint. The Specify distance to other axis or [Rotation]: prompt then appears. If you specify the other axis distance, AutoCAD draws the ellipse. If you specify Rotation (by typing **R** and pressing Enter), AutoCAD prompts for an angle and then completes the ellipse.

- **Center.** If you choose the Center option, the Specify center of ellipse: prompt appears, at which you specify the center point. The Specify endpoint of axis: prompt appears next. Specify an endpoint. Then the Specify distance to other axis or [Rotation]: prompt appears. If you specify the other axis distance, AutoCAD draws the ellipse. If you specify Rotation (by typing **R** and pressing Enter), AutoCAD prompts for an angle. The angle specifies the ratio of the major axis to the minor axis. An angle of 0 defines a circle. The maximum angle that's acceptable is 89.4, which yields a "flat" ellipse.

- **Arc.** If you choose the arc option (by typing **A** and pressing Enter), the `Specify axis endpoint of elliptical arc or [Center]:` prompt appears, which requests the same information as the prompt for a full ellipse. After you answer the prompt sequence for the full ellipse, the `Specify start angle or [Parameter]:` prompt appears. Specify a point to define the start angle of the arc, and the `Specify end angle or [Parameter/Included angle]:` prompt appears. Specify an end angle to draw the arc. Specifying **I**, for Included angle, enables you to specify an included angle for the arc, beginning with the start angle.

NOTE

In reckoning angles for elliptical arcs, the direction of the first point of the major axis is considered 0 degrees. If the system variable ANGDIR is set to 0 (the default), angles for the elliptical arc are measured counterclockwise; if ANGDIR is set to 1, angles are measured clockwise. If the minor axis is defined first, the major axis zero point is 90 degrees in a counterclockwise direction. If you choose the Included angle option, the angle is measured from the start point, not the 0 degree point.

INSIDER   **T**IP

When you're specifying elliptical arc angles, it is helpful to set the coordinate display on the status bar to indicate polar coordinates. You cycle through the coordinate display modes by pressing the F6 key.

In the following exercises, you practice drawing ellipses in a three-view mechanical drawing. Throughout the exercises, you will use the object snap techniques you learned in Chapter 6, "Accuracy in Creating Drawings with AutoCAD 2000."

In this exercise, you first use a full set of construction lines to draw an ellipse in one view, and then a reduced set of construction lines provides the information you need to draw an ellipse in another view.

DRAWING ELLIPSES IN A THREE-VIEW DRAWING

1. Open the drawing Ellipse.dwg on the accompanying CD-ROM. This drawing, shown in Figure 7.15, shows an unfinished three-view drawing of a mechanical mounting bracket. A shaded isometric view is included. The hole in the angled portion of the bracket has already been projected onto the Front view. You will use the Object Snap Tracking feature of AutoCAD 2000 (discussed in Chapter 6) to draw the ellipse and the elliptical arc representing the hole in the Top view.

Figure 7.15

An incomplete three-view drawing of a mounting bracket.

2. First, establish the settings you will need for Object Snap Tracking. Right-click on the OTRACK button on the mode status line at the bottom of the display and select Settings from the shortcut menu.

3. In the Drafting Settings dialog box, on the Object Snap tab, choose Object Snap On and Object Snap Tracking On. Under Object Snap Modes, select Endpoint, Midpoint, Quadrant, and Intersection (see Figure 7.16). Click OK to close the dialog box.

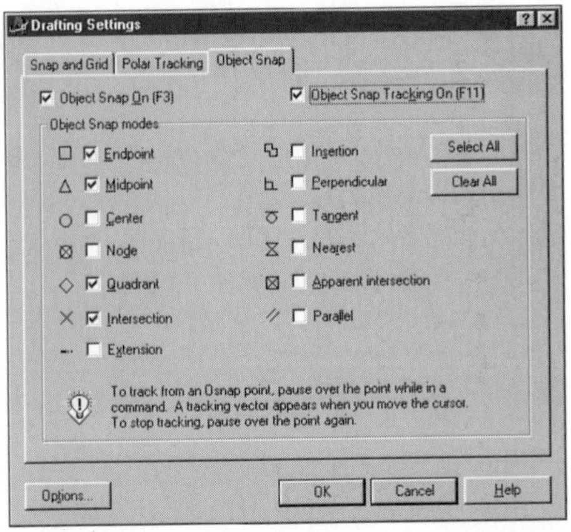

Figure 7.16

The settings for Object Snap Tracking.

4. To zoom to a closer view, open the View menu and choose Named Views. In the View dialog box, select view AAA, select Set Current, and click OK to close the dialog box and establish the new view as shown in Figure 7.17.

Figure 7.17

A close-up of the Top, Side, and Front views of the mounting bracket.

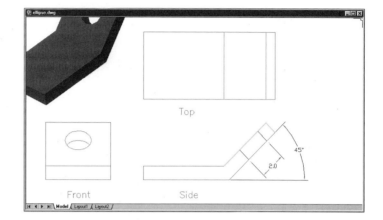

5. Referring to Figure 7.17, you will use the intersections of the hidden lines with the surface of the bracket at ① and ② and the midpoint of the top edge at ③ to establish Auto Tracking points to accurately position the ellipse in the Top view. From the Draw menu, choose Ellipse, and then select Axis, End.

6. At the `Specify axis endpoint of ellipse or [Arc/Center]:` prompt, move the cursor over ① in Figure 7.17 and hold it stationary until the auto track symbol appears (as shown in Figure 7.18A).

7. Move the cursor up into the Top view and hold it over ③ until the Midpoint Auto Track symbol appears. Then move the cursor back to the left until the tracking from ① appears. Auto Track will indicate the acquired point as Intersection <90, Midpoint <180, as shown in Figure 7.18B. Pick this point as the axis endpoint of the ellipse.

8. At the Specify other endpoint of axis: prompt, move the cursor over ② in Figure 7.17 and hold it stationary until the Auto Tracking symbol appears, as shown in Figure 7.18C.

9. Now drag the cursor up into the Top view again until the Auto Tracking point is acquired. Auto Tracking will report `Endpoint 6.2889 < 90`, as shown in Figure 7.18D. Click on this point to establish the second axis endpoint. AutoCAD draws a tentative ellipse using the axis endpoints supplied thus far. Note that the ellipse center point is now established.

Figure 7.18

Auto Tracking points used to place the ellipse.

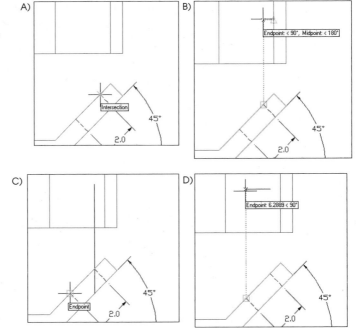

10. At the `Specify distance to other axis or [Rotation]:` prompt, type **1** and press Enter. AutoCAD completes the ellipse. This distance is referred to as the "ellipse center point," and the dimension in the Side view gives the diameter of the hole as 2 units, or a radius of 1 unit. Your drawing should now resemble Figure 7.19.

11. Keep this drawing open for use in the next exercise.

In the following exercise you use the Arc option of the `ELLIPSE` command to draw a partial ellipse, or an elliptical arc, to complete the ellipses in the Top view of the mounting bracket drawing.

Figure 7.19

The completed Top view ellipse.

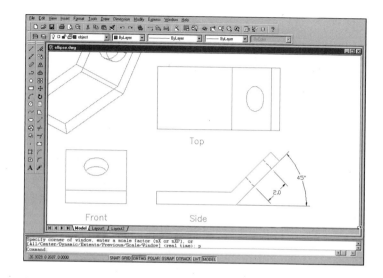

DRAWING ELLIPTICAL ARCS

1. Continue in the drawing of the mounting bracket from the preceding exercise. You will now place an elliptical arc "inside" the arc you drew in the last exercise, again using Auto Tracking to place the arc.

    Right now, the drawing now should resemble Figure 7.19. When you have completed this exercise, the drawing will resemble Figure 7.22. You will use the same Auto Tracking settings you used in the last exercise.

2. From the Draw menu, choose Ellipse and then Arc. At the `Specify axis endpoint of elliptical arc or [Center]:` prompt, rest the cursor over ① in Figure 7.20A until the tracking symbol appears.

3. Move the cursor straight up into the Top view and then to the right to acquire the Midpoint of the bracket edge, as shown in Figure 7.20B.

4. Slowly move the cursor to the left until the Auto Track symbol appears, as shown in Figure 7.20C. Select that point.

Figure 7.20

*Auto Tracking points used
to draw the elliptical arc.*

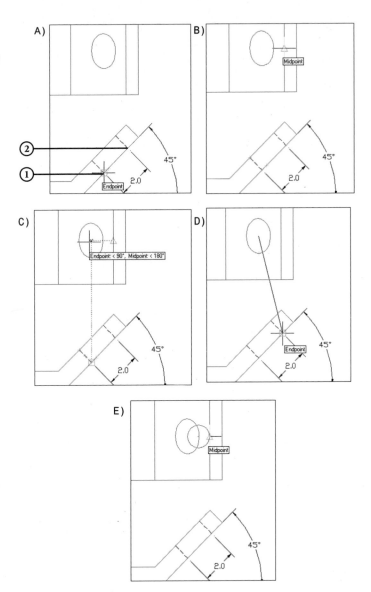

5. At the `Specify other endpoint of axis:` prompt, move the cursor over ② in Figure 7.20A until you acquire the tracking point as shown in Figure 7.20D.

6. Move the cursor back into the Top view to acquire the Midpoint again. Select this point as shown in Figure 7.20E. AutoCAD draws a tentative ellipse based on the endpoints you've supplied thus far.

7. At the `Specify distance to other axis or [Rotation]:` prompt, type **1** and press Enter. AutoCAD draws the complete ellipse. At the `Specify start angle or [Parameter]:` prompt, carefully place the cross hairs at ① in Figure 7.21 and pick. Then drag the cross hairs around the ellipse in a clockwise direction to ② and pick. This completes the elliptical arc.

The full ellipse and the elliptical arc should resemble those shown in Figure 7.22. This completes your work in this drawing.

Figure 7.21

Specifying the included angle for the elliptical arc.

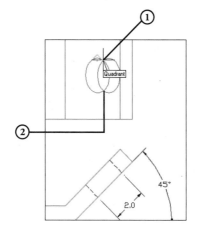

Figure 7.22

The completed baseplate fixture with ellipse and elliptical arc.

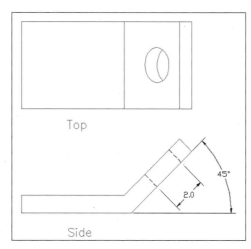

Summary

In this chapter, you learned to use the commands AutoCAD provides for drawing basic objects—from simple lines to more complicated arc segments. Mastering their use forms the basis of the range of skills required to use AutoCAD effectively.

Although the LINE command offers few options, when it's used in combination with the other basic objects and drawing aids (such as ORTHO and object snaps), it is a fundamental component of most AutoCAD drawings.

When you're drawing circles and arcs, several methods are available. The method you select depends on the information you have available. You can often use more than one of the methods to accomplish the task. Understanding how and when to use each method enables you to quickly construct complex designs.

Polygon objects are common figures found in many AutoCAD drawings. Knowing how to construct them quickly and accurately increases your efficiency.

You can create true mathematical ellipses and elliptical arcs in AutoCAD. Ellipses have true center and quadrant points to which you can snap. These objects are also frequently used to represent circular objects viewed in axonometric views.

8

CREATING POLYLINES AND SPLINES

In the previous chapter, you learned about lines and arcs and how to use them to draw straight line segments and circular arcs. Lines and arcs are separate entities, even if they are connected end to end. A box drawn with the LINE *command, for example, is really four separate line segments whose endpoints are shared with other line segments. Polylines, however, are multi-segmented objects; they can be composed of multiple straight or curved segments. No matter how many segments a polyline is composed of, it acts as a single multi-segmented line.*

In most AutoCAD drawings, you use traditional elements, such as lines, arcs, polylines, and circles. Sometimes, however, you may want to draw smooth or irregular curves. AutoCAD provides the spline object for drawing free-form irregular curves. Splines are useful when you need to draw map contours, roads, walkways, or other smooth, flowing objects.

This chapter covers the following topics on polylines and splines:

- *Polylines versus lines*

- *Creating polylines*

- *Polyline types*

- Editing polylines
- Creating true splines
- Controlling splines with SPLINEDIT

Polylines Versus Lines

Polylines are different from the line segments created by AutoCAD's LINE command. Polylines are treated as single objects and can include both line and arc segments connected at their vertices. AutoCAD stores information about the vertices, and you can access this information and edit the appearance of the polyline.

Polylines offer two advantages over lines. First, polylines are versatile; they can be straight or curved, thin or wide, and even tapered. Figure 8.1 shows some of the various forms a polyline can take.

Figure 8.1

Polylines can assume various useful forms.

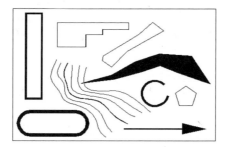

Second, editing polylines is easier: You can select any segment of a polyline, and all other segments will be also selected because all segments are connected. This makes editing operations, such as moving and copying, faster and more accurate. Objects drawn with lines and arcs may appear to be connected but, depending on how they were drawn, may actually have gaps or discontinuities that make it difficult to use them as boundaries for cross hatching.

Creating Polylines

Polylines are created using the PLINE command. The PLINE command enables you to draw two basic kinds of polyline segments: straight lines and arcs. Some PLINE command prompts, therefore, are the same as those you find in the LINE and ARC command prompts. If, for example, you draw straight polyline segments, you will find options such as Specify Next Point, Close, and Undo. You see these options in the standard polyline prompt for line segments:

```
Specify next point or [Arc/Close/Halfwidth/Length/Undo/Width]:
```

In addition, certain prompt options, such as Width, are specific to polylines. Those prompt options include the following:

- **Arc.** Switches from drawing polylines to drawing polyarcs and issues the polyarc options prompt.

- **Close.** Closes the polyline by drawing a segment from the last endpoint to the initial start point and exits the PLINE command.

- **Halfwidth.** Prompts for the distance from the center to the polyline's edge (half the actual width). For more information, read about the Width option.

- **Length.** Prompts for the length of a new polyline segment. AutoCAD draws the segment at the same angle as the last line segment or tangent to the last arc segment. The last line or arc segment can be that of a previous polyline, line, or arc object.

- **Undo.** Undoes the last drawn segment. It also undoes any arc or line option that immediately preceded drawing the segment. It does not undo width options.

- **Width.** Prompts you to enter a width (default 0) for the next segment. Enables you to taper a segment by defining different starting and ending widths. AutoCAD draws the next segment with the ending width of the previous segment. Unless you cancel the PLINE command prior to drawing a segment, the ending width is stored as the new default width.

- **Specify Start Point / Specify Next Point.** Prompts for the starting point or the next point of the current line segment. After you begin a new polyline, Specify Next Point is the default option.

If you select the Arc option, the Arc mode options prompt appears:

```
[Angle/CEnter/CLose/Direction/Halfwidth/Line/Radius/Second pt/Undo/
Width]
```

This prompt contains some of the same options as the ARC command and others specific to the drawing of polylines. The arc options include the following:

- **Angle.** Prompts for an included angle. A negative angle draws the arc clockwise.

- **Center.** Prompts you to specify the arc's center.

- **Close.** Closes the polyline by using an arc segment to connect the initial start point to the last endpoint and then exits the PLINE command.

- **Direction.** Prompts you to specify a tangent direction for the segment.

- **Halfwidth.** Prompts for a halfwidth, the same as for the Line option.

- **Line.** Switches back to the line mode.

- **Radius.** Prompts for the polyarc's radius.

- **Second pt.** Selects the second point of a three-point polyarc.

- **Undo.** Undoes the last drawn segment.

- **Width.** Prompts you to enter a width, the same as in line mode.

- **Specify Endpoint of Arc.** Prompts for the endpoint of the current arc segment. This is the default option.

INSIDER TIP

You can also close a polyline of two or more segments after the fact by using the PEDIT command's Close option. Using the PEDIT Close option draws a line between the last point of the last segment drawn and the start of the first segment. The PEDIT command is covered later in this chapter.

Although using the PLINE command to draw lines and arcs is similar to using the LINE and ARC commands to draw similar objects, there are several important differences:

- You get all the line or arc mode prompts every time you enter a new polyline vertex.

- Prompt options for the Halfwidth and Width control the width of the segment.

- You can switch back and forth from line segments to arc segments as you add segments to the polyline.

- You can apply linetypes continuously across vertices.

- You can apply the MEASURE and DIVIDE commands to polylines.

- You can use the AREA command to report the total length of a polyline and to calculate the area enclosed by certain polylines.

In the following exercise, you practice drawing a single polyline using many of the options for both the Line and Arc mode options of the POLYLINE command.

PRACTICING WITH THE POLYLINE COMMAND OPTIONS

1. Create a new drawing named chap08.dwg using this chapter's IAC801.DWT on the accompanying CD as a template. (See Chapter 2, "Starting a Drawing in AutoCAD 2000," for a discussion of template drawings.)

2. Start the POLYLINE command by typing **PL** and pressing Enter. The initial polyline prompt Specify start point: appears. Respond by entering the point **2.5,1.0**. The Line mode options prompt appears.

3. Use the default endpoint option by entering the relative polar coordinate **@5<90**. AutoCAD draws the first segment of the polyline from ① to ② in Figure 8.2. The Line mode options prompt reappears.

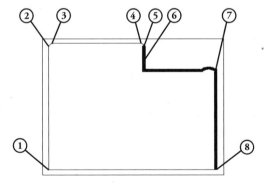

Figure 8.2

Drawing a multisegment polyline.

4. Switch to the Polyarc mode by typing **A** and pressing Enter. The Arc mode options prompt appears.

5. Use the default Specify Endpoint of Arc: option by typing **@.25<45** and pressing Enter. AutoCAD draws the polyarc to ③. The Arc mode options prompt reappears.

6. Switch back to the Line mode by choosing the Line option. Type **L** and press Enter. The Line mode options appear. Choose the Length option by entering **L**. Then, at the `Specify length of line:` prompt, type **@3<0** and press Enter. AutoCAD draws the next segment 3 units long, to ④. Now switch back to the Arc mode by entering **A**. The Arc mode options prompt appears.

7. Choose the angle option by typing **A** and pressing Enter. At the `Specify included angle:` prompt, type **-90** and **E**. This specifies a 90-degree clockwise included angle to the point at ⑤. The `Specify endpoint of arc or [Center/Radius]:` prompt appears.

8. Choose the Radius option by typing **R** and pressing Enter. When you're prompted to specify the radius of the arc, enter the value **0.125**. Respond to the `Then Specify direction of chord for arc:` prompt by typing **315** and pressing Enter.

9. Switch to the line mode by entering **L**. Choose the Width option by entering **W**.

10. Respond to the `Specify starting width:` prompt by typing **0.1** and pressing Enter. Accept the Ending Width <0.1>: value by pressing Enter. Respond to the Line mode's `Specify next point:` prompt by entering **@1<-90**. AutoCAD draws the next segment with a uniform width of 0.1 units ⑥.

11. Now at the `Specify next point:` prompt, enter the relative coordinate **@2,0**. AutoCAD draws the next segment at the current width of 0.1 units.

12. Again, switch to the Arc mode by entering **A**. Respond to the Arc mode prompt by typing **CE** and pressing Enter. At the `Specify center point of arc:` prompt, enter **@0.25,-0.25** to specify the center of the next arc section.

13. Respond to the `Specify endpoint of arc or [Angle/Length]:` prompt by entering **A**. Specify an included angle of **-90** (see ⑦).

14. Switch to the Line mode (type **L** and press Enter) and enter the relative polar coordinate **@4.052<270**. AutoCAD draws the next line segment at the current 0.1 width ⑧.

15. Now change the width for the next segment by typing **W** and pressing Enter. Respond to the `Specify starting width:` prompt by entering **0**. Then accept the default ending width by pressing Enter.

16. The standard `Specify next point or [Arc/Close/Halfwidth/Length/Undo/Width]:` prompt appears. Choose the Close option by entering **C**. AutoCAD draws the next segment to the start point of the first segment of the series with a 0 width ①.

17. Your drawing should now resemble Figure 8.2. You will continue using this drawing in the next exercise. For now, press Ctrl+S to save the changes you have made.

NOTE

Polylines can consist of a number of segments, and it's possible for significant changes to take place in the polyline's characteristics from segment to segment. The endpoint of one segment is the start point of the next. Later, in the discussion on editing polylines, these points are referred to collectively as "vertices" or singly as a "vertex."

As you saw in the preceding exercise, you can easily switch back and forth between the Line mode and the Arc (Polyarc) mode within the PLINE command. Each mode has its own set of prompts that repeat after you draw each segment. You also saw that both line and arc segments can have widths other than zero and that when you specify a new width, it becomes the default width for the next segment. In other words, both the mode (Line versus Polyarc) and the width remain in effect unless and until you explicitly change them. This facilitates drawing a long series of either straight line or curved arc segments.

In the following exercise, you construct an arc leader using both the Line and Arc modes. You will also take advantage of the capability to vary the width of a single polyline segment.

DRAWING AN ARC LEADER WITH A POLYLINE

1. Continue in the drawing from the preceding exercise. Refer to Figure 8.3 for this exercise.

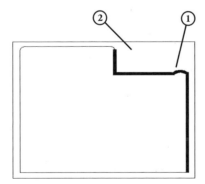

Figure 8.3

Picking the points for a PLINE *arc leader.*

2. Begin the PLINE command by choosing the Polyline tool from the Draw menu. The Specify start point: prompt appears.

3. Pick a point near ① in Figure 8.3. At the Specify next point: prompt, choose the Width option by typing **W** and pressing Enter.

4. Specify a starting width of **0.0** and an ending width of **0.1**.

5. Respond to the `Specify next point:` prompt by entering **@.2<115**. AutoCAD draws the first segment with a tapered width. You may not see the taper until the next step is complete.

6. At the `Specify next point:` prompt, enter **W** again.

7. Specify a starting width of **0** and an ending width of **0**.

8. Respond to the Line mode prompt by choosing the Arc option.

9. The Arc mode prompts appear. Note that the arc drags as you move the cursor near ② Pick a point near ②, and AutoCAD draws the arc. Press Enter to exit the `PLINE` command.

10. Your drawing should resemble Figure 8.4. Save this drawing.

Figure 8.4

The completed polyline arc leader.

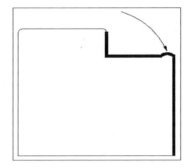

The preceding exercise demonstrates the versatility of polylines. Not only can polylines have varying widths, but each segment can have different starting and ending widths. The current polyline width is stored in the system variable `PLINEWID`.

Controlling Polyline Appearance with `FILL`

A drawing that consists of a large number of polylines with widths other than zero can significantly increase the time it takes AutoCAD to redraw the screen or to plot the drawing. AutoCAD provides the `FILL` command to enable you to control the visibility of the filled portion of wide polylines. When you turn `FILL` off, AutoCAD displays or plots only the outline of filled polylines. You must regenerate the drawing in order to see the effect of the `FILL` command. Figure 8.5 shows the effect of having turned `FILL` on and off. The `FILL` command also controls the appearance of all hatches and of objects created using the `SOLID`, `TRACE`, and `MLINE` commands.

Figure 8.5

You can turn fill on (left) or off by using the FILL command.

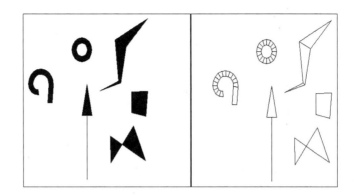

> **N**OTE
>
> The FILL command controls the setting of the system variable FILLMODE. A setting of 1 is equivalent to having FILL turned on; a setting of 0 is equivalent to having FILL turned off. You can also control the setting of FILLMODE in the Options dialog box's Display tab, under the Apply Solid Fill option.

Polyline Types

In AutoCAD Release 13 and earlier, polylines were generated and stored in AutoCAD's database differently. The current PLINE command produces a "leaner," optimized polyline, sometimes referred to as a "Lightweight Polyline." Some of the functionality and control available in the older 2D polyline objects (such as arc fit curve data, spline fit data, and curve fit tangent direction data) are not available in the current 2D optimized polyline.

To provide compatibility with the 2D polyline objects AutoCAD pre-Release 14, the system variable PLINETYPE is provided. PLINETYPE specifies whether AutoCAD uses the newer optimized 2D polylines. It controls both the creation of new polylines with the PLINE command and the conversion of existing polylines in drawings from previous releases. PLINETYPE can have one of three settings:

0	Polylines in older drawings are *not* converted when opened; PLINE creates old-format polylines.
1	Polylines in older drawings are *not* converted when opened; PLINE creates optimized polylines.
2	Polylines in older drawings are converted when opened; PLINE creates optimized polylines. This is the default setting.

An optimized polyline can have the following characteristics:

- Straight line segments

- Arc segments

- Constant and variable width

- Thickness

NOTE

PLINETYPE also controls the polyline type created by using the following commands: BOUNDARY (when object type is set to Polyline); DONUT; ELLIPSE (when PELLIPSE is set to 1); PEDIT (when selecting a line or arc); POLYGON; and SKETCH (when SKPOLY is set to 1).

You also can manually convert the older 2D polylines by using the CONVERT command, which is described next.

CONVERT Command

The CONVERT command allows you to "manually" optimize 2D polylines created in AutoCAD Release 13 and earlier. The prompts for the CONVERT command are as follows:

```
Enter type of objects to convert [Hatch/Polyline/All] <All>:
```

You enter **H** for hatches, **P** for polylines, or **A** for both. The next prompt then appears:

```
Enter object selection preference [Select/All] <All>:
```

Enter **S** to select objects or **A** to convert all candidate objects in the drawing. Depending on your response to these two prompts, AutoCAD displays one or both of the following messages:

```
number hatch objects converted.
number 2d polyline objects converted.
(Where number is the number of objects converted.)
```

In most cases, you do not need to convert polylines with the CONVERT command because the PLINETYPE system variable (described in the previous section) specifies that polylines are updated automatically whenever you open an older drawing.

However, older, non-optimized polylines might be created in your AutoCAD 2000 drawing by third-party applications or they may be part of an older drawing that is inserted into your current drawing and then exploded.

NOTE
> Polylines that contain curve fit or splined segments always retain the old-style format, as do polylines that contain extended entity data.

The **3DPOLY** Command

The **3DPOLY** command produces three-dimensional polylines. 3D polylines are not as versatile as the standard (2D) polylines produced with the **PLINE** command because they can contain only straight line segments with continuous linetype and no width information. They are more versatile than 2D polylines, however, because their vertices can be placed in 3D space. That is, you can draw them with a non-zero Z coordinate in addition to the required X and Y coordinates. 3D polylines are discussed in more detail in Chapter 28, "Drawing in 3D AutoCAD."

Editing Polylines

As you have seen so far in this chapter, polylines are complex objects consisting of a collection of arc and line segments, each possessing the additional capability of containing width information. AutoCAD, therefore, provides the **PEDIT** command, a command devoted to editing these complex entities. **PEDIT** does not differentiate between the newer, optimized polylines, and the older, pre-Release 14 polylines.

Editing Entire Polylines with **PEDIT**

PEDIT contains a large number of subcommands or options for the various polyline properties. To manage this large number of options, AutoCAD divides them into two groups of editing functions. The primary group operates on the polyline as a whole, while a secondary group is devoted to the vertices that mark the beginnings and ends of polyline segments. Several editing options are available for both 2D and 3D polylines. The following list outlines the primary group of PEDIT options:

■ **Close/Open.** Adds a segment (if required) and joins the first and last vertices to create a continuous polyline. If the polyline is open, the prompt shows Close; if the polyline is closed, the prompt shows Open. A polyline can be open even if the first and last points share the same coordinates. A polyline is open unless the polyline Close option is used when you draw it or you later use the Close option to close it.

■ **Join.** (2D only) Enables you to add selected arcs, lines, and other polylines to an existing polyline. Endpoints must be exactly coincident before you can join them. You can join lines, arcs, 2D polylines, and lightweight polylines to lightweight polylines or 2D polylines:

   ■ If you are editing a lightweight polyline, AutoCAD converts all joined segments to a single lightweight polyline at the end of the command.

   ■ If you are editing an old-style 2D polyline, AutoCAD converts all joined segments, as in previous releases. This would be the case for 2D polylines that were not converted when the drawing was opened.

■ **Width.** (2D only) Prompts you to specify a single width for all segments of a polyline. The new width overrides any individual segment widths already stored. You can edit widths of individual segments by using a suboption of the Edit Vertex option.

■ **Edit Vertex.** Presents a prompt for a set of options that enable you to edit vertices and their adjoining segments.

■ **Fit.** (2D only) Creates a smooth curve through the polyline vertices. AutoCAD converts lightweight polylines to 2D polylines before computing the curve.

■ **Spline curve.** Creates a curve controlled by, but not necessarily passing through, a framework of polyline vertices. AutoCAD converts lightweight polylines to 2D polylines before computing the curve.

■ **Decurve.** Undoes a Fit or Spline curve, restoring it back to its original definition. The Decurve option has no effect on lightweight polylines because they do not support curve or spline fitting.

- **Ltype gen.** (2D only) Controls whether linetypes are generated between vertices (Ltype gen OFF) or between the polyline's endpoints (Ltypes gen ON), spanning vertices (see Figure 8.6). AutoCAD ignores this option for polylines that have tapered segments.

- **Undo.** Undoes the most recent PEDIT function.

- **eXit.** Exits the PEDIT command. (This is the default <X>.)

Figure 8.6

The effect of turning Ltype Gen on and off.

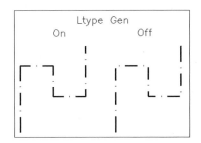

When PEDIT prompts Select polyline:, you can pick a polyline line, polyarc, or other polyline object. The PEDIT command operates on only one object at a time. Before you select a wide polyline, you must select either an edge or a vertex. You can use a Window or Crossing selection, but you must first enter **w** or **c** because PEDIT does not support the implied windowing selection feature. For convenience, you also can use the Last, Box, Fence, All, Wpolygon, and Cpolygon (but not Previous) selection methods. Selection ends as soon as PEDIT finds a line, arc, or polyline. If your selection method includes more than one valid object, PEDIT selects only one. If the first object you select is not a polyline but is capable of being converted into one (if it's a line or arc, for example), AutoCAD asks if you want to turn it into one.

In the following exercise, you practice using some of the options of the primary PEDIT command options.

USING THE PRIMARY OPTIONS OF THE PEDIT COMMAND

1. Start a new drawing named Parking.dwg, using the CH08b.DWG on the accompanying CD as a template (see Figure 8.7).

Figure 8.7

Editing entire polyline segments.

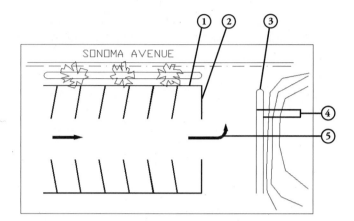

2. You will first join two separate polylines. Start the PEDIT command by typing **PE** and pressing Enter. At the Select polyline: prompt, pick the line at ①. The primary PEDIT prompt appears.

   ```
   Enter an option [Close/Join/Width/Edit vertex/Fit/Spline/Decurve/
   Ltype gen/Undo]:
   ```

3. Right-click to display the PEDIT shortcut menu, then choose the Join option. At the Select objects: prompt, pick the polyline at ② and close the selection process by pressing Enter. AutoCAD joins the two lines into a single polyline, and the primary prompt returns.

4. Right-click again and choose the Width option from the shortcut menu. Answer the Specify new width for all segments: prompt by typing **9** and pressing Enter.

5. Note that the polyline changes to a new width of 9 inches and the prompt returns. The line is too wide. Choose Undo from the shortcut menu. This undoes the previous editing operation. Repeat step 5, specifying a width of 3. Then right-click and choose Cancel to cancel the PEDIT command.

6. Zoom into the area around ③. Next, you convert an arc object into a polyarc and join it to two other polylines. Restart the PEDIT command. At the Select polyline: prompt, pick the arc object at ③. The following prompts appear:

   ```
   Object selected is not a polyline

   Do you want to turn it into one? <Y>
   ```

7. Accept the default option (<Y> for Yes) by pressing Enter. The primary PEDIT prompt appears. Right-click and choose the Join option. At the Select objects: prompt, pick the two polylines at ④. AutoCAD joins the three polylines. Press Enter to end the PEDIT command.

8. Next, you will explode a polyline, using AutoCAD's EXPLODE command. To start the EXPLODE command, type **EXPLODE** and press Enter. The Select objects: prompt appears.

9. Pick the arrow at ⑤ and press Enter. Note that the width information for this polyline disappears after it is exploded. Actually, AutoCAD destroys the polyline, demoting it to a Line object.

10. Restore the polyline arrow with the U command by choosing Undo from the right-click menu.

11. You will use this drawing in the next exercise. For now, press Ctrl+S to save your changes.

In the preceding exercise, you saw that you can work with one polyline at a time. The primary PEDIT prompt with its several options returns after each edit operation on the assumption that you may want to edit another polyline parameter. You must specifically dismiss the prompt by accepting the default eXit option or by pressing Esc to cancel the command or by choosing the Cancel option from the right-click menu. Also note that several of the options in the primary prompt undo other options. For example, after performing a Fit (curve) edit, you can undo the operation with the Decurve option. The Undo option undoes the last edit operation and returns the primary prompt. The EXPLODE command destroys a polyline and reduces it to a lower order object—either a line or arc.

I NSIDER TIP

You can produce a wide polyline with an apparent mitered end by using a trick. After specifying the last vertex, set the width to taper from the current full width to zero, and then draw another very short segment using a typed relative polar coordinate. The "miter" will appear perpendicular to the angle you create.

For example, enter @0.00001<45 to miter the top of a vertical wide polyline to an angle of 135 degrees (45 + 90). The end of the last segment is actually pointed, but the extremely short length has the effect of ending the previous segment with a miter.

Using the PEDIT Fit and Spline Options

PEDIT provides two options for making a polyline that passes through or is influenced by control points (see Figure 8.8). A fit curve actually passes through vertex points and consists of two arc segments between each pair of vertices. A spline-fit curve interpolates between control points, but the curve doesn't necessarily pass through the points.

To help you visualize a spline-fit curve, AutoCAD provides the system variable SPLFRAME. If you set SPLFRAME to a value of 1, the reference frame with control points appears. Figure 8.8 shows only the control points. In the case of the original polyline, the control points are coincident with the vertices of the polyline. In the instance of the fit curve example, the straight line segments between control points (vertices) have been replaced with arc segments, but still pass through the control points. The spline-fit curve uses the control points as guides to influence the shape of curve.

Figure 8.8

Creating curves from straight polylines.

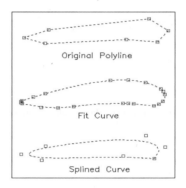

AutoCAD can generate two types of spline-fit polylines: a quadric b-spline and a cubic b-spline. The system variable SPLINETYPE controls the type of curve generated. A SPLINETYPE value of 5 approximates a true quadric b-spline; a value of 6 approximates a true cubic b-spline. In addition, the system variable SPLINESEGS controls the fineness of the b-spline. The numeric value of SLINESEGS sets the number of line segments in the control frame.

In the following exercise, you use both the Fit and Spline options of PEDIT to generate curves from polylines.

GENERATING CURVES WITH PEDIT

1. Continue in the drawing from the previous exercise.

2. First, zoom in to the contour lines area of the parking lot as shown in see Figure 8.9.

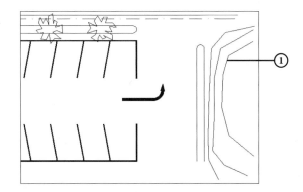

3. You will smooth the contour line at ① first. Start the PEDIT command by typing **PE**
    and pressing Enter. At the `Select polyline:` prompt, pick the polyline at ①. The
    primary PEDIT options appear. Type **F** (for Fit) and press Enter.

4. AutoCAD performs a fit curve smoothing on the polyline, and the prompt returns. This
    does not smooth the curve as you want, so right-click and choose the Undo option
    from the shortcut menu. AutoCAD undoes the fit curve operation. The PEDIT prompt
    returns.

5. Now right-click again and choose the Spline option. AutoCAD spline-fits the polyline.
    Note that this curve more closely approximates the contour. Exit the PEDIT command
    by pressing Enter.

6. By turning on the spline frame feature, you can examine the original data points for
    this new curve. At the command prompt, enter **SPLFRAME**, and then respond to the
    prompt by typing **1** and pressing Enter.

7. For the spline frame to be displayed, you must regenerate the drawing. At the
    command prompt, type **REGEN** and press Enter. The spline frame appears. Note that
    with an open polyline such as this contour line, the spline-fit curve passes through the
    spline frame at the start and end points.

8. Turn the spline frame off by repeating step 6 with the SPLFRAME variable set to 0. Then
    perform another regen to clear the frame.

9. You will use this drawing in the next exercise. For now, save the drawing by pressing
    Ctrl+S.

In the preceding exercise, you saw how the PEDIT command takes data points in the
form of polyline vertices and transforms them into a close approximation of a true
b-spline curve. In many instances, these polyline spline-fit curves are adequate for
representing data such as contour lines. At other times, the smoothing procedure of
the fit-curve procedure will suffice to remove the angles present at polyline vertices.

NOTE

> Optimized polylines do not support either of the spline-fit options of the PEDIT command. Whenever you choose either of these options, if necessary, AutoCAD converts optimized polylines into the older-style 2D polyline and then carries out the transformation to a curve. If the curve is subsequently changed back to its original shape using the Decurve option of the PEDIT command, AutoCAD converts the 2D polyline back into an optimized polyline.

Editing Polyline Vertices with PEDIT

Each polyline segment belongs to and is controlled by the preceding vertex. The Edit Vertex option of the primary PEDIT set of options displays another prompt with a separate set of options. When you use these options, AutoCAD marks the current vertex of the polyline with an X to show the vertex you are editing. Move the X (by pressing Enter to accept the <N>, Next, option) until the X marks the vertex you want to edit.

```
Enter a vertex editing option
[Next/Previous/Break/Insert/Move/Regen/Straighten/Tangent/Width/
eXit] <N>:
```

The Edit Vertex option of the PEDIT command takes the following options:

- **Next/Previous.** Moves the X marker to a new current vertex. (Next is the initial default.)

- **Break.** Splits the polyline in two or removes segments of a polyline at existing vertices. The first break point is the vertex on which you invoke the Break option. Use Next/Previous to access another vertex for the second break point. The Go option performs the actual break.

- **Insert.** Adds a vertex at a point you specify, following the vertex currently marked with an X. You can combine this option with the Break option to break between existing vertices.

- **Move.** Changes the location of the current (X-marked) vertex to a point you specify.

- **Straighten.** Removes all intervening vertices from between the two you select and replaces them with one straight segment. This option also uses the Next/Previous and Go options.

- **Tangent.** Sets a tangent to the direction you specify at the currently marked vertex to control curve fitting. You can see the angle of the tangent at the vertex with an arrow, and you can drag it with the screen cursor or enter the angle at the keyboard.

- **Width.** Sets the starting and ending width of an individual polyline segment to the values you specify.

- **eXit.** Exits vertex editing and returns to the primary PEDIT prompt.

INSIDER TIP

It is usually easier to edit the position of a polyline vertex by using AutoCAD's Grips feature. This is especially true for spline-fit polylines. Chapter 11, "Advanced Geometry Editing," covers grips editing.

In the following exercise, you perform vertex editing on polylines.

EDITING POLYLINE VERTICES WITH PEDIT

1. Continuing in the drawing from the previous exercise, move the first vertex of the polyline contour at ① (see Figure 8.10). Begin by starting the PEDIT command, then pick the contour line at ①.

Figure 8.10

Moving a polyline vertex.

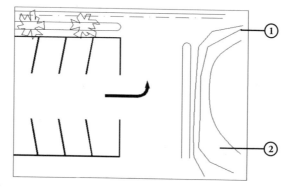

2. At the primary PEDIT prompt, choose the Edit Vertex option by typing **E** and pressing Enter. Note that an X appears at the endpoint and first vertex of the line, and the Edit vertex: prompt appears.

3. If the vertex you want to move is already selected (marked with an X), respond to this prompt by typing **M** and pressing Enter. Respond to the `Specify new location for marked vertex:` prompt by typing **@0,_12!** and pressing Enter. (Note: Watch the vertex when you press Enter.)

4. The vertex moves 12 units in the –Y direction. The `Edit vertex:` prompt returns.

> **I**NSIDER **T**IP
>
> In the next step, if you go too far, type **P** and press Enter to return to the previous vertex. Keep in mind, too, that all the prompt options are available from the PEDIT shortcut menu.

5. For the purposes of this exercise, assume you want to insert a new vertex between the current fourth and fifth vertices, as shown at ② in Figure 8.10. Step the current vertex down the line by pressing Enter to accept the default Next (vertex) option. (You'll need to press Enter three times.) The X is now at vertex 4 at ③ in Figure 8.11.

Figure 8.11

Inserting a new polyline vertex.

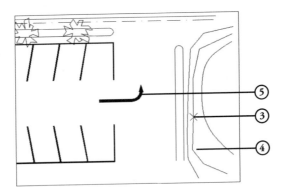

6. Now choose the Insert option by typing **I** and pressing Enter. Answer the `Enter location of new vertex:` prompt by picking a point near ④. AutoCAD inserts a new vertex, and the `Edit vertex:` prompt returns.

7. Exit the `Edit vertex:` prompts by typing **X** and pressing Enter. The primary PEDIT prompt returns. Select the Spline option by typing **S** and pressing Enter. AutoCAD spline-fits the curve.

8. Close the PEDIT command by pressing Enter.

9. Restart the PEDIT command by pressing the spacebar. At the primary PEDIT prompt, pick the polyline at ⑤. You will change the width of the vertex at the base of the arrowhead.

10. Choose the Edit Vertex option of the primary PEDIT prompt and choose Next until the active vertex is at the base of the arrowhead. This is the third vertex.

NOTE

In the next step, observe the width of the arrowhead when you press Enter.

11. Choose the Width option by typing **W** and pressing Enter. At the `Specify starting width for next segment:` prompt, enter the new value by typing **20** and pressing Enter. AutoCAD changes the width of the arrowhead base. At the `Specify ending width for next segment:` prompt, type **0** and press Enter.

12. Exit the Edit vertex: prompt by typing X and pressing Enter. Then exit the PEDIT command by pressing Enter again. Your drawing should now resemble Figure 8.12. You are finished with this drawing.

Figure 8.12

The finished parking lot drawing.

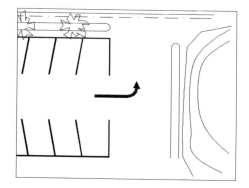

In the preceding exercise, you saw how to make changes to an existing polyline by editing parameters at its vertices. When combined with the primary editing option, the Edit vertex option provides a great degree of editing capability for polylines.

Creating True Splines

To create true spline curves in AutoCAD, you use the SPLINE command. Splines can be either 2D or 3D objects. You draw splines by specifying a series of fit-data points (vertices) through which the curve passes. The fit-data points determine the location of the spline's control points. Control points contain the curve information for the spline. AutoCAD's spline objects are true splines, unlike the spline approximations formed by spline-fit polylines. The SPLINE command draws non-uniform rational B-splines (*NURBS*). AutoCAD NURBS are mathematically more accurate than spline-fit polylines are. And even though spline objects are more accurate than spline-fit polylines, they actually require less memory for storage and result in smaller drawings, other factors being equal.

You can use the SPLINE command to convert 2D and 3D spline-fit polylines into true splines. Unlike spline-fit polylines, which can be either quadric or cubic spline approximations depending on how the SPLINETYPE system variable is set, the SPLINETYPE system variable does not affect the true spline objects produced by the SPLINE command.

SPLINE command offers the following options:

- **Specify first point or [Object].** The default option of the main prompt specifies the starting point of the spline. After you specify a starting point, AutoCAD prompts you to specify a second point. Spline objects must consist of a minimum of three points.

- **Object.** This option enables you to convert existing spline-fit polylines to true spline objects. After you specify this option, AutoCAD asks you to select objects.

- **Specify next point or [Close/Fit tolerance] <start tangent>:** AutoCAD displays this prompt after you specify a second point. The default option is to continue to specify additional data points for the spline that you are drawing. If you press Enter, AutoCAD prompts you to specify the tangent information for the start and endpoints and then ends the command.

- **Close.** This option causes the start and end of the spline to be coincident and to share vertex and tangent information. When you close a spline, AutoCAD prompts only once for tangent information.

- **Fit Tolerance.** This option controls how closely the spline curve follows the data points. The distance of the Fit Tolerance is expressed in current drawing units. The smaller the tolerance, the closer the spline fits the data points. When the value is 0, the spline follows the data points exactly.

- **(Undo).** Although this option does not appear in the prompt, you can enter **U** after any point to undo the last segment.

In the following exercise, you use the SPLINE command to draw the outline of a mechanical part.

CONSTRUCTING A SPLINE

1.   Begin a new drawing called Spline.dwg using IAC803.DWG on the accompanying CD as a template (see Figure 8.13).

Figure 8.13

Fitting a spline to data points.

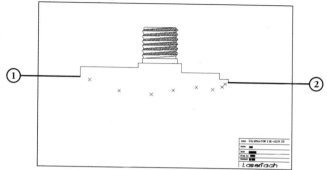

In the next step, you use the pre-positioned data points shown by Xs in the drawing. You need to set the Node and Endpoint running Osnaps so you can easily snap to the data points.

2. From the Draw menu, choose Spline to start the SPLINE command. The `Object/ <Specify first point>:` prompt appears.

3. Use the default option of specifying a first point. Snap to the endpoint at ①. Then enter the first point by clicking. The `Specify next point:` prompt appears.

4. Continue to specify points, snapping to each successive X node at each `Specify next point:` prompt. Finally, specify the last point by snapping to the endpoint at ②.

5. Press Enter three times to end the SPLINE command. Your drawing should now resemble Figure 8.14.

6. You will use this drawing in the next exercise. For now, save your work by pressing Ctrl+S.

Figure 8.14

The completed spline curve.

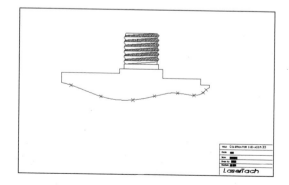

In the preceding exercise, you used pre-positioned points to help construct the spline. Depending on the type of work you want to do, you usually base splines on some form of preliminary data points rather than just drawing the curve in free-form style, although both methods are possible with AutoCAD. At best, splines are "tricky" objects to construct, and after you draw one, you frequently need to alter or refine it.

Controlling Splines with SPLINEDIT

The SPLINEDIT command enables you to edit a spline's control points and, if present, fit-data points. When you draw a spline, you pick fit-data points, which AutoCAD uses to calculate the location of the spline's control points. You can add additional control or fit-data points or move existing ones. You can change the weight or influence of control points, as well as the tolerance of the spline. You also can close or open a spline and adjust the tangent information of the start and endpoints.

Control points usually are not located on the spline curve (except at the start and endpoints), but they control the shape of the spline. AutoCAD uses the fit-data points to calculate the position of the control points. After AutoCAD determines the control points, it no longer needs the fit-data points. If you remove the fit-data from a spline, however, you cannot use any of the fit-data editing options of the SPLINEDIT command to further edit the shape of the spline.

When you select a spline for editing, AutoCAD displays its control points just as it does if you use grips editing, although grips editing is not available through the SPLINEDIT command. The SPLINEDIT command works on only one spline object at a time.

The SPLINEDIT command has the following options:

- **Fit Data.** Enables you to edit the fit-data points for spline objects that have them, in which case, AutoCAD displays another prompt of Fit Data options, which are described following this list.

- **Close.** Closes an open spline. Adds a curve that is tangent between the start and end vertices for splines that do not have the same start and endpoints. If the spline does have the same start and endpoints, the Close option makes the tangent information for each point continuous. If the spline is already closed, the Close option is replaced by the Open option.

- **Open.** Opens a closed spline. If the spline did not have the same start and endpoints prior to being closed, this option removes the tangent curve and removes tangent information from the start and endpoints. If the spline shares the same start and endpoint before you close it, the Open option removes the tangent information from the points.

- **Move Vertex.** Enables you to move the control vertices of a spline. You specify a vertex to edit by moving the current vertex to the next or previous vertex.

- **Refine.** Displays suboptions that enable you to add control points and adjust the weight of control points. You can add individual control points in areas where you want finer control of the curve. Performing any refine operation on a spline removes fit-data from the spline. You can reverse the effect of the Refine option and restore the fit-data with the Undo option before ending the SPLINEDIT command. The following list describes the Refine options:

  - *Add control point.* Enables you to add a single control point to a spline. AutoCAD locates the new control point as close as possible to the point you pick on the spline. Adding a control point does not change the shape of the spline.

  - *Elevate Order.* Elevates the order of the spline's polynomial, which adds control points evenly over the spline. This option does not change the shape of the spline. The order of the polynomial cannot be reduced after it has been increased.

  - *Weight.* Controls the amount of tension that pulls a spline toward a control point.

  - *eXit.* Returns to the main SPLINEDIT prompt.

  - *rEverse.* Changes the direction of the spline.

  - *Undo.* Undoes the most recently performed SPLINEDIT option.

  - *eXit.* Ends the SPLINEDIT command.

The following are the suboptions of the Fit Data option for editing spline object fit-data. When you choose the Fit Data option, the grips-like boxes change to highlight the fit-data points.

- **Add.** Adds additional fit-data points to the curve. Adding fit-data points changes the shape of the spline curve. Added fit-data points obey the current tolerance of the spline.

- **Close.** Performs the same function as the control point Close option using fit-data points.

■ **Open.** Performs the same function as the control point Open option using fit-data points. The Open option replaces the Close option if the spline is already closed.

■ **Delete.** Removes fit-data points and redraws the spline to fit the fit-data points that remain.

■ **Move.** Enables you to move fit-data point vertices of a spline. You specify a vertex to edit by moving the current vertex to the next or previous vertex. You cannot edit fit data information with AutoCAD's grips editing feature.

■ **Purge.** Removes all fit data from the spline.

■ **Tangents.** Enables you to change the tangent information of the start and endpoints of a spline.

■ **toLerance.** Changes the tolerance of the spline's fit-data points and redraws the spline. A spline loses its fit data if you change the tolerance and move a control point or open or close the spline.

■ **eXit.** Returns to the control point editing prompt.

In the following exercise, you edit the spline you drew in the preceding exercise using some options of the SPLINEDIT command. First, you reduce the number of fit-data points, and then you add additional control points to the spline by changing its order.

EDITING A SPLINE

1. Continuing from the previous exercise, remove the running Node osnap by right-clicking on the OSNAP window on the status line at the bottom of the display. Choose Settings and in the Drafting Settings dialog box, remove the check next to the Node option. Click OK to exit the dialog box.

2. Press F3 to disable the OSNAP function. From the Modify menu, choose Spline to start the SPLINEDIT command. Select the spline you drew in the preceding exercise. The control points appear (see Figure 8.15). Note that the control points do not necessarily fall on the spline curve itself. The following prompt appears:

   `Enter an option [Fit Data/Close/Move Vertex/Refine/rEverse/Undo]:`

Figure 8.15

SPLINEDIT *displays a spline's control points.*

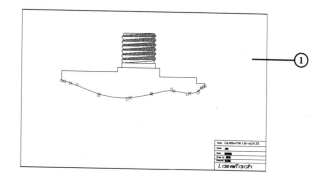

3. Right-click to display the SPLINEDIT shortcut menu. Choose the Fit Data option, and AutoCAD changes the control points to show the fit-data points. Notice that the fit-data points are not the same as the control points. The Fit Data prompt appears.

   ```
   Enter a fit data option
   [Add/Close/Delete/Move/Purge/Tangents/toLerance/eXit] <eXit>:
   ```

4. Right-click and choose the Delete option, then pick a couple of points. Note that the points disappear as you pick them. Press Enter after you remove the points. The prompt returns. Choose the Tangents option. The Specify start tangent or [System default]: prompt appears.

5. Press Enter to keep the current tangent. Then at the Specify end tangent or [System default]: prompt, pick a point near ①, as shown in Figure 8.15.

6. When the prompt returns, press Enter to return to the main control point prompt. The control points are displayed, and the control point prompt appears.

7. Right-click and choose the Refine option, then at the new prompt, right-click again and choose the Elevate Order option.

8. At the Enter new order <4>: prompt, type **6** and press Enter. This elevates the order of the polynomial and adds control points. The prompt returns. Respond by pressing Enter to exit to the main prompt.

9. Press Enter again to exit the SPLINEDIT command.

10. From the Layer Control box on the Object Properties toolbar, turn off the layer Frame. Your drawing should now resemble Figure 8.16, depending on which points you removed in step 4. You are finished with this drawing.

Figure 8.16

Figure 8.16

The completed spline fit curve after modification.

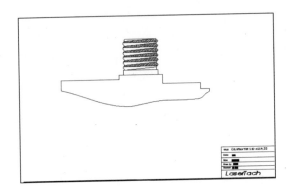

The options and sub-options of the SPLINEDIT command offer a great deal of control. In this exercise, you had the opportunity to investigate several ways you can modify and "tweak" a spline object. Splines are quite complex, but they are also quite accurate and flexible.

INSIDER TIP

As with polylines, Spline objects can be modified using AutoCAD's the grips editing feature. Chapter 11 tells more about grips editing.

Summary

In this chapter, you explored the versatility of polylines. You saw how you can edit polylines in a variety of ways. You also saw how to convert polylines into two different types of curves. You learned about the versatility and accuracy of true NURB splines and the many ways you can edit and shape them into complex smooth curves. Many of the shapes you may be required to draw in AutoCAD are not composed of straight lines, and the capability to fit polylines and splines to complex curves is an important skill.

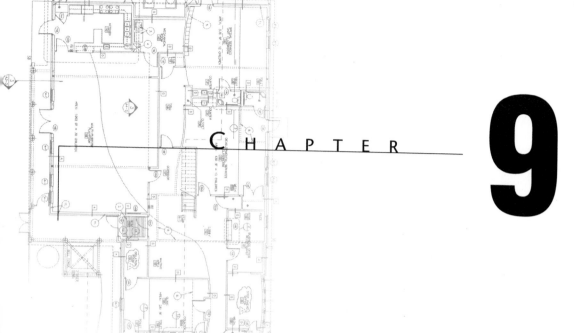

CHAPTER 9

UNDERSTANDING THE QUERY FEATURES IN AUTOCAD 2000

To get the most out of the power of AutoCAD, you must be able to extract information from AutoCAD objects. When an object is created, AutoCAD does more than just draw the object on the computer screen. It creates a list of object data and stores this data in the drawing's database. This data includes not only the layer, color, and linetype of an object, but also the X,Y,Z coordinate values of an object's critical elements, such as the center of a circle, or the endpoint of a line. The data can include the names of blocks, as well as their X,Y,Z scale and rotation angles. Information about block attributes and their text values can be extracted from the drawing into a text file. The two-dimensional area of closed polygons, as well as three-dimensional volumes of objects can be determined. By querying AutoCAD's objects, you can extract a wealth of information pertinent to your work, and you can query important data that AutoCAD creates automatically.

This chapter discusses the following topics:

- Querying information from the Object Properties toolbar
- Querying for 2D and 3D distances
- Querying for areas in blocks and xrefs
- Creation of block attributes
- Block and data extraction
- The ATTEXT command
- Block and attribute extraction formats
- Report templates
- Controlling the CDF file delimiters
- Specifying field width and numeric precision
- Extraction data types

Obtaining Object Information

The ability to query for object and drawing data is a valuable feature of AutoCAD. With AutoCAD 2000, querying tools are conveniently grouped together in the pull-down menus for easy, intuitive access. Additionally, the Object Properties toolbar makes identifying the most common properties of an object as easy as selecting the object itself. Let's start with the Object Properties toolbar.

Object Properties Toolbar

NEW for R2000 In AutoCAD 2000, the Object Properties toolbar automatically displays the selected object's layer, color, linetype, lineweight, and plot style, of which the last two are new to AutoCAD 2000. When the selected objects have different properties, such as different layers, the property value is left blank.

The following exercise demonstrates the querying capabilities of AutoCAD's Object Properties toolbar.

QUERYING OBJECTS WITH THE OBJECT PROPERTIES TOOLBAR

1. Open the 9DWG02.DWG drawing file found on the accompanying CD. Notice that the Object Properties toolbar lists the current layer 0, the default color Bylayer, and the default linetype Bylayer. This represents AutoCAD's current object-creation mode. If an object were created now, it would be assigned these properties.

2. Choose the blue dashed contour line (the sixth line from the top). AutoCAD displays the grips along the polyline (see Figure 9.1). Notice that the properties displayed in the Object Properties toolbar now reflect the properties of the selected object.

Figure 9.1

The selected object's properties are displayed in the Object Properties toolbar.

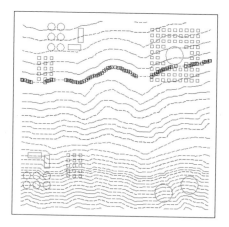

3. Choose the dashed contour line above the one you just chose. AutoCAD displays grips along the polyline (see Figure 9.2). Notice that AutoCAD no longer displays any properties in the Object Properties toolbar. This occurs because the two objects reside on different layers, and have different color and linetype settings.

4. Leave the drawing file open for the next exercise.

INSIDER TIP

The DDMODIFY command has been changed in AutoCAD 2000 to provide you with all the information shown in the Object Properties toolbar, plus a great deal more information. The command can be started by choosing Modify, Properties or by typing **DDMODIFY** at the command prompt. DDMODIFY is a modal dialog box, so you can select different objects while it is still open to see the properties.

Figure 9.2

Figure 9.2

No properties are
displayed in the Object
Properties toolbar when
the two objects have no
common properties.

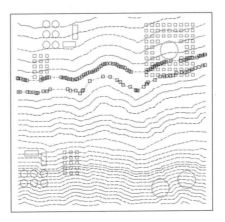

Inquiry Tools

The *inquiry tools* in AutoCAD provide you with a set of tools to find out information
about objects in your drawing. This information can include the area, length, point,
mass properties, and even a list of all the points in the object. In AutoCAD 2000, the
querying tools are conveniently grouped together in a single location, the Tools,
Inquiry pulldown menu (see Figure 9.3). To access one of the tools, simply click
on it.

Figure 9.3

Accessing the querying
tools from the Inquiry
menu on the Tools pull-
down menu.

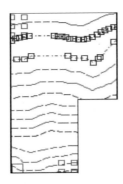

Distance

The DIST command is used to measure the distance between two points in an
AutoCAD drawing. When you use the DIST command to query lengths, it's important
to realize that this command measures points three-dimensionally. If you pick two
points that are not on the same plane, the overall distance will be based on a 3D

vector. To ensure that the distance is based on the current two-dimensional UCS, use X,Y,Z point filters when you query distance from 3D objects.

The following exercise demonstrates how to use X,Y,Z point filters to measure a distance two-dimensionally.

MEASURING DISTANCES WITH X,Y,Z POINT FILTERS

1. Continue with the 9DWG02.DWG file from the previous exercise.

2. Press the Esc key twice to clear the grips if you did not reload the drawing.

3. From the Tools menu, choose Inquiry, Distance. The command name for this is `dist`.

4. Using endpoint snaps, snap to the left end of the top blue contour. Then snap to the left end of the blue line below it (four lines down). AutoCAD displays the following data:

    ```
    Distance = 3767.7248, Angle in XY Plane = 270,
    Angle from XY Plane = 2 Delta X = 0.0000,
    Delta Y = -3766.3975, Delta Z = 100.0000
    ```

    Notice that AutoCAD indicates that the angle from XY plane = 270. This is the angle measured up from the XY plane in the Z direction. This data tells you that the distance is a 3D vector, caused by the two contours not being on the same XY plane. The first contour has an elevation of 100; the second contour has an elevation of 200. Next, you snap to the same two points while using X,Y,Z point filters.

5. From the Tools menu, choose Inquiry, Distance.

6. Type **.XY** (the period in front of the XY is necessary).

7. Using endpoint snaps, snap to the left end of the top blue contour

8. Type **0** when prompted for the Z value.

9. When AutoCAD prompts for the second point, type **.XY** again.

10. Snap to the left end of the second blue line.

11. Type **0** when prompted for the Z Value. AutoCAD displays the following data:

    ```
    Distance = 3766.3975, Angle in XY Plane = 270
    Angle from XY Plane = 0 Delta X = 0.0000,
    Delta Y = -3766.3975, Delta Z = 0.0000
    ```

    Notice that the measured distance is slightly smaller than the first distance you measured. This is the result of using the X,Y,Z point filters and setting the value to 0. This distance represents the true horizontal distance.

NOTE

> The last distance queried by using the DIST command is saved as a system variable. To view it, type **DISTANCE** at the command prompt.

Querying for Areas in Blocks and Xrefs

The AREA command is useful for finding the area of many AutoCAD objects. AutoCAD can find the area of circles, ellipses, splines, regions, closed polylines, or polygon objects. It also quickly finds the length of an open polyline. Using the AREA command's Object option, AutoCAD calculates and lists the object's area and perimeter length.

WARNING

> The AREA command provides both the total length and the total area of an open polyline object. Although the length is accurate, the calculated area is not.

If you select an object that is inserted as a block or xref, however, AutoCAD warns that the selected object does not have an area. How can you calculate the area of objects inserted as blocks or xrefs? The answer is to use the BOUNDARY command. You can use this command to create a temporary region or polyline boundary from which you can quickly determine the area of the xref objects. Otherwise, you would have to bind the xref objects and then explode the resulting block to accomplish this, which defeats the purpose of using either xrefs or blocks.

The next exercise demonstrates how to calculate the area of objects contained within blocks and xrefs.

DETERMINING THE AREA OF XREF OBJECTS

1. Open the 9DWG03.DWG drawing file found on the accompanying CD. The drawing opens and displays four objects. The rectangle is part of the current drawing; the other three are an xref.

2. From the Draw menu, choose Boundary. The Boundary Creation dialog box appears.

3. From the Object Type drop-down list, select Region.

4. Click on the Pick Points button. The dialog box will dismiss for point selection.

5. Pick inside the smaller circle that lies inside the octagon. AutoCAD determines the boundary from the circle object and highlights it.

6. Continue selecting the interior of the remaining xref objects. Pick inside the octagon, but outside the contained circle. Pick the area shared by the octagon and the left circle. Finally, pick inside the left circle, but outside the octagon. When you finish picking inside the xref objects, all objects are highlighted as shown in Figure 9.4.

Figure 9.4

The xref objects are highlighted.

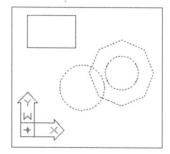

7. Press Enter to end object selection.

   AutoCAD notes that the **BOUNDARY** command creates five regions. It created two regions for the circle inside the octagon—one because you picked inside the circle and the second because you picked inside the octagon but outside the circle. This occurs because Island Detection was enabled in the Boundary Creation dialog box. After you create the region objets, you can use the **AREA** command to calculate their area and perimeter. You can also create a single composite region of the four objects and calculate its area. This is accomplished by using Boolean operations, as described in the following steps.

8. From the Modify menu, choose Solids Editing, Union.

9. When prompted to select objects, type **F**. This begins the fence selection method.

Figure 9.5

The FENCE selection method is used to select the region objects.

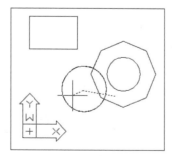

10. Select all the region objects except the circle inside octagon by picking inside the octagon as shown in Figure 9.5.

11. Drag the fence line left and pick inside the circle.

12. Press Enter when you have finished.

    AutoCAD creates a new composite region made up of the three smaller regions and then it erases the three smaller regions. You can calculate the new region's area and perimeter using the AREA command. Next, you subtract the remaining circle from the composite region.

13. From the Modify menu, choose Solids Editing, Subtract. AutoCAD prompts you to select the objects from which to subtract regions.

14. Choose the composite region and press Enter. You are then prompted for the regions to subtract.

15. Use the fence method to select the small circle region and press Enter. AutoCAD subtracts the circle region from the composite region, creating a new composite region. Now you can calculate the area.

16. From the Tools menu, choose Inquiry, Area.

17. When prompted, type **0**, for object, and then choose the composite region. AutoCAD calculates the region's area and displays it as follows:

    ```
    Area = 405708.1938, Perimeter = 4060.4512
    ```

By using this technique, you can quickly determine the area and perimeter of inserted block and xref objects.

Understanding Block Attributes

Block attributes are an additional feature of blocks that are very useful. Block attributes store informational data. This data can be defined as a constant value, or can be input by a user at the moment the block is inserted, or edited afterward.

INSIDER TIP

There is no limit to the number of attributes that can be associated with a block. I have attached 20 or 30 attributes to title sheets, for example. When the title sheet block is inserted into the current drawing, the user is prompted for various values: the sheet number, title, project engineer's name, CAD technician's name, and so on. This is useful for guaranteeing that appropriate data is added to a drawing and not accidentally overlooked.

When creating attributes for a block, it is important to control the sequence by which a user is prompted for data. For example, if a block will prompt for a series of data, and this data appears onscreen in alphabetical order, it makes sense to prompt the user for the data in the same order in which it appears on-screen.

To demonstrate how to control the sequence, AutoCAD prompts for attribute values, the following exercise will create two block definitions from a circle object that has five attributes. For the first block, the attributes will be selected from top to bottom. For the second, the attributes will be selected from bottom to top. Finally, the two blocks will be inserted so that you can observe the order in which you are prompted to define values for the attributes.

DETERMINING THE ORDER ATTRIBUTES PROMPT FOR VALUES

1. Open the 13DWG06.DWG drawing file on the accompanying CD.

   The drawing already contains the circle and five attributes you will use to define the two blocks.

2. From the Draw menu, choose Block, Make. The Block Definition dialog box appears.

3. In the Name list box, type **C1**.

INSIDER TIP

AutoCAD 2000 allows you to use extended symbol names when naming blocks. This feature provides the ability to use upper- and lowercase characters, as well as spaces, in block names.

4. Click the Pick Point button. The Block Definition dialog box is temporarily dismissed.

5. Using Center Osnap, select the circle. AutoCAD picks the circle's center as the block's base (insertion) point. The dialog box reappears.

6. Click the Select Objects button. The Block Definition dialog box is again temporarily dismissed.

7. Select the circle object first, and then select each attribute from the top down, then press Enter. Once again the dialog box appears.

8. In the Objects area, click the Retain option button, and then click OK.

   This completes the first block. Next, you create the second block.

9. From Draw, choose Block, Make. The Block Definition dialog box appears.

10. In the Name list box, type **C2**.

11. Click the Pick Point button. The Block Definition dialog box is temporarily dismissed.

12. Using Center Osnap, select the circle. AutoCAD picks the circle's center as the block's base point and the dialog box returns.

13. Click the Select Objects button. The Block Definition dialog box is temporarily dismissed.

14. Select the circle object first, and then select each attribute from the bottom up, then press Enter. The dialog box reappears.

15. In the Objects area, ensure that the Retain option button is still selected, then click OK.

   AutoCAD creates the second block, and deletes the objects used to define the blocks. Next, you insert the two blocks to observe the order AutoCAD prompts to fill in the attributes.

16. From the Insert menu, choose Block. The Insert dialog box opens.

17. Choose C1 from the Name drop-down list, if it is not already displayed.

18. In the Insertion Point area, be sure the Specify On-Screen option is selected. In the Scale and Rotation areas, be sure the Specify On-Screen option is cleared.

19. Click OK to close the Insert dialog box.

20. Choose a location near the center of the screen to insert the block. AutoCAD prompts for the attribute values at the command line.

21. When AutoCAD prompts for the first attribute value, type **1**. At each subsequent prompt, type the numbers **2**, **3**, **4**, and **5**, respectively.

   AutoCAD inserts the block and its attributes. The numbers 1, 2, 3, 4, and 5 appear in numerical order from top to bottom. Next, you insert the second block.

22. From the Insert menu, choose Block. The Insert dialog box opens.

23. Click on the Block button.

24. Choose C2 from the Name drop-down list.

25. Click OK to close the Insert dialog box.

26. Choose a location on the right side of the screen to insert the block.

27. When AutoCAD prompts for the first attribute value, type **1**. At each subsequent prompt, type the numbers **2**, **3**, **4**, and **5**, respectively.

    AutoCAD inserts the block. Notice this time, however, that the numbers 1, 2, 3, 4, and 5 appear in reverse order, as shown in Figure 9.6. This occurs because you selected the attributes in reverse order when you defined the second block.

Figure 9.6

The effect of the order in which attributes are selected.

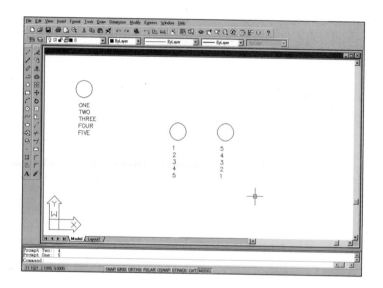

NOTE

The order in which attributes prompt for data is affected by the order in which they are selected when being defined. Therefore, their originally defined order is important when using the ATTREDEF command to redefine blocks with attributes.

INSIDER TIP

To determine the proper order to select attributes when redefining a block, use the LIST command to list one of the block insertions. When redefining the block, the attributes should be selected in the order in which they appear because this is the order in which they were originally defined.

Finding and Replacing Attributes

NEW for R2000 AutoCAD 2000 introduces a new tool that allows you to find and replace attribute text values in a drawing. To use this new feature, from the Edit menu, choose Find to display the Find and Replace dialog box shown in Figure 9.7. To locate a text value, enter the value in the Find Text String list box. If you want AutoCAD to replace the found text string with a new one, enter the new text value in the Replace With list box; otherwise leave it blank.

Figure 9.7

The new Find and Replace dialog box allows you to locate text values in a drawing.

To specify that AutoCAD should search only block attributes for a listed text value, click the Options button to display the Find and Replace Options dialog box, then clear all options except for Block Attribute Value, as shown in Figure 9.8. From the Find and Replace Options dialog box, you can also tell AutoCAD to match the upper- or lowercase spelling of the search word. Additionally, you can instruct AutoCAD to find the whole word, and not compound words that are partially composed of the search word.

After the find and replace words are indicated, and the options selected, to find the listed word or phrase, click the Find Next button in the Find and Replace dialog box (refer to Figure 9.7). To replace the found word with the listed replacement word or phrase, click the Replace or Replace All button. When AutoCAD finds an occurrence of the listed search word, it displays the listed word, and the phrase in which it's embedded, in the Context area. When a word is found, you can zoom to its location by clicking the Zoom To button.

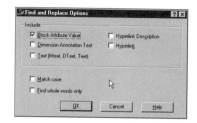

Figure 9.8

*The Find and Replace
Options dialog box allows
searching for text values in
block attributes only.*

Extracting Block and Attribute Data

Blocks and attribute object definitions contain a great deal of data. AutoCAD
automatically creates some of the data, including data that defines the block, such
as the block's name, its insertion coordinates, its insertion layer's name, its X,Y,Z
scale factors, and its X,Y,Z extrusion direction. This wealth of information can easily
be extracted into a text file.

Attribute data is user-defined. The data that AutoCAD extracts consists of one
element, which is either a character string or a numeric value. The attribute value
can be anything the user wants it to be, and the number of attributes that can be
attached to a block is unlimited.

By choosing the particular data records of blocks and the attributes you need, you
can easily extract an abundance of important information from your drawing.

Using the ATTEXT Command

The command used to extract block and attribute data has been around for several
releases of AutoCAD and has not changed. The ATTEXT command displays the
Attribute Extraction dialog box, and is shown in Figure 9.9. The Attribute Extraction
dialog box creates an ASCII text file (by default, a TXT file) containing the extracted
information.

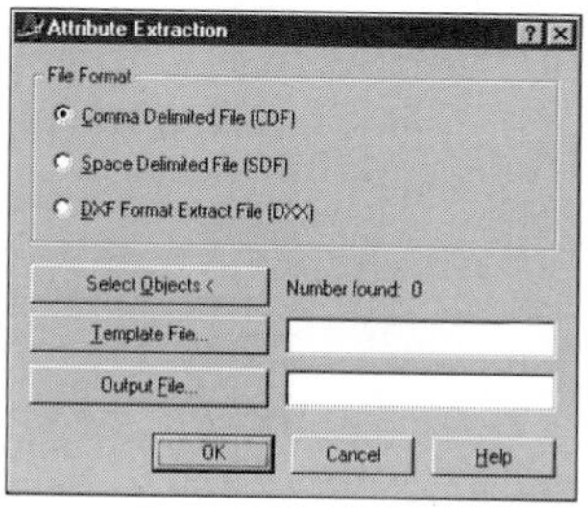

Figure 9.9

*The Attribute Extraction
dialog box.*

This command tells AutoCAD which block and attribute information to extract and how the extracted information will be arranged. The arrangement of the information is determined by a template file (discussed later in this chapter) and the file format you select, as discussed in the following section.

NOTE

You can extract and link attribute data to external databases. For more information, refer to Chapter 24, "Using External Databases."

Extraction Formats

The first item AutoCAD requests via the Attribute Extraction dialog box controls the extraction file format. The selected format determines the way each field within each record is separated and stored in the ASCII text file. AutoCAD provides three types of extraction file formats:

■ **Comma Delimited File (CDF).** The file format writes one record for each block on a separate line. Each data value in a record is separated from the next by a comma, with text strings enclosed in apostrophes, as follows:

```
'Sewer','Manhole', 36
'Storm Drain','Manhole', 48
'Storm Drain','Manhole', 36
```

■ **Space Delimited File (SDF).** The SDF file format also writes one record for each block on a separate line, and each data value in a record occupies a predefined field width. If the string or numeric value does not use the entire space allotted, AutoCAD fills the remainder of the field with spaces, as follows:

```
Sewer          Manhole      36
Storm Drain    Manhole      48
Storm Drain    Manhole      36
Sewer          Manhole      36
```

■ **Drawing Interchange File (DXF).** The DXF file format writes block data in AutoCAD's standard drawing interchange file format. An excerpt from a DXF file created with the ATTEXT command follows:

```
    0
INSERT
    2
MANHOLE
   10
5.115973
   20
5.442408
   30
0.0
    0
ATTRIB
    1
Sewer
    2
OBJECT_CATEGORY
    0
ATTRIB
    1
Manhole
    2
```

Figure 9.10 shows a drawing with several block insertions. Each insertion has three attributes. In the following three sections, the attribute data is extracted and the data is displayed in each format.

The CDF, SDF, and DXF file formats provide the capability for extracting block and attribute data into an ASCII text file. The CDF and SDF file formats are the most useful, enabling you to extract just the data you need, arranged in the order you want. The DXF file format, in contrast, is useful only when you need a copy of the DXF group code of the selected block objects.

Report Templates

To extract block and attribute data, the ATTEXT command requests the name of a template file. *Template files* are simple ASCII text files that list the data you want AutoCAD to extract. For example, a particular block may have 25 attributes attached to it. If you need to extract the data from only three attributes, the template file would indicate which three to extract.

Figure 9.10

Inserted block objects,
each with three attributes.

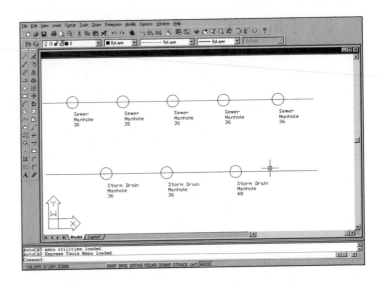

The following exercise demonstrates how to create a template file and then use it to write specific block and attribute data out to a text file in the CDF file format.

INSIDER TIP

In the following exercise, I use the MS WordPad program, which comes with both Windows 95/98 and Windows NT. You can also use any other text editor such as NotePad, which also comes with both Windows 95/98 and Windows NT, and which automatically saves files as ASCII text files.

CREATING AND USING A TEMPLATE FILE TO EXTRACT BLOCK AND ATTRIBUTE DATA

1. Open the 13DWG07.DWG drawing file found on the accompanying CD-ROM.

   The drawing opens, displaying several blocks. Each block represents a manhole, and also has attributes attached that uniquely describe it. For this exercise, you will extract each block's X,Y,Z insertion coordinates. You will also extract the attributes that indicate the block's diameter, and whether this is a sewer or storm drain manhole.

2. From the Start button on the Windows taskbar, choose Programs, Accessories, WordPad. WordPad opens.

3. In WordPad, type the following lines, using spaces to align the columns:

   ```
   BL:X                N010004
   BL:Y                N010004
   BL:Z                N010004
   OBJECT_CATEGORY     C015000
   OBJECT_SIZE         N004000
   ```

INSIDER TIP

To make aligning the columns easier, be sure to select Courier New (Western) from the Font drop-down list.

In step 3, the first column contains the field name. In the field name column, block data to be extracted begins with BL: and is followed by the descriptor that indicates the data to extract. In this example, the block's X,Y,Z insertion coordinates are being extracted. Attribute data is extracted by specifying the attribute's tag in the field name column. In this example, the tag names are OBJECT_CATEGORY and OBJECT_SIZE, and were defined when the attribute was created.

The second column specifies whether the field will contain numeric or character values. This is discussed in detail later in the chapter.

4. In WordPad, choose File, Save. The Save As dialog box opens.

5. From the Save as Type drop-down list, select Text Document – MS DOS Format, as shown in Figure 9.11. This saves the file as an ASCII text file.

Figure 9.11

*Choose Text Document –
MS-DOS Format to save
the text file in ASCII
format.*

6. Save the file in the ACAD2000\SAMPLE directory and name it **TEST01.TXT**, as shown in Figure 9.11. If WordPad prompts for the file's document type, select Text Document from the Save as Type drop-down list. WordPad saves the file as an ACSII text file.

7. Close WordPad.

Now that the template file is created, you will return to the AutoCAD drawing that you already opened to extract its data.

WARNING

When you create a template file, it is important to ensure that the file is saved as an ASCII text file with the file extension .TXT. This is the file type and extension that AutoCAD looks for.

8. Return to AutoCAD and type **ATTEXT** at the command prompt. The Attribute Extraction dialog box opens.

9. In the File Format area, select Comma Delimited File (CDF).

10. Click the Select Objects button, and then select the blocks individually. Start at the upper-left corner of the top row, and select across from left to right. Then continue with the bottom row, selecting from left to right. After selecting all the blocks, press Enter to exit object selection. The Attribute Extraction dialog box should indicate that eight objects were selected.

11. Click the Template File button, and open the TEST01.TXT file you saved in the ACAD2000\SAMPLE directory.

    The TEST01.TXT filename appears in the text box, as shown in Figure 9.12.

Figure 9.12

The Attribute Extraction dialog box shown with the proper settings to extract block and attribute data.

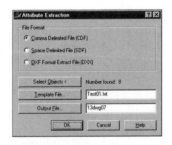

12. Click the Output File button and go to the ACAD2000\SAMPLE directory. Then click Save.

    The 13DWG07.TXT filename appears in the text box, as shown in Figure 9.12.

13. Click OK. AutoCAD creates the file and indicates that eight records exist in the extract file.

    Next, you will open the 13DWG07.TXT extract file in WordPad and view it.

14. From the Start button on the Windows Taskbar, choose Programs, Accessories, WordPad.

15. Choose File, Open to display the Open dialog box.

16. From the Files of Type drop-down list, select Text Documents – MS-DOS Format (*.txt).

17. From the ACAD2000\SAMPLE directory, open the 13DWG07.TXT extract file. The extract file should contain the following data, in the order shown:

```
67.8188, 111.6738, 0.0000, 'Sewer', 30
101.1619, 111.6738, 0.0000,'Sewer', 30
134.0559, 111.6738, 0.0000,'Sewer', 36
167.7358, 111.6738, 0.0000,'Sewer', 36
203.8855, 111.6738, 0.0000,'Sewer', 36
89.4862, 65.2266, 0.0000,'Storm Drain', 36
129.5653, 65.2266, 0.0000,'Storm Drain', 36
175.3699, 65.2266, 0.0000,'Storm Drain', 48
```

The first three fields represent the X,Y,Z insertion coordinates of each block's insertion point. The last two fields are extracted from the Object_Category and Object_Size attributes, respectively.

Controlling the CDF File Delimiters

The previous exercise created a Comma Delimited File (CDF). In this format, commas separate the fields, and text strings are enclosed in apostrophes. Although this is very useful, commas and apostrophes might not be the delimiters you need. Fortunately, AutoCAD provides the capability to specify the characters used to delimit CDF files.

The C:DELIM template field indicates to AutoCAD which character to use as the field delimiter. The C:QUOTE template field indicates to AutoCAD which character to use to enclose text strings. Both of these template fields must be entered at the beginning of the template file.

For example, in the previous exercise, you could have indicated to AutoCAD that you wanted the extract file's fields separated by semicolons, with text strings enclosed in quotation marks. To do this, you would add the following lines to the beginning in the template file:

```
C:DELIM              ;
C:QUOTE              "
BL:X                 N010004
BL:Y                 N010004
BL:Z                 N010004
OBJECT_CATEGORY      C015000
OBJECT_SIZE          N004000
```

WARNING

To specify delimiters, you must specify characters that are not used as values in the fields; specifically, the field-delimiter character must not appear in the numeric field values. Therefore, 0–9 and periods must not be used to separate fields. Similarly, the text-string delimiter character must not appear in any of the text strings.

When you use this template file, it creates an extract file that contains the same information as before, but with the new delimiters, as follows:

```
67.8188; 111.6738; 0.0000;"Sewer"; 30
101.1619; 111.6738; 0.0000;"Sewer"; 30
134.0559; 111.6738; 0.0000;"Sewer"; 36
167.7358; 111.6738; 0.0000;"Sewer"; 36
203.8855; 111.6738; 0.0000;"Sewer"; 36
89.4862; 65.2266; 0.0000;"Storm Drain"; 36
129.5653; 65.2266; 0.0000;"Storm Drain"; 36
175.3699; 65.2266; 0.0000;"Storm Drain"; 48
```

Notice that the numeric and text string values are the same as before. The only difference is that the newly specified delimiters are used.

NOTE

AutoCAD automatically uses the comma and apostrophe as default delimiters. Therefore, it is not necessary to specify these values.

Specifying Field Width and Numeric Precision

In the previous template file examples, the second column contained one of two character sets, which looked like the following:

C015000

N004002

These two values indicate to AutoCAD the type of information the field value represents. The character set that begins with a C indicates a text string value, whereas the N indicates a numeric value. The next three characters tell AutoCAD the maximum field width. The last three characters indicate how many decimal places to use when extracting numeric values (two decimal places in the previous example).

Because you set these values in the template file, you need to know what type of data—numeric or text string—you are extracting, and its field length. You must then set these values accordingly. For example, if you are extracting a numeric value whose number is 1,000,000, and you want this number to be extracted to four decimal places, you would specify the following character set as a minimum:

N012004

This value tells AutoCAD that the field being extracted is a numeric field that will occupy a maximum of 12 spaces and have a decimal precision of 4. The number one million, carried out four decimal places (with no commas), looks like this:

1000000.0000

Notice that this number occupies 12 spaces. If the number were longer than 12 digits, it would be necessary to adjust the field length accordingly. Otherwise, AutoCAD would simply truncate the extracted value.

To show the effects of setting the numeric and text string character length too short, the template file from the previous exercise has been modified as follows:

```
C:DELIM              ;
C:QUOTE              "
BL:X                 N002001
BL:Y                 N002001
BL:Z                 N002001
OBJECT_CATEGORY      C005000
OBJECT_SIZE          N001000
```

Notice that the field width values and decimal place values are too short to extract the block and attribute values correctly. When this template is applied to the previous drawing file, the extract file results are as follows:

```
67;11;0.;"Sewer";3
10;11;0.;"Sewer";3
13;11;0.;"Sewer";3
16;11;0.;"Sewer";3
20;11;0.;"Sewer";3
89;65;0.;"Storm";3
12;65;0.;"Storm";3
17;65;0.;"Storm";4
```

As you can see, even though the extract file used the same set of blocks, the data extracted does not correctly represent the true values of the blocks and attributes in the drawing.

Additionally, when ATTEXT was executed with the modified template file, it issued the following warnings when extracting the data:

```
** Field overflow in record 1
** Field overflow in record 2
** Field overflow in record 3
** Field overflow in record 4
** Field overflow in record 5
** Field overflow in record 6
** Field overflow in record 7
** Field overflow in record 8
8 records in extract file.
```

As demonstrated, it is important that you know in advance what type of data you are extracting, and the field widths necessary to obtain the true value of the block or attribute.

Extraction Data Types

The tag name is the only available extraction data type defined for attributes. Blocks, on the other hand, have a variety of data that can be extracted. To extract each type of block data, you must enter the appropriate field type in the template file. Each block data type begins with BL: and is followed by the character set that specifies the type of block data to be extracted. The following is a list of the various block data types, their definitions, and an example of each. To provide an example of each of the block extraction data types, the data types were added to the template used in the last exercise, and then the data was extracted.

- **BL:LEVEL N002000.** This value indicates the level of block nesting. Added to the beginning of the template file, the extract file looks like this:

```
1; 67.8188; 111.6738; 0.0000;"Sewer"; 30
1; 101.1619; 111.6738; 0.0000;"Sewer"; 30
1; 134.0559; 111.6738; 0.0000;"Sewer"; 36
1; 167.7358; 111.6738; 0.0000;"Sewer"; 36
1; 203.8855; 111.6738; 0.0000;"Sewer"; 36
1; 89.4862; 65.2266; 0.0000;"Storm Drain"; 36
1; 129.5653; 65.2266; 0.0000;"Storm Drain"; 36
1; 175.3699; 65.2266; 0.0000;"Storm Drain"; 48
```

The BL:LEVEL field is the first field. Notice that all records indicate that each block's nesting level is 1. If these blocks were nested inside other blocks, this value would represent the nested level occupied by the manhole block. For example, if the manhole block were nested inside another block, the record value would look like this:

```
2; 135.2779; 87.4341; 0.0000;"Sewer"; 30
```

- **BL:NAME C015000.** This value represents the block's name. Added to the beginning of the template file, the extract file looks like this:

```
"MANHOLE"; 67.8188; 111.6738; 0.0000;"Sewer"; 30
"MANHOLE"; 101.1619; 111.6738; 0.0000;"Sewer"; 30
"MANHOLE"; 134.0559; 111.6738; 0.0000;"Sewer"; 36
"MANHOLE"; 167.7358; 111.6738; 0.0000;"Sewer"; 36
"MANHOLE"; 203.8855; 111.6738; 0.0000;"Sewer"; 36
"MANHOLE"; 89.4862; 65.2266; 0.0000;"Storm Drain"; 36
"MANHOLE"; 129.5653; 65.2266; 0.0000;"Storm Drain"; 36
"MANHOLE"; 175.3699; 65.2266; 0.0000;"Storm Drain"; 48
```

The BL:NAME field is the first field. Notice that all records indicate the block definition's name, which in this case is MANHOLE.

- **BL:X, BL:Y, and BL:Z.** These values represent the block's insertion coordinates and are always expressed as WCS values. This is true even with nested blocks.

- **BL:NUMBER N002000.** This value represents the number of the current extracted block. Added to the beginning of the template file, the extract file looks like this:

```
1; 67.8188; 111.6738; 0.0000;"Sewer"; 30
2; 101.1619; 111.6738; 0.0000;"Sewer"; 30
3; 134.0559; 111.6738; 0.0000;"Sewer"; 36
              4; 167.7358; 111.6738; 0.0000;"Sewer"; 36
5; 203.8855; 111.6738; 0.0000;"Sewer"; 36
6; 89.4862; 65.2266; 0.0000;"Storm Drain"; 36
7; 129.5653; 65.2266; 0.0000;"Storm Drain"; 36
8; 175.3699; 65.2266; 0.0000;"Storm Drain"; 48
```

The BL:NUMBER field is the first field. The number is simply a counter, and indicates the order in which the block was selected. As each block's record data is extracted, AutoCAD increases this number in increments of 1.

- **BL:HANDLE C008000.** This value represents the value of the block's handle. Added to the beginning of the template file, the extract file looks like this:

```
"2B"; 67.8188; 111.6738; 0.0000;"Sewer"; 30
"30"; 101.1619; 111.6738; 0.0000;"Sewer"; 30
"3"; 134.0559; 111.6738; 0.0000;"Sewer"; 36
"1C"; 167.7358; 111.6738; 0.0000;"Sewer"; 36
"21"; 203.8855; 111.6738; 0.0000;"Sewer"; 36
"26"; 89.4862; 65.2266; 0.0000;"Storm Drain"; 36
"17"; 129.5653; 65.2266; 0.0000;"Storm Drain"; 36
"12"; 175.3699; 65.2266; 0.0000;"Storm Drain"; 48
```

The BL:HANDLE field is the first field. The handle value, which AutoCAD sets automatically for all objects, remains constant. Consequently, this value can be used to identify the insert objects when you write AutoLISP routines to manipulate these objects.

- **BL:LAYER C015000.** This value represents the block's insertion layer value. Added to the beginning of the template file, the extract file looks like this:

```
"LAYER1"; 67.8188; 111.6738; 0.0000;"Sewer"; 30
"LAYER1"; 101.1619; 111.6738; 0.0000;"Sewer"; 30
"LAYER2"; 134.0559; 111.6738; 0.0000;"Sewer"; 36
"LAYER2"; 167.7358; 111.6738; 0.0000;"Sewer"; 36
"LAYER2"; 203.8855; 111.6738; 0.0000;"Sewer"; 36
"LAYER3"; 89.4862; 65.2266; 0.0000;"Storm Drain"; 36
"LAYER3"; 129.5653; 65.2266; 0.0000;"Storm Drain"; 36
"LAYER4"; 175.3699; 65.2266; 0.0000;"Storm Drain"; 48
```

The BL:LAYER field is the first field. The layer value indicates the layer on which the block is currently inserted. If the block is moved to a new layer, and the block information is extracted again, the value is updated to the new layer. For nested blocks, the layer value is the layer that the nested block is inserted upon within the higher level block.

- **BL:ORIENT N010006.** This value represents the block's rotation angle. Added to the beginning of the template file, the extract file looks like this:

```
0.000000; 67.8188; 111.6738; 0.0000;"Sewer"; 30
0.000000; 101.1619; 111.6738; 0.0000;"Sewer"; 30
0.000000; 134.0559; 111.6738; 0.0000;"Sewer"; 36
0.000000; 167.7358; 111.6738; 0.0000;"Sewer"; 36
0.000000; 203.8855; 111.6738; 0.0000;"Sewer"; 36
0.000000; 89.4862; 65.2266; 0.0000;"Storm Drain"; 36
0.000000; 129.5653; 65.2266; 0.0000;"Storm Drain"; 36
0.000000; 175.3699; 65.2266; 0.0000;"Storm Drain"; 48
```

The BL:ORIENT field is the first field. The rotation angle value is expressed in decimal degrees, even when the angle units are set to another format. If the block is nested in another block, the rotation angle is the sum of its angle and the angle of the higher-level block in which it is nested.

- **BL:XSCALE, BL:YSCALE, and BL:ZSCALE N010001.** These values represent the block's X, Y, Z scale factors. When added to the beginning of the template file, the extract file looks like this:

```
10.0; 10.0; 10.0; 67.8188; 111.6738; 0.0000;"Sewer"; 30
10.0; 10.0; 10.0; 101.1619; 111.6738; 0.0000;"Sewer"; 30
10.0; 10.0; 10.0; 134.0559; 111.6738; 0.0000;"Sewer"; 36
10.0; 10.0; 10.0; 167.7358; 111.6738; 0.0000;"Sewer"; 36
```

```
10.0; 10.0; 10.0; 203.8855; 111.6738; 0.0000;"Sewer"; 36
10.0; 10.0; 10.0; 89.4862; 65.2266; 0.0000;"Storm Drain"; 36
10.0; 10.0; 10.0; 129.5653; 65.2266; 0.0000;"Storm Drain"; 36
10.0; 10.0; 10.0; 175.3699; 65.2266; 0.0000;"Storm Drain"; 48
```

The BL:XSCALE, BL:YSCALE, and BL:ZSCALE fields are the first three fields, respectively. In this particular drawing, the blocks were inserted with an X,Y,Z scale factor of 10. If a block is nested in another block, the scale factor is the product of its scale and the higher-level block in which it is nested.

■ **BL:XEXTRUDE, BL:YEXTRUDE, and BL:ZEXTRUDE N010001.** These values represent the block's X,Y, Z extrusion (3D orientation) directions. Added to the beginning of the template file, the extract file looks like this:

```
0.0; 0.0; 1.0; 67.8188; 111.6738; 0.0000;"Sewer"; 30
0.0; 0.0; 1.0; 101.1619; 111.6738; 0.0000;"Sewer"; 30
0.0; 0.0; 1.0; 134.0559; 111.6738; 0.0000;"Sewer"; 36
0.0; 0.0; 1.0; 167.7358; 111.6738; 0.0000;"Sewer"; 36
0.0; 0.0; 1.0; 203.8855; 111.6738; 0.0000;"Sewer"; 36
0.0; 0.0; 1.0; 89.4862; 65.2266; 0.0000;"Storm Drain"; 36
0.0; 0.0; 1.0; 129.5653; 65.2266; 0.0000;"Storm Drain"; 36
0.0; 0.0; 1.0; 175.3699; 65.2266; 0.0000;"Storm Drain"; 48
```

The BL:XEXTRUDE, BL:YEXTRUDE, and BL:ZEXTRUDE fields are the first three fields, respectively. In this particular drawing, the blocks were inserted with an X,Y,Z in the WCS. Consequently, the X,Y,Z extrusion directions are 0,0,1, respectively. If a block is nested in another block, the extrusion directions represent the actual values in the WCS.

As you can see from this section, extracting attribute and block data from AutoCAD drawings in not overly difficult once you know what can be extracted and how to format that information.

Summary

In this chapter, you learned how to quickly query for object data from the Object Properties toolbar, and how to query properly for 2D distances and areas in blocks and xrefs.

Quickly querying objects for data that AutoCAD automatically creates, such as layer, color, and linetype, increases your productivity by providing information you frequently need during an editing session. By querying data that users assign, such as attribute data, you can increase your productivity by automatically extracting large amounts of information you need to complete your work, such as when you need to create a bill of materials.

You also learned about how to handle additional data that is associated with AutoCAD objects, whether that data is block attributes or general data such as the color or linetype of an object. You learned about using the DDATTEXT command for block and attribute extraction, and about the different extraction formats. You found out how to create report templates, and how to control CDF file delimiters for block data extraction. This chapter showed you how to specify each field width and numeric precision, and told you about the different data extraction types for blocks and attributes.

By understanding how blocks and attributes work, and how to properly manage blocks and extract their data, you have learned how to make AutoCAD do tedious, repetitious drafting work automatically, and increase your productivity.

10

BASIC OBJECT EDITING

It is estimated that more than 70% of your time using AutoCAD will be spent editing existing objects. With this in mind, it is critical that you understand and efficiently implement the different methods for editing. Editing commands are grouped into two classes: editing commands that can be used on a variety of objects, and editing commands that are designed for a specific type of object. This chapter concentrates on the selection methods, standard editing commands, and processes. Chapter 11, "Advanced Geometry Editing," concentrates on enhanced editing methods and object-specific editing commands.

This chapter discusses the following skills:

■ *Selecting objects*

■ *Removing objects from a selection set*

■ *Undoing changes made in the drawing*

■ *Resizing objects*

■ *Relocating and duplicating objects*

■ *Adding chamfers and fillets to objects*

Assembling a Selection Set

Many of the editing commands start by displaying the Select Objects: prompt. The Select Objects: prompt signals the beginning of the process in which you can assemble a selection set by selecting the desired objects using a variety of methods. Most of the selection options covered in the following list are invoked by typing a letter or two at a Select Objects: prompt. The typical selection process is open-ended, which means that you can invoke any of the options listed, as many times as you want and in any order that you want. When an object is selected, it is highlighted on the screen as a visual confirmation. When you finish selecting objects for any given command, press the Enter key or spacebar, or right-click on the input device. Then you will pass the selection on to the current command that is active.

NOTE

The highlighting of objects is enabled by default. You can control this feature with the HIGHLIGHT system variable. However, some third-party software may disable the highlight variable when a routine is canceled. The HIGHLIGHT variable is set at the command line: With a setting of 1 it is on, and with 0 it is off.

The typical selection process provides you with the following options, which are discussed in detail in the sections that follow:

- Picking the objects directly
- Using an implied window, window, and crossing window
- Selecting the last object
- Selecting all objects
- Using a fence
- Using a window and crossing polygon
- Selecting the previously selected objects
- Using the multiple option
- Undoing the last selection option
- Removing and adding objects to the selection
- Using object cycling

Picking Objects Directly

When you're prompted to select objects, the normal pointer is replaced with a box cursor, which is referred to as the "pickbox." To select an object directly, position the pickbox over the object and select it. The size of the pickbox is controlled through the Selection tab in the Options dialog box (see Figure 10.1).

Figure 10.1

The Selection tab in the Options dialog box offers options for controlling the size of the pickbox.

Using Implied Windowing, Window, and Crossing Window

The basic method for selecting large groups of objects is to create a rectangular window around the objects. The window boundary method selects only items that are totally enclosed within the window. In the case of the crossing window method, objects enclosed or crossed by the boundary window itself are selected. Initializing a type of window is best done with implied windowing.

Implied Windowing

When you position the pickbox over an empty portion of the drawing and pick a point, the system assumes you want to place the first corner of a rectangular selection window at that point. You determine its size by moving the cursor to the opposite corner and then picking a second point (the opposing diagonal corner point relative to the initial point). When the window is defined from left to right, all objects completely enclosed in the window are selected. On the left of Figure 10.2, using the window method would select just the circle and vertical line.

When the window is defined right to left, it is referred to as a "crossing window." In a crossing window, all objects that are completely enclosed in the window or that merely cross the boundaries of the crossing window are selected. A crossing window is drawn with a dotted line, whereas a window is drawn with a continuous line. As you can see on the right side of Figure 10.2, using a crossing window selects the circle and all the lines. If you disable the Implied Windowing setting in the Selection tab of the Options dialog box, this feature is disabled.

Figure 10.2

A window selection is defined from left to right; a crossing window is defined from right to left.

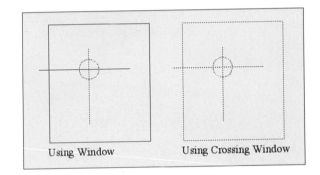

Using Window   Using Crossing Window

N O T E

By default, the Implied Windowing selection option on the Selection tab of the Options dialog box is enabled. If it's disabled, the only way you can define a window or a crossing window is to use the Window or Crossing Window options explicitly. This feature is disabled for backward-compatibility with previous versions of AutoCAD.

Explicitly Using the Window or Crossing Window Method

Window type selection methods include the typical window and crossing window. They are accessed by typing **W** or **C** at the Select Objects: prompt. When you use the Window option, you explicitly define a window with which to select objects. Unlike an implied window, the first point selected does not have to be located in an empty portion of the drawing because you establish it via point selection. Furthermore, it does not matter whether the window is defined from left to right or right to left. Using an explicit window or crossing method is superior to using an implied window when you deal with a crowded drawing and encounter difficulties finding an empty area of the drawing in which to anchor the first point of the implied window.

NOTE

> All window type selections are relative to the display, not to the current UCS. This means that you can not select objects in isometric views using a skewed isometric window.

Selection Modes Available for Selecting Objects

To display the Selection tab in the Options dialog box (shown in Figure 10.3), choose Options from the Tools menu and click the Selection tab. In this dialog box, you find the settings for controlling various aspects of the selection process. The following sections discuss these controls in more detail.

Figure 10.3

Selection Modes and Pickbox Size options in the Selection tab of the Options dialog box.

Understanding Noun/Verb Selection

The first option in the Object Selection Settings dialog box is Noun/Verb Selection, which is enabled by default. With this setting enabled, you have the option to select the objects to be manipulated prior to invoking a command. When the Noun/Verb option is disabled, you must invoke a command first and then select the objects to be modified. This option affects only those commands that begin with the `Select Objects:` prompt (such as the `ERASE` and `LIST` commands).

INSIDER **T**IP

> Working with the enabled Noun/Verb option can be confusing. You should practice using the option until you are comfortable with the processes of selecting objects and using the various editing commands. If you leave Noun/Verb enabled and accidentally select objects before choosing a command, press the Esc key once to release the selected objects. Press the Esc key once more to clear the grips, which are blue by default. (Grips are discussed in detail in Chapter 11.)

Most of the controls from Release 14's Object Selection Settings dialog box have been incorporated into the Options dialog box's Selection tab.

Replacing and Adding Selected Objects with the Use Shift to Add Option

The Use Shift to Add selection mode is disabled by default. Therefore, when you're selecting additional objects, the objects are automatically added to the current selection set. If you enable the Use Shift to Add option, any selection of objects during the same edit routine that occurs after the initial object(s) have been selected replaces those objects rather than adding to them. To add more objects to the current selection set, you must hold down the Shift key as you select the additional objects.

INSIDER TIP

This option is provided for compatibility with the way other Windows 95 applications deal with selecting objects. In AutoCAD, pressing the Shift key to select additional objects is typically an unnecessary step. Therefore, you should leave this option disabled. This feature is controlled via the PICKADD system variable.

Using Press and Drag

By default, the Press and Drag option on the Selection tab of the Options dialog box is disabled. Consequently, when you define a rectangular window (whether it is an implied window, window, or crossing window), you do so by picking the first corner of the window and then picking another point as the location of the opposing corner point. When Press and Drag is enabled, you first pick the initial corner point and then hold and press the pick button as you drag to the opposing corner of the rectangular selection window. You establish the location of the second corner point by releasing the pick button. Enabling this option makes the process of selecting objects with a rectangular window in AutoCAD similar to the process of using a window to select objects in Windows NT or Windows 95 itself.

INSIDER TIP

Using the Press and Drag option may be faster than using implied windowing. With implied windowing, if you miss the intentional selection of an object and pick nothing, an implied window will be started. With Press and Drag enabled in the same situation, you can simply continue to select objects with the standard pickbox.

Other Useful Selection Options

In some cases a typical selection method will not suffice. Fortunately, AutoCAD provides several more methods of selecting objects. The following list describes these secondary selection methods. For each one, the character in parentheses can be entered to invoke the respective option.

- **Last (L).** The Last option automatically selects the last object drawn that is visible in the display. This option can select an unexpected object, so you should use it only when you are working in a contained area.

- **ALL (ALL).** The All option selects all objects not residing on a locked or frozen layer. This option selects objects even if they are not visible in the current view.

- **Fence (F).** This option enables you to define a series of crossing line segments, which is referred to as a "fence." All objects the fence intersects or crosses are selected. The fence path is drawn as dotted lines (as shown in Figure 10.4). In Figure 10.4, only the lines and not the circle would be selected.

Figure 10.4

Using Fence to quickly select objects in a confined area to define a path.

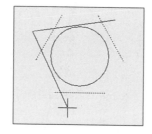

- **Wpolygon (WP).** The Wpolygon (Window Polygon) option is similar to the Window option, except that you can define an irregular polygon-shaped window as opposed to a rectangular window. Figure 10.5 illustrates using the Window Polygon option to select just the circle and a single line. You can define the window polygon with as many points as necessary. The Wpolygon option automatically draws the closing segment back to the beginning point.

Figure 10.5

The Window Polygon option allows for precise selection.

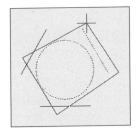

- **Cpolygon (CP).** The Cpolygon (Crossing Polygon) option is similar to the Crossing option, except that you define an irregular polygon-shaped crossing window instead of a rectangular window. Figure 10.6 illustrates using the Cpolygon option to select the circle and two of the three lines.

Figure 10.6

The Crossing Polygon option allows crossing selection by a polygonal area.

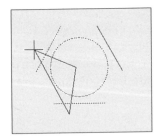

- **Previous (P).** Use this option to reselect the objects in the previous selection set, which was created during the most recent editing command.

- **Group (G).** The Group option enables you to specify the name of a pre-defined group. Groups are discussed in Chapter 11.

- **Undo (U).** When you enter U at the `Select Objects:` prompt, AutoCAD undoes the last selection option performed. Choosing the Undo tool cancels the current command when it's chosen at the `Select Objects:` prompt.

NOTE

Instead of typing the letter U at the Select Objects: prompt to undo the previous selection, if you modify the Standard toolbar Undo button's function to contain only the letter U (and not the Cancel characters of ^C), you can use that tool to undo the last selection. This also applies to reselecting objects again after they've been removed from the selection. Refer to Chapter 21, "Customizing Without Programming," to learn about customizing toolbar buttons. Figure 10.7 shows the Undo button you can modify.

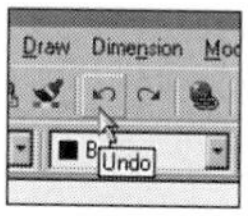

Figure 10.7

The Undo button on the Standard toolbar.

In addition to the options listed above, you can use several other options, including BOX, AUto, and Single. Programmers commonly use these options for AutoLISP and ARX-based programs or menu and toolbar macros.

NOTE

When you use Multiple option (invoked by typing **M** at a Select Objects: prompt), the selected objects are not highlighted until you press the Enter key or the spacebar. In addition, other selection options such as Previous, Last, All Window Types, Remove, and Undo do not function when the first object has been picked in multiple selection mode. You must press Enter to finish the multiple selection mode and highlight the objects.

The following exercise illustrates some alternative selection methods available in AutoCAD 2000.

USING A VARIETY OF SELECTION OPTIONS TO EDIT OBJECTS

1. Open the drawing chap10-1 from the accompanying CD-ROM.

2. Choose Named Views from the View pull-down menu. Then select the view named OFFICE-D, click the Set Current button in the View Control dialog box, then click OK. (See Figure 10.8.)

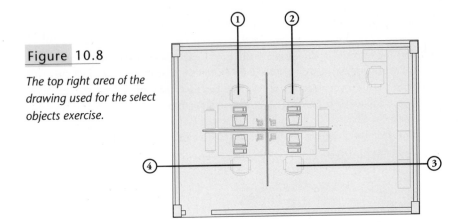

Figure 10.8

*The top right area of the
drawing used for the select
objects exercise.*

3. Use the MOVE command to relocate items in the room. Start the MOVE command and type **ALL** to select everything in the drawing. Notice that all objects in the drawing are now highlighted. Although this is a useful selection method, for our purposes we don't want to move everything in the drawing.

4. To undo the previous selection, type **U** and press Enter.

5. Now use the Crossing Polygon option to select all the chair and desk objects in the center of the room. Type **CP** at the Select Objects: prompt and pick the approximate centers of the four chairs. Select the points in a circular pattern at ①, ②, ③, and ④, but do not cross over the center with the polygonal selection box.

6. You should now have a highlighted group of objects including the four chairs and the desks in the center. Let's explore another method to select the chairs. Press the Esc key once to cancel the command.

7. Press Enter to start the MOVE command again. At the Select Objects: prompt, type **F** to use the Fence selection method. Select ① through ④ again.

8. Now you have the chairs and a similar selection of desk objects. However, we don't actually need to move anything, so press Esc to cancel the command.

9. As you can see, there are many methods of selecting objects for editing. Feel free to explore the other methods such as Previous, Last, and Window Polygon. You can leave this drawing open for the following exercise.

Refining the Selection Set

It is often impossible to get your initial selection set to include exactly the objects needed. To better control the object selection set, you can use a few tools AutoCAD offers for refining your selection.

NOTE

> The selection options previously discussed are only available if you choose the command first and respond to the command's prompt to select objects. The exceptions to this are implied windowing, shift to remove, object cycling, and the normal pickbox selection.

By default, when you're selecting objects, you work in the Add mode so that any objects selected are automatically added to the current selection set. How to remove objects from a selection set, the use of the Shift key, and object cycling are discussed in this section.

Removing Objects from the Selection Set

The Remove option switches you from the default Add mode to the Remove mode. In this mode, all objects selected are removed from the selection set. Undo is often used to remove the objects just selected from the selection set, but the Remove option enables you to select the specific objects you want to remove from the selection set. You remain in the Remove mode until you either end the selection process (by pressing the Enter key or the spacebar) or invoke the Add option by pressing A.

Holding Down the Shift Key

Instead of using the Remove option to deselect objects, you can hold down the Shift key and click on objects already in the selection set (already highlighted). This removes those objects from the current selection set. You can hold down the Shift key in combination with any of the aforementioned methods of selecting objects. When you release the Shift key, you are immediately placed back into the current mode.

N OTE

The Shift key method of deselecting objects works only in the Add mode; it will not add objects while you're in the Remove mode. To add objects you've removed from the selection set, simply release the Shift key. In addition, the Shift key method does not support the Window Polygon or Crossing Polygon (WP or CP) selection option.

Using Object Cycling

In a dense drawing, it can be difficult to select an object directly without inadvertently picking another nearby object. In such cases, you can zoom in on the area, making it easier to select the required object. You also can use object cycling to speed this process.

To use object cycling, start an edit command such as MOVE and position the pickbox over a dense area in the drawing so your cursor is on or touching more than one object. While holding down the Ctrl key, pick that location, then release the Ctrl key. This starts object selection cycling, so only a single object occupying the area of the pickbox is highlighted. If more than one object was found in the area of the pickbox, <Cycle on> appears at the prompt line. The next time you left-click (without holding down the Ctrl key), another object occupying the area of the pickbox is highlighted. If the highlighted object is not the required object, you can pick again anywhere in the drawing area, and the next object found in the area of the original pick location is highlighted. Every time you left-click, the next object found in the area of the original pick location is highlighted, cycling among all objects in that original pickbox area. When the desired object is highlighted, you can end the cycling by pressing the Enter key or the spacebar, or by right-clicking.

N OTE

As you continue to left-click to cycle and highlight the separate objects, the physical location of the current pickbox is immaterial. The location of the pickbox at the time you initiate object cycling is what defines the area that is searched. Any transparent command can be used during this mode; for example, you can use ZOOM to magnify the display.

Recovering from Unintentional Edits

Often when you're using AutoCAD, you will need go back to an earlier state of the drawing either by disposing of unneeded objects or restoring removed objects. The following sections discuss methods of recovering edits made to the current drawing.

Recovering Erased Objects

You can use the ERASE command to remove selected objects from a drawing. The ERASE command is found on both the Modify toolbar and the Modify menu. After selecting the desired objects, press the Enter key or the spacebar or right-click to end the general selection process. Because the ERASE command does not require any further information, the objects are then erased.

INSIDER TIP

If Noun/Verb is enabled, you can select the objects first and then choose the ERASE command, and immediately the objects highlighted will be deleted. In addition, in Noun/Verb mode, pressing the Delete key on the standard keyboard will erase the selected objects.

If you erase any objects by accident, you can undo the ERASE command. A specific command also can be used to retrieve the most recent selection of erased objects. Use the OOPS command whenever you want to unerase objects removed with the last ERASE command without affecting any other edits you've performed since the last ERASE command.

INSIDER TIP

Using the OOPS command to "unerase" objects is preferable to using the UNDO command. OOPS simply restores the last erased objects without undoing non-erase commands. The next section explains the UNDO command and its options. You may even try using this to clarify an area temporarily by erasing objects in your way, working as needed, then using OOPS to bring them back into the drawing.

Undoing Changes

In previous sections, you learned to use the Undo tool on the Standard toolbar to issue the U command that will undo the effects of the last command. A more powerful version of the U command also exists: the UNDO command, issued by typing

UNDO at the Command: prompt. The following list outlines the undo options and their functions:

- **Number.** With Undo, you can specify the number of commands to be undone by typing the number of commands you want to undo at the prompt. The REDO command undoes the effects of the UNDO command regardless of the number of options you specify within a single undo .

- **Auto.** Auto enables you to undo a complete menu selection as a single command sequence (this is also reversible with a single U command keystroke). Undo Auto inserts an Undo Begin at the start of each menu section—if a menu section is not already active—and inserts an Undo End upon exiting from the menu section.

- **Control.** Using Control, you can limit AutoCAD's ability to undo commands to just one command. Typically, the only time you must deal with the options available through Control is when you are critically short of drive space (because keeping track of commands takes up hard drive space). In such situations, it is better to allocate more free drive space than to limit AutoCAD's ability to undo commands.

- **Begin/End.** The Begin option begins the process of grouping a series of commands. All commands following that option become part of the group until you use the End option to close the group. Undo and U both treat grouped commands as a single operation.

- **Mark/Back.** Use the Mark option of the UNDO command to mark (much like a bookmark) a place in the Undo information file maintained by AutoCAD 2000. Later, during the same drawing session, you can use the Back option to undo all commands issued since the last Mark option was specified.

  In addition to undoing the commands, the Back option also removes the last mark. You can issue the Mark option as many times as you want during a drawing session to place multiple "bookmarks" throughout your drawing process.

INSIDER TIP

Issue the Mark option when you think you might need to make changes to the drawing. Then if you decide the changes weren't necessary, you can issue the UNDO command and use the Back option. Alternatively, you can save the drawing before you make the changes, and if you want to discard the changes, you can issue the OPEN command, discard the current changes, and open the same drawing over again.

Understanding the functionality of the UNDO command can be difficult. The following exercise demonstrates the power of the UNDO command.

USING UNDO TO RECOVER UNINTENTIONAL EDITS

1. Open CHAP10-1.dwg from the CD if it's not open from the previous exercise. Choose Named Views from the View pull-down menu. Then select the view named OFFICE-D, click the Set Current button in the View Control dialog box, and click OK.

2. Use the LINE command to draw four lines from ① through ④ as shown in Figure 10.9. Press Enter to exit the LINE command.

Figure 10.9

The office area with chairs and desks.

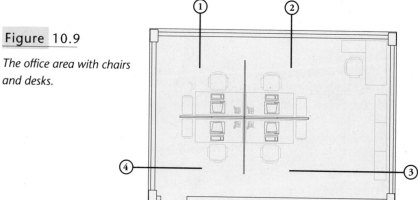

3. Execute the UNDO command by typing **UNDO** at the command line. Then type **M** for Mark and press Enter. This puts a marker in the AutoCAD system for use later.

4. Using the LINE command again, put an X in by picking points ① to ③. Press Enter twice, then pick ② and ④. Then press Enter to exit the command.

5. Reissue the UNDO command, type **B** for the Back option, then press Enter. This removes the X series of lines. Notice the following command prompt:

    ```
    LINE LINE
    Mark encountered
    ```

    This indicates that two LINE commands were undone and were followed by an UNDO Mark hit. At this point, the Undo sequence stops.

6. Now type **REDO** and press Enter to restore the X objects. The two lines reappear.

7. Using the UNDO command again, type **1** and press Enter. The last line drawn disappears. This numbering option of the UNDO command allows you to go back a specified number of steps.

8. Use the UNDO command once more. This time type **2** and press Enter. Only the last line disappears and the note `Mark encountered` appears. Even though you specified two steps back, AutoCAD halts when it reaches an undo marker.

9. Use the UNDO command again, type **1**, and press Enter. The four lines around the chairs disappear, and your drawing is restored to its original state.

10. Leave this drawing open for the following exercise.

If the objects you have created are not correct, it's often a better solution to change the appearance of these objects than to erase and re-create them. The following section covers various methods of resizing drawing objects.

Resizing Objects

A number of commands can be used to modify existing objects. The commands that can be used to resize objects are SCALE, STRETCH, LENGTHEN, TRIM, EXTEND, and BREAK, all of which are covered in this section. These commands are located on both the Modify toolbar and the Modify pull-down menu.

Scaling Objects

The SCALE command is used to scale objects up or down in size. This command employs the general selection process, which gives you many options for selecting the objects. After selecting the objects to be scaled, you are prompted to pick a base point. You then can enter a scaling factor or graphically pick a distance, or you can specify the Reference option. When you graphically scale the selection set, the length of the rubberbanding line is used as the scaling factor.

NOTE

Setting the scale factor by picking a point is very difficult. If the point you select is one unit away from the base point, your scale would be 1x and would not change. As you move farther away, you increase the object's scale factor. As you move closer to the base point, you decrease the scale factor. Picking a point to scale from other than the center point of the selected object(s) also moves the selection set by scaling the distance between that point and the base point.

The Reference option of the SCALE command provides a very useful control. After you request that option, you are prompted to specify a reference length. You usually specify it graphically along an existing object or distance. You are then prompted for a new length value. This makes it very easy to scale an unknown distance to a known distance.

Stretching Objects

The STRETCH command is used to stretch an object's length by relocating a portion of the object. Although the command does issue the general Select Objects: prompt, you must select the desired objects using one of the crossing selection methods (an implied crossing window, a crossing window, or Cpolygon). You can use only one crossing window per occurrence of the STRETCH command. If you define more than one crossing window in a single STRETCH command sequence, only the objects selected with the last crossing window are stretched.

After you select the objects, you are prompted to select a base point or enter a displacement. If you choose to pick a base point, you also must specify a second point for the new location of the base point. As an alternative to picking a base point, you can specify a displacement.

The displacement is defined as the delta-X, delta-Y, and delta-Z—or the distance and angle from the start point to the end point, which is essentially the distance the object(s) are to be stretched and the direction you want to apply to the objects. If you know the exact displacement you want to use, you can enter the displacement at the prompt for the base point and press Enter twice. The displacement you enter can be an absolute Cartesian coordinate, a relative distance from the base point, or a polar coordinate. The STRETCH command will move all objects that are completely enclosed in the crossing window. Any objects *not* completely enclosed within the crossing window are stretched by repositioning those endpoints inside the crossing window while maintaining the position of those endpoints outside the crossing window.

Note

The STRETCH command cannot be used to stretch circles or ellipses; those objects are resized using grips. For more on using grips, see Chapter 11.

Trimming Objects

With the TRIM command, you begin the trimming process by selecting the object(s) that will define the "cutting edge," then selecting the object(s) to be trimmed against the selected cutting edge(s), selecting those objects which are to be trimmed away or removed. If you want to select more than one object at a time, you can use the Fence option to select multiple cutting edges or multiple objects to be trimmed. The TRIM command is effective only if an object is left over; otherwise, the ERASE command should be used.

INSIDER TIP

Using the Fence option can return incomplete results. This may be due to the display scale, the object's linetype, any running Osnap modes, or the selection of the object(s) to be trimmed more than once. If the AutoCAD 2000 Fence line does not cross each object at a point where the object is displayed (not the gaps in a dashed linetype), the command cannot find the objects to trim. In addition, running Osnaps sometimes interferes when they don't apply to the type of objects selected. In all cases, performing several passes of the process or increasing or decreasing the display scale around the objects usually resolves the problem.

Any edge object, such as a line or a circle, can be used as a cutting edge or can be the object to be trimmed. However, an Mline object can be selected as a cutting edge but cannot be trimmed. It's worth mentioning that when you're trimming out a segment of a circle, after the first trim, the object is converted into an arc object. When you use the TRIM command, the result depends on the point you selected on the object being trimmed (see Figure 10.10).

Figure 10.10

The result of TRIM depends on the point you pick to trim against.

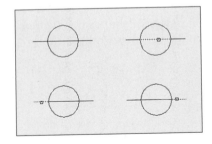

Starting from the point that is used to select the object, use the TRIM command to proceed in one direction along the object until you encounter either an endpoint or a cutting edge. Then the TRIM command proceeds from the original pick point in the opposite direction until it encounters either an endpoint or another cutting edge. The resulting defined portion of the object is then removed. Under no circumstances can an object be trimmed in such a way that nothing is left of the object. This condition exists when you trim a circle with a cutting edge that does not cross the circle completely.

INSIDER TIP

If you press Enter without selecting any cutting edges, all edge objects on the screen are automatically selected as valid cutting edges but are not highlighted. In addition, any object that is selected as a cutting edge can be trimmed (if permissible) with the same TRIM command.

INSIDER TIP

To use the internal objects of a block as a cutting or boundary edge, use the Express Tools command BTRIM. See Appendix B, "The Express Tools," to learn more about their functionality.

Extending Objects

The EXTEND command is used to elongate an edge object to an existing boundary (see Figure 10.11).

Figure 10.11

Using the EXTEND
*command is very helpful
to quickly lengthen
existing geometry.*

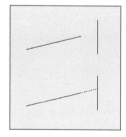

EXTEND is the complement to the TRIM command, so it has the same options. Instead of prompting you to select the cutting edge(s), the EXTEND command prompts you to select the boundary edge(s). The Project and Edge options are settings saved and shared by the TRIM and EXTEND commands.

INSIDER **T**IP

When working with an arc or partial ellipse object, you cannot extend any endpoint of the object to a point that would cause it to close on itself. If you attempt such a move, AutoCAD 2000 returns the prompt Object does not intersect an edge and then asks for another object selection.

Using the Edge Option to Extend the Cutting Edges

By default, the object to be trimmed must physically intersect the cutting-edge object. You can bypass this requirement with the Edge option. Choosing the Extend mode of the Edge option extends the cutting edges so the object(s) being trimmed need not intersect the cutting edge.

Choosing the Edge option to Extend sets the EDGEMODE system variable to 1. This option controls just how the TRIM and EXTEND commands find cutting and boundary edges. With a setting of 0, it uses the selected edge without any implied extension. With a setting of 1, it extends or trims the selected object to an implied extension of the selected cutting or boundary edge. This system variable can be used with the TRIM and EXTEND commands. When the setting has been made in either command, it affects the operation of both.

Breaking Objects

To remove a portion of an object, consider using the BREAK command. BREAK offers two advantages over TRIM for removing a portion of an object. First, you do not need any cutting objects to use BREAK. Second, the BREAK command can be used to break a non-closed object into two objects without removing any part of the original single object.

After you select the object to be broken, the default option requests a second point on the object. Then the portion of the object between the point used to select the object and the second point is removed. Notice that when you first select the object to break, it's not necessary to press Enter to go to the next prompt.

Sometimes, however, the point used to select the object is not where you want to begin the break. In such a case, you would use the First option to specifically define the beginning point of the break and the second point of the break.

Note

> When you're breaking curved edge objects, such as a circle, the removal process always proceeds from the first point to the second point in a counter-clockwise direction.

When you use BREAK, sometimes the second point that you selected for the end of the break (or the two points you pick for the First option) does not actually lie on the object to be broken. In this case, the point is projected perpendicularly back to the object, and the projected point is used as the end of the break (see Figure 10.12).

Line to be broken

Figure 10.12

The First option of the BREAK *command enables you to determine the starting point of the break.*

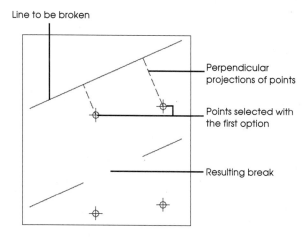

Perpendicular projections of points

Points selected with the first option

Resulting break

If you simply want to break an object into two objects without actually removing a portion of the object, define the second point at the same location as the first point of the break. The easiest way to do this is to enter @ as the second point. When you enter @, AutoCAD passes the last point recorded directly into the current request for a point location.

In the following exercise, you explore the various methods of resizing objects in AutoCAD. These commands will enable you to edit existing objects instead of erasing and creating new ones.

EDITING EXISTING OBJECTS

1. Open CHAP10-1.dwg from the CD if it's not open from the previous exercise. Choose Named Views from the View pull-down menu. Then select the view named OFFICE-D, click on the Set Current button in the View Control dialog box, and click OK to display the view shown in Figure 10.13.

Figure 10.13

The area of the drawing used in the edit exercise.

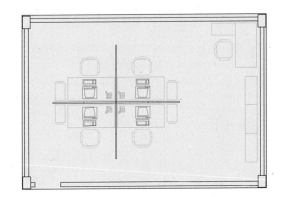

2. To use the UNDO command and place a marker with the Mark option, type **UNDO** at the command prompt, press **M**, and press Enter. This will enable you to restore the drawing after the exercise is complete.

3. From the Modify pull-down menu, select the Scale menu option. At the `Select Objects:` prompt, window the collection of chairs and desks in the center of the room.

4. At the `Specify base point` prompt, choose the intersection of the blue walls at the center of the room. It is not critical to choose the exact center; just eyeball the point.

5. At the `Specify scale factor or [Reference]` prompt, type in a scale of **1.2**. This will enlarge the object collection 120%.

6. From the Modify pull-down menu, select the **STRETCH** command. At the `Select Objects:` prompt, pick a point near ①, followed by ②, as shown in Figure 10.14. This selects the end of the wall at the bottom of the room.

Figure 10.14

The points need to stretch the wall.

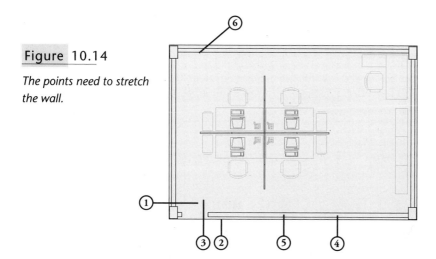

7. At the `Specify base point or displacement` prompt, pick at ③. Then, at the `Specify second point of displacement` prompt, type **@15'<0** to shorten the wall to the column to the right.

8. From the Modify pull-down menu, select the **EXTEND** command. At the `Select boundary edges` prompt, press Enter. For this exercise, you will not select objects; instead, you will have AutoCAD select all objects for use.

9. At the `Select object to extend or [Project/Edge/Undo]` prompt, pick the two lines that make up the wall to the right. Choose at point ④, and then press Enter. The wall lines now extend to close the wall.

10. From the Modify pull-down menu, select the **TRIM** command. At the `Select cutting edges` prompt, press Enter. You will again use all objects for trim edges.

11. At the `Select object to trim or [Project/Edge/Undo]` prompt, chose the two lines at ⑤. The wall lines will once again open the room.

12. From the Modify pull-down menu, choose Break.

13. At the `Select Objects:` prompt, chose the inside wall line at the top of the room. Pick a point at ⑥. This selects the object to be broken.

14. At the `Specify second break point or [First point]` prompt, type **F**. This allows you to fully define the points at which to break.

15. At the `Specify first break point` prompt, use the Center osnap and choose the upper-left chair in the room.

16. At the `Specify second break point` prompt, use the Center osnap again to choose the upper-right chair in the room. A portion of the wall is removed using the X coordinates of the two chairs.

17. To see the power of the UNDO command again, enter **UNDO** and **BE** for begin, and all changes you made in this exercise will be undone. You can leave this drawing open for the following exercise.

Sometimes the problems with your objects are not their physical properties but their locations. The following section covers commands for repositioning objects.

Relocating Objects Using MOVE and ROTATE

The MOVE and ROTATE commands allow you to relocate and/or re-orient selected objects. MOVE and ROTATE are found on both the Modify pull-down menu and the Modify toolbar.

Moving Objects

When you use the MOVE command to relocate selected objects to a new location, after you select the objects, you must determine the base point for the selection set. For the base point, you typically choose a point on one of the objects being moved. You then pick a second point, which is the new location of the base point.

In reality, the MOVE command simply calculates the distance and direction from the first point to the second point and then uses that information to move the objects. Picking the base point on one of the objects being moved can make it easier for you to visualize the end result of the MOVE command. As an alternative to picking a base point, you can specify a displacement.

The *displacement* is defined as the delta-X, delta-Y, and delta-Z—or the distance and angle from the base point to the second point. Essentially, this is the amount of movement you want to apply to the objects. If you know the exact displacement desired, you can enter the displacement at the prompt for the base point. Figure 10.15 shows the results of the different methods of displacement entry.

Figure 10.15

This figure shows the similar effects of the different types of displacement entry you can use to duplicate objects in AutoCAD.

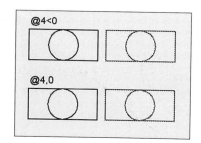

You can enter the displacement as an absolute Cartesian coordinate or a polar coordinate. You can force the MOVE command to interpret the numbers as a displacement by pressing Enter at the prompt for the second point. (In other words, do not define a second point.)

Rotating Objects

You use the ROTATE command to rotate selected objects about a particular point— the base point of the rotation. After you pick the base point, the default option enables you to specify a rotation angle by typing the rotation angle, picking a point to graphically rotate the objects, or selecting the Reference option. If you pick a point, the angle of the rubberbanding line is used as the rotation angle.

Using the Reference Option for the ROTATE Command

A valuable feature of the ROTATE command is the Reference option. Occasionally, you might draw an object at an incorrect or unknown angle. You can use the Reference option to correct the angle without having to investigate it.

To use the Reference option, first you select the objects and specify the base point, then you type **R** for reference. AutoCAD asks for a reference angle. At this point, you can enter the angle if you know it, or you can pick two points on-screen to graphically specify the unknown angle. You are then prompted for a new angle, at which point you can either graphically place a point or enter the desired angle for the selected objects.

Duplicating Objects

Depending on the specific command you use, you can create exact duplicates using the COPY, OFFSET, MIRROR, and ARRAY commands—and even the Clipboard—to make copies of selected objects.

Copying Objects

With the COPY command, you can make exact duplicates of selected objects. After you select the objects to be copied, you are prompted to specify the base point of the displacement and a second point. The distance and direction from the first point to the second point are calculated and used to locate the new copied objects. To help you visualize the results, pick a base point on one of the objects to be copied (for example, the center of a circle). The second point then becomes the point on the copies that corresponds to the first point on the originals.

Just as you can use the displacement function with the MOVE command, if you know the exact displacement, you can enter it at the prompt for the base point when you're using the COPY command. You force the COPY command to interpret your entry as a displacement by pressing Enter again at the prompt for the second point. (In other words, you do not define a second point.)

By default, the COPY command makes one copy of the selected objects. You can, however, use the Multiple option to make multiple copies of the selected objects. After you select the Multiple option and choose an initial base point, the COPY command repeatedly prompts you to select a second displacement point to locate the copies. Press Enter to end the multiple copy process.

The following exercise illustrates using the MOVE, COPY, and ROTATE commands.

EDITING THE FLOOR PLAN WITH BASIC EDITING COMMANDS

1. Open CHAP10-1.dwg from the CD if it's not open from the previous exercise. Select Named Views from the View pull-down menu. Then select the view named OFFICE-D, click on the Set Current button in the View Control dialog box, and click OK to see the view as shown in Figure 10.16.

Figure 10.16

The area of the building used for the Move, Copy and Rotate exercise.

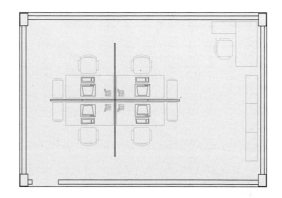

2. To use the UNDO command and place a marker, type **UNDO** at the command prompt, press **M**, and press Enter. This will enable you to restore the drawing after the exercise is complete.

3. From the Modify pull-down menu, select the Move menu option. At the `Select Objects:` prompt, use Window to select the chair and desk collection in the center of the room.

4. At the `Specify base point or displacement` prompt, type **170',80'**. This establishes the start point for the MOVE command.

5. At the `Specify second point of displacement or <use first point as displacement>` prompt, type **@40,10** and press Enter.

6. From the Modify pull-down menu, select the ROTATE command. At the `Select Objects:` prompt, type **P** and press Enter. AutoCAD will use the previous selection set for the objects to edit.

7. At the `Specify base point` prompt, type **173',89'** and press Enter. This point is the approximate intersection of the blue walls.

8. At the `Specify rotation angle or [Reference]` prompt, type **90** and press Enter. AutoCAD then rotates the chair and desk selection set 90 degrees using a point near the middle of the collection.

9. From the Modify pull-down menu, choose the Copy option. From the `Select Objects:` prompt, choose the two left chairs in the center of the room. These chairs are blocks, so selecting them requires a single pick for each. Press Enter to end object selection mode.

10. At the `Specify base point or displacement, or [Multiple]` prompt, type **-8'6,0** and press Enter twice. This uses a displacement entry to determine a start point and uses the values as the displacement distances for both the X and Y distances. The minus sign moves the objects in a leftward (negative) X distance.

11. To restore your drawing, type **UNDO** and **BE** (for begin) and press Enter. All changes in this exercise are removed. You can leave this drawing open for the following exercise.

When the objects you have are valid and all you need are more copies of them, using the COPY and OFFSET can certainly help you out.

Duplicating Objects with OFFSET

With the OFFSET command, you can create a copy of the selected object and have AutoCAD offset it a specified distance from the original object. At the initial prompt, you have the choice of entering the offset distance or using the Through option. To enter a specific offset distance, type the distance (or pick two points on the screen) at the `Specify offset distance` prompt. Thereafter, you can select one object at a time to create an offset from the duplicate and choose the side of the original on which you want the duplicate made.

If you choose the Through option, you pick a point the offset object is to go through after you select the object you want to copy. The distance along a perpendicular from the point that you pick to the original object serves as the offset distance. The copy made by the OFFSET command might or might not be an *exact* duplicate of the original. Table 10.1 lists the various types of objects you can choose with the OFFSET command and the shape of the resulting copy. The differences between the sizes and lengths of the resulting copies can be attributed to the side of the original object specified for the offset copy.

Table 10.1

Objects and Resulting Duplicates Created with OFFSET

Original Object	Resulting Duplicate
Arc	The new arc is created so it has the same included angle and center point as the original arc, but the arc length will change.
Circle, ellipse	The new circle or ellipse is created so it has the same center point as the original circle or ellipse. The radius of the new circle on the axis lengths of the new ellipse will be different from the original object's radius on axis lengths.

Original Object	...
Line, ray, xline	The ne...
Lwpolyline	The lengths ... lwpolyline are a... are located along a ... sponding endpoints on... intermediate vertex point, ... along a direction that bisects ... on either side of the vertex point.
Spline	The length and shape of the new spline... endpoints of the new spline are located alo... perpendicular to the corresponding endpoints... open spline.

Creating a Mirror Image

With the MIRROR command, you can create a mirror image copy of the selected objects. After you select the objects to be mirrored, you are prompted to pick two points to define the mirror line. The mirror line is the line, or axis, about which the mirror image is created. The mirror line itself does not have to be a physical line in the drawing.

The only option you have with the MIRROR command is whether or not the original objects should be deleted. The default is to not delete the original objects.

NOTE

When a block is mirrored, it is assigned a negative X or Y scale factor, depending upon the mirror line position. This may prevent the block from being exploded for editing of its individual objects.

By default, the copy of text and mtext objects will appear backward, as if you were holding a page of text up to a mirror. To prevent text from being reversed in the mirrored objects, set the system variable MIRRTEXT to 0 before you begin with the MIRROR command.

so the
circular

ompted to
ws, and the

Resulting Duplicate

line, ray, or xline is an exact duplicate of the original.

of the line and arc segments of the new
justed so the endpoints of the new
direction perpendicular to the new polyline
the original open lwpolyline to the corre-
the new vertex points are located
he angle between the segments
are adjusted so the
ng a direction
on the original

General... however, specify the
distances with a window ... king the two corner
points of the window at the Unit cell or ... ws (−) prompt. The
height of the window is used as the distance between ... and the width of the
window is used as the distance between columns.

If you enter a negative distance for the distance between columns, the columns of
the array are created in the negative direction along the X axis; otherwise, they are
created in the positive X direction. Likewise, if you enter a negative distance for the
distance between rows, the rows are created in the negative direction along the Y
axis; otherwise, they are created in the positive Y direction. If you choose to use a unit
cell to specify the distances, the direction in which the rows and columns are created
is determined by the direction from the first window point to the second window
point.

In the next exercise, you create a rectangular array. You then use the MIRROR and OFFSET commands to duplicate the objects to the drawing.

CREATING A RECTANGULAR ARRAY OF DUPLICATES

1. Start AutoCAD 2000 and open the drawing file CHAP10-1.DWG from the accompanying CD-ROM. This drawing may currently be open from a previous exercise.

2. Choose Named Views from the View pull-down menu. Then select the view named OFFICE-C, click the Set Current button in the View Control dialog box, and click OK.

3. Choose Array from the Modify toolbar or the Modify pull-down menu. Then select the desk and chair and press Enter.

4. Type **R** for the Rectangular option and press Enter.

5. Type in **3** for the number of rows and **4** for the number of columns (see Figure 10.18).

Figure 10.18

Creating a three-row and four-column array of the desk and chair using ARRAY.

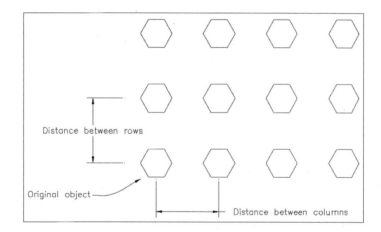

6. Type in **10'** for the distance between rows and **-12'** for the distance between columns. After you enter the final input for the distance between columns, AutoCAD creates the rectangular array.

7. From the Modify pull-down menu, select the MIRROR command. Select the cabinets, as shown in Figure 10.19.

Figure 10.19

The cabinets used in the MIRROR *exercise.*

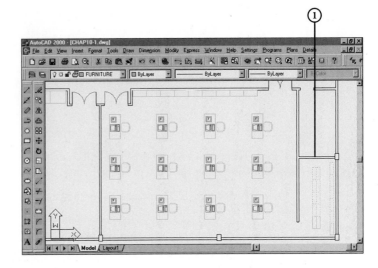

8. At the `Specify first point of mirror line` prompt, use the Endpoint osnap and pick a point near ①.

9. At the `Specify second point of mirror line` prompt, type **@1<0** to define the second point about which to mirror. AutoCAD duplicates the cabinets into the room adjacent to the current one.

10. Choose Named Views from the View pull-down menu. Select the view named OFFICE-B, click the Set Current button in the View Control dialog box, and click OK.

11. In this room, you need to increase the size of the conference table. From the Modify pull-down menu, choose Offset. At the `Specify offset distance or [Through]` prompt, type **12**.

12. At the `Select object to offset or <exit>` prompt, choose anywhere on the circle edge. Then at the `Specify point on side to offset` prompt, pick a point outside of the circle. This indicates which side of the object you want to offset toward.

13. At this point, you can close this drawing without saving.

Creating a Polar Array

If you choose to create a polar array, you are prompted to specify the center point about which the copies are made, the number of items (or copies) to be created (including the original), and the angle to fill, as shown in Figure 10.20.

Figure 10.20

Creating a polar array consisting of a circular pattern of copies.

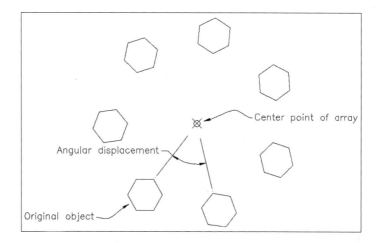

The angle to fill is the angle you want to occupy with your copies. AutoCAD uses the value you enter for the angle fill to determine the angular separation between adjacent items. For example, if you specify six items and enter 180 degrees as the fill angle, the angular separation between adjacent items is 180 divided by 6, or 30 degrees. If you specify a positive fill angle, the copies are made in a counterclockwise direction; otherwise, the copies are made in a clockwise direction by default.

INSIDER TIP

If you do not supply the number of items or the angle to fill and just press Enter, you will be prompted to specify the angle to be used as the angular separation between adjacent items in the array.

The final prompt of the polar array gives you the choice of rotating or not rotating the copies. If you answer Y (the default), the copies are rotated about the specified center point of the array. If you answer N, the copies are not rotated about the reference point of the selection set. The reference point of the selection set is determined from the last object selected. If a window of some type is used to select the objects, the last object in the selection set is picked arbitrarily: The reference point that's selected is based on the type of object (see Table 10.2).

Table 10.2

Point on Object Used As the Reference Point for a Polar Array

Object	Reference Point Used
Block insertion, text, mtext	Insertion point
Dimension objects	One of the definition points of the dimension object
Lines, rays, traces, mlines	One of the endpoints
Arcs, circles, ellipses	The center point
Lwpolylines, splines	The first vertex point
Xlines	The point connecting an imaginary line perpendicular to the xline with the center point of the polar array

As long as you use the default setting for rotating the copies, the resulting polar array will appear to be symmetrical regardless of the objects selected.

Chamfering Corners

If your design requires you to draw a beveled corner, use the CHAMFER command. The CHAMFER command is used to bevel corners formed by two nonparallel lines, rays, xlines, or the joined line segments of a single polyline. To issue this command, you choose Chamfer from the Modify pull-down menu or toolbar. To use the CHAMFER command, you first set the parameters defining the bevel to be generated and then select the two line segments that form the corner.

Defining the Bevel

To obtain the desired bevel, you first define one of two sets of parameters. One set of parameters, accessed with the Distances option, enables you to define the beveling operation with two distances—one along the first selected line and the other along the second selected line. Both distances are measured from the corner, or intersection, of the two lines (see Figure 10.21).

Figure 10.21

The Distance option enables you to define the bevel with distances measured from the intersection of two selected lines.

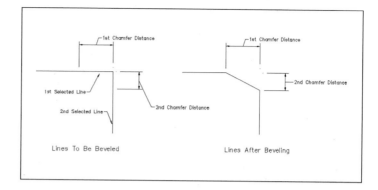

The other set of parameters, accessed with the Angle option, consists of a distance measured from the corner point along the first selected line and the angle of the new line relative to the first selected line (see Figure 10.22).

Figure 10.22

The Angle option enables you to define the bevel with a distance and an angle.

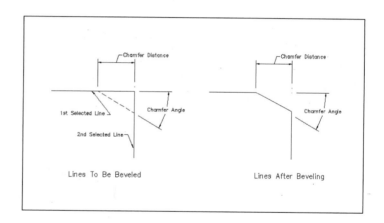

You can use either one or both the Distances and Angle options, depending on what design information is available to you. The CHAMFER command uses the most recently defined set of parameters. If both sets of parameters are defined, you can switch between them by using the Method option.

I N S I D E R   T I P

When you select either the Distances or the Angle option and set the parameters, the CHAMFER command ends. You must repeat the command and select the two line segments to produce the bevel. Remember, a quick way to repeat the last command issued is to press the spacebar or Enter at the Command: prompt.

The two lines you bevel do not have to intersect at a corner point. CHAMFER automatically trims or extends the two selected lines to an intersecting point before generating the bevel line. A quick way to trim or extend two lines to a corner point is to use the CHAMFER command with the distances set to zero (see Figure 10.23).

Figure 10.23

Using CHAMFER *with zero distances trims or extends two lines to a corner point.*

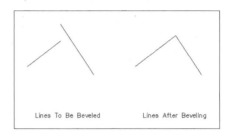

Lines To Be Beveled   Lines After Beveling

INSIDER TIP

When you use CHAMFER (or FILLET) to trim or extend two lines to a corner point, make sure the Trim option is set to Trim rather than No Trim.

If the two lines selected are on the same layer and have identical color and linetype properties, the new bevel line is drawn with the same properties. If there is a difference in a particular property of the two selected objects, the bevel line takes on the drawing's current object property value. For example, if the two selected lines are drawn on different layers, the new bevel line is drawn on the current layer. If the two selected lines are drawn with a different color, the bevel line is drawn with the current color property. If the two selected lines are drawn with a different linetype, the bevel line is drawn with the current linetype property.

NOTE

If two objects are drawn on two different layers and are displayed in two different colors, it does not mean that the color property of the two objects is different. If the two layers have different colors assigned to them and the color property of the two objects is BYLAYER, the two objects are drawn with the color assigned to the layer the objects reside on. Obviously, if the two layers have different assigned colors, the BYLAYER color setting causes the objects to be drawn in two different colors; however, both objects have the identical BYLAYER color property. The BYLAYER setting also affects the linetype used to display objects in the same manner.

Dealing with Polylines in the CHAMFER Command

To bevel all the corners of a polyline simultaneously, specify the Polyline option and select the target polyline. Be aware, however, that when you generate a bevel line at any angle other than 45 degrees relative to the selected lines, the result will not be symmetrical (see Figure 10.24).

Figure 10.24

Using the Polyline option simultaneously bevels all corners of a rectangle drawn with RECTANG, but the result can be asymmetric.

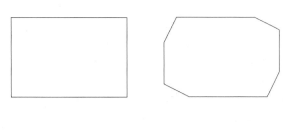

Lines To Be Beveled   Lines After Beveling

This asymmetric result is produced because the polyline segments are processed in the order in which they are drawn. To produce a symmetrically beveled shape, you must bevel one corner at a time. By explicitly selecting the first and second line segments, you control how much each segment is trimmed.

To Trim or Not to Trim

As previously stated, by default, CHAMFER extends or trims the lines to a corner point before applying the chamfer distances and/or angle. If, however, you want to draw the bevel line without any modifications to the original lines, choose the Trim option. At this point, you can choose between the Trim and No Trim settings. If you do not want the original lines modified, choose the No Trim setting. In the following exercise, you use the CHAMFER command to bevel the corners of a rectangle.

BEVELING THE CORNERS WITH CHAMFER

1. Open the drawing CHAMFILL.DWG on the accompanying CD. This drawing contains Plan and Elevation views of a part. Using CHAMFER, you are going to bevel the corners in the Plan view.

2. Select Chamfer from the Modify toolbar or drop-down list, then use the Angle option to set the chamfer distance to **1** and the chamfer angle to **45** degrees.

3. Repeat the CHAMFER command, but this time choose the Polyline option and select the rectangle in the Plan view. Note that all the corners are beveled in one operation.

4. Choose Undo from the Standard toolbar to undo the CHAMFER command, and the rectangle is restored to its original shape.

5. Repeat the CHAMFER command, selecting the two lines that form the upper-left corner of the rectangle (see Figure 10.25). Then repeat the CHAMFER command again and select the two lines that form its upper-right corner. The two top corners are now beveled at a 45-degree angle.

6. Repeat the CHAMFER command, but this time specify the Distances option. Set the first distance to **1.0** and the second distance to **0.5**.

7. Repeat the CHAMFER command and select the lines that form the lower-left corner with ① and ②. Then repeat the CHAMFER command and select the lines that form the lower-right corner with ③ and ④. Remember, the order in which you select the lines is important.

8. Save the drawing. Your rectangle should resemble the one in Figure 10.25. (This drawing is used in the next exercise, so keep it open.)

Figure 10.25

Using CHAMFER *to bevel the corners of the rectangle.*

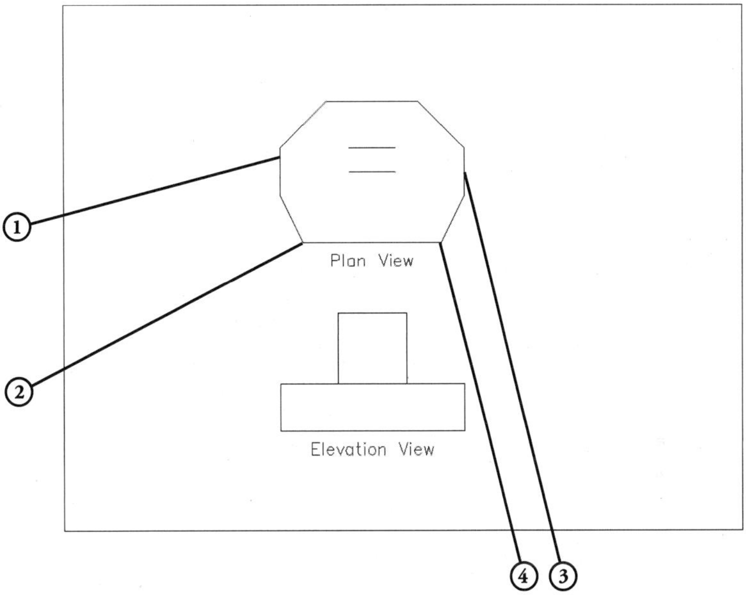

Filleting Objects

If your design includes rounded corners, use the FILLET command. To issue FILLET, you choose FILLET from the Modify pull-down menu or toolbar. With FILLET, you not only create rounded corners between two lines, rays, xlines, or line segments of a polyline, but also draw an arc segment between any combination of two lines, rays, xlines, circles, ellipses, arcs, elliptical arcs, or splines. The generated arc is always drawn so that it starts and ends tangent to the two selected objects.

Creating an Arc Using FILLET

To draw the arc, you first use the Radius option to set the radius, then you select the two objects. As with CHAMFER, if the two objects are nonparallel lines, the lines are trimmed or extended to a corner point, and the arc is drawn so the tangent lengths are equal (see Figure 10.26).

Figure 10.26

FILLET draws an arc joining two nonparallel lines.

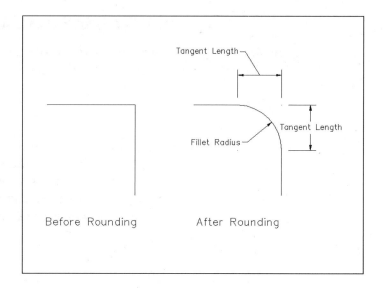

IN S I D E R   **T**I P

After you choose the Radius option and set the radius, the FILLET command (like the CHAMFER command) ends. To select the objects, you must repeat FILLET. An easy way to do this is to press the spacebar or the Enter key.

To cause AutoCAD to repeat FILLET (or any command), enter MULTIPLE at the Command: prompt and then invoke the FILLET command. The command will repeat after the completion of each filleted corner or option selection. Press Esc to cancel the command.

With the FILLET command (unlike the CHAMFER command), the two lines do not have to be nonparallel lines. If the lines are parallel, FILLET automatically draws a semicircle between the ends of the two lines, using the endpoint of the first selected line to determine how far to trim or extend the second selected line (see Figure 10.27). The radius of the generated semicircle is set automatically to half the distance between the two parallel lines.

Figure 10.27

FILLET *draws a half circle connecting the ends of two parallel lines, using the endpoint of the first line to determine where to trim the second line.*

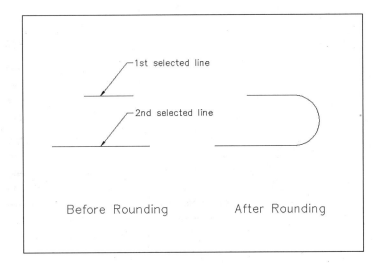

As mentioned earlier, you can use FILLET for more than just working on lines. Figure 10.28 shows some of the possible combinations of objects on which you can use FILLET, as well as the effect of the command.

Figure 10.28

FILLET *can be used with many objects other than lines.*

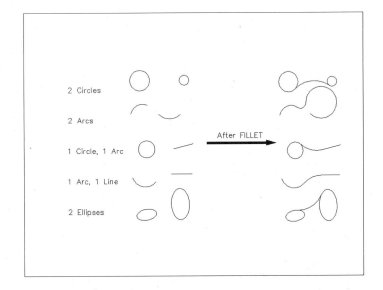

Using FILLET with any objects other than line objects (such as arcs) can produce surprising results (see the two arcs in Figure 10.28). The governing rule is that the generated arc must be drawn in such a way as to start and end tangent to the two selected objects.

If the two selected objects reside on the same layer and have identical color and linetype properties, the new arc is drawn with those properties. If there is a difference in a particular property of the two selected objects, the arc takes on the drawing's current object property value. For example, if the two selected objects are drawn on different layers, the new arc is drawn on the current layer. If the two selected objects are drawn with different colors, the arc is drawn with the current color property. If the two selected objects are drawn with different linetypes, the arc is drawn with the current linetype property.

INSIDER TIP

A quick and easy way to extend or trim two lines to a corner point is to use FILLET with a zero radius. This method also requires that the Trim mode option be current (as opposed to No trim).

NOTE

If you want to round all the corners of a polyline simultaneously, choose the Polyline option and then select the polyline. If an arc segment separates two line segments, the arc segment is automatically removed and replaced by a new arc based on the current FILLET radius setting.

Generally, if you use FILLET on two objects that are not closed (such as on any object other than a circle or ellipse), the two objects are trimmed or extended as necessary so that the arc can be drawn correctly. If you do not want the original objects to be trimmed, choose the Trim option, then choose No Trim. This Trim option is the same as the Trim option in the CHAMFER command. This setting is common to both commands, so setting Trim in FILLET affects CHAMFER, and vice versa.

In the following exercise, you use the FILLET command to round off the sharp corners in the drawing Chamfill.

USING FILLET TO ROUND SHARP CORNERS

1. Continue to use the drawing CHAMFILL.DWG. Choose Fillet from the Modify toolbar or Modify pull-down menu.

2. Specify the Radius option and type **0.5**.

3. Repeat the FILLET command. Specify the Polyline option and pick ① (see Figure 10.29).

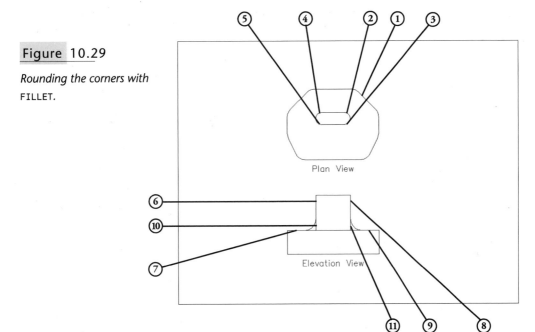

Figure 10.29

Rounding the corners with
FILLET.

4. Repeat the FILLET command and pick ② and ③. Then repeat the FILLET command and pick ④ and ⑤.

5. Repeat the FILLET command. Use the Trim option and choose the No Trim setting, then pick ⑥ and ⑦.

6. Repeat the FILLET command, but this time pick ⑧ and ⑨.

7. Choose Trim from the Modify toolbar or pull-down menu. Select (as the cutting edges) the last two arcs you drew with the FILLET command. Trim the two vertical lines by picking ⑩ and ⑪.

8. Save the drawing and close the file.

Summary

In this chapter, you learned the general commands and tools used to select objects and edit them. For the most flexibility in selecting objects, you should use the command-line version of the various editing commands. In addition to the editing operations you can use, AutoCAD offers a number of other editing commands, such as TRIM and EXTEND. The next chapter covers the remaining editing commands not covered in this chapter and some of the more advanced editing methods.

11

ADVANCED GEOMETRY EDITING

In Chapter 10, "Basic Object Editing," you learned the basic commands and tools needed to make changes to existing objects. In this chapter, you build on that foundation and learn about the following topics:

- *Using cut and paste*

- *Using drag and drop*

- *Grip editing commands*

- *Understanding the Object Properties Manager*

- *Using the Matchprop tool*

- *Using Quick Select*

- *Using object selection filters*

- *Creating and editing groups*

- *How to explode objects*

- *Specialized object editing*

- *Lengthening and shortening objects*

- *Aligning objects*

- *Renaming and purging named objects.*

Windows Functionality in AutoCAD

There are many advantages to opening several drawings in a session of AutoCAD, including two that relate to blocks. Along with the introduction of the Multiple Document Editor (MDE), AutoCAD 2000 also introduces two new features that take advantage of multiple open drawings. These new features allow you to either cut and paste, or drag and drop objects from one drawing to another. Additionally, you are given the option to insert the objects as a block.

Copying with the Clipboard

To copy using the clipboard, choose Copy from the Edit pull-down menu. This will copy selected objects to the clipboard. Choose Copy Link to copy the current view to the clipboard. Copy Link copies all objects in the drawing and preserves the current view of the drawing. As an alternative, you can use the CUT command to copy objects to the clipboard and remove them from the drawing.

A new addition to the Copy options is *Copy with Base Point*. This option allows you to define a coordinate and save it with the copy stored in the clipboard. This is then matched with a *Paste to Original Coordinates* option that allows you to paste this data using the stored base point. This is very useful in transferring data from drawing to drawing while maintaining a specific location (see Figure 11.1).

<u>Figure</u> 11.1

The new Copy with Base Point option on the Edit pull-down menu.

Cut and Paste Block Insertion

The phrase "cut and paste" refers to the process of selecting an object or group of objects, and cutting (or copying) them to the Windows clipboard. When selected objects are cut, they are copied to the clipboard and erased from the original document. In contrast, when you copy objects, they are copied to the clipboard, and the selected objects are left untouched in the original document.

Cut and paste block insertion is not really new to AutoCAD, but its capabilities are greatly enhanced. For example, AutoCAD 2000 allows you to identify the base point of an object when copying it to the clipboard. This feature provides you the control to specifically identify the new insertion point of the selected object, and is very powerful.

Also new to AutoCAD 2000 is *Paste as Block*. This is essentially the same as the R14 Paste option. When this feature is used, you can later explode the block to remove the arbitrary block name assigned by the PASTE AS BLOCK command.

If you choose Paste from the Edit menu in an AutoCAD drawing, the contents of the clipboard are inserted as individual objects. This is a change from R14, where it would come in as a randomly named block.

You also can paste an entire drawing into the current drawing by dragging the icon of the file from within Windows Explorer into the current drawing.

NOTE

You cannot use Paste Special when the contents you want to paste are taken from another AutoCAD drawing.

NOTE

You can even browse Web sites for blocks to insert into your drawing. For more information, see Chapter 25, "Publishing on the Web."

In the following exercise, you are taken through the steps to use for the Copy with Base Point feature from the EDIT command.

COPYING AND PASTING BETWEEN DRAWINGS

1. Open a drawing from which to copy existing objects, then open another drawing (or a new one) into which you wish to paste objects.

2. When both drawings are open, from the Window menu, choose Tile Vertically. AutoCAD tiles the two open drawing windows side by side.

3. When in a drawing that contains objects, select the objects to highlight them, then right-click to display the shortcut menu.

4. From the shortcut menu, choose Copy with Base Point. AutoCAD prompts you to specify the base point.

5. Select the base point using any AutoCAD pick-point method.

6. Move the cursor to the other drawing, and click in the drawing window. The drawing window acquires the focus.

7. Right-click to display the shortcut menu.

8. From the shortcut menu, choose Paste as Block (see Figure 11.2). The object's silhouette appears in the drawing, with the selected base point at the center of the cursor's crosshairs.

9. Pick the insertion point for the block object. AutoCAD inserts the new object as a block.

Figure 11.2

The shortcut menu has many copy/paste options on it available from a simple right-click of the mouse.

When you insert the block from the clipboard, you can either choose to paste it using a selected base point, or you can paste it using the block's original coordinates. The Paste to Original Coordinates option found on the shortcut menu copies the coordinate location of the objects in the original drawing, and then pastes the objects in the new drawing using those same coordinates. This option is useful for copying objects from one drawing to another when both drawings use the same coordinate system. You must have previously saved a base point and be in MDE to have access to the Paste to Original Coordinates option.

N OTE

To use the Copy with Base Point feature, you must be in MDE mode. If you only use Single Drawing Interface, the PASTE TO ORIGINAL COORDINATES command will be unavailable.

Drag and Drop Block Insertion

When you drag and drop objects, you are moving them from one place to another. When you drag and drop objects within the same AutoCAD drawing, the result is the same as using the MOVE command to move the object. When you drag and drop from one drawing to another, the result is similar to copying the object from the original drawing to the target drawing.

The drag and drop feature is useful for quickly moving or copying objects. However, this method does not provide a method for accurately selecting the base point for pasting the objects as a block. Consequently, to select objects in one drawing and paste them as a block in another while controlling the new block's base point, use the copy and paste feature described in the previous section.

The following is a listing of the options available on the shortcut list when right-clicking on a selection set and dragging and dropping into either the same drawing or a different drawing:

- **Move Here.** This option appears when the selected objects are dragged and dropped within the same drawing.

- **Copy Here.** This option appears when objects are dragged and dropped within the same drawing or between two drawings.

- **Paste as Block.** This option appears when objects are dragged and dropped within the same drawing or between two drawings.

- **Paste to Orig Coords.** This option appears only when objects are dragged and dropped between two drawings.

- **Cancel.** This option appears when objects are dragged and dropped within the same drawing or between two drawings.

OTE

> You can also drag and drop files from Windows Explorer into a drawing.

The drag and drop feature is useful for quickly moving or copying objects. However, this method does not provide a method for accurately selecting the base point for pasting the objects as a block. Consequently, to select objects in one drawing and paste them as a block in another while controlling the new block's base point, use the copy and paste feature described in the previous section.

Grip Editing

The usage of grips at first can be confusing because the grips appear so often, but after grips are understood and utilized, they can be extremely helpful and efficient at editing existing geometry.

NOTE

> With the Implied Window setting disabled, you will still be able to select objects with an implied window at the command prompt for use with the grip commands or with the Noun/ Verb setting.

Grip editing is a facility that integrates object snap points with the most commonly used editing commands and then places the combined capabilities literally at your fingertips. With grips, it is possible to edit objects and select specific object snap points without ever having to pick a tool, use a menu command, or type a command. In the following sections, you will learn how to enable the grips function, activate grips, and make use of the various options available with grips.

Enabling Grips

Grips are an optional facility that you can choose to use. By default, grips are enabled. You can disable grips with the Enable Grips toggle in the Selection tab of the Options dialog box (see Figure 11.3), which is displayed by choosing Options from the Tools pull-down menu.

Figure 11.3

The Grip options found on the Selection tab in the Options dialog box.

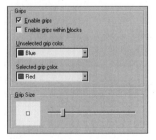

With grips enabled, you start the process of using the grip editing modes by selecting the objects you want to edit at the command prompt. In other words, you do not initiate any commands. Instead, you simply select the objects by picking them or by using implied windowing. After you have selected the objects, the object's grips are displayed as blue squares. The color and size of these *unselected* grips are set with the Unselected button in the Grips dialog box. The displayed grips correspond to the control points of the objects, and for the most part, the grip locations are the same as the object snap points for the various types of objects. The major exceptions to this rule are presented in Table 11.1.

Table 11.1

Specific Grip and Object Snap Discrepancies

Object	Description
Arc	Only three grips exist for an arc: its two endpoints and its midpoint. In contrast, object snap points include the center point and any valid quadrant points. Grip editing on an arc can be used to shorten to an intersection.
	Note: when moving a grip on an arc, it will change the geometry unless the new point placement results in the same radius and center coordinate.
Block Insertion	By default, only one grip is displayed at the insertion point of each block insertion. However, if you enable the Enable Grips Within Blocks setting from the Selection tab in the Options dialog box, then the grips of all the component objects are also displayed. Grip editing a block will relocate the insertion point.
Elliptical arc	Grips correspond to the arc's endpoints, midpoint, and center points but not to its visible quadrant points. Grip editing an ellipse will relocate it or resize it about its center.
Mline	Grips exist at the points used to locate the mline object. In contrast, endpoint and midpoint object snap points can exist on each visible segment. Grip editing an mline will change the vertex points.
Mtext	Four grips exist on an mtext object—one at each corner of the imaginary box that surrounds an mtext object. In contrast, only one insertion object snap point can be shown on an mtext object. Grip editing an mtext object can be used to relocate or resize the bounding box effecting the paragraph appearance.
Spline	A grip exists at every point used to define the spline, known as the spline's control points. Object snap points include only the endpoints. Grip editing can be used to redefine the curves as well as the start and end points of the spline.

As with object snap, grips enable you to easily choose a very specific point on an object. After the grips are displayed, you can choose one grip to activate the grip editing modes.

Activating the Grip Editing Modes

When you select one or more objects, grips are displayed. You may then pick any grip location and initiate the grip edit mode for the selection set. Selecting a grip affects the cursor much like osnaps do: The grip acts as a magnet and pulls the cursor to the grip. By default, the unselected grip box color is blue.

After a grip is selected, by default it is displayed as a red box and is referred to as a hot or selected grip. The color used to fill in the grip box is set from the Selection tab of the Options dialog box. The selected grip subsequently is used as the base point for the various grip editing modes: Stretch, Move, Rotate, Scale, and Mirror. Initially, the Stretch grip mode is activated, but you can press Enter or the spacebar to cycle through the other grip commands. Alternatively, right-click and pick the desired grip mode from the shortcut menu that appears (see Figure 11.4). The various editing mode options are discussed in the following sections.

Figure 11.4

*The shortcut menu
presented when a hot grip
is used with a right-click
press.*

Deactivating the Grips

When you select objects at the command prompt, the grips of the objects are displayed and the objects are highlighted. The highlighting indicates the objects that have been selected. If you press the Esc key, the objects will be deselected (no longer highlighted) but the grips will still be displayed. To cancel the display of the grips, simply press the Esc key one more time. In previous versions of AutoCAD, a common procedure that was employed was to select objects and press the Esc key once so that the object's grips could be selected (much like snap points) during a grip edit sequence but not affect the objects themselves. You could also selectively deselect highlighted objects by pressing the Shift key and selecting the highlighted objects, thereby leaving the grips displayed. These two procedures still work in AutoCAD 2000, but the Autosnap feature makes them irrelevant because Autosnap automatically displays the snap points on nearby objects.

Another common problem that users experience using grips is that they accidentally select objects and activate a grip editing mode by selecting one of the grips. To exit a grip editing mode, just press the Esc key. Remember that in AutoCAD 2000, pressing the Esc key always cancels the current operation. To deselect the objects and clear the display of the grips, press the Esc key two more times.

The first grip edit mode to discuss is the Stretch mode. The next section covers this valuable grip editing feature.

Using the Stretch Mode

The default edit mode when working with grips is *Stretch*, which enables you to relocate the selected grip. This in turn affects only the object or objects defined by the selected grip. For example, if the selected grip is the endpoint of a line (as shown in Figure 11.5), then that endpoint of the line can be stretched to the new position.

Figure 11.5

Using selected grips to stretch multiple objects.

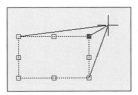

If the selected grip is the endpoint at which two lines meet, then both lines are stretched to the new endpoint location. As you decide on the new location of the selected grip, notice that the rubberband line is anchored at the selected grip. Thus, the selected grip is referred to as the base point of the stretch.

I NSIDER TIP

The Stretch grip editing mode offers two advantages over the STRETCH command. The Copy option of the Stretch grip mode enables you to scale and make copies of the selected objects simultaneously. In addition, STRETCH cannot be used to stretch circles or ellipses, whereas the Stretch grip mode can.

Stretching Multiple Points at the Same Time

If you want to stretch more than one point on the selected object(s) at a time, you must initiate a modified procedure to activate grips. First, you must hold down the Shift key while selecting all the grips you want to edit during the stretching procedure. Then, after releasing Shift, pick the grip that you want to use as the base point (the hot grip) of the stretch. This activates the grip edit modes on the prompt line.

NOTE

When using the grip Stretch and Move modes and/or their Copy option, if you know the exact delta-X, delta-Y, delta-Z, or distance and angle you want to apply to the selected grip, you can specify relative or polar coordinates rather than picking the new location for the edit. You also can define the distance and direction of the stretch with direct distance entry.

Using the Move Mode

Use the *Move* grip mode simply to move the selected objects to the new location. Unlike the Stretch grip editing mode—in which only the selected objects controlled by the selected grip are affected—all selected objects are moved with the grip's Move editing mode (see Figure 11.6).

Figure 11.6

The Move grip edit mode will relocate all selected objects.

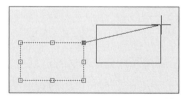

Using the Rotate Mode

The *Rotate* grip editing mode enables you to rotate the selected objects about the selected grip (see Figure 11.7).

Figure 11.7

The Rotate grip mode will
rotate all selected objects.

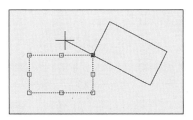

You can specify the amount of rotation to apply to the selected objects graphically with the "rubberband" line or by typing the specific value. The angle entered is relative to the drawing's 0 degree angle set in Units. Alternatively, you can specify the Reference option.

To use the Reference option, you first specify a reference angle by picking two points that define that angle or typing an angular value. Then, you specify the desired angle the reference line is to be rotated by dragging or typing the angle.

INSIDER **T**IP

The Reference option is useful when you know the desired angle for the object(s) but do not know the exact amount of rotation needed.

Using the Scale Mode

The *Scale* grip mode enables you to scale the selected objects about the selected grip. You can either type the scale factor or pick a point using the rubber-band line. Picking a point is subsequently used as the graphic specification of the scale factor. The grip point is the static point about which the objects expand or contract. Similar to the Rotate grip mode, the Scale grip mode has a Reference option.

To use the Reference option, you specify a reference length by picking two points to define that length or typing a known length value. Then, you specify the desired length to which you want the reference line to be scaled. The second length can be defined by entering the desired length or picking two points to define that length.

INSIDER **T**IP

One advantage that Scale grip edit mode has over the SCALE command is that grip edit mode enables you to use the Copy option to scale and make copies of the selected objects simultaneously.

Using the Mirror Mode

The *Mirror* grip edit mode enables you to mirror the selected objects about the mirror line that is anchored at the selected grip (see Figure 11.8).

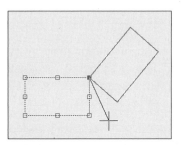

Figure 11.8

The Mirror grip mode will mirror all selected objects about the axis specified.

The *mirror line* is the imaginary line about which all the selected objects are flipped. Text and mtext objects also are flipped so that they appear backward. By default, the MIRRTEXT system variable is set to On, which produces backward text objects during mirroring. If you want the text and mtext objects to remain readable, type **MIRRTEXT** at the command prompt, and type **0** to turn off the mirroring of text objects.

Invoking the Grip Editing Base Point Option

The base point option of the grip edit modes enables you to relocate the anchor point of the rubberband line. In the Stretch grip edit mode, relocating the base point does not affect the grip that is stretched. A base point option exists in each grip edit mode. This option is very useful in the mirror grip edit mode when either of the mirror line points do not coincide with a grip location.

Invoking the Grip Editing Copy Option

A Copy option also exists in each of the five grip editing modes. When this option is invoked, the original objects are left unchanged and any changes are made to copies of the original. An alternative when using the Copy option is to hold down the Shift key after you have placed the first copy. Be aware, however, that if you continue to press the Shift key, AutoCAD uses the distance and direction between the original object and the first copy point to create a set of invisible snap points. For the STRETCH, MOVE, and SCALE commands, the snap points are arranged into a grid, with one of the grid axes running from the base point to the first selected point (see Figure 11.9).

Figure 11.9

The Shift key can be used to place copies with temporary invisible snap points that are arranged into a snap-like grid. (Invisible snap points shown for clarity.)

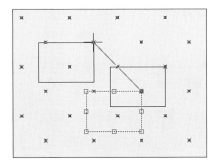

For the Rotate and Mirror grip modes, the snap points are arranged into a circular arrangement such that the angular displacement between adjacent snap points is equal (see Figure 11.10). When used with the Shift key, this process presets the available angles in increments equal to the first angle selected.

Figure 11.10

The Shift key also can be used to place copies with temporary snap angles that are arranged into a polar configuration.

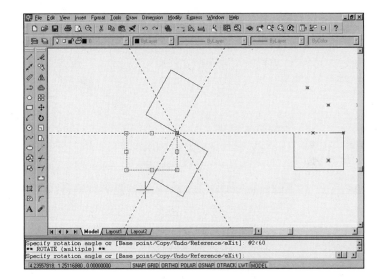

In the following exercise, you use grips to make changes and additions to the office layout in the drawing CHAP11-1.dwg. These changes include rotating and duplicating a chair in the office layout and stretching the cabinet.

USING GRIPS TO MAKE CHANGES AND ADDITIONS

1. Open the drawing CHAP11-1.dwg.

2. Choose Named Views from the View pull-down menu, select the view named OFFICE-A. Click the Restore button in the View Control dialog box, and click OK.

3. At the command prompt, pick the chair located below the desk and the other chair (see Figure 11.11). Each chair is a block, which explains why only one grip is displayed.

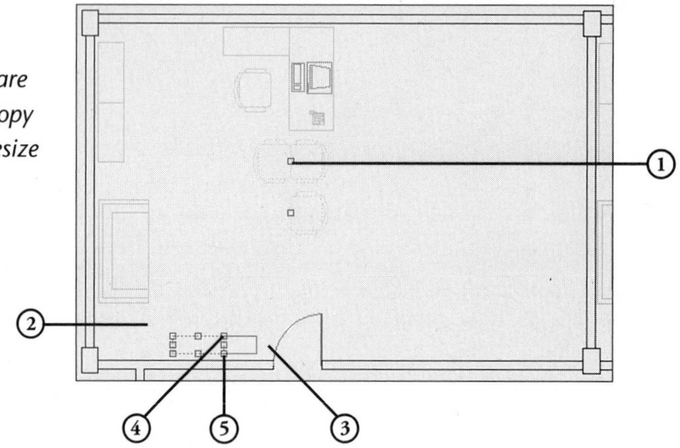

Figure 11.11

In this drawing, grips are used to relocate and copy a chair block and to resize a file cabinet.

4. Select the grip at ①. You have just activated the grip editing modes and the default mode of Stretch is current. Right-click and choose Rotate from the shortcut menu. Type **180** to rotate the chair 180 degrees.

5. Select the same grip, and press the spacebar once to cycle to the Move grip mode.

6. Type **C** to specify the Copy option, then type **@3'<270**. Press Enter to exit the Move grip mode. Press Esc to remove the selected grips on screen.

7. At the command prompt, use Implied Windowing to pick at ② and ③ to select the cabinet. Because the cabinet was drawn with four lines, it displays grips at the endpoints and midpoints.

8. While holding down the Shift key, pick ④ and ⑤ to select the multiple grips to stretch.

9. Release the Shift key, and pick ④ to activate the grip modes. Type **@2'<0** to stretch the rectangle 2' to the right and exit the command.

10. Press the Esc key twice to clear the selection and the grips.

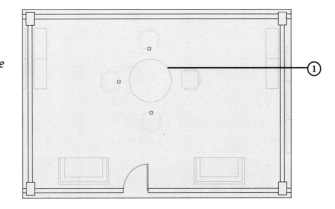

Figure 11.12

In this drawing, grips are used to array copies of the chair around the table.

11. Refer to step 1 and restore the view OFFICE-B. Select the single chair (refer to Figure 11.12), and pick the grip to enable the grip editing modes.

12. Right-click and choose Rotate, then right-click again and choose Base Point.

13. Move your cursor to a point that's not on a grip, hold the Shift key and right-click the mouse, then select CENter from the Object Snap shortcut menu. Then pick the desk at ①.

14. Right-click and choose Copy. Then type **90**, **180**, and **270** to make three copies at the three respective angle positions. Press the Enter key to exit the Rotate grip mode.

15. Restore the view OFFICE-E, then select the office cubicles on the left side of the room with an implied crossing window by picking ① and ② (see Figure 11.13).

Figure 11.13

In this drawing, grips are used to mirror a set of room objects about an axis line.

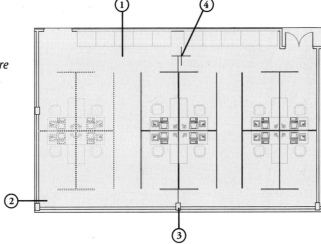

16. Pick one of the displayed grips, then right-click and pick Mirror, then right-click and pick Copy. Now right-click and choose Base Point.

17. Use Midpoint object snap and pick ③. Turn on Ortho and pick ④. By turning on Ortho, you ensure that you create a horizontal or vertical mirror line.

18. Press Enter to exit Mirror grip edit mode. You do not need to save the changes.

So far, this chapter has discussed how to use grips to modify objects. The following section covers AutoCAD 2000's object modification tools.

Changing an Object's Properties

The properties of an object are defined as its layer, color, and linetype and, for most objects, also include its object linetype scale and/or thickness. You can use the Object Properties toolbar, the Properties tool off the Object Properties toolbar, or the Match Properties tool from the Standard toolbar to change an object's properties (see Figure 11.14).

Figure 11.14

The Standard and Object
Properties toolbar.

Understanding the Object Properties Manager

NEW
for R2000

The *Properties* dialog box is the next generation of a properties editor (see Figure 11.15). With it comes everything from the power to change a simple layer setting to manipulating individual dimension variables of a selected set of dimensions. The Properties dialog box can either be accessed from within the Tools pull-down menu under Properties, by selecting the Properties toolbar button, or by selecting an object and using the right-click shortcut menu item Properties.

Figure 11.15

The new Properties dialog box has controls for all object properties.

The Properties dialog box is structured around two primary tabs: Alphabetic and Categorized. In the Alphabetic tab, all options are listed in an alphabetical order. This is useful if you know the name of the control you want to change. The Categorized option essentially breaks the same information into groups, typically General and Geometry for a single or like objects.

When you select multiple objects, Properties will filter the available options down to those that are shared. For instance, selecting two circles would allow editing of the radius. But selecting a line and circle would limit you to standard appearance settings such as layer and color.

At the top of the Properties dialog box is a drop-down list that provides a listing of the type of object(s) selected. Additionally, it will allow you to modify similar objects from within a multiple selection. For example, if you selected a circle and two lines, this list would allow you to change all general properties but also to choose to modify the circle properties independently from within the circle selection. You could then choose to change the two lines and have the edit values shown accordingly.

NOTE

In the Properties dialog box, if the text in an edit box is blank, you can simply type in new values. Some edit boxes will expand to a list box for their value options and some edit boxes are unavailable. Lastly, edit boxes that are blank generally indicate that the objects selected do not share identical values for that property.

The Properties dialog box can be docked, which enables the user to place it permanently on-screen. In Figure 11.16, you can see the many different user settings found in the pull-downs and toolbars. Additionally, you have multiple UCS control options that can come in handy.

Figure 11.16

The Properties dialog box in a "no selected object" state.

The last item in the Properties dialog box, the filter + lightning tool (Quick Select) in the upper-right corner, is covered later in this chapter.

By using Properties, you can very quickly edit multiple objects to share command settings. In those cases where the editing is more specific, you may find the Match Properties tool more applicable.

The Match Properties Tool

NEW for R2000

The MATCHPROP command has been enhanced in AutoCAD 2000 to be more dynamic and customizable. Accessed from the Match Properties tool on the Standard toolbar and in the Modify pull-down menu, this command allows the user to copy the properties of one object (the source), then paste any similar parameters to selected objects (the destination objects). When selecting the destination objects, you can use any of the object selection methods available. Table 11.2 outlines the properties that can be pasted and what objects will accept the change.

Table 11.2

Object Properties Changed by MATCHPROP

Property	Application
Layer	Matches the layer of the destination object(s) to that of the originating source object. This applies to all objects except OLE objects.
Color	Matches the color of the destination object(s) to that of the originating source object. This also applies for all objects except OLE objects.
Lineweight	Matches the lineweight of the destination object(s) to that of the source object. Available for all objects.
Linetype	Matches the linetype of the destination object(s) to that of the source object. This can applied to all objects except for attributes, hatches, mtext objects, OLE objects, points, and viewports.
Linetype Scale	Matches the linetype scale factor of the destination object(s) to that of the source object. This applies for all objects except attributes, hatches, mtext objects, OLE objects, points, and viewports.
Thickness	Matches the thickness of the destination object(s) to that of the source object. This applies only to arcs, attributes, circles, lines, points, 2D polylines, regions, text objects, and traces.
Plot Style	Matches the plot style of the destination object(s) to that of the source object. However, if color-dependent plot style mode is active (PSTYLEPOLICY is set to 1), this control is not applicable. This applies for all objects except OLE objects.
Text	Matches the text style of the destination object(s) to that of the source object. This applies only for attribute, text, and mtext objects.
Dimension	Matches the dimension style of the destination object to that of the source object. Available only for dimension, leader, and tolerance objects.
Hatch	Matches the hatch pattern of the destination object(s) to that of the source object. This applies only for hatch objects (both associative and non-associative).

In the following exercise, you will experience firsthand the power of the MATCHPROP command.

USING THE MATCHPROP COMMAND

1. Open the drawing CHAP11-2.dwg from the CD that accompanies this book. This drawing contains a variety of object types that you might use every day (see Figure 11.17).

Figure 11.17

The drawing used for the
MATCHPROP *exercise.*

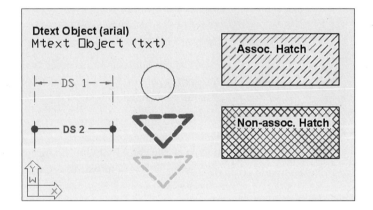

2. Locate and choose the Match Properties tool found on the Standard toolbar. It looks like a paintbrush above a color strip.

3. At the `Select objects` prompt, choose the text object in the top left of your drawing. This text uses Arial for its font property.

   Pause for a moment to examine the Settings options found in the MATCHPROP command.

4. Type **S** to display the Property Settings dialog box shown in Figure 11.18.

Figure 11.18

The Settings dialog box for the MATCHPROP *command controls the variety of object types and how their properties can be "painted" to others.*

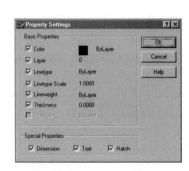

5. The default settings in this dialog box are generally preferred to speed using the MATCHPROP command. In some cases you may need to change one or more of these options. However, for this exercise, click OK to close the dialog box.

6. When the paintbrush pickbox is active, it indicates that you will be "painting" properties to any objects you select. Pick the word Mtext to paint the Dtext properties on to it.

   After pasting, you can continue to paste properties to any additional objects. For this exercise, however, stop and restart the command.

7. Press Enter twice to exit and restart the MATCHPROP command.

8. Select the dimension DS 2 to establish a dimension as the source object, then choose the dimension DS 1. The DS 2 dimension properties will then be applied to the DS 1 dimension as well as the DS 2 layer setting.

9. Press Enter twice to exit and restart the command.

10. Select the hatching in the top right of the display, then choose the non-associative hatch object at the midddle right in the drawing to paste the hatch and layer settings from the top hatch to the bottom.

11. Press Enter twice to exit and restart the command.

12. Select the green dashed polygon at the bottom of the display as the source object. Properties garnished from this object include color, layer, linetype, linetype scale, and lineweight.

13. Now, instead of choosing one by one, use implied windowing by picking a point to the bottom left of the green polygon, then use the window to enclose all three polygons. The upper two will then inherit the original polygon's properties, including layer and color.

14. Press Enter to exit the command and close the drawing without saving changes.

Using the MATCHPROP command is highly recommended over other methods of general object editing. When you need to select objects on a broader scale, using filters can be very helpful. The following section exposes new AutoCAD 2000 tools to help you select objects prior to editing.

Using Quick Select

NEW
for R2000   When editing a drawing, often the task of selecting the objects to change is more work than the actually change itself. This is where object filtering becomes crucial to your work. Imagine having a convention center drawing where you need to

change the layer and color of a circle with a radius of 12". Now compound the problem by increasing the number of circles to be changed to hundreds and the layers they reside on to include nearly all layers in the drawing. Zooming and panning around and selecting these circles among other circles and layers would be a huge task.

With the Quick Select feature, this could be done with one visit into the Quick Select dialog box and setting the proper parameters. In Figure 11.19, you see the standard settings for the QSELECT command dialog box.

Figure 11.19

The Quick Select dialog box contains controls for many basic object properties in which you can filter to a new selection.

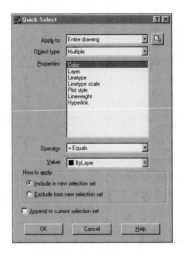

The first thing to understand about the Quick Select dialog box is where it can be used. It is not a transparent command, so it cannot be used at any Select objects: prompt. It works with the Properties dialog box because it is "modeless," meaning that it's active all the time. So to utilize the QSELECT command, you must initiate it before the command is started that would use its selection.

When the QSELECT command is executed, your first task is to define the parameters of the filter selection. As you modify the settings in the dialog box, you build the criteria that objects must meet in order to be selected. When complete, exit the dialog box; the drawing database is filtered to match those parameters. These controls are covered in the following sections.

Specifying Objects to be Filtered with Apply To

The Apply To control is very simple to understand. By default, the setting of the Apply To drop-down list is set to Entire Drawing. If you click the Select Objects tool to its right, you can choose a set of objects using standard selection techniques. The selection set would then be used to filter against. If you do select a group of objects or if you have selected objects prior to opening the Properties dialog box, the drop-down list for Apply To displays Current Selection. You may then switch between that selection and the entire drawing at your leisure.

The Object Type Drop-Down List

The Object Type control allows you to specify which object types are to be considered when filtering through the selection made in the Apply To drop-down list. If only one type of object exists in the drawing, that single object will be your only choice. But if other object types exist, each type will be displayed in the drop-down list from which you can choose one. This control will determine what properties to list in the Properties option.

The Properties Option

This control displays a categorized listing of the properties of the object(s) currently being filtered. For example, if a line is the current object type, this control would show all properties that lines have. If you change the object type to circle, then Properties would show all settings unique to circles, such as a radius. This is where you get specific beyond simple object type filtering.

The Operator Option

With this control, you create conditional statements that the objects must meet in order to be selected. Table 11.3 outlines these conditions.

Table 11.3

Quick Select Conditional Operands

Operand	Definition
=	Equal To. With this operand, the data in the field must be matched perfectly to be valid.
<>	Not Equal To. With this operand, the data in the field must not match to be valid.

continues

Table 11.3, continued

Quick Select Conditional Operands

Operand	Definition
>	Greater Than. With this operand, the data in the field must be greater in value to be valid.
<	Less Than. With this operand, the data in the field must be smaller in value to be valid.
*	Wildcard Match. This is used only with text fields that can be edited by the user.

NOTE

Not all operands are available with all objects. As you define different object types, the Operator list will change automatically to the available options for that type of object.

Using the Options in How to Apply

This option box control is where you add and remove objects from the current selection set. Either one of the two settings, Include or Exclude, specifies what AutoCAD is to do with the objects that meet the filter criteria.

The Include option adds all matching objects to the selection set when the user exits QSELECT. By choosing Exclude, you can then select all non-matching objects and apply them to the current selection set.

The Append to Current Selection Set Control

The last item in the Quick Select dialog box is the Append to Current Selection Set toggle. This toggle will determine if the selection set created from the QSELECT command adds to the current drawing selection set or if it simply replaces it. After you have completed the QSELECT command, the objects will be selected and the grips displayed (if grips are on) and ready for immediate use. You then can proceed with editing or, if needed, use QSELECT again to further filter your object selection set.

The QSELECT command is a very easy-to-use filtering method for building selection sets. Another method that has been in AutoCAD for several versions is the FILTER command. The following section examines the use of this feature.

Using Object Selection Filters

Object filtering enables you to search for objects based on certain attributes. For example, you could use object filtering to select all circles in a drawing with a specific radius. To invoke object filtering, type the command **FILTER** at the Select Objects: prompt. This displays the Object Selection Filters dialog box (see Figure 11.20).

Figure 11.20

The Object Selection Filters dialog box is a robust filtering system with the added ability to save filter lists for later use.

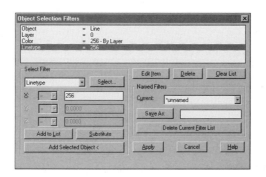

You can assemble a list of the properties, also known as *filter criteria*, with which you want to conduct the search. Then, by clicking the Apply button, you can select a group of objects within which you want to find those objects that meet your list of characteristics. The following sections discuss how to define your list of filters.

Defining Simple Selection Criteria for Filters

A filter can be a type of object, a characteristic of that type of object, or defined from an object property. For example, you can search for arcs in general or arcs that have a specific radius. The list of available filters is extensive and is displayed in the Filters drop-down list. If you choose a characteristic of an object, you also must supply the specific value of that characteristic that you seek within the X edit box, located below the filter list. For some filter selections, you can click the Select button to choose the specific value from a list of existing or valid values. For other properties, you must type that value in the edit box.

After you select the filter and its associated value (if any), click the Add to List button to add the selected filter to the list at the top of the dialog box. To select the objects to which your filter criteria will be applied, click the Apply button.

To remove a filter from the list, choose the filter and click Delete. To edit the specific value of a filter in the list, select the filter and click Edit Item. After changing the value of the property, click Substitute to replace the old property with the revised property.

Defining a Complex Selection Criteria for Filters

The search criteria employed can be a complex set consisting of multiple filters. By default, when you assemble a list of filters, only objects that meet all the individual filters in the list are selected. For example, you could choose to select only arcs that reside on the layer CURVES by choosing the Arc and Layer filters. In doing so, you assemble a list of properties that must be met; this is referred to as an AND conditional. When you assemble a list of properties, the system assumes that you are assembling an AND conditional filter list. Other options do exist, however.

The most common option is to create an OR conditional filter list. In an OR conditional, the objects must meet only one of the conditions, not all of them. For example, you could assemble a list of properties such that any object that is an arc *or* that resides on the CURVES layer is selected. You begin an OR conditional by choosing the **Begin OR filter. Then you assemble the various properties in which you are interested. You end the list of properties with the **End OR filter.

The list of filters can consist of AND and OR conditionals nested within each other, but for most users a simple search criteria consisting of a single conditional filter is enough.

INSIDER TIP

To gain an idea of the properties that are available for a particular object, click the Add Selected Object button and select an object in your drawing. All the relevant filters and their specific values for the selected object automatically are assembled into a list. You then can delete the filters you do not need, leaving only the properties for which you want to search.

Saving and Restoring the Criteria for Filters

To save a list of filters you have assembled so the list can be reused at a later date or in another drawing, type a name in the Save As edit box and click Save As. The next time you want to use that filter, simply select its name from the Current drop-down list. To delete a named filter, select the name from the Current drop-down list and click Delete Current Filter List. Named filter lists are saved in the file FILTER.NFL, which is created in the current working directory when you initially click the Save As button.

USING THE FILTERS TO ASSEMBLE SELECTION SETS

1. Open the CHAP11-1.dwg from the CD that accompanies this book. This office plan includes many object types for using filters.

2. From the Tools pull-down menu, choose the Quick Select menu option. The QSELECT dialog box will appear.

3. From the Object type list box, choose Line. Then click OK to close the command. The system will then highlight 336 line objects in the drawing. Now we need to refine this selection to fewer objects.

4. Press Enter to restart the QSELECT command. From the Properties list box, choose Layer. Then in the Value list box choose 1FL_WALL. Click OK to close the dialog box.

5. AutoCAD will then replace the 336-object selection set with a 274-object selection set and highlight it for you. You're not done, so press Enter to restart the QSELECT command again.

6. Set the Object type list box to Line. Then from the Properties list box, choose Start Y. Change the Operand to > Greater Than. In the Value edit box, type **77'3"**. Then click OK to close the dialog box.

7. AutoCAD then selects and highlights all the line objects on layer 1FL-WALL with a Y start point greater than 77'-3". These objects are now available for general editing such as a COPY or MOVE command.

   If you need to save and restore a selection set, you must use the FILTER command. The rest of the exercise demonstrates this method.

8. Type **Filter** at the command line and press Enter.

9. In the Select Filter area, choose Line from the list box and click the Add to List button. This adds a filter for line objects only.

10. From the Select Filter area, choose Line Start. Change the X and Z operands to * from their list box and type **0** in each of the edit boxes. Change the Y operand to > and in its edit box type **77'3"**. Then click the Add to List button. This adds a filter for coordinates in any X and Z location but only points greater than 77'-3" in the Y direction.

11. From the Select Filter area, choose Layer. Click the Select button and choose 1FL_WALL from the listing; then click OK. Click Add to List to add this required layer name to match against. In the Named Filters area, locate the edit box to the right of the Save As button. Type **North Walls** and click the Save As button. The current filter name then changes from *unnamed to North Walls.

12. Click the Apply button at the bottom of the Objects Selection Filters dialog box. This closes the dialog box and prompts you to select objects. Type **ALL** and press Enter. Then press Enter again to end the Select Objects request. This then applies the filters to all the objects in the drawing and prepares a specific selection set matching your North Walls filter criteria.

13. Press Enter to restart the FILTER command. You will notice that your filter parameters are still available and the name set. Click the Clear List button. The filter parameters will disappear.

14. Now choose North Walls from the Current name list. Notice that the filters criteria reappears in the list area. Click the Delete Current Filter List button to remove the saved list and clear the filter area. Then click Cancel to exit the dialog box.

15. Now you may exit this drawing; there is no need to save it.

In addition to searching for objects that share certain properties, you can also gather up objects and place them in named groups for later retrieval. The next section explains this process in detail.

Creating and Editing Groups

You can link disparate objects on different layers into what is referred to as a group. After a group is created, all the member objects of the group can be selected by selecting one member of the group or by naming the group. Assembling the objects into a group, however, does not prevent you from editing the member objects individually. To create and edit a group, you use the GROUP command, which you initiate by typing **Group** at the command line (see Figure 11.21).

Figure 11.21

*The Object Grouping
dialog box of* GROUP
*enables you to create and
edit a group.*

The following sections discuss how to use the GROUP command for specific tasks.

Creating a Group

Every group must have a name. To create a group, you first type a name in the Group
Name edit box. Then, click New and select the objects you want to include in the
group. To complete the creation of the group within the drawing, you must click OK
in the Object Grouping dialog box. If you do not want to name the group, enable the
Unnamed option, and AutoCAD will give the group an arbitrary name that begins
with an asterisk. Unnamed groups also are created when you duplicate a group using
commands such as COPY or ARRAY. To include unnamed groups in the list of groups
displayed in the dialog box, enable the Include Unnamed option.

By default, any group you create is selectable. This means that the group of objects
can be selected by name or by selecting a member. If you turn off the Selectable
option before you create a group, the group will not be selectable. The individual
group members still will be listed as members of the group, but they will be
selectable only as individual objects. You might want to create a non-selectable
group, for example, if you want to associate various objects together for use with
custom programs (created by you or a third-party developer) that interact with the
drawing database but are not for use with AutoCAD editing commands. The typical
user does not have an application for non-selectable groups; so as a rule, always
make your groups selectable.

A group can have as many members as you desire, and an individual object can be
a member of more than one group. The group description is an optional piece of
information that you use to better describe the contents of the group or the
relationship between the member objects.

Selecting a Group to Edit

After you create a selectable group, you can select all members of the group simply by selecting one group member or by naming the group. The Object Grouping setting controls the selection of all members of a group when one member is selected. This setting is found in the Settings tab of the Options dialog box. The Object Grouping setting can also be enabled or disabled with the Ctrl+A key sequence. Even with the Object Grouping setting disabled, the members of a selectable group can be selected by typing **G** at the `Select objects` prompt, then entering the group name.

Inquiring About a Group's Membership

If you ever forget whether an object is a member of a group or which objects are members of a particular group, you can use the following two buttons to find this information when in the Object Grouping dialog box:

■ **Find Name.** Use the Find Name button to determine the group, if any, to which a selected object belongs. This allows you to select an object within a group and report back the group name.

■ **Highlight.** Select a group name from the list of group names, and click the Highlight button to highlight all the members of the selected group on-screen.

NOTE

You also can use the LIST command to see the contents of a group. When listing a group, all the group objects are highlighted and descriptions of the objects contained within are listed.

Modifying an Existing Group

To modify the makeup of a particular group, first select the group name from the list of groups. The following list shows the buttons you use to modify the group you select (refer to Figure 11.21):

- **Remove and Add.** You can use these buttons to remove an object from or add an object to an existing group.

- **Rename and Description.** You can rename a group or change the group's description by selecting the group name, typing in the new name or description, and then selecting the corresponding button.

- **Selectable.** Use this button to change the selectable status of the selected group.

- **Re-Order.** Selecting this button displays the Order Group dialog box, which enables you to change the order in which the member objects are arranged in a group. You can use this option to visually control how the objects in the group are ordered internally.

Deleting a Group

To remove or undefine a group, click Explode in the Object Grouping dialog box (refer to Figure 11.21). Exploding a group dissolves the associations between the member objects but does not erase the member objects.

The previous sections have discussed the various ways to select an object or objects for editing. After you have selected the object(s), you can edit the properties, as discussed in the following section.

Exploding Compound Objects

Several objects are considered *compound objects*—meaning the objects themselves are composed of other AutoCAD objects. Compound objects can be *exploded*, or broken down, into their constituent parts with the EXPLODE command. You usually explode a compound object to modify one or more of its constituent objects in a way that you cannot do with the compound object itself.

EXPLODE is issued by choosing Explode from the Modify pull-down menu or toolbar. Table 11.4 lists the types of 2D compound objects covered in this book (with appropriate chapter references), and describes briefly how EXPLODE affects the objects, and some reasons why you would consider exploding the object.

Table 11.4

2D Compound Objects and EXPLODE

Object Type	Result of Explode
Block insertions	An insertion of a block is replaced with duplicates of the block's component objects. Component objects originally drawn on Layer 0 are redrawn onto Layer 0.

A block insertion is usually exploded because you want to modify the component objects themselves. This is usually, but not always, done in the context of redefining the block definition. See Chapter 13, "Creating and Using Blocks," for more information. |
Dimensions	A dimension is replaced by a combination of lines, mtext, points, solids, and block insertions. Dimensions usually are exploded so that you can further manipulate their component objects. Generally, because exploded dimensions are no longer associative, you should avoid exploding dimensions. For information about dimensions, see Chapter 17, "Productive Dimensioning," and Chapter 18, "Advanced Dimensioning."
Hatch	Hatch is replaced by its component lines. An exploded hatch is no longer associative. Again, because of the loss of associativity, exploding a hatch is normally not a good idea. Hatching is covered in Chapter 16, "Drawing Hatch Patterns."
Mline	An mline (multiline) is replaced by its component lines. In this way, you can work around editing commands, such as EXTEND and TRIM, that don't work with mlines. By replacing the Mline object with its component lines, you then can trim or extend those lines. Mlines are covered in Chapter 8, "Creating Polylines and Splines."
Polylines	A polyline is replaced by a series of lines and arcs. If the polyline has a width, the replacement lines and arcs will have no width. Polylines are drawn with the PLINE, POLYGON, RECTANG, and DONUT commands, which are covered in Chapter 7, "Creating Elementary Objects," and Chapter 8, "Creating Polylines and Splines."
Region	A region is replaced by the edge objects (such as lines and circles) that define the loops (closed shapes) in the region. Regions are covered in Chapter 28, "Drawing in 3D AutoCAD."

An exploded object can only be returned to its original unexploded form by using the U or the UNDO command. The U or UNDO command must be the next command after EXPLODE for this to take place.

An additional option to the standard EXPLODE command is XPLODE. This command allows the user to control what happens to the objects after being exploded. You can opt to apply the changes individually or globally. Properties that can be controlled are color, layer, lineweight, and linetype. These properties can also be gathered from the object being exploded.

Common components of the block object type are attributes. The next section discusses the tools used to modify and control these objects.

Specialized Editing Commands

Within AutoCAD 2000 exist numerous commands that have been provided to edit very specific object types. These unique objects have characteristics that can be exposed through specialized commands made just for them.

Editing Attribute Values

There are two editing commands available that are used specifically on attributes contained within an attributed block. The commands are DDATTE and ATTEDIT, both of which are discussed in the following sections.

Using DDATTE on Attributes

If you want to change the text values of a variable attribute that is part of an inserted block, use DDATTE. This command is issued by choosing Single from the Attribute submenu. After selecting the block, the Edit Attributes dialog box is displayed. It shows the attribute prompts and the current text values of the attributes (see Figure 11.22).

Figure 11.22

The Edit Attributes dialog box is displayed by the DDATTE *command.*

If more attributes exist than can be displayed in the dialog box, use the Next and Previous buttons to display the additional sets of attributes.

Using ATTEDIT on Attributes

Whereas DDATTE enables you to change the text values of attributes, the ATTEDIT command enables you to change other properties of inserted attributes. ATTEDIT is issued by selecting Global from the Attribute submenu. You are prompted whether you want to edit attributes one at a time. If you answer No, you can perform a text search-and-replace on the text string of the selected attributes. If you answer Yes to editing attributes one at a time, you can change the value, position, height, rotation angle, style, and color of the selected attributes.

Whether you answer Yes or No, you also have the option of filtering the selected attributes by block name, attribute tag name, or attribute value. The default value for all three filters is an asterisk (*), which indicates that no filters should be used and that the attributes the user selects are to be accepted.

If you are not familiar with attributes, see Chapter 9, "Understanding the Query Features in AutoCAD 2000," for complete coverage of attributes and their use with blocks.

Editing External References

There are two editing commands available that are to be used specifically on external references: XBIND and XCLIP, both of which are discussed in later chapters. For additional information about blocks and external references, see the respective Chapters 13 and 14, "Creating and Using Blocks" and "Working with Drawings and External References Productively."

Editing Raster Images

There are three editing commands available that are to be used specifically on images that are typically inserted as raster images: IMAGECLIP, IMAGEADJUST, and TRANSPARENCY. In addition to the commands, the system variables IMAGEFRAME and IMAGEQUALITY affect the display of images. The commands and system variables are discussed in the following sections.

Clipping Images

You can clip portions of an image just as you can clip the display of an external reference. The equivalent of XCLIP (used for xrefs) is IMAGECLIP, which is designed for use on images. To issue the IMAGECLIP command, choose Image Clip from the Object submenu. With IMAGECLIP you can define a new rectangular or irregular polyline clipping boundary. You can also use the command to turn on or off the clipping boundary. To display the clipping frame of all images, turn on the system variable IMAGEFRAME by choosing Frame from the Image submenu. If the frame is not displayed, you cannot select the boundary object.

Adjusting the Image

Several additional editing commands are available in the Image submenu. Choosing Adjust issues the IMAGEADJUST command and displays the Image Adjust dialog box (see Figure 11.23), in which you can adjust the brightness, contrast, and fade settings of the selected image.

Figure 11.23

The Image Adjust dialog box is used to modify the appearance of raster images inside AutoCAD 2000.

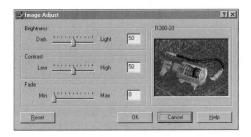

You can accelerate the display of images by setting the system variable IMAGEQUALITY to the Draft setting. IMAGEQUALITY, accessed by choosing Quality from the Image submenu, affects only the display of raster images, not the plotting of images; raster images are always plotted at the high quality setting.

Controlling Transparency

Some raster image file formats support a transparency setting for pixels. When transparency is enabled, the graphics on the display show through the transparent pixels of the overlaid raster image. By default, images are inserted with transparency off. You can turn this setting on or off for the selected images by using the TRANSPARENCY command, issued by choosing Transparency from the Image submenu.

Editing Multilines

The MLEDIT command is designed specifically to enable you to perform specialized editing operations on mline objects. To issue the MLEDIT command, choose Multiline from the Objects submenu. Figure 11.24 shows the Multiline Edit Tools dialog box.

Figure 11.24

The Multiline Edit Tools dialog box is used to trim Mlines in various configurations.

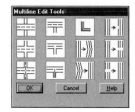

With MLEDIT, you can clean up various types of intersections of two mlines, remove or add a vertex point in an mline, and insert or heal breaks in an mline. Mlines are covered in detail in Chapter 8.

Editing Polylines

The PEDIT command is designed for the editing of polylines and is issued by choosing Polyline from the Object submenu. With PEDIT, you can accomplish the following tasks:

■ Create a polyline from a selected line or arc.

■ Close an open polyline (Close option) or open a closed polyline (Open option).

■ Join additional segments to the selected polyline (Join option).

■ Change the polyline's width (Width option).

- Set the polyline's Ltype generation setting (Ltype gen option).

- Fit a curve to the polyline (Fit option).

- Fit a spline to the polyline (Spline option).

- Delete the curve or spline fitted to the polyline (Decurve option).

- Move, delete, or add vertex points in the polyline (Vertex option).

Polylines are covered in detail in Chapter 8.

Editing Splines

The SPLINEDIT command is designed for the editing of splines and is issued by choosing Spline from the Objects submenu. With SPLINEDIT, you can accomplish the following tasks:

- Edit the fit points of the spline (Fit Data option).

- Open or close a spline (Open and Close options).

- Move the vertex points of the spline (Move option).

- Control the number or weighting of the control points (Refine option).

- Reverse the direction of the spline (Reverse option).

Splines are covered in detail in Chapter 8.

Editing Text and Mtext

The DDEDIT command enables you to edit text and mtext objects (as well as the value of associative dimensions). The DDEDIT command is issued by choosing Text from the Objects submenu. If a text object is selected, a single-line text editor dialog box is displayed. If an mtext object is selected, the Multiline Text Editor dialog box is displayed. The drawing and editing of text is covered in detail in Chapter 15, "Text Annotation."

Lengthening and Shortening Objects

Any open object, such as a line or an arc, can be lengthened or shortened with the LENGTHEN command. The following listing details the options available at the initial prompt:

- **Select Object.** The default option involves selecting an object. When an object is selected, its length is displayed and the initial prompt is re-displayed. The length value is shown using the current units setting for both style and precision. However, this value can contain round-off error.

- **DElta.** Use this option to specify the length by which the object is to be lengthened or shortened. Enter a positive value to lengthen the object or enter a negative value to shorten the object. If the object to be affected is an arc, you have the option of entering a change in the arc length (the default) or a change in the included angle.

- **Percent.** Use this option to define the change as a percentage, where 100 percent is the original length. Enter a percentage greater than 100 percent to lengthen the object or a percentage less than 100 percent to shorten the object.

- **Total.** Use this option when you know the final length you want to the object to have.

- **DYnamic.** Use this option to dynamically drag the endpoint to the desired location. In dragging the endpoint of the object, the alignment of the object cannot change.

    After defining the amount of change to be applied, pick the object to be affected. The endpoint nearest the point used to select the object is the endpoint that is moved, so pick closer to the endpoint that you want to affect when selecting.

As a general rule, when using the DElta, Percent, or Total option, pick a point on the portion of the line to which the edit is to be applied.

Aligning Objects

The ALIGN command initially was conceived as a 3D editing command, which explains why it is found in the 3D Operation submenu of the Modify pull-down menu. In 2D work, however, ALIGN can also be very useful. In effect, it is a combination of the MOVE, ROTATE, and SCALE commands. ALIGN typically is used to align one object with another object (see Figure 11.25).

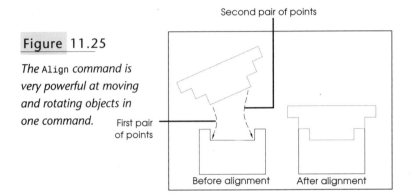

Second pair of points

Figure 11.25

The Align *command is very powerful at moving and rotating objects in one command.*

First pair of points

Before alignment   After alignment

After selecting the objects to be aligned, you are prompted to specify up to three pairs of points. Each pair consists of a source point and a destination point. The source point is a point on the object to be aligned, and the destination point is the corresponding point on the object to which you want to align.

As you can see in Figure 11.25, you must specify only two pairs of points in 2D work—simply press Enter when prompted for the third pair. The selected objects are moved from the first source point to the first destination point. Then the objects are rotated such that the edge defined by the first and second source points is aligned with the edge defined by the first and second destination points.

Finally, you have the option to scale the objects such that the length defined by the first and second source points is adjusted to be equal to the length defined by the first and second destination points. In effect, this scaling option serves the same function as the Reference option of the SCALE command.

EDITING WITH LENGTHEN AND ALIGN

1. Open drawing CHAP11-1.dwg that accompanies the CD with this book.

2. Use the VIEW command, choose the view OFFICE-E, and set it current.

3. From the Modify pull-down menu, choose 3D Operation, Align. This initiates the ALIGN command for use.

4. At the Select objects, type **C** and press Enter. At the `Specify first corner` prompt, type **point 98',65'** and press Enter. At the `Specify opposite corner` prompt, type **79',67'** and press Enter. Then press Enter to end selection of objects. This selects the first series of five file drawers in upper part of the room.

5. Turn on a running Osnap Endpoint if it is not active. At the `Specify first source point` prompt, pick at ①. At the `Specify first destination point` prompt, pick at ②. This establishes the first set of transformation points.

6. At the `Specify second source point` prompt, pick at ③. At the `Specify second destination point` prompt, pick at ④. This establishes the second set of transformation points. (See Figure 11.26.)

Figure 11.26

The office room used for the ALIGN *and* LENGTHEN *exercise.*

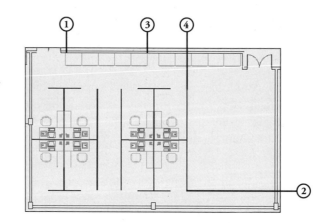

7. At the `Specify third source point or <continue>` prompt, press Enter to accept the default. Do the same at the `Scale objects based on alignment points` prompt (press Enter to accept the default).

8. The file drawers then align with the workstation panels starting at ② with an angle through ④.

9. Type **Copy** and press Enter, then select the two vertical wall lines on the right side of the room and press Enter to end the selection. At the `base point` prompt, type **-10',0** and press Enter twice. Refer to Figure 11.27.

10. Now use LENGTHEN to adjust the wall. From the Modify pull down menu, choose Lengthen. At the Select an object or [DElta/Percent/Total/DYnamic] prompt, type **T** and press Enter. At the Specify total length or [Angle] prompt, type **20'** and press Enter.

11. At the Select an object to change or [Undo] prompt, pick a point at the top of each of the two new lines near ①. Press Enter to exit the command. As you select each line, it shortens to a total length of 20' from the opposite end selected.

Figure 11.27

The modified file drawers and new interior wall.

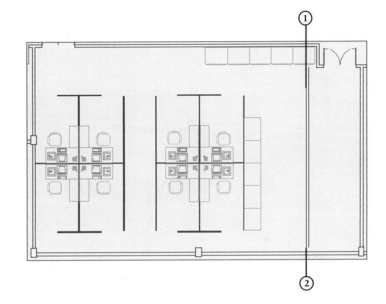

12. Press Enter to restart the LENGTHEN command. At the Select an object or [DElta/Percent/Total/DYnamic] prompt, type **DE** for a delta distance. At the Enter delta length or [Angle] prompt, type **9"** and press Enter. Now pick a point on each of the two new lines near ②. Press Enter to exit the command. Because this value is positive, the lines grow in length. If you had typed a negative number, the line would shorten in length.

13. You may now close the drawing; it is not needed to save.

As you work in your drawings, you may find the need to cleanse your drawing of unneeded data types. In the following sections, you will be exposed to renaming and purging objects from the current drawing.

Renaming Named Objects

AutoCAD objects fall into two inclusive categories: named and unnamed objects. *Named objects* are items that you name when you create them and are referred to by their assigned names. Examples of named objects include layers, block definitions, and text styles. *Unnamed objects* are objects such as lines, circles, and arcs, and cannot be assigned individual names.

Sometimes you need to rename a layer or a block because of changing conditions or simple typographic errors committed when you initially created the objects. To rename a named object, you can use the Rename dialog box (see Figure 11.28), which is invoked by choosing Rename from the Format pull-down menu.

Figure 11.28

The Rename dialog box is used to rename named objects.

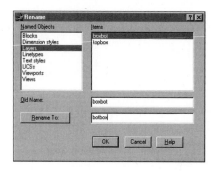

After you choose the named object to be renamed, a list of the existing objects of that type is displayed. To change a name in the Items list, you first select the specific object to be renamed and its name appears in the Old Name edit box. Type the new name in the edit box to the right of the Rename To button, then click Rename To to queue the name change.

NOTE

Layer 0 is the only layer that cannot be renamed, which accounts for why this layer is never displayed as part of the list of layers that can be renamed. However, you may rename any default objects named Standard.

Any changes entered into the Rename dialog box will not be actually processed until you click OK and the dialog box closes. Every valid modification you make will visually change in the dialog box, but they will not actually occur if you exit the dialog box by clicking the Cancel button. Consequently, you cannot rename one item to the name of previously renamed item because it would not be unique to the RENAME command session.

Deleting Named Objects

Sometimes you will find unneeded layers or linetypes; you should delete these objects from the drawing to clean up the drawing database.

The act of removing a named object from the database is referred to as *purging* the object. This action is performed with the PURGE command, which is invoked by choosing Purge from the Drawing Utilities submenu of the File menu (see Figure 11.29). From the pull-down menu, you can choose to purge all named objects or limit the command to a specific type of named object, such as text styles.

Named objects that are not used, such as a layer with no objects drawn on it, are referred to as unreferenced objects. Only unreferenced objects can be purged from a drawing. Whenever PURGE finds a named object suitable for deletion, you are prompted to confirm the deletion prior to the object being deleted.

Figure 11.29

The many options from the PURGE *cascade menu item.*

All
Layers
Linetypes
Text Styles
Dimension Styles
Multiline Styles
Blocks
Plot Styles
Shapes

NOTE

Layer 0 can never be purged, even if it is unreferenced and unused.

Although saved User Coordinate Systems, views, and viewport configurations are named objects and can be renamed with the RENAME command, PURGE does not give you the option of deleting these types of objects. Instead, if you want to remove these objects, you must use the command that manages them. For example, you cannot use PURGE to delete a named view. Instead, you must use the shortcut menu item Delete in the View dialog box to delete a named view. Use UCSman to delete a named UCS and use Vports to delete named viewport configurations.

I N S I D E R   T I P

An additional method to "purge" a drawing of all unreferenced objects (except saved UCSs, views, and viewport configurations) is to use the EXPORT command (see Chapter 25). The EXPORT command enables you to create a new drawing file and specify the asterisk (*) wild-card character as the block name to be exported.

The * option specifies both that the entire drawing should be exported to the new drawing file and that all unreferenced named objects should not be saved to the new drawing. The name of the new drawing created can be the same as the current drawing. In this case, you essentially replace the current version of the drawing with a new purged version. If you have given the new drawing the same name as the current drawing, don't save changes when you exit the current drawing or you will overwrite the new drawing that has been cleaned up.

In the following exercise, you will purge an unreferenced layer and rename another.

RENAMING BLOCKS AND PURGING LAYERS

1. Open the drawing CHAP11-3.DWG found on the accompanying CD-ROM.

2. Choose Rename from the Format menu, and choose Blocks from the Named Objects list.

3. Choose boxbot from the Items list. This will fill in boxbot automatically into the Old Name edit box.

4. Type **BOTBOX** in the Rename To edit box as shown in Figure 11.30, then click Rename To.

5. Click OK to exit the Rename dialog box and apply the name change to the block.

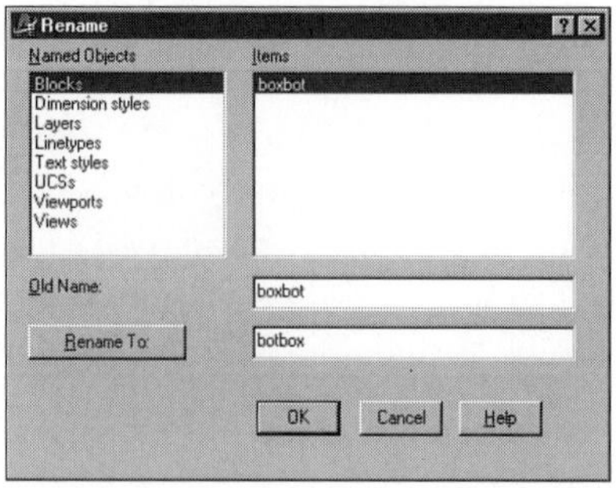

Figure 11.30

The Rename dialog box allows quick access to rename Named Objects such as Layers.

6. To purge layer TOPBOX from this drawing, choose the File pull-down menu, then Drawing Utilities, Purge, and Layers.

7. At the `Enter name(s) to purge <*>:` prompt, press Enter to accept the default *.

8. At the `Verify each name to be purged? [Yes/No] <Y>:` prompt, press Enter to accept the default.

    Note the command response `No unreferenced layers found`. Because this drawing has objects on the existing Layers 0, BOXBOT, and TOPBOX, and no other empty layers exist, the `PURGE` command could not purge anything. To successfully accomplish the purging of a layer, you need to remove these objects and purge the layers again.

9. Select the `ERASE` command from the Modify pull-down menu and type **ALL** at the `Select objects:` prompt. Press Enter to remove all drawing objects and exit the command.

10. Repeat steps 2 to 4 to purge all layers in the drawing. Answer Yes to all confirmations.

    Note that you were not asked to purge TOPBOX. This is because that layer is current and not available for purging. Additionally, the layer BOXBOT did not purge. This is because a previously existing block is using that layer.

11. Set layer 0 to be current by selecting it from the Layer drop-down list. This will now enable you to purge the layer TOPBOX since the `PURGE` command will not purge the layer that's current.

12. Repeat steps 2 to 4 and purge the TOPBOX layer. Answer Yes to all confirmations. The layer is now removed from the drawing. You may then exit this drawing without saving changes.

As seen in the exercise, renaming and purging objects in your drawings is an easy task to accomplish. Regular usage of these commands will keep drawings clean and maintain minimal file sizes.

Summary

This completes the discussion of the advanced editing commands available in AutoCAD 2000. This chapter introduced you to grip editing and the available object-specific editing commands. To learn more about how and when to create and edit the objects discussed with the object-specific editing commands, please refer to the chapters cited in the text. In the next chapter, you learn how to create and use blocks, an important productivity tool.

12

APPLICATIONS FOR THE NEW AUTOCAD DESIGNCENTER

The power of AutoCAD lies in its ability to reuse existing data. Objects such as blocks and xrefs, as well as layers, text styles, and linetypes, can be used repeatedly once they are defined. By using existing data and placing it into your drawing, you avoid duplicating tasks, which saves time and increases productivity.

AutoCAD 2000 introduces a new feature called AutoCAD DesignCenter, which allows you to quickly locate, view, and import a variety of existing AutoCAD objects into the current drawing. In essence, you can look inside a drawing to see the blocks it contains, and even identify its xrefs. You can view its defined text styles, dimension styles, and linetypes. You can also identify its layers and layouts. After the desired objects are located, AutoCAD DesignCenter allows you to place duplicates of the objects into the current drawing, thereby instantly populating your drawing with valuable data from other drawings. By using AutoCAD DesignCenter, you take advantage of AutoCAD's real power—the power to reuse existing, valuable data.

In this chapter, you will learn about the following subjects:

- Understanding the AutoCAD DesignCenter interface
- Loading content into DesignCenter
- Adding content to drawings

Understanding the AutoCAD DesignCenter Interface

AutoCAD *DesignCenter* is primarily composed of two windowpanes, as shown in Figure 12.1. The pane on the left is the navigation pane or the Tree View interface, and the pane on the right is the content pane or palette interface. The Tree View allows you to locate source objects, and the palette allows you to view the content of the source objects. For example, in Figure 12.1, the Tree View is used to navigate to the My Computer folder, and the folder's contents are displayed in the palette. By using the Tree View and the palette, you can locate and view source objects.

Figure 12.1

DesignCenter is composed of the Tree View and palette windowpanes.

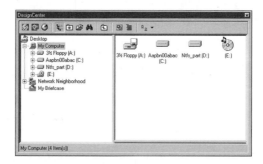

In the following two sections, you explore the Tree View and the palette interfaces.

Exploring the AutoCAD DesignCenter Tree View

DesignCenter's *Tree View* allows you to easily navigate through a directory structure. It works similarly to Windows Explorer, allowing you to expand or collapse folders to control the display of subfolders. By using Tree View, you can navigate to the desired location.

Although Tree View allows you to easily view and navigate a directory structure, you are not required to use it. For example, you can turn off the Tree View display by clicking the Tree View Toggle button, as shown in Figure 12.2. Toggling off the Tree

View display is useful after you have located the desired folder, and no longer need the Tree View. By toggling off the Tree View, the palette automatically expands, making the viewing of source objects easier. Once you have used the Tree View to locate source objects, you may toggle it off to display only the palette.

Figure 12.2

You can toggle off Tree View's display.

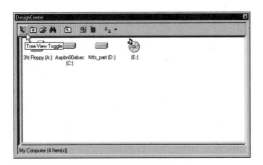

NOTE

You can navigate through directories using the palette by double-clicking a folder to display its contents, or by clicking the Up button to move up one level in the directory.

INSIDER **T**IP

Although you can use the palette to navigate through a directory, it's better to use Tree View because Tree View makes it easier to identify your location in a directory structure. By clicking the plus sign (+) or minus sign (–) button, you can open or close a directory's contents, respectively.

Tree view can display views in four different modes. Using a particular mode can assist you in locating the desired content source more quickly. The four modes are as follows:

- **Desktop View.** Allows you to locate source data on local or network drives.

- **Open Drawings View.** Lists all opened drawings in the current AutoCAD session.

- **History View.** Displays the last 20 locations of source objects accessed through DesignCenter.

- **Custom Content View.** Lists the currently registered applications used to create custom objects, if custom objects are present.

By selecting the proper mode, you can quickly find the locations that contain the desired source objects.

> **N**OTE
>
> The Custom Content button is displayed only when there are applications currently registered with your AutoCAD 2000 application. When applications that contain custom content are registered with AutoCAD 2000, such as Object ARX applications, DesignCenter displays the Custom Content button, allowing you to locate and view the registered application's content.

You can switch to the desired mode by choosing the appropriate view button. The buttons are displayed when the Tree View is toggled on, and are located in the upper-left corner of DesignCenter, as shown in Figure 12.3. The current mode in Figure 12.3 is History, which lists the most recent drawings from which source objects were queried. By clicking the proper button, you can more quickly display the locations of desired source objects.

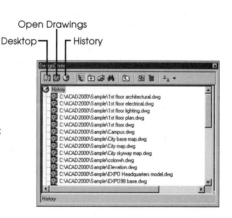

Open Drawings

Desktop ┐ ┌ History

Figure 12.3

Tree view's different display modes are accessed from the buttons in the upper-left corner.

> **N**OTE
>
> In History mode, DesignCenter automatically turns off the palette. This mode is intended to allow you to quickly locate the most recent locations from which you copied source objects. To redisplay the palette, double-click one of the locations displayed in Tree View.

By using DesignCenter's Tree View, you can easily navigate through a directory structure to the desired location of source data. In the next section, you learn about DesignCenter's palette interface, which allows you to view source objects.

INSIDER TIP

You can refresh the Tree View and palette display by right-clicking in the palette, then selecting Refresh from the shortcut menu.

Exploring the AutoCAD DesignCenter Palette

DesignCenter's palette displays the source objects found in a particular location. For example, when a location is selected using Tree View, the location's source objects are displayed in the palette, as shown in Figure 12.4. By using the palette, you can easily view the available source objects.

Figure 12.4

The palette displays the source objects using Large Icons view.

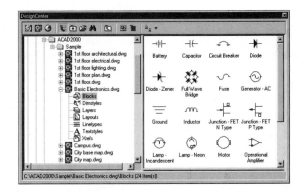

The palette can display source objects in one of four views. The view you may prefer to select largely depends on the source objects you are viewing. For example, when viewing blocks in a drawing, it is appropriate to use the Large Icons view to better see each block's thumbnail image, as shown in Figure 12.4. However, when viewing drawing files in a folder, choosing the Details view may be more desirable, as shown in Figure 12.5. The four available views are as follows:

■ **Large Icons.** Displays source objects using large object icons and uses thumbnail images, if available.

■ **Small Icons.** Displays source objects using small object icons, and does not use thumbnail images even if they are available.

■ **List.** Displays source objects as a simple list, without file detail information.

■ **Details.** Displays source objects as a list, and includes file information such as each file's size and type, if available.

By selecting the desired view, you can preview the source objects in an appropriate format.

Figure 12.5

The palette displays source objects using Details view.

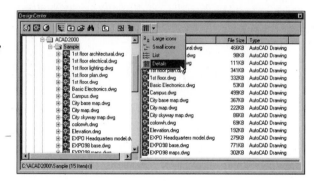

By right-clicking in the palette, you can select the desired view display by selecting View from the shortcut menu. Alternatively, you can select the desired view display by clicking successively on the Views tool.

You can control the sort order of objects displayed in the Details view by clicking the button at the top of each column. For example, in Figure 12.5, if you click the File Size button at the top of the palette, you can sort the objects in the list by file size in ascending order. By clicking the button a second time, you can re-sort the objects by size in descending order.

By using the DesignCenter's palette, you can easily view source objects in a format that you find useful. In the next section, you are introduced to two additional panes that provide additional information about the selected source object.

Viewing Images and Descriptions of Source Objects

There are two additional windowpanes you can open in DesignCenter. These panes display an image of the selected source object and its description, if such information was saved with the source object. By using these panes, you can better identify the contents of a source object before its contents are copied to the current drawing.

The *preview* pane allows you to display an image of the selected object, and is activated by clicking the Preview button, as shown in Figure 12.6. The preview pane is resizable, and can be expanded to better view the source object's image. By using the DesignCenter's preview feature, you can visualize the source object prior to inserting it into the current drawing.

Figure 12.6

The palette displays source objects using Details view.

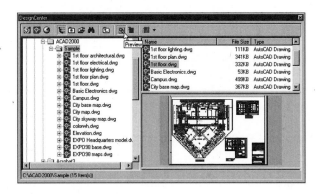

NOTE

> You can automatically generate preview images for blocks that do not have preview images by using the BLOCKICON command, which will generate preview images for block references defined in the current drawing.

The *description* pane displays text that describes the selected source object. When you click the Description button, if a description was provided, the description pane displays the description below the palette, as shown in Figure 12.7. By using the DesignCenter's description feature, you can better determine whether the selected source object is the one you need to copy into the current drawing.

Figure 12.7

The palette displays source objects using Details view.

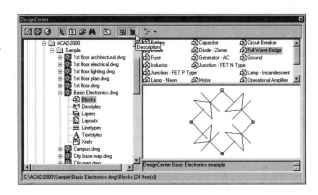

By using the preview and description features provided in DesignCenter, you can better identify the contents of a source object before its contents are copied to the current drawing. In the next section, you learn about other techniques for displaying source objects in the DesignCenter's palette.

Loading Content into DesignCenter

When you use the Tree View to locate source objects and then display those objects in the palette, you are actually loading content into the palette. Using Tree View, you can load content into the palette using the Desktop, Open Drawings, History, and Custom Content modes. By using Tree View's simple interface, you can load content into the palette from different locations.

Although Tree View's simple interface can load content into the palette, its capabilities are limited. For example, Tree View does not allow you to define the file type you wish to locate when browsing for source objects. Additionally, Tree View does not provide an automated find feature that locates content based on a key word search. Tree View's features for locating source objects are useful, but limited.

To compensate for Tree View's limited abilities for locating source objects, DesignCenter has additional methods for loading content that are very powerful. For example, you can locate drawings using a feature similar to AutoCAD's Select File dialog box, which allows you to browse for files. The Load DesignCenter Palette feature allows you to indicate the file type for which you are searching, and displays a preview image of the selected file.

You can also use the powerful Find feature, which can search local and network drives for files, as well as source objects within files, using search criteria. By using these features, you can more easily locate the desired source objects, especially when you're not sure where to look.

In the following two sections, you learn how to use the Load DesignCenter Palette feature and the Find feature to more easily locate the desired source objects.

Using the Load DesignCenter Palette Feature

DesignCenter provides a feature for loading content into the palette that works similarly to AutoCAD's Select File dialog box. By using the *Load DesignCenter Palette* dialog box, you can browse for files on local and network drives, in your Favorites folder, or over the Internet. You can also use this feature to automate searching for a particular file based on its name or its file type. By using the Load DesignCenter

Palette dialog box, you can use specific tools to locate, preview, and load content into the palette.

The Load DesignCenter Palette dialog box is opened by clicking the Load button located between the Favorites and Find buttons in DesignCenter, as shown in Figure 12.8. After you click the Load button, the Load DesignCenter Palette dialog box appears, as shown in Figure 12.9. Once you've opened this dialog box, you can use the various features of the Load DesignCenter Palette to locate files.

Figure 12.8

DesignCenter's Favorites, Load, and Find buttons.

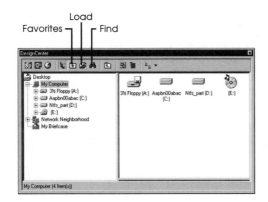

Figure 12.9

The Load DesignCenter Palette dialog box displays source files.

In the following exercise, you use the Locate feature of the Load DesignCenter Palette dialog box.

LOCATING FILES WITH THE LOAD DESIGNCENTER PALETTE DIALOG BOX

1. Create a new folder on your computer called Find Files.

2. Copy the 12DWG01.dwg, 12DWG01a.dwg, and 12DWG01b.dwg files from the accompanying CD to the Find Files folder.

After copying the files, right-click the *.dwg files and select Properties, then clear the Read-only attribute.

Next, you use the Locate feature to find the files.

3. Start a new drawing in AutoCAD.

4. From the Standard toolbar, select AutoCAD DesignCenter. AutoCAD opens DesignCenter.

5. From DesignCenter, select Load. AutoCAD displays the Load DesignCenter Palette dialog box.

6. From the Load DesignCenter Palette dialog box, click Find File. AutoCAD displays the Browse/Search dialog box (see Figure 2.10).

7. Select the Search tab.

8. In the Search Pattern text box, type **12DWG01***. (Be sure to include the asterisk at the end of the text string.)

9. In the Search Location area, click the Drives option button, then select the drive on which you created the Find Files folder.

10. Click Search. AutoCAD searches the selected drive using the 12DWG01* search pattern, and displays the results in the Files list, as shown in Figure 12.10.

Figure 12.10

The Browse/Search feature of the Load DesignCenter Palette dialog box locates files based on search patterns.

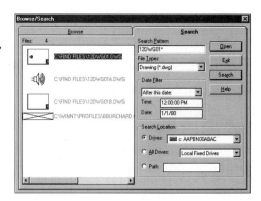

11. From the Files list, select the 12DWG01.dwg file, then click Open. AutoCAD displays the file's location in the Tree View, and displays its content in the palette, as shown in Figure 12.11.

Figure 12.11

The found file's location is displayed in the Tree View, and its contents are displayed in the palette.

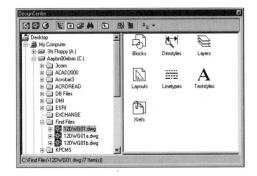

12. You may close DesignCenter, and close the drawing without saving changes.

The Load DesignCenter Palette dialog box allows you to locate files by browsing local and network drives, and by browsing the Internet. You can also locate files using its Browse/Search dialog box.

NOTE

You can also load content into the palette using Windows Explorer by dragging a file from Explorer to DesignCenter's palette.

In the next section, you use the Find feature to locate content within files.

Searching for Content Using the Find Feature

DesignCenter provides a very powerful search feature that allows you to locate the source objects you need. For example, you can search for drawing files by name, or by keyword or description. You can also search inside drawings for a variety of source objects including blocks, layers, linetypes, and text styles. By using DesignCenter's *Find* feature, you can locate the source objects you need, even if they reside within a drawing.

INSIDER **T**IP

You can make drawings and blocks easier to find using two new features available with AutoCAD 2000. To make drawings easier to find, add keywords to the current drawing by using the Drawing Properties dialog box, which appears by selecting Drawing Properties from AutoCAD's File menu. To make blocks easier to find, AutoCAD 2000 allows you to add a description to the block in the Block Definition dialog box. By adding keywords and descriptions to drawings and blocks, you can use DesignCenter's Find feature to quickly locate the desired source object.

In the following exercise, you use DesignCenter's Find feature to locate a specific block that resides inside a drawing.

NOTE

The following exercise uses drawing files copied to the Find Files folder, as instructed in steps 1 and 2 of the previous exercise located in the section titled, "Using the Load DesignCenter Palette Feature."

LOCATING FILES WITH DESIGNCENTER'S FIND FEATURE

1. Start a new drawing in AutoCAD.

2. From the Standard toolbar, select AutoCAD DesignCenter. AutoCAD opens DesignCenter.

3. From DesignCenter, click the Find button. AutoCAD displays the Find dialog box.

4. From the Look For list, select Drawings.

5. From the In list, select the drive on which you created the Find Files folder.

6. From the Drawings tab, in the Search for the Word(s) list, type ***.dwg**. This instructs AutoCAD to search for words that end with .dwg.

7. From the In the Field(s) list, select File Name.

8. From the Advanced tab, in the Containing list, select Block name.

9. In the Containing Text list, type **ALARM**, then click Find Now. AutoCAD searches the selected drive for any drawing files that contain a block named ALARM, and displays the results as shown in Figure 12.12.

Figure 12.12

Figure 12.12

The Find dialog box locates source objects, such as blocks, within drawing files.

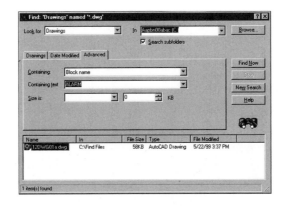

10. In the list of found files, right-click the 12DWG01a.dwg file, then select Load into Palette from the shortcut menu. AutoCAD displays the file's location in the Tree View, and displays its content in the palette.

11. You may close DesignCenter, close the Find dialog box, and close the drawing without saving changes.

The Find dialog box allows you to locate files and source objects within files by entering search criteria. You can use its three tabs to locate files by type, by date modified, or by specific text. You can search for a variety of object types, such as blocks, layers, layouts, and xrefs, and you can search for objects based on text values for block names, drawing and block descriptions, and attribute tags and values. By using DesignCenter's Find feature, you have access to a powerful set of tools that help you pinpoint the source objects you need.

INSIDER TIP

You can avoid searching for frequently accessed source objects by right-clicking the source object and selecting Add to Favorites from the shortcut menu. AutoCAD adds a shortcut to the selected source object in the Autodesk Favorites folder. The source object can then be loaded into the palette by clicking the Favorites button in DesignCenter, and then selecting the source object's shortcut icon.

In the previous sections, you learned how to use DesignCenter's various tools for locating content. In the next section, you learn how to load content into the current drawing.

Adding Content to Drawings

The purpose of DesignCenter is to make locating existing AutoCAD objects easy. Consequently, DesignCenter provides several methods for locating and identifying pre-made source objects. As discussed in previous sections, by using the features available in DesignCenter, you can quickly locate existing sources of AutoCAD objects to copy into the current drawing.

After you have located a desired source object, you must copy it into the current drawing. Once copied into the current drawing, the object becomes a part of the current drawing, and can be used just as if it were originally created in the current drawing. Therefore, objects like blocks and xrefs, layers and layouts, and text styles and dimensions styles can be copied into the current drawing from DesignCenter's palette.

Typically, after you've identified a source object and displayed it in DesignCenter's palette, you can copy the object to the current drawing by simply dragging it from the palette into the current drawing's window. Objects you can simply copy by dragging from the palette to the current drawing include the following:

■ Dimstyles

■ Layers

■ Layouts

■ Linetypes

■ Textstyles

You can select multiple source objects of the types shown in the list. After they are copied, the object(s) become part of the current drawing. By dragging the desired source object(s) from the palette into the current drawing, you can quickly add content to the current drawing.

Not all individual objects can be simply dragged into the current drawing. Source objects such as drawings, blocks, images, and xrefs can be only copied one at a time. Additionally, you must define their scale, rotation, and insertion point. Therefore, when inserting drawings, blocks, images, and xrefs, you must tell AutoCAD their scale, rotation, and location.

In the following exercise, you use DesignCenter to locate source objects, and insert them into the current drawing.

NOTE

The following exercise uses drawing files copied to the Find Files folder, as instructed in
steps 1 and 2 of the exercise located in the section "Using the Load DesignCenter Palette
Feature."

LOADING CONTENT INTO THE PALETTE

1. Start a new drawing in AutoCAD.

2. From the Standard toolbar, select AutoCAD DesignCenter. AutoCAD opens
    DesignCenter.

3. In Tree View, navigate to the Find Files folder, then click the plus sign to expand the
    folder. The three drawing files in the Find Files folder appear in the Tree View.

Next, you use DesignCenter to attach an xref to the current drawing.

4. In Tree View, click the plus sign next to the 12DWG01.dwg file to display its source
    objects.

5. In Tree View, select the Xrefs source object. The palette displays the two xrefs that are
    attached to the 12DWG01.dwg drawing, as shown in Figure 12.13.

Figure 12.13

The attached xrefs are
displayed in the palette.

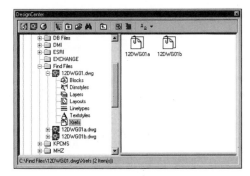

6. In the palette, right-click the 12DWG01a xref.

7. From the shortcut menu, select Attach Xref. AutoCAD displays the External Reference
    dialog box.

8. In the Insertion Point area, clear the Specify On-Screen check box, then click OK.
    AutoCAD attaches the xref to the current drawing.

WARNING

DesignCenter will not copy an object if an object with an identical name already exists in the current drawing. To copy the object using DesignCenter, you must change the name of the object that already resides in the current drawing.

Next, you use DesignCenter to copy a block definition into the current drawing.

9. In Tree View, click the minus sign next to the 12DWG01.dwg file to collapse the display of its source objects.

10. In Tree View, click the plus sign next to the 12DWG01a.dwg file to display its source objects.

11. In Tree View, select the Blocks source object. The palette displays the block definitions that are stored in 12DWG01a.dwg drawing, as shown in Figure 12.14.

Figure 12.14

The selected drawing's block definitions are displayed in the palette.

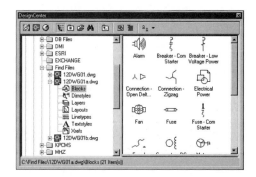

12. In the palette, right-click the Alarm block definition.

13. From the shortcut menu, select Insert Block. AutoCAD displays the Insert dialog box.

    At this point, you could specify the insertion values to use to insert the block into the current drawing's model space. For this exercise, you will click Cancel to close the Insert dialog box without inserting a block reference.

14. Click Cancel. AutoCAD saves the block definition in the current drawing, then closes the Insert dialog box.

NOTE

By clicking Cancel to close the Insert dialog box, you insert a block definition into the current drawing without actually inserting a block reference into the current drawing's model space. The block definition can then be used at a later time to insert a block reference using the INSERT command.

Next, you use DesignCenter to copy named layers into the current drawing.

15. In Tree View, select the Layers source object. The palette displays the named layers that are stored in 12DWG01a.dwg drawing, as shown in Figure 12.15.

Figure 12.15

The selected drawing's named layers are displayed in the palette.

16. In the palette, starting in the upper-left corner, drag a window around all the layers to select them. DesignCenter highlights all the named layers.

17. Right-click over one of the highlighted layers, then select Add Layer(s) from the shortcut menu. DesignCenter adds the highlighted layers to the current drawing.

18. You may close DesignCenter, and close the drawing without saving changes.

By using DesignCenter, you can easily locate source objects and copy their content into the current drawing. When copying objects such as blocks and xrefs, you can only copy the objects one at a time. When copying objects such as layers, linetypes, and text styles, however, you can select multiple objects and copy them simultaneously.

Summary

In this chapter, you learned how to use DesignCenter to locate source objects, and copy their content into the current drawing. You used DesignCenter's Load and Find features to search for source objects using search criteria. You also learned how to use the Tree View to locate source objects, and how to display the content of source objects in the palette. You experienced how to drag different types of content from the palette, and copy them into the current drawing. In this chapter, you learned how to use DesignCenter to find and use existing data, which allows you to work more productively by reusing existing AutoCAD objects located in other drawings.

13

CREATING AND USING BLOCKS

Blocks are a very powerful feature of AutoCAD 2000. They enable you to define an object or collection of objects that can be inserted into a drawing over and over, without having to create the object or objects again from scratch. They also can significantly reduce a drawing's file size. More importantly, although a drawing may contain hundreds of insertions of a particular block, if it becomes necessary to edit the blocks, AutoCAD requires only that you edit a single block definition. When that block is redefined, the hundreds of instances of the inserted block will automatically be updated. The new changes will appear instantly. Additionally, attributes containing user-defined textual information can be attached to a block, providing a means to create, locate, and then extract useful data unique to a particular block insertion.

To use the power of blocks to their fullest potential, it is necessary to first understand the nature of blocks. If you understand how blocks work and how to properly manage them, you will learn how to make AutoCAD 2000 do tedious, repetitive tasks automatically, thereby increasing your everyday productivity.

This chapter discusses the following subjects:

- Defining and inserting blocks
- Modifying blocks with the new in-place reference editing feature
- Using nested blocks
- Managing blocks effectively

Understanding Blocks

A *block* is a collection of individual objects combined into a larger single object. Think of the block as the parent of a family, and think of the individual objects as the parent's children. Although the children have identities of their own (color, layer, lineweight, and linetype), they are also under the control of their parent, which has its own color, layer, lineweight, and linetype properties.

The fact that both the block (parent) and its individual objects (children) have their own properties makes it important to understand how these properties are affected by certain conditions. For example, assume that a block has been created from several child objects and that each child object was originally created on its own layer. The layers on which the child objects were created can be frozen individually. If one of these layers is frozen, the child object that resides on that layer is also frozen and becomes invisible. However, the other child objects in the block remain visible because the layers they are on are still thawed. In contrast, if the parent block is inserted on a layer and that layer is then frozen, all its child objects will become frozen. This is true even when the layers on which the child objects reside are on and thawed.

For example, Figure 13.1 shows an inserted block made up of three objects: a rectangle, a triangle, and a circle. The block (parent) is inserted on the layer Parent. When the block was defined, the rectangle, triangle, and circle objects (children) were on the layers Rectangle, Triangle, and Circle, respectively.

When the Triangle layer is frozen, as shown in Figure 13.2, only the triangle object disappears, and all other objects remain visible. This is true even though the triangle is part of another object—the inserted block object. In other words, because the Triangle child's layer is frozen, only it is affected. None of the other children or the parent is affected.

Figure 13.1

The parent block is made up of three child objects.

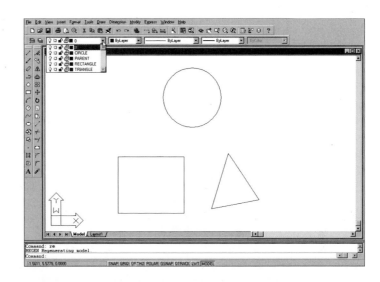

Figure 13.2

The parent block with only the Triangle layer frozen.

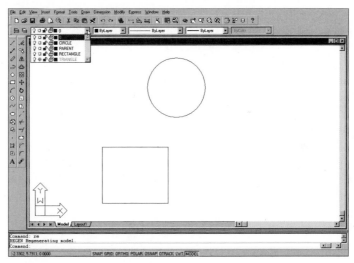

In contrast, all the objects disappear when the Parent layer is frozen, as shown in Figure 13.3. This demonstrates the difference between freezing a child object's layer and freezing its parent layer.

Figure 13.3

The parent block and its child objects disappear when the Parent layer is frozen.

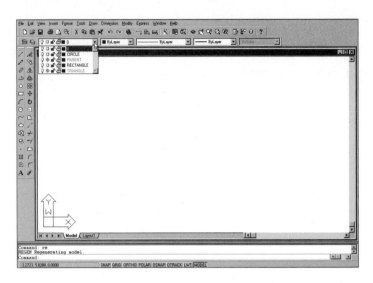

This example is just one of several conditions that can influence the behavior and appearance of an inserted block. Understanding the rules that govern these conditions is essential to implementing the power of blocks and increasing your productivity.

The New Block Definition Dialog Box

NEW for R2000 The Block Definition dialog box is the most common method used to create new blocks. AutoCAD 2000 has updated the dialog box, adding new features and enhancing its functionality. You access the new Block Definition dialog box, shown in Figure 13.4, from the Draw pull-down menu by choosing Block, Make.

Figure 13.4

The updated Block Definition dialog box.

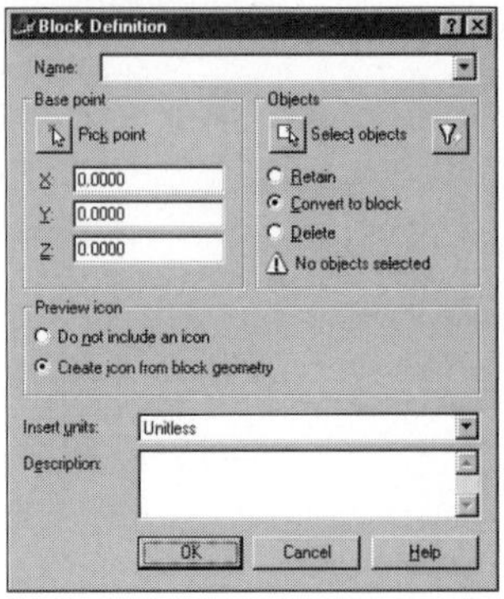

The following list describes the dialog box's features:

- **Name.** This is where you specify the name of the block. To assign a new name, type the name in the edit box.

  This feature is improved over its predecessor by the addition of a drop-down list. The list displays the names of all currently defined blocks. In addition to displaying block names, by selecting a name, you can display all its current settings and then redefine any or all of its values.

- **Base Point.** Allows you to define the X,Y,Z insertion coordinates for the block. You can enter the coordinate values in the appropriate edit boxes, or you can click the Pick Point button and specify the insertion base point by selecting a point on screen.

  The base point value is saved with the block and represents the point in the block that AutoCAD 2000 uses to define the block's position when it's inserted in the drawing.

- **Objects.** This area controls various options when selecting objects that define a new block, and it displays the number of objects selected.

  If you click the Select Objects button, you can then choose the objects that make up the block definition on-screen.

  Clicking the Quick Select button displays the Quick Select dialog box shown in Figure 13.5, which allows you to select objects based on filter criteria. For example, you can select all CIRCLE objects whose color is blue.

Figure 13.5

The new Quick Select dialog box.

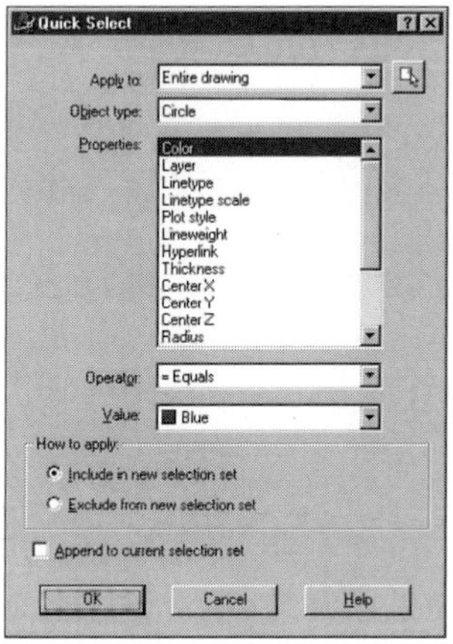

Refer to Chapter 11, "Advanced Geometry Editing," for more information on using the Quick Select options.

The Retain, Convert to Block, and Delete option buttons tell AutoCAD what to do with the selected objects after the block is defined. When you retain the objects, they are left in the drawing and are not converted to a block after AutoCAD 2000 uses them to define the new block. When you convert the objects to a block, the original objects are erased and then reinserted as a single block in their original positions in the drawing. When you delete the objects, AutoCAD erases them from the drawing after the new block is defined.

- **Preview Icon.** This new feature allows you to control whether AutoCAD 2000 creates an image of the new block and saves it with the block definition. You can display the image when viewing blocks by selecting a block name or by using the new AutoCAD DesignCenter (discussed later in this chapter).

- **Insert Units.** This new feature specifies the units to which the block is scaled when it's inserted from the new AutoCAD DesignCenter. You can choose from numerous unit types including feet, inches, or millimeters. This feature is discussed in the AutoCAD DesignCenter section later in this chapter.

- **Description.** This new feature allows you to provide a detailed description of the block definition. The description is displayed when it's selected in the block command and when blocks are viewed using the new AutoCAD DesignCenter, as discussed later in this chapter.

Defining Blocks

What happens inside a drawing when a new block is defined? If you have created xblocks before, you know that when you select the child objects that make up the block, they all disappear from the screen. This happens because AutoCAD automatically erases them after they have been used to define a block.

INSIDER TIP

Use the OOPS command to unerase the objects. The OOPS command can always be used to unerase the most recently erased selection set. This is true even if several other commands have been executed since the object was erased.

N OTE

I always thought it silly that AutoCAD erases a block's child objects. After all, I typically create the objects where I need them in the first place. I was only trying to make a copy of the objects to put someplace else in my drawing. Why, then, would it erase them? The following paragraph explains.

There is a logical reason why AutoCAD erases the objects. The BLOCK command is more than another COPY command; it enables you to make copies of a collection of child objects that uses less file space. It minimizes the file size of an AutoCAD drawing by storing each child object's property data in a place AutoCAD calls the *Block Table*. It stores this information under the name of the parent block. When you insert a block into AutoCAD, instead of duplicating the property data of each child object (as the COPY command does), AutoCAD simply refers to the property data stored in the Block Table. It then draws the child objects based upon this data. This enables AutoCAD to store each child object's property data in just one place, the Block Table. You can, therefore, insert multiple copies of a block, duplicating the child objects where needed. In each case, AutoCAD refers back to the Block Table for the data it needs to draw the child objects. Consequently, AutoCAD erases the original objects after they are used to define a block because it assumes you will want to reinsert those objects as a block to reduce the file size of your drawing.

The Effect of the Current UCS on Block Definitions

When you create a block, you must define its insertion base point. This point's coordinates are relative to the block object and are set to its 0,0,0. Consequently, when you define a block's insertion base point, even though the current *UCS (User-defined Coordinate System)* coordinates may be 100,100,100 when you pick them, AutoCAD ignores these values and stores the block's insertion base point as 0,0,0. This is true in both paper space and model space. If you were then to export this block out as its own drawing using the WBLOCK command, the insertion base point would be at 0,0,0 of the *WCS (World Coordinate System)* in the new drawing. This feature enables predictable insertion of blocks.

INSIDER TIP

AutoCAD remembers the series of commands you enter at the command prompt. Therefore, you can recall the previously entered commands by pressing the Up arrow on your keyboard. Each time you press the Up arrow, you move back through the previous commands. You can also press the Down arrow to move forward through the previous commands. When the desired command is displayed at the command prompt, press Enter to execute the command.

NOTE

AutoCAD ignores the current UCS coordinate values in paper space and model space when defining a block's insertion base point.

INSIDER TIP

When you're defining the insertion base point of a new block, simply imagine that AutoCAD is temporarily redefining the UCS origin to the point you pick.

In addition to understanding how AutoCAD deals with the current UCS's coordinates when defining a block, you must also understand the effect the current UCS's X-axis orientation has on the angle a block assumes when it is inserted into a drawing.

When creating a block, AutoCAD uses the current UCS to determine its insertion angle. This angle is oriented relative to the current UCS's X-axis.

To demonstrate the effect of the current UCS's orientation, the following exercise walks you through inserting two different arrowhead blocks into an existing drawing.

EXAMINING THE EFFECT OF THE CURRENT UCS'S ORIENTATION

1. Open the 13DWG03.DWG drawing file on the accompanying CD.

    The drawing contains two sets of objects that appear on the right side of your screen. Both sets are made up of a closed polygon in the shape of an arrowhead with a text object inside. The first set was used to create a block definition called AR1. The second set was used to create a block definition called AR2.

It is important to note the X-axis orientation relative to the two arrowheads. Both arrowheads were defined as blocks with the same UCS orientation. As a consequence, when you insert each block during this exercise, you will see the effect the current UCS orientation has on the inserted objects.

Now you will insert the AR1 block.

2. From the Insert menu, choose Block. The Insert dialog box opens.

3. Choose AR1 from the Name drop-down list if is not already displayed.

4. In the Insertion point area, be sure the Specify On-screen option is selected. In the Scale and Rotation areas, make sure the Specify On-screen option is cleared.

5. Click OK to close the Insert dialog box. The dialog box closes, and the AR1 Insert object appears. Notice that the arrowhead is oriented in the same direction as the original AR1 object that appears on the lower-right side of your screen.

6. Choose a location in the lower-left portion of the drawing to insert the arrowhead.

    Now, you will insert the AR2 block.

7. From the Insert menu, choose Block to open the Insert dialog box.

8. Choose AR2 from the Name drop-down list.

9. Click OK to close the Insert dialog box. The dialog box closes, and the AR2 Insert object appears. Notice that the arrowhead is oriented in the same direction as the original AR2 object that appears on the upper-right side of your screen.

10. Choose a location in the upper-left portion of the drawing to insert the arrowhead. Your drawing should look similar to Figure 13.6.

    Next, you change the rotation of the WCS about its Z axis. Then you redefine the AR2 block to see the effect the new UCS has on the block's rotation.

11. From the Tools menu, choose New UCS, and then choose Z.

12. At the `Specify rotation angle about Z axis <90>:` prompt, type **45**.

    Notice that the UCS's X axis arrow is now rotated parallel to the AR2 objects in the upper-right corner.

13. From the Draw menu, choose Block, Make. The Block Definition dialog box opens.

14. From the Name drop-down list, choose AR2.

15. In the Base Point area, click the Pick Point button. The Block Definition dialog box temporarily disappears, allowing you to pick an insertion point for the block.

16. Using an Endpoint snap, select the tip of the AR2 arrowhead object in the upper-right corner. AutoCAD captures the coordinates for the pick point and displays the values in the Block Definition dialog box.

Figure 13.6

The two arrowhead blocks are inserted

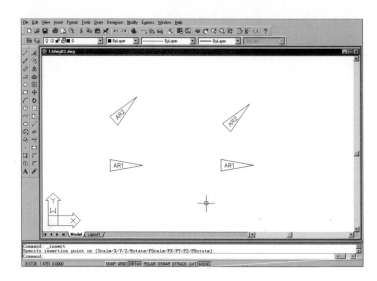

17. In the Object area, choose the Select Objects button. The Block Definition dialog box temporarily disappears, allowing you to select the objects.

18. Select the two AR2 objects in the upper-right corner and press Enter. AutoCAD displays the Block Definition dialog box, noting that two objects are selected.

19. Click OK. AutoCAD displays a message noting that the AR2 block is already defined and asks if you want to redefine it.

20. Choose Yes to redefine the AR2 block and close the warning dialog box.

     AutoCAD redefines the AR2 block definition using the current UCS's X-axis orientation and regenerates the drawing. If the AR2 object set was erased from your screen, enter OOPS at the command prompt to unerase it.

     Next, you will set the UCS back to the WCS and insert the AR2 block.

21. From the Tools menu, choose New UCS, World.

22. From the Insert menu, choose Block to open the Insert dialog box.

23. Choose AR2 from the Name drop-down list.

24. Click OK to close the Insert dialog box. The dialog box closes, and the AR2 Insert object appears. Notice that the arrowhead is now oriented in the same direction as the WCS's X axis.

25. Choose a location near the center of the drawing to insert the arrowhead. Your drawing should look similar to Figure 13.7. Notice that both AR2 block insertions align parallel to the WCS's X axis.

26. Close the drawing without saving it.

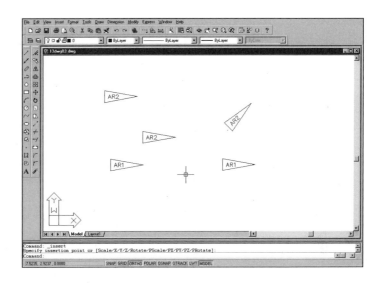

Figure 13.7

The redefined AR2 block is inserted.

This exercise shows how the current UCS affects a block's orientation when it is created and then inserted into a drawing. By understanding this behavior, you can better control how blocks are inserted into drawings, and thereby maintain a higher level of productivity.

I NSIDER TIP

When using the command-line version of the Insert command, you can preset the scale and rotation of a block before it is inserted. This feature is useful when you want to see the effect of a scale or rotation angle before inserting the block. To take advantage of this feature, type **-INSERT** at the command prompt and then select the block to be inserted. When AutoCAD prompts for the insertion point, type **S** to preset the scale or **R** to preset the rotation.

Inserting Blocks

Several commands can be used to insert blocks. Understanding the unique features of these commands is important in selecting the right tool for a particular task.

INSERT and -INSERT

The INSERT and -INSERT commands are used to insert blocks. The INSERT command prompts for insertion information using the Insert dialog box, whereas -INSERT prompts for information at AutoCAD's command line. The Insert dialog box interface makes it easy to select blocks already stored in the current drawing's Block Table. The Insert dialog box also makes it easy to search for blocks stored outside the current drawing by choosing the Browse button.

INSIDER TIP

When you use script files to perform repetitious commands, AutoCAD automatically uses the command line version of the commands. Therefore, you can use the -INSERT command to understand the series of options the script file will need to address to ensure the script functions correctly.

NOTE

To use the standard command alias of the INSERT command, at the command prompt, simply type I to open the Insert dialog box. Type -I at the command prompt to start the command-line version of the Insert command.

MINSERT versus ARRAY

Sometimes it may be necessary to insert a block as a rectangular array. Two options exist to accomplish this. You can use MINSERT or ARRAY.

The MINSERT Command

First, the MINSERT command combines the INSERT and ARRAY commands. When executed, the first command-line prompts are the typical ones for inserting a block. After that, the typical command-line prompts for creating an array appear. The exception is that MINSERT can only create rectangular arrays. Therefore, no option is available for selecting a polar array.

One drawback to this command is that the MINSERT object cannot be exploded, nor can its individual objects be moved or edited. The advantage to using this command, however, is that less file space is required to define the MINSERT object, which reduces the file size of your drawing. It is important to note that the reduction in file size can be dramatic. For example, a simple block inserted as an array of 100×100 using the MINSERT command will have little, if any, impact on the file's size. In contrast, the same number of blocks inserted using the ARRAY command can increase the file's size by 1/2MB or more.

If you need to insert an array of blocks and you will not need to explode or edit the objects, I suggest that you use the MINSERT command. Otherwise, use the ARRAY command discussed in the next section.

The ARRAY Command

The ARRAY command accomplishes the same thing as the MINSERT command, but it affords you more control over the inserted objects. With the ARRAY command, you can choose between rectangular and polar arrays. Also, after the array is created, you can explode the inserted objects individually or move them independently of the other Insert objects. To use the ARRAY command with a block, however, you must first use the INSERT command to create the first object; then you can use the ARRAY command to create the desired array.

The disadvantage of using the ARRAY command is that multiple insertions of the block object are made, which therefore, increases your drawing's file size.

MEASURE and DIVIDE

The MEASURE and DIVIDE commands provide two methods of inserting a block along a path.

MEASURE Command

The MEASURE command enables you to insert a block in multiple places along a line, arc, or polyline at a given distance. To demonstrate, the next exercise shows you how to create a series of rectangles along the centerline of a street design. By creating a block of a rectangle and inserting it at the appropriate distances along a centerline path, you can quickly create a series of viewport guides. For this particular drawing, the guides can be used to define the various Plan View sections for street improvement plans.

USING MEASURE TO SET A SERIES OF BLOCKS ALONG A PATH

1. Open the 13DWG04.DWG drawing file on the accompanying CD. This file contains a typical street centerline with right-of-way lines. A block called Viewport exists in the Block Table. This block consists of a rectangle with an insertion base point located in the center of the rectangle. The rectangle is 400 feet wide by 1,000 feet long.

You will use the MEASURE command to insert this block every 800 feet along the centerline.

2. From the Draw pull-down menu, select Point, Measure. AutoCAD prompts for the object to measure.

3. Select the red centerline.

4. At the `Specify length of segment or [Block]:` prompt, type **B** to select block, and then press Enter.

5. At the `Enter name of block to insert:` prompt, type the block name **Viewport**, and then press Enter.

6. At the `Align block with object? [Yes/No] <Y>:` prompt, type **Y**, and then press Enter.

7. At the `Specify length of segment:` prompt, type a segment length of **800**, and then press Enter. AutoCAD creates many Viewport blocks along the centerline path, placing one every 800 feet, as shown in Figure 13.8.

Figure 13.8

The MEASURE command places the Viewport blocks along a path.

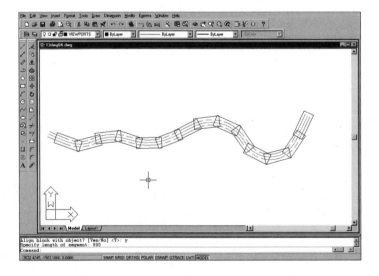

DIVIDE Command

The DIVIDE command allows you to insert a block multiple times along a line, arc, or polyline any given number of times. Suppose you must draw a series of manholes along the street centerline in the previous example. After you create the Manhole block, you can use the DIVIDE command to insert 30 copies of it along the centerline path.

USING DIVIDE TO INSERT 30 MANHOLE BLOCKS ALONG A PATH

1. Continuing with the previous drawing, open the 13DWG04a.DWG drawing file on the accompanying CD.

2. From the Draw pull-down menu, select Point, Divide. AutoCAD prompts for the object to divide.

3. Select the red centerline.

4. At the `Enter the number of segments or [Block]:` prompt, type **B** to select block, and then press Enter.

5. At the `Enter name of block to insert:` prompt, type the block name **Manhole**, and then press Enter.

6. At the `Align block with object? [Yes/No] <Y>:` prompt, type **Y** to align the block with the selected object, and then press Enter.

7. At the `Enter the number of segments:` prompt, type a segment number of **30**, and then press Enter. AutoCAD draws 30 evenly spaced Manhole blocks along the centerline path, as shown in Figure 13.9.

8. You can close the drawing without saving.

Figure 13.9

The DIVIDE *command evenly spaces the Manhole blocks along a path.*

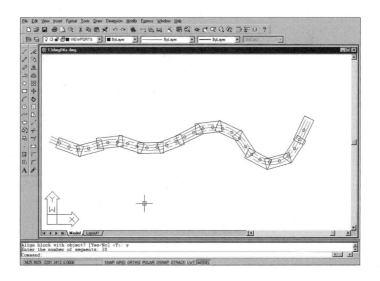

When you're inserting blocks into a drawing, it is important for you to remember that AutoCAD aligns the block's WCS parallel to the current UCS. This feature not only affects the insertion angle of the block, but also affects the rotation angle. If the rotation angle is assigned when a block is inserted, the rotation angle is relative to the current UCS. This is true in both paper space and model space.

Windows-Based Insertion Features

AutoCAD 2000 introduces a new feature called *Multiple Document Environment (MDE)*, which allows you to open multiple drawings in a single AutoCAD session. This feature works in the same fashion as other Windows applications, such as Microsoft Word and Excel.

There are many advantages to opening several drawings in a session of AutoCAD, and two of them relate to blocks. Along with MDE, AutoCAD also introduces two new features that take advantage of multiple open drawings. These new features allow you to either cut and paste or drag and drop objects from one drawing to another. Additionally, you are given the option of inserting the objects as a block.

Cut and Paste Block Insertion

The phrase "cut and paste" refers to the process of selecting an object or group of objects and cutting or copying them to the Windows Clipboard. When you cut selected objects, they are copied to the Clipboard and erased from the original document. In contrast, when you copy objects, they are copied to the Clipboard, but the selected objects are left untouched in the original document.

Cut and paste block insertion is not really new to AutoCAD, but its capabilities are greatly enhanced. For example, AutoCAD 2000 allows you to identify the base point of an object when copying it to the Clipboard. This very powerful feature provides you with the control to specifically identify the new insertion point of the selected object.

When you insert the block from the Clipboard, you can paste it using either a selected base point, or the block's original coordinates. The Paste to Original Coordinates option, found on the shortcut menu, copies the coordinate location of the objects in the original drawing and then pastes the objects in the new drawing using those same coordinates. This option is useful for copying objects from one drawing to another when both drawings use the same coordinate system. You must have previously saved a base point to have access to the Paste to Original Coordinates option. For more information, refer to Chapter 10, "Basic Object Editing."

NOTE

> You can browse Web sites for blocks to insert into your drawing. For more information, refer to Chapter 25, "Publishing on the Web."

Drag and Drop Block Insertion

When you drag and drop objects, you are moving them from one place to another. When you drag and drop objects within the same AutoCAD drawing, the result is the same as using the MOVE command to move the object. When you drag and drop from one drawing to another, the result is similar to copying the object from the original drawing to the target drawing.

The drag and drop feature is useful for quickly moving or copying objects. However, this method does not provide a method for accurately selecting the base point for pasting the objects as a block. Consequently, to select objects in one drawing and paste them as a block in another while controlling the new block's base point, use the copy and paste feature described in the previous section. For more information, refer to Chapter 10.

NOTE

> You can also drag and drop files from Windows Explorer into a drawing.

Block Reference

When you insert a block, you are actually creating an Insert object. The Insert object references a particular set of block data in the Block Table. This is called a *Block reference*. AutoCAD uses the Block reference to find the data stored in the Block Table. It uses this data to draw the child objects that make up the Insert object.

Although only one set of data in the Block Table is used to define a block, multiple block references can refer to that data. In fact, there is no limit to the number of Insert objects you can create. In each case, AutoCAD uses the Block reference to find the data it needs to draw the Insert object.

Behavior of Block Properties

There are three properties of blocks that behave in different ways depending on their settings when the block is defined. The color, linetype, and lineweight properties can behave in different but predictable ways when defined on the 0 layer as opposed to other layers. In addition, you can define these properties explicitly by selecting particular values, or you can define them implicitly as BYLAYER or BYBLOCK.

The Effect of Creating Blocks on Layers Other Than 0

The simplest way to control the appearance of a block is to define it on a particular layer and explicitly define its color, linetype, and lineweight. For example, suppose you have created a circle object on a layer called Circles. To explicitly define its color, open the Modify menu and choose Properties. When AutoCAD displays the Properties window, select the circle. When the Properties window displays the circle's properties, select a color from the Color property drop-down list, or choose the Other option from the list to display the Select Color dialog box. The Properties window now lists the color you chose as the property of the circle and changes the circle object's color to reflect the modified property. You have just defined the color value explicitly. As a consequence, if you use the circle object to define a block and the block is inserted into the drawing, its color will be constant. It will always be the color you explicitly defined.

In contrast, if you implicitly define an object's color, linetype, and lineweight by choosing BYLAYER, altering the layer properties the original object was on when it was defined as a block will change the object's appearance in the block. For example, suppose the circle object in the previous example is used to define a block. Also suppose the circle's color, linetype, and lineweight are defined as BYLAYER, and the circle object is on a layer called Circle. When the block containing the circle object is inserted into the drawing, altering the color, linetype, or lineweight of the Circle layer will change the circle object's color, linetype, or lineweight. This is true no matter what layer the block is inserted on. When a child object's color, linetype, and lineweight properties are set to BYLAYER, those properties are determined by the values of the child object's original layer.

The Effect of Creating Blocks on Layer 0

Layer 0 has a unique feature. When a block is defined from child objects created on the 0 layer, AutoCAD assigns special properties to that block if its color, linetype, and lineweight properties are set to BYLAYER or BYBLOCK. This feature can be very powerful.

NOTE

> Another property that may be set to BYLAYER or BYBLOCK is the Plot Style property. The Plot Style property is discussed in Chapter 20, "Productive Plotting."

If BYLAYER is used to define a child object's color, linetype, and lineweight, the layer on which the block is inserted controls the child object's color, linetype, and lineweight properties.

The following exercise demonstrates the effects of inserting a block whose color, linetype, and lineweight properties have been set to BYLAYER.

INSERTING A BLOCK WITH **BYLAYER** PROPERTIES

1. Open the 13DWG05. DWG drawing file on the accompanying CD. The screen is blank, containing no objects. In this drawing file, two blocks are already defined. The block C1 is a circle created on layer 0 with its color, linetype, and lineweight properties set to BYLAYER. The block C2 is a circle created on layer 0 with its color, linetype, and lineweight properties set to BYBLOCK.

   Note that on the Object Properties toolbar, the current layer is BLUE, and the layer's color, linetype, and lineweight properties are set to BYLAYER.

2. From the Insert pull-down menu, choose Block. The Insert dialog box appears.

3. From the Name drop-down list, choose the C1 block.

4. In the Insertion Point area, be sure the Specify On-Screen option is selected. In the Scale and Rotation areas, make sure the Specify On-Screen option is cleared.

5. Click OK to close the Insert dialog box.

6. Choose a location on the left side of the screen where you want to insert the block. The C1 block is inserted and assumes the color, linetype, and lineweight of the BLUE layer's property values. Remember, this occurs because the block's child objects were created on the layer 0, and their property values for color, linetype, and lineweight were set to BYLAYER.

In contrast, if BYBLOCK is used to define a child object's color, linetype, and lineweight, the current Object Creation values control the child object's color, linetype, and lineweight values. This is true no matter which layer the block is inserted on. These values are controlled from the Object Properties toolbar.

The following exercise demonstrates the effect of inserting the C2 block whose color, linetype, and lineweight properties have been set to BYBLOCK.

INSERTING A BLOCK WITH **BYBLOCK** PROPERTIES

1. Continue with the 13DWG05.DWG drawing file. From the Object Properties toolbar, change the Color property to Magenta, change the Linetype property to Hidden2, and change the Lineweight property to 0.020 inches.

2. From the Insert menu, choose Block. The Insert dialog box appears.

3. From the Name drop-down list, choose the C1 block.

4. Click OK to close the Insert dialog box.

5. Choose a location on the right side of the screen to insert the block.

Your screen should look similar to Figure 13.10. Notice that the C1 block acquired the color, linetype, and lineweight property values based on the layer's values, whereas the C2 block acquired the color, linetype, and lineweight property values set via the Object Properties toolbar.

Figure 13.10

The effects of BYLAYER and BYBLOCK on inserted blocks.

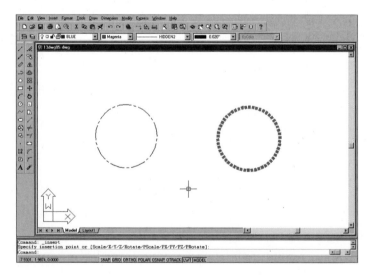

NOTE

DEFPOINTS is another layer that AutoCAD deals with uniquely. AutoCAD automatically creates this layer any time you draw associative dimensions. The unique property of this layer is that objects residing on this layer will not be plotted.

WARNING

Objects that would not plot have occasionally frustrated me, even though I could see them on-screen. The problem was that the objects, including blocks, were accidentally placed on the DEFPOINTS layer.

Redefining Blocks with In-Place Reference Editing

The ability to redefine blocks with In-Place Reference Editing is new with AutoCAD 2000. This feature allows you to edit an inserted block, altering its child objects and automatically redefining all block insertions. Although this feature allows you to edit inserted blocks, its real power is found in its ability to edit attached external references in the current drawing and save the changes to the original drawing (for more information, see Chapter 14, "Working with Drawings and External References Productively"). Nonetheless, you can use it to quickly edit an inserted block without having to explode the block. The following exercise shows you how.

EDITING A BLOCK WITH IN-PLACE REFERENCE EDITING

1. Open the 13DWG10.DWG drawing file on the accompanying CD. The drawing opens and displays four insertions of the same block.

2. From the Modify menu, choose In-Place Xref and Block Edit, Edit Reference. AutoCAD prompts you to select the reference to edit.

3. Choose the block in the upper-left corner named Terri. AutoCAD displays the Reference Edit dialog box. Notice the block's name is listed as Circle in a Square.

4. Select the Display Attribute Definitions for Editing option, as shown in Figure 13.11, because the name in the center of the block insertion is an attribute. Selecting this option allows you to edit the block's attribute.

Figure 13.11

The Reference Edit dialog box allows you to edit inserted blocks.

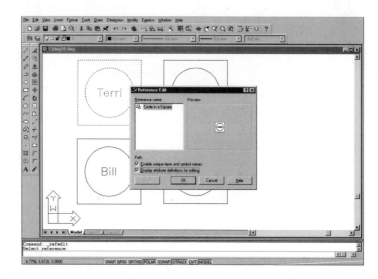

5. Click OK. AutoCAD prompts you to select nested objects.

6. Select the circle in the block named Terri, and then press Enter. The circle is added to the list of objects to edit. AutoCAD then displays the Refedit toolbar, as shown in Figure 13.12. There is no need to try to select the attribute.

Figure 13.12

The Refedit toolbar.

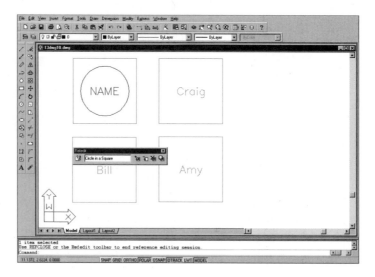

7. Choose the circle. AutoCAD highlights the circle and displays its grips.

8. Choose the grip in the bottom quadrant of the circle, and then drag the grip down to the bottom line in the square. Use the midpoint snap to snap the circle to the midpoint of the line. The circle's radius increases.

9. Right-click anywhere in the drawing area and choose Deselect All from the shortcut menu. The highlighted circle is unselected.

10. Choose the attribute, and then drag and drop it towards the lower half of the circle. Notice the enlarged circle object appears in all the blocks. However, the attribute you moved toward the lower half of the circle appears to not have changed, as shown in Figure 13.13. This occurs because changes in edited attributes do not change in previously inserted blocks, but only relocate in new block insertions.

Figure 13.13

The circle object is updated in all inserted blocks, but the block's attribute is not updated.

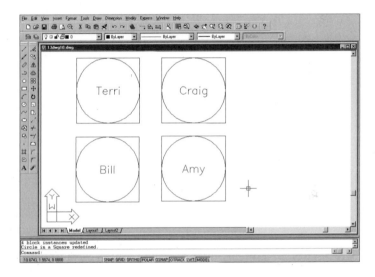

11. From the Insert menu, choose Block. The Insert dialog box displays.

12. Make sure the Circle in a Square block is selected in the Name drop-down list, click OK, and insert the block on the right side of the drawing. Then enter your name when prompted. AutoCAD inserts the revised block. Note that the attribute appears in its modified position in the lower half of the circle, as shown in Figure 13.14.

Figure 13.14

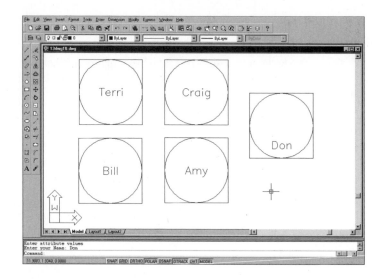

The redefined block attribute appears in its new position, but with new block insertions.

Using Nested Blocks

As was indicated earlier in this chapter, two significant reasons exist for using blocks. The first is to reduce a drawing's file size. The second is to quickly update all the insertions of a particular block. For example, suppose you have a block that is made up of a circle with a text object in its center, and you have inserted this particular block hundreds of times. If the text value is currently the letter M but needs to be changed to S, you can simply redefine the block with the correct letter. After you redefine it, the hundreds of block insertions are instantly updated with the S text value. This is a very valuable feature that can save you hours of editing time.

The previous example demonstrates a powerful feature of blocks. This power can be expanded through the use of nested blocks. A *nested block* is simply a block that contains other blocks and objects.

Nested blocks increase the power of blocks by making it easier for you to redefine blocks. For example, suppose you have a large block made up of numerous objects. Also suppose that one object in the large block occasionally changes color. Instead of redefining the large block and all its objects every time the object changes color, you can create a small block consisting of the one object and insert it as a nested block in the large block. Then, when it becomes necessary to change the object's color, you can redefine it in the small block. When you redefine it, the small block is automatically updated in the large block. The important point in this example is that the large block reflects the new color of the nested block object, but the large block does not have to be redefined.

One problem you must be aware of exists when you redefine nested blocks. To redefine a nested block, you must redefine it explicitly in the current drawing. If you redefine a nested block in its parent block outside of the current drawing and then use the -INSERT command to redefine the parent block in the current drawing, the nested blocks won't be updated. AutoCAD redefines only the parent block when you use the -INSERT command. The nested block definitions in the current drawing always take precedence over nested block definitions inserted from another drawing. The nomenclature for this is blockname=filename.

Using the -INSERT command with = is a technique that enables you to redefine a nested block. Simply WBLOCK the updated nested block to its own drawing, and then use the -INSERT command to redefine the nested block in the necessary drawing.

Managing Blocks Effectively

As you learn how to take advantage of the power of blocks, you will eventually develop hundreds of blocks, possibly more. You can further enhance the power of blocks by managing those blocks in a fashion that enables you and other users to quickly find the desired block definition. If you do not do this, productivity will be lost in one of two ways. First, it will take significant time to simply find the appropriate block. Second, if the block can't be found, it will take time to re-create the block from scratch. It is therefore necessary to establish criteria that everyone must follow to properly create and store blocks for future use.

WBLOCK Command

When you're creating a block library, the most important component is the block itself. Chances are you probably already have a wealth of predefined blocks residing in existing drawing files. These existing files are the first place you should go to develop your block library because they probably contain blocks your organization frequently uses.

Once you find useful predefined blocks in an existing drawing, you must export them as individual drawings. The WBLOCK command is a convenient way to quickly extract blocks from the current drawing.

When you type WBLOCK at the command prompt, the new Write Block dialog box appears (see Figure 13.15). This dialog box makes the process of exporting a block very intuitive. You can export an existing block by selecting the Block option, exporting the entire drawing, or selecting a group of objects and exporting them as a new block. When you have identified the desired block or objects, you can assign a new filename, determine the location in which to save the new block, and select its Insert Units. After selecting the desired options, you click the OK button, and AutoCAD exports the data and creates the new drawing. The new drawing file can then be inserted as a block into any drawing.

Figure 13.15

*The new Write Block
dialog box.*

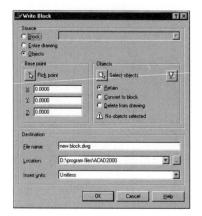

Organizing Blocks

The key to managing your block library is to organize the block locations using a well thought-out path structure. Store blocks in a standard location on each computer or on a network server, such as on the C drive under a subdirectory called WORK\BLOCKS. You can further organize blocks into classes and subclasses. The organizational structure should reflect a class structure used in your industry. For example, in civil engineering, it may be useful to organize standard storm drain junction structures using the following path structure:

```
C:\WORK\BLOCKS\STANDARDS\ORANGE_COUNTY\STORM_DRAIN\
JUNCTION_STRUCTURE-201A\STD-OC-SD-JS-201A.DWG
```

With this type of structure, a CAD technician could easily follow the path to find a particular block. If the block cannot be found in this path structure, the block probably has not been created yet. In such a case, it could be created in the current drawing and then WBLOCKed out to the appropriate path location.

AutoCAD DesignCenter

NEW
for R2000 AutoCAD 2000 introduces *AutoCAD DesignCenter (ADC)*, a new and powerful drawing content management tool. ADC helps you manage drawing content by providing tools for searching for, locating, and viewing blocks created in other drawings. Using these tools, you can quickly locate a desired block from among hundreds of drawings and insert it into your current drawing.

The important point to understand that makes this new feature so powerful is that ADC actually looks "inside" AutoCAD drawings for the desired block. For example, suppose you need to use a block of a sewer manhole, and you know that the block already exists in another drawing. Also suppose you do not know which drawing the block is in, and you must search hundreds of drawings. By using ADC's Find feature, you can quickly search through all drawings for a block whose name or description contains the word MANHOLE.

AutoCAD DesignCenter allows you to view blocks inside the selected drawing and displays both the block's graphic image and its description if they exist, as shown in Figure 13.16. When you find the desired block, you can drag and drop it into the current drawing. Additionally, if the block definition includes an Insert Units value and the current drawing's units are also defined in the Drawing Units dialog box, AutoCAD will automatically scale the block to its proper size in the current drawing.

Figure 13.16

The new AutoCAD DesignCenter makes finding blocks embedded in a drawing very easy.

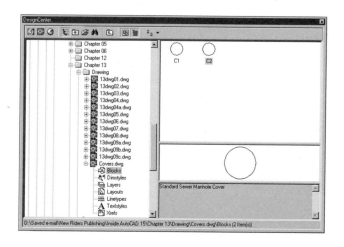

AutoCAD DesignCenter provides powerful tools for managing blocks. However, its capabilities go beyond simply managing blocks; they allow you to manage other drawing content such as external references, text styles, dimension styles, and more. For detailed information on ADC's features, refer to Chapter 12, "Applications for the New AutoCAD DesignCenter."

Summary

Blocks are a very powerful feature of AutoCAD. This chapter has shown you how to extract the power of blocks by explaining the nature of blocks. You learned what happens to AutoCAD's database when a block is defined and how the current UCS affects a block when it's being defined or inserted. You learned how AutoCAD stores a block definition in the Block Table and how it references the Block Table to create the Insert object. You saw the effects of defining blocks on a normal layer and on layer 0 and the difference between explicitly and implicitly defining the color, linetype, and lineweight properties of a block. This chapter also outlined the advantages of creating complex blocks from simpler blocks and the steps for redefining nested blocks with the -INSERT command. In addition, it presented several techniques for managing block libraries, which enable you to quickly find the block you need.

14

WORKING WITH DRAWINGS AND EXTERNAL REFERENCES PRODUCTIVELY

AutoCAD 2000 introduces several new features that enhance how you work with drawings and external references (xrefs). The Partial Open and Partial Load enhancements give you the ability to load only the portions of a drawing you need to edit. Another new feature allows you to edit external references from the current drawing. Understanding how to use these new features can increase your productivity.

This chapter shows you how to use these new features, and also provides an in-depth review of AutoCAD's external references. This chapter discusses the following subjects:

■ *AutoCAD's new Partial Open and Partial Load features*

■ *When you should use xrefs rather than blocks*

■ *Attaching versus overlaying xrefs*

■ *Permanently binding xrefs to the current drawing*

- Clipping xref boundaries
- Demand loading, and layer and spatial indexes
- Managing xrefs
- AutoCAD's new In-Place Reference Editing feature

Working with Drawings Productively

In previous releases of AutoCAD, to edit a drawing you simply opened it. Although this technique works fine in many editing situations, it can be a slow, tedious process if you're working with large drawing files. As a consequence, many technicians have developed procedures that help limit a drawing file's size, thereby increasing AutoCAD's response time when opening drawings and executing commands. One of these techniques included separating a large drawing into a group of smaller drawings. In some situations, a drawing was divided into a tiled grid, and each grid exported as its own drawing file. In other situations, a drawing was isolated by different layers, with each layer and all its objects saved as a single drawing file. Whichever method was used, the intent was the same: to decrease the drawing's file size and thereby increase productivity through faster response by AutoCAD.

The new Partial Open and Partial Load features provide the ability to simulate the advantages achieved when separating a drawing into smaller files without the need to divide the original drawing into groups of smaller drawings. These new features allow you to open only a portion of a drawing, thereby loading only the elements you need to edit. Objects can be loaded based on selected layers by choosing a predefined view, or by windowing in on an area. When you've finished, simply save the drawing normally. This new feature enables you to maintain a high level of productivity even while working on large drawings, and it avoids the management problems encountered by separating a single drawing into many smaller drawings.

AutoCAD 2000's New Partial Open Feature

NEW
for R2000   The new *Partial Open* feature allows you to open a portion of a drawing by either selecting the drawing's extents or the last view when the drawing was saved, or by selecting a predefined view if one exists. After you select the desired view option, you identify the object geometry you wish to load by selecting the layer(s) on which they reside.

The following exercise demonstrates how to use AutoCAD's new Partial Open feature.

USING THE NEW PARTIAL OPEN FEATURE

1. From the File menu, choose Open. The Select File dialog box appears.

2. From the accompanying CD, select the 14DWG01.DWG drawing file.

    The drawing appears in the Preview window as shown in Figure 14.1. Next, you load only a portion of the object geometry from the drawing.

Figure 14.1

The Partial Open feature is accessed from the Select File dialog box.

3. Click the Partial Open button. AutoCAD displays the Partial Open dialog box.

4. In the View Geometry to Load area, choose Area 1. This instructs AutoCAD to load objects that lie within or pass through the predefined view named Area 1.

5. In the Layer Geometry to Load area, select the check boxes next to layer names BUILDING, CONTOURS-INDEX, and CONTOURS-NORMAL, as shown in Figure 14.2. This instructs AutoCAD to load objects on the selected layers.

6. Save your changes.

Figure 14.2

The Partial Open dialog box allows you to identify the object geometry to load by selecting the view and the layers in which the objects reside.

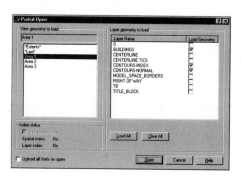

AutoCAD opens the drawing, loading only the objects that lie within or pass through the view, and that reside on the selected layers, as shown in Figure 14.3. At this point, you can edit the loaded geometry, create new objects, and zoom or pan the drawing. You can also create and modify data outside the area you opened. You are not limited by the initial view when working with partially opened drawings.

Figure 14.3

The Partial Open feature loads only the objects that lie within or pass through the selected view, and that reside on the selected layers.

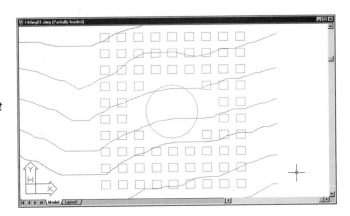

When you used the Partial Open feature in the previous exercise, you selected a view and three layers. However, it is not necessary to select layers. You can select a view, but leave all the check boxes next to the layer names cleared. If you do, when you click Open, AutoCAD issues a warning that no objects will be loaded. However, AutoCAD does load all the layers, and also loads all the other named objects such as blocks, text styles, dimension styles, and linetypes. Once the drawing is partially opened, it is possible to use these named objects to create new object geometry in the drawing without actually loading any existing geometry.

Another behavior unique to the new Partial Open is feature occurs when you save and then reopen a drawing that was partially opened. When you reopen the drawing, AutoCAD displays a warning noting that the drawing was partially opened when last saved. This warning, and the options it presents, is described in the next section.

AutoCAD 2000's New Partial Load Feature

NEW
for R2000   The new *Partial Load* feature allows you to load additional geometry into a drawing that is already partially opened. By using this feature, you can further refine the selection set of objects you load into the current editing session.

The following exercise demonstrates how to use AutoCAD's new Partial Load feature.

USING THE NEW PARTIAL LOAD FEATURE

1. From the File menu, choose Open. The Select File dialog box appears.

2. From the accompanying CD, select the 14DWG02.DWG drawing file.

   The drawing was created at the end of the previous exercise by saving the partially opened 14DWG01.DWG drawing file. Notice that the drawing's image does not appear in the Preview window. This is because the drawing was saved while only partially opened.

3. Click the Open button. AutoCAD displays a warning noting that the drawing was partially opened when last saved, as shown in Figure 14.4.

   AutoCAD presents three options for handling the file. By clicking the Fully Open button, you load all the drawing's object geometry. This is how AutoCAD normally opens a drawing. By clicking the Restore button, you partially open the drawing using the previous Partial Open settings. By clicking the Cancel button, you stop AutoCAD from loading the drawing and create a new drawing instead.

Figure 14.4

AutoCAD displays a warning when you select a file that was partially opened when last saved.

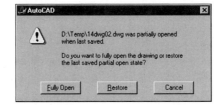

4. Click the Restore button. AutoCAD partially opens the drawing using the previous Partial Open settings that were saved with the drawing.

5. From the File menu, choose Partial Load. AutoCAD displays the Partial Load dialog box.

   This dialog box is almost identical to the Partial Open dialog box. The main difference is the Partial Load dialog box includes the Pick a Window button, which allows you to drag a selection window around the area from which to load objects.

6. In the Layer Geometry to Load area, select the check box next to the CENTERLINE layer name. This instructs AutoCAD to load objects on the selected layer.

7. Click the Pick a Window button, as shown in Figure 14.5. When AutoCAD temporarily removes the dialog box, create a window selection around the circle, after which AutoCAD redisplays the Partial Load dialog box.

8. Click OK. AutoCAD loads the objects within the defined area and on the CENTERLINE layer, as shown in Figure 14.6.

Figure 14.5

The Partial Load dialog box allows you to pick an area from which to load named objects.

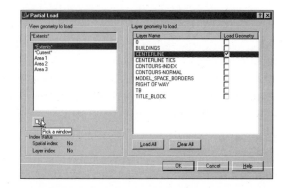

Figure 14.6

The objects within the defined area and on the CENTERLINE layer are partially loaded.

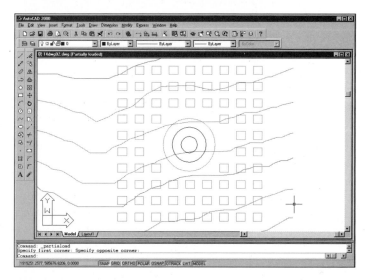

AutoCAD's new Partial Open and Partial Load features allow you to load specific objects into the current editing session. By using these features, you can reduce the time it takes to open a drawing and to execute AutoCAD's commands, and thereby increase productivity.

Working with External References Productively

External references, or *xrefs*, represent a powerful feature of AutoCAD. They provide the capability to create a composite drawing using other saved drawings, even while those other drawings are being edited. In a multidisciplinary work environment, you can attach another discipline's drawings to see the impact their design will have on your design. The drawings can be attached temporarily, or inserted permanently as a block. You can permanently insert the entire xref, or just its named objects, such as text styles or dimension styles. You can attach an entire xref or just the portions you need to review. You can even define an irregularly shaped polygon as the clipping boundary for the portion of the xref you want to attach. By attaching small clipped portions of an xref, you can dramatically reduce regen times.

Additionally, AutoCAD 2000 introduces a new feature called In-Place Reference Editing, which allows you to edit an attached xref from the current drawing, and save the changes back to the original drawing file. These versatile features make AutoCAD's xrefs a very powerful tool.

Using Xrefs Versus Blocks

External references have behavior that is similar to blocks. They can be inserted or "xreffed" into a drawing and used to display a group of objects as a single object. They can be copied multiple times, and all the insertions of a block or an xref can be changed by editing the original reference file. The only real difference between the two is that blocks are inserted permanently into the current drawing, becoming part of the drawing, whereas xrefs exist externally as independent files that are only attached to the current drawing.

So, if xrefs behave like blocks, then when should you use xrefs rather than blocks? One situation in which you should use xrefs is when the objects in external drawings that you need to view are undergoing change. When edits are made to an externally referenced file, you can reload the xref to update it to reflect the most recent condition of the xref. Additionally, AutoCAD automatically loads the latest version of an xreffed drawing when you open your drawing. This is not true with blocks.

Another reason to use xrefs instead of blocks is when the xreffed drawing is large. Not only can you keep the current drawing's file size low by attaching large drawings as xrefs, you can also instruct AutoCAD to only load a small portion of an xref instead of the entire xreffed drawing. This reduces the number of objects in the current drawing and therefore reduces file size and regen times.

Inserting an Xref: Attach Versus Overlay

You can link an xref to the current drawing in two different ways. You can either attach it or overlay it. Both methods enable you to turn layers on and off, or to freeze and thaw layers. Both enable you to change the color, linetypes, and lineweights of layers of xreffed drawings. Both methods are virtually identical, with one exception: *Attached* xrefs appear when nested in other xreffed drawings, whereas *overlays* do not.

The following exercise demonstrates the difference between attaching and overlaying an xref.

ATTACHING VERSUS OVERLAYING AN XREF

1. Open the 14DWG03c.DWG drawing file on the accompanying CD to display a Tentative Tract Map consisting of right-of-way lines, property lines, street centerlines, and proposed building pads.

   Next, you insert two xrefs. One you attach, and the other you overlay.

2. From the Insert menu, choose Xref Manager, and then click the Attach button. The Select Reference File dialog box opens.

3. From the Select Reference File dialog box, open the 14DWG03a.DWG drawing file. AutoCAD displays the External Reference dialog box.

4. In the External Reference dialog box, under Reference Type, choose Overlay.

5. In the Insertion Point area, Scale area, and Rotation area, clear any checked Specify On-Screen check boxes, as shown in Figure 14.7.

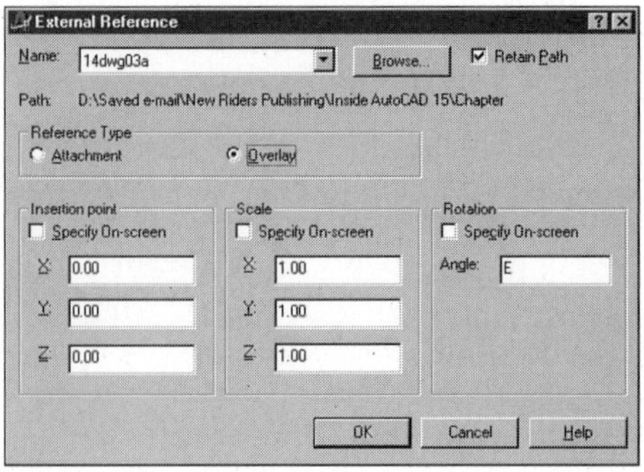

Figure 14.7

The Overlay option is selected in the External Reference dialog box.

6. Click OK. AutoCAD overlays the drawing and displays its existing contours.

7. From the Insert menu, choose External Reference. The Select Reference File dialog box opens.

8. From the Select Reference File dialog box, open the 14DWG03b.DWG drawing file. AutoCAD displays the External Reference dialog box.

9. In the External Reference dialog box, under Reference Type, choose Attachment.

10. In the Insertion Point area, Scale area, and Rotation area, clear any checked Specify On-Screen check boxes.

11. Click OK. AutoCAD attaches the drawing and displays its existing trees, as shown in Figure 14.8.

Figure 14.8

One xref is attached, and the other is overlaid in the current drawing.

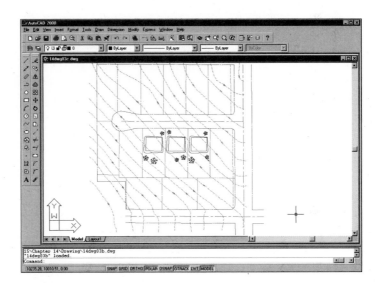

12. Save the file in the ACAD2000\SAMPLE directory.

13. Close the 14DWG03c.DWG drawing file.

14. Open the 14DWG03d.DWG drawing file on the accompanying CD. AutoCAD displays the drawing, which displays the building plans.

    Next, you insert the Tentative Tract Map drawing, with its two xrefs.

15. From the Insert menu, choose External Reference. The Select Reference File dialog box opens.

16. From the Select Reference File dialog box, open the 14DWG03c.DWG drawing file from the ACAD2000\SAMPLE directory. AutoCAD displays the External Reference dialog box.

17. In the External Reference dialog box, under Reference Type, choose Attachment.

18. In the Insertion Point area, Scale area, and Rotation area, clear any checked Specify On-Screen check boxes.

19. Click OK.

20. You may now exit the drawing without saving your changes.

AutoCAD attaches the drawing, as shown in Figure 14.9. It's important to realize that the existing Contours and the existing Trees drawings are already referenced in the Tentative Tract Map drawing, and are therefore nested xrefs. Note that the Trees xref appears, but that the Contours xref does not. This occurs because the Contours drawing was overlayed, whereas the Trees drawing was attached to the Tentative Tract Map drawing.

Figure 14.9

The nested trees xref appears, but the nested contours xref does not.

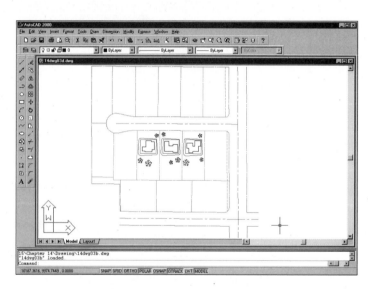

By using the attach and overlay features as shown in the preceding exercise, you can more easily manage the visibility of xreffed drawings.

NOTE

If the xref file you attach or overlay has objects organized with the DRAWORDER command, the objects will not appear in their proper drawing order. This is because the DRAWORDER command only works on objects in the current drawing, and not on objects in xrefs.

INSIDER TIP

You can force xref objects to appear in their desired drawing order by opening the xref and using the DRAWORDER command to arrange objects as desired, and then using the WBLOCK command to write the entire xref out as a new drawing. AutoCAD retains the desired drawing order when the xref is re-created using the WBLOCK command.

Unloading and Reloading Xrefs

After you have attached or overlaid xrefs, the xrefs can be unloaded and then reloaded as desired. This ability allows you to temporarily remove xrefs from a drawing so AutoCAD does not spend time calculating the positions of xref objects during regens. When you unload an xref, AutoCAD removes the xref from the current drawing, but leaves its path. To display the xref in the drawing again, you can reload the xref.

In addition to reloading xrefs that have been unloaded, you can also reload xrefs that are already loaded. This is useful when you know that an xreffed drawing is being edited, and you want to refresh the drawing's display to see any new changes that have taken place since you originally loaded the xref.

INSIDER TIP

Loaded xrefs can significantly increase regen times. If you are editing a drawing and do not need to see a loaded xref, use the UNLOAD command to remove it temporarily from the drawing. This will increase your productivity.

Permanently Inserting an Xref: Bind Versus Xbind

Occasionally, you may need to make an xref drawing a permanent part of the current drawing. When archiving files for permanent storage, for example, or when submitting a file to another technician, you may find it useful to make xrefs a part of the drawing to which they are attached, thereby combining all the drawings into a single dwg file. By combining the xrefs into a single drawing, you ensure that all the drawing data exists in a single file. You can make an xref a permanent part of another drawing by *binding* it to the drawing, which inserts the entire xref into the drawing as a block.

When you choose to bind an xref to the current drawing, AutoCAD prompts you to select the type of bind to use: Bind or Insert. When the Bind option is selected, AutoCAD inserts the xref into the current drawing, and prefixes all named objects with the xref's drawing name. Therefore, named objects such as layers, blocks, and text styles are prefixed by the xref's drawing name, and then inserted into the current drawing. However, if you choose the Insert option, AutoCAD inserts the drawing as a normal block, and does not prefix named objects with the xref's drawing name. Consequently, any duplicate named objects in the xref are ignored, and the named objects in the current drawing hold precedence.

This means, for example, that if a block in the xref has the same name as a block in the current drawing, the block in the current drawing will take precedence and will be substituted in place of all same name block insertions in the xref. Although this feature eliminates the redundancy of duplicate layer names, it may give unexpected results if you are not aware of duplicate named objects.

NOTE

When you attach an xref to a drawing, the xref's drawing name prefixes its layer names, which are separated by the pipe (|) symbol. When you bind the xref to the drawing, the pipe symbol is replaced by 0, where the zero represents the first instance of a bound xref. If another xref with the same name as the first is also bound to the drawing, the zero increments to one, and appears as 1. This feature avoids potential problems when binding xrefs from different departments or companies that may coincidentally use the same xref name.

While binding an xref into the current drawing is useful under certain conditions, there are occasions when it is more useful to only bind an xref's named objects. You can accomplish this with the XBIND command.

Suppose, for example, that you have attached an xref to the current drawing. You intend to leave the xref attached for a short time only, and then detach it. After the xref is attached, you notice that some of its text objects are using a text style that you want to use in the current drawing. You can easily insert the text style in the current drawing with the XBIND command.

The following exercise demonstrates how to use XBIND to attach an xrefs-dependent text style.

XBINDING A DEPENDENT TEXT STYLE

1. Start a new drawing from scratch. Next, attach an xref drawing that contains the Simplex text style.

2. From the Insert menu, choose External Reference. The Select Reference File dialog box opens.

3. From the Select Reference File dialog box, open the 14DWG04.DWG drawing file on the accompanying CD.

4. In the External Reference dialog box, under Reference Type, choose Attachment.

5. In the Insertion Point area, Scale area, and Rotation area, clear any checked Specify On-Screen check boxes.

6. Click OK. AutoCAD attaches the xref, and the text appears in the current drawing.

    Next, use **XBIND** to insert the dependent text style.

7. From the Modify menu, choose Object, External, Reference, Bind. The Xbind dialog box appears.

8. Double-click on the highlighted xref name.

    AutoCAD displays the five named object headings in the xreffed drawing. Notice that a small box containing a plus (+) sign is next to two of the named object headings.

9. Click on the box with the plus sign next to the Textstyle heading. AutoCAD displays two dependent text style objects.

10. Choose the 14DWG04|SIMPLEX text style object. The selected text style symbol is highlighted.

11. Click the Add button. The highlighted text style object appears in the Definitions to Bind text box, as shown in Figure 14.10.

Figure 14.10

The XBIND *command allows you to insert named objects such as text styles from xreffed drawings into the current drawing.*

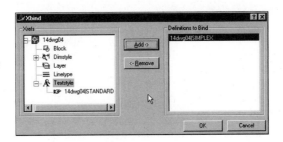

12.   Click OK. AutoCAD binds the text style object to the current drawing.

13.   From the Format menu, choose Text Style. The Text Style dialog box opens.

14.   Under Style Name, open the drop-down list and look at the available style names.

Notice that the text style 14DWG04$0$SIMPLEX is listed as a selection, as shown in Figure 14.11. AutoCAD always prefixes bound named objects with their original drawing's filename.

15.   You may exit the style command and quit the drawing without saving changes.

Figure 14.11

The text style is inserted from the xref file.

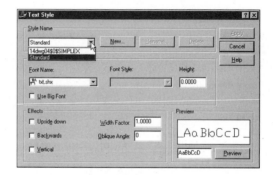

N O T E

XBIND does not permit you to load view objects from the attached drawing.

By using AutoCAD's Bind and Xbind features, you can permanently insert the entire xref, or just insert specific named objects, such as text styles and linetypes.

Clipping Boundaries

The XCLIP command allows you to use rectangles and irregularly shaped polygons to define clipping boundaries for xrefs. The polygons can be created on the fly or by selecting an existing 2D polyline. After the clipping boundary has been chosen, AutoCAD removes from display any portion of the xref that lies *outside* the clipping boundary.

The following exercise demonstrates how to use the Select Polyline feature of the XCLIP command to define the xref clipping boundaries with an irregular polygon.

USING THE SELECT POLYLINE FEATURE OF THE XCLIP COMMAND

1. Open the 14DWG05b.DWG drawing file on the accompanying CD. The 14DWG05a.DWG drawing file is already attached as an xref.

2. From the Modify menu, choose Clip, Xref.

3. Select the xref and press enter.

4. Press enter again to accept the default for a new boundary.

5. Type **s** to choose Select Polyline.

6. Select the large, green polyline.

   AutoCAD determines the limits of the clipping boundary and redisplays only the portion of the xref that is inside the clipping boundary, as shown in Figure 14.12.

7. Keep the drawing open for a following exercise.

Figure 14.12

The xref is clipped using the polyline.

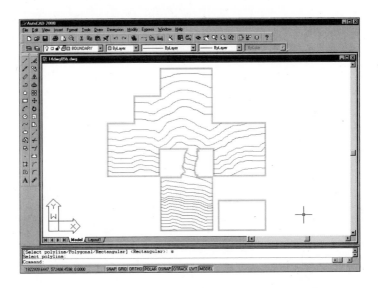

The preceding exercise demonstrated how to use the Select Polyline feature of the XCLIP command. In some cases, however, defining only one clipping boundary for the xref may not be enough. The following section leads you through the necessary steps to create multiple boundaries.

Creating Multiple Clipping Boundaries

One limitation of the XCLIP feature is that an xref can have only one clipping boundary. But what if you want to clip the same xref with more than one polygon? How do you create multiple clipping boundaries? One answer is to insert the same xref more than once.

The following exercise demonstrates how to use two separate polygons to create two clipping boundaries for the same xref.

CREATING MULTIPLE CLIPPING BOUNDARIES FOR THE SAME XREF

1. Continue with the 14DWG05b.DWG drawing from the previous exercise.

2. Choose the Copy command from the Modify pull-down menu and select the xref 14DWG05a that has been clipped.

3. At the `Specify base point or displacement, or [Multiple]:` prompt, type @ and press enter twice.

4. AutoCAD "attaches" the xref again, creating a duplicate xref on top of the existing clipped xref.

   Next, use the Select Polyline feature of the XCLIP command to clip the xref by selecting the small rectangular polygon.

5. From the Modify menu, choose Clip, Xref.

6. Select one of the xrefs in the large area and then press enter.

   Because the first xref has been clipped, it can be selected only from inside the large polygon.

7. Press enter to accept the new boundary default.

8. Type **S** to choose Select Polyline.

9. Select the small, green rectangle.

10. You may now close the drawing without saving.

AutoCAD determines the limits of the clipping boundary and then redisplays only the portion of the copied xref that is inside the small rectangular clipping boundary, as shown in Figure 14.13.

Figure 14.13

The same xref is inserted twice, and each xref is clipped separately.

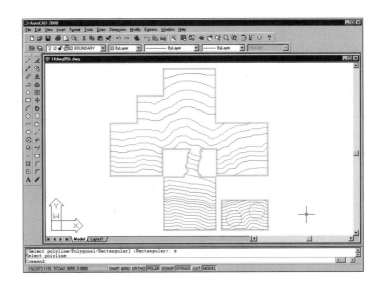

INSIDER TIP

As an alternate method of inserting a copy of an xref, you could use the RENAME command to rename the original xref insertion, then insert the xref again, and xclip the new insertion. This method would then create two uniquely named xrefs, which is useful for modifying different xref layer properties.

INSIDER TIP

The xref can be renamed from the Xref Manager dialog box. Simply highlight the xref to be renamed, then press F2. After you change the name, press Enter.

Demand Loading

Demand Loading works in conjunction with layer and spatial indexes, and reduces regen times. By enabling Demand Loading when using xrefs, AutoCAD loads only specific objects from the xref into the current drawing. By loading only a portion of the xref's objects, the number of objects in the current editing session is minimized, thereby increasing AutoCAD's performance.

Demand Loading is controlled by a system variable named XLOADCTL, which controls how AutoCAD uses layer and spatial indexes that may exist in xrefs. By enabling Demand Loading (setting XLOADCTL to either 1 or 2), AutoCAD loads only objects on layers that are thawed when the xref has layer indexes, and loads only objects within the clipping boundary when the xref has spatial indexes. The following table shows the variable's three settings and their effects.

Table 14.1

The Demand Loading Settings

Setting	Effect
0—Disabled	Turns off Demand Loading.
1—enabled	Turns on Demand Loading, and prevents other users from editing the drawing file while it is xreffed.
2—enabled with Copy	Turns on Demand Loading, and creates a copy of the drawing that it xrefs. This allows other users to edit the xref's original drawing.

In most networked environments, a setting of 0 is preferred. With today's newer systems, the time-savings provided by setting 1 is negated by the problems with xreffing drawings that others have open or xreffed. Setting 2 can be useful because of its time-savings, but can result in increased hard disk activity by the duplication of the dwg file.

N O T E

> The XLOADCTL system variable's settings can be controlled through the Options dialog box, from the Open and Save tab. For more information, refer to Chapter 3, "Controlling the AutoCAD 2000 Drawing Environment," in the section "External References."

Layer and Spatial Indexes

In the previous section, you learned about the system variable that controls Demand Loading. AutoCAD has another system variable, called INDEXCTL, that controls layer and spatial indexing, and works in conjunction with the Demand Loading system variable, XLOADCTL.

When *layer indexing* is enabled, AutoCAD does not load xref objects residing on layers that are frozen in the external reference drawing. When *spatial indexing* is enabled, AutoCAD will not load xref objects that reside outside the clip boundary. In both cases, fewer objects are brought into the current drawing, and regen times are reduced.

By enabling the INDEXCTL system variable, AutoCAD's performance can be enhanced by reducing the regen times of drawings with xrefs. The following table shows the variable's four settings and their effects.

Table 14.2

The layer and spatial index Settings

Setting	Effect
0—None	Both layer and spatial indexing are disabled.
1—Layer	Only layer indexing is enabled.
2—Spatial	Only spatial indexing is enabled.
3—Layer & Spatial	Both layer and spatial indexing are enabled.

NOTE

Setting the INDEXCTL system variable to a value other than 0 enables layer or spatial indexing (or both). Consequently, when the drawing is saved, AutoCAD adds to it the additional layer and spatial index data, thereby increasing the drawing's file size.

Spatial indexes work three dimensionally by defining a front and back clipping plane. The front and back clipping planes are defined via the XCLIP command's clipdepth option. By creating a clipping boundary and specifying the clipdepth, you can greatly limit the xref objects that AutoCAD loads into the current drawing session.

Layer and spatial indexes are created in a drawing when the INDEXCTL system variable is set to the desired value and the drawing is then saved. If INDEXCTL is set to 3, for example, both layer and spatial indexes are created when the current drawing is saved. The indexes are saved with the drawing file. Consequently, if you attach the drawing as an xref to a new drawing that has Demand Loading enabled, AutoCAD uses the xref's layer and spatial indexes to load only those objects that are on thawed layers and lie within the clipping boundary.

NOTE

Layer and spatial indexes are available only with Release 14 and AutoCAD 2000 drawings. Previous releases of AutoCAD do not create layer and spatial indexes when drawings are saved.

INSIDER **T**IP

Leave the INDEXCTL system variable set to its default value of 0 to help keep the drawing's file size minimal. Only set the variable to a value other than 0 when the file you are saving is to be used as an xref, and the layer and spatial indexes will be used by the Demand Loading feature.

Managing Xrefs

The advantage of using xrefs is that they provide the capability to create composite drawings that have relatively small file sizes and are easily updated. Unfortunately, on large projects involving multiple disciplines, keeping track of xref drawings can be difficult. Proper xref management is critical to ensure that composite drawings can find the latest versions of xrefs on stand-alone stations or over networks. Features available in AutoCAD can make managing xrefs easier.

The Xref Manager

The *Xref Manager* makes the task of managing xrefs easier. The dialog box's diagrams and intuitive button commands are great visual aids, as is its display of such pertinent data as the xref's name and path, current load status, whether the xref is attached or overlayed, and the xref's file size and last modification date.

Displaying Xrefs with List View Versus Tree View

When the *Tree View* feature is selected, it displays any nested xrefs that may exist and a diagram of the hierarchy of xrefs. This feature makes it easy to see which xrefs have been attached and how they relate to one another.

NOTE

The Tree View feature instantly displays a visual diagram of xrefs and any nested xrefs. More importantly, the nested xrefs are actually shown attached to their parent xref.

The following exercise demonstrates the Tree View feature.

ACCESSING TREE VIEW DISPLAY

1. Open the 14DWG06a.DWG drawing file on the accompanying CD.

   The drawing contains two xrefs, each of which also contains two xrefs. When the drawing opens, the hierarchy of the xrefs and nested xrefs appears on screen, as shown in Figure 14.14.

Figure 14.14

The hierarchy of the xrefs and nested xrefs.

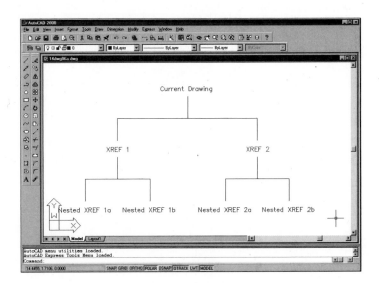

2. From the Insert menu, choose Xref Manager. The Xref Manager dialog box opens. Initially, it opens in List View mode. Two buttons appear in the upper-left corner of the dialog box. The one on the left, the List View button, is grayed. The one on the right is the Tree View button.

INSIDER TIP

> In *List View* mode, you can sort the xrefs in the display box in ascending or descending order. This is true for any of the displayed data. To sort, choose a column's title bar. AutoCAD sorts the data in ascending order based on the selected column. Select the column's bar again to sort the data in descending order.

3. Click on the Tree View button.

   The text box below the buttons changes and now displays the hierarchy of the xrefs, as shown in Figure 14.15. From this display, you can easily manage the xrefs. For example, you can unload a nested xref that is no longer needed.

Figure 14.15

The Xref Manager in Tree View mode.

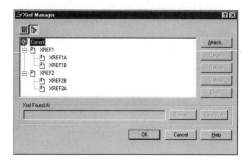

4. In the Xref Manager, choose XREF1A. Several buttons in the Xref Manager become active, and the xref's path and drawing filename appear, as shown in Figure 14.16.

Figure 14.16

The Xref Manager's buttons activate when XREF1A is selected.

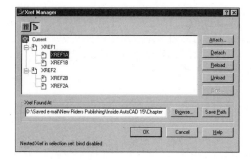

5. Click the Unload button, then click OK.

   AutoCAD unloads the nested xref XREF1A and redisplays the drawing, as shown in Figure 14.17.

Figure 14.17

*The Xref Tree View
illustrating the condition
after XREF1A is unloaded.*

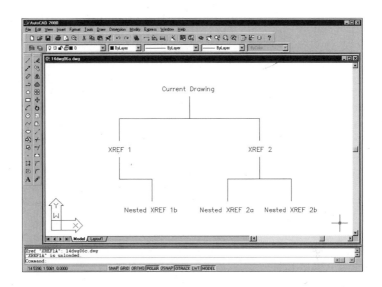

INSIDER TIP

The best way to eliminate display of unwanted nested xrefs is to overlay an xref, but you can achieve the same effect—reducing regen time—by unloading an unwanted nested xref.

NOTE

In previous releases, xref-dependent layer names in the current drawing could be only 31 characters long. Because AutoCAD would add the xref's drawing name to its layer names, if the layer's names were long, AutoCAD would abort loading the xref. With AutoCAD 2000, layer names can be 255 characters long. More importantly, the xref's drawing name does not count toward the 255-character limit.

WARNING

It is not recommended that you use long layer names if the data is to be used by R14 or earlier. Even though AutoCAD 2000 supports long names, these names cannot be read properly by older versions.

Explicit and Implicit Xref Paths

An xref's path can be defined explicitly or implicitly. *Explicit paths* include the entire directory path and end with the xref's filename. *Implicit paths* contain only a partial subdirectory path and the xref's filename. AutoCAD saves both explicit and implicit path data with the drawing.

There is an advantage to saving the xref paths implicitly. If the drawing is opened on another workstation, AutoCAD will successfully resolve the xref as long as the implicit path hierarchy exists at the new workstation. In contrast, if the path is explicitly defined, AutoCAD will probably not find the xref file.

For example, suppose that a drawing lies in the following directory:

```
G:\WORK\JOB-ONE\14DWG07A.DWG
```

Also, suppose that this drawing has an xref attached that lies in the following directory:

```
G:\WORK\JOB-ONE\XREFS\14DWG07B.DWG
```

Both of these xref paths are explicitly defined. Notice that the entire drawing's path is shown, including its root directory. This means that while you edit the 14DWG07a.DWG file at the workstation on which it resides, AutoCAD can successfully resolve the xref because it will find it in the explicit path. In other words, the xref file is still located on the G drive, and in the subdirectory shown.

But what happens if the drawing and xref are moved to another workstation? Suppose that the files are moved to the following hard drive and directory:

```
C:\ACAD2000\SAMPLE\14DWG07A.DWG
C:\ACAD2000\SAMPLE\XREFS\14DWG07B.DWG
```

The 14DWG07a.DWG file can still be opened in AutoCAD on the new workstation after it is located, but if the xref's path is not in the explicitly defined path, AutoCAD issues the following error message:

```
Resolve Xref XREF1: D:\WORK\JOB-ONE\XREFS\14DWG07B.dwg
Can't find D:\WORK\JOB-ONE\XREFS\14DWG07B.dwg
```

AutoCAD indicates that it can't find the xref indicated by the explicitly defined path. Consequently, AutoCAD opens the 14DWG07a.DWG drawing without resolving the attachment of the xref (which it could not find). To avoid the problem of unresolved xrefs, you can redefine the xref's path implicitly, as described in the following exercise.

IMPLICITLY DEFINING AN XREF'S PATH

1. Create a new directory folder called XREFS in the ACAD2000\SAMPLE subdirectory.

2. Copy the 14DWG07a.DWG drawing file on the accompanying CD into the ACAD2000\SAMPLE subdirectory.

3. Copy the 14DWG07b.DWG drawing file on the accompanying CD into the ACAD2000\SAMPLE\XREFS subdirectory.

4. Open the 14DWG07a.DWG drawing file from the ACAD2000\SAMPLE directory.

    The drawing opens, and then issues the warning that it can't find the xref. (By pressing F2, you can toggle on the AutoCAD Text Window and view the information.)

5. From the Insert pull-down menu, choose Xref Manager. The Xref Manager appears, as shown in Figure 14.18. Notice that the XREF1 drawing file's status is Not Found. Also notice that AutoCAD looked for the xref in the explicitly defined path location listed in the Saved Path column.

Figure 14.18

AutoCAD cannot find the xref using its explicitly defined path.

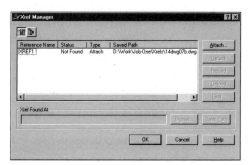

6. Select the reference name XREF1. The Xref Found At text box becomes active.

7. Click the Browse button. The Select New Path dialog box opens.

8. Open the 14DWG07b.DWG drawing file from the ACAD2000\SAMPLE\XREFS directory.

    The display returns to the Xref Manager. The xref's path is now displayed in the Xref Found At text box, as shown in Figure 14.19. Notice that the XREF1 status is still Not Found.

9. Click the Reload button. The XREF1 status changes to Reload.

    Next, you redefine the xref's path implicitly.

10. In the Xref Found At text box, highlight the beginning portion of the path, from the root directory listing up to the Xrefs folder, as shown in Figure 14.20.

Figure 14.19

The XREF1 file's location is displayed in the Xref Found At text box.

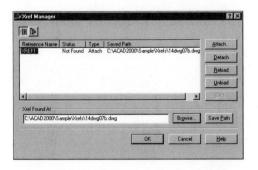

Figure 14.20

The beginning portion of the XREF1 file's path is selected, then deleted.

11. Press the Delete key. AutoCAD deletes the highlighted portion of the path.

12. Press Enter to save the modified path as the implicit path. AutoCAD redefines the path as implicit, and displays it in the Saved Path column, as shown in Figure 14.21.

Figure 14.21

The XREF1 file's path is redefined as implicit.

13. Click OK.

14. You may close the drawing without saving your changes.

AutoCAD resolves the xref, and loads it into the current drawing. AutoCAD was able to resolve XREF1 using the implicit path because the 14DWG07a.DWG and the XREFS folder were in the same folder. In the exercise, both were in the SAMPLE folder.

With the xref's path now implicitly defined and saved with the drawing, if the 14DWG07a.DWG file is moved to a different folder, and the 14DWG07b.DWG is moved and placed in a subfolder named XREFS, AutoCAD will resolve the xref when the 14DWG07a.DWG is opened. This is true as long as the 14DWG07a.DWG and the XREFS subfolder are placed in the same folder.

By using the preceding technique to define xref paths implicitly, you can avoid the problem of unresolved xrefs when transferring drawing files from one workstation to another.

INSIDER TIP

> You can use the PROJECTNAME system variable to assign xref search paths to your workstation. By assigning the search paths to a project name, you can resolve xrefs although their paths are defined explicitly or implicitly. For more information, see the section "Using PROJECTNAME to Specify Xref Search Paths."

Circular Xrefs

Circular xrefs occur when two drawings are inserted as xrefs into each other. For example, suppose you have drawing A and drawing B. A circular xref occurs when drawing A is attached as an xref into drawing B, and then drawing B is attached as an xref into drawing A.

In releases prior to Release 14, AutoCAD would issue a warning about the circular reference and abort the XREF command. Now, AutoCAD loads the xref up to the point where the circularity exists. It stops at the point of circularity because a drawing cannot load itself as an xref.

WARNING

> A circularity anomaly introduced into AutoCAD 2000 can cause problems in certain file naming techniques. If a drawing has a period in its name other than the one separating the name and dwg suffix (filename.dwg), attaching xrefs will be halted if they share the same name up to the first period. For example: A2.10.dwg could not attach xref A2.10-2.dwg because AutoCAD 2000 would assume circularity at the A2. and halt attachment.

Using PROJECTNAME to Specify Xref Search Paths

The PROJECTNAME system variable allows you to assign a project name to a drawing. The project name can also be declared in AutoCAD on each workstation, and assigned search paths for xrefs. By assigning xref search paths to a project name on a workstation, you can load a drawing that has the same project name assigned to its PROJECTNAME variable, and thereby use the workstation's search paths to resolve xrefs.

AutoCAD saves the project name in the workstation's system Registry, and includes the search paths assigned to the project name. AutoCAD also saves the project name to the current drawing, but does not save the search paths in the drawing. What this means is that a particular project name can be assigned to a drawing that has xrefs attached, and each CAD technician can assign different xref paths to the same project name on his workstation. When the drawing is opened, no matter what xref paths are defined in the drawing, each workstation will resolve the drawing's xrefs. This feature avoids the problem of managing xref paths, either explicitly or implicitly, in order to resolve xrefs.

This feature also enables you to create multiple project names on your workstation, each of which can contain a specific set of xref search paths. This means you can have many project names defined for your workstation, each with its own set of xref search paths.

NOTE

When AutoCAD searches for xrefs, it searches first for xrefs in the current drawing's folder, then it searches using explicitly and implicitly defined paths. Next, it searches using the current project name search paths, and finally, it uses AutoCAD's default search paths.

The following exercise demonstrates how to add, remove, and modify project name search paths.

ADDING, REMOVING, AND MODIFYING PROJECT NAME SEARCH PATHS

1. Start a new drawing.

2. From the Tools menu, choose Options, then select the Files tab.

3. Double-click on the Project Files Search Path title. A subdirectory appears beneath the title. If you have not yet defined any project names, the only subdirectory listed is Empty.

4. To create a project name, choose the Project Files Search Path folder so it is highlighted, then click the Add button. AutoCAD creates a new folder with the title Project1. This name is ready to be edited.

5. Type a new project name, **Path One**, and press Enter. AutoCAD creates the new project name, as shown in Figure 14.22.

Figure 14.22

The new Path One project name is created.

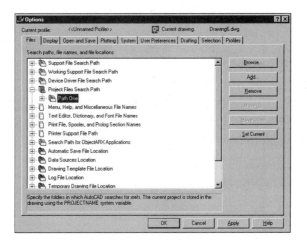

6. With the Path One project name still highlighted, click the Add button. AutoCAD creates a blank search path directory. You can either type in a search path, or browse for one.

7. Click the Browse button. The Browse for Folder dialog box appears.

8. Browse to the ACAD2000\SAMPLE subdirectory, open the Sample folder, and click OK. AutoCAD returns to the Options dialog box and displays the selected path, as shown in Figure 14.23.

9. To save the project name and its search paths, click the Apply button, then click OK.

10. You may close the drawing without saving your changes.

NOTE

It is recommended that you compare the speed of the loading xrefs via the PROJECTNAME variable and the Support File Search path from the Files tab in the Options dialog box. Some conditions may result in slower load times either way.

Figure 14.23

The xref path is assigned to the Path One project name.

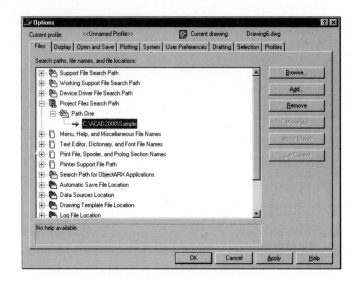

You can add as many paths as necessary to each project name, and you can create as many project names as you need.

When a project name is highlighted as shown in Figure 14.24, by clicking the Set Current button, you set the current drawing's PROJECTNAME variable to the highlighted project name. The highlighted project name's search paths then become the current paths AutoCAD uses to find xrefs.

Figure 14.24

Highlighting the project name and clicking the Set Current button sets the drawing's PROJECTNAME system variable.

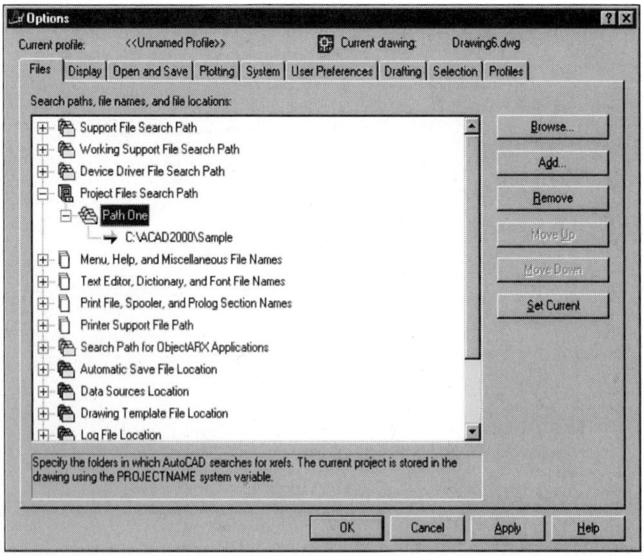

Xref Layers, Colors, Linetypes, and Lineweights

When an xref is attached to the current drawing, AutoCAD duplicates the xref's layer names in the current drawing. AutoCAD prefixes the layer names with the xref's name, followed by the pipe symbol (|). Then, AutoCAD assigns these new layers the same colors, linetypes, and lineweights as those in the xref drawing.

The only time AutoCAD does not assign the same colors, linetypes, and lineweights as those in the xref is when the objects are created on layer 0 in the xref. Just like blocks, these xref objects have special properties. If their color, linetype, and lineweight properties are set to BYLAYER, they assume the color, linetype, and lineweight of the layer on which the xref is inserted. If their color, linetype, and lineweight properties are set to BYBLOCK, they assume the color, linetype, and lineweight properties that are currently defined for the creation of new objects in the current drawing, as displayed in the Object Properties toolbar. Finally, if their color, linetype, and lineweight properties are explicitly defined in the xref, those properties remain fixed.

Except for colors, linetypes, and lineweights assigned explicitly in the xref, you can change the color, linetype, and lineweight of an xref's layers from the Layer Manager. These changes appear in the current drawing and do not affect the color, linetype, and lineweight in the original xref file. After you exit the drawing, however, any changes to the color, linetype, and lineweight properties are lost. When the drawing is opened again, the colors, linetypes, and lineweights assume the settings in the original xref.

INSIDER TIP

To save changes you make to an xref layer's color, linetype, and lineweight properties with the current drawing, set the system variable VISRETAIN to 1. When you open the drawing, the changes you made to the xref layer's color, linetype, and lineweight properties in a previous editing session are restored.

The New In-Place Reference Editing Feature

NEW
for R2000

AutoCAD 2000 introduces a powerful feature called *In-Place Reference Editing*. This new feature allows you to edit objects in an inserted xref file from the current drawing, and save the changes back to the xref file. You can use In-Place Reference Editing to quickly edit an inserted xref without the need to open the xref file.

In-Place Reference Editing is intended to allow you to make modest edits to an xref file from the current drawing. Although you can make significant changes to the xref file from the current drawing, it is more efficient to open the xref file to directly perform significant edits. Using In-Place Reference Editing to make significant changes to xref files can temporarily increase the current drawing's file size, thereby increasing regen times and slowing productivity. Therefore, use this new feature to quickly make modest edits to xrefs.

After you select the xref, you specify the objects you want to edit. AutoCAD temporarily brings the selected objects into the current drawing for modification and makes them part of a working set. After the objects are modified, the working set of objects is saved back to the xref file.

The following exercise demonstrates how to use In-Place Reference Editing.

EDITING AN XREF WITH IN-PLACE REFERENCE EDITING

1. Copy the files 14DWG08a.DWG and 14DWG08b.DWG from the accompanying CD to the ACAD2000\SAMPLE subdirectory. Before you continue with the exercise, you must clear the read-only attribute to edit and save changes back to the files.

2. From Windows Explorer, select the 14DWG08a.DWG and 14DWG08b.DWG drawing files in the ACAD2000\SAMPLE directory, then right-click to display the shortcut menu.

3. From the shortcut menu, choose Properties. The Properties dialog box appears.

4. From the Properties dialog box, clear the Read-Only check box, then click OK. The read-only attribute is cleared from the files.

    Next, you start a new drawing and insert the 14DWG08a.DWG file as an xref.

5. From AutoCAD, start a new drawing from scratch.

6. From the File menu, choose Save. AutoCAD displays the Save Drawing As dialog box.

7. Name the file MYFILE, and save it to the ACAD2000\SAMPLE subdirectory.

8. From the Insert menu, choose External Reference. The Select Reference File dialog box appears.

9. Open the 14DWG08a.DWG drawing file from the ACAD2000/SAMPLE directory. AutoCAD displays the External Reference dialog box.

10. In the External Reference dialog box, under Reference Type, choose Attachment.

11. In the Insertion Point area, Scale area, and Rotation area, clear any checked Specify On-Screen check boxes.

12. Click OK. AutoCAD attaches the drawing and displays two text objects inside a
     rectangle object.

     The upper text object is located in the 14DWG08a.DWG xref file. The lower text object
     is located in the 14DWG08b.DWG file, and is a nested xref.

13. Zoom in close to the objects to view them better.

14. From the Modify menu, choose In-Place Xref and Block Edit, Edit Reference.
     AutoCAD prompts you to select a reference.

15. Select the lower text object. AutoCAD displays the Reference Edit dialog box, which
     shows the two xref filenames.

     Because the 14DWG08b.DWG file is nested within the 14DWG08a.DWG file, and you
     selected the text object that's in the nested xref, AutoCAD displays both names. At this
     point, you select the file whose objects you wish to edit.

16. In the Reference Name area, choose the 14DWG08b.DWG file. AutoCAD highlights the
     selected xref name, as shown in Figure 14.25.

Figure 14.25

*The Reference Edit dialog
box allows you to select
the xref to edit.*

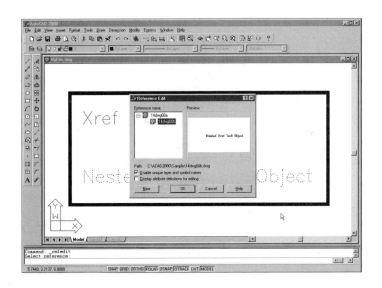

17. Be sure the Enable Unique Layer and Symbol Names check box is selected, and that
     the Display Attribute Definitions for Editing check box is cleared.

NOTE

AutoCAD assigns temporary layer names to the current drawing when the Enable Unique
Layer and Symbol Names check box is selected.

18. Click OK. AutoCAD prompts you to select the nested objects.

19. Choose the lower text object, then press Enter to end object selection. AutoCAD
    visually moves the selected object into the current drawing, and displays the Refedit
    toolbar.

    Notice that AutoCAD fades objects that are not being edited, as shown in Figure 14.26.
    This makes it easier to identify the objects you selected for editing.

Figure 14.26

*AutoCAD fades objects
that are not being edited.*

NOTE

> You can adjust the fading intensity from the Display tab found on the Options dialog box,
> which is displayed from the Tools menu by choosing Options.

Next, you edit the lower text object, and save the changes back to its xref.

20. Select the lower text object. AutoCAD highlights the object.

21. Right-click to display the shortcut menu, then choose Text Edit. AutoCAD displays the
    Text Edit dialog box.

22. In the text box, replace the highlighted text with the word **MODIFIED**.

23. Click OK, then press Enter to end object selection. AutoCAD modifies the text object.

24. Click the Save Back Changes to Reference button, as shown in Figure 14.27. AutoCAD
    issues a warning noting that all reference edits will be saved.

Figure 14.27

Figure 14.27

The edits to xref objects are saved back to their original xref file.

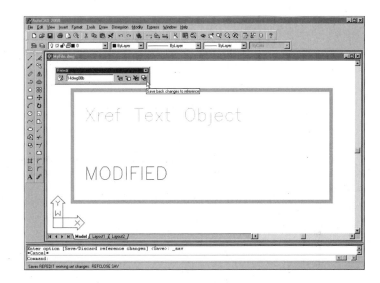

25. Click OK. AutoCAD saves the changes back to the xref file, then exits the reference edit mode.

26. You may close the drawing without saving your changes.

At this point, if you open the 14DWG08b.DWG drawing from the ACAD2000\SAMPLE directory, you will notice that the text object is changed to MODIFIED.

AutoCAD allows you to add or remove additional objects to the working set. This is done by clicking the Add or Remove Objects from the Working Set buttons, located on the Refedit toolbar. If you decide you don't want to save edits back to the original xref, you can click the Discard Changes button.

While in the reference edit mode, if you create new objects, they are almost always added to the working set. There are some situations in which this is not true, such as when AutoCAD generates an arc object during the fillet command.

Although AutoCAD fades objects that are not part of the working set, the objects can still be edited, so caution should be taken. For example, if the MyFile drawing contained another text object, you could edit its text string. The changes you make to it, however, would only be saved in the current drawing.

Summary

In this chapter, you learned about AutoCAD's new Partial Open and Partial Load features, and about the new In-Place Reference Editing feature. You also learned about the differences between attaching and overlaying xrefs, and about the differences between binding and xbinding xrefs. You reviewed how to create clipping boundaries, and you learned how to increase productivity with Demand Loading and spatial and layer indexes. The way AutoCAD deals with circular xrefs was covered, as was the PROJECTNAME system variable, and the way it stores xref's paths. You also learned about the Xref Manager, and how it is used to manage xrefs and nested xrefs.

AutoCAD's xref capabilities are powerful. You can save regen time and increase your productivity by using these xref features to better manage xrefs.

P A R T   IV

ANNOTATING, DIMENSIONING, AND PLOTTING

15

TEXT ANNOTATION

Text is a very important part of any drawing. On any given drawing, you may need to draw a single word, a single sentence, or even paragraphs of text. Being able to efficiently draw and edit text directly affects your productivity. In this chapter, you learn how to do the following:

■ *Draw and edit single lines of text*

■ *Define and use text styles to control the appearance of your text*

■ *Draw and edit paragraphs of text*

■ *Perform a spelling check on your drawing*

■ *Invoke Quick Text mode, mapping fonts, and the Clipboard*

Drawing Single-Line Text

A single line of text can consist of a single character, a word, or a complete sentence. The easiest way to draw such text is to use the DTEXT command. To insert a single line of text, open the Draw menu and choose Text, Single Line Text. The initial prompt displayed in the command window presents several options:

```
Specify start point of text or [Justify/Style]:
```

The default option is to specify the lower-left corner, otherwise known as the *start point*, of the new line of text. After picking the start point, you are prompted to supply the height (unless the height is set in the style being used), the rotation angle of the text, and the new text to be drawn. As you type the text, it is displayed on your drawing. If you make a typographical error, you can use the Backspace key to delete the error and retype the text. You signify the end of the line of text by pressing the Enter key, at which point you can begin a new line of text immediately below the line of text just created. To stop adding lines of text, press the Enter key without typing any new text. You can also relocate the next line of text by picking a point with the cursor.

NOTE

AutoCAD 2000 replaces the TEXT command with the DTEXT command. Therefore, when you type TEXT at the command prompt, you are actually starting the DTEXT command.

When you enter text, you can take advantage of the command line buffer to repeat previously entered text. You use the up and down arrow keys to scroll through the buffer.

INSIDER **T**IP

The spacing between successive lines of text is fixed at a factor of approximately 1.67 of the text height. This spacing is normally fixed; however, each line of text created with the DTEXT command is a separate object. As such, you can use the MOVE command to rearrange the lines. You also can pick a new justification point at the Text: prompt before typing the new line of text; this overrides the default line spacing.

Typing the text you want to create is the easy part. It is also important to know how to format the text according to your needs. The following sections discuss how to choose the correct text height, justification, and text style. You also learn how to continue text below the previous line, use special formatting codes and symbols, and edit text.

In the following exercise, you use DTEXT to add several lines of text to a site drawing.

DRAWING SINGLE-LINE TEXT USING DTEXT

1. Open the drawing 15dwg01.dwg from the accompanying CD. This is a site drawing set up in paper space with a model space scale in which 1 drawing unit is equal to 100 feet (1:100 scale).

2. Make sure you are in paper space. Choose Named Views from the View menu to restore the view TITLE_BLOCK. Make sure the layer named TEXT is current.

3. From the Draw menu, choose Text, Single Line Text. Using the Style option, set the current style to STANDARD. Using the Justify option, set the justification option to Center and pick the point 29,2.5 as the center point. Specify a height of 0.3 and a rotation angle of 0.

   Type **ACME Engineering** and press the Enter key twice.

4. Repeat the DTEXT command. Pick the point 26.75,2 as the start point. Remember, the default justification is left-justified text, but that is what we want now. Use a height of 0.2 and a rotation angle of 0.

   Type **Bakersville Project** and press the Enter key once. Type **Legend & General Notes** and press the Enter key twice.

5. Repeat the DTEXT command. Type **M** at the start point prompt to specify Middle as the justification setting.

   You can bypass the Justify option and set the justification directly at the initial prompt. Pick the point 29.5,1 as the middle point. Use a height of 0.2 and a rotation angle of 0.

   Type **L100** and press the Enter key twice.

6. Repeat the DTEXT command. Type **R** at the start point prompt to specify Right justification.

   Pick the point 27.8,0.6 as the right point. Use a height of 0.1 and a rotation angle of 0.

   Type **1"=100'** and press the Enter key twice.

7. Restore the view ALL. Make the model space viewport active (choose the Model tab).

8. Issue the DTEXT command. Pick the point 855,1290 as the start point.

Use a text height of 50, which at a 1:100 plot scale will produce 1/2" text. Use a rotation angle of 10 degrees.

Type **Route 101** and press the Enter key twice.

9. Choose the Layout 1 tab. You can close the drawing without saving your changes. Figure 15.1 shows the outcome.

Figure 15.1

The single-line text added with the DTEXT *command.*

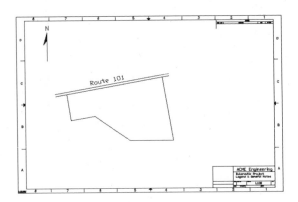

Now you know how to create new text in your drawing. The following section provides details on how to change text styles in accordance with your needs.

Choosing the Correct Text Height

The hardest part of drawing text is deciding on the correct text height for the scale for which the drawing is set up. Unfortunately, because AutoCAD does not have a built-in mechanism for storing and using the drawing scale to set the correct text height for full-size drawings, it is necessary to take into account the drawing scale when specifying the text height. Use Tables 15.1 and 15.2 to help you determine the correct text height. To use these tables, go to the row associated with your drawing scale, and then move along the row to the column associated with the height you want your text to have on your plot.

Table 15.1

Text Heights for Architectural Scales

Drawing Scale	Plotted Text Heights				
	3/32"	*1/8"*	*3/16"*	*1/4"*	*3/8"*
1/16"=1'	18"	24"	36"	48"	72"
3/32"=1'	12"	16"	24"	32"	48"
1/8"=1'	9"	12"	18"	24"	36"
3/16"=1'	6"	8"	12"	16"	24"
1/4"=1'	4.5"	6"	9"	12"	18"
1/2"=1'	2.25"	3"	4.5"	6"	9"

Table 15.2

Text Heights for Decimal Scales

Drawing Scale	Plotted Text Heights				
	3/32"	*1/8"*	*3/16"*	*1/4"*	*3/8"*
1:10	0.9375 d.u.*	1.25 d.u.	1.875 d.u.	2.5 d.u.	3.75 d.u.
1:20	1.8750 d.u.	2.50 d.u.	3.750 d.u.	5.0 d.u.	7.5 d.u.
1:50	4.6875 d.u.	6.25 d.u.	9.375 d.u.	12.5 d.u.	18.75 d.u.
1:100	9.3750 d.u.	12.50 d.u.	18.750 d.u.	25.0 d.u.	37.5 d.u.

*d.u. stands for drafting units

Choosing a Justification

The default option of DTEXT is to specify the left endpoint, or the start point, of the line of text. Specifying the Justify option at the initial DTEXT prompt displays the following prompt:

```
Enter an option [Align/Fit/Center/Middle/Right/TL/TC/TR/ML/MC/MR/BL/
BC/BR]:
```

Figure 15.2 shows the various justification options and their corresponding locations.

Figure 15.2

The possible justification points for a line of text.

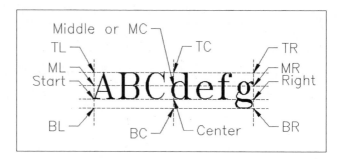

Unlike the justification options illustrated in Figure 15.2, the Align and Fit options require you to define two points.

Use the Align option when you want to specify the left and right endpoints of the text and do not care about the resulting height. The text height is automatically set to make the text fit between the specified points. Also, the angle from the first point to the second point is used as the rotation angle of the text.

Use the Fit option when you want to specify the left and right endpoints and the height of the text. To make the text fit between the specified points, AutoCAD varies the height-to-width ratio of the text characters. Therefore, you may end up with skinny-looking characters on one line and very fat-looking characters on the next.

I N S I D E R   T I P

You can enter the desired text justification option when the DTEXT command prompts for the Start point, which eliminates the need for first selecting the Justify option.

When the text is initially drawn with one of the alternate justification options specified, it is drawn left justified, as if the default justification were being used. When the DTEXT command ends, however, the text is redrawn with the correct justification.

N O T E

You can snap to the justification point of an existing line of text using the INSERT object snap mode.

This concludes the discussion of text justification options. The next section deals with the topic of text styles.

Choosing a Text Style

The appearance of the text drawn by DTEXT is controlled via a named group of settings referred to as a *Text Style*. The default text style supplied in the template drawings ACAD.DWT and ACADISO.DWT is STANDARD. In other template drawings, several text styles are predefined for you. Use the Style option to set the style you want to use to display text with the new style. The process of actually defining new styles and modifying existing ones is discussed in the section "Defining Text Styles," later in this chapter.

Continuing Below the Previous Line

If, after you end the DTEXT command, you want to draw an additional line of text below the last line drawn, you can easily do so by issuing the DTEXT command and pressing the Enter key instead of picking a new start point. DTEXT will then draw the new line of text right below the last one, using the style, height, and rotation angle of the previous line.

INSIDER **T**IP

> To help you spot the last line of text drawn, that line is highlighted when you begin DTEXT. The highlighting, however, may not be apparent if the text is too small on the screen.

Using Special Formatting Codes and Symbols

You can do a limited amount of formatting with the DTEXT command. For instance, you can add a line under or above the text simply by adding the codes %%u (for underlining) and %%o (for overlining) to the text as you enter it. The codes act as toggle switches; the first time you include the code in a line of text, it turns that effect on and is applied to the successive text characters. The second time you enter the code in the same line of text, the effect is turned off. If you do not enter the code a second time in the line of text, the effect is continued to the end of the text line but is not continued to the next line. For example, to draw the text shown in Figure 15.3, you would type this line of text: `%%uUnderlining%%u and %%oOverlining%%o can be used separately or %%o%%utogether.`

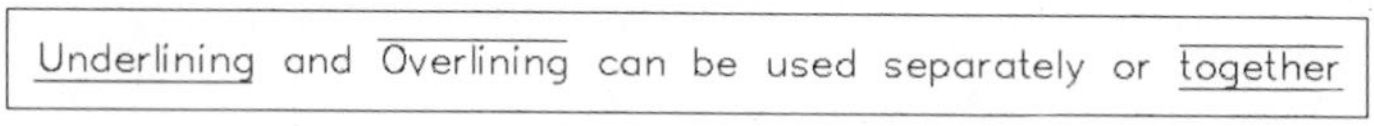

Figure 15.3

*Using underline and
overline formatting codes.*

Underlining and Overlining can be used separately or together

In addition to underlining and overlining, you also can draw symbols that are in the font file but are not on the keyboard. Table 15.3 shows several formatting codes and the resulting symbols.

Table 15.3

Additional Formatting Codes

Formatting Code	Symbol	Meaning
%%c	Ø	diameter
%%d	°	degree
%%p	±	plus/minus

The codes are not case-sensitive. In addition to the codes in Table 15.3, you can enter the code **%%nnn**, where **nnn** is a three-digit integer, to draw any character in a font file.

A much easier way of drawing a symbol is to use the Windows Character Map program. To use the Character Map program in place of the %%nnn code, simply start the Character Map program (usually found in the Accessories group of programs) and select the font file you have specified in the current text style. Then select the character you want to draw and copy it to the Clipboard. You can then paste the character into the text you are typing.

WARNING

Not all font files contain the same characters, which is why it is important that the font file you choose to copy from in the Character Map program is the same font file specified in the text style you are drawing with in AutoCAD. What the Character Map program actually copies when you copy a character to the Clipboard is the character's position number in the font chart. When you paste that character into AutoCAD, the character corresponding to the position number recorded in the Clipboard is drawn. Therefore, if you are using a different font file in AutoCAD, you may end up with a different character altogether.

After drawing and formatting the initial text, you may want to change the wording or appearance of the text. The following section covers the commands you will need to do this.

Editing Single-Line Text

Two commands are of particular use for editing existing text: DDEDIT and PROPERTIES. DDEDIT is easier to use than PROPERTIES when all you want to do is change the text string. PROPERTIES is more powerful than DDEDIT in that it displays the new Properties dialog box, which enables you to change several properties of the selected text.

Using DDEDIT

From the Modify menu, choose Text to issue the DDEDIT command. Select the text object to be changed, and the Edit Text dialog box appears, displaying the selected text (see Figure 15.4).

Figure 15.4

The Edit Text dialog box.

Initially, the entire line of text is highlighted and will be replaced by whatever you type. If you want to edit a specific portion of the text, position the cursor at the desired point in the text and pick it. You can then use the Insert, Delete, and Backspace keys to add and delete characters.

If you want to replace a portion of the text displayed in the Edit Text dialog box, highlight the portion to be replaced, and then type the new text. The highlighted portion is replaced with the text you type.

Using Properties

NEW
for R2000 Choose Properties from the Standard toolbar or the Modify menu to launch the new
Properties dialog box shown in Figure 15.5. The Properties dialog box allows you to
change the text string, style, justification point, and various settings that control the
appearance of the text object.

Figure 15.5

*The new Properties
dialog box.*

See "Defining Text Styles" later in this chapter for a clearer explanation of the text
settings you can change.

In the following exercise, you use DDEDIT and PROPERTIES to change some text in a
drawing.

EDITING SINGLE-LINE TEXT WITH DDEDIT AND PROPERTIES

1. Open the 15dwg02.dwg drawing from the accompanying CD. This is a site drawing set
    up in paper space with a model space scale of 1 drawing unit equal to 100 feet (1:100
    scale).

2. Choose Named Views from the View menu. Restore the view TITLE_BLOCK.

3. From the Modify menu, choose Text and select the text "Bakersville Project." High-
    light "ville" and type **field**. Click OK to make the change. Then press Enter to exit the
    DDEDIT command.

4. Choose Properties from the Object Properties toolbar. Select the text "L100." Press the Enter key to end the selection process. Change the Height property from 0.20 to 0.30, then press Enter to effect the height change. The text should look like that shown in Figure 15.6.

Figure 15.6

The text is modified with the DDEDIT *command and the new Properties dialog box.*

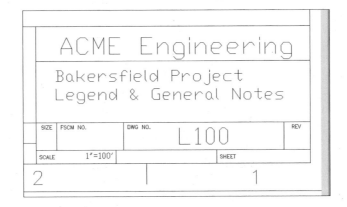

5. Close the drawing without saving your changes.

Defining Text Styles

A *text style* is a named group of settings that controls the appearance of text in a drawing. If you define several text styles, you can quickly select the text style you need for a particular text object, thereby automatically assigning such properties as font type and text height. By creating and using text styles, you can easily control the way your text looks.

The default text style (the only defined style) in the templates ACAD.DWT and ACADISO.DWT is named STANDARD. You can, however, define as many text styles as you want in a drawing (each of the other template files provided with AutoCAD has several predefined styles). Text styles are defined and modified with the STYLE command, which you issue by choosing Text Style from the Format menu. Figure 15.7 shows the Text Style dialog box. The various settings within the Text Style dialog box are explained in more detail in the following sections.

Figure 15.7

The Text Style dialog box.

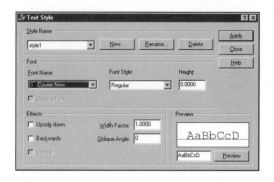

To create a new style, you actually begin by making a copy of the current style. If the current style is not the style you want to begin with, select the desired style from the list of existing styles (thereby making it the current style).

Click the New button. Specify a name for the new style, and a duplicate style is created from the selected style. To rename an existing style, select the style from the list of existing styles, click the Rename button, and enter a new name. To delete an existing style, highlight the name from the list of existing styles and click the Delete button. The Standard text style cannot be renamed or deleted.

NOTE

> When a text object is created, the style it is created with is recorded with the object. A text style can be deleted only if no existing text objects reference the style.

Text styles are stored in the drawing in which they are defined. If you want multiple styles to be available in a new drawing immediately, define the styles in your template drawings. If you want to import a style from another drawing, use AutoCAD's new DesignCenter. For more information on importing object tables into the current drawing, refer to Chapter 12, "Applications for the New AutoCAD DesignCenter."

When defining a new style or modifying an existing style, you must choose a font file, the special effects you want enabled, a text height, a width factor, and an oblique angle. Choosing these settings and previewing the results of these settings are covered in the following sections.

Previewing the Text Style Settings

The character Preview area enables you to view a sample of the selected style and the results of changing the various settings. To view your own sample text, type your sample text in the text edit box and click the Preview button.

Choosing a Font and Style

The font file is the file that contains the information that determines the shape of each character. Table 15.4 lists the various types of font files supplied with AutoCAD.

Table 15.4

Various Types of Font Files

File Name Extension	Font Type
SHX	AutoCAD's native font file, known as a shape file
TTF	TrueType font file

In addition to the TrueType font files supplied with AutoCAD, the TrueType fonts supplied with Windows and other Windows applications can also be used.

You can use PostScript files in AutoCAD. To do so, you must first use the COMPILE command to compile the PostScript (.pfb) font file into a shape file.

AutoCAD supports TrueType font families, which means that for some TrueType fonts, you can choose a font style such as regular, italic, bold, or bold italic. Note that not all TrueType fonts have more than the regular style defined.

Two system variables affect the plotting of text drawn with TrueType fonts: TEXTFILL and TEXTQLTY. When TEXTFILL is disabled, the characters are plotted in outline form only. If TEXTFILL is enabled, the characters are filled in. The value of TEXTQLTY affects the smoothness of the characters at plot time. The value of TEXTQLTY can be set from 0 to 100, with the default value set to 50. The higher the value, the better the resolution of the characters, but it will take longer to process the drawing for plotting. Both system variables can be typed at the Command: prompt and then set to the desired value.

INSIDER TIP

Using the simplest shaped characters will minimize the drawing size and speed up opening and working with the drawing file. Simpler shaped characters are those that use very few elements, or line segments, to define a character's shape. The characters in the Simplex and Romans font files are quite simple in appearance and are similar to the simplex characters used in board drafting. Some shape files contain the alphabet of foreign languages, such as GREEKS.SHX, or even symbols, such as SYMUSIC.SHX.

After you change the font file associated with an existing style, when you apply the change, all text that has already been drawn with the modified style is updated to reflect the change. If you want to draw text with more than one font file, you must create one style per font file and switch between the styles as you draw the text.

Setting a Height

Also found in the Font area of the Text Style dialog box is the text Height setting. The default height of 0 dictates that the user sets the text height at the time the text is drawn. A height other than 0 sets the text height for that particular style to that height. The style is then referred to as a fixed height style, and the text height prompt for the DTEXT command is suppressed.

Changing the text height setting of an existing style does not affect the appearance of existing text objects.

Specifying Special Effects

The Effects section of the Text Style dialog box contains the Upside Down, Backwards, Vertical, Width Factor, and Oblique Angle settings. These settings are covered in detail in the following sections.

Upside Down, Backwards, and Vertical Text

In the Effects area, you can enable the Upside Down, Backwards, and Vertical settings. See Figure 15.8 for an example of how these settings affect the appearance of text.

Figure 15.8

The effects of Upside Down, Backwards, and Vertical text settings.

Although the Upside Down and Backwards options work with all font files, the Vertical setting works with SHX files only.

INSIDER TIP

If you want to draw text upside down, you don't have to enable the Upside Down option. Instead, you can specify a text rotation angle of 180 degrees.

The Backwards option is useful if you want to plot text on the backside of a transparent plot sheet so that the text is readable when viewed from the front.

The Vertical option is useful when you need to draw text down the side of a vertical surface, such as a building.

Unlike the font file setting, the Upside Down and Backwards settings for an existing style can be changed without affecting text that has already been typed in that style; the text will not be automatically updated to reflect setting changes. Changing the Vertical setting, however, does affect existing text objects, so you may want to create a new style before changing the Vertical setting.

Setting a Width Factor

The Width Factor determines the width-to-height ratio of the drawn characters. A factor of 1 results in the characters being drawn with the width-to-height ratio defined in the font file used. A factor greater than 1 results in fatter characters; a factor less than 1 results in skinnier characters. Figure 15.9 illustrates the effects of using different width factors. All three lines were drawn with the same text height.

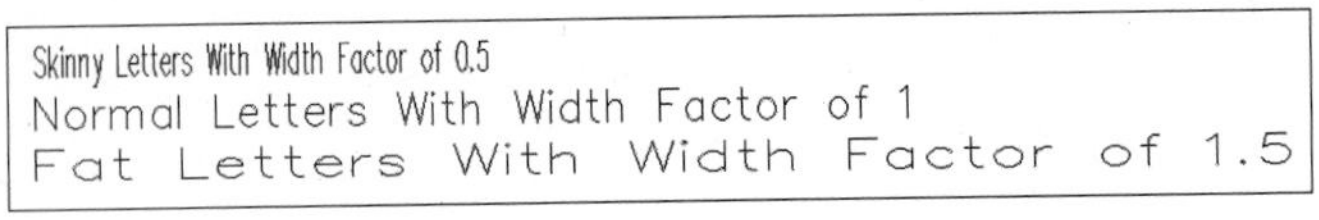

Figure 15.9

The effects of the Width Factor setting on a line of text.

```
Skinny Letters With Width Factor of 0.5
Normal Letters With Width Factor of 1
Fat Letters With Width Factor of 1.5
```

INSIDER TIP

Drawing text with a width factor that is less than I may make it easier to squeeze text into an already crowded drawing, while keeping the text readable.

Setting an Oblique Angle

The Oblique Angle setting affects the slant of the characters. It is often used to draw italic text when the characters in the font file being used are not naturally italic. Unlike the text rotation angle, the oblique angle of 0 refers to a vertical direction (see Figure 15.10). A positive text value makes the letters lean to the right, and a negative value makes the letters lean to the left.

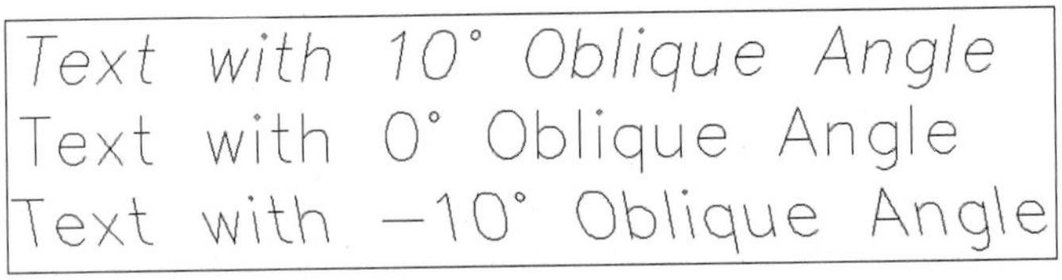

Figure 15.10

The effects of the Oblique Angle setting on a line of text.

```
Text with 10° Oblique Angle
Text with 0° Oblique Angle
Text with −10° Oblique Angle
```

In the following exercise, you use the STYLE command to modify an existing style and to create a new style.

MODIFYING AND CREATING TEXT STYLES

1. Open the drawing 15dwg03.dwg from the accompanying CD.

2. Issue the STYLE command by choosing Text Style from the Format menu. In the Text Style dialog box, make sure STANDARD is the current style.

3. Select the ROMANS.SHX font file. Click the Apply button and close the dialog box. In Figure 15.11, notice that the "ACME Engineering" text is revised to reflect the font file change.

Figure 15.11

*Changing the text style's
font modifies the
appearance of text.*

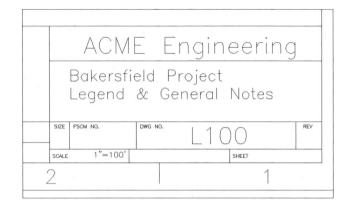

ACME Engineering

Bakersfield Project
Legend & General Notes

| SIZE | FSCM NO. | DWG NO. | | REV |

L100

| SCALE | 1"=100' | | SHEET |

2   1

4. Repeat the **STYLE** command. Click the New button, name the new style **NOTES**, and click OK. Initially, NOTES is a duplicate of STANDARD, the style that was current at the time you clicked the New button.

5. Choose the TrueType font Courier New, which is a font file that offers several font styles. If Courier New does not appear in your list of available fonts, choose an alternate font. Choose Bold as the Font Style. Click the Apply button and close the dialog box. The text style NOTES is now the current text style.

6. You can close the drawing without saving your changes.

Drawing Paragraphs of Text with **MTEXT**

Whereas the **DTEXT** command can be used to draw multiple lines of text, each line is drawn as a separate object. Sometimes you will want to draw multiple lines of text as a single unit, such as a paragraph of text. At such times, you can use the **MTEXT** command, which you issue by choosing either Text from the Draw toolbar or Multiline Text from the Text submenu of the Draw menu.

After you issue the **MTEXT** command, you are prompted to select the first corner point of a window. This window is used to determine the direction in which the mtext object is drawn. When the window is dragged to the right, the mtext object is drawn to the right; when the window is dragged to the left, the mtext object is drawn to the left. Within the window, the mtext object is drawn with a top left justification. If you want, you can change the justification type to one of eight others: TC (Top Center), TR (Top Right), ML (Middle Left), MC (Middle Center), MR (Middle Right), BL (Bottom Left), BC (Bottom Center), or BR (Bottom Right). These justification types are similar to those available with the **DTEXT** command (refer to Figure 15.2), except that they apply to the whole mtext object frame and not just a single line of text.

If you want, you can also choose to use the first window point as the justification point by specifying the Justify option and choosing a justification option. You then choose the Width option and numerically enter the desired width of the mtext window rather than graphically specifying its width. A width of zero disables the word wrap feature of the Multiline Text Editor. With that setting, you will have to press the Enter key every time you want to begin a new line of text.

Several other command-line options appear, but these are easier to set through the Multiline Text Editor dialog box (see Figure 15.12). The Multiline Text Editor is divided into two parts. The bottom part is the screen editor, and the top part is divided into four tabs: Character, Properties, Line Spacing, and Find/Replace, which are described in detail in the following sections.

Figure 15.12

The Multiline Text Editor dialog box.

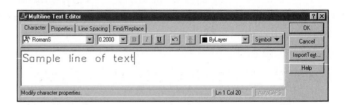

If you have text in an existing ASCII or RTF file, use the Import Text button to import the file into the editor, then you can edit the text as you want.

Using the Character Tab

The Character tab controls the text's properties. The settings can be used in one of two ways. First, the settings control the appearance of the text you type. You also can change the properties of selected text through these settings, thereby creating various special effects. To select text, position the cursor at the beginning of the text, left-click, then drag the cursor to the end of the text you want to select. You can select a word by double-clicking in the word, or you can select the entire body of text by triple-clicking anywhere in the text.

Changing MTEXT's Font File and Text Height

After selecting the text to be affected, you can change the font file to be used and even the height of the text. The text height drop-down list is actually a combination drop-down list and text edit box. You can enter a new text height in the text edit box, or you can select a height that was previously entered from the drop-down list.

Setting the Bold, Italic, and Underline Text Properties

The Bold and Italic buttons enable you to bold or italicize the text, but only if the chosen font file is a TrueType font. You can use the Underline button to underline any selected text regardless of the font file used. All three buttons act as toggles, and you can turn their properties on or off by simply selecting the desired text and clicking the appropriate button.

Stacking and Unstacking Fractions

The Stack/Unstack button is an improved feature in AutoCAD 2000 that is used to stack or unstack selected text. For example, you can designate selected text to be stacked by using a carat (^), a forward slash (/), or a pound sign (#) character between the characters you want stacked. The text to the left of the character is stacked on top of the text to the right of the character. To unstack stacked text, select it and then click the Stack button.

AutoCAD 2000 provides for three stacked text types based on which of the following characters is used:

- **Carat (^):** Converts selected text to left-justified tolerance values.

- **Forward Slash (/):** Converts selected text to center-justified text separated by a horizontal bar.

- **Pound Sign (#):** Converts selected text to a fraction separated by a diagonal bar.

You can edit stacked text and change the stack type, its alignment, or the size of stacked text in the Stack Properties dialog box, shown in Figure 15.13. To display the Stack Properties dialog box, from the Multiline Text Editor dialog box, select the stacked text, right-click, and choose the Properties option from the shortcut menu.

Figure 15.13

The new Stack Properties dialog box.

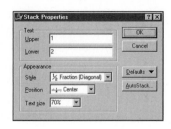

When you first create stacked text, AutoCAD displays the AutoStack Properties dialog box, which allows you to control default settings for stacked text, as shown in Figure 15.14. Ideally, you should set the values for enabling AutoStacking, removing leading blanks, and creating horizontal versus diagonal stacking as desired, then you should select the check box to keep the AutoStack Properties dialog box from appearing each time you create stacked text. If you need to change settings, you can display the AutoStack Properties dialog box by clicking the AutoStack button from the Stack Properties dialog box.

Figure 15.14

The new AutoStack Properties dialog box.

Color Settings

The Text Color list allows you to set the color for selected text. You can set the color to ByLayer, ByBlock, or any one of AutoCAD's other 255 colors.

Using Special Symbols

Use the Symbol drop-down list to insert the degree, plus/minus, or diameter symbol (see Figure 15.15). To insert any other symbol, choose Other from the list to invoke the Character Map program. Inserting a non-breaking space prevents the Multiline Text Editor from making a break at that point when it decides where to break the line of text (word wrap feature) and continue to the next line.

Figure 15.15

The Symbol list allows you to insert special characters.

Using the Properties Tab

Choosing the Properties tab enables you to set the text style, justification option, width, and rotation angle of the overall mtext object. Remember that if you use a window to define the location of the mtext object, the justification used is TL, or Top Left, and that the width of the window is the width used for the mtext object. By using the settings on the Properties tab, you can modify these values.

Using the Line Spacing Tab

From the Line Spacing tab, you control line spacing for new or selected mtext. You control line spacing by selecting the desired line spacing properties from two lists. The first list determines whether the selected line spacing is exactly as indicated, or at least the spacing indicated. The second list determines the line spacing value, which can have one of three settings: a single line space, a 1.5 line space, or a double line space. By using these two lists together, you control the spacing between lines of text.

Using the Find/Replace Tab

Use the Find/Replace tab to search for a specific combination of characters and even to replace the found text with a replacement text string. If the Match Case setting is enabled, AutoCAD finds only text that exactly matches the case of the find string. If the Whole Word setting is enabled, AutoCAD finds only words that exactly match the find string; otherwise, even words that contain only a fragment of the find string are located. After you specify the settings you want, use the Find button to start the search.

In the next exercise, you use MTEXT to add notes to a drawing.

USING MTEXT TO DRAW PARAGRAPHS OF TEXT

1. Open the drawing 15dwg04.dwg from the accompanying CD.

2. Issue the MTEXT command by choosing the Multiline Text tool from the Draw toolbar.

   Specify the point 26,18 as the first corner point. Type **@4,-1** for the opposite corner point. The Multiline Text Editor dialog box is displayed. On the Character tab, type in a height of **0.25**. Type **Notes** and press the Enter key twice.

3. Type the following text: **The information on this drawing reflects information gathered as of 2/2/97**. Press the Enter key twice.

4. Type: **This drawing is a preliminary drawing and should not be used for engineering purposes**. Press the Enter key twice.

5. Highlight the text "Notes," then click on the Underline button. Click OK to close the dialog box. Your drawing should look similar to Figure 15.16.

6. Close the drawing without saving your changes.

Figure 15.16

You can add notes to a drawing using MTEXT.

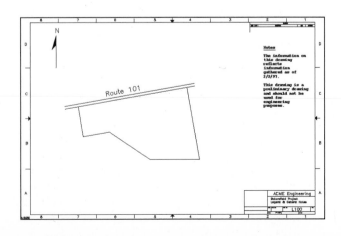

Editing Mtext Objects

You can edit mtext objects by choosing Text from the Modify menu and choosing the mtext text object you want to edit. When you start the command, AutoCAD prompts you to select the text object. If you choose an mtext object, AutoCAD displays the Multiline Text Editor. You can then modify the text in the mtext object or use the Multiline Text Editor's various properties to modify the mtext object's appearance.

Additionally, you can use grips to move or change the width of the mtext object. When you select the grip point that corresponds to the justification point, you can move the mtext object. If you select any other grip point, you will stretch the width of the mtext object.

Performing a Spelling Check

To check spelling within your text and mtext objects, issue the SPELL command by choosing Spelling from the Tools menu. When you start the command, AutoCAD prompts you to select the text objects to check. If the SPELL command encounters an unknown word, the Check Spelling dialog box appears, and you must choose to replace the word, ignore the discrepancy, or add the word to your supplemental dictionary. If no errors are found, a message box appears, informing you that the spell check is complete.

The following exercise shows you how to use the SPELL command.

CHECKING THE SPELLING IN YOUR DRAWING

1. Open the drawing 15dwg04.dwg from the accompanying CD.

2. Issue the SPELL command by choosing Spelling from the Tools menu.

   Use the All option to select all objects, then press Enter. SPELL stops at any word it does not recognize.

INSIDER TIP

If you use abbreviations very often, be sure to add them to your supplemental dictionary.

3. The only words in the example drawing that SPELL does not recognize are Bakersfield and the acronym FSCM. When it stops for these words, choose Ignore to leave their spelling unchanged and to continue checking the spelling of the remaining text

objects. AutoCAD finishes the spelling check and displays a message stating that the spelling check is complete.

4.   Click OK to dismiss the message dialog box.

5.   Close the drawing without saving your changes.

NOTE

If you want to check the spelling of text in model space, you must repeat the SPELL command when the model space viewport is current.

Specifying the Dictionaries

The SPELL command looks up words in as many as two dictionaries at any given time: a main dictionary and a supplemental dictionary. Several main dictionaries are supplied with AutoCAD; the default is the American English Dictionary. The default supplemental dictionary is SAMPLE.CUS (SAMPLE.CUS contains a number of AutoCAD command words and terms). To change the dictionaries used by SPELL, issue the OPTIONS command. In the Options dialog box, select the Files tab, then change the Main Dictionary and Custom Dictionary File settings located under Text Editor, Dictionary, and Font File Names.

Unlike the supplemental dictionary, the main dictionary file cannot be modified or added to. You can, however, add words to update the current supplemental dictionary or to select a new supplemental dictionary.

Creating a Supplemental Dictionary

A *supplemental* dictionary file is a text file that contains the additional words you want SPELL to use when checking for correct spelling. The supplemental dictionary is an ASCII text file that contains one word per line. You can create as many supplemental dictionaries as you want, but you can use only one at time. When you create a supplemental dictionary, be sure to use a .CUS filename extension and place it in one of the folders listed in the Support Files Search Path setting in the Options dialog box.

Looking at Additional Text Options

The following sections cover several optional text handling features that may prove useful to you. These features will enable you to speed up the display of text, handle missing font files, and insert text files into the current drawing.

Enabling the Quick Text Display

When AutoCAD opens or regenerates a drawing, if the drawing contains numerous text objects, it may take quite some time to complete the regeneration process, especially if the text is drawn with complex fonts. If you want to speed up the regeneration of the drawing and you do not need to actually see the existing text, enable the Quick Text mode. To enable the Quick Text mode, access the Display tab of the Options dialog box and select the Show Text Boundary Frame Only check box. When Quick Text is enabled, text and mtext objects are displayed as simple rectangles that contain no characters. If you enable Quick Text mode after opening a drawing, issue the REGEN command to redisplay the text as empty rectangles.

NOTE

Even with Quick Text enabled, new text objects are displayed as text characters—instead of as rectangles—while the DTEXT and MTEXT commands are active, which makes it easier to add text.

Specifying an Alternate Font File

Font files are not stored with the drawing file. If a font file that is referenced in the drawing is not available when the drawing is opened, an error message is displayed. You are then prompted to choose a replacement font file. If you want to bypass all such error messages, you can specify a font file that is automatically used whenever a needed font file cannot be found. You specify this *alternate font file* in the Alternate Font File setting under Text Editor, Dictionary, and Font File Names in the Files tab of the Options dialog box. The default alternate font is simplex.shx.

WARNING

A couple of problems can occur when you use an alternate font. If the missing font file contains special characters that the alternate font file does not have, the text on the drawing may end up incomplete. Furthermore, because the space that a line of text occupies depends on the font file used to generate the text, you may find that when the alternate font is applied, the text on the drawing looks out of place or does not fit properly. The best solution is to obtain the correct font files and use them unless you are sure you have a suitable alternative font file.

Mapping Fonts

If you need to specify more than one alternate font file, specify a font mapping file. A *font mapping* file is a text file in which each line in the file specifies the font file to be replaced and its substitute font file (separated by a semicolon). The default font map file is ACAD.FMP. You can identify a different font map file by changing the Font Mapping File setting under Text Editor, Dictionary, and Font File Names in the Files tab of the Options dialog box.

Drawing Text as Attributes

An alternate method to drawing text objects that are to be incorporated into block definitions is to draw attributes. Attributes behave much like text objects but have additional functions beyond displaying text. Attributes are discussed in more detail in Chapter 9, "Understanding the Query Features in AutoCAD 2000."

Dragging and Dropping Text Files

In Windows, you can drag a text file from the desktop or from Windows Explorer and drop it into your drawing. AutoCAD will automatically insert the file as an mtext object, using the current text settings for the text height, rotation angle, and text style.

Copying Text Using the Clipboard

You also can copy text from any application to your Clipboard and paste the contents into your drawing. If you use the PASTE command, the contents are dropped into your drawing as an embedded object. If you use the PASTESPEC command, you can choose to paste the Clipboard contents as text, in which case the text is drawn as an mtext object.

The Clipboard operations depend on OLE (Object Linking and Embedding). For more information on AutoCAD's OLE features, refer to Chapter 23, "Effective Applications for OLE Objects in AutoCAD 2000."

Creating Your Own Shape File

You have the option of creating your own shape file containing the characters you want to use for text objects. Creating each character is a laborious procedure because you have to break each character into a series of short line segments and enter the codes for those line segments into the new font file. In earlier versions of AutoCAD that did not support the use of TrueType fonts, defining your own shape file was the only way to add to the font files supplied with AutoCAD. However, since Release 14, AutoCAD supports TrueType font families, which are supplied with Windows. Using TrueType fonts is much easier than creating your own fonts from scratch. You can also purchase additional fonts from a number of software vendors at a very low cost.

Using the Express Text Routines

AutoCAD 2000 provides several useful text-related tools. These tools are actually bonus tools, which you access via the Express menu by choosing Tools. The tools enable you to create some very interesting effects with text, including aligning text to an arc and masking objects below text.

You should explore the features of the Express menu's text tools, as well as the other Express tools AutoCAD provides. Appendix B, "The Express Tools," contains a list of the various Express tools you can use for text, as well as several short exercises relating to the text features. You can learn about the Express tools by choosing Help from the Express menu.

Summary

AutoCAD provides a variety of tools that deal with drawing and editing text. This chapter covered the basic steps for creating and working with single lines of text in your drawings, as well as how to add multiple paragraphs of text using the MTEXT command. The chapter also provided detailed information on editing text and defining and changing text styles to control the appearance of text.

16

DRAWING HATCH PATTERNS

When you need to fill an area with a repetitive pattern or a solid fill, you can use the BHATCH *command to create a hatch object. In this chapter, you will learn to do the following:*

■ *Specify the pattern to be used and the parameters governing the generation of the hatch.*

■ *Define the boundaries of the area to be filled.*

■ *Edit a hatch pattern.*

■ *Control the visibility of hatch objects.*

■ *Create your own custom hatch pattern.*

■ *Use the* BOUNDARY *command to create outlines of complex areas.*

Creating Hatch Patterns Using BHATCH

You draw hatch patterns, *including solid fills*, to highlight an area of your drawing, to visually separate areas of your drawing that share common boundaries, or to convey information about an area of your drawing. For example, you might have a map in which you use a hatch pattern to identify a type of terrain, or you use slightly different patterns to separate contiguous land plots. Figure 16.1 shows several examples of using hatch patterns.

Figure 16.1

Examples of the uses of hatch objects.

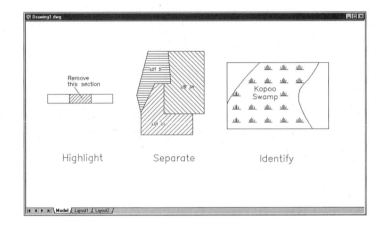

You use the BHATCH command to draw hatch patterns. This section introduces the BHATCH command and also discusses specifying hatch patterns, defining hatch boundaries, setting attributes, working with boundary islands, and using the BHATCH command's advanced settings.

To issue the BHATCH command, from the Draw toolbar, choose Hatch. The Boundary Hatch dialog box appears (see Figure 16.2).

To add a hatch to an object, you first specify a pattern and its parameters and then define the limits of the area to be hatched.

Figure 16.2

BHATCH *command's*
Boundary Hatch
dialog box.

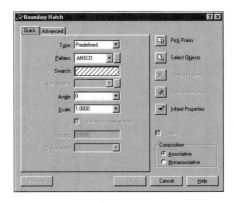

Specifying a Pattern

When selecting a hatch pattern, you have several choices. First, you can choose from any of the predefined patterns that come with AutoCAD. Second, you can make a basic line pattern on the fly using the current linetype. Last, you can select a pattern that is defined in any custom .PAT file that you have added to the AutoCAD search path. All of these methods will be discussed in the following sections.

Predefined Patterns

AutoCAD comes with a large number of predefined patterns. A number of these are standard patterns established by the American National Standards Institute (ANSI) and are used widely in North America. Another group of predefined patterns is derived from patterns established by the International Standards Organization (ISO), the organization that sets international drafting standards in all fields except electrical and electronics. Yet a third group of predefined patterns includes many useful and traditional patterns used worldwide. Figure 16.3 shows a sampling of these patterns.

To select a predefined hatch pattern, in the Quick tab of the Boundary Hatch dialog box, make sure that Predefined is selected from the Type drop-down list (refer to Figure 16.2). In the Pattern drop-down list, select a pattern name. Notice that a representation of the selected pattern is displayed in the Swatch display box. You can also select a pattern by type (ISO, ANSI, and so on) by clicking the ellipses (…) button next to the Pattern drop-down list. This displays the Hatch Pattern Palette dialog box (see Figure 16.4). You can select a pattern from any of the tabs by either double-clicking on the pattern or by selecting the pattern and closing the dialog box by clicking OK.

Figure 16.3

Some sample predefined hatch patterns supplied with AutoCAD.

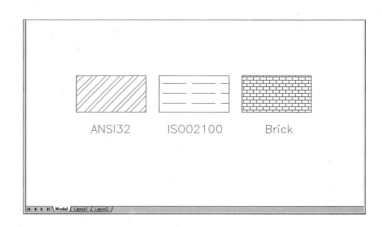

Figure 16.4

Hatch Pattern Palette dialog box of BHATCH.

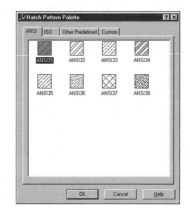

Choosing Scale and Angle Settings

After you choose a pattern, you can also adjust the Angle and Scale settings as desired in the Boundary Hatch dialog box. The Angle setting allows you to change the orientation of the pattern by rotating it. The Scale setting provides a scaling factor used to scale the pattern's size, much as LTSCALE is used to control the generation of linetypes. Figure 16.5 shows the effects of changing scale and rotation.

Some of the predefined patterns are intended to represent real-world materials and are defined with appropriate dimensions. Drawing these patterns at a scale factor at or near 1.0 will yield realistic results in full-scale drawings. The pattern AR-B88, for example, represents 8"×8" building blocks; when drawn at a scale of 1.0, the blocks measure 8 inches by 8 inches. Other patterns, such as ANSI31, are simply standard drafting hatching symbols and can be scaled to give the best visual results consistent with the plot or dimension scale factor for which the drawing is set up.

Figure 16.5

Effects of changing hatch pattern scale and rotation.

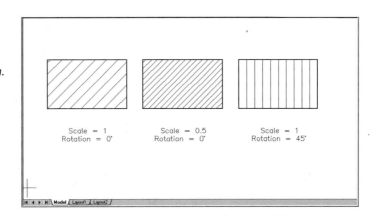

Insider Tip

If you set the scale of a pattern too small, it will take an inordinate amount of time to generate and may plot unsatisfactorily. If you set the scale to an overly large value, the pattern may be so large that it doesn't appear in the area being hatched. Use the Preview feature of the BHATCH dialog box to visually fine-tune the pattern's usable scale.

In the following exercise, you use the BHATCH command to carry out some basic hatch placements.

HATCHING AREAS WITH BHATCH

1. Open the drawing chap16.dwg. The layer BODY will be current. Perform a ZOOM/All. Your screen should resemble Figure 16.6.

2. From the Draw menu, choose Hatch. In the Boundary Hatch dialog box's Quick tab, ensure that the pattern type is Predefined and the pattern is ANSI31. Confirm the settings for Angle 0 and Scale 1.0000.

3. From the right side of the dialog box, click Pick Points and in the drawing pick ① (refer to Figure 16.6). Notice that BHATCH automatically determines and highlights the boundary. Right-click to display the BHATCH shortcut menu. Notice that you can change many of the BHATCH parameters in the shortcut menu. Choose Preview. The completed hatch pattern previews. Right-click again to return to the dialog box. You can now either accept the hatch pattern as previewed or change the pattern parameters.

Figure 16.6

You can pick a point and let AutoCAD determine the hatching boundary.

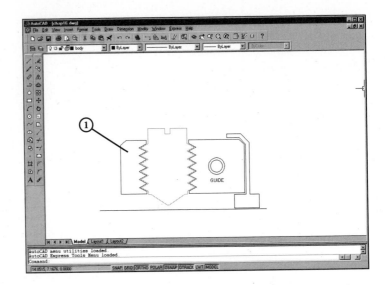

4. Display the preset values in the Scale input box by choosing the down arrow and choose 0.7500 scale factor. Likewise, in the Angle input box choose an angle of 90.

5. Choose Preview to view the effect of the new scale factor and angle. Right-click or press Enter to return to the dialog box and then click OK to accept the hatch object.

6. Save your work. You will continue work in this drawing in a later exercise in this chapter.

ISO (Metric) Patterns

The ISO hatch patterns are designed to be used with metric drawings. These patterns begin with the prefix ISO. They appear alphabetically in the drop-down list of predefined patterns and can be viewed on the ISO tab of the Hatch Pattern Palette dialog. These patterns are defined with the millimeter as the unit of measure. Choosing an ISO pattern enables the ISO pen width input box and drop-down list on the Quick tab of the Boundary Hatch dialog box. Choosing a pen width sets the initial value for the pattern's scale setting equal to the pen width. You can, of course, override this initial scale setting.

User-Defined Patterns

You can define a simple line hatch pattern on the fly by choosing the User-Defined option from the Type drop-down list in the Boundary Hatch dialog box. This disables the Pattern and Scale input boxes and enables the Spacing input box and the Double check box. User-defined patterns are simple and consist of either one or two sets of parallel lines. The spacing and angle of the lines are set in the Spacing and Angle input boxes, respectively. If you check the Double check box near the lower-right side of the Boundary Hatch dialog box, a second set of parallel lines perpendicular to the first will be generated. The spacing of the second set is the same as the first set.

Although user-defined patterns lack a great deal of variety, their simplicity and the speed with which they can be drawn make them useful for quickly hatching an area.

Custom Patterns

You can define additional patterns similar to the patterns supplied with AutoCAD. You can add these additional pattern definitions to the ACAD.PAT file (or ACADISO.PAT file for metric patterns), or you can save each definition as an individual .PAT file. These individual hatch pattern files are referred to as *custom pattern* files. To access one of these custom pattern files, choose Custom from the Type drop-down list on the Quick tab of the Boundary Hatch dialog box. This enables the Custom pattern input box where you enter the name of the custom pattern you want to use. The Scale and Angle parameters for a Custom pattern function as they do for a standard predefined pattern.

Procedures for creating your own custom hatch pattern are discussed in the section "Customizing Hatch Patterns," near the end of this chapter.

Inherit Properties Button

By clicking the Inherit Properties button on the right side of the Boundary Hatch dialog box, you can copy the parameters of an existing hatch object to other objects in the drawing. After clicking this button, the dialog box is temporarily dismissed and a special "inherit" pick box and icon appear in the drawing as shown in Figure 16.7. Select the hatch pattern whose properties you want to duplicate. Another special "painter" crosshair and icon appear. Use these crosshairs to select an internal point of the area to which you want to apply the hatch pattern (see Figure 16.7).

INSIDER **T**IP

After selecting the hatch object whose properties you want the new hatch object to inherit, you can right-click and use the shortcut menu to toggle between the Select Objects and Pick Internal Point options to create boundaries.

Figure 16.7

Two distinctive inherit properties and transfer properties icons.

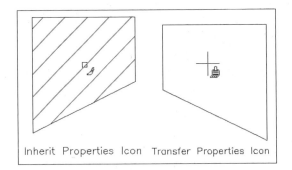

Inherit Properties Icon   Transfer Properties Icon

Associative Versus Non-Associative Hatch Objects

By default, BHATCH generates an associative hatch object. An *associative* hatch object is one that conforms to its boundary object(s) such that modifying the boundary objects automatically adjusts the hatch. If, for example, the boundary object(s) defining an associative hatch are edited, the hatch object's size is automatically adjusted to fill the new boundary area.

INSIDER **T**IP

Unless there is a compelling reason to generate a non-associative hatch object, use the default associative hatch generation method. Associative hatch objects offer the significant advantage of allowing you to edit the boundary object without having to re-select the boundary and re-create the hatch.

Defining Hatch Boundaries

After selecting a hatch pattern and specifying its parameters, you need to define the area or areas you want to fill with the pattern. The area must be completely enclosed by one or more objects.

In Figure 16.8, a single closed object—a circle—defines the boundary of area A. A series of lines and curves that meet end-to-end defines the boundary for area B. Two lines and two arcs define the boundary for area C. The lines and arcs of area C overlap and do not meet end-to-end but, together, they define an enclosed area. Objects that define the area to be filled are called *boundary objects*.

Figure 16.8

Closed areas that define permissible areas to hatch.

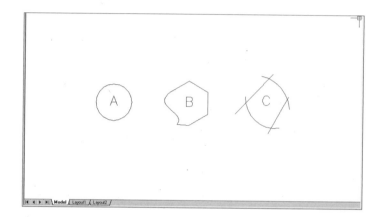

With the BHATCH (boundary-hatch) command, you can define the boundaries of the area you want hatched by either choosing a point or points within the desired boundary or by selecting an object or objects that define an outer boundary.

Using Pick Points

When you click the Pick Points button in the Boundary Hatch dialog box, the overall hatch boundary can be automatically calculated by BHATCH. You merely pick a point that lies within the area that you want filled. This point is referred to as an *internal point*. Using this method of establishing a hatch boundary offers a major advantage: If multiple objects are involved in establishing the boundary, the boundary objects do not have to meet end-to-end (recall area C in Figure 16.8).

Selecting Objects

Another method for indicating the boundary of an area you want to hatch is provided by clicking the Select Objects button in the Boundary Hatch dialog box. With this method, you select the individual boundary objects that define the area to be hatched. This method is adequate for simple areas bounded by a single closed object, such as a circle, but if more than one object will make up the boundary, this method requires that the objects meet end-to-end, as shown in area B of Figure 16.8. Using the Select Objects method with an intended boundary such as area C in Figure 16.8 will yield erroneous results because the boundary objects do not meet end to end.

I N S I D E R   T I P

If the area you want to hatch is enclosed by a single boundary object and no areas within the boundary need be excluded from hatching, the Select Objects method may be faster than picking an internal point. In all but the simplest situations, however, picking an internal point and letting the BHATCH command calculate the boundary generally yields the best results.

Dealing with Islands

It is not uncommon to have enclosed areas within the overall hatching area. These areas are referred to as *islands*. There can even be islands within islands. Text and Mtext objects lying within an area to be hatched can behave like islands.

If you use the Pick Points method of defining the hatch boundary, AutoCAD automatically detects islands. This is one of the advantages of using the Pick Points method. On the other hand, if you use the Select Objects method, you must explicitly indicate those internal boundary objects that you want to be considered islands—otherwise, BHATCH will not recognize their presence. One or more objects can define islands in the same way boundary objects define the overall hatch area.

The ways islands are detected and treated by BHATCH are controlled by settings found on the Advanced tab of the Boundary Hatch dialog box (see Figure 16.9).

On the Advanced tab, under Island Detection Style, you control the way BHATCH treats successive levels of nested islands. The three styles are Normal, Outer, and Ignore. Figure 16.10 shows how the same outer boundary and inner islands are treated using these three detection styles.

Figure 16.9

*The Advanced tab of
the Boundary Hatch
dialog box.*

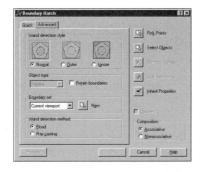

Figure 16.10

*The three styles of island
detection.*

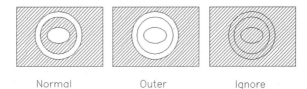

Normal   Outer   Ignore

- **Normal.** Hatches inward from the outermost boundary. Hatching is turned off at first internal island then turned at the next detected island, hatching alternate areas.

- **Outer.** Hatches inward from the outermost boundary. Hatching is turned off and remains off at first detected island.

- **Ignore.** Hatches all of the area within outermost boundary ignoring all internal islands.

The default style is Normal and is applicable in most situations. The Outer detection style is useful if you want to hatch overlapping islands with different patterns. Figure 16.10 shows how this can be done. Using the Outer style, pick in area 1 and apply a pattern. Next, repeat BHATCH and, again using the Outer style, pick island 2 and apply a different pattern. Continue with this method until all islands are hatched. In Figure 16.11, islands 2 and 3 have different patterns applied; the outer area and island 4 have the same pattern with a different angle setting applied.

Figure 16.11

*Use the Outer style to
hatch overlapping areas.*

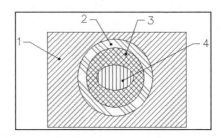

BHATCH can also be used on regions. Islands within a region are detected by BHATCH and treated according to the current setting of the island detection style. A benefit of using a single region is that it effectively saves the boundary set into an object that can be selected quickly for later use. Regions are discussed in Chapter 30, "Solid Modeling."

I NSIDER TIP

The Normal, Outer, and Ignore options are also available from a shortcut menu by right-clicking in the drawing area after you specify points or select objects to define your boundaries.

Defining the Boundary Set

Normally, the Pick Points method of defining the boundary set of an area to be hatched examines all of the objects in the current viewport. You can, however, click the New button under Boundary Set on the Advanced tab of the Boundary Hatch dialog box and explicitly select a smaller set of object to be examined for valid hatch boundaries. This option is useful when you have a crowded drawing and want to speed up the search mechanism by restricting the number of objects examined.

If you use the New button to create a new set of objects to be examined, the drop-down list under Boundary Set will list an existing set in addition to Viewport. There can be a maximum of two search sets at any time: the entire viewport, which is the default set and is always available, and an existing set, if you have defined one. Defining a new set replaces any pre-existing set.

Retaining Boundaries

When hatch area boundaries and internal islands are defined, AutoCAD uses temporary polylines to delineate these areas. These polylines are normally removed after the hatch object is generated. By checking Retain Boundaries under Object Type on the Advanced tab of the Boundary Hatch dialog box, the temporary polylines are not removed but retained on the current layer. You can save them as either closed polylines or as regions, depending on the option you select from the drop-down list.

Enabling the Retain Boundaries option is useful when the hatching area is delineated by multiple objects and you want polylines or regions to represent the hatch area. If you subsequently use the AREA command on the resulting polylines, or the MASSPROP command on the resulting region, you can easily measure the hatched area.

Detecting Islands

The controls located under Island Detection Method on the Advanced tab of the Boundary Hatch dialog box allow you to turn island detection on or off. There are two choices:

- **Flood.** Includes islands as boundary objects.

- **Ray Casting.** Runs a line from the point you specify to the nearest object, then traces the boundary in a clockwise direction, excluding islands as potential boundary objects.

If you use the Ray Casting method, you must be careful where you pick because AutoCAD casts a ray to the *nearest* object. In Figure 16.12, for example, point A is a valid point, whereas point B is not. The object nearest point A is a line that qualifies as part of a potential boundary of which point A is *inside*. Point B, however, is closest to a line that qualifies as a part of a potential boundary of which B is *outside*. Point B will cause BHATCH to issue an error message as shown in Figure 16.12.

Figure 16.12

Selecting valid points with the Ray Casting option.

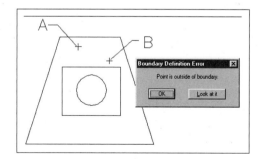

Other Boundary Hatch Controls

There are several other buttons shared by both the Quick and Advanced tabs of the Boundary Hatch dialog box:

- **Remove Islands.** Allows you to remove individual islands from the boundary set when you use Pick an Internal Point. You can also remove an island by pressing the Ctrl key and picking inside the selecting island.

- **View Selections.** Displays the currently defined boundaries with highlighted boundary objects. This option is unavailable when you have not yet specified points or selected objects.

- **Preview.** Displays the currently defined boundaries with the current hatch settings. This option is not available when you have not yet specified points or selected objects to define your boundaries.

In the following exercise, you continue drawing hatch objects in chap16.dwg.

HATCHING AREAS WITH BHATCH (CONTINUED)

1. Continue in or reopen chap16.dwg. Set the layer LOCK-SCREW current. Start the BHATCH command by opening the Draw menu, and choosing Hatch. On the Quick tab of the Boundary Hatch dialog box, select pattern ANSI33. Check that the Angle is set to 0 and the Scale is set to 1.000.

2. Click the Select Objects button. The lock screw is drawn on its own layer and is composed of a pair of mirrored polylines with ends meeting, forming an enclosed space. Pick the two polylines at ① and ② of Figure 16.13.

Figure 16.13

Select the two polylines that compose the lock screw.

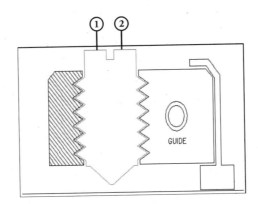

3. Right-click and choose Preview from the shortcut menu. Right-click to return to the Boundary Hatch dialog box and select a scale of 0.75. Click Preview in the lower-left corner of the dialog box. Right-click and click OK to apply the hatch object. Notice that the hatch is drawn on the current layer. Your drawing should resemble Figure 16.14.

Figure 16.14

Hatching the lock-screw.

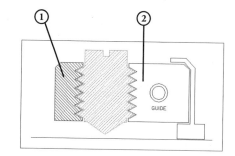

4. Set layer BODY current. Restart the BHATCH command and on the right side of the dialog box, click Inherit Properties. In the drawing, place the "inherit" cursor in the area you hatched earlier and pick ① (refer to Figure 16.14).

5. Right-click and select Pick Internal Point from the shortcut menu. Place the cursor of the "transfer to" cursor in the body to the right of the lock-screw at ② and pick. BHATCH calculates and highlights the boundary and internal islands. Right-click and choose Preview. Notice that the text object is treated as an island and excluded from hatching.

6. Assume you do not want the inner circle representing a guide bar to inherit the current hatch properties. Right-click to return to the dialog box and click Remove Islands. In the drawing, pick the inner circle to remove it from the boundary set. Right-click and choose Preview. Right-click and choose OK to accept the hatch.

7. Right-click and choose Repeat BHatch from the shortcut menu. In the Boundary Hatch dialog box, under Type, select User-Defined from the drop-down list. In the Spacing input box, type 0.1. Select the Double option check box.

8. Click Pick Points and in the drawing pick inside the inner circle. Right-click and choose Preview. Right-click and click OK to accept the new hatch. Your drawing should resemble Figure 16.15.

Figure 16.15

Figure 16.15

Hatching the guide bar with a user-defined pattern.

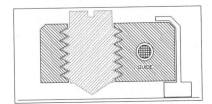

9. Right-click and repeat the BHATCH command. In the Type drop-down list, select Predefined. In the Pattern drop-down list, select the Solid pattern. Notice that there are no Angle or Scale parameters available with the Solid pattern.

10. Click Pick Points, and in the drawing pick inside the bracket on the right of the assembly. Right-click and Preview the boundary set. Right-click and click OK to accept the solid hatch. Your drawing should now resemble Figure 16.16.

11. Save your work. If you plan to continue immediately with the next section, leave your drawing open.

Figure 16.16

Hatching the mounting bracket with a solid pattern.

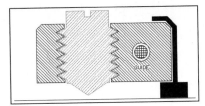

NOTE

The BHATCH command is also available on the Draw toolbar and by typing **BHATCH** on the command line.

Editing Hatch Patterns

The HATCHEDIT command lets you modify hatch patterns or replace an existing pattern with a different one. Hatch objects drawn as associative hatch objects (the default type) automatically adjust to modifications in the boundary that defines them.

Using HATCHEDIT

With HATCHEDIT, you can change the pattern of a hatch object or the parameters that control the generation of the pattern. To issue the HATCHEDIT command, choose Hatch from the Modify menu. The Hatch Edit dialog box is identical to the Boundary Hatch dialog box with several settings disabled and unavailable (see Figure 16.17).

Figure 16.17

The Hatch Edit dialog box.

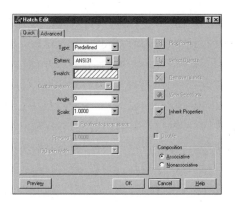

In the following exercises, you perform an edit on a previously drawn hatch object and investigate the behavior of associative hatches.

EDITING A HATCH PATTERN

1. Continue in or open chap16.dwg. Start the HATCHEDIT command: From the Modify menu, choose Hatch. Select the solid hatch pattern by picking anywhere inside the hatch object.

2. In the Hatch Edit dialog box, notice that the name and parameters of the pattern you just selected are now displayed in the appropriate edit and drop-down boxes.

3. In the Pattern drop-down list, select ANSI31. click the Preview button.

4. To further modify the pattern, right-click to return to the dialog box. Set the Angle to 30 and the Scale to 0.500. Click Preview. Right-click and click OK to accept the edits. Your drawing should resemble Figure 16.18. You will continue in this drawing in the next section.

Figure 16.18

Modifying a hatch pattern with HATCHEDIT.

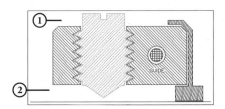

Editing Hatch Boundaries

If you stretch or otherwise modify the scale or shape of the boundary objects defining the overall area of an associative hatch object, the hatch object automatically adjusts to fit the modified boundaries. If you move, delete, or stretch any of the islands within the overall hatch boundary, the hatch object is also adjusted.

If you delete any of the boundary objects defining the overall hatch area or islands (resulting in an open rather than a closed area), however, the associative property is removed from the hatch object and the hatch loses the capability to adjust to modifications to the boundary. In the following exercise, you see how associative hatch objects automatically adjust to changes in their boundaries.

It is impossible to "repair" an associative hatch pattern after editing removes the associative property, or associativity. However, you can use the Undo U command to correct a drafting mistake immediately afterward.

UNDERSTANDING HATCH ASSOCIATIVITY

1. Continue in chap16.dwg. From the Modify menu, choose Stretch and pick first at ① then ② (refer to Figure 16.18). Right-click to end the object selection process.

2. Type in the displacement –1,0 and press Enter twice to carry out the stretch. Notice that the hatch pattern automatically adjusts to fill the new boundary geometry.

3. Save your work. You will continue in this drawing in the next section.

Other Hatching Considerations

There are several other considerations to keep in mind when creating and working with hatch objects. These include the *hiding*, or turning hatching off; exploding hatch objects into their constituent lines; and controlling whether associative hatch objects include their boundaries when selected for an editing operation.

Aligning Hatch Objects

Areas hatched with the same pattern and with the same scale and angle parameters will have the corresponding elements in the pattern lined up in adjacent areas. All hatch patterns are referenced to the snap origin, which usually coincides with the drawing's 0,0. If you want to re-align a hatch pattern, change the snap origin before drawing the hatch. The snap origin is controlled by the system variable, SNAPBASE, which stores the value of a point. Set SNAPBASE to a point other than 0,0, by picking a point such as the corner of a rectangular area, to cause the next hatch object drawn to align with the current snap origin.

The reason for this stems from the fact that families of lines in the pattern were defined with the same base point and angle and this is true no matter where the patterns appear in the drawing. This causes hatching lines to line up in adjacent areas. All hatch patterns are referenced to the snap origin, which by default is the drawing's 0,0 origin.

Exploding Hatch Objects

You can explode a hatch object into its constituent lines with the EXPLODE command. Exploding a hatch object removes any associativity. Additionally, the grouped set of line objects that make up the pattern replaces the single hatch object. Although exploding a hatch object does enable you to edit the individual lines of the hatch, in most cases you lose more productivity than you gain.

NOTE

Because a hatch object is composed of lines, you can use the same object snap modes (such as endpoint and midpoint) on the individual lines in hatch objects, associative or exploded, as you use on line objects.

Controlling Visibility with FILLMODE

You can control the visibility of all hatch objects in a drawing by setting the FILLMODE system variable to 0. With FILLMODE off (set to 0), all hatch objects become invisible regardless of the status of the layers on which the hatch objects reside. You must issue the REGEN or REGENALL command after changing FILLMODE for the change in visibility to take effect.

The disadvantage of using FILLMODE to control hatch object visibility is that FILLMODE also controls the fill of other objects such as wide polylines and multilines. If you wish to hide hatching more selectively, place hatching objects on separate layers so that the layers can be turned on and off without affecting other elements of the drawing.

Selecting Hatch Objects and Their Boundaries

Usually, you will want to select both an associative hatch and its boundary for editing operations such as moving, mirroring, or copying. By default, however, AutoCAD treats the two elements separately during the object selection process. To speed hatch and boundary selection, you can change the PICKSTYLE system variable from its default value of 1 to a value of 3. The PICKSTYLE system variable controls the selection of groups and hatch elements. A setting of 0 or 1 disables simultaneous hatch and boundary element selection. A value of 2 or 3 enables simultaneous hatch and boundary selection.

Using Point Acquisition with the HATCH Command

The older version of the BHATCH command is HATCH . Although BHATCH replaced HATCH in functionality and especially the ability to calculate boundaries, HATCH is still supported. The principle disadvantage of the HATCH command is that it can create only non-associative hatch objects.

Despite its drawbacks, HATCH does have an option that you may find useful: the Direct Hatch option. The Direct Hatch option enables you to define an area to be hatched on the fly, negating the necessity to draw boundary objects before drawing the hatch object. The Direct Hatch option, or point acquisition method, is useful when you want to "suggest" large hatch areas by hatching only a few representative patches. This method is shown in the following exercise.

UNDERSTANDING HATCH ASSOCIATIVITY

1. Return to chap16.dwg. Start the HATCH command by typing **HATCH** at the Command prompt. Press Enter to accept the default ANSI31 hatch pattern.

2. At the next two command-line prompts, type **0.75** for the pattern scale and then press Enter to accept the default of 0 for the pattern angle.

3. At the Select Objects prompt, press Enter to indicate that you will be specifying points instead of objects.

4. Type **N** to indicate that you want to discard the polyline boundary after the hatch is completed.

5. Referring to the left portion of Figure 16.19, use an Endpoint osnap to pick 1 and then pick points 2 through 9. Use an Endpoint osnap to pick point 10, then type **C** and press Enter to create and close the polyline boundary on the fly.

6. The hatching is completed. Your drawing should resemble the right portion of Figure 16.19.

7. Save your work and close the drawing.

Figure 16.19

Using the HATCH command and direct hatching.

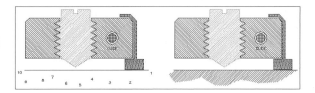

Customizing Hatch Patterns

It is possible to add new patterns to the ones supplied with AutoCAD. You can add these new patterns (called *custom hatch patterns*) to the file ACAD.PAT (or ACADISO.PAT for metric patterns), or you can define each new pattern and assign it to its own .PAT file. ACAD.PAT and ACADISO.PAT are found in the \ACADR15\SUPPORT folder of a standard AutoCAD installation. If you choose to store each custom pattern in its own .PAT file, the file must have the same name as the pattern. The new custom pattern files should be placed in one of the directories/ folders defined in your installation's support file search path (see the OPTIONS command). Because hatch pattern files are ASCII files, a text editor is all you need to create these custom pattern files and to add them to the ACAD.PAT file.

NOTE

If you choose to add custom hatch patterns to the ACAD.PAT file, you should first make a backup copy of this file. This will allow you to revert to a functional file should ACAD.PAT become corrupted. Creating a folder under your \ACAD2000 installation called SAFE, for example, provides a convenient place to locate such backup files.

A hatch pattern consists of one or more *families* of parallel pattern lines. The rules for defining a pattern line are the same as those for defining a new linetype except that no text or shapes can be included in the definition of a hatch pattern line (refer to Chapter 5, "Using Linetypes and Lineweights Effectively," for information on linetypes). A pattern definition can be broken down into two components: the header and the definition body. These will be explained in the next section.

NOTE

Although the rules for defining a hatch pattern are relatively straightforward, implementing the rules can take time, effort, and patience. A much easier and more cost-effective solution might be to purchase any of several third-party hatch pattern sets. If you definitely want to define your own pattern, read on.

Defining the Header Line

The first line in any pattern definition is called the *header line*. The format for the header line is as follows:

```
*Pattern-name [, description]
```

The pattern name cannot contain any blank spaces. As shown, the description and the preceding comma are optional and are used only by the HATCH command.

INSIDER **T**IP

Although the description portion of the header line is optional, you may want to always include a descriptive phrase. This is especially helpful when working in the ACAD.PAT file, where the pattern names are frequently short and non-descriptive.

The header line is followed by one or more pattern line descriptors, one for each family of lines. A pattern line has the following syntax:

```
Angle, x-origin, y-origin, delta-x, delta-y [,dash-1, dash-2, …]
```

The following line descriptor, for example, would result in the hatch shown on the left in Figure 16.20:

```
*L45, 45 degree lines @0.25 units
45,0,0,0,0.25
```

Figure 16.20

The L45 and TRIANG patterns.

L45 TRIANG

Each family of lines starts with one line, and the line's angle and origin are specified by the first three numbers of the line descriptor. In the L45 example, the first line is drawn at a 45-degree angle through the point 0,0. The family of lines is generated by offsetting each successive line by delta-x and delta-y offsets with delta-x measured along the line and delta-y measured perpendicular to the lines. In L45, each succeeding line is offset 0 in the x direction and 0.25 in the y direction. With no other *dash* specifications included in the definition, AutoCAD draws the lines with the current linetype.

The pattern shown on the right in Figure 16.20 is one found in AutoCAD's ACAD.PAT file. It has the following definition:

```
*TRIANG, Equilateral triangles
60, 0,0, .1875,.324759526, .1875,-.1875
120, 0,0, .1875,.324759526, .1875,-.1875
0, -.09375,.162379763, .1875,.324759526, .1875,-.1875
```

In this example, the pattern consists of three families of lines: one family drawn at 60 degrees, another drawn at 120 degrees, and a third drawn at 0 degrees. The dash specifications (the last two numbers of each line) indicate that each line is to consist of a 0.1875 dash and a 0.1875 space repetitive pattern.

Using BOUNDARY to Delineate Areas and Islands

As you saw earlier in this chapter, when calculating the boundary for a hatch object using the pick internal point(s) method, the BHATCH command constructs a polyline or region to delineate the boundary set. The BOUNDARY command is a variation of the BHATCH command and creates objects delineating an overall area and the islands, if any, within that area. BOUNDARY also offers the choice of creating region objects from the calculated polylines. The Boundary Creation dialog box is nothing more than the Advanced tab of the BHATCH Boundary Hatch dialog box (see Figure 16.21). You use the BOUNDARY command when you want to delineate an area and its internal islands without applying hatch objects.

Figure 16.21

The Boundary Creation dialog box of the BOUNDARY *command.*

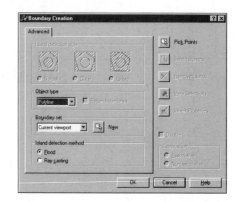

Summary

Hatching is a powerful tool for clarifying the meaning of your drawing or for conveying information to the reader. Effective use of hatching is one of the more powerful features of computer-aided design. Hatching is easy to apply using the BHATCH command and just as easy to edit with the HATCHEDIT command. Creating associative hatch objects lets you modify the hatched area easily after its creation. You can even design your own hatch patterns and add them to those that are supplied with AutoCAD.

17

PRODUCTIVE DIMENSIONING

When working in a production environment, one of the more time-consuming and critical challenges is the need to dimension a drawing quickly and accurately. Then, if necessary, you must also be able to modify and correct existing dimensions just as quickly and accurately.

This chapter and Chapter 18, "Advanced Dimensioning," introduce you to various techniques necessary to dimension a drawing quickly and easily. The techniques are the same, regardless of the type of drawing, whether it is architectural, civil, or mechanical in nature.

This chapter focuses on how to become more productive when dimensioning by using AutoCAD's basic dimensioning tools. Chapter 18 focuses on how to modify existing dimensions quickly. In particular, this chapter focuses on the following topics:

■ *Linear dimensions*

■ *Other dimension types*

■ *Leader dimensions*

■ *Layout window and model space dimensioning*

Becoming Proficient at Productive Dimensioning

To become proficient at dimensioning a drawing, you need a little practice and a little understanding about some of the various options made available to you by AutoCAD. The most commonly used dimensioning type is linear dimensioning.

Linear Dimensioning

Linear dimensions, of course, define a specific length, whether it is horizontal, vertical, or aligned to the object you are dimensioning. AutoCAD provides you with five different linear dimensioning commands, including DIMLINEAR, DIMCONTINUE, DIMBASELINE, DIMALIGNED, and DIMROTATED. Each of these commands can be accessed through either the pull-down menu (see Figure 17.1), the Dimensioning toolbar (see Figure 17.2), or entered at the command prompt. You should access this command using the method you are most comfortable with. For example, DIMLINEAR is the command prompt command for a linear dimension, whereas it appears as Linear on the pulldown and toolbar. All are the same command.

Figure 17.1

The Dimension pull-down menu, where you can access all of the dimensioning commands available in AutoCAD 2000.

Figure 17.2

The Dimension toolbar, where you can select dimensioning commands instead of using the pull-down menu.

The base linear command, DIMLINEAR, is fairly straightforward and easy to use. But, you may not be aware of one or two options of the command, which are covered in the next section.

Linear Options

The DIMLINEAR command is based on selecting three points to create the dimension. These points are the starting and ending points of the dimension, and the location of the dimension line. When choosing the first two points for the linear dimension, you are prompted to select the first and second extension line origins on the object(s) being dimensioned.

An alternative method is to press Enter when prompted to select the first extension line origin. At that point, you can select the line, polyline, circle, or arc you want to dimension. Then, all you have to do is place the dimension. When selecting a line or are using this method, the endpoints of the dimension are automatically determined. This alternate method works well when you are dimensioning a single line, arc, circle, or polyline segment that is precisely the length you need it to be. When this method is applied to a multi-segmented polyline, only the segment you select will be dimensioned. If you use this method with a circle, you can dimension the diameter of the circle with a linear dimension. DIMLINEAR will recognize objects that it cannot dimension and will issue the following informational message: Object selected is not a line, arc, or circle. Figure 17.3 shows you some example dimensions created with two clicks.

Figure 17.3

Examples of using DIMLINEAR *with selected objects on various types of geometry.*

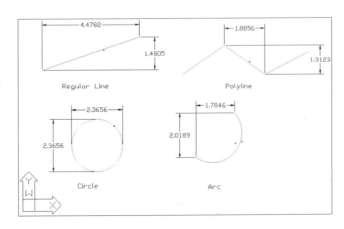

The following exercise gives you a taste of how to use the DIMLINEAR command.

DIMENSIONING WITH DIMLINEAR

1. Load the file 17TUT05.DWG from the accompanying CD. This file has three objects—two circles and a rectangle—that you will dimension.

2. From the Dimension pull-down menu, select Linear.

3. At the command prompt, you will be prompted to select the first extension line or select by object. Press Enter to choose Select by Object.

4. Click on the bottom line of the rectangle. You will immediately see a linear dimension of that edge of the rectangle.

5. Move the mouse down and pick a position for the dimension line a comfortable distance away from the rectangle.

   Now, let's see how to manually create a linear dimension.

6. Press Enter to bring the command back up again.

7. When prompted for the first extension line, type **CEN** for center point snap, press Enter, then click on the left circle.

8. You will then be prompted for the second extension line. Again, type **CEN**, press Enter, then select the right circle.

9. When you do, you will see the dimension line appear. If you move the cursor up and down and left to right, you will see that you can create either a horizontal or vertical dimension for the two circles, simply based on where you place the dimension line. Place the line to the right of the rectangle and you are finished.

10. You may close this drawing without saving.

The DIMLINEAR by selection option, however, does not solve every situation for linear dimensions. You may still need to resort to using construction lines in conjunction with object snap modes. In these cases, AutoCAD 2000's new tracking feature is very helpful. See Chapter 6, "Accuracy in Creating Drawings with AutoCAD 2000," for more information on how to use tracking.

Ultimately, to get more productivity when creating linear dimensions, you need to explore a few more commands—in particular, DIMBASELINE and DIMCONTINUE. Both commands are used after creating an initial linear dimension to quickly create additional dimensions. These commands are discussed in the following sections.

Baseline Dimensions

Baseline dimensions are used to quickly and easily create a series of dimensions from a single basepoint. If you want to dimension various objects along a wall, but want all the dimensions to measure from one end of the wall, for example, baseline is the method to use.

To make use of the baseline command, you must create a linear, aligned, or rotated dimension before using the baseline command. After you have the initial dimension, choose Baseline from the Dimension pull-down menu or the toolbar. When inside the command, select the endpoint of the next dimension. Each dimension is then automatically placed next to or above the previous dimension with a user-specified spacing. When using DIMBASELINE and DIMCONTINUE, AutoCAD remembers the position of the last dimension placed.

N OTE

You can perform any non-dimensioning command between the use of DIMLINEAR and DIMBASELINE and not lose the last dimension for use by the command.

I NSIDER TIP

If you want to baseline a dimension that was not the most recently based dimension, you can press the Enter key at the Specify a second extension line origin or (<select>/Undo): prompt. This will enable you to select the dimension you want to baseline. This will work with the continuous dimension type as well.

Figure 17.4 shows you the click points necessary to create a series of dimensions using the baseline command.

Figure 17.4

A set of baseline dimensions and the mouse clicks that created them.

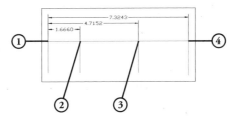

The following exercise shows you how to dimension a steel plate quickly and efficiently using baseline dimensions.

CREATING LINEAR DIMENSIONS BY USING BASELINES

1. Load the drawing 17TUT01.DWG from the accompanying CD.

2. Create a linear dimension by using the **DIMLINEAR** command from the left end of the block to the center point of the first circle, as shown in Figure 17.5.

Figure 17.5

The block with the first linear dimension applied.

3. Choose Dimension, Baseline from the pull-down menu or the Dimension toolbar.

4. When prompted for the second extension line, select a center object snap mode and select the center of the second circle.

5. Continue using center snap modes and select the center of the rest of the circles, moving from left to right.

6. When you are finished with the circles, select the endpoint of the upper-right corner of the block. Figure 17.6 shows you the block with all the dimensions applied.

7. Close this drawing without saving, or undo these dimensions and leave open for a following exercise.

Figure 17.6

The block dimensioned using baseline dimensions.

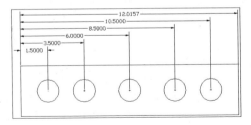

As you can see from this exercise, after you have created the first linear dimension, regardless of whether the dimension was created using DIMLINEAR, DIMALIGNED, or other linear commands, the block is dimensioned quickly with a minimal amount of mouse operations.

To further test the baseline command, try rotating the plate 45 degrees before you create the first dimension. Then, create a DIMALIGNED dimension for the first dimension. When you use the baseline command again, you will see that it works perfectly.

Quick Dimensions

NEW
for R2000   Before looking at other dimensioning commands available in AutoCAD 2000, let's take a quick look at quick dimensions. *Quick dimensions*, or *QDIM*, is an automated system for quickly dimensioning a series of objects. It works by selecting the objects you want to dimension, then placing the dimension line. To illustrate this, let's run through the previous exercise again, but this time use QDIM to create the dimensions.

DIMENSIONING A BLOCK WITH QDIM

1. Continue from the previous exercise or reload the file 17TUT01.DWG from the accompanying CD.

2. Choose Dimensions, QDIM from the pull-down menu.

3. Select all of the objects in the scene and press Enter.

4. Click above the block to place the dimensions, and you're done. Figure 17.7 shows you the block.

5. Close the drawing—there is no need to save.

Figure 17.7

The block after using QDIM to create the dimensions.

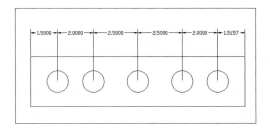

As you can see from the previous exercise, QDIM is very quick and easy to use to create a set of linear dimensions. As you work with AutoCAD 2000, you will find that this command is a great time saver.

Continue Dimensions

Continue dimensions are very similar to baseline dimensions with one exception: rather than basing all the dimensions off a single point, they are based off the endpoint of the last dimension drawn. Continue dimensions automatically line up the dimension lines to create crisp, clean dimensions. For example, a wall is generally dimensioned from centerline to centerline of the components of the wall, such as doors and windows. Using the continue dimension makes this very easy.

If you have to create a series of dimensions, one after the other on a single dimension line, use the continue command, because it automates the placement of additional dimensions, much like the baseline command did. Figure 17.8 shows you an example of a continue dimension.

Figure 17.8

A set of dimensions showing the use of the continue command.

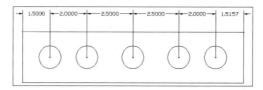

Like baseline dimensions, continue dimensions rely on having one linear dimension type already created, followed by the continue dimension command.

For an exercise on how to use this command, repeat the baseline exercise, but use the continue command instead. Both commands work the same way, but produce different results. As you may have guessed, in a lot of ways, QDIM can replace continue dimensions, but there will still be instances in which it will be easier to use continue.

Aligned and Rotated Dimensions

The last two linear dimension types are aligned and rotated. Both of these types are similar to each other in the fact that they are not horizontal or vertical dimensions. Aligned and rotated dimensions are the only linear dimensions in which the dimension line is not horizontal or vertical.

Aligned dimensions arrange the dimension line to match the angle produced between the start and endpoints of the dimension. *Rotated dimensions* have the dimension line rotated a specific angle amount before the start and endpoints are selected. Figure 17.9 shows you examples of both types of dimensions.

Figure 17.9

*Two dimensions, showing
the difference between an
aligned and a rotated
dimension.*

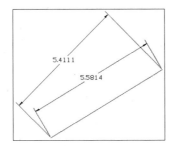

As you can see in Figure 17.9, you can use the rotated command to create linear dimensions with any orientation. The aligned command, however, is forced to align itself along the start and endpoints of the dimension. Also note that a different dimension is measured because of the dimension angle, even though both dimensions use the same endpoints.

The aligned dimension command may be accessed through the pull-down menu, toolbar, or entered at the command prompt. The rotated command, however, is only available at the command prompt. Simply type **DIMROTATED** to access the command.

The following exercise shows you how to use the rotated command to create a few dimensions. The exercise also shows you why you need to be careful when using this dimension type, because a rotated linear dimension may end up with a different measured length than the original.

CREATING A ROTATED DIMENSION

1. Load the file 17TUT02.DWG from the accompanying CD. This drawing shows three circles that you are going to dimension from center point to center point.

2. At the command prompt, type the command **DIMROTATED**.

3. When prompted for an angle, type **38**, which sets the angle of the dimension line.

4. Select the center of the left circle as the start point.

5. Select the center of the middle circle as the end point. Pick a point above and to the left to position the rotated dimension. The distance between the left and middle circles should measure out to 4.000.

6. Press Enter to bring up the rotate command again. This time, enter an angle of **315** (45 degrees down and to the right).

7. Select the center point of the middle circle as the start point.

8. Select the center point of the circle on the right. Figure 17.10 shows you the three circles dimensioned.

Figure 17.10

A 38-degree and a 45-degree rotated dimension showing what happens when you use the rotate command on a linear dimension.

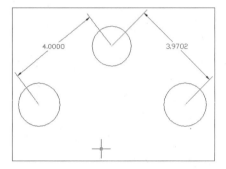

9. When you are finished with the rotate command, type **exit** to return to the standard AutoCAD command prompt. Close the drawing without saving.

Other Dimensions

Several other dimensioning types are worth mentioning. These dimension types are not linear and serve specific purposes. Depending on your discipline, you may have a use for some of these types. For example, a mechanical part designer will make heavy use of radius and diameter dimension types, whereas a civil engineer will make use of datum dimension types.

Radius and Diameter Dimensions

Radius and *diameter* dimensions are used to dimension the size of an arc or circle, regardless of the type of object. If you create a polyline with an arc in it, for example, you can use either dimension type to dimension the arc. If you select the Center Mark check box in the Dimension Styles dialog box, the center mark will automatically be used with radius and diameter dimensions when the dimension text is placed outside the circle or arc. Other than that, the placement of radius and diameter dimensions is relatively straightforward. With these dimension types, you simply pick the arc or circle to dimension, then the dimension line location. Features of the Dimension Style dialog box will be presented in Chapter 18.

Angular Dimensions

Angular dimensions are used to dimension the angle between two non-parallel lines. Of course, when you dimension angles between two lines, four angles are possible: one on each side of the intersection point of the two lines. Where you place the dimension line determines which angle is measured. Like radius and diameter dimensions, angular dimensions are straightforward.

NOTE

Angular dimensions cannot use other arcs, dimensions, or block entities to develop the boundary edges for the angle. You may on occasion need to create construction objects to draw the angular dimension and then dispose of them.

The following exercise demonstrates how to make use of the DIMANGULAR and DIMRADIUS commands.

DIMENSIONING ANGLES AND RADII

1. Load the file 17TUT06.DWG from the accompanying CD. This file contains a simple filleted triangular object that you will dimension.

2. To start, choose Dimension, Radius to activate the DIMRADIUS command.

3. You will be prompted to select a circle or an arc. Select one of the filleted corners of the object.

4. You will immediately see the dimension appear. By moving the mouse around, you can see different looks for the dimension. Place the dimension outside the triangular area.

5. Now, select Dimension, Angular to invoke the DIMANGULAR command.

6. You will be prompted to select a line, arc, or circle or a first vertex. Click on the left vertical line of the shape.

7. You will then be prompted to select a second line. Click on the angled line on the top of the shape.

8. Now, move the mouse around in a circle around the upper-left corner of the shape. You will see that you have four possible dimensions. Place the dimension inside the shape so it measures the angle as 57 degrees.

9. Close this drawing without saving.

Ordinate Dimensions

Ordinate dimensions are used to dimension a specific coordinate, such as a point from a civil survey. For example, a civil survey relies upon a set of three-dimensional data points on which to base a topography. These coordinates are labeled using an ordinate dimension type, which labels the point's exact X and Y coordinates.

When using ordinate dimensions, you may dimension the X or Y axis points, called *datums*. You also have the option to create a leader-like ordinate dimension that has text before or after the coordinate. Figure 17.11 shows you an ordinate dimension.

Figure 17.11

An ordinate dimension showing both X and Y datums.

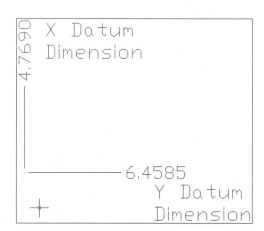

The ordinate dimension command can be accessed on the pull-down menu, on the toolbar, or by typing **DIMORD** at the command prompt. When you select this command, you are prompted to select the feature, or the coordinate, to dimension. After you select the coordinate, you can select the type of ordinate dimension you want to use.

The four types of ordinate dimensions are X datum, Y datum, Mtext, and Text. The X and Y datum points produce the corresponding coordinate. Mtext pops up the Multiline Text Editor dialog box so you can add text before and after the Datum dimension. The datum dimension appears as <> in the Multiline Text Editor dialog box. In fact, the first set of <> are used by all dimensions to produce the default dimension value. Figure 17.12 shows you the Multiline Text Editor dialog box when used with the ordinate Mtext option. The Text option enables you to modify the text of the Datum dimension, without having to use the Multiline Text Editor.

Figure 17.12

The Multiline Text Editor dialog box showing text before and after the ordinate dimension.

WARNING

You should not delete this <> marker, or the actual coordinate will not appear in the dimension.

The following exercise shows you how to use ordinate dimensions to dimension several survey points. In this exercise, the PDMODE system variable has been set so that points appear as crosses.

USING ORDINATE DIMENSIONS

1. Load the file 17TUT03.DWG from the accompanying CD.

2. Choose Ordinate from the Dimension pull-down menu or toolbar if it is open.

3. Using a node object snap mode, click on one of the crosses and place the dimension to the right of the point. Make sure you use the Polar Snap feature to place the dimension along the X axis.

4. Repeat steps 3 and 4, but place the dimension above the cross this time.

5. Repeat steps 3 through 5 for several other crosses so you get a little practice. Figure 17.13 shows you this file with a few ordinate dimensions added.

6. Close the drawing without saving it.

Figure 17.13

Figure 17.13

The points dimensioned
with ordinate dimensions.

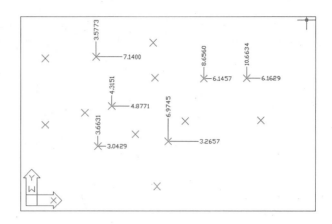

Tolerance Dimensions

Another dimension type is the tolerance dimension. *Tolerances* are used to provide constraints within which you can construct the drawn object. For example, you might construct a mechanical part and specify that its length may be 2.0 cm + or − 0.001 cm.

AutoCAD provides you with methods of creating tolerance dimensions. One method is to specify the tolerances in the Dimension Styles dialog box. The tolerances are then automatically added to the dimension text as you place dimensions. The second method is to use the tolerance command and place tolerance symbols on the drawing. The second method is the method discussed in the following section. Figure 17.14 shows a standard tolerance symbol inside of AutoCAD.

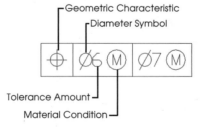

Figure 17.14

The tolerance dimension
and its parts.

Placing Tolerance Symbols in a Drawing

Under the Dimension menu and toolbars, you find a Tolerance option. Choosing this option displays the Geometric Tolerance dialog box, shown in Figure 17.15. The

Geometric Tolerance dialog box is used to select the appropriate type of tolerance you want to use, through the use of industry standard tolerance symbols.

Figure 17.15

The Geometric Tolerance dialog box enables you to specify the tolerances.

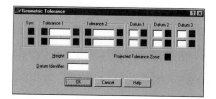

In the Geometric Tolerance dialog box, you can specify values for tolerances 1 and 2, as well as round symbols. You can also specify up to three datums, such as a material condition and a value for that condition. You can also specify height, projected tolerance zones, and datum identifiers.

At the far left of the Geometric Tolerances dialog box, you will find two black boxes for symbols. If you click on one, you will see the Symbols dialog box (see Figure 17.16). In this dialog box, notice the several different symbols, each representing a different geometric characteristic. When you choose one of the symbols, the selected tolerance method is then placed in the tolerance dimension itself. After you click on a geometric tolerance type, you are transferred back to the Geometric Tolerance dialog box where you may then enter the values for the tolerances.

Figure 17.16

The Symbol dialog box, in which you can select the type of tolerance you want to use.

Creating Annotation with a Leader

Leaders are the most popular method of adding notes and pointing out specific aspects of a drawing. A leader is a line with an arrowhead pointing to a specific feature with some sort of text or graphics at the end of the line. For example, you might create a wall section of a house and use leaders to point out specific materials in the section.

A leader is easily created by selecting the Leader command from the Dimension pull-down menu. When prompted for the first point, select the point where you want the arrowhead of the leader to appear. Then, you simply draw as many straight leader segments as you like. When you are done, press Enter, enter your text, and press Enter twice more to exit the command. This chapter will focus on several more advanced features of leaders, such as using the Multiline Text Editor dialog box to enter multiline text and using splines instead of straight line segments in your leaders.

Leader Options

When you select the Leader command, you are prompted for a point. This point is, of course, the location of the arrowhead. After you select the start point and then the second point, you are presented with the options for the Leader command. Usually, you type in a single line of text to complete the Leader command. Occasionally, however, you may want to select one of the three options available to you. These options are as follows:

- **Format.** This option enables you to specify a variety of formats for the leader, such as using splines instead of straight line segments, or whether you need to have an arrowhead.

  - *Splines.* A spline is a smooth curved line, instead of straight line segments. When you select this option, your leader line is drawn using the AutoCAD Spline command. Note that this is not a smooth polyline, but a true spline.

  - *Straight.* The Straight option creates a series of straight line segments. You may select either straight or spline, but you cannot have both. AutoCAD does not enable you to draw a leader line with both straight and curved segments. Figure 17.17 shows you one leader with splines and another leader with straight lines.

  - *Arrow.* The Arrow option defines whether an arrowhead is drawn. If you want to change the arrowhead to something other than a standard arrow, you must do so in the Dimension Styles dialog box, discussed in Chapter 18.

  - *None.* This option removes all formatting, including arrowheads, and draws straight line segments.

Figure 17.17

A leader with splines
versus one without splines.

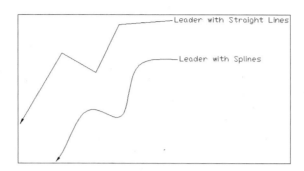

I NSIDER TIP

Each of the format options must be set each time you use the Leader command.

- **Annotation.** This option, which is the default, enables you to control how you place you text in the Leader command.

- **Undo.** This option removes the last line segment you drew in the Leader command.

Annotation Options

The *annotation* options provide you with some control over what is placed at the end of the leader line. When you select the Annotation option, you are presented with five options at the command line: Tolerance, Copy, Block, None, and Mtext, which is the default. All text in leaders is now placed using Mtext. If you select this option, you are presented with the Multiline Text Editor dialog box, where all the options of formatting Mtext are available to you. See Chapter 15, "Text Annotation," for more information about the Mtext command.

Three of the four other annotation options enable you to place a variety of objects rather than text at the end of the leader. You can place a tolerance dimension, copy an object from somewhere else in the drawing, or insert a block. Selecting one of these options launches the respective command. The last option is None, which removes all formatting.

NOTE

AutoCAD 2000 now has a QLEADER command that is very similar to a QDIM command. With QLEADER, many of the options are not available to you. You simply place the arrow point and second point, right-click, and then enter the text to complete the command. It saves you roughly one or two mouse clicks and one or two keystrokes versus a regular LEADER command. When possible, you should try to use the QLEADER command. It is the leader command that appears on the Dimension toolbar.

The following exercise shows you how to create leaders on a simple architectural wall section.

CREATING LEADERS IN AUTOCAD 2000

1. Load the file 17TUT04.DWG from the accompanying CD. Figure 17.18 shows you how the drawing should appear at the end of this exercise. Use it as a reference for completing this exercise.

Figure 17.18

The wall section as it will appear at the end of the exercise.

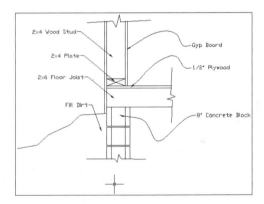

2. On the left side of the wall, create straight leaders by choosing the Leader command from the Dimension pull-down menu or toolbar.

3. When asked for the first point, select a point close to the arrowhead location of the 2 × 4 Wood Stud leader.

4. Select the second point of the leader, as shown in Figure 17.18.

5. At this point, you are presented with the leader options at the command prompt. Press Enter to accept the default Annotation Option, which enables you to add text to your leader.

6. Type in **2 × 4 Wood Stud** and press Enter to complete the leader.

7. Repeat steps 3 through 5 for the rest of the straight leaders shown in Figure 17.18.

8. For the spline leaders shown in Figure 17.18, again enter the Leader command.

9. Select your start point and a second point so you are presented with the options for the command.

10. Type **F** for the format options.

11. Type **S** for spline. Now the line is a spline. Draw the rest of the line and enter the appropriate text.

12. The detail is now complete. Close the drawing without saving it.

Increasing Productivity with Third-Party Programs

At this point, you have seen most of the options available to you for creating standard AutoCAD dimensions. By practicing and using the options that are available to you, you can increase your productivity to some degree in terms of dimensioning. The standard AutoCAD dimensioning commands are by no means slow, but you can increase your speed with a little help.

Many users today make use of third-party programs to help increase productivity in their respective professions. Many of these programs provide automated methods for creating these same dimensions.

An architectural modeling program, for example, enables you to create with one click all the necessary dimensions for a wall, including intersecting wall, door, and window locations, as well as overall dimensions. Then, all you have to do is correct any errors, if they exist. Both Autodesk's Architectural Desktop and Ketiv's ArchT are excellent examples of programs that automate the dimensioning process.

Other disciplines, such as civil engineering, may make use of programs such as Autodesk's Land Survey Desktop or Eagle Point Software's civil software. Both packages again automate dimensioning tasks.

In some programs, such as Mechanical Desktop, dimensions are a critical aspect of using the program correctly. In Mechanical Desktop, you must add enough dimensions to the object to fully *constrain* (define) it . After the object is constrained, the dimensions are *parametric*, meaning if you change the value of the dimension, the geometry also changes.

This list of third-party programs goes on and on. If you are using a third-party program, explore its dimensioning commands and compare how much faster or easier its commands are versus the standard AutoCAD commands.

Dimension Placement in the Drawing

When looking at productivity in terms of dimensioning a drawing, one other factor to consider is where you are placing your dimensions. You have two choices in AutoCAD: model space and paper space. Each space has pros and cons.

Pros and Cons of Dimensioning in Model Space

Most users today dimension their drawings in model space as opposed to placing dimensions in a paper space layout. The concept and features involved with layouts is covered in Chapter 19, "Paper Space Layouts." Dimensioning in model space comes naturally because the drawing is actually created in model space. The advantages and disadvantages are listed and briefly described.

The following are some advantages of creating dimensions in model space rather than in the layout window.

- You can use quick intuitive dimensioning directly on the drawing.

- When using associative dimensioning, you can stretch both the geometry and dimensions at the same time, enabling both the geometry and the dimensions to update at the same time.

- You can use the object selection dimensioning method. This is a simple selection, such as selecting a line to dimension, rather than picking points.

The following are some disadvantages of creating dimensions in model space rather than in the layout window.

- If you have a sheet with drawings created at different scales, you must use different scale dimensions as well using different layers.

- For dimensions to plot correctly, all dimensions must be scaled by a scale factor that is equivalent to the output plot scale.

Overall, the biggest reason to place your dimensions in model space is if you do not understand the layout window and how it works. Until you feel comfortable working in the layout window, create your dimensions in model space.

INSIDER **T**IP

If you work in an environment in which you constantly create drawing sheets with varying drawing scales, you should strongly consider using the layout window and its associated dimensioning methods.

Pros and Cons of Layout Dimensioning

When dimensioning in the layout environment, you are separating them from the drawing objects being dimensioned. Like model space, dimensioning in a paper space layout also has advantages and disadvantages.

The following are some advantages of creating dimensions in the layout window rather than using model space.

- Layout dimensions are separate from the drawing, which makes it easy to switch over to model space and view a clean drawing.

- All layout dimensions make use of the same dimension scale factor: 1.

- Dimensions can be placed on sheets more easily with multiple scales.

The following are some disadvantages of creating dimensions in the layout window rather than using model space.

- You cannot stretch layout dimensions and model space geometry at the same time.

- You cannot use the object selection dimensioning method.

- You have to adjust linear scaling factors to show the true model space dimension distance.

Ultimately, the decision of whether to use layout window dimensioning depends on your comfort with and understanding of the layout window itself. If you are not comfortable with it, continue to place dimensions in model space.

Improving Productivity: Tips and Techniques

The following are a few techniques to help you increase your dimensioning speed when you are creating dimensions. Editing dimensions is covered in the Chapter 18.

■ Create keyboard shortcuts for most of the dimension commands. For example, `DIMLINEAR` can be shortened to `DL`, which obviously is much quicker to type in. See Chapter 21, "Customizing Without Programming," for more information about keyboard shortcuts.

■ Create a chart of dimension scales for standard plot scales. That way, you create consistency in your drawing throughout your drafting operations.

■ Create a variety of dimension styles and save them to AutoCAD 2000 template files. Then, all you have to do is assign the appropriate style as the current one and begin dimensioning.

■ Whenever possible, use QDIM (Quick Dimension) for dimensioning because you can simply select the objects to be dimensioned.

■ If you are going to create a series of dimensions, consider using baseline or continue dimensions to help automate and speed up the process.

■ If you have a third-party program, consider using that program's dimensioning routines, if it has any. These routines will probably be quicker than the standard AutoCAD commands.

■ If you want to create a series of leaders, all using splines, consider writing either a script or LISP routine to enable you to create spline-based leaders quickly and easily. Otherwise, you must set the spline option each time.

Summary

Overall, AutoCAD 2000's dimension commands are fairly productive and much quicker than dimensioning by hand. The key things to remember are as follows:

■ Be familiar with all your dimensioning options. Many times, using a different command such as continue is quicker that using `DIMLINEAR`.

■ Consider using third-party programs to help increase dimensioning speed. You can also consider writing your own dimensioning routines in LISP.

■ When possible, use the object selection dimensioning method. Otherwise, you will have to pick the start, end, and dimension line points. In many cases, you may need to create temporary construction lines for dimensioning purposes.

The next chapter delves further into the world of dimensions and covers topics such as dimension styles, as well as editing existing dimensions, where AutoCAD is extremely fast.

18

ADVANCED DIMENSIONING

One of AutoCAD's best features is its capability to control and create dimensions in a drawing. In other words, AutoCAD 2000 provides you with several tools for editing dimensions, as well as controlling how a dimension appears in the drawing. This chapter focuses on the following topics:

■ *Dimension styles*

■ *Style options*

■ *Modifying dimensions*

Defining Dimension Styles

Dimension styles are your primary methods for controlling how a dimension appears. By creating a dimension style, you define exactly how that dimension is going to appear in the drawing. This includes the dimension scale, the types of arrowheads, whether or not the dimension lines appear and, if so, what color the dimension lines are.

AutoCAD allows you to control dimension styles through the use of Dimension Variables (DIMVARS). You can control these variables in two different ways. You can use the DDIM Dimension Style dialog box to access many of the variables using a graphical interface, or you can type the variable at the command prompt or `DIM:` prompt and assign it a new value. There are 68 dimension variables in AutoCAD 2000. Most of the time, adjusting the dimension variables through the Dimension Styles dialog box is the best method to use (see Figure 18.1). You can access this dialog box by choosing Dimension Styles from the Dimension toolbar or by choosing Dimension Style Manager from the Dimension menu.

Figure 18.1

The Dimension Style Manager dialog box enables you to control how a dimension is drawn.

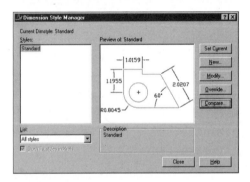

The Dimension Style Manager allows you to set the current dimension style, create a new style, modify an existing style, override part of the current style, or even compare two existing styles in the same drawing. To make it even easier for you to make changes, the Style Manager gives you a graphical preview of what the currently selected dimension style will look like when used in the drawing.

Dimension Style Options

Dimension styles provide you with a method for saving different sets of dimension variables for the various types of drawings you might create. You have many options for defining how a dimension looks. To help you understand some of these options,

Figure 18.2 shows you a standard linear dimension with all the parts of the dimension labeled.

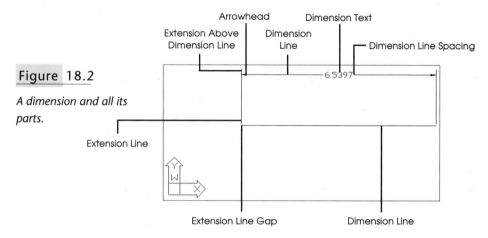

Figure 18.2

A dimension and all its parts.

To edit a dimension style, you simply open the Dimension Style Manager, select the style you want to edit, and click the Modify button. To create a new style, you can choose New in the Style Manager. In the dialog box that appears (see Figure 18.3), you can name the style and base it on an existing style.

Figure 18.3

In the Create New Dimension Style dialog box, you can give the style a name, select the base style, and specify how the dimension style will be used.

Regardless of whether you choose to modify an existing dimension style or create a new one, the Dimension Style dialog box shown in Figure 18.4 appears, in which you can edit the individual parts of the style.

Figure 18.4

*In the Dimension Style
dialog box, you can
change the settings for
each individual part of the
dimension.*

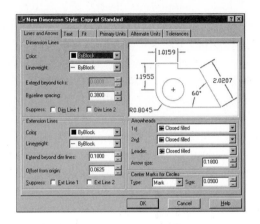

The following exercise shows you how to create and/or edit dimension styles.

CREATING A NEW DIMENSION STYLE

1. Start a new drawing in AutoCAD.

2. From the Dimension pull-down menu, select Style. This launches the Dimension Style dialog box, in which you can create, edit, and even compare dimension styles.

3. All drawings start with the Standard dimension style, on which you can base new dimension styles. To create a new style, click on the New button. This opens the Create New Dimension Style dialog box.

4. Under New Style Name, enter a name for the style using a name that you will recognize easily. This can be any name you like.

5. Under Start With, select the dimension style you want to base the new style on. The Standard style already exists in this drawing, so you can create another style based on it.

6. In the Use For drop-down list, select the types of dimensions you want to use the style for. If you select an option other than All, the new dimension style can be used with only the type of dimension you choose.

7. Click OK, and the New Dimension Style dialog box appears. You can make any changes you need to the style.

8. In the Arrowheads area, click in the drop-down list for 1st Arrowhead and choose Closed Blank. Then click OK to return to the Dimension Style dialog box.

9. In the list on the left, you will now see the name of the new style you just created. To edit the dimension style, make sure it is still highlighted and click on the Modify button. This returns you to the Modify Dimension Style dialog box, where you can make further changes.

10. To compare two dimension styles, click the Compare button. This launches the Compare Dimension Style dialog box.

11. At the top of this dialog box, you will see two drop-down lists. In the Compare drop-down list, select the first dimension style.

12. In the With drop-down list, select the second style. You will immediately see a list of variables that differ between the styles (if there are any).

13. Click Close in each dialog box to return to the drawing.

The Dimension Style dialog box contains a tabbed interface for each set of controls for the style. A preview window accompanies each tabbed page to show you exactly what the dimension style looks like based on the current settings. This preview window enables you to make a change to the style so you can immediately see the effect of that change. The tabs in this dialog box are listed below and explained in the following sections:

- Lines and Arrows

- Text

- Fit

- Primary Units

- Alternate Units

- Tolerances

Lines and Arrows Tab

The selections found on the Lines and Arrows tab (refer to Figure 18.4) enable you to control all the dimension system variables related to the geometry of the dimension, except for the text. This tab is broken down into four distinct areas: Dimension Lines, Arrowheads, Extension Lines, and Center Marks for Circles.

The Dimension Lines section controls the appearance of the dimension line. In a linear dimension, this is the line beside or below the dimension text. In certain circumstances, you may want to create a dimension without the dimension line. For example, you may have a short dimension with large text centered inside of the dimension line. In this situation, you can suppress the first or second dimension line or both. When the dimension text is above the dimension line, the suppression options have no effect. The location of the dimension text is controlled by the Format options, which are covered in the next section.

The Extend Beyond Ticks option, which is grayed out by default, is used in conjunction with certain arrowhead types. In particular, the oblique and architectural tick arrowheads make use of this option. When one of these two arrowheads is active, you can adjust the extension of the dimension line beyond the extension lines.

A commonly used dimension line option is that of color. The default color of the dimension line is BYBLOCK, which means the line will take on the color of the dimension as a whole. The only reason to change this color is if you want a different line width for the dimension line. For example, you could have a thinner line for the dimension line versus the extension lines.

NEW for R2000

Another way to control the thickness of the plotted lines is to use lineweights. You can control extension or dimension lineweights via the Dimension Style Manager to apply to all same name dimension styles. Additionally, it should be noted that lineweights set at the dimension level override any settings to the layers or object directly. Refer to Chapter 5, "Using Linetypes and Lineweights Effectively," for more information about using lineweights.

The options in the Extension Lines area of the dialog box perform the same functions as those under Dimension Lines. The notable exception is the Offset from Origin option. When you create a dimension, such as a linear dimension, you select two points for the dimension. These points are considered the extension line origin points. The origin offset defines the distance from these points that the extension line is started.

The Arrowheads section of the Lines and Arrows tab provides you with complete control over the arrows. AutoCAD 2000 provides you with standard arrowheads, including closed filled, open 30, dot blanked, box filled, and many others. Even with all these arrowheads, you may want to create your own. To create your own arrowheads, in the 1st and 2nd drop-down lists, select the User Arrow option. This option enables you to select any block for use as an arrow, as long as that block is already defined in the current AutoCAD drawing. The arrowhead block should be created with an overall size of one unit so it will be correctly scaled when used in the dimension. It also should be created for use at the right-hand end of the dimension. The block will be rotated for the opposite end.

INSIDER TIP

When you create a custom arrowhead, you should save the arrowhead as a block in a template file so it is available to all drawings based on that template.

Figure 18.5 shows you the dialog box in which you can enter the block name for the arrowhead.

Figure 18.5

In the Select Custom Arrow Block dialog box, you can select any block for use as the arrowhead in your dimensions.

The following exercise shows you how to create your own arrowheads.

CREATING YOUR OWN ARROWHEADS

1. Start a new drawing from scratch.

2. Create an octagon using the polygon command. Make the radius of the polygon one unit.

3. Make a block of the polygon with an insertion point at the center of the polygon. Name the block P1.

4. From the Dimension pull-down menu, choose Style.

5. In the Dimension Style dialog box, select the Standard style and click on the Modify button.

6. In the Lines and Arrows tab, select User Arrow from the 1st drop-down list.

7. In the User Arrow dialog box, enter P1 as the arrow name.

8. Click on OK to close the Select Custom Arrow Block dialog box.

9. Click on OK to close the Geometry dialog box and return to the Dimension Styles dialog box.

10. Click Close to save the dimension style changes to Standard and exit the dialog box.

11. Create a linear dimension. Figure 18.6 shows a linear dimension created with a custom arrowhead.

12. You can now close the drawing without saving it.

Figure 18.6

A linear dimension with a custom arrowhead.

The last section of the Lines and Arrows tab controls center marks and scaling. The Center options define how center marks appear when used with radius and diameter dimensions.

Text Tab

The Text tab, shown in Figure 18.7, enables you to control how the text is displayed in your dimensions. In the Text Style drop-down list, you can select any previously defined text style. (See Chapter 15, "Text Annotation," for more on how to define a text style.) You could also create a new text style by clicking on the button to the right of the Text Style drop-down list. This launches the Text Style dialog box, where you can create the new style.

Figure 18.7

The Text tab of the Dimension Style dialog box. Here you can control how and where the text appears in your dimensions.

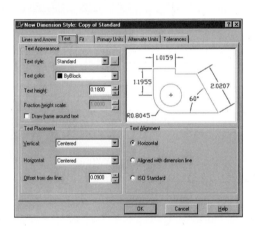

After you select a text style, you can apply other properties, such as height and color. The Height option, in particular, depends on how the text style is defined. If the text style is defined with a fixed height, that height will be used. If the originating text style's height is set to 0, the height specified in the Text tab will be used instead.

In addition to selecting the text style, you can control the placement of the text around the dimension line, as well as the alignment of the text in the drawing.

Fit Tab

The Fit tab of the Dimension Styles dialog box (see Figure 18.8) enables you to control how the text is placed when the dimension is too small for the text to fit between the extension lines.

Figure 18.8

In the Fit tab of the Dimension Style dialog box, you can control what happens to text when there isn't room for it.

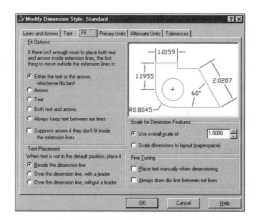

The Fit Options section contains the following six options:

- **Either the Text or the Arrows, Whichever Fits Best.** When this option is selected, AutoCAD will try to determine the best method to use to create the most readable dimension. This is the default option.

- **Arrows.** When this option is selected, only the arrows will be forced inside of the extension lines. Text may appear outside the extension lines when the distance between the lines is too small for the text to fit otherwise.

- **Text.** When this option is selected, only text will be forced inside the extension lines. Arrows can be pushed outside the extension lines when the distance between the lines is small enough.

- **Both Text and Arrows.** When this option is selected, both the text and arrows will be forced inside the extension lines, even when there is not enough room for them.

- **Always Keep Text Between Ext Lines.** When this option is selected, the text will always be placed between the extension lines of the dimension, regardless of whether or not it will fit.

- **Suppress Arrows If They Don't Fit Inside the Extension Lines.** This option enables you to suppress the drawing of the arrows on a dimension when the text is forced inside of the extension lines.

The Text Placement options enable you to control where the text is placed in relation to the dimension line when the text is not in the default position. You can choose from three ways of handling this: You can place the text beside the line, over the line with a leader, or over the line without a leader.

INSIDER TIP

In the architectural field, dimension text is typically above the dimension line. If you adjust an existing dimension with this property by using the Grip feature and drag the dimension to the side, however, a leader appears underneath the text. This can be undesirable and annoying. A quick fix to this is to use the DimOverRide command. When you use this command, the system asks you for a dimension variable to override. Type **DIMTAD** (DIMension Text Above Dimension), set it to 1, and then select the newly moved dimension with the incorrect leader format. When you finish, the dimension settings will be returned to normal.

Probably the most important options in the Fit tab of the Dimension Style dialog box are the Scale options. There are two scale options: Overall Scale and Scale to Layout. The Overall Scale controls how large all the features of the dimension (such as arrowheads) will appear in the drawing. This scale is directly related to the final plot scale for the drawing. For example, if you are plotting at an architectural scale of 1/4 inch = 1'–0", your Overall Scale factor should be 48. You obtain this value by inverting the desired plot scale. In another instance, a scale such as 1:50 equates to 1/50 = 1, so the overall scale factor is 600.

When you set the scale factor, you define a scale multiplier by which all dimension size variables are multiplied. For example, arrowheads default to 0.18 units in size. If you have a scale factor of 48, the 0.18 is multiplied by 48 to arrive at the current size, correctly scaled for plotting.

If you are going to dimension in a paper space layout, you can leave the Overall Scale factor set to 1, or you can turn on the Scale to Layout option. The Scale to Layout option sets the dimension variable DIMSCALE to 0. In layout, a default value of 1.0 will be used. In this situation, when you are working in a model space viewport in layout, you can create a dimension in either space, and it will be scaled correctly. This assumes that you have used the Zoom command to correctly scale the geometry in the model space viewport. See Chapter 19, "Paper Space Layouts," for more information about layouts and working with model space viewports.

Primary Units Tab

The Primary Units tab (shown in Figure 18.9) is used to define the units that dimensions will use in their text. Unfortunately, AutoCAD does not automatically set the dimension units to match your Units setting in AutoCAD. Therefore, you must correctly define the units for your dimensions separately.

Figure 18.9

In the Primary Units tab, you can define the units that are displayed in your dimensions.

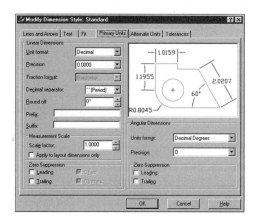

NOTE

One reason AutoCAD does not automatically use the Units setting from the drawing is because additional unit types are available to you in the dimensions that are not supported in the Units setting.

In the Linear Dimensions section of the tab, you can select the type of units, precision of the display, and even prefixes and suffixes. For example, if you select architectural units, you can select the precision with which the units will be displayed, how fractions are drawn (horizontal, slanted, or not stacked), and whether you want to append FT or IN to the dimension as a suffix. One important option in this section of the dialog box is the Round Off option, which enables you to define the increment to which the dimension measurements are rounded off.

The Measurement Scale option is used to adjust how the distance between the start and end points of the dimension is measured. Most of the time, this option is used when dimensions are drawn in a layout. When you place a dimension in a layout, it measures the dimension in layout units, not model space units.

In a viewport that is scaled to 1/4" = 1'–0", for example, a 4-foot line will measure 1 inch. This is because the underlying scale factor differs 1/48 between layout and model space. Just as you have to adjust the overall scale factor of a dimension style for model space, you must adjust the linear scale to match layout. It is calculated in the same way as the overall scale factor. In the above example, a linear scale of 48 is correct.

Zero Suppression is used to control when a 0 appears in a dimension. For example, 6' is a valid dimension in architectural units. However, 6' is easily confused with 6", especially if the blueprint of the drawing is not very good. In both cases, the leading or trailing zeros have been suppressed. These dimensions read much easier as 6'_0" and 0'_6". You can set this up by disabling zero suppression for feet and inches. You can also control zero suppression for leading and trailing zeros such as 0.6 and 6.000.

Lastly, you can set the options for angular dimensions. Here you can define what unit format angles are read back and the precision of the angle measurements. Like linear dimensions, angles also have a setting for zero suppression.

Alternate Units Tab

The Alternate Units tab enables you to display alternate units in your drawing. For example, you might have drawings with architectural units and metric units as alternate units. Figure 18.10 shows an example of alternate units used in a dimension.

Figure 18.10

A dimension showing alternate units.

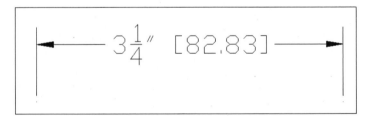

When alternate units are enabled, the controls for this tab of the Dimension Style dialog box are the same as those found in the Primary Units tab.

Tolerances Tab

The Tolerances tab (shown in Figure 18.11) of the Dimension Style dialog box enables you to add tolerances to the end of the dimension text. These tolerances are different from those related to the Tolerance command discussed in Chapter 17, "Productive Dimensioning."

Figure 18.11

In the Tolerances tab of the Dimension Style dialog box, you can set up tolerances to be displayed with your dimensions.

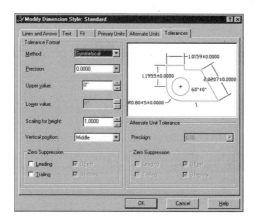

Actually, there are five different types of tolerances, each of which is briefly described in the following list:

- **None.** No tolerances are used in the dimension.

- **Symmetrical.** The tolerance is applied with a high and low limit that are the same. For example, 1.00 +/– 0.1 is a symmetrical tolerance.

- **Deviation.** The tolerance is applied with a high and low limit that can differ. As long as the object is manufactured within the limit, it is acceptable.

- **Limits.** The tolerance completely replaces the dimension. As long as the object is manufactured within the tolerances, it is acceptable.

- **Basic.** No tolerance is used, but a box is drawn around the dimension to help emphasize it.

After you select the tolerance method, you can apply an upper and lower value, as well as justification of the text in the dimension line. Figure 18.12 shows a dimension with a symmetrical tolerance applied.

Figure 18.12

A dimension showing the use of symmetrical tolerances.

The following exercise ties together all the information you have learned in this chapter so far. It shows you how to quickly and easily set up a complete dimension style for use in AutoCAD.

CREATING A DIMENSION STYLE FOR A MECHANICAL DRAWING

1. Start a new drawing.

2. From the Dimension menu, choose Style.

3. In the Dimension Style dialog box, click on New and give the new style the name **MECH1**.

4. Click on Continue. Then click on Modify to change the style.

5. In the Center Marks for Circles area of the Lines and Arrows tab, select Line.

6. In the Arrowheads area, select Dot for 1st arrowhead. The 2nd arrowhead will automatically change to match the 1st.

7. In the Extension Lines area, select Red as the color.

8. Click on the Text tab.

9. In the Text Placement section, set the Vertical option to Above.

10. In the Text Alignment area, turn on Aligned with Dimension Line.

11. Click on the Primary Units tab and, in the Linear Dimension area, set the Precision to 0.00.

12. In the Angular Dimensions area, set the Precision to 0.0.

13. Set the Text dimension color to green.

14. Click on the Tolerances tab and set the Tolerance Format Method to Symmetrical.

15. Set the Upper Value to 0.2.

16. Click on OK to close the Dimension Style dialog box.

17. Click on the MECH1 style, and then click the Set Current button in the upper-right portion of the dialog box.

18. Click Close to save and exit the Dimension Style dialog box and return to AutoCAD.

19. Create a couple of linear dimensions in this style. Figure 18.13 shows a few possibilities you could create using the MECH1 dimension types.

Figure 18.13

A few dimensions created with the MECH1 dimension style.

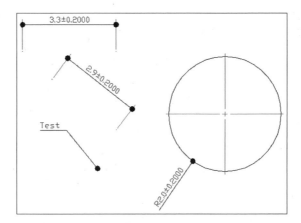

Now you know about the processes and steps for working with dimension styles. The following section introduces some important tips that will help you optimize your dimension styles.

Tips for Creating Effective Dimension Styles

The following list offers a few tips and techniques concerning dimension styles:

- Create all necessary styles and save them in a drawing template. That way, you never have to re-create the same styles and can easily load them into new drawings.

■ Give your styles names that make sense to you and to others. For example, ARCH48 is more easily recognized as an Architectural dimension style for a ¼" drawing than is a name such as STYLE1.

■ Make use of families when you need your dimension styles to change slightly when you're using different dimension types. This saves you from having to set dimension styles every time you change dimension types such as linear or angular.

Modifying Dimensions

After you have created your dimension styles and created a variety of dimensions in your drawing, eventually you may need to modify the dimensions. Some reasons you might need to modify existing dimensions include the following:

■ The drawing plot scale changes.

■ You make a change to dimensioned geometry.

■ You want to override the AutoCAD measurement for the dimension.

■ You want to re-position the dimension text for the purpose of clarity.

■ You want to change the settings for some elements of a dimension without having to re-create the dimension.

The sections that follow discuss the various techniques for modifying existing dimensions.

NOTE

The rest of this chapter assumes that Associative Dimensioning is turned on. This is controlled through the DIMASO dimension variable, which should be set to On. Without associative dimensioning, you cannot update or modify your dimensions because they are broken down into individual entities and are not considered an individual dimension entity after they are created. To check the DIMASO setting, type **DIMASO** at the command prompt. It will be either On or Off. DIMASO is set to On by default.

Leaders, of course, do not make use of associativity and, therefore, are slightly different when it comes to dimension editing. In most cases, you will simply edit leaders as normal AutoCAD entities.

Grip Editing

One of the most powerful methods of editing in AutoCAD is *grip editing*. Just as you can grip edit most objects in AutoCAD, you can grip edit dimensions as well. However, you can use grip editing only if the variables PICKFIRST and GRIPS are enabled and set to a value of 1.

To grip edit a dimension, click on the dimension to highlight it. If the dimension is associative, the five grip boxes will appear on a linear dimension, as shown in Figure 18.14.

Figure 18.14

You can use grip boxes to edit a linear dimension.

Of course, the exact location and the effect of each grip differs from dimension type to dimension type. Figure 18.15 shows the grip layout for a radius dimension.

Figure 18.15

The dimension grips for a radial dimension.

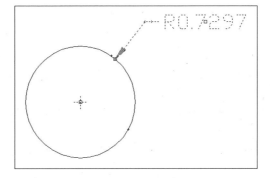

To edit a grip, click on one of the blue grip boxes. The box turns red to indicate that it is selected. Then right-click on the box to view the grip editing pop-up menu shown in Figure 18.16.

Figure 18.16

The right-click menu that appears when you right-click on a grip to edit a dimension.

With the enhanced right-click capabilities in AutoCAD 2000, you will find that not only can you choose options for working with the selected grip, you can also find options for editing the dimension itself. This enables you to control options such as the placement of the dimension text, the precision of the measurement, and even the dimension style itself.

Most of the time, you will use the Move option to reposition the dimension text, the dimension line, or the start or end points of the dimension. After you select the option you want, simply grip edit the dimension just as you would any other object. See Chapter 11, "Advanced Geometry Editing," for more information on grip editing.

You might encounter a couple of problems when editing dimensions with grips:

■ If you select the grip that is nearest to the dimension text and select Rotate, the dimension will rotate around the text. The text itself does not rotate. You must use a special dimension editing command (DIMEDIT) if you want to rotate the text and not the dimension line.

■ If you are working with a radius or diameter dimension, you can grip edit the center point of the dimension. If you reposition the center point, the dimension text will change. AutoCAD does not maintain a link between the dimensioned object's center and the dimension itself. Always make sure you move the point back to the center of the dimensioned object.

NOTE

PICKFIRST and GRIPS must both be enabled. They are enabled by default in AutoCAD; if you have disabled them, re-enable them for this exercise.

The following exercise shows you how to make use of grip editing with dimensions.

GRIP EDITING A DIMENSION

1. Load the file 18TUT01.DWG from the accompanying CD-ROM, and then turn on a running object snap mode of Endpoint.

2. Click on the dimension to highlight it and show the grips.

3. Click on the lower-right grip to highlight it.

4. Right-click on the same grip and choose Copy from the pop-up menu.

5. Select each corner going to the right to create three more dimensions.

6. Press Enter once.

7. Click on the dimension farthest to the right.

8. Select the grip at the intersection of the dimension and extension lines and move the dimension up into position, as shown in Figure 18.17.

Figure 18.17

The first dimension is in position, but the copies overlay it.

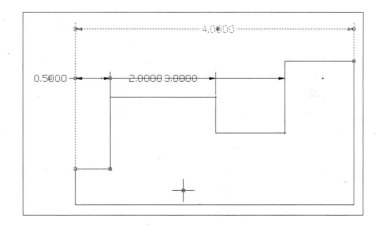

9. Repeat steps 2–10 for the other two dimensions. Figure 18.18 shows you the final dimensioned drawing.

10. Close the drawing without saving.

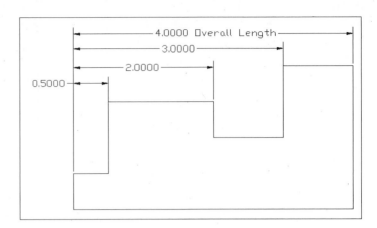

Editing Dimension Text

One of the most common editing tasks for a dimension is changing the dimension text after the dimension has been created. The easiest way to edit the text is to choose Text from the Modify pull-down menu. This executes the DDEDIT command. If you select the dimension object, the Multiline Text Editor appears, as shown in Figure 18.19.

The only thing that appears in the dialog box is <>. This symbol indicates the measured AutoCAD value. To replace the measured value, delete the <> and replace it with the value you want. Otherwise, add the text before and/or after the symbol as you see fit. Pay attention to the amount and size of the text for the dimension. You don't want to put in more information than there is room for.

When it comes to leaders, the DDEDIT command works just fine for editing the text.

In addition to changing the value of the text in a dimension, you can also rotate and reposition the text. The fastest and easiest way to reposition text is to simply grip edit the dimension. Alternatively, you can use the DIMTEDIT command, which you access by clicking on the Dimension Text Edit button on the Dimension toolbar or by choosing Align Text from the Dimension pull-down menu. For the pull-down menu version, each DIMTEDIT option is listed individually on the Align Text cascade menu.

`DIMTEDIT` enables you to reposition the text and to align it to the left or right side of the dimension. If you make a mistake, `DIMTEDIT` also has a Home option you can use to move the text back to its original position. The last `DIMTEDIT` option is Rotate, which enables you to rotate the text of a dimension without rotating the dimension itself.

The following exercise shows you how to edit the text of a dimension.

EDITING THE DIMENSION TEXT

1. Load the file 18TUT02.DWG from the accompanying CD.

2. Choose Text from the Modify pull-down menu and click on the 4.000 dimension. AutoCAD displays the Mtext dialog box.

3. After the < > symbol, type the text **Overall Length**.

4. Click OK to close the Mtext dialog box. Figure 18.20 shows the resulting dimension.

Figure 18.20

The dimension with the modified text.

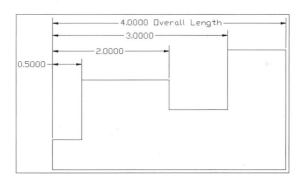

5. Now suppose you want to rotate the text of the dimension 45 degrees. You can accomplish this with the `DIMTEDIT` command.

6. From the Dimension pull-down menu, select Align, Angle.

7. Select the dimension you just modified.

8. Enter a value of **45** to rotate the text, and then press Enter.

9. If you make a mistake when editing the position and rotation of the dimension text with DIMTEDIT, or if you simply want to return the dimension to its original condition, you can use the Home option to restore it. Choose Dimension, Align, Home.

10. Select the dimension and press Enter. The text is returned to its original position.

11. You can close the drawing without saving it.

Updating Dimensions

Another popular dimension editing task is updating an existing dimension to the current dimension style. This is often necessary when a user creates drawings with many different dimension styles. When you use many dimension styles in a drawing, it is very easy to create a dimension in the wrong style by accident. AutoCAD offers three ways to update the style of a dimension:

- Modify the style
- Update the dimension with DIMSTYLE
- Revise the dimension with Update

If you modify a dimension style that is currently in use in the drawing, when you save the style and exit the Dimension Style dialog box, all dimensions using that style will automatically be updated with the new settings. In some instances, you may have to refresh the screen to see the changes.

If you want to change a dimension to a differently named style, you must first set the active current style to the new style desired. You can do this in the Dimension Style dialog box, or you can use the DIMSTYLE system variable. After resetting the current style, you can choose Dimension, Update or use the Dimension Update tool on the Dimension toolbar. Then select the dimension, and it will be updated to match the new style.

The following exercise shows you how to update AutoCAD dimensions.

UPDATING DIMENSIONS IN AUTOCAD

1. Open the file 18TUT03.DWG from the accompanying CD-ROM.

2. Choose Dimension, Style to open the Dimension Style dialog box.

3. Set the style 18TUT3 as the current style.

4. Click OK to close the Dimension Style dialog box.

5. Choose Dimension, Update.

6. Select all the dimensions in the drawing and press Enter. The dimensions are updated, as shown in Figure 18.21.

Figure 18.21

The updated dimensions.

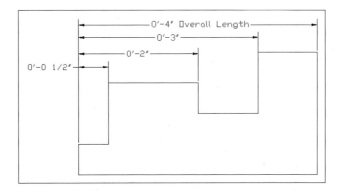

7. Save the files as 18TUT05.DWG on your hard drive for use in the next exercise.

Using DIMEDIT

DIMEDIT is another AutoCAD dimension editing tool. To use this command, you type DIMEDIT at the command prompt, or select the Dimension Edit tool from the Dimension toolbar. It is not available from the Dimension pull-down menu.

DIMEDIT enables you to reposition the dimension text back to the home position, rotate the text, and replace the dimension text, just as DIMEDIT does. What is unique about DIMEDIT is its capability to add an obliquing angle setting to a dimension. An obliquing angle forces the vertical extension lines off from vertical by the angle specified. This is more of a cosmetic adjustment you might use to make a dimension look more interesting. Obliquing a dimension does not affect the text, dimension line, arrowheads, or origin points. It affects only the extension lines.

The following exercise shows you how to use DIMEDIT.

USING DIMEDIT ON A DIMENSION

1. Continue from the last exercise, or load the file 18TUT04.DWG from the accompanying CD-ROM.

2. Open the Dimension toolbar if it is not open already and select the Dimension Edit tool.

3. At the command prompt, type **O** for Oblique.

4. Select all the dimensions in the drawing and press Enter.

5. Enter **85** as the oblique angle and press Enter. Figure 18.22 shows the resulting drawing.

Figure 18.22

The drawing with oblique dimensions.

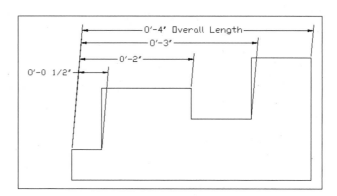

Overriding Dimension Variables

A lesser-known method of modifying a dimension is to override a dimension variable. When you are creating a dimension in a specific style, it is possible to override one or more dimension variables in the current style. For example, you may want to change the color of the dimension text for a couple of dimensions and then revert back to the original if you so desire.

There are several ways to implement a dimension variable override. The easiest way is to override the dimension variable when you are creating the dimension. Unfortunately, to do this, you must know the name of the dimension variable you want to override. When you start the dimension command, such as DIMLINEAR, enter the name of the dimension variable you want to override. Give it the new value, and that value will be used until you clear the override. For example, DIMASZ controls the size of the arrowheads. You can override this variable with a larger or smaller value than that found in the dimension style.

To clear a dimension override, you can use the DIMOVERRIDE command, which is available on the Dimension pull-down menu as Override. At the command prompt, you will be asked for the dimension variable to override. You can type **Clear** at this prompt to clear all overrides and revert to the original style definition. Alternatively, you can enter any dimension variable, override it, and apply it to existing dimensions.

Alternately, and probably more conveniently, you can override dimension style variables from the Dimension Style dialog box. To do so, select the style you want to override and click on the Override button. The Modify dialog box appears. Override any styles you like. Then click OK to return to the Dimension Style dialog box, and you will see the Dimension style listed in an outline format with a Style Overrides listing below it. To remove the overrides, right-click on the listing and choose Delete. You can also choose to rename those overrides or to incorporate them into the style permanently.

Overrides stay valid until you execute the CLEAR command, choose a new style, or change the override to another value.

To help you make effective use of the override command, Table 18.1 lists all the dimension variables and what each does.

Table 18.1

Dimension Variables and Meanings

Variable	Function
DIMADEC	Lets you control angle precision.
DIMALT	Enables the use of alternate dimensions units.
DIMALTD	Controls the decimal places used in alternate units.
DIMALTF	Controls the alternate unit scale factor.
DIMALTRND	Controls the alternate unit roundoff.
DIMALTTD	Indicates the number of decimals in a tolerance in an alternate unit.
DIMATTZ	Toggles suppression of zeros for tolerances.
DIMALTU	Controls unit format for alternate units except for angular dims.
DIMALTZ	Controls suppression of zeros for alternate units.
DIMAPOST	Allows you to specify the text prefix or suffix for alternate dimensions except angular.
DIMASO	Enables associative dimensions.
DIMASZ	Controls the arrowhead sizes.
DIMATFIT	Controls Fit: Arrows and Text.
DIMAUNIT	Specifies angle format for angular dimensions.
DIMAZIN	Indicates Angle Zero Suppression.
DIMBLK	Lets you specify the name of the block to be drawn instead of a regular arrowhead.
DIMBLK1	Allows the use of a user-defined arrowhead 1.
DIMBLK2	Allows the use of a user-defined arrowhead 2.

continues

Table 18.1, continued

Variable	Function
DIMCEN	Enables use of center marks.
DIMCLRD	Sets the color of the dimension line.
DIMCLRE	Sets the color of the extension line.
DIMCLRT	Sets the color of the dimension text.
DIMDEC	Controls the number of decimal places for primary tolerances.
DIMDLE	Controls extension of dimension line when oblique or architectural tick arrowheads are used.
DIMDLI	Controls dimension line spacing for baseline dimensions.
DIMDSEP	Indicates decimal separator.
DIMEXE	Allows you to specify the distance extension lines extend beyond the dimension line.
DIMEXO	Controls the extension line offset.
DIMFIT	Indicates placement of arrows and dimension lines inside of extension lines.
DIMFRAC	Specifies Dimension Fraction Format.
DIMGAP	Controls the gap around dimension text.
DIMJUST	Allows you to specify horizontal dimension text position.
DIMLDRBLK	Controls the Leader Arrow Block.
DIMLFAC	Sets the global scale factor for linear measurements.
DIMLIM	Generates dimension limits as default text.
DIMLUNIT	Sets units for all dimension types except Angular.
DIMLWD	Controls Dimension Line Lineweight.
DIMLWE	Controls Dimension Line Extension Lineweight.
DIMPOST	Allows you to specify a prefix or suffix for text.
DIMRND	Sets dimension rounding value.
DIMSAH	Enables use of user-defined arrowheads.
DIMSCALE	Indicates overall scale factor.
DIMSD1	Controls first dimension line suppression.

Variable	Function
DIMSD2	Controls second dimension line suppression.
DIMSE1	Controls first extension line suppression.
DIMSE2	Controls second extension line suppression.
DIMSHO	Controls redefinition of dimension when dragged.
DIMSOXD	Suppresses drawing of dimension lines outside extension lines.
DIMSTYLE	Indicates current dimension style.
DIMTAD	Allows you to control vertical position of text in relation to the dimension line.
DIMTDEC	Sets number of decimals in a tolerance.
DIMTFAC	Indicates scale factor for text height in tolerances.
DIMTIH	Controls position of text inside extension lines.
DIMTIX	Draws text between extension lines
DIMTM	Lower tolerance limit.
DIMTMOVE	Controls Fit: Text movement.
DIMTOFL	Forces drawing of dimension line.
DIMTOH	Indicates position of text outside of extension lines.
DIMTOL	Appends tolerances to text.
DIMTOLJ	Allows you to specify vertical justification of tolerances.
DIMTP	Sets upper tolerance limit.
DIMTSZ	Indicates size of oblique dimension arrowheads.
DIMTVP	Lets you set vertical position of text.
DIMTXT	Controls text height.
DIMTXTSTY	Indicates text style for the dimension.
DIMTZIN	Sets zero suppression of tolerance values.
DIMUNIT	Controls unit format for dimensions except angular.
DIMUPT	Specifies cursor functionality for user-positioned text.
DIMZIN	Controls suppression of primary unit value.

For most dimension variables, you may need to look up exactly what values can be used. Many are simply 1 or 0 (on and off); others, such as DIMSTYLE, accept text strings. If you are going to use overrides, though, you need to know which variables you want to override and how you want to override them.

The following exercise shows you how to make use of dimension overrides.

OVERRIDING DIMENSION VARIABLES

1. Load the file 18TUT05.DWG from the accompanying CD-ROM.

2. Turn on the ENDPOINT running OSNAP if it's not already active.

3. Choose Linear from the Dimension pull-down menu and create an overall dimension.

4. Select DIMLINEAR again by pressing Enter.

5. At the First Extension line prompt, type **DIMBLK** and press Enter.

6. Enter the string value of **ARCHTEXT** to set a new arrowhead format.

7. Dimension the smaller horizontal lengths of the block, as shown in Figure 18.23.

Figure 18.23

The drawing with correctly placed dimensions.

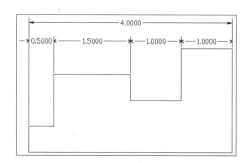

8. Select DIMLINEAR.

9. Enter **DIMBLK** again and set it back to Closed Filled by entering just a period (.). That is a quick way to revert to a standard filled arrowhead.

10. Dimension the right vertical edge of the block. Figure 18.24 shows you the final drawing.

Figure 18.24

The drawing with four overridden dimensions.

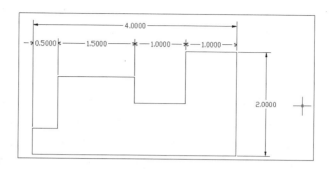

Figure 18.24

The drawing with four overridden dimensions.

Summary

AutoCAD provides you with a fair amount of control over dimensions through dimension styles. By making good use of templates, you can save your dimension styles so you don't have to re-create them.

After you create dimensions, of course, you need to be able to edit them. The primary methods for editing dimensions are grip editing, DDEDIT, and DIMTEDIT. Each method gives you various ways of editing the dimension, from editing text to positioning text.

19

PAPER SPACE LAYOUTS

Paper space layouts provide the ability to plot a model space drawing without cluttering the drawing with objects that are needed only for plotting purposes, such as title blocks and sheet borders. You can create a standard size sheet border in a layout, insert a view of your model, and plot it at a 1:1 scale. By creating multiple viewports of the model space objects, you can view the objects from different angles. After establishing the views, you can move and arrange the viewports in the layout to any necessary position inside the sheet border. You can accomplish all this without compromising the purity of the model space drawing by allowing the project's design model to exist separately from objects needed only for plotting sheets. By using layouts properly, you can quickly and easily design the sheets you need to plot model space objects.

This chapter discusses the following subjects:
- *The basics of paper space*
- *Using paper space layouts*
- *New AutoCAD 2000 features*

Using Paper Space Layouts

AutoCAD 2000 introduces a new feature called *layouts*. This is probably one of the most significant enhancements of the new release because it makes working in paper space easy to understand. Layouts provide a preview of what your plotted sheet will look like, and they make working with paper space intuitive. Layouts simulate the piece of paper your model will be plotted on and accurately reflect the plotted sheet's scale factor, the paper orientation, the current lineweight setting of objects, and the layout's current plot style settings.

Layouts help prevent the confusion many CAD technicians experienced when dealing with model space and paper space in previous releases. Because of the layout's WYSIWYG approach, it is easy to visualize what it is designed to do. Specifically, as shown in Figure 19.1, layouts make it easy to visualize how your model space objects are plotted on a sheet of paper.

Figure 19.1

Layouts make paper space easier to visualize.

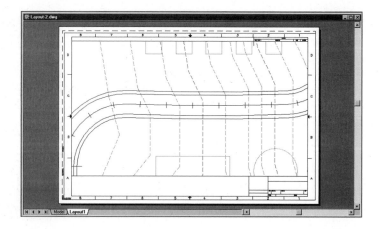

NOTE

In AutoCAD 2000, the paper space feature has been broadened to allow you to work in not just one paper space, but as many paper spaces as you desire and that are named however you want. The term *paper space* now refers to the multiple layouts that can be created and used. *Layout* refers to an individual "plot space" of the paper space for any given drawing.

Creating Layouts

When you start a new drawing from scratch, AutoCAD automatically creates a single Model tab and two Layout tabs, as shown in Figure 19.2. The Model tab is where your model space drawing is created and edited. The Model tab itself cannot be renamed or deleted. Extra Layout tabs beyond one, however, are not a requirement and can be renamed or deleted entirely. They are available to allow you to easily assemble the paper sheets you use to plot your drawing.

Figure 19.2

When you start a new drawing from scratch, AutoCAD automatically creates a single Model tab and two Layout tabs.

NOTE

AutoCAD does not require you to plot from a layout. You can plot your drawing from model space, but some new AutoCAD 2000 features are not supported in that case. However, it's easier to visually create a plot through the layouts' WYSIWYG display, so they are preferred for creating plots.

Although AutoCAD automatically creates two Layout tabs, you may need to create more. AutoCAD provides the following three methods for creating layouts:

■ Create layouts from scratch

■ Create layouts from templates

■ Create layouts with wizards

In the following exercise, you create a layout from scratch and save it as a layout template.

CREATING A LAYOUT FROM SCRATCH

1. Launch AutoCAD and start a new drawing from scratch. AutoCAD creates a new drawing with a single Model tab and two Layout tabs.

   When you select a Layout tab for the first time, AutoCAD's default system settings instruct it to automatically prompt for a Page Setup to apply to the layout and to create a single viewport. For this exercise, you will disable these features.

2. From the Tools menu, choose Options, then choose the Display tab.

3. In the Layout Elements area, clear the Show Page Setup Dialog for New Layouts option, then clear the Create Viewport in New Layouts option, as shown in Figure 19.3.

Figure 19.3

You can stop AutoCAD from automatically creating a viewport in a layout and from prompting for a Page Setup by deselecting those options in the Options dialog box.

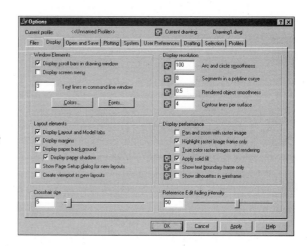

4. Choose Apply and click OK. Next, you will create three additional layouts.

5. Move the cursor over the Layout2 tab and right-click. AutoCAD displays the shortcut menu.

6. From the shortcut menu, select New Layout. AutoCAD creates a new layout, automatically naming it Layout3.

7. Repeat step 6 two more times until you have five Layout tabs.

INSIDER TIP

Layouts can be created, imported from a template, deleted, renamed, moved, copied, set up, or plotted from the shortcut menu with a simple right-click.

8. To rename a Layout tab, move the cursor over the Layout3 tab and right-click. AutoCAD displays the Layout shortcut menu.

9. From the shortcut menu, choose Rename. The Rename Layout dialog box appears.

10. Type **First Layout** in the dialog box and click OK. AutoCAD renames the layout.

NOTE

You can name layouts using most keyboard characters except the following:

< > / \ " : ; ? * | . = '

This allows you to use names that provide very clear descriptions of your layouts.

---

11. Repeat step 10 two more times, renaming Layout4 and Layout5 to **Second Layout** and **Third Layout**, respectively (see Figure 19.4).

Figure 19.4

The last three tabs have been renamed.

12. To delete the two original Layout tabs supplied by AutoCAD, hold the Shift key, choose the Layout1 tab, then choose the Layout2 tab. Both tabs are highlighted.

13. Move the cursor over either highlighted Layout tab and right-click. AutoCAD displays the shortcut menu.

14. From the shortcut menu, select Delete, as shown in Figure 19.5. AutoCAD issues a warning noting that the selected layouts will be deleted permanently.

15. Click OK to permanently delete the two Layout tabs. Only the three Layout tabs you created and renamed remain.

Keep this .dwg file open for the following exercise, or close it without saving.

Figure 19.5

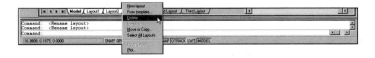

The first two Layout tabs are selected for deletion.

As you can see, creating layouts from scratch is simple. After you create a layout, you can save it in a template file and insert it into new drawings. This is a useful method for creating a set of predefined layouts and sharing them with others to insert into their drawings.

In the following exercise, you save the layouts you created in a template and insert them into a new drawing

CREATING A LAYOUT FROM SCRATCH AND SAVING IT AS A TEMPLATE

1. Continuing from the previous exercise, open the File menu and choose Save As.

2. In the Save Drawing As dialog box, choose the Save As Type drop-down list and select AutoCAD Drawing Template File (*.dwt).

3. Name the drawing Layouts, then save it to the AutoCAD 2000/Template subdirectory, as shown in Figure 19.6. AutoCAD displays the Template Description dialog box.

Figure 19.6

Save the drawing with the new layouts as a template file that you can insert into other drawings.

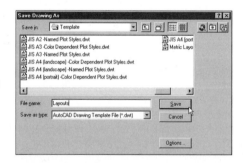

4. In the Description text box, type **My Layouts**. Note that the Measurement setting can be set to English or Metric; select English and click OK. AutoCAD saves the drawing as an AutoCAD template file.

    Next, you will use the template file to insert a new layout from a template.

5. From the File menu, choose New and create a new drawing from scratch.

6. Move the cursor over the Layout2 tab and right-click.

7. From the shortcut menu, select From Template. AutoCAD displays the Select File dialog box.

8. From the Select File dialog box, choose the Layouts template file you saved in step 4 from the AutoCAD 2000\Template folder, then click Open. AutoCAD displays the Insert Layout(s) dialog box.

INSIDER TIP

You can use AutoCAD Design Center to browse drawing files and to drag-and-drop Layouts from these outside files directly into the current drawing. For more information on AutoCAD Design Center, refer to Chapter 12, "Applications for the New AutoCAD DesignCenter."

9. From the Insert Layout(s) dialog box, choose Third Layout from the Layout Names list (as shown in Figure 19.7), and click OK. AutoCAD inserts the Third Layout from the template you created in the previous exercise.

NOTE

You cannot replace a layout with another of the same name from a template. If you attempt such a task, AutoCAD 2000 will prefix the inserted layout with Layout# - when it's created. You should delete an existing layout before inserting another layout with the same name.

Figure 19.7

You can insert predefined layouts from template files.

If you use the technique demonstrated in this exercise, you can spend a little time at the beginning of a project setting up all the project's desired layouts and saving them as a template file. Then you can insert the layouts into new project drawings as needed.

Understanding the Limitations of Layouts

It's important that you understand the limitations of working in a paper space layout. Because layouts are intended to make creating plots easier, certain commands that are available in model space do not work when you are in a layout.

For example, the Layout tabs are intended to display the contents of two-dimensional environments. In model space, however, not only can you create three-dimensional objects, but also you can modify the model space view to look at these objects from different perspectives. Consequently, model space is where your project design work should be performed.

Remember that the Layout tab is intended as the environment in which you compose the plotted sheets of your model space project. It is not intended for modeling. Therefore, use model space to design your project and use the Layout tab(s) to define your project's plots.

Controlling Output Through Page Setup

NEW
for R2000

The Page Setup feature is a powerful new tool that controls certain paper and plotter configuration information and links it to the current Model or Layout tab. By using Page Setup, you can define certain characteristics of the sheet of paper on which you plot your drawing. You can also associate a specific plotter configuration, which indicates the printer or plotter that plots your drawing. With Page Setup, you control values that define such things as the plot device, paper size, scale factor, plot orientation, XY offset values, and more.

A single drawing may contain several layouts, and each layout can be assigned a page setup. In a single layout, you can switch between numerous page setups. When a page setup is selected, AutoCAD redefines the paper size, scale factor, and all other page setup properties.

In previous releases of AutoCAD, when you wanted to change your plot configuration to either plot to a different plotter or plot at a different scale and still maintain proper lineweights, you had to spend time adjusting the plot parameters and/or loading PC2 files. However, in AutoCAD 2000, you can select the appropriate page setup, and you won't need to redefine the plot configuration file. For example, if you need to plot a full scale drawing to a large format plotter, you can set up a unique page setup defined for the large format plotter. Then, in the same drawing, you can create a second page setup to plot the same drawing to a LaserJet printer on an 8 1/2 × 11 sheet of paper. Because both page setups can exist in the same drawing simultaneously, you can quickly switch between the two to plot to the desired device. Additionally, when you choose the appropriate page setup, your drawing is plotted to the desired paper size, at the proper scale, using the appropriate lineweights, and you never have to redefine the plot parameters. This is a tremendous time saver.

Note

Using page setups, you can assign plot styles to layouts, floating paper space viewports, and individual objects. For more information, refer to Chapter 20, "Productive Plotting."

Not only does the ability to associate a unique page setup with a specific layout save you time when creating different plots of your drawing, it also saves you time by allowing you to save a page setup configuration and insert it into another layout. You learned in the previous exercise how to save time when creating new drawings by inserting predefined layouts from a template file; in the same way, you can save time by inserting predefined page setups into the current drawing.

The Page Setup dialog box contains two tabs, as shown in Figure 19.8. On the Plot Device tab, you select the plotter or printer device to send plots. You can also assign a plot style table, which defines the pen assignments that control lineweights and line colors. On the Layout Settings tab, you define settings such as paper size, plot area, drawing orientation, and plot scale. If you are familiar with AutoCAD's Plot dialog box, you may notice that the Layout Settings tab is the same as the Plot dialog box's Plot Settings tab. This emphasizes that Page Setup allows you to predefine plot settings, which means you do not have to make any adjustments to the Plot Settings tab if you already selected the appropriate page setup. For detailed information on using page setup to control plot parameters, refer to Chapter 20.

Figure 19.8

The new Page Setup dialog box allows you to define paper and plotter settings and link them to the current Layout tab.

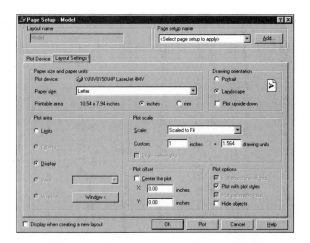

At the top of the Page Setup dialog box, notice the areas that specify the current layout's name and the page setup name. The Layout Name area indicates which tab the current Page Setup values are linked to. In Figure 19.8, the Page Setup is linked to the Model tab. From the Page Setup Name area, you can select a predefined page setup from the drop-down list. Alternatively, by clicking the Add button, you can add the current page setup values to the drop-down list. When you click the Add button, the User Defined Page Setups dialog box is displayed (see Figure 19.9). In that dialog box, you can name, rename, delete, or import page setups from other drawings.

NOTE

When you save a page setup, it is saved in the current drawing only; it cannot be saved as a unique file type. Therefore, if you want to import a saved page setup, you must locate the drawing that contains the desired page setup and use the Import option in the User Defined Page Setups dialog box.

Figure 19.9

From the User Defined Page Setups dialog box, you can import predefined page setups from other drawings.

NOTE

The PSETUPIN command allows you to insert page setups from other drawings, templates, and DXF files, and is executed at AutoCAD's Command: prompt.

Also, when PSETUPIN is called from AutoLISP, you can insert as many page setups as desired from outside files. For example, by entering the following AutoLISP code, you can find my-page-setups.dwg and read in saved page setups named Fullsize and Halfsize:

```
(command "psetupin" "my-page-setups" "Fullsize,Halfsize")
```

Working with Viewports in a Layout

Viewports (Mviews) created in a layout have unique settings for controlling the appearance of your project's model. If you control layer visibility, hidden line removal, and model-to-paper space scale, your finished plot can display objects precisely as needed. More importantly, you can control these properties on a viewport-by-viewport basis, even when you have several viewports on a single sheet. The capability to control how your model space project appears through these viewports is a powerful feature.

AutoCAD 2000 introduces new features that greatly enhance the usefulness of floating viewports. For example, you can now create non-rectangular viewports. You can also clip a viewport and resize it to any shape by using grips. Additionally, you can lock the display scale of a viewport so it is not accidentally modified when you zoom or pan in the viewport.

This section discusses the differences between tiled viewports and floating viewports and explores using floating viewports in layouts. It also reviews new viewport features available with AutoCAD 2000.

Tiled Viewports Versus Floating Viewports

NEW
for R2000

Tiled viewports are created when you are working in model space. Untiled, or *floating*, viewports are created when you are working in paper space. When you create a viewport, AutoCAD automatically determines the type of viewport to create based on which space you are currently working in. Therefore, tiled viewports are automatically created when the Model tab is active, and floating viewports are automatically created when a Layout tab is active.

Tiled viewports, as the name implies, appear as tiles on the screen. They subdivide the original model space viewport (which is a single tiled viewport) into multiple viewports, as shown in Figure 19.10. They are fixed and cannot be moved. They never overlap, and their edges always lie adjacent to the surrounding viewports. Their usage is primarily for helping to view the model during its the creation. The currently selected tile can be further divided into more tiles or joined with another tiled viewport to create a new larger one.

In contrast, floating viewports neither subdivide the screen nor remain fixed. Additionally, they can be copied, resized, and moved, just like any other AutoCAD object. They can even overlap each other, as shown in Figure 19.11.

Figure 19.10

*Model space viewports
subdivide the screen into
smaller tiled viewports
that cannot overlap.*

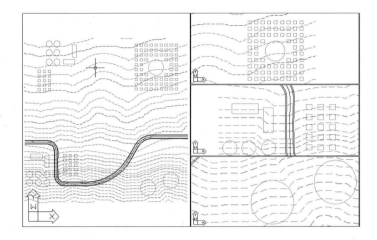

Figure 19.11

*Paper space viewports can
be copied, resized, and
can overlap.*

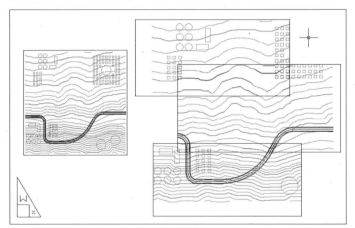

The New Viewports Toolbar

**NEW
for R2000**

AutoCAD 2000 provides a new toolbar that makes creating viewports very easy. The Viewports toolbar, shown in Figure 19.12, allows you to insert a single viewport, define a polygonal- or non-rectangular viewport, and clip an existing viewport. Additionally, you can set the scale for model space objects displayed in a viewport, and you can display the new Viewports dialog box, which allows you to create multiple viewports by selecting the desired predefined viewport configuration.

Figure 19.12

The new Viewports toolbar makes creating viewports very easy.

Figure 19.13

You can display the Viewports toolbar by selecting it from the shortcut menu.

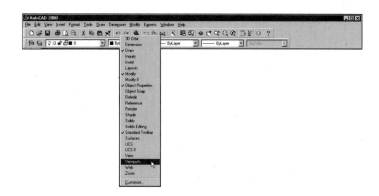

Creating Non-Rectangular Floating Viewports

NEW for R2000

For years, AutoCAD technicians have dreamed of the day they would be able to create non-rectangular viewports. With the release of AutoCAD 2000, that day has finally arrived. The Polygonal Viewport button allows you to create irregularly shaped viewports like the one shown in Figure 19.14.

When you choose the Polygonal Viewport button from the Viewports toolbar, AutoCAD prompts you to specify the start point. Then the feature works much like the PLINE command, continuing to prompt for additional points to define the polygon viewport's vertices. Also similar to the PLINE command, you can switch between a line segment and an arc segment, as well as close the polygon or undo the last point selected. After creating the polygon viewport, you can even edit the pline with several options from the PEDIT command.

Figure 19.14

The Polygonal button allows you to create irregularly shaped floating viewports.

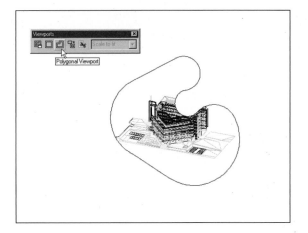

INSIDER TIP

After you create a floating viewport, you can modify its shape by selecting the edge of the viewport to display its grips, selecting the grips, then moving them to new positions.

WARNING

If you wish to hide the display of a viewport's boundary, do not freeze the layer the viewport is on; turn it off instead. If the viewport's layer is frozen, it does not display the model space objects as desired. However, the objects will be displayed properly if the viewport's layer is turned off. It is recommended that you create specific layers on which to place your viewports.

Converting Objects to Floating Viewports

NEW
for R2000

Another handy new feature that comes with AutoCAD 2000 allows you to convert an existing AutoCAD object into a floating viewport. Any closed object such as a circle or a closed polyline can easily be converted to a floating viewport. For example, if you click the Convert Object to Viewport button shown in Figure 19.15, a circle object can be selected and converted into a viewport, as shown in Figure 19.16.

Figure 19.15

The Convert Object to Viewport button allows you to select a closed object and convert it into a floating viewport.

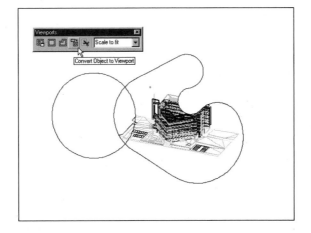

Figure 19.16

This circle has been converted into a floating viewport.

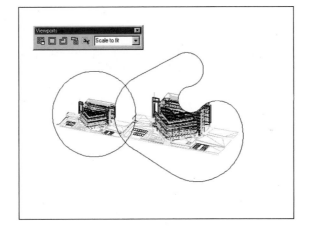

Insider Tip

You can convert a region object to a clipped viewport. By creating composite regions, you can define a region object with holes or voids, which can be used to blank model space areas in the viewport, as shown in Figure 19.17. This is a great way to show notes on top of a viewport. Simply create the composite region in the desired shape, then convert it to a viewport.

Figure 19.17

The viewport, shown in bold, was created from a composite region object, which consists of the irregularly shaped polygon and the circle.

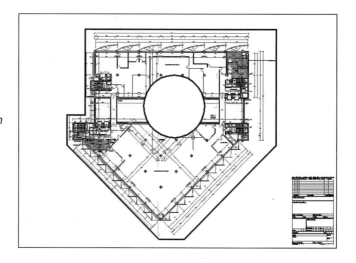

Clipping Existing Floating Viewports

NEW for R2000

AutoCAD 2000 provides a new feature that seemingly clips an existing floating viewport. While the phrase "clip" may conjure visions of AutoCAD's TRIM command, this feature does not actually clip—or trim—an existing viewport. Instead, it replaces an existing viewport with a new clipped viewport.

What makes this feature useful is that you can replace an existing viewport with a new closed object that assumes the current properties of the existing viewport. So, to quickly revise an existing viewport's shape while retaining its properties (such as the model's view position and scale in the viewport), use the new viewport clip feature.

To clip a viewport, click the Clip Existing Viewport button on the Viewports toolbar. AutoCAD then prompts you to select the viewport you want to clip. Next, AutoCAD prompts you to select the clipping object. When you do, AutoCAD converts the clipping object into a viewport and deletes the existing viewport.

The following exercise demonstrates how to create a composite region object and use it to clip an existing viewport.

CLIPPING FLOATING VIEWPORTS

1. Open the 19DWG02.DWG drawing file on the accompanying CD. When the drawing opens, it displays a single floating viewport (as shown in Figure 19.18), as well as a polyline and a circle object, both of which are in paper space.

    Next, you convert the polyline and the circle into regions.

Figure 19.18

The existing viewport, along with the polyline and circle objects.

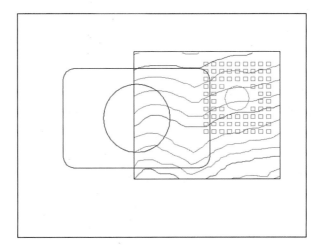

2. From the Draw menu, select Region. AutoCAD prompts you to select the objects to convert into regions.

3. Select the polyline and the circle, then press Enter. AutoCAD converts the two objects into region objects.

    Next, you convert the two region objects into a single composite region.

4. From the Modify menu, choose Solids Editing > Subtract. AutoCAD prompts you to select the regions to subtract from.

5. Select the polyline and press Enter. AutoCAD prompts you to select the regions to subtract.

6. Select the circle and press Enter. AutoCAD subtracts the circle region from the polyline region and creates a single composite region in their place.

    Next, you use the composite region object to clip the existing viewport.

7. Right-click over any toolbar button to display the shortcut menu.

8. From the shortcut menu, choose Viewports to display the Viewports toolbar.

9. On the Viewports toolbar, click the Clip Existing Viewport button. AutoCAD prompts you to pick the viewport you want to clip.

10. Choose the existing viewport, and AutoCAD prompts you to select the clipping object.

11. Select the composite region. AutoCAD clips the existing boundary, replacing it with the composite region, as shown in Figure 19.19. Notice that the model space view does not display through the circle. This effect is achieved by using composite regions.

Figure 19.19

The existing viewport is clipped by the composite region object.

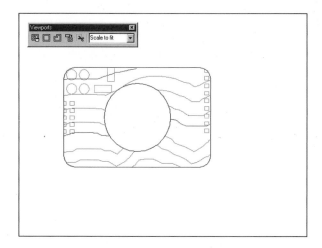

Controlling a Viewport's Scale

NEW
for R2000

Another welcome feature introduced with AutoCAD 2000 is the ability to easily scale your model in a floating viewport. In previous releases, to set the proper scale of your model, you had to calculate the viewport's scale ratio and then use the Zoom XP command. Now you can quickly select the desired scale ratio from the Viewports toolbar.

For example, suppose you are plotting your drawing from a layout, and you are displaying your model in a single floating viewport. If your plotted sheet's scale must be 1" = 40', you would choose the 1:40 option from the Viewport Scale Control.

INSIDER TIP

To set a floating viewport's scale ratio manually, double-click inside the viewport to switch to model space mode, then execute the ZOOM command. At the Command: prompt, type in the scale ratio value followed by **XP**. For example, to manually set the viewport's scale ratio to 1" = 40', execute the ZOOM command and type **1/40XP** at the Command: prompt.

The Viewport Scale Control comes with more than 30 predefined scale ratios and includes the most common model-to-paper space ratios, as shown in Figure 19.20. To change an existing viewport's scale, select the viewport, then choose the desired scale ratio from the drop-down list. To set the desired ratio for new viewports as you create them, choose the desired ratio without selecting any objects.

Figure 19.20

The Viewport Scale Control allows you to quickly set the scale for a floating viewport.

INSIDER TIP

You can double-click inside or outside a viewport to switch between the layout environment and model space.

The New Viewports Dialog Box

In the previous section, you learned about the various features of the Viewports toolbar. The only feature not discussed was the Display Viewports Dialog button, shown in Figure 19.21. When you click this button, AutoCAD displays the Viewports dialog box shown in Figure 19.22.

Figure 19.21

The Display Viewports Dialog button displays the new Viewports dialog box.

Figure 19.22

The Viewports dialog box.

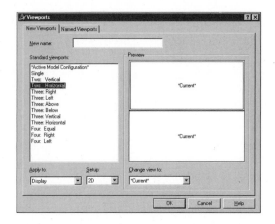

The Viewports dialog box allows you to create and edit both tiled and floating viewports. You can select from a list of standard viewport configurations, define new configurations, and assign saved Views to each viewport in a configuration. If you are in the Model tab, you can name a defined configuration and save it for later use.

The Viewports dialog box contains two tabs: the New Viewports tab and the Named Viewports tab. The options displayed in each tab vary depending on whether the Model tab is current or a Layout tab is current. The New Viewports tab (shown in Figure 19.22) shows the options available when the Model tab is current.

When the Model tab is current, the New Viewports tab allows you to select a viewport configuration from the Standard Viewports list and to apply it to the display or insert it into an existing viewport. If you apply the configuration to the display, the Model tab's current viewport configuration is replaced by the new configuration. If you insert the configuration into an existing viewport, the original viewport configuration is retained, and the new configuration is inserted into the Model tab's current viewport. You can also indicate whether the configuration is a 2D or a 3D setup. A 2D setup allows you to define each viewport's view by selecting defined views from the Change View To drop-down list. In contrast, when you select a 3D setup, AutoCAD allows you to define each viewport's view by selecting from a set of standard orthogonal 3D views in the Change View To drop-down list. After you create the desired viewport configuration, you can name the configuration and save it for later use.

In contrast, when a Layout tab is current, the options available in the New Viewports tab (see Figure 19.23) are slightly different from those available in model space. For example, although you can select a viewport configuration from the Standard viewports list, you can only apply it to the display. You cannot insert it into an existing viewport. However, unlike with tiled viewports created in the Model tab, you can indicate the viewport spacing, which defines the amount of space to apply between viewports when they are created. Additionally, when you insert a new configuration in a layout, AutoCAD allows you to select the location to insert the viewports.

NOTE

You can only create viewport configurations when the Model tab is active. You cannot create viewport configurations when a Layout tab is active.

Figure 19.23

These options are available in the New Viewports tab when a Layout tab is current.

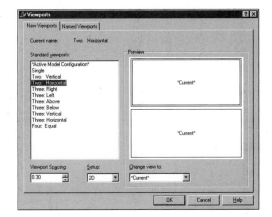

The Named Viewports tab, shown in Figure 19.24, allows you to select a named viewport configuration to insert. Although named viewports must be created in the Model tab, they can be inserted in either the Model tab or a Layout tab. The options available in the Named Viewports tab are the same for both Model and Layout tabs.

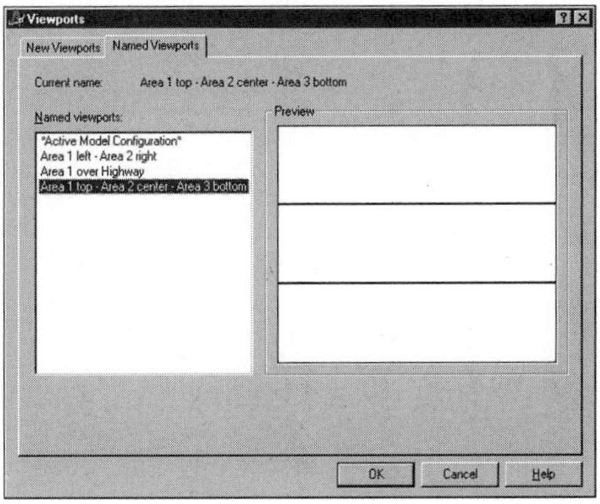

Figure 19.24

The Named Viewports tab allows you to select a named viewport configuration to insert.

Accessing Viewport Commands Through the Shortcut Menu

AutoCAD 2000 allows you to access many commands through the shortcut menu. You access these commands with a right-click, and they are context sensitive. The options displayed on the shortcut menu vary depending on the cursor's position in the drawing, whether objects are selected, and whether a command is currently in progress. For example, if you are in a Layout tab and a floating viewport is selected, a right-click of your mouse provides the wide selection of options shown in Figure 19.25.

Figure 19.25

When a floating viewport is selected, a right-click of your mouse displays many options, several of which are related to floating viewports.

Among these options, the following are three related to floating viewports:

- **Display Viewport Objects.** This option allows you turn on or off the visibility of objects in a viewport. When it's turned off, the objects in the viewport are not displayed and will not be plotted.

- **Display Locked.** This option allows you to lock the viewport so that its model space scale cannot be altered during zooms and pans. When you turn this option on, any zooms or pans occur in paper space, and not in the viewport, thereby ensuring that the proper model space scale is maintained.

- **Hide Plot.** This option allows you to remove hidden lines from objects in floating viewports when they're plotted. Basically, hidden lines are the lines on the back of 3D objects. When you view a 3D object such as a sphere in wireframe mode, AutoCAD allows you to see the lines in the back of the object, as well as those in the front. In essence, the lines in back of the object show through the object and are not hidden.

To remove the lines from view, you turn the Hide Plot option on. When the 3D objects in the floating viewport are plotted from the layout, AutoCAD hides any lines in the back of the object so they do not show through. In Figure 19.26, the left viewport has Hide Plot turned off, and the right viewport has Hide Plot turned on. Notice that the hidden lines show through the sphere in the left viewport but are hidden in the right viewport.

NOTE

AutoCAD provides two methods for removing hidden lines. The Hide Objects option found in the Plot Options area of the Plot dialog box removes hidden lines from objects plotted from the Model tab and from objects in a Layout tab that are not displayed in a floating viewport. The Hide Plot feature, however, removes hidden lines only from objects displayed in floating viewports.

Figure 19.26

When the Hide Plot option is turned on, hidden lines are removed and do not show, as you can see in the sphere on the right.

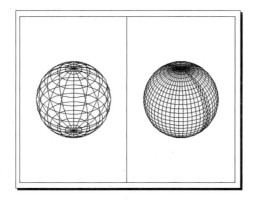

Aligning Objects in Floating Viewports

Floating viewports can be edited in several ways. You can use grips to scale, move, or resize viewports. Viewports can be copied or erased. You can even create an array of viewports.

Although creating multiple viewports is easy, aligning objects in different viewports can be difficult unless you take advantage of the MVSETUP command.

The following exercise demonstrates how to use the MVSETUP command to align objects in two different viewports.

ALIGNING OBJECTS IN TWO DIFFERENT FLOATING VIEWPORTS

1. Open the 19DWG03.DWG drawing file on the accompanying CD.

    When the drawing opens, it displays two floating viewports in a layout. Each viewport shows a different view of the same model space objects. It is important to note that both viewports have the same scale.

2. Type **MVSETUP** at the Command: prompt, and AutoCAD initializes the MVSETUP routine.

3. Type **A** to start the Align feature.

4. Type **H** to start the Horizontal feature. AutoCAD prompts for the basepoint. The view in the other viewport will be aligned with this point. If the lower-right viewport is not already highlighted, pick inside it to make it current.

5. With the lower-right viewport current, use endpoint snap to snap the small rectangle (as shown in Figure 19.27).

Figure 19.27

Align objects in two different viewports using the MVSETUP command. First, snap to the endpoint of an object that appears in both viewports.

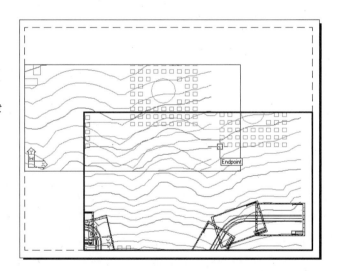

6. When AutoCAD prompts for the other point, pick inside the upper-left viewport to make it current.

7. With the upper-left viewport current, use endpoint snap to snap the small rectangle as shown in Figure 19.28. AutoCAD moves the view in the upper-left viewport down and aligns the two small rectangles.

Figure 19.28

Finish the MVSETUP *command by snapping to the same endpoint of the same object in the other viewport.*

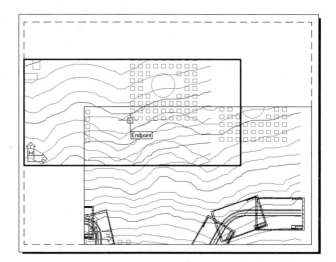

8. Type **V** to start the Vertical feature. Once again, AutoCAD prompts for the basepoint. Pick inside the lower-right viewport to make it current.

9. With the lower-right viewport current, use endpoint snap to snap the same small rectangle shown in Figure 19.27.

10. When AutoCAD prompts for the other point, pick inside the upper-left viewport to make it current.

11. With the upper-left viewport current, use endpoint snap to snap the same small rectangle shown in Figure 19.28. AutoCAD moves the view in the upper-left viewport to the right and aligns the two small rectangles, as shown in Figure 19.29.

12. Press Enter twice to end the command.

13. Close the drawing without saving.

Figure 19.29

The MVSETUP command aligns the objects in the two viewports.

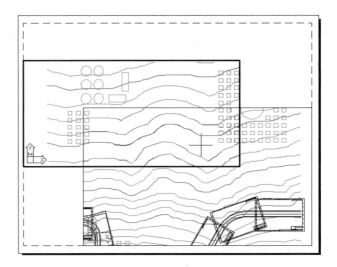

Notice that the MVSETUP command was started in paper space but exited in a model space viewport. Also note that the objects in these two viewports aligned perfectly because the two viewports have the same scale.

Controlling Layer Visibility in Floating Viewports

With floating viewports, you can freeze and thaw layers individually, independent of other viewports. This means you can make a given object in model space invisible in one viewport by freezing its layer, but that object can remain visible in another viewport where its layer is thawed. You can accomplish this within the Layer Properties Manager or by using the VPLAYER command.

The advantage of using the Layer Properties Manager is that you can simply choose the Freeze/Thaw in Current Viewport icon to toggle the layer visibility. The disadvantage to using the Layer Properties Manager is that the settings affect the current viewport only. Consequently, to apply the same layer freeze/thaw properties to multiple viewports, you must select each viewport individually to make it current, and choose the desired settings. The advantage of using the VPLAYER command is that you can apply the desired freeze/thaw settings to multiple viewports simultaneously. However, because VPLAYER does not have a dialog box interface, you must type in the layer names manually.

WARNING

Although you can control a layer's freeze/thaw property in the current viewport, the global freeze/thaw value can override a specified viewport's setting. If a particular layer is thawed in a viewport but frozen globally, for example, the model space objects on the frozen layer will not appear in any viewport.

The following exercise demonstrates the usefulness of the Layer Properties Manager and the VPLAYER command.

CONTROLLING LAYER VISIBILITY IN FLOATING VIEWPORTS

1. Open the 19DWG04.DWG drawing file on the accompanying CD. The drawing opens in Layout1 and displays two floating viewports. At this point, it is obvious that some layers are not visible in the viewport on the right.

   Next, you determine which layers are frozen in the viewport on the right.

2. Click the Layers button on the Object Properties toolbar. The Layer Properties Manager opens, displaying the list of layers (see Figure 19.30). Notice that the icons in the Active VP Freeze column indicate that all layers are thawed.

Figure 19.30

The Active VP Freeze column indicates all layers are thawed.

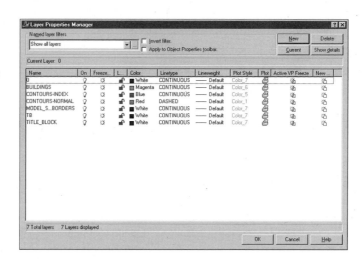

3. Click OK to close the dialog box.

4. Double-click in the right viewport. AutoCAD switches from paper space to model space, and the right viewport becomes active.

5. Click the Layers button on the Object Properties toolbar. The Layer Properties Manager opens, displaying the list of layers (see Figure 19.31). Notice that the icons in the Active VP Freeze column indicate that three layers are frozen in the current viewport.

Figure 19.31

The Active VP Freeze column indicates that three layers are frozen in the current viewport.

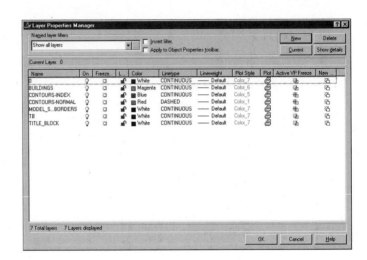

6. Click OK to close the dialog box.

7. Double-click outside of the floating viewports, and AutoCAD switches from model space to paper space.

   The next part of this exercise uses the VPLAYER command to list the frozen layers in the two viewports.

8. Type **VPLAYER** at the Command: prompt.

9. Type **?** at the Command: prompt, and AutoCAD prompts you to select a viewport.

10. Select the right viewport, and the following information is displayed:

    ```
    Layers currently frozen in viewport 3:
    CONTOURS-INDEX
    CONTOURS-NORMAL
    MODEL_SPACE_BORDERS
    ```

    AutoCAD lists the layers frozen in the selected viewport.

11. Type **?** at the Command: prompt.

12. Choose the left viewport, and you see the following information:

    ```
    Layers currently frozen in viewport 2:
    MODEL_SPACE_BORDERS
    ```

NOTE

Notice that the VPLAYER command listed the first viewport selected as viewport 3 and the second as viewport 2. Although only two paper space viewports appear in this drawing, the Layout's view is considered viewport 1.

The next steps use the global freeze/thaw layer settings to set both viewports' current freeze/thaw layer settings.

13. Press Enter to end the VPLAYER command.

14. Click the Layers button on the Object Properties toolbar.

15. Freeze all the layers except layer 0 in the New VP Freeze column, as shown in Figure 19.32.

INSIDER **T**IP

To view a column's entire heading, click and drag the line separating column titles to the right until the heading is visible. You can also stretch the dialog box wider to display more information.

Figure 19.32

All the layers except layer 0 are frozen in the New VP Freeze column.

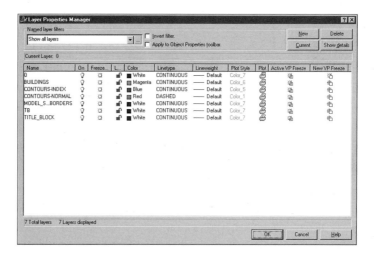

16. Click OK to accept the changes and close the dialog box.

17. Type **VPLAYER** at the Command: prompt.

18. Type **R** for reset.

19. Type ***** to reset all layers to the current values in the New VP Freeze column.

20. Type **S** for Select.

21. Select the two viewports, then press Enter to end object selection.

22. Press Enter to end the **VPLAYER** command.

The two viewports' Active VP Freeze values are set equal to the New VP Freeze column's current values. Consequently, only the road alignment is visible (see Figure 19.33).

Figure 19.33

The Active VP Freeze values for both viewports are automatically set equal to the New VP Freeze column's current values using the VPLAYER command's Reset option.

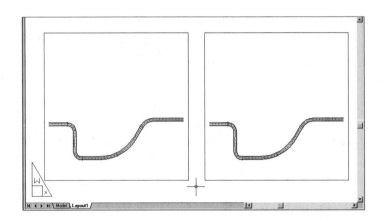

When you need the same Active VP Freeze values in multiple viewports, use the technique of setting the New VP Freeze values to the desired values in the Layer Properties Manager. Then use the VPLAYER's Reset option to select the viewports and automatically update their Active VP Freeze values.

NOTE

You might have experienced a problem with retaining changes you made to layer values for xref objects after you closed the drawing and reopened it. If you make changes to the layer values of xrefs and you want those values to be saved with the drawing, set the VISRETAIN system variable to 1. This instructs AutoCAD to save any changes you make to xref-dependent layers with the drawing. This feature is also controlled from the Options dialog box's Open and Save tab; in the External References area, toggle the Retain Changes to Xref Layers check box.

Summary

This chapter covered paper space layout basics and why you should use layouts to plot your drawings. You learned about the `TILEMODE` system variable and the difference between tiled and untiled, or floating, viewports. You compared model space to paper space and examined the differences between the Hide Plot and Hide Objects features. You also learned about new layout features in AutoCAD 2000 and how to use the `MVSETUP` command to align viewport objects relative to model space coordinates. Finally, you learned how to quickly change the Active VP Freeze values in multiple viewports simultaneously.

This chapter showed you how to productively use the layouts and paper space features in AutoCAD 2000. By using the techniques discussed, you can easily control the appearance of your final drawings and ease the time-consuming process of plotting your drawings, thereby increasing your productivity.

20

PRODUCTIVE PLOTTING

The ultimate goal of most AutoCAD drawings is the final plot because the plots are what your client uses to build the model you created inside AutoCAD. Consequently, when beginning a project, it is important to consider the form your final output must take to meet the needs of your client. By considering the form of the final output at the beginning of a project, you take an important step towards minimizing the amount of time spent re-editing a nearly complete project just so the final output meets your client's needs.

AutoCAD 2000 introduces new features that make the process of creating output very easy. You can assign page setups to paper space layouts, which determines the printer or plotter the layout is sent to, and how it will appear. You can control plot-specific information at the layout level, the layer level, or the object level by assigning them unique page setups. Plots can even be created in digital form using the new ePlot feature, which generates DWF files.

By understanding the plotting features available in AutoCAD 2000, you can ensure a high level of productivity, and provide a final product that is useful to your client.

This chapter discusses the following subjects:

- Configuring a plotter
- Defining plot styles
- Creating page setups
- Plotting from AutoCAD 2000
- The AutoCAD Batch Plot utility
- AutoCAD's ePlot feature

The following sections step you through the process of creating a plot, starting with configuring a printer and a plotter, then proceeding to defining plot styles and page setups, and finishing with plotting the drawing. The exercises do not require you to have access to a printer or plotter.

Configuring a Plotter

The first step in plotting drawings from AutoCAD is configuring the plot devices intended for plotting. By configuring the printers and plotters to which AutoCAD will plot, you can predefine certain output properties, and later refine them with plot styles and page setups.

AutoCAD supports many printers and plotters, and ships with a variety of drivers. The drivers allow AutoCAD to communicate with the printers and plotters, including those that support raster and PostScript file formats. The device drivers support many plotting devices, including Hewlett-Packard, Xerox, and Océ plotters. Additionally, AutoCAD plots to Windows system printers, which is any device that is listed in the Windows Printer Folder, including Adobe Acrobat PDFWriter, which allows you to create PDF files.

NOTE

The Windows Printer Folder, is accessed from the Windows Start menu by choosing Settings, Printers.

The New Autodesk Plotter Manager

NEW
for R2000

The new Autodesk Plotter Manager allows you to easily configure non-system and Windows system plotter and printer devices. You can use it to configure AutoCAD to use local and network plotters and printers, and you can use it to predefine non-default output settings for Windows system devices.

AutoCAD 2000 stores information about media and plotting devices in plot configuration files, called PC3 files. If you have used previous releases of AutoCAD, you are probably familiar with PCP and PC2 files. The PC3 files are similar to the earlier versions, except they do not store any pen settings information.

NOTE

> *Pen settings* information exists separately from PC3 files, and is stored with the plot styles.

The Autodesk Plotter Manager steps you through the process of creating PC3 files, as shown in the following exercise.

CONFIGURING PRINTERS AND PLOTTERS

1. From the File menu, select Plotter Manager. AutoCAD displays the Plotter Manager folder, as shown in Figure 20.1. This folder is where AutoCAD stores PC3 files, and where you access the Add-A-Plotter Wizard.

Figure 20.1

The Autodesk Plotter Manager stores PC3 files, and is where you access the Add-A-Plotter Wizard.

2. Double-click the Add-A-Plotter Wizard. The wizard displays the Add Plotter - Introduction page.

3. Click the Next button. The wizard displays the Add Plotter - Begin page.

The Begin page is where you indicate whether you want to use a local, network, or system printer. There are three choices:

- **My Computer.** Configures plotter driver settings to be managed by your computer.

- **Network Plotter Server.** Configures plotter driver settings to be managed by the network plotter server.

- **System Printer.** Configures a Windows system driver that already resides in your computer's operating system. It allows you to set default print/plot parameters that apply only when plotting from AutoCAD.

4. Select the My Computer option button, then Click Next. The wizard displays the Add Plotter – Plotter Model page. The Plotter Model page is where you select the printer/plotter manufacturer and model type.

5. From the Manufacturers list, select Hewlett-Packard.

6. From the Models list, select DesignJet 755CM C3198A, as shown in Figure 20.2, then click Next.

Figure 20.2

The Plotter Model page is where you select your plotter's manufacturer and model.

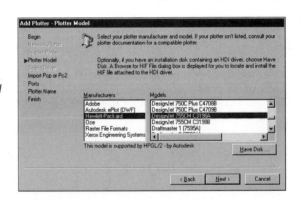

The wizard issues a warning if you have not already installed the HP DesignJet Windows system printer supplied on the AutoCAD 2000 installation CD. This driver is developed by Hewlett-Packard and is optimized for use with AutoCAD 2000. If the wizard issues a warning, click Continue.

The wizard displays the Add Plotter – Import PCP or PC2 page. This page allows you to import certain PCP and PC2 file information into the PC3 file.

NOTE

AutoCAD allows PC3 files to import certain PCP and PC2 information such as pen optimization, plot to file configurations, paper size and orientation, resolution, device name, and plot destination.

7. Click Next. The wizard displays the Add Plotter – Ports page. This page is where you indicate whether you want your plot to be sent to a port (serial, parallel, or network), to a file (PLT), or to AutoCAD's AutoSpool directory.

8. Click the Plot to File option button, then click Next. The wizard displays the Add Plotter – Plotter Name page. This page is where you indicate the name to assign the PC3 file.

NOTE

Although you can use special characters when naming a plotting device, it is recommend that you not use a space when doing so. Aspects of plotting with scripts are complicated when devices have spaces in their names.

9. In the Plotter Name text box, type **DesignJet 755CM - Plot to File**, as shown in Figure 20.3, then click Next.

Figure 20.3

The Plotter Name page is where you assign a name to the PC3 file.

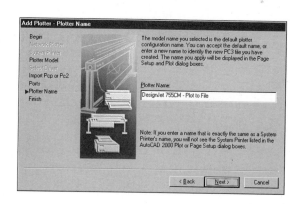

The wizard displays the Add Plotter – Finish page. This page notes that the PC3 file is installed, and allows you to edit the PC3 file settings, and to calibrate your file for the plotter.

10. Click Finish. The PC3 file is created and saved in the Plotter Manager folder, and is now available for use as a plotter configuration.

Next, you create another PC3 file configured for a LaserJet printer.

11. If the Plotter Manager folder is not visible, select Plotter Manager from the File menu. AutoCAD displays the Plotter Manager folder.

NOTE

The Plotter Manager folder display is independent from AutoCAD. Consequently, you can leave it open on your desktop, even after you end your AutoCAD session.

12. Double-click the Add-A-Plotter Wizard. The wizard displays the Add Plotter - Introduction page.

13. Click Next. The wizard displays the Add Plotter - Begin page.

14. Select the My Computer option button, then click Next. The wizard displays the Add Plotter – Plotter Model page.

15. From the Manufacturers list, select Hewlett-Packard.

16. From the Models list, select LaserJet 4MV, as shown in Figure 20.4.

Figure 20.4

The Hewlett-Packard LaserJet 4MV is selected.

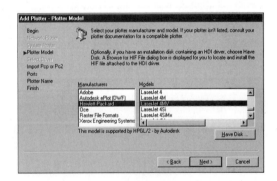

NOTE

The Add Plotter – Plotter Model page allows you to install drivers not found in the list. Click the Have Disk button and the wizard prompts you to identify the driver to install.

17. Click Next. The wizard displays the Add Plotter – Import PCP or PC2 page.

18. Click Next. The wizard displays the Add Plotter – Ports page.

19. Click the Plot to File option button, then click Next. The wizard displays the Add Plotter – Plotter Name page.

20. In the Plotter Name text box, type **LaserJet 4MV - Plot to File**, as shown in Figure 20.5, then click Next. The wizard displays the Add Plotter – Finish page.

Figure 20.5

*The PC3 file is named
LaserJet 4MV - Plot to File.*

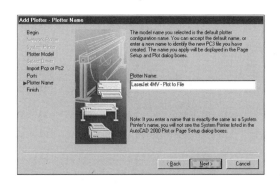

21. Click Finish.

The second PC3 file is created and saved in the Plotter Manager folder, and is now available for use as a plotter configuration.

INSIDER TIP

You can set a PC3 file as the default output device for new drawings, and for earlier version drawings first opened in AutoCAD 2000. From the Options dialog box, in the Plotters tab, select the desired PC3 file from the Use as Default Output Device list.

INSIDER TIP

You can display the Plotter Manager folder in any of the following four ways:

■ From AutoCAD's File menu, select Plotter Manager.

■ From AutoCAD's Options dialog box, in the Plotting tab, click the Add or Configure Plotters button.

■ At AutoCAD's command line, type **PLOTTERMANAGER**.

■ From the Windows Control Panel, double-click the Autodesk Plotter Manager.

Creating PC3 files is easy with the new Add-A-Plotter Wizard. You can create as many PC3 files as you need, and share them with others. Later in this chapter, you use the PC3 files you created and apply them to page setups.

Next, you use the Plotter Configuration Editor to modify one of the PC3 files.

The New Plotter Configuration Editor

NEW
for R2000   You can create AutoCAD 2000 Plotter Configuration (PC3) files to predefine the print device to which your drawing is sent. You can create as many PC3 files as you need to meet all your plotting conditions. By creating the PC3 files you need, you can quickly switch to the proper PC3 file to plot your drawing to the desired device.

It is not necessary to create PC3 files using the Add-A-Plotter Wizard. For example, you can create a new PC3 file by copying an existing file, then modifying its settings. In this manner, you can quickly define a new PC3 file.

INSIDER TIP

> To quickly create a copy of a PC3 file, select Plotter Manager from the File menu. Then right-click the desired PC3 file and drag it to a blank area in the Plotter Manager folder. When prompted, select Copy Here. Finally, right-click the copy and select Rename, then rename the copy.

The new Plotter Configuration Editor allows you to modify your PC3 files. It has features that allow you to provide a description of the PC3 file, switch the port to which drawings are plotted, and control device and document settings such as the media source and custom paper sizes. By using the Plotter Configuration Editor, you can quickly edit your PC3 files, as shown in the following exercise.

This exercise uses a PC3 file created in the previous exercise. Alternatively, you can copy the DesignJet 755CM - Plot to File.pc3 file from the accompanying CD to the Plotter Manager folder. After copying the file, be sure to right-click the PC3 file and select Properties, then clear the Read-only attribute.

NOTE

> When copying PC3 Plotter files, be sure to copy any attached PMP files from the \Acad2000\Drv directory. A PMP file is where AutoCAD 2000 stores any changes or additions to the paper sizes for a given plotter. A PMP can be reattached to the PC3 files after they have been copied to the new location.

EDITING AUTOCAD 2000 PLOTTER CONFIGURATION (PC3) FILES

1. From the File menu, select Plotter Manager. AutoCAD displays the Plotter Manager folder.

2. Double-click the DesignJet 755CM - Plot to File.pc3 file. The Plotter Configuration Editor appears.

3. From the General tab, in the Description box, type **Configured for Plots on Translucent Bond**, as shown in Figure 20.6.

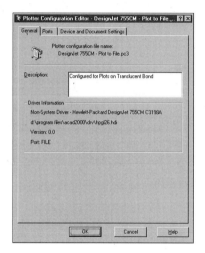

Figure 20.6

The PC3 file's description is given.

The Ports tab allows you to select the port to send your plot. The DesignJet 755CM - Plot to File.pc3 file is currently set to Plot to File. This instructs AutoCAD to create a plot file of the drawing, instead of sending the drawing to a plotter device.

4. Select the Device and Document Settings tab.

   The Device and Document Settings tab allows you to define many of the PC3 file's settings. These include the paper source and size; custom properties settings for the device, if available; and plotter calibration files. You can also define custom paper sizes, adjust the paper's printable area, and identify the type of media to use, such as opaque bond or high-gloss photo.

5. In the tree view window, under the Media branch, select Media Type. The Media Type list appears.

6. From the Media Type list, select Translucent Bond, as shown in Figure 20.7.

Figure 20.7

The PC3 file's media type is set to Translucent Bond.

7. Click OK. The Plotter Configuration Editor modifies the PC3 file, and saves the changes.

8. Close the Plotter Manager folder.

The Plotter Configuration Editor makes modifying PC3 files very easy. This is especially useful when you want to create several nearly identical PC3 files whose settings vary slightly. For example, by creating a single PC3 file using the Autodesk Plotter Manager, then copying the PC3 file, you can use the Plotter Configuration Editor to quickly make minor changes to the PC3 file copy. This saves time by duplicating all the settings from the original PC3 file, and allows you to change the one or two settings necessary to customize the file.

In the next section, you continue the process of creating a plot by defining plot styles.

Defining Plot Styles

NEW
for R2000 AutoCAD 2000 introduces a new feature called plot styles, which allow you control how objects in drawings appear when plotted. Through a plot style, you can tell AutoCAD to override and plot certain objects with a wide line, a different color, or even a different linetype than what is assigned to the object in the drawing. With plot styles, you can easily vary the way objects look when plotted, no matter how they look in the drawing.

Plot styles allow you to control several object properties when you plot a drawing. You can control the object's color, linetype, and lineweight. You can also control values for dithering, gray scale, and screening. You can set pen assignments and define object fill styles. You can also control how line endpoints appear, as well as how they appear at joint points. With plot styles, you can create from a single drawing many plots that appear different, without actually modifying any objects in the drawing.

If you have used prior releases of AutoCAD, you may be familiar with controlling linetypes and lineweights by assigning pen settings in the Print/Plot Configuration dialog box. The limitation with this feature is that you can assign linetypes and lineweights only globally, to all objects in the plotted drawing. With plot styles, however, the pen settings are assigned by layer or by object. This means you can control linetypes and lineweights by groups of layers or groups of objects. More importantly, you can also control other properties, such as object screening and fill styles, as noted earlier.

Plot styles are saved in a *plot style table*, and a plot style table can have as many plot styles as needed. To assign a plot style to a layer or an object, you must attach a plot style table to the Model or Layout tab. After the plot style table is attached, you can assign its various plot styles to layers or to objects. Additionally, you can assign different plot style tables to the Model and Layout tabs. The ability to assign different plot styles to layers and objects, and to then attach different plot style tables to the Model and Layout tabs, provides you with a tremendous amount of flexibility on how your plotted drawings appear.

The New Plot Style Manager

The new Plot Style Manager provides a location to store your plot style tables. Similar in design to the Autodesk Plotter Manager, the Plot Style Manager also provides access to the Add-A-Plot Style Table Wizard, which steps you through the process of creating plot style tables, as demonstrated in the following exercise.

CREATING A PLOT STYLE TABLE

1. From the File menu, select Plot Style Manager.

   AutoCAD displays the Plot Style Manager folder, as shown in Figure 20.8. This folder is where AutoCAD stores color-dependent plot style tables and named plot style tables, and where you access the Add-A-Plot Style Table Wizard.

Figure 20.8

The Plot Style Manager
folder stores color-
dependent and named
plot style tables, and is
where you access the Add-
A-Plot Style Table Wizard.

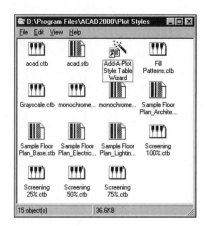

2. Double-click the Add-A-Plot Style Table Wizard. The wizard displays the Add Plot Style Table - Introduction page.

3. Click Next. The wizard displays the Add Plot Style Table - Begin page.

    The Begin page is where you indicate whether you want to create a plot style table from scratch, or from an existing file. There are four choices:

    ■ **Start from Scratch.** Creates a new plot style table.

    ■ **Use an Existing Plot Style Table.** Creates a new plot style table from an existing plot style table, duplicating all the defined plot styles.

    ■ **Use My R14 Plotter Configuration (CFG).** Creates a new plot style table by importing pen assignments stored in the acadr14.cfg file.

    ■ **Use a PCP or PC2 File.** Creates a new plot style table by importing pen assignments stored in a PCP or PC2 file.

4. Click the Start from Scratch option button, then click Next. The wizard displays the Add Plot Style Table – Pick Plot Style Table page.

    The Plot Style Table page is where you select the type of plot style table to create:, either color-dependent or named. These two types of plot style tables are discussed in the section following this exercise.

5. Click the Named Plot Style Table option button, then click Next. The wizard displays the Add Plot Style Table – File Name page. This page is where you indicate the name to assign the plot style table file.

6. In the File Name text box, type **IA-2000**, as shown in Figure 20.9, then click Next.

Figure 20.9

The File Name page is where you assign a name to the plot style table file.

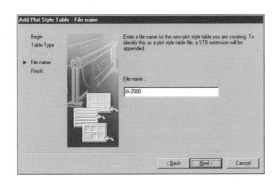

The wizard displays the Add Plot Style Table – Finish page. This page notes that the plot style table is created, and allows you to edit the file settings.

7. Click Finish.

8. Close the Plot Style Manager folder.

The plot style table is then saved in the Plot Style Manager folder. With the plot style table created, you can now define plot styles in the table. Then, the Plot Style Table can be attached to the Model or Layout tab and its plot styles assigned to layers or objects in the drawing.

Before you proceed to defining plot styles in the plot style table, it is important to understand the differences between color-dependent and named plot style tables. The next section reviews the differences between these two types of tables.

Choosing the Plot Style Table Type

AutoCAD provides two types of plot style tables: *color-dependent* and *named*, and both types behave similarly. For example, both types allow you to control the appearance of objects when plotted, including controlling the object's color, linetype, and lineweight. Both types can be attached to the Model and Layout tabs, and both can assign plot styles by layer or by object. So, if both types are so similar, then why have two?

Although similar, there are two important differences between the plot style table types. One difference is the number of plot styles each table type can hold. A color-dependent plot style table has a maximum of 255 color designations, which means you can define only 255 different plot styles per table. In contrast, a named plot style table can have an unlimited number of plot styles because the plot styles in each table are assigned unique names.

The other—and perhaps more important—difference, is how each type assigns plot styles to objects. As its name implies, color-dependent plot styles are based on the color of the object, or the color of the layer on which the object resides. Consequently, you must be careful when selecting an object's color to ensure that it appears as desired when plotted.

If you have plotted drawings from prior releases of AutoCAD, then you are probably familiar with using colors to define an object's lineweight or linetype. If you have plotted drawings from prior releases of AutoCAD, then you have used color-dependent plot styles, whether you realized it or not.

Named plot styles, however, are not based on object color. Named plot styles assign properties by name. Therefore, you can assign objects any color and control properties such as lineweight and linetype regardless of their color. This provides a new flexibility when creating objects never before available because you no longer need to use colors to control an object's linetype or lineweight. With named plot styles, color is just another independent property like lineweight and linetype. A basic example of this use is a drawing in which all content is red in color, but because of name plot style usage, each object and layer could be plotted differently.

There is one very important feature to understand about color-dependent and named plot styles. A drawing can use only one type, and cannot switch between the two types. When you create a drawing, the plot style table type is automatically assigned to the drawing, and is permanent. Therefore, you must determine which type you will use *before* you create your drawing.

NOTE

The default plot style table type is set in the Options dialog box's Plotting tab by clicking either the Use Color Dependent Plot Styles option button, or the Use Named Plot Styles option button. Once changed, the new default plot style table type takes effect on new drawings, or drawings created in earlier versions of AutoCAD that haven't yet been saved using AutoCAD 2000.

INSIDER **T**IP

Although a drawing's plot style table type is permanently set to color-dependent or named, you can simulate changing a drawing from one type to the other. To do so, copy all the objects in the current drawing into a new, blank drawing whose plot style table is set to the type you wish to use.

In the next section, you use the Plot Style Table Editor to add two plot styles to an existing plot style table.

Adding Plot Styles to Plot Style Tables

Plot styles reside in plot style tables, and provide the ability to control an object's appearance when plotted. You can control color, linetype, and lineweight, as well as other properties. By using plot styles, you control how an object looks when plotted without changing the object's appearance in the drawing.

After a named plot style table is created, you can add new plot styles, and you can edit or delete existing plot styles by using the Plot Style Table Editor. After you add plot styles to a plot style table, the table can be attached to the Model or Layout tab, and its plot styles can be assigned to layers or objects.

NOTE

> Plot styles can be added to or deleted from named plot style tables only. Color-dependent plot style tables have 255 predefined plot styles, whose "names" are based on colors, and whose values can only be edited.

The following exercise shows how to add and edit plot styles in a named plot style Table. The exercise uses the named plot style table file created in the previous exercise. Alternatively, you can copy the IA-2000.stb file from the accompanying CD to the plot styles folder. After copying the file, be sure to right-click the STB file and select Properties, then clear the Read-only attribute.

ADDING PLOT STYLES TO A NAMED PLOT STYLE TABLE

1. From the File menu, select Plot Style Manager. AutoCAD displays the Plot Style Manager.

2. Double-click the IA-2000.stb file. The Plot Style Table Editor appears.

   The Plot Style Table Editor has three tabs. The General tab allows you to provide a description for the table. The Table View and Form View tabs display property information for the selected plot style. They display the same information but in different formats.

3. From the General tab, in the Description box, type **Plot styles configured for D Size sheets**, as shown in Figure 20.10.

Figure 20.10

The plot style table's description is set.

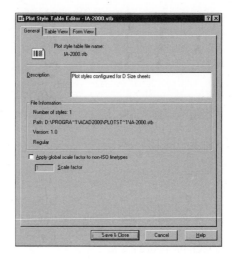

4. Select the Form View tab.

    The Form View tab displays the property information for the Normal plot style, as shown in Figure 20.11. Notice that only the Normal plot style is displayed in the Plot Styles list. The Normal plot style is automatically created as the default plot style in a table, and cannot be edited or deleted.

Figure 20.11

Every named plot style table has the default Normal plot style.

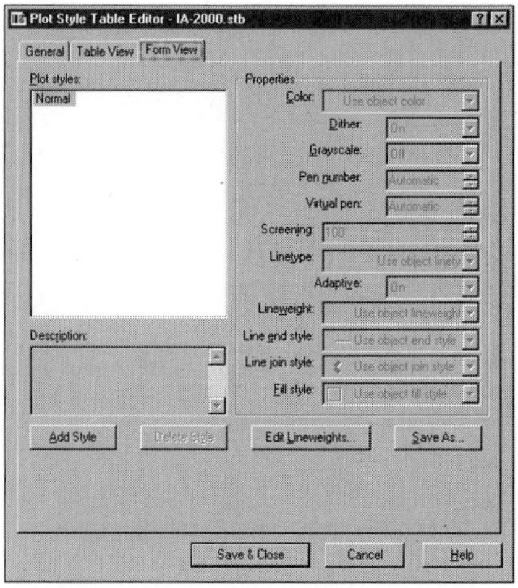

5. To add a plot style to the table, click Add Style. The Add Plot Style dialog box appears.

6. In the Plot Style text box, type **Contours - Normal**, then click OK. The Contours - Normal plot style is created and added to the Plot Styles list.

    The Properties area displays the properties you can edit for the selected plot style. When you assign the Contours - Normal plot style to an object's plot style property, the Contours - Normal plot style's property values will override the object's properties when plotted.

    Next, you will edit several properties of the Contours - Normal plot style.

7. From the Color list, select Black. The selected color is the color the plotter uses to draw the object.

8. In the Screening scroll box, type **30**.

    The screening value specifies a color intensity setting, which controls the amount of ink the plotter uses to draw a color. The lower the screening value, the less ink is used to draw the object, and the lighter—or less intense—the object appears when plotted. The range of screening values is 0 through 100. Selecting 100 displays the color at its full intensity.

9. From the Lineweight list, select 0.1000mm.

10. In the Description text box, type **Objects are screened to 30%**, as shown in Figure 20.12. The new plot style is complete.

Figure 20.12

The Contours - Normal plot style is defined.

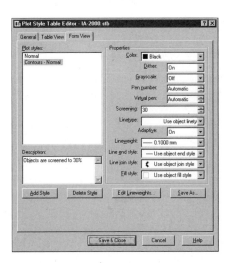

11. Select the Table View tab. Notice that the plot style properties are the same as those displayed in the Form View tab. They are simply arranged differently. Both forms allow you to control identical properties, and the form you use is up to you.

12. Click Add Style. A new plot style column is created and assigned the default name Style 2.

13. In the name row, type **Contours - Index** to rename the plot style.

14. Select the Description box in the Contours - Index column. The description box is highlighted.

15. In the Description box, type **Objects are screened to 70%**.

16. From the Color list, select Black.

17. In the Screening scroll box, type **70**.

18. From the Lineweight list, select 0.2000mm, as shown in Figure 20.13. The new plot style is complete.

Figure 20.13

The Contours - Index plot style is defined.

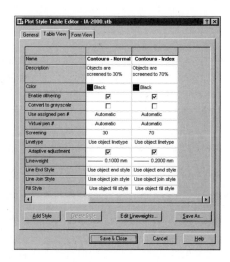

19. Click Add Style. A new plot style column is created and assigned the default name Style 3.

20. In the name row, type **Buildings** to rename the plot style.

21. Select the Description box in the Buildings column. The description box is highlighted.

22. In the description box, type **New fill style applied to objects**.

23. From the Color list, select Black.

24. From the Fill Style list, select Solid, as shown in Figure 20.14. The new plot style is complete.

Figure 20.14

The Buildings plot style is defined.

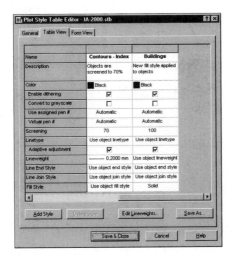

25. Select Save As to save the new plot styles to a new plot style table. The Save As dialog box appears.

26. Name the table **D Size Sheets**, then click Save. The plot style table is saved using the new name.

    Next, you complete the exercise by modifying the current plot style table and saving it as a new table.

27. From the General tab's Description box, type **Plot styles configured for A Size sheets**.

28. From the Form View tab, select the Buildings plot style.

29. From the Fill Style list, select Horizontal Bars.

30. Click Save As to save the plot styles to a new plot style Table.

31. Name the table **A Size Sheets**, then click Save. The plot style table is saved using the new name.

32. Click Save & Close to save the new plot style table, and close the Plot Style Table Editor.

The two new plot style tables are saved to the Plot Style Manager folder. The tables are now available for use with drawings, and can be attached to the Model or Layout tab. Then their plot styles can be assigned to layers and objects.

As you just experienced, creating and editing plot styles is very easy. By using the various properties provided, you can alter the appearance of plotted objects, creating numerous versions of your drawing when plotted, without actually changing any object properties in the drawing.

In the next section, you create page setups that use the plot style table you created.

Creating Page Setups

Page setups are a new feature of AutoCAD 2000, and provide the ability to control certain paper and plotter configuration information. Page setups work similarly to PC2 files in that they allow you to store certain plot settings and restore them when needed. Plot settings such as plot device, paper size, scale factor, and plot orientation may be saved, as well as a plot style table that contains plot styles used in the current drawing.

What makes page setups especially powerful is the ability to assign different page setups to the Model and Layout tabs in your drawing. Consequently, a single drawing can have numerous page setups, with a particular page setup recalled and assigned to the current Model or Layout tab, which can then produce the desired results when plotted. Ultimately, this means you no longer have to worry about restoring prior plot and pen settings to duplicate a previous plot. All plot settings are saved with the drawing, and are instantly recalled by selecting the desired Model or Layout tab, and assigning the appropriate page setup. For more information on the versatility of page setups, refer to Chapter 19, "Paper Space Layouts," in the section titled, "Controlling Output Through Page Setup."

The following exercise shows how to create page setups. This exercise uses the Plotter Configuration (PC3) files and named plot style tables created in previous exercises in this chapter. Alternatively, you can copy the following files from the accompanying CD to the designated folders:

- DesignJet 755CM - Plot to File.pc3 to the Plotter Manager folder
- LaserJet 4MV - Plot to File.pc3 to the Plotter Manager folder
- A Size Sheets.stb to the Plot Style Manager folder
- D Size Sheets.stb to the Plot Style Manager folder

After copying the files to their folders, be sure to right-click on each one and select Properties, then clear the Read-only attribute.

CREATING PAGE SETUPS

1. Open the 20DWG01.DWG drawing file, found on the accompanying CD. The drawing opens, displaying a D size sheet border and a single viewport that displays model space objects.

2. Right-click over the Layout1 tab, then select Page Setup. The Page Setup dialog box displays.

3. From the Plot Device tab, in the Plotter configuration area, select the DesignJet 755CM - Plot to File.pc3 file from the name list. This is the PC3 created in a previous exercise in this chapter, and indicates the device to which AutoCAD plots.

4. In the Plot style table (Pen Assignments) area, from the Name list, select D Size Sheets.stb, as shown in Figure 20.15. This is the plot style table that contains the plot styles created in a previous exercise in this chapter, and which controls the appearance of objects when plotted.

Figure 20.15

The PC3 file and Plot style table are selected for the current page setup.

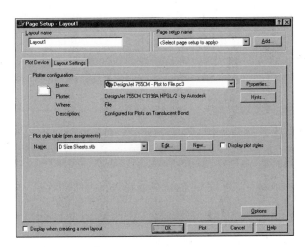

5. From the Layout Settings tab, in the Paper Size and Paper Units area, be sure the ANSI expand D (34.00 × 22.00 Inches) paper size is selected.

6. In the Drawing Orientation area, click the Landscape option button. This instructs AutoCAD to use the long edge of the paper as the top of the page.

7. In the Plot area, click the Extents option button. This instructs AutoCAD to calculate the plot area based on all objects in the current space—in this case, paper space. Extents does not include the layout's paper image and shadow, which appears in the background and is provided for appearance only.

8. In the Plot Scale area, be sure the Scale is set to 1:1. Typically, in the case of layouts, the paper background represents your drawing's paper sheet, and is set at the sheet's actual size. In this case, the sheet size is 34.00 × 22.00 inches. Therefore, the scale is set to 1:1—one unit equals one inch.

9. In the Plot Scale area, be sure the Scale Lineweights check box is selected.

   Lineweights specify the line width of plotted objects, and are normally plotted using the lineweight's value, regardless of the plot scale. This means that if an object's lineweight is set to 0.1000 inches, the object's lineweight will always be plotted at 0.1000 inches. This is true even if the plot scale is to 1:2. By selecting Scale Lineweights, if the drawings scale is set to a value other than 1:1, the lineweights are proportionally scaled based on the scale factor. In the case of a 1:2 plot scale, for example, if the lineweight is set to 0.1000 inches, AutoCAD re-scales the plotted object's lineweight to 0.0500 inches.

Note

> The Scale Lineweights option is only available in a paper space layout. This is another valid reason to do all sheet plotting from paper space rather than model space.

10. In the Plot Offset area, be sure the Center the Plot check box is selected. This ensures that the plotted objects are centered on the sheet when plotted.

11. In the Plot Options area, be sure the Plot with Plot Styles check box is selected. This instructs AutoCAD to use the plot styles in the D Size Sheets.stb plot style table attached to the page setup in step 4.

    Next, you save the settings of the Plot Device and Layout Settings tabs as a named page setup.

12. In the Page Setup Name area, click Add. The User Defined Page Setups dialog box appears.

13. In the New Page Setup Name text box, type **D Size Plots**, then click OK. AutoCAD names the page setup as shown in Figure 20.16.

Figure 20.16

The current settings are stored in the D Size Plots page setup.

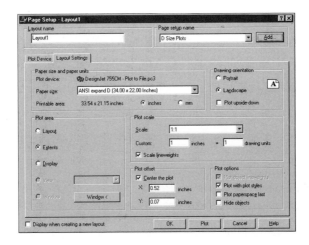

The current settings of the Plot Device and Layout Settings tabs are saved as a named page setup called D Size Plots. The settings are saved in the current drawing, and can be recalled anytime by selecting D Size Plots from the Page Setup Name list.

INSIDER TIP

You can insert named page setups from other drawings by clicking Import in the User Defined Page Setups dialog box. This is also available by the command PSETUPIN.

Next, you will define one more page setup.

14. From the Plot Device tab, in the Plotter Configuration area, select the LaserJet 4MV - Plot to File.pc3 file from the Name list. This is the second PC3 file created in a previous exercise in this chapter.

    AutoCAD displays a warning noting the paper size in the layout is not supported by the selected plot device, and that the layout will use the paper size specified by the plot device.

15. Click OK to dismiss the warning message.

16. In the Plot Style Table (Pen Assignments) area, from the Name list, select A Size Sheets.stb.

    This is the second plot style table that contains the plot styles created in a previous exercise in this chapter. The only difference between the two plot style tables is that the Buildings plot style in the A Size Sheets.stb displays fills using the Horizontal Bars fill style, whereas the Buildings plot style in the D Size Sheets.stb displays fills using the Solid fill style.

17. From the Layout Settings tab, in the Paper Size and Paper Units area, be sure the ANSI A (8.50 × 11.00 Inches) paper size is selected.

18. In the Drawing Orientation area, click the Landscape option button.

19. In the Plot area, click the Extents option button.

20. In the Plot Scale area, from the Scale list, select Scale to Fit (you may need to scroll to the top of the list).

WARNING

You may not get the desired results when using the Scale to Fit plot scale size if the Layout option is selected in the Plot area. Therefore, when using the Scale to Fit plot scale size, select the Extents option.

21. In the Plot Scale area, be sure the Scale Lineweights check box is selected.

22. In the Plot Offset area, be sure the Center the Plot check box is selected.

23. In the Plot Options area, be sure the Plot with Plot Styles check box is selected.

24. In the Page Setup Name area, click Add. The User Defined Page Setups dialog box appears.

25. In the New Page Setup Name text box, type **A Size Plots**, then click OK. AutoCAD names the page setup as shown in Figure 20.17.

Figure 20.17

The current settings are stored in the A Size Plots page setup.

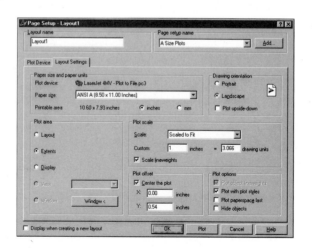

26. Click OK to accept the page setup changes.

AutoCAD saves the page setups to the current drawing, where they can be assigned to the Model or Layout tab, or to any new Layout tabs. By right-clicking the Model or Layout tab, then selecting Page Setup, you can assign the tab a saved page setup, or create a new page setup.

Recall that when you clicked OK in the Page Setup dialog box, the currently selected Page Setup—A Size Plots—redefined the drawing's paper size and scale. This is one of the big benefits of page setups. Without the need to reset any scale values, you can instantly change the plot device, pen assignments, sheet size, and scale of the current tab by selecting the desired page setup.

Now that the plot style tables are assigned to the page setups, the only step remaining is to take advantage of the plot styles pen settings by assigning them to layers in the drawing, as demonstrated in the next exercise.

CREATING PAGE SETUPS

1. Continue from the previous exercise.

2. Select the Layers tool on the Object Properties toolbar. AutoCAD displays the Layer Properties Manager.

3. Select the Normal plot style for the BUILDINGS layer. AutoCAD displays the Select Plot Style dialog box.

4. Select the Buildings plot style, then click OK. AutoCAD assigns the Buildings plot style to the BUILDINGS layer.

5. Select the Normal plot style for the CONTOURS-INDEX layer. AutoCAD displays the Select Plot Style dialog box.

6. Select the Contours - Index plot style, then click OK. AutoCAD assigns the Contours - Index plot style to the CONTOURS-INDEX layer.

7. Select the Normal plot style for the CONTOURS-NORMAL layer. AutoCAD displays the Select Plot Style dialog box.

8. Select the Contours - Normal plot style, then click OK. AutoCAD assigns the Contours - Normal plot style to the CONTOURS-NORMAL layer, as shown in Figure 20.18.

Figure 20.18

The current settings are stored in the A Size Plots page setup.

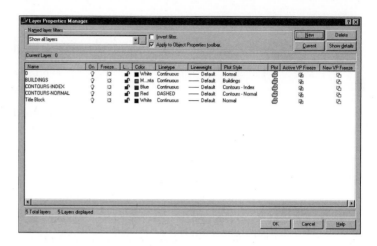

9. Click OK to close the dialog box and keep the assignments.

   With the plot styles now assigned to the appropriate layers, you can preview the effect a page setup will have on a plotted drawing.

10. From the File menu, select Plot Preview.

    The plot preview of the A Size Plots page setup is shown in Figure 20.19. Notice that the contours (the jagged polylines) are displayed in shades of gray, and the fill style of the buildings is horizontal bars. In the drawing, the colors used to depict the polylines are red and blue, and the fill is solid and magenta. This demonstrates the effect plot styles have on the current Model or Layout tab.

Figure 20.19

The effect of the A Size Plots page setup is previewed.

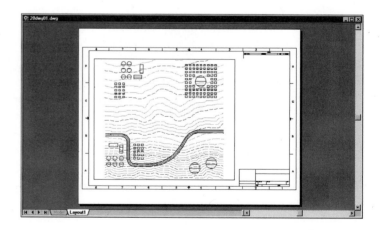

Next, you preview the D Size Plots page setup.

11. Right-click in the plot preview, then click Exit. AutoCAD closes the plot preview.

12. Right-click the Layout1 tab, then select Page Setup. The Page Setup dialog box appears.

13. In the Page Setup dialog box, select D Size Plots from the Page Setup Name list, then click OK. AutoCAD automatically switches to the D size sheet size, and re-scales the drawing to the correct size.

14. From the File menu, select Plot Preview. AutoCAD displays a preview of the drawing, as shown in Figure 20.20.

Notice that the contours are displayed in shades of gray, just as they were in the A Size Plots preview. However, the fill style of the buildings is now solid. This occurs because the two plot style tables use the same plot style names. In other words, when the A Size Plots page setup is selected, the A Size Sheets plot style table is used, whose Buildings plot style uses the Horizontal Bars fill style. In contrast, when the D Size Plots page setup is selected, the D Size Sheets plot style table is used, whose Buildings plot style uses the Solid fill style.

Figure 20.20

The effect of the D Size Plots page setup is previewed.

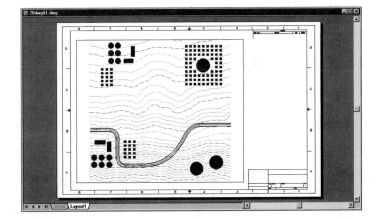

15. Exit Plot Preview, and close the drawing.

By defining multiple page setups, and assigning the desired PC3 files and plot style tables to each one, you can quickly switch a drawing plot settings, and achieve different output results when the drawing is plotted.

INSIDER TIP

An easy way to access stored page setups is to create one drawing that contains all your standard page setup combinations, and save the drawing as pagesetupfile.dwg. Then create a custom toolbar button that executes the following string:

```
'(command "psetupin" (findfile "pagesetupfile.dwg")'
```

When you click the new toolbar button, AutoCAD automatically locates the drawing, allowing you to select the page setups you wish to load.

Plotting from AutoCAD 2000

AutoCAD 2000 provides several methods for plotting drawings, with the most traditional method being the Plot dialog box. Additionally, AutoCAD provides a powerful batch plotting utility that allows you to select many drawings, and define different plot settings for each one, then automatically plot all the files.

There is also the capability to produce and publish electronic drawing files to the Internet using the ePlot feature.

These methods of producing plotted drawings, combined with the new page setup and plot style features, present a broad variety of options that ensures your ability to produce output that meets your needs.

New Features of the Plot Dialog box

NEW for R2000

The *Plot* dialog box is updated to take advantage of the new Plot Configuration (PC3) files, plot styles stored in plot style tables, and page setups as discussed previously in this chapter. Additionally, there are several other improvements of which you should be aware.

When you execute the `plot` command, AutoCAD displays the new Plot dialog box, as shown in Figure 20.21. Notice that the Plot dialog box resembles the Page Setup dialog box (refer to Figure 20.15). The main difference between the two is the additional options available in the What to Plot and Plot to File areas.

Figure 20.21

The new Plot dialog box is similar to the Page Setup dialog box.

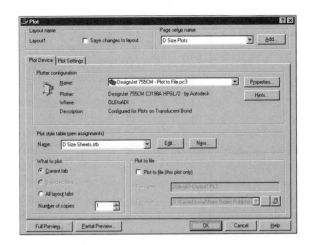

In the What to Plot area, you can choose to plot the current tab, selected tabs, or all tabs. When plotting selected tabs or all tabs, AutoCAD automatically uses the page setup assigned to the tab. Therefore, it is good practice to define the page setup options for each tab when the tab is created.

Another very useful feature in the What to Plot area is the new Number of Copies control. This feature allows you to define the number of copies AutoCAD should plot on the current or selected tab.

One other new feature is found on the Plot Settings tab. The new Plot Paperspace Last option found in the Plot Options area allows you to force AutoCAD to define objects to plot in model space viewports first, then define paper space objects. This avoids problems encountered in previous releases of AutoCAD where model space objects were plotted "on top" of paper space objects, which could produce undesired effects.

The AutoCAD Batch Plot Utility

The AutoCAD Batch Plot Utility provides a method for plotting many drawings automatically. By using the utility, you can define a list of AutoCAD drawings that you want to plot. The list can be saved as a batch plot list (BP3) file, and later recalled to plot the drawings in the list. By using the AutoCAD Batch Plot Utility, you can send complete sets of drawings to different plot devices with a single click of a button.

NOTE

You access the AutoCAD Batch Plot Utility from the Windows Taskbar by selecting Start, Programs, AutoCAD 2000, Batch Plot Utility.

The AutoCAD Batch Plot Utility main applications window allows you to easily identify the drawings to plot, and provides the ability to set various plot parameters, as shown in Figure 20.22. This window provides the following capabilities related to the drawings to be batch plotted:

■ Indicate the layout, the page setup, and the plot device used when drawings are plotted.

■ Add or remove drawings from the list, create a new list, and/or append lists to the current plot list.

■ Perform a plot test, which allows you to check to see if there are missing xrefs, fonts, or shapes.

■ Enable logging, which keeps track of who plotted a drawing, or any errors encountered during the plot process.

■ Specify scaling, the area to plot, and which layers to plot.

■ Indicate that drawings are to be plotted to a file.

Figure 20.22

The AutoCAD Batch Plot Utility allows you to plot many drawings automatically, and predefine their plot settings.

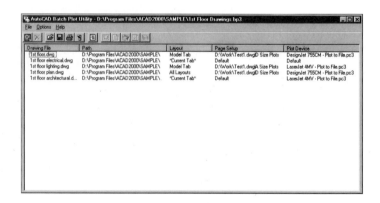

By using AutoCAD's Batch Plot Utility, you can create and save predefined lists of drawings in BP3 files, and automatically plot large sets of drawings without the need to attend the plot process. You can plot many drawings overnight, or over the weekend, and retrieve the finished plots the following morning.

AutoCAD's ePlot Feature

AutoCAD 2000 includes a feature called *ePlot*, which allows you to publish electronic drawing files on the Internet. You create an ePlot file by plotting your drawings using a PC3 file configured from the Autodesk ePlot (DWF) plot device. DWF (Drawing Web Format) files can be opened, viewed, and plotted by anyone from the Internet using an Internet browser and the Autodesk WHIP! 4.0 plug-in. DWF files support real-time panning and zooming, and allow the viewers to control the display of layers and named views. You can also include embedded hyperlinks in DWF files.

For detailed information on the ePlot feature and DWF files, see Chapter 25, "Publishing on the Web."

Summary

In this chapter, you learned about configuring a plotter, the new Autodesk Plotter Manager, and the new Plotter Configuration Editor. You created plot styles and saved them in plot style tables, and reviewed the difference between color-dependent and named plot style tables. You learned how to create page setups. You also reviewed AutoCAD's new plotting features, the AutoCAD Batch Plot Utility, and AutoCAD's ePlot feature.

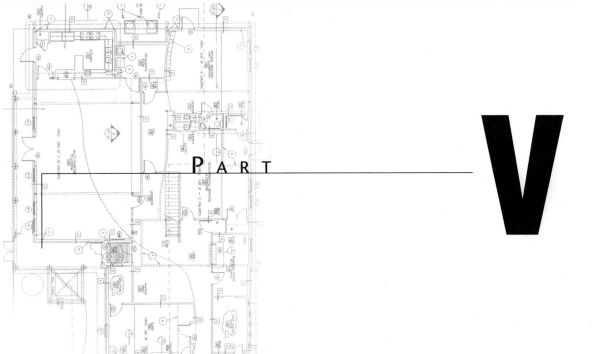

PART V

CUSTOMIZING AND ADVANCED CONCEPTS

CUSTOMIZING WITHOUT PROGRAMMING

One of AutoCAD's greatest assets is the degree to which this program can be personalized. Users with little or no formal programming knowledge or skills can learn to customize AutoCAD.

Customizing AutoCAD to suit your needs is one of the best ways to increase your productivity. If you can make AutoCAD work in a manner that facilitates your needs, you obviously will be more productive. In fact, AutoCAD is so easy to customize that in a matter of hours, you can tailor this program to match your working environment.

The first part of this chapter focuses on topics that allow you to customize the accessing of AutoCAD commands. This chapter does not, however, discuss the process of adding new commands to AutoCAD. (Adding new commands is covered in Chapter 22, "Introduction to AutoLISP Programming"). The topics of writing AutoCAD scripts and making slide libraries will be the focus of the second half of the chapter.

This chapter covers the following topics:

- Creating command aliases
- Customizing toolbars
- Customizing menus
- Scripts and slides

Creating Command Aliases

The most basic type of AutoCAD customization involves creating *command aliases*, which are one- or two-key combinations that provide a "shortcut" keyboard access to an AutoCAD command. Command aliases offer a powerful way to increase your productivity. For example, when you work with AutoCAD, one of your hands is almost always on the mouse or tablet puck. Because one hand is free for typing, command aliases offer a quick, alternate way to initiate commands.

After they are started, many AutoCAD commands offer one or more options or *sub-commands* that are answered with short one- or two-letter keyboard entries. The PEDIT command is a case in point. After you start the PEDIT command and select a polyline, AutoCAD presents the following options at the command line:

```
Enter an option [Close/Join/Width/Edit vertex/Fit/Spline/Decurve/
Ltype gen/Undo]:
```

There is no default option; one of the eight options must be entered at the keyboard. It is often convenient, therefore, to use the keyboard to initiate the command as well. Command aliases provide this convenience.

There are a large number of command aliases already defined in a special text file located in the \Support folder of a standard AutoCAD installation. This file is named the ACAD.PGP file (PGP stands for ProGram Parameters). This file is often referred to as "the PGP file." In AutoCAD 2000 there are, in fact, some 178 predefined command aliases in the PGP file. The ACAD.PGP file is actually divided into two main sections: the External Command section and the Command Alias section. In a modern Windows-type environment, the External Command section is largely redundant. This chapter examines the Command Alias section. A portion of the Command Alias section is shown here:

```
3A,        *3DARRAY
3DO,       *3DORBIT
3F,        *3DFACE
```

```
3P,       *3DPOLY
A,        *ARC
ADC,      *ADCENTER
AA,       *AREA
AL,       *ALIGN
AP,       *APPLOAD
AR,       *ARRAY
ATT,      *ATTDEF
-ATT,     *-ATTDEF
ATE,      *ATTEDIT
-ATE,     *-ATTEDIT
ATTE,     *-ATTEDIT
B,        *BLOCK
-B,       *-BLOCK
BH,       *BHATCH
BO,       *BOUNDARY
```

A short inspection of this excerpt shows the basic scheme of defining a command alias:

```
;    <Alias>,*<Full command name>
```

`<Alias>` represents the one-, two-, or three-letter keyboard combination that can be typed as a substitute for the official command name. A comma character must immediately follow the alias. Next you enter the full name of the AutoCAD command for which the alias will stand. This name must be immediately preceded by an asterisk (*) character. There can be any convenient number of spaces between the comma and the asterisk. These spaces are inserted solely to visually separate the alias from its command so that the list is easier to read.

Although the pre-defined aliases are quite extensive, you may want to edit a pre-defined alias to suit your own needs or add an alias for a command not included in the pre-defined list. In the following exercise, you edit the alias for the 3DARRAY command.

NOTE

You should make a backup copy of the ACAD.PGP file before loading it into any editing application, just to be safe.

Editing a Command Alias in the **ACAD.PGP** File

1. With AutoCAD running, start the Notepad text editor. You can also start Notepad from the command prompt by typing **Notepad** and pressing Enter.

2. In the \ACAD2000\SUPPORT folder of your ACAD installation, find and load the ACAD.PGP file.

3. Scroll down to find the Command Alias section and the list of command aliases. Find the line containing the definition of the alias for the **3DARRAY** command.

4. Edit the alias, changing it from 3A to **3DA**, and save the file.

5. Exit Notepad and return to AutoCAD.

   (You can edit the ACAD.PGP file without AutoCAD running. In that case you would *not* need to perform the following re-initializing step (step 6) because AutoCAD will read your changes the next time it is started. However, because the preceding steps were performed while AutoCAD was running, you need to alert AutoCAD of the change to the .PGP file.)

6. To re-initialize the PGP file, run the REINIT command by typing **REINIT** and pressing Enter. AutoCAD displays the Re-initialization dialog box as shown in Figure 21.1

Figure 21.1

The Re-initialization dialog box of the REINIT *command.*

7. In the Re-initialization dialog box, select PGP File and click OK. AutoCAD will read the edited PGP file and load it into memory.

8. In AutoCAD, type **3DA** and press Enter to test the new alias. Check that AutoCAD's 3DARRAY command starts. Press Esc to cancel the command.

Note

Command aliases only initiate commands; they cannot be used to specify command options. To automate both command initiation and subsequent options selection, you need to build simple AutoLISP keyboard macros. Such macros are discussed in Chapter 22, "Introduction to AutoLISP Programming."

Customizing AutoCAD Toolbars

Modifying AutoCAD's toolbars or creating a new toolbar of your own offers another way to increase your AutoCAD efficiency. Toolbars themselves can be great time-savers because they group a set of related tools—AutoCAD commands—in a single unit that can be repositioned on screen and even reshaped to fit a particular screen work area. Unlike menu pull-downs, the individual tools on a toolbar are visible (if the toolbar is visible) and easy to point to.

You can modify standard AutoCAD "factory" toolbars by rearranging the default tool layout, removing tools, or adding new tools. If you add new tools, they can be either from a library of standard AutoCAD tools and icons or "new" commands or macros that you have put together yourself. Figure 21.2 shows AutoCAD 2000 and its Draw, Modify, Standard, and Object Properties command toolbars in their "out-of-the-box" default positions.

Figure 21.2

AutoCAD 2000's "out-of-the-box" toolbar arrangement.

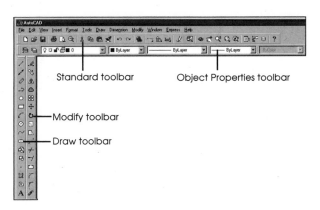

Standard toolbar   Object Properties toolbar

Modify toolbar

Draw toolbar

Modifying an Existing Toolbar

The ability to modify toolbars is one of AutoCAD's most powerful customization features. Adding a tool (icon) is easy to do. The following exercise demonstrates how to add the Polar Array tool and icon to the Modify toolbar.

WARNING

Modifying toolbars causes the modifications to be written to several AutoCAD menu files. It is advisable that you copy these files to a separate folder prior to modifying any toolbars, just in case. Assuming that your current menu is the ACAD menu, you need to copy the ACAD.MNU, ACAD.MNS, and ACAD.MNR files found in the \SUPPORT folder. If you follow the steps in the next two exercises, the changes you make will be undone.

ADDING AN ICON TO A TOOLBAR

1. Start AutoCAD 2000. In AutoCAD's default configuration, the Modify toolbar should be located on the left side of the screen as shown in Figure 21.2.

2. Right-click on any toolbar button to display the toolbar status menu (see Figure 21.3). The toolbar status menu displays all the available toolbars from the current loaded menu and indicates their current On/Off status. A check beside the toolbar name indicates that the toolbar is displayed, or on. You can turn a toolbar on or off by clicking its name.

Figure 21.3

Right-clicking on any toolbar displays the toolbar status menu.

3. Make sure Modify is checked on the toolbars status menu. Select Customize to display the Toolbars dialog box (see Figure 21.4).

Figure 21.4

The Toolbars dialog box allows you to control several aspects of toolbars.

4. Click Customize. The Customize Toolbars dialog box appears, as shown in Figure 21.5.

Figure 21.5

The Customize Toolbars dialog box is displayed from the Toolbars dialog box.

5. In the Customize Toolbars dialog box, select the down arrow on the Categories drop-down list, then scroll down to find and select the Modify category. The icons for the Modify toolbar are displayed as shown in Figure 21.6.

6. Find and select the icon for the Polar Array tool. A description for the tool appears in the Description box at the bottom of the dialog box (see Figure 21.6).

Figure 21.6

Tool icons available for placement on the Modify toolbar are shown together.

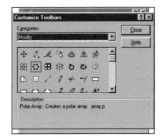

7. Drag the Polar Array icon onto the Modify toolbar near the location where you want the button to appear. The new Polar Array button appears on the toolbar, as shown in Figure 21.7.

Figure 21.7

The new Modify toolbar with the Polar Array tool and icon added.

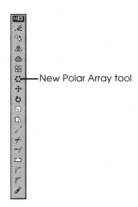

New Polar Array tool

8. Click Close in the Customize Toolbars dialog box. Then click Close in the Toolbars dialog box. AutoCAD writes the new toolbar configuration to the menu files.

INSIDER TIP

To bypass the toolbar status right-click menu and display the Toolbars dialog box directly, from the View menu, select Toolbars.

You have just customized the standard Modify toolbar. On the assumption that you use the Polar option of the ARRAY command frequently, this modification will make starting the ARRAY command with its Polar option easier, quicker, and more efficient. The following exercise shows you how to remove icons from a toolbar.

NOTE

In some cases, it may not be a good idea to modify AutoCAD's standard toolbars, making them no longer "standard." This is especially true if others are using the same installation of AutoCAD with the modified menu that toolbar modifications produce. Instead, consider making your own toolbar(s) with a collection of tools you find helpful for your work. Creating your own customized toolbars is covered later in this chapter.

To save a toolbar configuration in a profile, refer to Chapter 3, "Controlling the AutoCAD 2000 Drawing Environment."

REMOVING AN ICON FROM A TOOLBAR

1. Right-click on any toolbar to display the toolbar status menu and select Customize to display the Toolbars dialog box as shown in Figure 21.4.

2. In the Toolbars dialog box, select Customize to display the Customize Toolbars dialog box as shown in Figure 21.5.

3. Drag the tool icon you want to remove from the toolbar (in this example, the Polar Array tool icon you added in the previous exercise) and release it on any portion of the drawing area. This removes the icon and its tool from the toolbar.

4. Close the Customize Toolbars dialog box, then close the Toolbars dialog box. AutoCAD writes the new toolbar configuration to the (MNS) menu file.

INSIDER **T**IP

Referring to the previous exercise, after you have activated the Customize Toolbars dialog box (step 2), you can move, or rearrange, individual icons on any toolbar with a drag operation. Be careful not to drag (and release) an icon into the drawing area or it will be deleted from the toolbar. After an icon is deleted, it must be added again manually. The UNDO command is not of any use for any user interface modifications while the Customize Toolbars dialog box is open. To maintain uniformity, you may not want to rearrange icons on AutoCAD's standard toolbars if others are sharing the same installation of AutoCAD.

Creating Your Own Toolbar

In AutoCAD, you not only can customize existing toolbars, but you also can create your own toolbars. You can place your new toolbar anywhere on the screen or even on other toolbars as a flyout. The following exercise demonstrates the steps used in the process of creating a customized toolbar.

CREATING CUSTOMIZED TOOLBARS

1. Right-click on any button on any toolbar, or select the View menu, then Toolbars. The Toolbars dialog box appears, as shown previously in Figure 21.4.

2. Click on the New button to display the New Toolbar dialog box (see Figure 21.8).

Figure 21.8

Name the new toolbar in the New Toolbar dialog box.

3. Type **Favorites** in the Toolbar Name field. This is the name of your new toolbar.

4. Click OK to create the toolbar. A blank toolbar appears at the top of the screen, as shown in Figure 21.9.

NOTE

The new, blank toolbar is small and may appear at the top of the AutoCAD screen superimposed on the Object Properties toolbar where it is often difficult to see. To make working with the new toolbar easier, drag it into the drawing area.

Figure 21.9

Drag the new toolbar into the drawing area to make it easier to work with.

5. Select Customize in the Toolbars dialog box.

6. Use the Categories drop-down list to find the command categories from which you can drag individual tools and their icons onto the new toolbar.

NOTE

If you don't know the commands represented by icons, click on the icon to display a description of the tool icon in the Description area of the Customize Toolbars dialog box. You can drag icons from more than one category onto the new toolbar.

7. When you have placed all the tools that you wish on the new toolbar, click Close in the Customize Toolbars dialog box. Then close the Toolbars dialog box; this saves the new toolbar and AutoCAD rewrites the appropriate menu files. The new toolbar will appear as a choice on the Toolbars section of the Toolbars dialog box. A possible configuration for the Favorites toolbar is shown in Figure 21.10.

NOTE

By carefully dragging an icon sideways on the new toolbar, you can cause a separator bar to be inserted next to the icon. A separator bar appears between the second and third tools in Figure 21.10.

Figure 21.10

After customizing, the
Favorites toolbar could
have a configuration
similar to this.

The process of creating new toolbars is relatively easy and straightforward and requires no special knowledge of menu or AutoLISP programming techniques. By making one or more toolbars that contain the AutoCAD commands you use most often in your work, you can significantly increase you efficiency.

You can further customize your toolbar environment by creating flyout toolbars, such as the UCS flyout toolbar found on AutoCAD Standard Toolbar, for example. You can also create tools and accompanying icons for commands or AutoLISP and DIESEL programming macros that you devise. See Chapter 22 of this book and either the online or printed versions of the "AutoCAD Customization Guide" for more detailed information about these customization topics.

Adding a Command to the Cursor Menu

Modifying AutoCAD's main menu is a common method of customizing AutoCAD. However, extensive modification of this menu requires advanced knowledge of AutoCAD's menu macro language, the DIESEL programming language, or the AutoLISP programming language. Although these topics are beyond the intent and scope of this book, simple modifications of the cursor menu, for example, are possible with only a basic understanding of AutoCAD's menu macro language. Figure 21.11 shows an unmodified Osnap menu.

Figure 21.11

Simple modifications to
the Osnap menu are
relatively easy to carry out.

The Osnap menu in AutoCAD 2000 is available by holding down the Shift key and clicking the right mouse button. The Osnap menu is often referred to as the Cursor menu because it appears at the current cursor position.

WARNING

> Before performing modifications to any AutoCAD menu file, make a backup copy and place the copy in a separate folder. You may want to consider establishing a dedicated folder in which to store copies of all the AutoCAD support files that you use in customization.

To perform any AutoCAD menu customization, you must first find and open the main AutoCAD menu source file. The menu source file is named acad.mns. In a standard AutoCAD installation it is placed in the \Support folder. This file is a plain text ASCII file and should be opened in a generic text editor program such as Notepad. To begin modification of this file, use Windows Explorer to navigate to the AutoCAD 2000 directory of your AutoCAD installation. In the \Support folder find and double-click on the acad.mns file to open it.

NOTE

> The original menu file acad.mnu is the only location where you can place custom changes (toolbar, pull-down, and so on) and have them available in spite of what changes a user may do. For instance, if a user damages the toolbars in the menu, reloading the acad.mnu will restore the settings prior to any user interface changes. As noted earlier, it is a good practice to keep a copy of this menu file in a safe location outside AutoCAD's search path.

NOTE

> During a standard AutoCAD installation, Notepad is automatically associated with the ACAD.MNS file. Double-clicking this file in Windows Explorer will cause it to be opened in Notepad or another file editor application that you have designated during installation.

In the text editor, scroll down to the ***POP0 section of the file. This section is near the beginning of ACAD.MNS, at or near line 42 of the file. POP0 is the menu designation for the Osnap menu section. The beginning portion of this menu section appears as follows:

```
***POP0
**SNAP
                   [&Object Snap Cursor Menu]
ID_Tracking        [Temporary trac&k point]_tt
ID_From            [&From]_from
ID_MnPointFi       [->Poin&t Filters]
ID_PointFilx         [.X].X
ID_PointFily         [.Y].Y
ID_PointFilz         [.Z].Z
                     [--]
ID_PointFixy         [.XY].XY
ID_PointFixz         [.XZ].XZ
ID_PointFiyz         [<-.YZ].YZ
                   [--]
ID_OsnapEndp       [&Endpoint]_endp
ID_OsnapMidp       [&Midpoint]_mid
ID_OsnapInte       [&Intersection]_int
ID_OsnapAppa       [&Apparent Intersect]_appint
ID_OsnapExte       [E&xtension]_ext
                   [--]
ID_Osn
```

The POP0 section is denoted by the ***POP0 line. The next line, **SNAP, denotes the name of the menu itself. (The next line is not used by the Osnap menu and can be disregarded.) There follows the nametags, labels, and command sequences for all the entries on the Osnap menu. To the left are the nametags, all beginning with ID_. These are unique tags for each line containing a function and are used for cross-referencing and for defining the Help strings that appear at the bottom of the screen on the mode status line. (For your purposes in this chapter, these nametags can be ignored.) After you carry out the modification to this file as you do in the exercise that follows, you will save the changes to this file.

In addition to the nametag, each operative line in the POP0 section contains a label and a command sequence. For example, the first operative line has the nametag ID_Tracking followed by the label Temporary trac&k point. The label is what actually appears on the displayed menu as shown in Figure 21.11. The label is enclosed in square brackets. The ampersand symbol (&) that appears in the label is used to designate the shortcut letter for the line and can be disregarded for the Snap menu. The command sequence follows the label. This sequence is encoded in menu macro language and represents the commands that are executed when you select the item on the menu with the mouse. In this case, the command sequence is _tt, which initiates a temporary tracking point during commands.

In the following exercise, you will edit the ACAD.MNS file and add the ability to initiate a transparent ZOOM/WINDOW command sequence to the Cursor (Osnap) menu.

ADDING A COMMAND TO THE CURSOR MENU

1. Using Windows Explorer, find and load the ACAD.MNS file in Notepad. If Windows reports that the file is too large to load in Notepad, click OK to load the file in Wordpad.

2. Find the section beginning at ***POP0 and find the following line:

   ```
   ID_PointFiyz          [<-.YZ].YZ
   ```

   Press Enter at the end of this line to create a new line.

3. Type the following entry on the new line:

   ```
   ID_CursorZoom         [ZoomW]'_zoom;_w;
   ```

This new line adds a new label to the menu and a transparent ZOOM/WINDOW command as shown in Figure 21.12

Figure 21.12

Adding a new entry to the cursor shortcut menu.

4. Save the file.

5. If necessary, start AutoCAD and at the Command prompt, type **MENU** and press Enter to display the Select Menu File dialog box (see Figure 21.13)

Figure 21.13

The Select Menu File dialog box allows you to load or reload menus.

6. Find the ACAD.MNS file, highlight it, and click Open. AutoCAD will recompile and reload the ACAD menu.

7. To test your cursor menu addition, return to (or launch) AutoCAD, start the LINE command, and begin drawing several random line segments similar to those shown in Figure 21.14. Do not end the LINE command.

Figure 21.14

Test the new cursor menu entry by drawing several line segments.

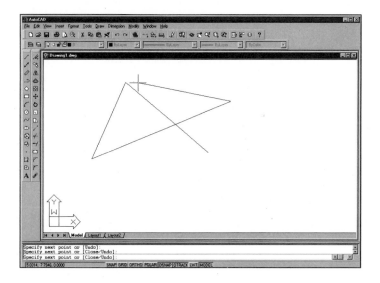

8. At the Specify next point or [Close/Undo]: prompt, display the cursor menu by Shift+right-clicking and selecting the new ZoomW entry (refer to Figure 21.12).

9. Verify that the ZOOM command Window option starts by observing the following prompt at the command line:

   >>Specify first corner:

10.   Specify a window near the current screen cursor position and verify that AutoCAD zooms to the specified window area.

11.   End the LINE command by picking a point and pressing Enter, or by pressing Esc.

One of the principal advantages of the cursor menu is that it is displayed at the area in your drawing where you are working. The new ZoomW entry allows you to quickly zoom closer to your work area transparently (such as while a command is in progress) without the need to divert your attention to make a selection from a toolbar or a pull-down menu.

Although it is not the purpose of this chapter to explore AutoCAD's menu macro language extensively, by studying the ACAD.MNS file and performing simple modifications such as that in the previous exercise, you can start customizing your menu structure to increase your efficiency. See Chapter 22 and either the online or printed version of the "AutoCAD Customization Guide" for more detailed information about these more advanced menu customization topics.

NOTE

> As stated earlier, you may not want to modify AutoCAD's standard menu structure. To undo the cursor menu modification, you must edit the ACAD.MNS file, removing the line you added in the preceding exercise then repeating steps 4–6 of the exercise. This will return the cursor menu to its default configuration.

Scripts and Slides

AutoCAD provides a *script* feature that executes AutoCAD commands read directly from a simple text file. Prior to the incorporation of Template drawings, plotting PCX files and user Profiles, scripts were often used to perform drawing and plotting setups and configurations. In the modern CAD environment offered by Release 15, the script facility is largely reserved for more advanced customization tasks and for displaying a continuously running demonstration of AutoCAD screen displays.

Scripts are created outside of AutoCAD in a standard text editor (such as Windows Notepad). You run a script using AutoCAD's SCRIPT command. To show a sequence or series of AutoCAD screen captures, AutoCAD's MSLIDE and VSLIDE (*make* slide and *view* slide) commands, create and view "captures" of an AutoCAD screen. This process is typically automated by placing the slide names and display commands in a script file. You can insert pauses into the script as well as have the script automatically repeat on a continuous basis.

In the following exercise, you use the MSLIDE command to create a series of four slides. You then use these slides in another exercise to help create a script to show the slides in a continuous loop fashion.

Because you will be saving .SLD files in the following exercise, it is important that you make a mental note of the folder where the files are being created so you can direct AutoCAD to that folder when you run the scripts.

MAKING SLIDES FOR A SCRIPTED SLIDE SHOW

1. Start AutoCAD and open Chap21.DWG from the accompanying CD-ROM. Your initial view should resemble that of Figure 21.15.

Figure 21.15

A view of three solid objects for use with the MSLIDE *command.*

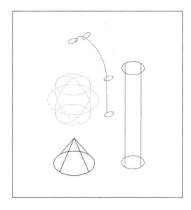

2. Start the MSLIDE command by typing **MSLIDE**. In the Create Slide File dialog box in the File Name input box, type **slide01** then click Save. AutoCAD creates the slide in the current directory.

3. Type **ISOLINES** and set the new value to **8**. Type **RE** to regenerate the drawing showing the increased number of boundary lines for the four solids.

4. Repeat step 1, giving the slide the name **slide02**.

5. Perform a Hide by typing **HI**.

6. Repeat step 1, giving the slide the name **slide03**.

7. Type **FACETRES** and set the new value to **2**. Perform another Hide.

8. Repeat step 1, giving the slide the name **slide04**.

In the following steps you open this chapter's script file to view it.

9.   Start Windows Notepad (or your setup's ASCII text editor) and navigate to the current directory. Find the file Chap21.scr and open it. The file should look like the following:

```
VSLIDE SLIDE01
DELAY 3000
VSLIDE SLIDE02
DELAY 3000
VSLIDE SLIDE03
DELAY 3000
VSLIDE SLIDE04
DELAY 3000
RSCRIPT
;END OF FILE
```

As you can see, each line in an AutoCAD script contains a single command—in this case the command VSLIDE and the name of the slide. The command DELAY is a special script command that delays execution of the script for a period of time expressed in thousandths of a second. The RSCRIPT command causes the entire script to repeat. AutoCAD's script reader disregards any line starting with a semicolon.

10. Close Notepad and return to AutoCAD.

11. From the Tools menu, select Run Script. In the Select Script File dialog box, find and select the script file Solid.scr. AutoCAD runs the script.

12. To halt the script, press the Backspace key (or Esc key). You will need to REGEN the drawing to erase whatever slide was on the screen when you halted the script.

13. Exit the drawing without saving changes.

NOTE

One other script-specific command you should be aware of is the RESUME command. Entering this command at the command prompt will restart a script halted with the Backspace key or by a script error.

The MSLIDE and VSLIDE commands combined with AutoCAD's script facility offer the ability to build self-running slide shows that can be quite complex. The more advanced uses of scripts for customization, however, are beyond the scope of this book. You should consult a source such as the "AutoCAD Customization Guide."

Summary

There are many ways to customize AutoCAD. Adding or changing command aliases in the .PGP file, creating toolbars, and modifying menus are among the most popular. As this chapter demonstrated, these methods do not require any advanced knowledge of programming techniques and are easy to learn. If you want to take a further step in customization, Chapter 22 introduces you to AutoCAD's most popular customization and programming interface: AutoLISP.

22

INTRODUCTION TO AutoLISP PROGRAMMING

One of AutoCAD's most powerful features is its programming interface. With support for AutoLISP, ADS, ObjectARX, and script programming, you can customize AutoCAD to just about any degree you want.

This chapter focuses on the basics of AutoLISP. Its intent is to introduce you to AutoLISP's capabilities. The chapter covers the following topics:

- *Introducing AutoLISP*

- *Using AutoLISP for keyboard macros*

- *Creating a simple AutoLISP routine*

- *Using ACAD.LSP and ACADDOC.LSP*

- *A brief look at Visual LISP*

Introducing AutoLISP

LISP is a programming language originally developed for use in the field of Artificial Intelligence (AI) in the early 1960's. In fact, with the possible exception of FORTRAN, LISP is the only surviving high-level programming language from the 1960s. There are some dozen dialects, or subsets, of LISP in use today. LISP is an acronym for *LISt Processor* and all of LISP's data are, indeed, contained in the form of lists.

AutoLISP is Autodesk's own subset of LISP. Due to AutoCAD's overall popularity, there are more worldwide users of AutoLISP today than of any other implementation of the popular LISP language. AutoLISP was introduced in an early version of AutoCAD and has remained a popular, although little-changed, feature. Some significant extensions to AutoLISP's capabilities and functionality became possible with the introduction of Visual LISP as an integral part of AutoCAD 2000.

Programming with AutoLISP is easier than you might think. In fact, a large number of AutoCAD users who program with AutoLISP had no programming experience before learning AutoLISP. In this chapter, you will be introduced to the basic concepts of AutoLISP programming.

If you have created menu macros before, you probably found them to be powerful tools but somewhat limited in flexibility and "brainpower." A macro is like a robot typist entering sequences of AutoCAD commands. AutoLISP turns your macros into a "thinking" typist capable of making calculations and logical decisions. Simple AutoLISP routines go a step further than macros and can act as custom AutoCAD commands that prompt, instruct, and provide choices. In this chapter, we will examine both AutoLISP macros and a simple AutoLISP routine.

The following is a sample of a simple AutoLISP macro:

```
(defun C:ZO ()
   (command "zoom" ".5X")
)
```

At first, this may look confusing but it is rather simple. All AutoLISP macros follow a basic formula and consist of two basic elements. First is a function definition, which is nothing more than a name for the macro. Next is a call to an AutoCAD command along with input to the command's prompts just as though you were typing from the keyboard. In the preceding macro, the `defun` function is used to state our intention to define a new function (a macro) and to declare its name. This macro will perform a quick zoom out so we gave it the name ZO, for zoom-out. If you prefix the name of the macro with a `c:` then the macro can be called directly from the command line by merely typing its name—**ZO**, in this case.

The next element of a standard AutoLISP macro is a call to a standard AutoCAD command. Logically enough, you use the AutoLISP function command to call AutoCAD commands. After the command is called, or started, you must make provision to answer all the prompts associated with the command. In the case of C:ZO the ZOOM command is started. The nine options to the ZOOM command are now available just as they would be at the command line. In the case of C:ZO, you want to issue a zoom with a choice of the Scale option. At the keyboard, you could type an **s** for Scale and then the scale factor or just enter the scale factor directly. Likewise in the C:ZO macro, we can directly submit a scale factor to the ZOOM command. C:ZO uses a scale factor of .5X—which will yield a zoom of one half the current screen size. Once defined, running the C:ZO macro merely involves typing **zo** followed by pressing Enter.

It would be difficult to create a macro simpler than C:ZO, yet such simple macros, once defined and loaded into memory, can save significant amounts of time for repetitive command sequences compared to typing the same sequence at the command line or even using a mouse to perform the same functions with picks from a displayed toolbar.

The trick to writing AutoLISP macros is knowing your AutoCAD commands and their options as well as the type of information the various prompts and options require. You can usually save time and reduce the number of errors in your macros by first "running" them conventionally from the keyboard. You can then either write down the exact input and response sequence or change to the text screen (press F2) to view the sequence as you compose the macro.

Understanding AutoLISP's Parentheses

Before moving on to a closer look at AutoLISP keyboard macros, you need to understand the matter of LISP parenthesis. We have said that the LISP programming language is based on lists and that all data in LISP is stored and presented as lists. In LISP, the lists are delimited with parentheses; a single list is begun with a left, or *opening*, parenthesis and is closed with a right, or *closing*, parenthesis. Lists can—and usually do—contain other lists, each of which must, in turn, be delimited with an opening and closing pair of parentheses. In the macro C:ZO, for example, there are three lists:

```
(defun C:ZO ()              ;line 1
   (command "zoom" ".5X")   ;line 2
)                                ;line 3
```

The parent list holds the other two lists and begins on line 1 with the (defun ... statement. The second list is an *empty* list—that is, it contains no data. It appears on line 1 also, immediately after the name of the macro: (). The reason for the appearance of this empty list goes beyond the scope of this chapter; suffice it to say it is required. The third list comprises line 2 of the code. It begins with the (command ... function. Line 3 of the code contains but one item: the closing, or *matching*, parenthesis for the very first (defun ... parenthesis. Although not required, it appears on a separate line and directly under its opposite parentheses for visual clarity.

In the case of C:ZO, there are two lists within the *parent*, or outer, list. When a list appears as an element within a larger list, it is called a *nested* list. The nesting of lists to a depth of several levels is common in AutoLISP. Nesting, however, often makes the matching of all the right and left parentheses more difficult. If an AutoLISP function—whether a simple macro or a complicated multi-line routine—contains unbalanced parentheses, an error message will result when the function is executed. Keeping track of parentheses is one of the less appealing aspects of programming in AutoLISP.

Using AutoLISP for Keyboard Macros

Many of the most useful AutoLISP macros are as simple as C:ZO, which was defined in the previous section. Other macros, although performing more involved tasks, are extensions of the simple macro model represented by C:ZO. An AutoLISP macro, for example, may call a series of commands as shown later in this section, start a command or provide pre-determined responses to one or more command prompts that allow the user to finish the command sequence interactively.

The following is an example of an AutoLISP macro that calls more than one AutoCAD command:

```
(defun C:RX ()
   (command "UCS""X""90")
   (command "PLAN" "C")
)
```

This macro, C:RX, could be useful in 3D work. It first rotates the UCS about the X axis by ninety degrees. It next calls the PLAN command and specifies the current, C, plan view. By typing **RX** and pressing Enter, you've used this macro to perform the work of 16 keyboard strokes.

NOTE

> To help you better understand the logic and sequence of these macros, you may want to open a drawing and run the command involved in AutoCAD as you follow the explanations.

The next AutoLISP macro shows an example of a macro that suspends command operation and allows the users to finish the sequence interactively.

```
(defun PB ()
(command "PURGE" "B" "*" "y")
```

As you can see, this macro, C:PB, starts the PURGE command and answers the first prompt of the command with a "B" for Blocks. The next PURGE command prompts you to name the blocks to offer for purging or to type a * for all blocks. The next prompt asks whether you want to verify each name to be purged. In the C:PB macro, this prompt is answered with a **Y** for "yes". At this point, the macro ends and allows the PURGE command to continue normally, offering candidate blocks, if any, for purging. At this point, you can accept or reject candidate blocks interactively as you would if the command had been entered manually.

WARNING

> Many AutoCAD commands offer defaults for some of their prompts. Often these defaults are based on a previous response to the prompt. You can accept a default value to any prompt by supplying a double quote (" ") in the macro—the equivalent to pressing Enter on the keyboard. However, you should form the habit of explicitly specifying the desired response to all prompts in your macros.

Creating a Single AutoLISP File with Multiple Macros

As you noticed, AutoLISP macros are typically very short with perhaps only two or three lines of AutoLISP code. It is useful to group a number of related macros together into a single file that can be loaded in one operation. No matter how many individual macros are contained in a parent file, they are all loaded into AutoLISP's memory when the file is loaded.

NOTE

AutoLISP code can be written using any standard ASCII text editor, such as Windows Notepad. Third-party, ASCII text editor programs can also be used. The important thing to remember is to use a non-formatting ASCII editor. AutoCAD 2000 also provides a full-featured, LISP-aware ASCII text editor as part of Visual LISP. We will look at the basic elements of Visual LISP later in this chapter.

A useful grouping of AutoLISP keyboard macros might have the manipulation of the UCS (User Coordinate System) as its theme and include a family of macros related to the C:RX macro from earlier in this chapter. The following group of eight macros is just such a grouping.

```
(defun C:RX ()
  (command "UCS" "X" "90")
  (command "PLAN" "C")
  (princ)
)

(defun C:RX- ()
  (command "UCS" "X" "-90")
  (command "PLAN" "C")
  (princ)
)

(defun C:RY ()
  (command "UCS" "Y" "90")
  (command "PLAN" "C")
  (princ)
)

(defun C:RY- ()
  (command "UCS" "Y" "-90")
  (command "PLAN" "C")
  (princ)
)
```

```
(defun C:RZ ()
  (command "UCS" "Z" "90")
  (command "PLAN" "C")
  (princ)
)

(defun C:RZ- ()
  (command "UCS" "X" "-90")
  (command "PLAN" "C")
  (princ)
)

(defun C:PW ()
  (command "UCS" "W")
  (command "PLAN" "W")
  (command "ZOOM" ".9X")
  (princ)
)

(defun C:ISO ()
  (command "VPOINT" "1,-1,1")
(princ)
)
```

These eight macros—as well as others related to 3D work—could be typed into a text editor and saved as a file with a descriptive name such as 3DUTILS.LSP. In fact, that is the name of the file that contains these macros found on the CD-ROM accompanying this book.

NOTE

Standard AutoLISP files have an .LSP file extension.

The following exercise demonstrates one method of loading files containing one or more AutoLISP macro definitions.

LOADING AND RUNNING AN AUTOLISP MACRO FILE

1. Start AutoCAD and open Chap22.DWG. The loaded drawing should resemble Figure 22.1

Figure 22.1

Opening view of Chap22.DWG.

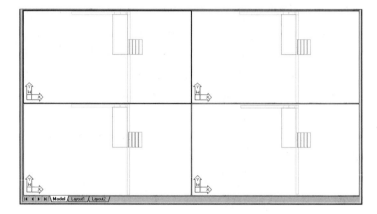

2. From the Tools menu, select Load Application to display the Load/Unload Applications dialog box as shown in Figure 22.2.

3. In the Look In portion of the dialog box, find this book's CD-ROM, then find and select the file 3DUTILS.LSP. Click the Load button and note that the 3DUTILS.LSP file is added to the top of the list of the Loaded Applications tab. Also note that an informational message is displayed in the message box near the bottom of the dialog box. Click Close to exit the dialog box.

Figure 22.2

The Load/Unload Applications dialog box.

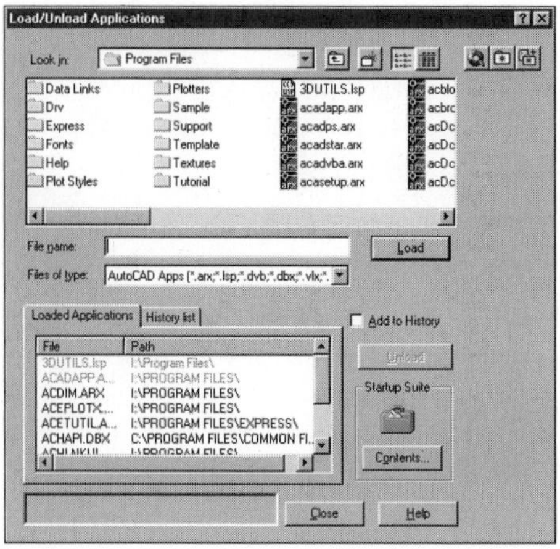

4. Pick in the upper-left viewport to make it active. Test the C:ISO macro by typing **ISO** and pressing Enter. Note the view in the current viewport changes to a standard isometric in accordance with the AutoLISP code in the C:ISO macro.

5. Set the upper-right viewport current. Test the C:RX macro by typing **RX** and pressing Enter. Note that the view changes to a plan view with the UCS rotated positive 90 degrees about the X axis.

6. Set the lower-right viewport current and test the C:RY macro. First, establish the same view as in the upper-right viewport by running the C:RX macro in this viewport. Then run the C:RY macro by typing **RY** and pressing Enter. Note that the view changes to a plan view with the UCS rotated 90 degrees about the X axis and 90 degrees about the Y axis.

7. With the lower-left viewport current, test the C:RZ macro by typing **RZ** and pressing Enter. Note that the view changes to a plan view with the UCS rotated 90 degrees about the Z axis.

8. Finally, with the lower-left viewport still current, test the C:PW macro by typing **PW** and pressing Enter. Note that the view changes to World UCS plan view with a 10 percent zoom-out factor.

9. Close Chap22.DWG.

Simple AutoLISP keyboard macros allow you to perform repetitive command sequences with a minimum number of keystrokes and they are relatively easy to write. In a later section of this chapter, you will see how AutoLISP routines and programs take over where macros leave off, offering the ability to receive input from the user and to make decisions based on that input.

Working with APPLOAD and the Load/Unload Applications Dialog Box

NEW
for R2000   In the previous exercise, you loaded an AutoLISP file using the Load/Unload Application dialog box. This dialog box provides the graphical interface for the APPLOAD command.

You used the APPLOAD command to load an AutoLISP file in the previous exercise. The APPLOAD command is used when you need to use applications that are not automatically loaded when you start AutoCAD. You can use APPLOAD to load and unload applications, store a history list of applications you've loaded, and create a startup list of applications to be loaded each time you start AutoCAD. The APPLOAD command was introduced in Release 12, and the graphical interface changed little in appearance and functionality until the appearance of the current Load/Unload Applications dialog box. The AutoCAD 2000 Load/Unload Applications dialog box adds significant functionality and a new visual appearance (refer to Figure 22.2). The main features of this new dialog box are outlined here:

- The options at the top of this dialog box are derived from the standard file selection dialog box common to many AutoCAD file operation dialog boxes in which you can navigate through your directory structure and select files to open.(Refer to Chapter 1, "What's New in AutoCAD 2000," for more details).

- **Load button.** Loads or reloads that applications that are selected in either the files list or the History List tab. The Load button is unavailable until you select a file that you can load. APPLOAD loads ARX, VBA, LSP, VLX , FAS and DBX applications

- **Load Applications tab.** Displays an alphabetical list, by file name, of currently loaded applications. LISP applications are displayed in this list only if you loaded them in the Load/Unload Applications dialog box.

- **History List tab.** Displays an alphabetical list, by file name, of applications that you previously loaded with Add to History selected.

- **Add to History check box.** Adds any applications that you load to the History List.

- **Unload button.** Unloads the selected applications. Unload is not available for all file types. You cannot unload LISP applications, for example.

- **Remove.** Removes the selected applications from the History List. Remove is available only when you select a file on the History List. Remove does *not* unload an application. The Remove option is also available from a shortcut menu by selecting the application on the History List then right-clicking to display the shortcut menu.

- **Startup Suite section.** Contains a custom list of applications that are started each time you start AutoCAD. Click the Startup Suite icon or Contents to display a secondary, Startup Suite dialog box, which displays the contents of the Startup Suite and allows you to add or remove files from the list. You can also add files to the Startup Suite by right-clicking an application in the History List tab and choosing Add to Startup Suite from the shortcut menu.

You can drag files into the Loaded Applications files list or into the History List from either the main files list (at the top of the dialog box) or from any application that allows dragging, such as Windows Explorer.

In addition to the Startup Suite available with the APPLOAD command, you can create a file named ACAD.LSP composed of AutoLISP functions and routines. AutoCAD will automatically load the contents of this file each time AutoCAD is started. The ACAD.LSP file is covered in a later section of this chapter.

Creating a Simple AutoLISP Program

Now that you have seen how to use AutoLISP in the relatively simple context of a keyboard macro, it is time to progress to a more complex example. AutoLISP *routines* lie a step above macros in complexity—and flexibility. Generally speaking, AutoLISP routines are distinguished by the fact that they will accept input from the user (or other routines) and are capable of branching in more than one direction based on the input they receive. AutoLISP routines, in other words, exhibit "intelligence"—or at least the ability to make simple decisions.

Functions, Routines, and Programs

Routines are composed of one or more AutoLISP functions—such as the Command function used in writing the 3DUTIL.LSP macros. AutoLISP functions are the building blocks of all AutoLISP code. If two or more routines are grouped together to accomplish some desirable task, the grouping is commonly referred to as a *program*. Programs are usually composed of routines. Some routines are rather specialized and are found in specialized programs. Other routines are of a basic, generalized nature and can be used—perhaps slightly modified—in a variety of larger programs. This *modular* use of routines provides the AutoLISP programmer with a library of routines that can be utilized over and over again, in various program contexts making the building of larger programs easier.

NOTE

> The distinction among the terms *function*, *routine*, and *program* is somewhat arbitrary. A routine by the definition of this chapter, for example, is itself a function composed of one or more other functions. This chapter uses these terms in a hierarchical sense rather than a strict functional one.

STAIR.LSP—A Simple AutoLISP Program

The AutoLISP program, STAIR.LSP, is an example of a modular program. STAIR.LSP is included on this book's CD-ROM. A listing of its AutoLISP code follows:

```
;;Get Information
;;Stairs.lsp
;;
;;Get Information

(defun Get-Info       ()
  (initget 1 "Standard Modern")
  (setq optn  (getkword "\nStair type: [S]tandard, [M]odern?  "))
  (setq wid   (getdist  "\nEnter step width in inches: "))
  (setq tread (getdist  "\nEnter tread in inches: "))
  (setq rise  (getdist  "\nEnter rise in inches: "))
  (setq num   (getint   "\nNumber of steps: "))
  (setq crnr  (getpoint "\nSpecify lower-left corner
                of bottom step: "))
 )
;
;insert proto-step

(defun Proto ()
  (command "zoom" "all")
  (command "vpoint" "-1,-1,1")
  (command "-insert" optn crnr "x" wid tread rise "0")
)
;
;copy steps

(defun Copy-Steps ()
  (repeat (1- num)
    (command "copy" "L" "" (list 0 tread rise) "")
    (command "zoom" "e")
  )
)
```

```
;
;make a command

(defun C:STAIRS   (/ optn tread wid rise num crnr)
  (get-info)
  (proto)
  (copy-steps)
  (princ)
)
```

NOTE

> With few exceptions, AutoLISP is case insensitive. The choice of upper or lower case is largely a matter of programming style or programmer's choice. Function names are often given an initial capital letter for visual clarity. Likewise, symbols and variables are treated differently by various programmers. Generally, you can disregard case. Punctuation and capitalization in prompts should conform to normal text practice because they are read by the user at the command prompt.

This program consists of three self-contained, modular routines:

■ **Get-Info.** Users supplies information required.

■ **Proto.** The first prototype object is drawn.

■ **Copy-Steps.** Additional items are drawn using information obtained in Get-Info module.

The purpose of STAIRS.LSP is to automatically draw a set of stairs in 3D. The user supplies the number of steps, as well as the width, tread, or depth, and the rise of each step. A typical set of steps drawn with STAIRS.LSP is shown in Figure 22.3.

Figure 22.3

3D stairs created with STAIRS.LSP.

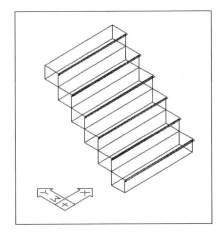

In the sections that follow, these three routines will be briefly discussed so that you can gain a basic understanding of how a number of AutoLISP functions operate, how functions go together to make routines, and how routines fit together to make a simple AutoLISP program. Keep in mind that it is the intent of this chapter to provide you with an introduction to AutoLISP, not an in-depth tutorial of AutoLISP program building.

Gathering Information with the Get-Info Routine

The first routine in STAIR.LSP, Get-Info, is intended to gather information by requesting input from the user and save that information in unique variables. After this information is gathered, the next sequence plugs the information in for the response at the appropriate commands. A series of prompts asks for the style of stair to draw, the tread of each step, the width of the stair, the rise of each step, the number of steps, and the position of the bottom step.

```
(defun Get-Info ()
 (initget 1 "Standard Modern")
 (setq optn  (getkword "\nStair type: [S]tandard, [M]odern?  "))
 (setq wid   (getdist  "\nEnter step width in inches: "))
 (setq tread (getdist  "\nEnter tread in inches: "))
 (setq rise  (getdist  "\nEnter rise in inches: "))
 (setq num   (getint   "\nNumber of steps: "))
 (setq crnr  (getpoint "\nSpecify lower-left corner
                          of bottom step: "))
)
```

AutoLISP functions in the get*xxx* family of functions are used to collect this data. Data specifying the dimensions of each step, for example, is collected via AutoLISP's getdist function. The getdist function accepts either typed distance input or distance input derived from screen picks. As with all of the get*xxx* functions, you can include a prompt as a quoted string. The first getdist function in the Get-Info routine prompts for the step width. The distance supplied in response to this prompt is stored as a *variable*—an arbitrary symbol—by the setq function. Although there are few rules governing the choice of symbols, using a symbol for the variable that somehow represents the data that the variable stores is helpful in following the sense of the routine. In this instance, the programmer chose the variable WID because the variable holds the value of the width of the stair.

In a similar manner, getdist functions, with appropriate prompts, are used to obtain the tread and rise distances. Again, a setq function stores the input distances of each parameter in the variables TREAD and RISE, respectively.

A different get*xxx* function is used to obtain the number of stairs to be drawn. Because the number of stairs is not represented by a distance but rather by a whole number, the getint (for "get integer") is used. Again, an appropriate prompt is included and the input is stored in the variable NUM (for "number") by the setq function.

Points are sets of three numbers representing the X, Y, and Z coordinates of a point. A getpoint function is therefore next used to obtain the lower-left starting point of the stairway. Points are usually supplied by picking a point on the screen although—like most of the get*xxx* functions—the data can be typed in on the command line. The point is stored in the variable CRNR (for "corner").

Often you may want to restrict the input to a particular get*xxx* function. For example, you may want to disallow a "zero," a negative number, or even a keypress of Enter. Or you may wish to restrict input to one of several permissible choices (usually strings). The initget function provides this flexibility. For example, an initget function is used in the Get-Info routine to obtain the name of the type of step. Because a block will be used by STAIRS.LSP to draw each individual step, it is important that the user knows the choices available and not enter an erroneous choice. Two styles of steps are available: Standard and Modern. The initget function, therefore, restricts the user's response to the very next get*xxx* function by setting up a list of permissible choices—Standard and Modern. Since the choices are specified with initial capital letters, the user can designate their choice by simply typing the capitalized letter rather than the entire name. This conforms with the convention used in AutoCAD prompts and is, therefore, assumed by users.

The initget function acts somewhat as a filter. Its restrictions apply only to the next get*xxx* function, which in the case of Get-Info is a getkword function. kword, in this context, stands for "keyword," and the keywords allowable in response to a getkword function are those initialized by the preceding initget. Get-Info offers two keywords: Standard and Modern. The user selects one of these in response to the getkword prompt and the choice is stored by the setq function in the variable OPTN (for "option"). When the Get-Info routine is completed, six pieces of data are stored in six variables. These variables will be used by the other two routines in the program.

Putting the Variables to Work with the Proto Routine

The *Proto* routine is little more than an AutoLISP macro. The big difference between Proto and a typical macro is that Proto uses data collected outside the routine itself. Proto is composed of three functions. In the following example, you will see that the first function executes AutoCAD's ZOOM command and specifies the All option. In a plan view, a ZOOM/All will zoom the drawing to either the drawing's limits or its extents, whichever is greater. In a 3D view, a ZOOM/All is equivalent to a ZOOM/ Extents. This zoom is included to provide adequate "room" in the drawing for the block insert. The second function in Proto is a specific change to a non-plan view in which the VPOINT command is called with a SW Isometric viewpoint vector.

```
(defun Proto ()
  (command "zoom" "all")
  (command "vpoint" "-1,-1,1")
  (command "-insert" optn crnr "x" wid tread rise "0")
)
```

The last function in the Proto routine calls the command line version of the INSERT command. The command-line version is required because AutoLISP cannot deal directly with dialog boxes. In AutoCAD 2000, to invoke the command-line version of the INSERT command, the name must be preceded with a hyphen.

NOTE

Prior to AutoCAD 2000, the command-line version of the INSERT command was either the only or the default version and was called with the name "insert." In Release 12, 13, and 14, the dialog box version was called with the name "ddinsert." In AutoCAD 2000, the dialog box version is the default version called with the name "insert" and the command line version is available with the name "-insert."

A review of the prompt sequence for the command-line version of the INSERT command in the above Proto example will make the third function's call to "-insert" clear. Here is the sequence of prompts with the responses used by the Proto routine:

```
Enter block name or [?]:
```

The variable OPTN is supplied here. It is not enclosed inside double quotes because the *getkword* function stores it as a string automatically. Specifically, variable OPTN will contain either the string "standard" or "modern". Therefore the drawing must also contain blocks by this name.

```
Specify insertion point or [Scale/X/Y/Z/Rotate/Pscale/...
```

The Get-Info variable CRNR is supplied in answer to this prompt.

```
Enter X scale Factor, specify opposite corner, or

[Corner/XYZ]...
```

You want to be able to specify different scale factors for X, Y, and Z during insertion of the Proto step block, so an X enclosed in double quotes (as a string) is supplied in response to this prompt.

```
Specify X scale factor or [Corner]...
```

The X scale factor corresponds to the stair width, which is held in the variable WID.

```
Specify Y scale factor...
```

The Y scale factor corresponds to the stair tread held in the variable TREAD.

```
Specify Z scale factor...
```

The Z scale factor is the rise of the Proto step and is held in the RISE variable.

```
Specify rotation angle...
```

The last prompt asks for rotation angle. This will always be 0 degrees. The value 0 is specifically quoted.

This completes the Proto routine. If the program were to halt at this point, you would see either the Standard or Modern block inserted with the lower left corner located at the point specified in the Get-Info routine. The block would be differentially scaled so that the width of the step would equal the value held by variable WID, the depth (or Y distance) of the step would equal the value held in variable TREAD, and the height of the step would equal the value held by variable RISE.

N O T E

To take advantage of the INSERT command's ability to scale differentially in the X, Y, and Z directions, the blocks used for STAIRS.LSP must be defined with a single unit height, width, and depth.

Building the Stairs with the Copy-Steps Routine

The *Copy-Steps* routine is at the heart of the STAIRS.LSP program. After the Proto routine has inserted the first step at the proper X, Y, and Z scale factor, the Copy-Step routine takes over to build the stairway.

```
(defun Copy-Steps ()
  (repeat (1- num)
    (command "copy" "L" "" (list 0 tread rise) "")
    (command "zoom" "e")
  )
)
```

Copy-Steps contains two functions, each enclosed by a repeat function loop. The number of "repeats" is equal to the number of stairs stored in the num variable minus 1—since the first step is already in place.

The first function enclosed in the repeat loop consists of a macro-like execution of the COPY command:

```
(command "copy" "L" "" (list 0 tread rise) "")
```

Again, a review of the COPY command's prompt sequence shows how Copy-Steps builds the stairway. Here is the sequence:

```
Select objects:
```

As with most AutoCAD EDIT commands, you can specify the Last object drawn at the Select objects: prompt. A quoted L is first supplied in answer to the prompt. This refers to the Last object added to the drawing, in this case, the block inserted in the Proto routine.

```
Select objects:
```

Close the repeating Select objects prompt by supplying the macro equivalent of a keyboard Enter—a double quote.

```
Specify base point or displacement, or [Multiple]:
```

You need to displace the copy by an amount equal to the stair tread and rise, that is the values held in variables TREAD and RISE. No displacement in the X direction is required. We can supply this displacement by listing an X value of 0, a Y value of TREAD and a Z value of RISE. In AutoLISP, the most direct method of supplying this displacement is to use AutoLISP list function:

```
(list 0 tread rise)
```

This response ID followed by a double quote to indicate a keypress of Enter to complete the displacement specification and end the COPY command.

The second function contained in the repeat loop is a straightforward execution of the ZOOM command with an Extents parameter. Performing this zoom after each call to the COPY command will ensure that all the copied steps are displayed in the current viewport. This is necessary because the Last option in the Select objects: prompt of the COPY command requires that the object be visible.

The Copy/Last and Zoom/Extents events are repeated a number of times equal to the value held in the variable NUM, minus 1, to yield the correct number of steps.

Lastly, we group the three routines inside STAIRS.LSP together:

```
(defun C:STAIRS (/ optn tread wid rise num crnr)
  (get-info)
  (proto)
  (copy-steps)
  (princ)
)
```

As with AutoLISP macros, a C: prefix to a user-defined function such as STAIRS, elevates the function or program to the level of an AutoCAD command that can be entered directly at any command prompt. Immediately following the naming of the program is a list of all the variables used in the constituent routines. Listing the variables in this manner effectively deletes them from AutoLISP's memory after the program ends, freeing the memory space for other variables. The last function in the C:STAIRS function is a call to another AutoLISP function: princ. The sole purpose of including this function is to eliminate the "nil" that would otherwise be printed to the command line upon completion of C:STAIRS.LSP. This "nil" is visually unwanted and intimidating to many users.

In the following exercise, you load and run STAIRS.LSP in Chap22.DWG.

OTE

STAIRS.LSP attempts to insert a block. The block must be defined in the drawing or the Proto routine will fail. The provided file Chap22.DWG contains all blocks required for this program.

LOADING AND RUNNING THE STAIRS.LSP PROGRAM

1. Open Chap22.DWG. Type **AP** then press Enter to start the APPLOAD command and display the Load/Unload Applications dialog box as shown in Figure 22.4.

Figure 22.4

The Load/Unload Applications dialog box.

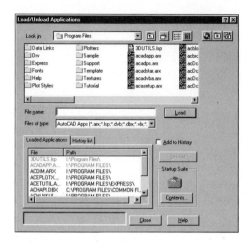

2. In the Look In portion of the dialog box, find this book's CD-ROM then find and select the file STAIRS.LSP. Click the Load button and note that the STAIRS.LSP file is added to the top of the list of the Loaded Applications tab. Also note that an informational message regarding the loading of this file is displayed in the message box near the bottom of the dialog box. Click Close to exit the dialog box.

INSIDER TIP

In the previous step, you could highlight the STAIRS.LSP file and drag it into the Loaded Applications list box.

3. If necessary, click in the upper-left viewport to set it current. To configure a single viewport, from the View menu, choose Viewports, 1 Viewport. Then, from the View menu, select Named Views. In the View dialog box, select view AAA and Set Current. Click OK to close the dialog box and restore view AAA. Your drawing should resemble Figure 22.5.

Figure 22.5

Chap22.DWG with view AAA restored.

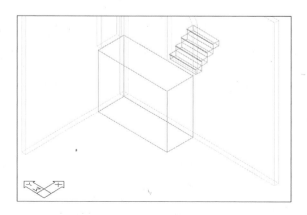

4. To test the STAIRS.LSP program loaded in step 2, type **STAIRS** then press Enter. Type responses the STAIRS.LSP prompts as follows:

```
Stair type: [S]tandard, [M]odern? S
Enter step width in inches: 36
Enter tread in inches: 8
Enter rise in inches: 6
Number of steps: 12
Specify lower-left corner of bottom step: 17',7'
```

5. Use the HIDE command (View, Hide) to obtain a hidden line view (see Figure 22.6).

Figure 22.6

*Stairs drawn with
STAIRS.LSP.*

6. Close Chap22.DWG.

STAIRS.LSP is useful here as an example of the kinds of sophisticated programming you can perform in AutoLISP. Several improvements, such as the ability to control the direction of the stairway, could be added to STAIRS.LSP to make it even more useful in a typical 3D modeling or drafting environment. But although STAIRS.LSP is not a complex program, its ability to accept user input places it ahead of the simpler, but useful, AutoLISP macros and shows why and how AutoLISP is such a popular means to customize and extend AutoCAD.

Understanding ACAD.LSP and ACADDOC.LSP

If you want to load a group of AutoLISP routines every time you start AutoCAD, you can place the routines in a standard (ASCII) text file and save the file with the name ACAD.LSP. When AutoCAD starts, it searches its library path for a file named ACAD.LSP. If it finds such a file, its contents are loaded into memory. By default, ACAD.LSP is loaded only once: upon starting AutoCAD. If you want to load a group of AutoLISP routines every time you start a new drawing (or open an existing drawing), you should create a file named ACADDOC.LSP and place it in AutoCAD's library path. Each time AutoCAD opens a drawing, it searches the library path for a file named ACADDOC.LSP and if a file with that name is found, it loads the contents of the file into memory.

You can have ACAD.LSP load with every drawing by selecting the Load ACAD.LSP with Every Drawing option on the System tab of the Options dialog box. If this option is not checked, only the ACADDOC.LSP file is loaded into all drawing files. Clear this option if you do not want to run certain LISP routines in specific drawing files. You can also control Load ACAD.LSP with Every Drawing by using the ACADLSPASDOC system variable.

By controlling the location of the ACAD.LSP and ACADDOC.LSP files in the AutoCAD library path, you can control whether or not these files are found (and loaded). AutoCAD will load the first ACAD.LSP and ACADDOC.LSP it encounters, so by utilizing AutoCAD profiles and project directories, you can control which among several ACAD.LSP files, for example, is found first and loaded. (Refer to Chapter 2, "Starting a Drawing in AutoCAD 2000," for more information about profiles and AutoCAD's library path.)

NOTE

If you move beyond basic AutoLISP programming, you will want to further investigate the uses of ACADDOC.LSP and ACAD.LSP in the multiple and single document environment. Refer to Chapter 4 of the *Visual LISP Developer's Guide*, available through AutoCAD 2000's on-line help.

A Brief Look at Visual LISP

With the release of AutoCAD 2000, Visual LISP is fully incorporated into AutoCAD. Visual LISP is a modern, updated implementation of AutoCAD's AutoLISP programming interface. It should not be viewed as a replacement for AutoLISP, but rather as an extension of AutoLISP's functionality with the addition of a fully integrated development environment (IDE) that makes it easier and faster for users to create, debug, and even package AutoLISP-based applications.

For AutoCAD users who already have a working—or even extensive—knowledge of AutoLISP, the introduction of Visual LISP will be virtually transparent. Not only are all the AutoLISP functions represented in Visual LISP, but also a significant number of new functions that extend the power of LISP within AutoCAD. Figure 22.7 show the Visual LISP IDE with some of its functional windows.

Figure 22.7

The new Visual LISP integrated development environment (IDE).

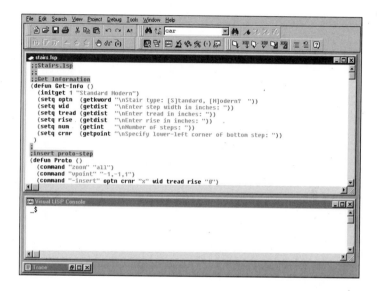

Even the beginning or casual AutoLISP user will be able to take advantage of many of Visual LISP's advanced features:

- An AutoLISP code editor with color-coded source display for easier-to-read, easier-to-debug code.

- A source code syntax checker to reduce errors.

- Autoformat and Smart Indent features that promote code writing standardization and readability.

- Dynamic symbol completion that saves time and reduces errors.

- Programmed structure navigation for easier program code editing.

- Direct LISP function evaluation that reduces code errors.

- Unlimited number of open source files with cut and paste capability to speed the writing of AutoLISP routines.

- A complete AutoLISP reference manual and other help features built into a sophisticated, useful Help facility.

AutoLISP users ranging from novices to veteran power users can take advantage of the features of Visual LISP to speed the learning and development of AutoLISP principals and techniques. Visual LISP represents the most significant advancement in AutoCAD's most popular customizing environment since the introduction of AutoLISP itself.

Summary

AutoLISP is one of the oldest and most popular programming interfaces in AutoCAD. Although a full-blown, modern programming language, AutoLISP is not difficult to learn. Even a basic understanding of its usage within AutoCAD can give you the ability to write simple programs and macros that can save significant amounts of time, and customize AutoCAD to the way you work.

EFFECTIVE APPLICATIONS FOR OLE
OBJECTS IN AUTOCAD 2000

When you work on a set of drawings, you typically are working on one element of a project. Other elements might include word processing documents, spreadsheet data, and graphics created in programs other than AutoCAD. All of these elements combined are required to complete the project's deliverables, and to meet your client's needs.

Quite often, data created in other applications must be duplicated in your AutoCAD drawing. Elements such as "General Notes" created in a word processing program, or a "Bill of Materials" created in a spreadsheet application, must be duplicated in your drawing to satisfy the project's final delivery requirements. By adding this data to your drawing, you make the drawing a complete project deliverable.

Developing compound documents using Object Linking and Embedding (OLE) is a powerful, simple way to create the final documents required for satisfying your client's needs. By inserting documents created from other applications into your AutoCAD drawing, you create a *compound document*, and take advantage of data already created in other applications. By simply dragging existing files into your drawing, you can insert data created in word processing applications such as Word or WordPerfect, as well as tabular data from spreadsheet programs such as Excel or Lotus, directly into your AutoCAD drawing. By using OLE, you make the process of completing a set of drawings easier by using existing data in its native format.

This chapter reviews AutoCAD OLE capabilities, and covers the following subjects:

■ Understanding object linking and embedding

■ Importing objects into AutoCAD using OLE

■ Exporting AutoCAD objects using OLE

Understanding Object Linking and Embedding

Object linking and embedding (OLE) is a feature provided by the Windows operating system. Whether or not an application takes advantage of OLE is up to its program developers. In the case of AutoCAD, the application is designed to take advantage of OLE technology, allowing you to interact with other OLE-compliant applications. By using OLE, you can insert files from other applications directly into AutoCAD drawings, and you can insert AutoCAD views and AutoCAD objects into other OLE-compliant applications.

Linking and embedding refer to two different ways you can insert a file from another application into your drawing. You can either insert an OLE object as a linked object or as an embedded object. A *linked* object inserts a copy of a file that references the original source file. A linked OLE object behaves similar to xrefs in that any modifications made to the source file are reflected in the linked OLE object when the link is updated in your drawing.

In contrast, although an *embedded* object also inserts a copy of a file into your drawing, it does not maintain a link to the source file. An embedded OLE object behaves similarly to a block inserted from another drawing in that the inserted file exists independent of the source from which it was copied, and may be edited independently without affecting the source file. More importantly, any edits made to the source file are never reflected in the embedded OLE object. Use linked objects when you want modifications to the source file to appear in your drawing, and use embedded objects when you want to insert a copy of a file, and do not want edits to the source file to appear in your drawing.

OLE objects inserted into AutoCAD drawings have certain limitations. Additionally, OLE objects typically appear in plotted drawings when plotted using devices configured as a Windows system printer or new HDI drivers. Another limitation is that OLE objects cannot be resized if they are rotated in your drawing. Even with these limitations, you will find object linking and embedding a very useful feature.

NOTE

You can use the OLESTARTUP system variable to optimize the quality of plotted OLE objects. The variable controls whether the source application of an inserted OLE object loads when plotting. Setting the value to 1 instructs AutoCAD to load the OLE source application when plotting. Setting the value to 0 instructs AutoCAD to not load the OLE source application when plotting.

Importing Objects into AutoCAD Using OLE

You can create compound documents in AutoCAD by linking or embedding objects from other applications. For example, you can insert a table from a spreadsheet application, a set of notes from a word processing application, and a graphic image from a paint program. By inserting the desired objects into your AutoCAD drawing, you create a compound document.

AutoCAD provides several options for linking and embedding objects in drawings, as described in the following sections.

Using the Insert Object Dialog Box to Insert OLE Objects

You can insert OLE objects into AutoCAD using the Insert Objects dialog box. This procedure allows you to insert linked or embedded objects from within AutoCAD by executing an AutoCAD command. From the Insert Objects dialog box, you can insert an object from an existing file, or create a new OLE object that exists only in the current drawing.

The Insert Object dialog box is opened from the Insert menu by choosing OLE Object. Once opened, the Insert Object dialog box presents a list of object types it can link or embed, as shown in Figure 23.1.

Figure 23.1

The Insert Object dialog box allows you to insert OLE objects from within AutoCAD.

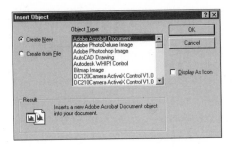

From the Insert Object dialog box, you select whether you want to create a new OLE object, or insert an OLE object from an existing file. The Create New option opens the selected application so you can create the object. Then, when the object is saved, the selected application is closed, and AutoCAD embeds the object in the current drawing.

In contrast, by choosing the Create from File option, the Insert Object dialog box changes its display, allowing you to browse for an object to link or embed, as shown in Figure 23.2. By selecting the Link check box, the selected object is inserted into AutoCAD and linked back to the original file.

Figure 23.2

The Insert Object dialog box allows you to browse for existing OLE object files to insert in AutoCAD.

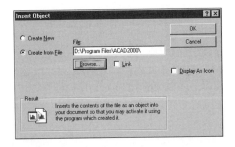

The Insert Object dialog box provides a straightforward method for inserting OLE objects. By giving you the option of browsing for existing OLE object files to insert, or creating new OLE objects by selecting the desired application, you can easily insert the needed OLE object into your AutoCAD drawing.

In the following exercise, you embed an OLE object into an AutoCAD drawing.

EMBEDDING AN OLE OBJECT

1. Open a new drawing in AutoCAD.

2. From the Insert menu, choose OLE Object. The Insert Object dialog box appears.

3. From the Object Type list, choose a word processing application type to insert into AutoCAD. The exercise in this book uses Microsoft Word Document, as shown in Figure 23.3.

Figure 23.3

The Microsoft Word Document is selected as the type of object to insert.

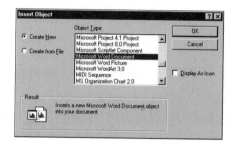

4. Be sure the Create New option button is selected, then click OK. The source application launches, allowing you to edit the newly inserted OLE object file.

5. In the source application, type **My Object**.

6. From the source application's File menu, choose Close & Return to DrawingX.dwg. The source file is saved and its modifications shown in the OLE Properties dialog box.

7. Click OK. The OLE object is now updated in the AutoCAD drawing.

8. You may close the drawing without saving.

Because AutoCAD launches the source application, the application may stay open, even after you close the file and return to the AutoCAD drawing. If so, you can close the source application.

Pasting OLE Objects into AutoCAD

You can insert OLE objects into AutoCAD by pasting them from the Windows Clipboard. This procedure is a very common way to insert OLE objects from one application to another. Using this feature, you can copy an object directly from its application to the Clipboard, then paste the Clipboard's contents into AutoCAD.

You paste objects from the Clipboard with either the PASTE command, or the PASTE SPECIAL command. These commands are accessed from AutoCAD's Edit menu. The PASTE command is also accessed from the shortcut menu, which is displayed by right-clicking in the drawing area. These commands are only available when the Clipboard contains objects.

NOTE

You can view or delete the contents of the Clipboard by using the Clipboard Viewer. You access the Clipboard Viewer from the Windows taskbar by choosing Start, Programs, Accessories, Clipboard Viewer. You view the Clipboard's contents by opening the Clipboard window, which appears as an icon in the Clipboard Viewer. To delete the Clipboard's contents, from the Clipboard Viewer's Edit menu, choose Delete.

Although both commands paste objects into the current drawing from the Clipboard, they differ in one important way. The PASTE command only embeds objects. The PASTE SPECIAL command allows you to either embed objects or insert them as linked objects.

When you choose the PASTE command, the object is immediately embedded into AutoCAD. Additionally, the OLE Properties dialog box appears if the Display Dialog Box When Pasting New OLE Objects check box is selected. The OLE Properties dialog box allows you to control the size of the OLE object, and is discussed in detail later in this chapter.

When you choose the PASTE SPECIAL command, AutoCAD displays the Paste Special dialog box. From this dialog box, you can choose either the Paste option, or the Paste Link option.

When you use the Paste option, the OLE object is embedded into the drawing. The difference between pasting an object from the Paste Special dialog box versus pasting it directly from the Edit or shortcut menus is that by using the Paste Special dialog box, you have more control over the OLE object type you are embedding.

When you choose the Paste option in the Paste Special dialog box, the available object types appear in the As list. The object types listed depend on the OLE object you are pasting from the Clipboard. For example, if the Clipboard contains a Microsoft Word document, you can embed the Clipboard's contents as one of several object types shown in Figure 23.4. The list only displays acceptable types for the particular object. Several other object types are described as follows:

- **Picture (Metafile).** Inserts the contents of the clipboard into your drawing as a vector-based picture.

- **AutoCAD Entities.** Inserts the contents of the clipboard into your drawing as circles, arcs, lines, and polylines. Text is inserted as text objects, with each line of text located in a paragraph in the source file converted to individual AutoCAD text objects.

- **Image Entity.** Inserts the contents of the Clipboard into your drawing as an AutoCAD raster image object.

- **Text.** Inserts the contents of the Clipboard into your drawing as an AutoCAD MTEXT object. Any line objects are ignored.

- **Package.** Inserts the contents of the Clipboard into your drawing as a Windows Package object. A *package* is an icon that represents embedded or linked information. The information may consist of a complete document, such as a Paint bitmap, or part of a document, such as a spreadsheet cell. You create packages using the Windows Object Packager, which is accessed from the Taskbar by choosing Start, Programs, Accessories, Object Packager.

- **Bitmap Image.** Inserts the contents of the Clipboard into your drawing as a bitmap image object.

Figure 23.4

The Paste Special command allows you to select an object's type when it is embedded.

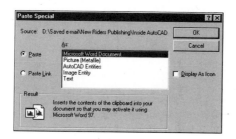

When you choose the Paste Link option, you can insert the OLE object only as its original object type. For example, if you choose the Paste Link option to insert a

Microsoft Word document, you can insert it only as a Microsoft Word document. This ensures that you can open and edit the source Word document to which the OLE object is linked.

INSIDER **T**IP

If you work in a black background in AutoCAD and paste an image from a word processing or spreadsheet application, the pasted image will appear with a white background in the drawing. If this is undesirable, change your background in either program to match the other.

By using the PASTE and PASTE SPECIAL commands, you can embed or link OLE objects in your AutoCAD drawing from the Clipboard. Next, you learn about another method for inserting OLE objects.

Using Drag and Drop to Insert OLE Objects

The Windows operating system provides the ability to drag selected objects from another application into an AutoCAD drawing. By selecting objects in an open application, then dragging the selected objects into AutoCAD, you, in effect, cut the objects from the application and embed them into the AutoCAD drawing. To copy the objects from the open application instead of cutting, hold down the Ctrl key while dragging the objects into the drawing.

INSIDER **T**IP

After you select objects in an application, drag them into AutoCAD by right-clicking with your pointing device. When you release, AutoCAD displays the shortcut menu, and allows you to either move the objects (Move here), copy the objects (Copy here), or insert the objects (Paste as block) into the AutoCAD drawing. You can also cancel the operation from the shortcut menu.

Additionally, you can drag objects from the Windows Explorer. If AutoCAD recognizes the object type, it embeds it into the drawing. If AutoCAD does not recognize the file type, or if the object type cannot be inserted as an OLE object, AutoCAD issues an error and cancels the function.

Controlling OLE Object Properties

AutoCAD provides specific tools for manipulating an OLE object because AutoCAD commands typically do not affect OLE objects. For example, you cannot select an OLE object and erase it with the ERASE command, nor can you resize it using the SCALE command. However, by using specific tools designed for manipulating OLE objects, you can control an OLE object's appearance in AutoCAD.

INSIDER TIP

When you select an OLE object in AutoCAD to display its grips, you can press the Delete key to delete the object.

Controlling OLE Object Size

AutoCAD provides the ability to manipulate an OLE object's size in a drawing through the OLE Properties dialog box. The dialog box allows you to control an object's size any one of three ways: by size, scale, or text size (see Figure 23.5). You access the dialog box by right-clicking over an OLE object, and selecting Properties from the shortcut menu.

Figure 23.5

The OLE Properties dialog box allows you to control an OLE object's size.

In the Size area, you control an OLE object's size by entering values in the height and width fields. If the Lock Aspect Ratio check box is selected in the Scale area, when one field value is changed, the other updates automatically, proportionally maintaining the OLE object's aspect ratio size. The units entered in the field are based on the drawing's current units setting. You can also set the OLE object back to its original size by clicking the Reset button in the Size area.

In the Scale area, you control the OLE object's size by entering a percentage of the object's size. As with the values in the Size area, if the Lock Aspect Ratio check box is selected, when one field value is changed in the height and width fields, the other value updates automatically.

A third method for controlling an OLE object's size is available in the Text Size area. If the OLE object contains text, you can enter a new text size value to adjust the object's size. The first field displays the list of font styles in the OLE object, and the second field contains a list of the selected font's sizes. By choosing the desired font style and size in the first two fields, you can control the object's overall size by entering the desired height of the text in the third field. For example, in Figure 23.5, the OLE object will be resized based on the 12 point Courier font being set to 0.10 drawing units.

NOTE

> It's important to understand that the three areas provided for controlling an OLE object's size work in unison. When one set of values is changed in one area, the values are automatically changed in the other two areas. The values in the three areas cannot be set independently of one another.

In the following exercise, you resize an OLE object.

RESIZING AN OLE OBJECT

1. Open the drawing 23DWG01 from the accompanying CD. The drawing displays an embedded OLE object that consists of a single line of text.

2. Select the object to display its object frame.

3. Right-click inside the object frame, then select Properties from the shortcut menu. AutoCAD displays the OLE Properties dialog box.

   You will resize the object from the Text Size area. To determine the proper size for text, multiply the text's font size by the scale at which the drawing will be plotted. For this exercise, assume the plotted drawing scale is 1:40 (1 inch equals 40 feet). Therefore, to calculate the text's size, multiply 0.10 by 40, which equals 4.0.

4. In the Text Size area, in the empty text box on the right, type **4.0** as shown in Figure 23.6, then click OK.

   AutoCAD resizes the OLE object based on the current text's size equaling 4.0. You may need to execute a Zoom Extents to see the OLE object.

5. You may close the drawing without saving your changes.

In this exercise, the calculations determined that the OLE object's text height must be converted to 4.0. This means that when the drawing is plotted at 1:40, the text's height will plot at 0.10 units high.

Figure 23.6

The OLE Properties dialog box allows you to control an OLE object's size.

In addition to controlling an OLE object's size, the OLE Properties dialog box provides the ability to control the plot quality of an OLE object. From the OLE Plot Quality list, you can choose one of the following five plot quality options:

- **Line Art.** Intended for plotting objects such as a spreadsheet

- **Text.** Intended for plotting objects such as a Word document

- **Graphics.** Intended for plotting objects such as a pie chart

- **Photograph.** Intended for plotting objects that are color images

- **High Quality Photograph.** Intended for plotting objects that are true-color images

The plot quality options are applied specifically to the selected OLE object. Therefore, you can insert a Word document that contains only text and set the plot quality to Text. Then, you can insert a true-color image, and set its plot quality to High Quality Photograph. By applying the desired plot quality to each OLE object, you can control an object's appearance when plotted.

Controlling OLE Objects Using the Shortcut Menu

After an OLE object is inserted into a drawing, you can control several object properties and perform edits through commands accessed from the shortcut menu. By using these commands, you can delete the OLE object, and copy it to the Clipboard. You can determine whether the object appears on top or below other objects in the drawing, and you can control whether or not it may be selected for editing. The shortcut menu offers these commands and more, providing useful control over OLE objects.

Cutting, Copying, and Clearing OLE Objects

When you right-click over an OLE object, AutoCAD displays the available OLE shortcut commands, as shown in Figure 23.7. The first three commands do the following:

- **Cut.** Erases the selected object from the drawing, and places a copy on the Clipboard. You can also execute the CUT command by pressing Ctrl+X.

- **Copy.** Leaves the selected object in the drawing, and places a copy on the Clipboard. You can also execute the COPY command by pressing Ctrl+C.

- **Clear.** Erases the selected object from the drawing without placing a copy on the Clipboard. You can also execute the CLEAR command by typing **E**, then pressing Enter.

Figure 23.7

Right-click over an OLE object to display the shortcut menu commands.

When you use the CUT or COPY commands on an OLE object, the object is placed on the Clipboard in its original object format, not as an AutoCAD object. For example, suppose a Word document resides in your drawing as an OLE object. If you use the COPY command to copy the Word document object from your drawing to the Clipboard, when you paste the object into another application, it is pasted as a Word document object.

Undoing OLE Object Edits

The next command on the shortcut menu is UNDO, which undoes edits made to the OLE object while in your drawing. For example, if you move or resize the object in your drawing, you can undo the edit by selecting Undo from the shortcut menu. By selecting the UNDO command repeatedly, you can undo a series of edits made to the object.

The UNDO command has one important limitation: It does not undo edits made to the OLE object in the object's source application. For example, if you paste a Word document object into your drawing, then edit the document object in Word by adding additional text, when you save your edits and return to your drawing, the edits made in Word cannot be undone in AutoCAD. In other words, the text added to the document from the Word application cannot be undone using the Undo command in AutoCAD.

NOTE

Don't confuse the UNDO command found on the OLE object shortcut menu with AutoCAD's UNDO command. The UNDO command (Ctrl+Z), which is accessed from AutoCAD's Edit menu, does not undo edits made to an OLE object while in your drawing, such as moving or resizing the object. However, AutoCAD's UNDO command will undo the command used to paste the object into your drawing, thereby removing the entire object from your drawing.

Controlling OLE Object Selectability

The next item on the shortcut menu is the Selectable property, which toggles the selectability of the OLE object. When this option is toggled on, a check appears next to the property, indicating that the OLE object can be selected, then moved or resized in your drawing. When the property is toggled off, the check is cleared, indicating that the object cannot be selected.

When you select an OLE object whose Selectable property is toggled on, an object frame and its sizing handles appear around the object. When you place your cursor inside the object frame, the cursor changes to the move cursor, which is an icon comprised of a cross with four arrows, as shown in Figure 23.8. The move cursor allows you to drag the object to a new position in your drawing.

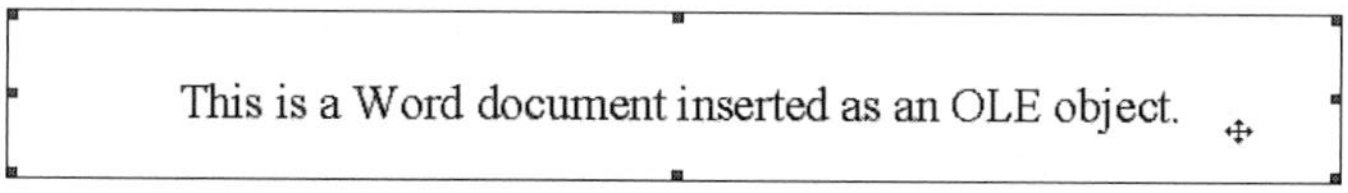

Figure 23.8

By moving your cursor inside the OLE object's frame, you can drag the object to a new position.

This is a Word document inserted as an OLE object.

The sizing handles are the small, solid squares that appear at the corners and midpoints of the object frame. When you place your cursor over a sizing handle, the cursor changes to a double-headed arrow. You can then resize the object by dragging the sizing handle. The sizing handles at the midpoints of the object frame stretch the object, distorting its appearance. The sizing handles at the corners of the object frame scale the object proportionally, maintaining the object's aspect ratio.

INSIDER TIP

The sizing square color is controlled by the unselected grip color. This can be changed in the Grips area of the Selection tab of the Options dialog box.

The three objects in Figure 23.9 are OLE objects inserted from a Word document, and provide an example of how stretching and resizing affects an object. The top object shows how all three objects appeared in their original size. The middle object is a copy of the top object, and was stretched by dragging its sizing handles at the midpoints on each side of the object frame. Notice that the height of the text is the same as in the original. Only the width of the text is changed. The bottom object is also a copy of the top object, and was resized by dragging its sizing handles in the corners of the object frame. Notice that although the text's height and width are larger than the original, their aspect ratio is maintained, and their overall size is correctly proportioned.

Figure 23.9

The original object is at the top, the stretched object is in the middle, and the resized object is at the bottom.

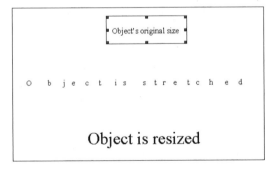

INSIDER TIP

To quickly duplicate an OLE object inserted in AutoCAD, select the object, then drag it while pressing the Ctrl key.

When the Selectable property is toggled off, you cannot select the object to display its object frame and sizing handles. This feature is useful to maintain an object's size and position in your drawing after it is set as desired. By clearing an OLE object's Selectable property, you ensure that the object will not be moved or resized in your drawing.

It's important to note that the Selectable property does not affect the other commands and properties on the shortcut menu. For example, although you cannot drag an OLE object's sizing handles when its Selectable property is cleared, you can resize the object through the OLE Properties dialog box. By right-clicking over the OLE object and choosing the Properties command from the shortcut menu, you display the OLE Properties dialog box. Any changes made to the object's size in the dialog box modify the object, even though its Selectable property is cleared. This is true for the shortcut menu's other commands, including CUT, COPY, CLEAR, and UNDO.

Controlling OLE Object Display Order

The next two properties are Bring to Front, and Send to Back. These two properties control an object's position in the drawing relative to other objects, and perform the same function as AutoCAD's Display Order tools. By right-clicking your cursor over an OLE object, then selecting Bring to Front or Send to Back from the shortcut menu, you place the object above or below other objects, as shown in Figure 23.10. These two properties are actually a toggle, and AutoCAD allows you to set only one or the other for each OLE object.

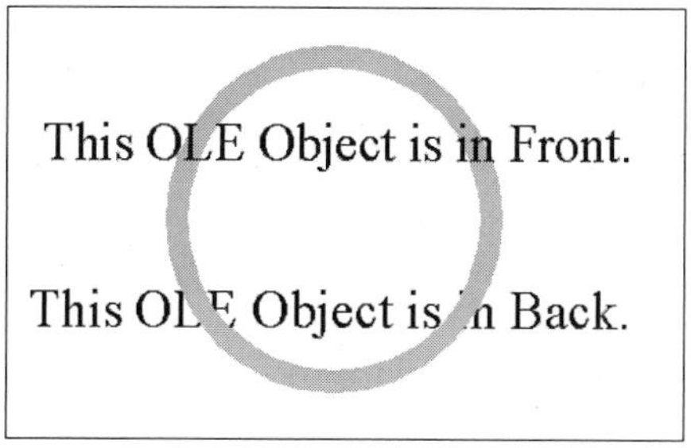

Figure 23.10

The OLE object at the top has its Bring to Front property set, whereas the object at the bottom has its Send to Back property set.

This OLE Object is in Front.

This OLE Object is in Back.

NOTE

Clicking inside an OLE object always selects it, even though it may be behind other AutoCAD objects. To select AutoCAD objects that lie within an OLE object's frame, clear the object's Selectable property.

Editing and Converting OLE Objects

The final item on the shortcut menu is the Object menu item. When selected, the Object menu item displays a cascading menu that provides access to the OLE object's source application through the EDIT and OPEN commands, allowing you to modify the object. Additionally, you can access the Convert dialog box, which specifies a different source application for the OLE object. From the Object item menu, you can modify an OLE object, or convert it to a different object type.

The name displayed in the shortcut menu changes depending on the type of OLE object selected when the menu is accessed. For example, the shortcut menu in Figure 23.7 indicates the type of object is a Document Object, specifically a Microsoft Word document object. If a Microsoft Excel worksheet is inserted as an OLE object and the shortcut menu is accessed, the object type is listed as a Worksheet Object, as shown in Figure 23.11.

Figure 23.11

The Object description changes to indicate that a Microsoft Excel Worksheet is selected.

The EDIT and OPEN commands launch the object's source application, displaying the object's source file, and allowing you to make modifications. In AutoCAD, both commands perform the same function. The reason the two commands perform the same function is a result of how AutoCAD interfaces with the Windows operating system when dealing with OLE objects.

In some applications other than AutoCAD, the EDIT command only opens a source application file window inside the current application, whereas the OPEN command launches the entire source application. For example, Figure 23.12 shows what happens when you modify a Word document object inserted in an Excel spreadsheet by accessing the EDIT command. Notice that the Word document window is inside the Excel spreadsheet. This allows you to make edits to the Word document from inside Excel without actually launching the Word application. In AutoCAD, the EDIT command launches the entire source application. Therefore, selecting either the EDIT or the OPEN command launches the source application, allowing you to make modifications.

Figure 23.12

The Edit *command allows you to modify a Word document object in Excel.*

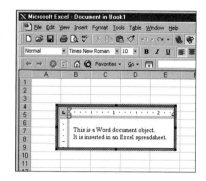

INSIDER TIP

You also can execute the object **Edit** command by double-clicking inside an object's frame.

The Convert command opens the Convert dialog box, which allows you to specify a different source application for an embedded object. By selecting the desired source application, then clicking OK, the object's source application type is changed to the new application type.

The different object types to which you can convert an object depend on the object selected. For example, when you select an embedded Word document object, then choose the Convert command, you are allowed to convert the document object to a Word picture object, as shown in Figure 23.13. The object types listed are those supported by the source application.

Figure 23.13

The Convert dialog box allows you to convert the selected object to a different object type.

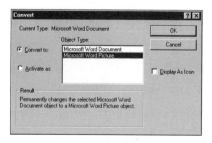

When you convert an object, you can choose from one of two options: Convert To, or Activate As. The Convert To option converts an embedded object to the type specified under Object Type. This means the object is actually converted to the new selected object type. For example, if you converted a Word document object into a

Word picture object, then right-clicked over the object, the shortcut menu would list the object as a picture object. This means that when you edit the object, you would edit it as a Word picture, not a Word document.

The Activate As option acts similarly to the Convert To option, except that it only temporarily converts the object during the editing process to the selected object type. After the editing is complete, the object returns to its original type. For example, you can edit a Word document object, temporarily activating it as a Word picture object. This means the document object opens as a picture object in the Word application, which allows you to modify the object using Word's picture editing tools. After you finish modifying the picture, and close and save the file, the modified object appears in AutoCAD in its original format as a Word document object.

If you look at Figure 23.13, you will notice that you can also convert the Word document object to a Word document object. This option is intended to maintain an object in its current type, while working in conjunction with the Display as Icon check box. For example, by choosing to convert the Word document object into a Word document object, and choosing the Display as Icon option, the document object maintains its current type, and changes its appearance to a Word document icon, as shown in Figure 23.14. To return the document object back to its original display, convert the Word document object into a Word document object, then clear the check box.

Figure 23.14

The Convert dialog box allows you to display an OLE object as an icon.

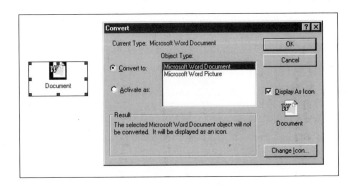

INSIDER TIP

Double-clicking the object icon launches the object's source application, and allows you to modify the file.

NOTE

When you select the Display as Icon option, the Change Icon button activates. When selected, this button displays the Change Icon dialog box, which allows you to select a new icon to appear as the object icon.

The OLE object shortcut menu provides several useful commands and options that allow you to control an OLE object's appearance and its behavior. Next, you learn about two features that allow you to control an OLE object's visibility.

Controlling OLE Object Visibility

When you insert OLE objects into your drawing, you may want to control their visibility. Whether objects are inserted only temporarily, or are used for drawing construction purposes the way you might use Construction Lines or Rays, you may want the visibility of OLE objects turned off in your drawing or on plotted sheets. By controlling OLE object visibility, you can use the objects to assist you in your work by displaying reference information, and not be forced to delete them to control their display.

AutoCAD allows you to control the visibility of OLE objects through two features. The first is to simply insert the OLE object on a layer that you turn off or on, or that you freeze or thaw. The second is to use a special command that allows you to globally control the visibility of all OLE objects. By using these two features, you can easily control the visibility of OLE objects inserted in your drawing.

Controlling OLE Object Layer Properties

Controlling object visibility from the layer on which it is inserted is a very common method for controlling whether or not an object appears in your drawing. One of the chief reasons for using layers to organize the objects in your drawing is to control the visibility of groups of objects that reside on a common layer. By inserting OLE objects on their own layers, you can easily control their visibility from the Layer Properties Manager.

INSIDER TIP

To move or copy an OLE object to a new layer, you must Cut or Copy the object to the Clipboard, make the layer current to which you want to move or copy the object, then Paste the object.

WARNING

When you cut or copy an OLE object from an AutoCAD drawing, then paste it back into the drawing, the object's size will revert to its original size, and any modifications to the object are lost. Therefore, the OLE object's size must be reset to the desired value after it is pasted back into the drawing. You can resize the OLE object from the Object Properties dialog box.

The Layer Properties Manager allows you to control more than just an OLE object's visibility. Specifically, OLE objects react to the following layer properties:

- **On/Off and Freeze/Thaw**. The On/Off and Freeze/Thaw layer properties control an OLE object's visibility, both on-screen and when plotted. By turning off or freezing the layer on which an OLE object resides, the object is no longer displayed in your drawing, either on-screen or when plotted. To restore the object's visibility, turn on or thaw the layer. To learn about the differences between the On/Off and Freeze/Thaw layer properties, refer to Chapter 4, "Organizing a Drawing with Layers," in the section "Turning Layers Off Versus Freezing Layers."

- **Lock.** The Lock property prevents the OLE object from being selected. It functions similarly to the OLE object's Selectable property, except that it does not allow any type of edits from the OLE object shortcut menu. For example, if an OLE object's Selectable option is turned off, you can still edit the object using commands from the shortcut menu such as PROPERTIES, and EDIT or OPEN. In contrast, when the layer on which an OLE object is inserted is locked, the OLE object shortcut menu cannot be invoked. The Lock property absolutely prevents the OLE object from being edited.

NEW for R2000
- **Plot.** The new Plot property allows an object to remain visible on-screen, but prevents it from plotting. This feature is useful if you need to display an OLE object during an editing session for reference information only, and do not want the object to appear when plotted. By turning off the Plot property, you ensure that the OLE object will not appear on plotted drawings.

NOTE

> The Plot option is new to AutoCAD 2000 and thereby not supported in older versions of AutoCAD. Do not rely on this functionality if you use the drawing in an older release.

By using the layer properties discussed in this section, you can control the behavior of an OLE object from the layer on which it resides. In the next section, you learn how to globally control OLE object visibility.

Globally Controlling OLE Object Visibility

AutoCAD provides a method to globally control OLE object visibility. The OLEHIDE command allows you to determine if OLE objects are visible in paper space and model space. By using the OLEHIDE command, you control the visibility of all OLE objects, and whether they appear in paper space or model space.

The OLEHIDE command is actually a system variable whose current setting is stored in your computer's system registry. This means that when you set a value for OLEHIDE, the setting affects all drawings in the current editing session, as well as in future sessions. To control the display of all OLE objects in all drawings, set the desired display value for the OLEHIDE system variable.

Typing **OLEHIDE** at the command prompt allows you to set the current OLEHIDE system variable value. There are four possible integer values you can set, described as follows:

- **0.** Makes all OLE objects visible, both in paper space and model space
- **1.** Makes OLE objects visible only in paper space
- **2.** Makes OLE objects visible only in model space
- **3.** Makes all OLE objects invisible, both in paper space and model space

By setting these values, you control the appearance of all OLE objects, both in paper space and model space.

NOTE

> If the OLEHIDE system variable is set to 1 or 2 when you insert a new OLE object, AutoCAD automatically changes the OLEHIDE system variable value to allow the new OLE object to appear in the current space. This will also cause all OLE objects in the current space to appear.

In the next section, you learn how to work with OLE objects that are linked to their original file.

Working with Linked OLE Objects

When you insert an OLE object and link it to its original file, the file can be edited in its source application, and the linked object automatically updated. This means that when a linked object is inserted in a drawing, and the object's original file is modified, the linked OLE object in AutoCAD automatically updates to reflect the modifications. This feature is very useful for ensuring that the latest version of an inserted OLE object appears in an AutoCAD drawing.

Although the ability to automatically update and display the latest version of a linked file is very useful, there will probably be occasions when you don't want the linked object to automatically update. For example, if you want to permanently save a set of drawings that represent a 50% completion set, then you do not want OLE objects to automatically update when the 50% completion set of drawings is re-opened for reference in the future. You need the ability to control whether or not linked OLE objects automatically update.

AutoCAD provides a tool that allows you to control whether or not linked OLE objects automatically update. By choosing the OLE LINKS command from the Edit menu, the Link dialog box appears, as shown in Figure 23.15. From the Links dialog box, you choose either the Automatic or Manual update option, which controls whether linked objects are automatically or manually updated. Additionally, from the Link dialog box, you can restore links lost because the original file can't be found, and you can associate the link to a different file. You can also break the link connection between the OLE object and the original file, which converts the linked object to an embedded object. From the Link dialog box, you control the link between an OLE object and the file to which it is linked.

Figure 23.15

The Links dialog box allows you to control the link between an OLE object and its source file.

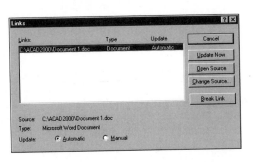

In the following exercise, you restore a lost link using the OLE LINKS command.

RESTORING LOST LINKS TO OLE OBJECTS

1. Create a new folder on your PC called OLE Links.

2. Copy the Document1.doc file from the accompanying CD to the OLE Links folder.

3. Open the drawing 23DWG02 from the accompanying CD. The drawing displays a linked OLE object that consists of a single line of text.

   When you open the drawing, AutoCAD displays a dialog box that asks if you want to update the linked OLE objects.

4. Click No to dismiss the dialog box.

   At this point, the OLE object is a linked object whose linked file is unavailable for update. Next, you restore the link between the OLE object and its original file.

5. From the Edit menu, select OLE Links. The Links dialog box appears.

6. Select the Document1.doc from the Links list. The link highlights, and the buttons on the Links dialog box activate, as shown in Figure 23.15.

7. From the Links dialog box, click the Change Source button. The Change Source dialog box appears.

8. From the Change Source dialog box, browse to the OLE Links folder and select the Document1.doc file, then click Open Source. The link to Document1.doc is restored and the new link path is displayed, as shown in Figure 23.16.

Figure 23.16

The updated link path is displayed.

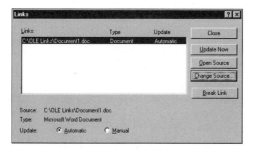

9. Close the Links dialog box. AutoCAD updates the link to the source file.

10. You may exit the drawing without saving your changes.

The Links dialog box allows you to select either an automatic or a manual link update. If you choose to manually update, the link can be updated by clicking the Update Now button on the Links dialog box. The Open Source button opens the linked file's source application, allowing you to edit the source file. The Change

Source button allows you to either locate a missing source file or select a new file. The Break Link button terminates the link between the OLE object and the source file, and it cannot be reestablished. After the link is broken, the OLE object permanently becomes an embedded object.

Exporting AutoCAD Objects by Using OLE

Just as you can insert files from other applications into AutoCAD, you can also insert AutoCAD drawings into other application files. By using certain commands created specifically for AutoCAD drawings and AutoCAD objects, you can either insert linked or embedded AutoCAD files into other application files. The OLE features in AutoCAD work both for inserting other application files into AutoCAD, and for inserting AutoCAD files into other applications.

Exporting AutoCAD objects into other application files as OLE objects involves determining whether the AutoCAD object's will be linked or embedded. Linked objects are based on a named view in AutoCAD. When the view is updated in the AutoCAD drawing, the link is updated and the modified view appears in the application's file. In contrast, embedded objects are AutoCAD objects selected in the drawing then copied to the Clipboard. After they are pasted from the Clipboard, the objects are inserted as independent objects with no association to the original AutoCAD objects. Therefore, if the original AutoCAD objects are edited in the drawing they were copied from, the objects embedded in the application will not be updated.

AutoCAD provides three commands for exporting AutoCAD information into other applications for linking and embedding, described as follows:

- **Cut.** Executes the CUTCLIP command, which copies AutoCAD objects to the Clipboard, erasing the selected objects from the drawing.

- **Copy.** Executes the COPYCLIP command, which copies AutoCAD objects to the Clipboard.

- **Copy Link.** Executes the COPYLINK command, which copies the current AutoCAD view to the Clipboard.

All three commands are located on AutoCAD's Edit menu.

When you use the CUT or COPY commands, AutoCAD prompts you to select objects if no objects are currently selected. Once the objects are selected, AutoCAD copies the selected objects to the Clipboard. If objects are selected prior to executing the commands, the selected objects are immediately copied to the Clipboard and the command ends. If the COPY LINK command is selected, AutoCAD copies all objects in the current view to the Clipboard, without prompting for object selection. Therefore, the main difference between the CUT and COPY commands and the COPY LINK command is that the CUT and COPY commands prompt you to select objects, the COPY LINK command does not.

When the AutoCAD objects are pasted into the target application, an object frame surrounds the objects, and represents the drawing's viewport display at the time the objects were copied. This is true for all three commands. Therefore, whether you use the CUT or COPY commands to select objects, or use the COPY LINK commands to automatically select objects, the AutoCAD OLE object pasted into the target application includes the visible area displayed in the current viewport.

When you paste an AutoCAD OLE object that was copied using the COPY LINK command, AutoCAD creates a named view representing the current viewport display. This is necessary to maintain the link and accurately update the OLE object when the drawing file is modified. By associating the OLE object with a named view, modifications to AutoCAD objects in the area of the drawing defined by the named view can be accurately updated to the AutoCAD OLE object and correctly displayed in the target application.

INSIDER **T**IP

> You can use the COPY LINK command to paste an existing named view to the Clipboard by setting the named view current immediately before executing the COPY LINK command.

In the following exercise, you use the COPY LINK command to copy AutoCAD objects and paste them into a target application.

INSERTING AUTOCAD OBJECTS INTO OTHER APPLICATIONS

1. Open the drawing 23DWG03 from the accompanying CD. The drawing displays two objects.

   Next, you launch the target application.

2. From the Windows Taskbar, choose Start, Programs, Accessories, WordPad. The WordPad application launches.

3. From the Named Views tab, in the View list, choose the view named OLE Object Area, then click the Set Current button, as shown in Figure 23.17.

Figure 23.17

The named view is used to define the AutoCAD objects copied to the Clipboard.

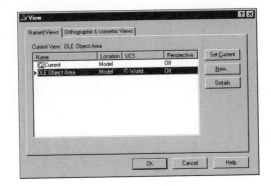

4. Click OK. AutoCAD restores the named view.

5. From the AutoCAD Edit menu, select Copy Link. AutoCAD copies the objects in the current view to the Clipboard.

    Next, you paste the AutoCAD objects in the target application.

6. From WordPad's Edit menu, select Paste Special. WordPad displays the Paste Special dialog box.

7. From the Paste Special dialog box, click the Paste Link option button, then click OK. WordPad pastes the AutoCAD OLE object into the current file, and links it to the named view in the AutoCAD drawing.

    After the OLE object is inserted in the WordPad file, you may need to resize the object to view it, as shown in Figure 23.18. You can resize the object using the object frame's sizing handles.

Figure 23.18

The linked AutoCAD OLE object in the WordPad application.

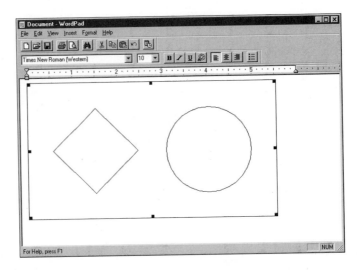

8. You may close the AutoCAD drawing and the WordPad file without saving changes. .

Often the main complaint with importing drawings into other applications is the lineweight control. In prior releases it was difficult to have weights that reflect an AutoCAD plot. However, in AutoCAD 2000, you can create drawings that provide their own means for showing wide lineweights for both line objects and text.

By using AutoCAD's commands for exporting AutoCAD drawing information into target applications, you can create compound documents in other applications using AutoCAD drawings.

Summary

In this chapter you reviewed how to insert OLE objects from within AutoCAD, paste OLE objects into AutoCAD from the Clipboard, and how to use drag and drop to insert OLE objects into AutoCAD drawings. You learned how to control various OLE object properties, including how to resize an OLE object and control its visibility. You also reviewed how to edit OLE objects, and how the Layer Properties Manager can affect certain Ole object properties. Finally, you learned how to export objects from AutoCAD into other applications, creating AutoCAD OLE objects.

By using the techniques discussed in this chapter, you can create compound documents by inserting OLE objects into AutoCAD. You can also create compound documents in other applications, by pasting AutoCAD OLE objects.

24

USING EXTERNAL DATABASES

External databases are files that store information. The files are typically composed of tables that look similar to a spreadsheet, with similar data organized in columns called fields, and each unique set of data stored in rows called records. When external databases are used to organize and store data, tremendous volumes of data can be created, edited, and retrieved.

AutoCAD 2000 provides tools that allow you to work with external database files. You can open a database table and view or edit its data. You can link database records to AutoCAD objects, such as lines, circles, and polylines. You can run queries, which retrieve a subset of records based on certain criteria. By using AutoCAD's tools, you can work with external database files from entirely within AutoCAD.

This chapter reviews AutoCAD's database tools and explains the steps for working with external database files from directly within AutoCAD. This chapter covers the following subjects:

■ Setting up AutoCAD to work with external databases

■ Working with database tables

- Working with data and objects
- Using queries

Setting Up AutoCAD to Work with External Databases

The first step in using external databases with AutoCAD 2000 drawings requires you to define information about the database files you are using. When you define the necessary information, AutoCAD can interface with external databases and link its data to objects in drawings. Defining the information AutoCAD needs to interface with external databases enables you to use the data in database files with your drawings.

After you define the external database information AutoCAD needs, you can access its data from AutoCAD. This is true even if you don't have the database application that originally created the database files installed on your PC. AutoCAD 2000 is designed to access external database files without using the originating database application. AutoCAD 2000 is designed to access data from the following database applications:

- Microsoft Access 97
- dBase V and III
- Microsoft Excel 97
- Oracle 8.0 and 7.3
- Paradox 7.0
- Microsoft Visual FoxPro 6.0
- SQL Server 7.0 and 6.5

If you have database files created in any of these database applications, you can access the data in the files directly from AutoCAD 2000.

NOTE

> Microsoft Excel is not a true database application and, therefore, contains no tables. Consequently, to access Excel data from within AutoCAD, you must first specify at least one named range of cells to act as a database table.
>
> A single Excel file can contain multiple ranges of cells, and AutoCAD treats each range as a unique table.

To define the information AutoCAD 2000 needs to access external database information, you must do two things. First, you must use the ODBC Data Source Administrator provided by the Windows operating system, which is a programming interface that enables AutoCAD to access data based on the database applications listed above. Second, you must use the Data Link Properties dialog box, which you access from AutoCAD 2000. The Data Link Properties dialog box creates a .UDL configuration file that points to the external database table you want to access. By using these two features, you create the information necessary for AutoCAD to successfully communicate with external databases.

NOTE

> ODBC stands for Open Database Connectivity, which is a standard protocol for accessing information in SQL (Structured Query Language) database servers, such as Microsoft SQL Server.

In the following two sections, you use the ODBC Data Source Administrator and the Data Link Properties dialog box to create the information necessary for AutoCAD to access data from an external database file.

Creating an ODBC Data Source File

To provide AutoCAD access to data in an external database file, you must first use the ODBC Data Source Administrator to create a data source file. The data source file identifies the type of database files you are accessing and identifies the folder in which the database files are located. This information is stored in the data source file and is used by AutoCAD to successfully access the database files. By using the ODBC Data Source Administrator, you can create a data source file that AutoCAD uses to access database files.

NOTE

If you use Microsoft Access, Oracle, or Microsoft SQL Server database management systems, you can use the direct database drivers they provide. If you use these direct drivers, you do not need to set up an ODBC data source file and can access the database files directly from an OLE DB configuration file.

For more information, refer to AutoCAD 2000's ASI Configuration Guide to the section titled "Bypassing ODBC Using an OLE DB Direct Driver." The Guide is located in the acad_asi.hlp file, which is stored in the Acad2000/Help folder.

In the following exercise, you use the ODBC Data Source Administrator to identify the location and file type of the external database files AutoCAD will access.

USING THE ODBC DATA SOURCE ADMINISTRATOR

1. Create a new folder on your PC called DB Files.

2. Copy the Manholes.dbf and Pipes.dbf files from the accompanying CD to the DB Files folder. After you copy the dBase files, be sure to right-click *.dbf files, choose Properties, and then clear the Read-Only attribute.

   Next, you create a data source file using the two *.dbf files.

3. From the Windows taskbar, choose Start, Settings, Control Panel. The Control Panel folder opens.

4. From Control Panel, double-click the ODBC icon. The ODBC Data Source Administrator appears.

5. In the ODBC Data Source Administrator, choose the User DSN tab.

NOTE

An ODBC data source stores information on how AutoCAD connects to database file. The three methods for defining a data source are described here:

■ The User DSN tab creates a data source that is visible to only you and that can be accessed only from the computer on which the data source is created.

■ The System DSN tab creates a data source that is visible to all users who have access rights to the computer on which the data source is created.

■ The File DSN tab creates a data source that can be shared with other users who have the same ODBC drivers installed on their computer systems.

6. Click Add, and the Create New Data Source dialog appears.

7. From the list of available database drivers, choose Microsoft dBase Driver (*.dbf), as shown in Figure 24.1.

Figure 24.1

The Create New Data Source dialog box identifies the database driver to be used with the database files you access from within AutoCAD.

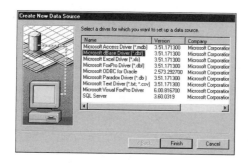

8. Click Finish, and the ODBC dBase Setup dialog box appears.

    The ODBC dBase Setup dialog box enables you to locate the database files you will access from AutoCAD and to assign a data source name and description that identifies the files.

9. In the Data Source Name text box, type **StormDrains**.

10. In the Description text box, type **Storm Drain Tables**.

11. In the Database area, choose dBase 5.0 from the Version list. This is the appropriate version to select because the database files you copied to the DB Files folder are dBase 5.0 files.

12. In the Database area, clear the Use Current Directory check box. The Select Directory button becomes active, as shown in Figure 24.2.

Figure 24.2

In the ODBC dBase Setup dialog box, you can locate and assign a data source name to the database files you use in AutoCAD.

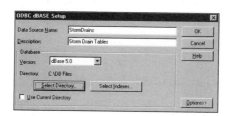

13. In the Database area, click the Select Directory button. The Select Directory dialog box appears.

14. In the Select Directory dialog box, browse to your DB Files directory, as shown in Figure 24.3.

Figure 24.3

The Select Directory dialog box allows you to locate the folder that contains the database files you use in AutoCAD.

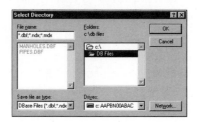

15. Click OK to dismiss the Select Directory dialog box, and then click OK to dismiss the ODBC dBase Setup dialog box. The ODBC Data Source Administrator displays the new StormDrains data source, as shown in Figure 24.4.

Figure 24.4

After you create the StormDrains data source, you can access it from AutoCAD.

16. Click OK. The data source is saved and can be accessed from AutoCAD.

17. Close the Control Panel folder.

Using the ODBC Data Source Administrator, you can create multiple data source files, with each data source file providing the information necessary for AutoCAD to access database tables. When you define the data source files, you tell AutoCAD what type of database application created the tables and where the tables are located on your PC, which allows AutoCAD to locate and access the database files. By using the ODBC Data Source Administrator to create a data source file, you can access data stored in database files from within AutoCAD.

NOTE

> The steps used in the preceding exercise are those necessary to create data source files for accessing dBase files. The steps for accessing database files created in other applications vary slightly. AutoCAD 2000 provides the acad_asi.hlp file, which contains information for configuring ODBC data source files for different database applications supported by AutoCAD. That help file is composed of AutoCAD's ASI Configuration Guide and is stored in the Acad2000/Help folder.

In the next section, you use the data source file you just created to configure an OLE DB file, which is the last component AutoCAD needs in order to access database files.

Creating an OLE DB Configuration File

An OLE DB configuration file contains information that AutoCAD uses to access data in database files. The configuration file is where you add information that identifies the ODBC data source filename. It also allows you to password-protect the connection, and it defines the location of the source database files. By creating an OLE DB configuration file, you give AutoCAD the information it needs to access database files.

The following exercise walks you through creating an OLE DB configuration file.

CREATING AN OLE DB CONFIGURATION FILE

1. From the AutoCAD Tools menu, choose dbConnect.

NOTE

> The dbConnect command located on the Tools menu is a toggle. When it's selected, AutoCAD loads the dbConnect menu and the dbConnect Manager and then places a check mark next to the dbConnect command. To remove the dbConnect menu and the dbConnect Manager, choose dbConnect from the Tools menu again to remove the check mark.

2. From the dbConnect menu, choose Data Sources, Configure. AutoCAD displays the Configure a Data Source dialog box.

3. In the Data Source Name text box, enter **Storm_Drain**, as shown in Figure 24.5. This is the name that appears in the dbConnect Manager, and which you select to connect to a database.

Figure 24.5

The Data Source Name is the name you select in the dbConnect Manager to connect to a database.

4. Click OK, and the Data Link Properties dialog box appears.

5. From the Provider tab, select Microsoft OLE DB Provider for ODBC Drivers, as shown in Figure 24.6. Then click Next. The Connection tab appears.

Figure 24.6

From the Provider tab, select the Microsoft OLE DB Provider for ODBC Drivers.

6. On the Connection tab, under Step 1, select the Use Data Source Name option button.

7. From the Use Data Source Name list, choose the StormDrains data source name (DSN). Then click the Reset button.

NOTE

The StormDrains data source name (DSN) was created in the exercise in the previous section "Creating an ODBC Data Source File."

8. Under Step 2 on the Connection tab, be sure the Blank Password check box is selected.

9. Under Step 3 on the Connection tab, choose the DB Files catalog from the list, as shown in Figure 24.7.

Figure 24.7

The Connection tab allows you to identify the data source name, to password-protect access to the database files, and to locate the folder (catalog) that holds the database files.

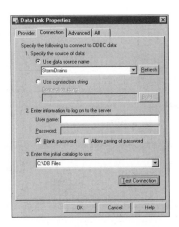

NOTE

In a database, a *catalog* refers to the folder that contains the database files.

10. At the bottom of the Connection tab, click the Test Connection button. AutoCAD performs a test to ensure it is successfully connected to the database files. If it is, it displays a message that the test connection was successful.

    If the test connection is successful, click OK to dismiss the dialog box. If the test connection fails, you must verify that you chose the correct data source name and catalog folder.

11. Click OK to dismiss the Data Link Properties dialog box.

After you close the Data Link Properties dialog box, the Storm_Drain OLE DB configuration file appears in the dbConnect Manager, as shown in Figure 24.8. This means that you successfully configured the database, and AutoCAD can now access the two tables located in the DB Files folder.

When you successfully configured the database for use with AutoCAD, a configuration file with the extension .UDL is created. This configuration file contains the information AutoCAD needs to access the configured database.

Figure 24.8

*The newly created
Storm_Drain OLE DB
configuration file appears
in the dbConnect
Manager.*

INSIDER TIP

By default, .UDL files are stored in the Data Links folder, which is located in the Acad2000 folder. However, you can specify a different location for .UDL files in the Options dialog box.

WARNING

There are some limitations to using AutoCAD's database connectivity feature because AutoCAD uses a limited subset of the ODBC and OLE DB database configuration utilities.

For more information, refer to AutoCAD 2000's ASI Configuration Guide to the section titled "Known Limitations of External Database Configuration." The Guide is located in the acad_asi.hlp file, which is stored in the Acad2000/Help folder.

In the preceding two sections, you created a data source for two database files and configured an OLE DB file to allow AutoCAD to access the database files stored in the DB Files folder. Next, you learn how to access the data in the database files.

Working with Database Tables

AutoCAD provides tools for working with external database files. By using these tools, you can view database tables and edit their data. When viewing tables, you can move, resize, and hide columns. You can specify a sort order for the table's records. You can edit or delete a record, and you can add a new record to a table. You can search the table for particular values and replace those values when you find them. By using AutoCAD's database table tools, you can control the display of table data and edit the data in tables.

Accessing Tables from the dbConnect Manager

The dbConnect Manager provides a simple visual way to review drawings linked to database files and the data sources to which they are linked. You can display links, labels, and queries defined in drawings. You can also display the tables associated to data sources. Through the dbConnect Manager, you can easily view the tables available on your system and the relationship between the tables and drawings to which they are linked.

The dbConnect Manager also allows you to connect to data sources. Once connected, you can select a table in the data source and view or edit its data. You can also create a new link template or a new label template, which is used to link objects in drawings to data in tables, and then label the objects using data extracted from the tables. You can also define a new query or execute an existing one. By using the dbConnect Manager, you can perform several useful functions on tables and their data.

To view the dbConnect Manager, either you can select dbConnect from the Tools menu, or you can type **DBCONNECT** at the command prompt. When the command executes, AutoCAD loads the dbConnect menu and the dbConnect Manager. The Manager is a dockable, resizable window that can float over your AutoCAD drawing windows. To close the Manager, either execute the dbConnect command again or click the Exit button (the small "X" button in the upper-right corner of the dbConnect Manager window). When the Manager is closed, both it and the dbConnect menu are removed.

In the following exercise, you use the dbConnect Manager to connect to a data source and view one of its tables.

Using the dbConnect Manager

1. From the AutoCAD Tools menu, choose dbConnect. AutoCAD loads the dbConnect menu and the dbConnect Manager.

2. Under Data Sources, right-click jet_dbsamples, and then choose Connect from the shortcut menu. The tables located in the jet_dbsamples folder appear, as shown in Figure 24.9.

Figure 24.9

When you connect to a data source, the dbConnect Manager displays its tables.

NOTE

If you did not install AutoCAD in its default directory, you may need to update the jet_dbsamples.udl configuration file before working with these tables. Updating the file is only necessary if AutoCAD cannot locate the files on your system.

3. Under the jet_dbsamples data source, choose the Employee table. The table becomes highlighted, and several tool buttons are activated on the dbConnect Manager, as shown in Figure 24.10.

Figure 24.10

When you select a table under a data source, the tool buttons are activated on the dbConnect Manager.

4. Choose the View Table button. The Data View window is displayed in read-only mode, as shown in Figure 24.11.

Figure 24.11

You access the Data View window from the dbConnect Manager.

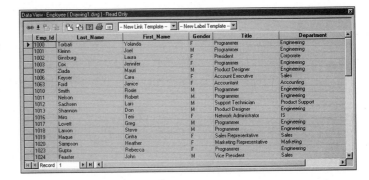

NOTE

When you click the View Table button, AutoCAD also displays the Data View menu, which appears in the list of AutoCAD menus.

5. Leave the Data View window open to continue with the next exercise.

The dbConnect Manager provides an easy way to display information about drawing links, labels, and queries and about data sources available on your system. From this window, you can access table data and define queries. Using the dbConnect Manager, you can quickly perform common database tasks.

In the next section, you use the Data View window to view data in a table.

Viewing Table Data with Data View

AutoCAD's Data View window allows you to manipulate its view to display data in the table the way you want. For example, you can hide and unhide columns. You can move columns to new positions in the table, changing their order. You can also sort the data in columns in either ascending or descending order. You can even control the appearance of the text displayed in the table by changing its font or font size. Through the Data View window, you can manipulate the display of a table to make viewing data easier.

In the following exercise, you learn about controlling the appearance of data in the Data View window.

MANIPULATING THE DATA VIEW WINDOW

1. Continuing from the previous exercise, choose the Title column's header. You may need to pan to the right in order to see the Title column.

   The column header is actually a button at the top of a column that displays the column's name. When you click the button, AutoCAD highlights the entire column.

2. Drag the column to the left side of the Gender column. When a red line appears between the First Name and Gender columns, release your mouse button to drop the column. AutoCAD places the. Title column to the left of the Gender column, as shown in Figure 24.12.

Figure 24.12

*You can highlight and
move a column by
choosing its header, which
displays the column's
name.*

You can resize a column as desired. By clicking and dragging the line between
header buttons, you can resize a column. Next, you use a feature that automatically
resizes the Last_Name column.

3. Move your cursor to the line between the Last_Name and First_Name columns and
    double-click. The Last_Name column is automatically resized to fit the longest name
    in the column, as shown in Figure 24.13.

Figure 24.13

*The Last_Name column is
resized.*

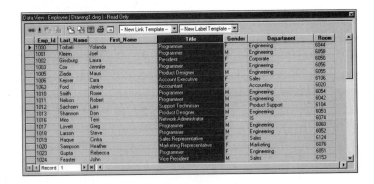

You can hide columns in the Data View, and you can unhide hidden columns. Next,
you hide and then unhide the First_Name column.

4. Choose the First_Name column's header. The column becomes highlighted.

5. Right-click over the First_Name column's header and choose Hide. The First_Name
    column is hidden, as shown in Figure 24.14.

Figure 24.14

The First_Name column is hidden from view.

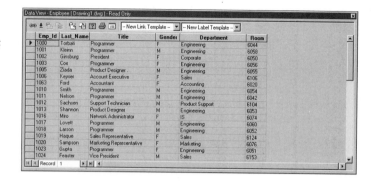

INSIDER TIP

By holding down the Ctrl key when choosing column headers, you can select and then hide multiple columns at the same time.

6. Right-click over the Emp_ID column, and then choose Unhide All. The First_Name column reappears.

    The Data View window allows you to sort the data in columns. In the Data View window, you can sort both numerically and alphabetically, and you can choose between sorting data in ascending or descending order. You can also execute sorts based on up to five columns at one time.

    Next, you sort two different columns at once.

7. Right-click over the Emp_ID column's header button, and then choose Sort. The Sort dialog box appears.

8. In the Sort By area, choose Emp_ID from the list. Be sure the Ascending option button is selected.

9. In the Then By area immediately below the Sort By area, choose Department from the list, as shown in Figure 24.15. Again, be sure the Ascending option button is selected.

10. Click OK. AutoCAD executes the sort and redisplays the data based on the sort results.

    As you work with large database files, some tables you display in the Data View window will contain many columns. To view these columns, you will need to drag the slide bar at the bottom of the window left or right. The downside to dragging the slide bar to view columns outside the window's current display is columns you are currently viewing will be moved out of view as you move the slide bar.

Figure 24.15

The Sort dialog box allows you to create up to five simultaneous sorts.

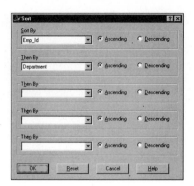

The Data View window allows you to freeze a column's position. This means that when you move the slide bar to view other columns, the frozen columns do not move from view, and their positions remain fixed. This feature allows you to drag the slide bar to view columns outside the current display, while always displaying the frozen columns.

Next, you freeze the Last_Name column and then drag the Data View window's slide bar to see the effects of the frozen column.

11. Right-click over the Last_Name column's header button. Then choose Freeze. AutoCAD automatically moves the Last_Name column to the far left side of the Data View window and freezes its position.

12. Resize the Data View window so that the Department and Room columns are hidden. To resize the window, move your cursor over the left or right edge of the window. When your cursor changes to a double-sided arrow, click and drag the window to make it smaller. The slide bar is now movable.

13. Drag the slide bar to the far right. Notice that the Department and Room columns are displayed, and the Emp_ID and First_Name columns are removed from view. More importantly, notice that the Last_Name column remains visible, as shown in Figure 24.16.

14. Right-click over the Last_Name column's header button, and then choose Unfreeze All. AutoCAD unfreezes the Last_Name column.

The Data View window allows you to control the alignment of text in columns and to change the font and font size of the text used to display a table's data.

Next, you change the text alignment of the Last_Name column, and then you change to a new font to display the data in the Data View window.

15. Drag the slide bar to the far left to display the Last_Name column, and then right-click over the Last_Name column's header button and choose Align, Right. AutoCAD right-justifies the text in the Last_Name column, as shown in Figure 24.17.

Figure 24.16

The Last_Name column is frozen and remains displayed at all times, even as the horizontal slide bar is moved.

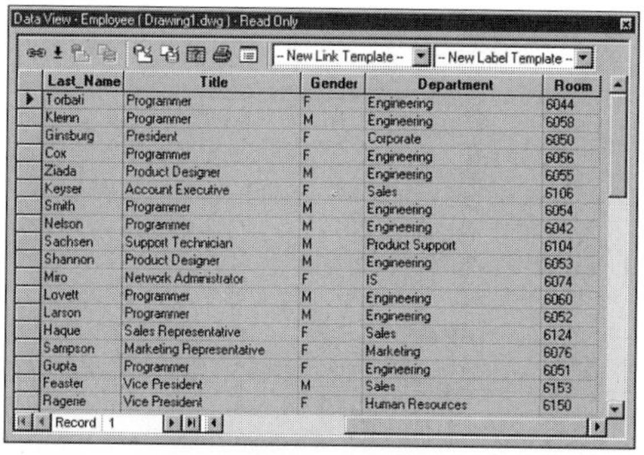

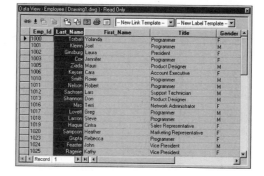

Figure 24.17

The Last_Name column's text is right-justified.

16. From the Data View pull-down menu, choose Format. AutoCAD displays the Format dialog box.

17. From the Font list, choose Arial.

18. From the Size list, choose 10, as shown in Figure 24.18. Then choose OK. AutoCAD changes the table's text to the Arial font with a point size of 10, as shown in Figure 24.19.

Figure 24.18

The Format dialog box allows you to change the font used to display text in the Data View window.

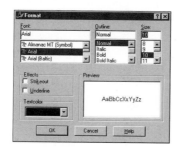

Figure 24.19

The new font and font size are used to display text in the Data View window.

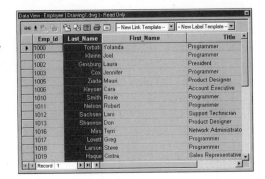

19. Close the Data View window and the dbConnect Manager by clicking the Exit button, which is the small button with an "X" in it, located in the upper-right corner of each window.

20. You can now exit AutoCAD without saving your changes.

The Data View window allows you to control its appearance. You can hide columns, change their positions, or lock their positions by freezing them. You can also sort the data using the Sort dialog box. In addition to these features, you can also control the appearance of the text displayed in the columns and rows. You can change their justification and their font size. By manipulating its display, you can modify the Data View window to display the data the way you want.

Editing Table Data with Data View

AutoCAD's Data View window has two modes. The first is read-only mode, and the second is edit mode. The read-only mode allows you to view data and manipulate its appearance in the Data View window. The edit mode also allows you to manipulate the window's appearance, but more importantly, it allows you to manipulate the table and its data. For example, in edit mode, you can edit, delete, and add new records to a table. You can also search the table for certain values and replace those values with new ones. By using Data View's edit mode, you can view, edit, and explore the data in database tables.

In the following exercise, you learn about the various features of the Data View window's edit mode.

NOTE

> The following exercise accesses a table whose type and location is defined in previous exercises. To perform the steps in the following exercise, you must first complete the two exercises located in the section "Setting Up AutoCAD to Work with External Databases."

USING DATA VIEW'S EDIT MODE

1. From AutoCAD's Tools menu, choose dbConnect. AutoCAD displays the dbConnect menu and the dbConnect Manager.

2. Right-click the Storm_Drain data source, and then choose Connect. AutoCAD connects to the data source and displays the two tables in its folder.

3. Choose the Pipes table, and then click the Edit View button. AutoCAD opens the Data View window in edit mode, as shown in Figure 24.20.

   From the Data View window, you can edit individual cells in the table. Next, you edit the DIA value for one of the records.

Figure 24.20

You can edit the Pipes table in the Data View window when it is in edit mode.

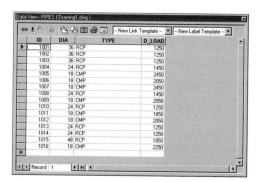

4. Select the cell that displays the 24 DIA field value for the record whose ID is 1008.

5. Type **36** for the new cell value and press Enter. AutoCAD replaces the old cell value with the new one, as shown in Figure 24.21.

Figure 24.21

*The cell in the DIA field
of record 1008 is changed
to 36.*

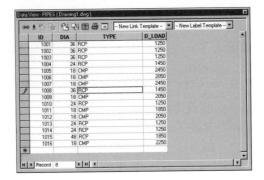

N OTE

When you enter a new value, AutoCAD instantly updates the table. Edits cannot be undone.

The Data View window allows you to add new records to an existing table. Next, you add a new record.

6. Select the record header whose ID value is 1010. (The record headers are the small buttons to the left of the ID column.) AutoCAD highlights the record.

7. Right-click the highlighted record header, and then choose Add New Record. AutoCAD adds a new blank record at the end of the list of records.

8. Enter the following values for the cells in the new record:

    ■ ID: Type **1017**. Then press Tab.

    ■ DIA: Type **24**. Then press Tab.

    ■ TYPE: Type **RCP**. Then press Tab.

    ■ D_LOAD: Type **1450**. Then press Enter.

    The Data View window should appear as shown in Figure 24.22.

    The Data View window also allows you to delete records from an existing table. Next, you delete a record.

9. Select the record header whose ID value is 1007. AutoCAD highlights the record.

10. Right-click the highlighted record header and choose Delete Record. AutoCAD displays a window asking you to verify that you want to delete the selected row.

11. Click Yes. AutoCAD deletes the selected record.

Figure 24.22

The new record 1017 is
added to the existing
table.

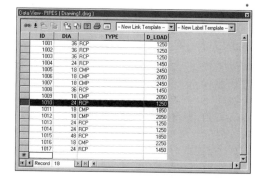

INSIDER TIP

By holding down the Ctrl key when choosing record headers, you can select multiple
records to delete at the same time.

The Data View window allows you to find specified values in selected columns. If you
choose a cell in the column whose values you want to search and then right-click and
choose Find from the shortcut menu, AutoCAD will search the column for the value
and highlight the cell in which it finds the value.

You can also search for a specified value and replace it with a new value. Next, you
search for values in the TYPE column and replace them with new values.

12. Select a cell in the TYPE field. AutoCAD highlights the cell.

13. Right-click over the cell and choose Replace from the shortcut menu. AutoCAD
     displays the Replace dialog box.

14. In the Find What text box, type **CMP**.

15. In the Replace With text box, type **RCP** as shown in Figure 24.23.

Figure 24.23

The CMP value will be
replaced by the RCP value.

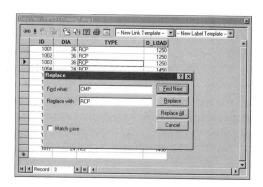

16. Click Replace All. AutoCAD replaces all instances of the CMP value in the TYPE column with RCP.

17. Click the Cancel button to dismiss the Replace dialog box. The Data View window displays the updated records, as shown in Figure 24.14.

Figure 24.24

The Data View window displays the table's updated records.

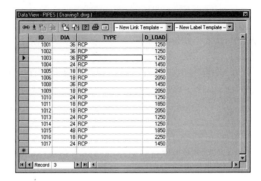

> **N**OTE
>
> AutoCAD searches for values only in the column indicated. AutoCAD cannot globally search all columns in a table for values.

18. Close the Data View window and the dbConnect Manager by clicking the Exit button (the small button with an "X" in it, located in the upper-right corner of each window).

19. You can now exit AutoCAD without saving your changes.

> **N**OTE
>
> In this example, modifications made to the table instantly updated the original table. Other databases do not instantly update the original table; rather, they allow you to choose whether you want to accept or reject your modifications before updating the original table.
>
> When you work with databases that allow you to accept or reject your modifications, you are prompted to either *commit* modifications or *restore* the table's original values by right-clicking the grid header and choosing the desired option from the shortcut menu. The grid header is the small button in the upper-left corner of the column and record headers.

The Data View window's edit mode allows you to edit an existing table. You can change cell values individually, or you can search and replace specified values instantly in an entire column. You can add new records to the table or delete existing ones. By using the Data View window's edit mode, you can easily modify a table's data.

Working with Data and Objects

AutoCAD allows you to create a link between records in a database table and objects in a drawing. Once you have established a link between an object and a record, you can use the link to locate objects by selecting the records to which they are attached, or to locate records in a table by selecting objects in a drawing. Additionally, you can extract the data values stored in a table and automatically insert it as a text label that is attached to its linked object. By using AutoCAD's ability to link data to objects, you can quickly locate linked objects and records and easily label objects by extracting the data to which they are linked.

Linking Data to AutoCAD Objects

AutoCAD provides a feature that allows you to connect data stored in external database files to objects in drawings. Using this feature, you can select a single record in a table and associate it to a graphic object in a drawing. With this feature, you can create links between the graphic objects in a drawing and the data stored in database tables.

To link data stored in database tables to objects in AutoCAD drawings, you must do two things. First, you must create a link template. Second, you must create the link. After you perform these two simple steps, you can associate a record in a table with an object in a drawing.

Creating a Link Template

Before you can link data in a table to objects in a drawing, you must create a link template. A *link template* identifies the field in a table used to link a record to an object. You create a link template so that AutoCAD knows which field to use to link data in a table to objects in a drawing.

In the following exercise, you create a link template.

CREATING A LINK TEMPLATE

1. Copy the 24DWG01.DWG file from the accompanying CD to the DB Files folder. (You created the DB Files folder in a previous exercise in the section "Creating an ODBC Data Source File.")

    After copying the drawing file, be sure to right-click the file, choose Properties, and then clear the Read-only attribute.

2. Open the drawing 24DWG01.DWG located in the DB Files folder. The drawing displays a series of polylines and circles that represent storm drain lines and manholes.

3. From the Tools menu, choose dbConnect. AutoCAD displays the dbConnect menu and the dbConnect Manager.

4. In the dbConnect Manager, right-click the Storm_Drain data source and choose Connect. AutoCAD connects to the data source and displays the two tables in its folder.

5. From the dbConnect pull-down menu, choose Templates, New Link Template. AutoCAD displays the Select Data Object dialog box.

6. In the Select Data Object dialog box, choose the PIPES table, as shown in Figure 24.25, and then click Continue. AutoCAD displays the New Link Template dialog box.

Figure 24.25

The Select Data Object dialog box identifies the table for which you will create a link template.

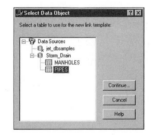

7. In the New Link Template Name text box, type **PipesLink** as shown in Figure 24.26. Then click Continue to display the Link Template dialog box. AutoCAD automatically creates the default link name by adding Link1 to the PIPES table name.

The New Link Template
dialog box allows you to
define the name for the
new link template.

8. In the Key Fields list, click the check box next to the ID key field, as shown in Figure
    24.27. Then click OK. AutoCAD defines the new link template for the 24DWG01.DWG
    drawing as indicated by the PipesLink connection displayed in the dbConnect
    Manager (see Figure 24.28).

Figure 24.27

The Link Template dialog
box allows you to identify
the key field for the new
link template.

Figure 24.28

The PipesLink Link
Template is defined for the
24DWG01.DWG drawing
and is displayed in the
dbConnect Manager.

9. Save your changes, but leave the drawing open for use in the next exercise.

Creating link templates allows AutoCAD to access the data in a table's field and link it to objects in drawings. Creating a link template and associating it with a drawing is necessary to creating links between records and objects. By creating link templates for drawings, you define the field in a table that AutoCAD uses to link records to objects.

Next, you use the link template you just created to link records in the PIPES table to polyline objects in a drawing.

Creating Links

After you have defined a link template for a drawing, you can link records in a table to objects in a drawing. You can link multiple records to a single object or link a single record to multiple objects. After a link is created, you can select an object to highlight the record to which it is attached, or you can select a record to highlight the object to which it is linked. a link template is defined for a drawing, you can link records to objects, and then view their link associations.

In the following exercise, you create links between records in a table and objects in a drawing. This exercise is a continuation of the previous one.

LINKING RECORDS TO OBJECTS

1. In the dbConnect Manager, choose the PIPES table. Then click the View Table button. AutoCAD displays the Data View window in read-only mode.

2. In the Data View window's New Link Template list, choose the PipesLink template.

3. In the Data View window, choose the record header for the record whose ID value is 1001. AutoCAD highlights the record.

4. From the Data View pull-down menu, choose Link and Label Settings, Create Links if it's not already checked. AutoCAD sets the link mode to create links.

5. From the Data View menu, choose Link. AutoCAD prompts you to select objects to which it should link the highlighted record.

6. Choose the polyline that connects the circle labeled 1 and the circle labeled 3, and then press Enter to end object selection. AutoCAD links the highlighted record to the selected polyline and changes the highlighted record's color to yellow.

7. In the Data View window, choose the record header for the record whose ID value is 1004. AutoCAD highlights the record.

8. From the Data View menu, choose Link. AutoCAD prompts you to select objects to which it should link the highlighted record.

9. Choose the polyline that connects the circle labeled 2 and the circle labeled 4, choose the polyline that connects the circle labeled 4 and the circle labeled 5, and then press Enter to end object selection. AutoCAD links the highlighted record to the selected polylines and changes the highlighted record's color to yellow, as shown in Figure 24.29.

Figure 24.29

In the Data View windows, the record 1004 is highlighted yellow when it is linked to an object in a drawing.

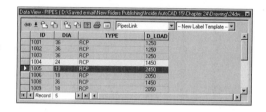

After creating links between records and objects, you can view the links either by selecting records to highlight the objects to which they are attached or by selecting objects to highlight the records to which they are linked.

Next, you use the link associations you just created to highlight records and objects.

10. In the Data View window, choose the record header for the record whose ID value is 1001. AutoCAD highlights the record.

11. From the Data View menu, choose View Linked Objects. AutoCAD selects the object to which the record is linked and zooms to display the object in the center of the drawing window, as shown in Figure 24.30.

Figure 24.30

The selected record is used to locate and highlight the object to which it is linked.

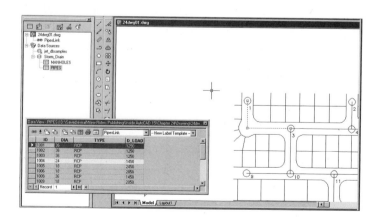

Next, you use an object to highlight a record.

12. Press Esc twice to deselect the polyline object.

13. Pan the view to display the polyline that connects to the circles labeled 4 and 5, and then select the polyline. AutoCAD highlights the polyline.

14. From the Data View menu, choose View Linked Records. AutoCAD displays only the record to which the object is linked in the Data View window, as shown in Figure 24.31.

Figure 24.31

The selected object is used to locate and display the record to which it is linked.

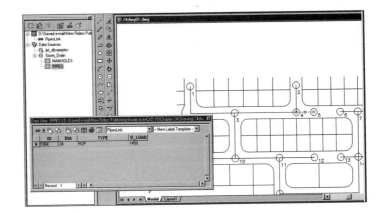

15. Save your changes, and then close the drawing.

By establishing links between objects and records, you can use the links to locate and highlight linked objects. You can select objects and locate the records to which they are linked, or you can choose records to locate and select the objects to which they are attached. By creating links between records and objects, you add intelligence to your drawing that you can use to locate and select records and objects.

Labeling Objects with Data from Tables

When you have established links between records in a table and objects in a drawing, you can use those links to label the objects. AutoCAD provides a labeling feature that allows you to use data in a table to place text in a drawing. By using AutoCAD's label feature, you can extract data from a table and use it to label the objects to which the data is linked.

NOTE

AutoCAD allows you to create freestanding labels, which are labels inserted in a drawing using data from tables, but that are not attached to an object in a drawing.

Creating labels from data linked to objects requires two steps. First, you must create a label template. Second, you must insert the label. After performing these two simple steps, you can insert a label into a drawing and attach it to an object in a drawing.

NOTE

The following exercise uses a drawing you modified in previous exercises. To perform the steps in the following exercise, you must use the drawing you modified in the two exercises in the section "Linking Data to AutoCAD Objects."

In the following exercise, you use the links created between records in a table and objects in a drawing to label the objects.

LABELING OBJECTS LINKED TO RECORDS

1. Open the 24DWG01.DWG file located in the DB Files folder.

2. If the dbConnect Manager is not displayed, open the Tools menu and choose dbConnect. AutoCAD displays the dbConnect Manager and the dbConnect menu.

3. From the dbConnect menu, choose Templates, New Label Template. AutoCAD displays the Select a Database Object dialog box.

NOTE

A label template requires a link template. You can create a label template only after you have created a link template.

4. In the Select a Database Object dialog box, be sure the PipesLink link template is selected, as shown in Figure 24.32. Then click Continue. AutoCAD displays the New Label Template dialog box.

Figure 24.32

In the Select a Database Object dialog box, you identify the link template to use with the label template.

5. In the New Label Template Name text box, type **PipesLabel**, as shown in Figure 24.33, and then click Continue. AutoCAD displays the label template.

Figure 24.33

In the New Label Template dialog box, you can enter a name for the new label template.

6. In the Label Template dialog box, choose the Label Fields tab.

7. From the Field list, choose DIA. Then click Add. The DIA field is added to the text window.

NOTE

The table field displayed in the text area represents the column from which AutoCAD will extract the value of the record that is linked to the selected AutoCAD object. You can add additional text to the text window that you want included in the label, such as a prefix or suffix.

8. In the text window after #(DIA), type a double quotation mark symbol (").

9. In the Label Template dialog box, choose the Properties tab.

10. From the Justification list, choose Middle Left ML. The text's insertion point is text to middle left.

11. In the Label Template dialog box, choose the Character tab.

12. Right-click in the text window and click Select All. The text is selected in the window.

13. In the Font Height list, type **10.0** (as shown in Figure 24.34), and then click OK. AutoCAD defines the new label template for the 24DWG01.DWG drawing as indicated by the PipesLabel symbol displayed in the dbConnect Manager (see Figure 24.35).

Figure 24.34

The field from which to extract the table data is defined, and a quotation mark symbol is added as a suffix to be included with the label.

Figure 24.35

The label template is defined for the 24DWG01.DWG drawing.

Next, you insert a label.

14. In the dbConnect Manager, choose the PIPES table and click the View Table button. AutoCAD displays the Data View window in read-only mode.

15. In the New Link Template list, be sure the PipesLink link template is selected.

16. In the New Label Template list, be sure the PipesLabel label template is selected.

17. In the Data View window, select the record whose ID value is 1003.

18. From the Data View pull-down menu, choose Link and Label Settings, Create Attached Labels. AutoCAD switches to Create Attached Labels mode.

19. From the Data View menu, choose Link, and then select the polyline that connects to the circles labeled 3 and 4. Then press Enter. AutoCAD links the record to the selected polyline object and then inserts the label at the midpoint of the polyline, as shown in Figure 24.36.

Figure 24.36

The selected record will be used to extract the label value.

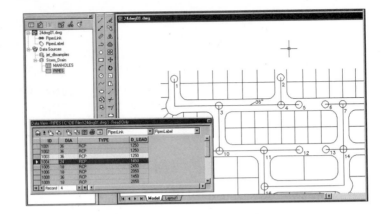

20. Save your changes. Then either leave this drawing open for the following exercise, or close the drawing.

AutoCAD creates a link between the selected record and the selected AutoCAD object, and then it extracts the cell value from the field indicated by the label template. The label's insertion point is controlled in the Label Template from the Label Offset tab and can be modified. Additionally, you can edit label templates by choosing Templates, Edit Label Template from the dbConnect menu.

INSIDER TIP

You can control the layer on which the label is inserted by switching to the desired layer before inserting the label.

By using AutoCAD's label feature, you can easily label objects in drawings by extracting values from data in tables. Using this technique, you can automate the process of labeling objects and insert text values accurately by extracting the text values directly from the linked database table. AutoCAD's labeling feature makes adding text to drawings easier. In the next section, you use AutoCAD's query features.

Using Queries

Databases can contain enormous amounts of data. They can be made of dozens of tables, with each table containing hundreds of records, and each record consisting of many fields. The amount of data in a database can be overwhelming.

The goal of any database is to provide a place to organize and store large amounts of information, which you can then query for subsets of data. A query consists of search criteria that you specify. You define the search criterion and run the query, and the query searches the entire database for data that matches the specified criteria. If matching data is found, the query returns only those records that contain the matching data. By defining and running queries, you can quickly extract the particular set of data you need.

AutoCAD allows you to create and run queries. You can create queries that search through a table for specified values. You can also define queries that search through the objects in a drawing, returning a selection set of records that meet the query criteria. Using AutoCAD's Query Editor, you can build and run queries that search through a drawing or a table for the data you need.

You create queries in AutoCAD using the Query Editor, which consists of four query tabs, as shown in Figure 24.37. The tabs, designed to build queries, are described in the following list:

- **Quick Query.** This tab allows you to define and run a query using basic operators such as IS Equal To and Is Greater Than.

- **Range Query.** This tab allows you to define and run a query based on a range of values. For example, you can query for all objects whose field value is greater than or eqaul to 18 and less than or equal to 36.

- **Query Builder.** The Query Builder tab allows you to define and run a query using multiple operators and ranges and allows you to use parentheses to group the criteria. Additionally, you can use Boolean operators such as AND and OR to further refine your query. This tab represents AutoCAD's primary query builder.

- **SQL Query.** This tab allows you to define and run a query by creating SQL statements that conform to Microsoft's implementation of the SQL 92 protocol. This tab allows you to build free-form SQL queries, in which you can construct queries that perform relational operations on multiple database tables using the SQL join operator.

Using AutoCAD's Query Editor, you can construct a variety of queries that range from the simple to the complex.

Figure 24.37

The Query Editor allows you to build queries that range from simple to complex.

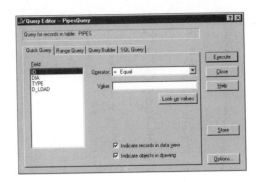

In the following section, you use the Query Editor to quickly define and run a simple query.

Querying Objects

The simplest way to create a query is to use the Query Editor's Quick Query feature. The Quick Query feature allows you to define a basic query that can find data using simple comparison operators such as Is Equal To or Is Greater Than. By using the Quick Query feature, you can easily define and run a query that searches your data and returns the values you need.

NOTE

The following exercise uses a drawing you modified in previous exercises. To perform the steps in the following exercise, you must use that drawing you modified in the exercises in the section "Working with Data and Objects."

In the following exercise, you use the Quick Query feature to build and run a query that searches for pipes with a diameter equal to 36 inches.

CREATING AND RUNNING A QUERY

1. Open the 24DWG01.DWG file located in the DB Files folder. If it's already open from the previous exercise, skip to step 4.

2. From the Tools menu, choose dbConnect. AutoCAD displays the dbConnect Manager and the dbConnect menu.

3. In the dbConnect Manager, right-click the Storm_Drain data source and choose connect. AutoCAD connects to the data source and displays the two tables in its folder.

4. From the dbConnect menu, choose Queries, New Query on an External Table. AutoCAD displays the Select Data Object dialog box.

5. In the Select Data Object dialog box, select the PIPES table as shown in Figure 24.38. Then click Continue. AutoCAD displays the New Query dialog box.

Figure 24.38

From the Select Data Object dialog box, you choose the table you will query.

6. In the New Query Name text box, type **PipesQuery** (as shown in Figure 24.39), and then click Continue. AutoCAD displays the Query Editor.

Figure 24.39

From the New Query dialog box, you define the name for the new query.

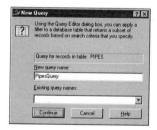

7. In the Query Editor, select the Quick Query tab.

8. In the Field list, choose DIA.

9. From the Quick Query tab's Operator list, choose = Equal.

10. In the Value text box, type **36**.

11. In the Quick Query tab, be sure the Indicate Records in Data View and the Indicate Objects in Drawing check boxes are selected, as shown in Figure 24.40.

Figure 24.40

The Quick Query is defined
and ready to run.

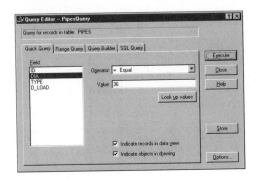

12. Click Execute. AutoCAD executes the query, returns the subset records that match the query criterion, and displays the records in the Data View window, as shown in Figure 24.41.

13. Exit AutoCAD without saving your changes.

Figure 24.41

The Quick Query returns
the subset of records that
match the query's
criterion.

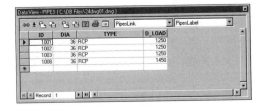

AutoCAD's Query Editor allows you to define and run a query. You can quickly define a query using the Quick Query tab, or you can create more complex queries using the Range Query, Query Builder, or SQL Query tabs. By using the Query Editor, you can easily define and execute a query that returns the data you need.

Summary

In this chapter, you reviewed how to use the ODBC Data Source Administrator provided by the Windows operating system to enable AutoCAD to access data in external databases. You learned how to use the Data Link Properties dialog box to create a .udl configuration file, which points to a file's location. You used the dbConnect Manager to access external database tables, and you used the Data View window to view and edit the information in tables. You learned how to link data to AutoCAD objects and how to label objects with data extracted from external database tables. Finally, you learned how to execute queries and query for objects either in AutoCAD drawings or in tables.

By using the techniques discussed in this chapter, you can associate external database files with your AutoCAD drawings and use the tools provided by AutoCAD to work with the data stored in database tables.

VI

CAD ON THE INTERNET

25

PUBLISHING ON THE WEB

With the rich integration of Internet access functionality into Release 2000, AutoCAD now offers a truly Web-enabled solution. At the same time, Autodesk's WHIP! technology continues the tradition to "CAD-enable" the Web. The merger of these two technologies delivers very powerful tools to Web-savvy designers. In this chapter, you learn how to integrate these exciting new capabilities into your current engineering practices. Useful information to help further your understanding of the Internet is also included. Exercises in this chapter help you learn how to use AutoCAD's Internet functionality to do the following:

- *Access DWG files located on remote Internet sites transparently from within AutoCAD 2000.*

- *Create DWF files using the new ePlot mechanism.*

- *View AutoCAD DWF files in your Web browser.*

- *Embed hyperlinks within drawings.*

- *Place DWF files into HTML pages.*

AutoCAD 2000: Where Design *Really* Connects

The World Wide Web has become a pervasive medium for computing. For many firms, the role of the Internet as a serious business tool has not yet been made clear, with numerous Web sites implemented strictly for marketing purposes. Yet, for creators and users of CAD data, the Internet provides an environment that greatly benefits the engineering community. From a CAD perspective, the Web is the ideal mechanism for facilitating collaborative design and real-time communication. As explained herein, the World Wide Web has propelled the growth of the Internet and allowed businesses to expand their reach significantly.

The Internet and the World Wide Web deliver powerful tools and new ways to enhance the virtual reach of your business. With these new Net tools, you can offer potential customers immediate access to technical drawing data, specifications, or other key project data. The explosive growth of the Internet in recent years has revolutionized the way people work and communicate in everyday life. More drawings than ever before are now made available to designers within local organization intranets, and to solution partners via the Internet. It is amazing to see the impact of the Web on businesses, both small and large. AutoCAD 2000 offers a rich and vastly expanded set of Internet features, with some exciting new functionality that empowers users by augmenting their reach across logical or physical boundaries.

The Internet, Intranets, and Extranets

The *Internet* is a global network made up of other networks that communicate with each other using well-defined protocols. People using the Internet can access services from other computers. Much of the resources available through the networks are free. The services available on the Internet include the following:

- **HTTP (Hypertext Transfer Protocol).** Used to receive hypertext content that links to other content on the Web.

- **FTP (File Transfer Protocol).** Used for downloading and uploading files.

- **Internet email.**

- **Usenet news groups and discussion forums.**

An *intranet* offers services similar to those previously noted, but is an internal corporate network. Rather than being hooked up to the entire world, an intranet is an internal corporate resource. The purpose of an intranet is to deliver internal information about the company's resources to each employee. Intranet access is secure and typically limited to designated employees, with external access prevented by a *firewall*.

An *extranet* is an extension of a company's intranet, which allows it to share business-related information with its suppliers and collaborators using secure protocols. Specifically, extranets are secure wide-area networks that facilitate organizations to work on projects of mutual interest using the same benefits as those afforded by intranets. Several companies have realized the strategic importance of extranets to achieve a competitive advantage by linking employees and key business partners.

Impact of the Internet on CAD

The Internet has a wide variety of uses, and new capabilities emerge on a daily basis. As previously noted, the Web is used for marketing, software distribution, retail sales, stock trading, entertainment, market research, email, and more. Companies with a presence on the Web (a Web site) deliver information to a global audience, saving time, the cost of materials, and shipping and handling. Web users get the benefits of rapid access to information they need at little cost. The Internet lends itself particularly well to communicating technical information (such as CAD drawing information) or data about sophisticated products (such as AutoCAD 2000). Most importantly, the Internet can deliver information targeted at an audience with interests similar to yours.

Manufacturers' information is becoming widely available online in electronic formats, ready to be inserted into a CAD drawing. Designers and manufacturers save time while improving accuracy and overall project quality. Online training programs improve the skills of designers while reducing the cost of keeping current with changing technologies.

Direct Benefits of the Net for CAD

With Internet-enabled AutoCAD 2000, multiple designers at various locations can view, redline, or edit your drawings in real time. This new technology is highly beneficial, facilitating the coordination of large or small projects. With AutoCAD 2000, you can access DWG files anywhere in the world at any time via the Internet. No more waiting for a drawing file to arrive by overnight courier! This immediate access reduces cycle time and travel costs while increasing quality through enhanced communications. Bids for new projects can be searched, solicited, and submitted online, opening up new opportunities for companies that may not have had the resources to previously participate in such processes. Questions and proposals are emailed, and the time saved is put to better use in refining the bid. A product portfolio of the firm's successful projects can be converted into a Web site. This expands the audience for your services, resulting in greater market exposure and potentially higher revenues.

Understanding the Capabilities of the Web-Oriented AutoCAD 2000

The Web enabling of AutoCAD actually began with the AutoCAD Release 13 Internet Publishing Kit (IPK). The IPK included some utilities for accessing DWG files across the Net of the WHIP! plug-in for Netscape Navigator, and the capability to create DWF files from inside Release 13. With Release 14, some key elements of the IPK were integrated into AutoCAD, resulting in a more Internet-friendly product. AutoCAD 2000 takes Internet functionality to new heights by offering a seamless and transparent integration for access to resources on remote sites.

System Requirements

The completely revamped Internet functionality in AutoCAD 2000 is built on lower-level services provided by the Windows operating system. The layer of software that implements Internet access in AutoCAD 2000 depends on the availability of certain system files, including WININET.DLL and SHDOCVW.DLL. In addition, certain other system files are required to enable features such as document hyperlinking, which will be discussed later. These files are installed as part of the Microsoft Internet Explorer (MSIE) setup. If you already have MSIE version 4.01 or higher present on your system, you have all the files required to activate the Internet features in AutoCAD 2000. If you have an older version, you will need to upgrade appropriately. If you decide to use the recently released MSIE version 5.0, please note that there are known compatibility problems as pointed out in the README file that accompanies the AutoCAD 2000 installation. AutoCAD 2000 was tested extensively with Microsoft Internet Explorer 4.x, and unless version 5.0 offers features that are indispensable to your work, it is strongly recommended that you continue to use a 4.x version.

NOTE

Internet functionality in AutoCAD 2000 will not be available in the absence of an appropriate version of Microsoft Internet Explorer. Browsers such as Netscape Navigator are not supported in AutoCAD 2000.

Help System

AutoCAD 2000 offers the capability to connect directly to the Autodesk Web site. In the Help pull-down menu, select Autodesk on the Web to display a submenu with several choices. When a selection is made, the system's configured Web browser is launched, and the system changes focus to your Web browser. Complete context-sensitive help for the AutoCAD 2000 Internet functionality is built in to the AutoCAD Help system.

Configuring Windows and AutoCAD for the Internet

AutoCAD 2000 has streamlined its Internet functionality by using the Internet properties of your personal computer—there is no separate command to configure the settings. In fact, AutoCAD 2000 retrieves the Internet configuration from your workstation and uses it in all remote file transfers.

To set up the Internet properties for your computer, click on the Start button located on the Windows taskbar, and select Settings. From the Settings submenu, select Control Panel. Finally, in the Control Panel window, double-click on the Internet icon to launch the corresponding applet.

The Internet Properties dialog box that subsequently appears is a consolidation of the Internet settings for your computer (see Figure 25.1). Select the Connection tab. If you know whether your connection to the Internet is via a proxy server, you will need to supply the appropriate information. If you are unsure about the Internet setup in your organization, contact your network administrator.

Figure 25.1

*The Connection tab of
the Internet Properties
dialog box.*

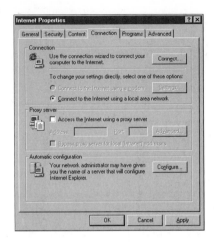

Select the type of access method used for logging on to the Internet.

- **Modem/Direct Connection.** If you connect to the Web through an *Internet Service Provider (ISP)*, typically via a phone dial-up function, select Direct Connection. Direct connections do not require that you perform proxy configuration.

- **Proxy Server.** A *proxy server* is a machine that serves as a gateway between a company's internal intranet and the external Internet. A proxy server typically runs on a firewall machine, providing secure access to the outside world for people inside the firewall. The proxy server provides various services, mainly caching of requests and a secure means of accessing data. If you don't know if you are using a proxy server, you can look at the proxy settings in your browser or contact your network system administrator. If you connect to the Internet through a proxy server, you will need to select the Proxy Server option and supply the appropriate details.

NOTE

> AutoCAD does not store your user name and password across sessions. Each new AutoCAD session requires you to enter the authentication information when accessing secure sites.

The INETLOCATION System Variable

AutoCAD's default, or start page, URL is stored in the profilable system variable INETLOCATION. You can store a different URL default for each saved profile. You can easily modify the default value (URL address) of this variable, which is used as the start page for the built-in browser. To change the URL invoked by the BROWSER command, type **INETLOCATION** at the command prompt. You will be prompted as follows:

```
New value for INETLOCATION <C:\Acad2000\Home.htm>:
```

Type the new URL you want to have your browser go to when launched by AutoCAD. This setting also applies to the built-in Web browser dialog box.

INETLOCATION can also be changed from Preferences in the Files tab of the Options dialog box, as seen in Figure 25.2.

Figure 25.2

The Files tab of the Options dialog box.

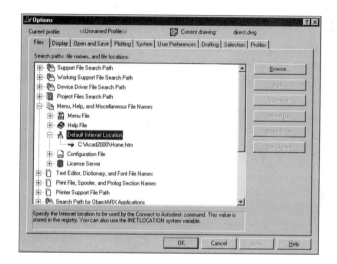

The following exercise takes you through the necessary steps to modify the browser's start page.

MODIFYING THE BROWSER'S START PAGE

1. From the Tools pull-down menu, choose Preferences.

2. Select the Files tab.

3. Scroll to the Menu, Help, and Miscellaneous File Names entry as shown in Figure 25.2.

4. Expand the selection by double-clicking it.

5. Select and expand Default Internet Location by double-clicking on the entry.

6. Choose Browse, enter a URL to the desired Internet location, and click OK. Alternatively, launch the Web Browser dialog box by clicking the Search the Web button and navigate to the Internet location that you want to use as the start page. A good URL for AutoCAD users could be either **http://www.augi.com** or **http://www.autodesk.com**.

7. Click OK.

The **BROWSER** Command

The **BROWSER** command launches the Internet Web browser that is associated with .HTM in the system Registry. This command is available from the Help pull-down menu (Autodesk on the Web) or the command prompt. When invoked from the pull-down menu, the **BROWSER** command does not prompt for a location (URL). The system variable **INETLOCATION** contains the URL address that the **BROWSER** command will initially display.

When the **BROWSER** command is issued at the command prompt, the command window shows the following:

```
Location <www.autodesk.com/acaduser>:
```

At this point, you can press Enter to accept the default location or type in a new address. AutoCAD then launches the Web browser, and your browser then goes to the specified location (URL).

INSIDER TIP

AutoCAD won't launch a new instance of your browser if the browser is already running. Your browser will go to the URL specified by AutoCAD's INETLOCATION system variable. You can use your browser's Back button to return to the location that was active prior to using the BROWSER command.

Viewing Design Data on the Web

It is essential to have the capability to view design data, such as drawing files, on the Web if you are going to add the Internet to your arsenal of design tools. With the extensive incorporation of the WHIP! technology into the AutoCAD 2000 graphics pipeline, Autodesk furthers your ability to accomplish this key task. AutoCAD 2000 incorporates built-in visual access to remote sites on the Internet by means of an integrated Web browser. In addition, Autodesk offers browser plug-ins that support viewing of DWG (Autodesk View) and DWF (WHIP! Release 4) files.

URLs as First-Class Citizens

In order to make the Internet access truly transparent in AutoCAD 2000, most of the intrinsic commands that either read a file or write to one have been enhanced to accept Uniform Resource Locators (URLs). This allows the user to specify remote sites on the Internet as the source or the destination of the command. Doing so offers an enormous potential in collaborative design. In addition, this has been accomplished without the introduction of new paradigms—the familiar user-interface elements have been extended to integrate seamless access to the Internet. However, there have been other additions to the program interface in order to facilitate a more convenient and intuitive extension of the desktop.

In addition to conventional pathnames, AutoCAD 2000 accepts the following URLs to identify and access files:

- **HTTP/HTTPS.** URLs identifying resources on local or remote servers that respond to requests sent via Hypertext Transfer Protocol.

- **FTP.** URLs pointing to servers that speak the File Transfer Protocol.

- **FILE.** URLs identifying local/network resources.

The most striking attribute of AutoCAD's Internet access is the complete transparency in file access: A URL can be specified in the same File Open/Save dialog box that accepts conventional pathnames. This reduces the learning curve dramatically—a user can simply enter a URL to an existing resource and work directly with it. There are several tools to make simplify the job further, and we shall discuss them in turn.

Opening a DWG File Directly from the Internet

AutoCAD 2000 offers multiple ways to access drawings located on remote servers on the Internet. Designers on the Internet functionality in AutoCAD 2000 wanted to ensure that users did not have to launch a separate application, be it a Web browser or a command-line utility, in order to access files located on remote Internet hosts.

Using the Select File Dialog Box

If you know the complete URL to the file you want to open, there's nothing faster and easier than using the familiar Select File dialog box, as shown in Figure 25.3.

Figure 25.3

The Internet-enabled Select File dialog box.

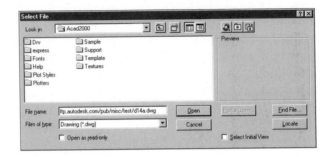

OPENING A DRAWING FROM THE INTERNET

1. Starting from within AutoCAD, choose the File pull-down menu, and select Open.

2. In the Select File dialog box that subsequently appears, enter **ftp.autodesk.com/ pub/misc/test/d14a.dwg** as the complete URL to the file in the File Name edit box. This specifies the protocol for the file transfer, as well as the file extension (see Figure 25.3).

3. Click the Open button on the dialog box, or press Enter.

4. The drawing will open. Leave this drawing open for the next exercise; saving is not required.

INSIDER TIP

If the URL you want to specify begins with the characters www or ftp, you may choose to omit the protocol specification; AutoCAD 2000 will assume HTTP protocol for the former and FTP for the latter.

Specifying a URL in the Text Window

AutoCAD 2000 also allows you to open files specified as URLs at the command line in the text window, in a manner similar to the Select File dialog box.

OPENING A DRAWING FROM THE INTERNET

1. At the command prompt, type **FILEDIA**.

2. Type in the value **0** to prevent the display of dialog boxes temporarily.

3. Type the command **Open**, press Enter, and specify the URL of the file when prompted for a file name (see Figure 25.4).

4. Press Enter. The file will be downloaded and opened in AutoCAD 2000.

5. Reset the FILEDIA variable to the value **1**.

6. Leave this drawing open for a following exercise; saving is not needed.

Figure 25.4

URLs are acceptable at the AutoCAD 2000 command line.

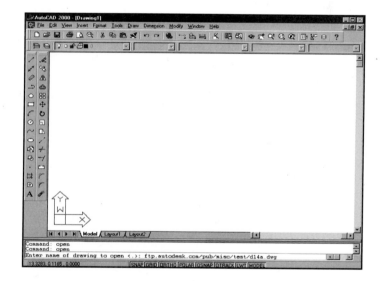

Using the Browse the Web Dialog Box

The Browse the Web dialog box is one of the most visually appealing enhancements in AutoCAD 2000, allowing direct and intuitive access to the Internet. Most users do not remember the URL of a file they wish to access. In situations like these, it is convenient to be able to navigate to a remote server and locate the desired resource interactively.

OPENING A DRAWING FROM A WEB SITE

1. Pull down the File menu and select Open.

2. Notice that the Select File dialog box now features three new buttons above the Preview area. Click the Search the Web button (the globe with magnify glass), which is the first of these three. This launches the Browse the Web dialog box (see Figure 25.5).

3. To navigate to a host on the Internet, specify a URL in the Look In edit box, and press Enter. If you don't have a specific Web site in mind, try the following:
   `ftp://ftp.autodesk.com/pub/misc/test`

4. When navigation to the remote host is complete, follow the links on the page as you would in your favorite Web browser to arrive at the page containing the link to the file you wish to open.

5. Click on the link identifying the desired file. Note that the complete URL of the selected file now appears in the File Name edit box at the bottom of the Browse the Web dialog box.

6. Click the Open button to open the drawing.

Figure 25.5

The Browse the Web dialog box in AutoCAD 2000 offers integrated visual access to sites on the Internet or on an intranet.

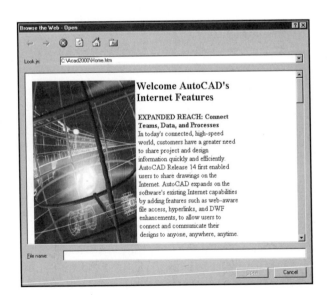

You can also use relative paths in the Browse the Web dialog box. For instance, after having navigated to an FTP site that contains a link to the file you wish to open, you can simply specify the name of that file in the File Name edit box and press Enter, or click the Open button (Figure 25.6). This information will be sufficient to enable AutoCAD 2000 to identify and download the file.

Figure 25.6

Using relative paths to remote files in the Browse the Web dialog box.

The MRU File List

If you have opened one or more drawings from the Internet, you may not need to specify the URL for a previously accessed file in a subsequent session of AutoCAD 2000. The *MRU (Most Recently Used)* list of files that appears in the File menu also captures URLs. This can be a real time-saver: if your URL appears in the MRU list, you can open the remote file without having to enter the URL at all!

OPENING A DRAWING FROM THE INTERNET

1. Continuing from within AutoCAD, select the File pull-down menu.

2. In the MRU list at the bottom of the menu, locate the URL of the file you wish to open. URLs in the MRU list will usually appear abbreviated for aesthetic reasons. See Figure 25.7.

3. Click on the URL to open the corresponding drawing.

4. Leave AutoCAD open for the following exercise.

Figure 25.7

The MRU list in AutoCAD 2000 keeps track of URLs accessed earlier.

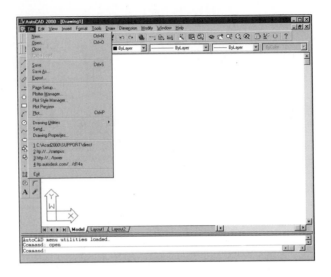

Saving a DWG to the Internet

The metaphor for saving files to remote locations on the Internet is no different from that for opening files—the same steps apply. AutoCAD 2000 attempts to present the Internet as a logical extension of your desktop that you can access transparently. Note, however, that you need the appropriate permissions on the destination host site to save files to it successfully.

SAVING A DRAWING TO A WEB SITE

1. From the File menu, select Save As.

2. Enter the complete destination URL to an Internet or intranet server that allows you to save files, including the filename as well as the extension.

3. Click the Save button, or press Enter.

NOTE

AutoCAD 2000 does not support the ability to save files to HTTP and HTTPS servers. To save a file to a remote host on the Internet, or to a local host on your intranet, you need to use the FTP or FILE protocol.

AutoCAD 2000 keeps track of files that were opened from the Internet. If you attempt to close a drawing that was opened from some remote site on the Internet, without saving the changes made to it, AutoCAD 2000 will offer to save the drawing back to the remote site, as shown in Figure 25.8.

Figure 25.8

AutoCAD 2000 can recognize files that were opened from the Internet, and prompts the user accordingly.

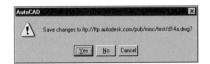

Canceling File Transfers

AutoCAD 2000 displays the progress for all inbound and outbound file transfers in a small dialog box that contains an animation and a progress meter with information about the estimated time remaining and the amount of data that has already been transferred. This dialog box also features a Cancel button that you can click to stop the file transfer (see Figure 25.9). This is useful in situations in which the file being transferred is too large, or the Internet connection is too slow. If the process is canceled while opening a drawing, the transfer will be aborted. If the process is canceled while saving a drawing, the transfer will cancel but leave you in the drawing.

Figure 25.9

File transfer progress is displayed simultaneously.

Favorites and Shortcuts

The design of the Internet-related features in AutoCAD 2000 was centered around the idea of enhancing user productivity by allowing seamless access to resources, regardless of their location. In this spirit, AutoCAD 2000 incorporates the concept of the Favorites folder, which can be used as a repository for links to frequently accessed files on a per-user basis. In other words, users can create links, or shortcuts, to files, folders, and URLs of their choosing. This can be done from within the Select File dialog box as well as the Browse the Web dialog box.

CREATING SHORTCUTS FOR FILES IN THE SELECT FILE DIALOG BOX

1. Pull down the File menu, and select Open.

2. Select one or more files, as shown in Figure 25.10.

3. From among the Internet buttons above the Preview area on the dialog box, click Add to Favorites at the right.

4. In the pop-up menu, choose Add Selected Items to Favorites. This creates the corresponding shortcuts in the Favorites folder.

5. Next, click the Look in Favorites button in the center. Notice that the dialog box displays the contents of your Favorites folder, with icons for the shortcuts you created in step 4. Figure 25.11 displays the Select File dialog box with the shortcuts in the Favorites folder. Note the corner arrow, which indicates that this is a shortcut to the real file location, not a copy of it.

6. Leave AutoCAD open for the following exercise.

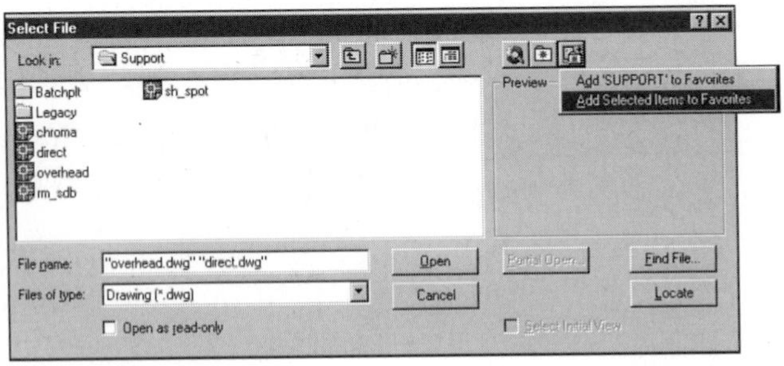

Figure 25.10

The Add to Favorites pop-up menu in the Select File dialog box.

Figure 25.11

The Favorites folder in the Select File dialog box.

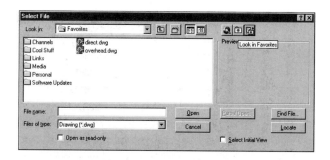

To create shortcuts to arbitrary URLs, follow the steps outlined below.

CREATING A URL SHORTCUT IN THE BROWSE THE WEB DIALOG BOX

1. From within AutoCAD, choose the File pull-down menu, and select Open.

2. Launch the Browse the Web dialog box by clicking on the Search the Web button.

3. Navigate to the Autodesk Home Page, `http://www.autodesk.com`, as shown in Figure 25.12.

4. Click on the Favorites button at the right end of the toolbar in the Browse the Web dialog box.

5. Select the Add To Favorites menu item.

6. In the dialog box that is subsequently displayed, accept the default name for the shortcut, or enter a name that you wish to assign to it.

7. Click on Save, or press Enter.

8. If you click the Favorites button again, you will see that it has been extended on the fly to include the shortcut you created in step 7 (see Figure 25.13). In a later session of AutoCAD 2000, you can simply select this shortcut in the Browse the Web dialog box and have it navigate immediately to the Autodesk Home Page.

9. You may now close the drawing and AutoCAD if desired.

Figure 25.12

Frequently accessed Internet sites can be added to the list of Favorites in the Browse the Web dialog box.

Figure 25.13

The Favorites pull-down menu in the Browse the Web dialog box.

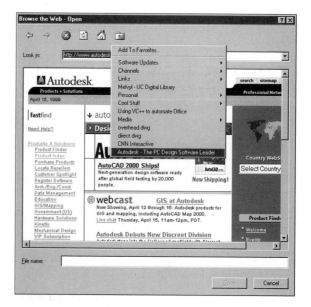

Understanding DWF Files

In essence, a *DWF file* is like an electronic plot: It facilitates the viewing of CAD drawings on the World Wide Web. DWF is a file format for viewing CAD data published to the Web through your Internet browser. DWF is not intended to be a

CAD file format used to create engineering documents, but to publish them. As previously explained, Autodesk (and other software companies) offers Web browser plug-ins that support viewing of DWG and DWF files. The DWFOUT command is superseded in AutoCAD 2000 by the PLOT command. The preconfigured ePlot printer drivers can be used to create DWFs with wide, patterned, and end-capped lines. ePlot is described in detail later in this chapter.

The Drawing Web Format was developed because the previous, widely varying, two-dimensional vector file standards did not address the needs of Internet-aware applications and because existing commercial formats are too closely tied to specific proprietary data structures to support the exchange of illustrations among systems.

Specifically, the Drawing Web Format was developed for the following purposes:

- To archive drawings in an openly accessible and application-independent format

- To transmit drawings over a variety of media, especially the Internet's World Wide Web

- To openly exchange drawings between DWF-generating applications and DWF-viewing applications

- To enable users of illustration applications to self-publish their work on the World Wide Web and to add functionality to their drawings by embedding hyperlinks (URLs)

What Is DWF?

DWF is intended for the efficient viewing of CAD drawing data on the Web (an electronic plot). DWF is not intended for the interchange of higher-level data between applications. DWF is a file format for the standardized description of two-dimensional, vector-based drawings and illustrations.

The primary features of DWF files are as follows:

- **Application independence.** Because DWF files incorporate a generalized two-dimensional vector format rather than using the data structure details of a specific application, DWF provides application independence.

- **Compatibility.** DWF files provide for compatibility by having established a common, extensible syntax for the exchange of two-dimensional graphical data between applications that generate drawings and viewing applications that read DWF files.

- **Simplicity.** Through the use of a flexible syntax that requires minimal information for simple cases while allowing a graceful escalation of information required for more complex drawing descriptions, DWF maintains simplicity.

- **Robustness.** Fully supported features of DWF include lines, polylines, polygons, polytriangles, markers, images, circles, arcs, wedges, ellipses, Bézier curves, text, visibility, Gouraud shading, texture mapping, 32-bit data precision, layer control, view control, clip regions, variable transparency, and international character sets.

- **Extensibility.** DWF delivers extensibility through the use of mechanisms built into the specification and through a set of rules for DWF file-reading programs that allow for unforeseen extensions.

- **Compact size.** Especially critical for Internet transmission, DWF includes a data compression method that minimizes duplication of geometric information.

- **Embedding mechanism.** DWF includes a mechanism for the attachment of any kind of data (with a link or an embed operation) to the format.

- **URL hyperlink support.** DWF supports the embedding of World Wide Web hyperlink URLs into the drawing data.

The preceding list summarized the main features of a DWF file. The primary benefits of using the DWF file type are described in the following section.

Benefits of DWF

You should note several benefits of using the DWF file format. The main advantages are summarized as follows:

- **Speed.** DWF allows rapid download and viewing.

- **Accuracy.** With 32-bit precision, drawing detail is maintained.

- **Security.** Proprietary drawing data can be kept safe.

- **Ease of Use.** Creating, publishing, and viewing DWF files is simple to do.

Speed

DWF files are vector-based, making them more efficient than bitmaps or other file formats for storing and displaying design information. In addition, DWF files are transmitted in compressed form, further reducing download time. As a result, DWF drawings are faster to download and faster to use. Panning and zooming are virtually instantaneous because there's no need to reload images or access the server.

Accuracy

AutoCAD 2000 supports creating DWF files with up to 32-bit precision, ensuring that your designs can maintain the detail you expect with AutoCAD. Within the DWF file, vector data is stored as lines, arcs, and circles, as opposed to the individual pixels found in bitmap file formats such as GIF and JPEG. Vector images are a more efficient and robust method for storing precise, detailed graphic information, such as technical illustrations and CAD drawings.

Security

DWF supports both secure and open data. For liability reasons, electronic transfer of engineering data has been fairly limited. DWF files don't expose all the drawing file data to the public. This means that you can showcase your work, yet maintain ownership of the intellectual property contained within the drawing file.

Ease of Use

Creating DWF files with AutoCAD 2000 is a simple matter, as shown later in the chapter. Publishing DWF files to the Web is quite easy as noted in the section titled "Publishing Your Drawings on the Web." Viewing DWF files with Autodesk's WHIP! browser tool is an intuitive and straightforward process.

Viewing DWG Files

Now that the DWF file format has been covered, it's time to discuss the role that DWG files have on the Web. First, it is important to reiterate that DWF does not supplant the DWG format. Remember that DWF is like an electronic plot file, containing only the information needed to convey the visual representation of the drawing. DWG files contain greater amounts of drawing data (object associations, xdata, styles, and so on) and in a higher order of precision. Both formats have their proper place on the Web.

The viewing and use of DWF files can be considered an important tool for the communication of drawing information on the Internet. DWG files are essential components of any corporate intranet. The bandwidth and performance constraints of the Internet do not necessarily apply to an intranet. Also, due to the inherently secure nature of an intranet, issues surrounding protection of the intellectual property contained in DWG files are minimized. In an intranet setting, the use of DWG files facilitates internal collaborative design work.

The following example illustrates the role each file format plays in the design process. During the initial phase of a project, the internal development team creates the basic product design by using AutoCAD 2000. An interdepartmental team reviews the initial design (DWG file) on the corporate intranet using their browsers and DWG viewing plug-ins. Comments are made via email or by directly editing the DWG file using AutoCAD. Once approved, ownership of the project is passed to the engineering department, which elects to subcontract various elements. The drawing file is converted to DWF, and a notice is placed on the company Web site soliciting bids for certain aspects of the project. Prospective bidders view the DWF file on the Web and submit their proposals accordingly.

Tools for Viewing DWG Files on the Web

Numerous tools are available for viewing DWG on the Internet. An enhanced version of the Autodesk View DwgX plug-in (Release 2.0) also supports redlining and other DWG viewing capabilities such as layer control. Version 2.0 of the DwgX plug-in requires that a client version of Autodesk View be installed on the host PC. The Autodesk View DwgX plug-in has an interface similar to that of WHIP!.

SoftSource's Vdraft plug-in adds support for viewing DXF in addition to DWG and DWF files.

WARNING

Be judicious about which DWG files you choose to publish on the Internet. Unlike DWF, the DWG file format is not "Web friendly." Features such as streaming and compression are the domain of DWF. Also please recognize that the average DWG file can be very large, resulting in lengthy load times for clients who access the Internet with a low-speed connection.

Viewing DWF Files with WHIP!

DWG has limitations that reduce its usefulness as an Internet-based design collaboration medium. To overcome this limitation, AutoCAD 2000 supports generation of DWF files. In this section, we will study WHIP!, Autodesk's DWF Web browser viewing tool. Again, remember that DWF does not replace DWG files.

The WHIP! Browser Tool

The WHIP! plug-in and ActiveX control are Autodesk's Internet tools for viewing DWF files on your Web browser. WHIP! Release 4 is written to the Win32 API specification, which means that the plug-in and control support the Windows 95 and Windows NT operating systems only. Support of other platforms has not been readily forthcoming from Autodesk. However, Autodesk does offer a developer's toolkit that enables independent developers to port the plug-in to other platforms.

How to Get the WHIP! Browser Tool

Autodesk makes WHIP! available for download at no charge from its Web site. You can obtain WHIP! Release 4 by pointing your browser to `http://www.autodesk.com/whip/`. The WHIP! home page contains download, installation, and user guide information.

About WHIP! Release 4

WHIP! Release 4 includes support for AutoCAD 2000 ePlots with an expanded set of opcodes. Multiple URLs and "friendly" URL names (for example, Autodesk Home Page, as opposed to `http://www.autodesk.com`) are also supported. Following are brief descriptions of some of the attractions WHIP! has to offer.

Named Views

Some DWG files have named views for use with AutoCAD. With AutoCAD 2000, the named views are passed along to the DWF file. Any named views that are present in the DWG file (when the DWF file is generated) are recorded in the DWF. For convenience, if the named view INITIAL is not already specified in the DWG, this named view is automatically placed in the DWF file. Named views of DWF files are available via a pop-up dialog box off the WHIP! right mouse button menu.

WHIP! incorporates support for named views into the right-click menu. Right-clicking a DWF file pops up the WHIP! menu. The Named Views menu option appears only when the loaded DWF file contains named views. Choosing Named Views from the right button menu displays a modeless dialog box that lists previously defined views to select from, as shown in Figure 25.14. This option appears only when the loaded DWF file contains named views. Double-clicking on the named view positions the browser to that view. You can also single-click a named view and then click OK to select that view and dismiss the dialog box. Alternatively, you can click Cancel to dismiss the dialog box.

Figure 25.14

The WHIP! Release 2 Named View selection box.

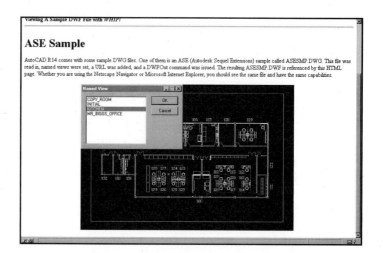

DWF View Coordinates

DWF file coordinates can be determined when viewing a DWF. Position the drawing to a desired view by panning and zooming. Issue the ABOUT WHIP! command from the right mouse button menu. One of the items listed, Current View Coordinates, is shown in Figure 25.15. These coordinates can be noted and used in HTML files.

Figure 25.15

*The WHIP! Release 2
About WHIP! dialog box
displays the DWF view
coordinates.*

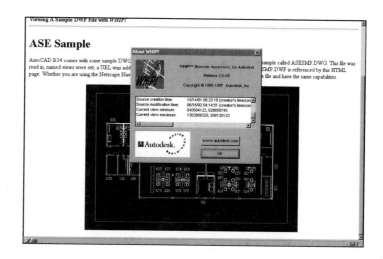

Pan and Zoom Features

By now you are familiar with the WHIP! display driver menu. When Fit to Window
is selected from inside an HTML document, the DWF file being viewed fills the entire
browser window. To return to normal viewing, select Back from either the WHIP!
menu or your browser's toolbar.

Highlighting URLs in DWF Files

When you right-click and toggle the Highlight URLs check item, WHIP! identifies all
the URLs in a drawing by highlighting a box over each URL region. This enables you
to see where URLs are before navigating. To avoid matching the color of the
background or geometry in the DWF file, the box is drawn in alternating light-gray,
dark-gray, and clear colors. Rendering in the clear color enables you to see the
geometry underneath the box. To remove the boxes, right-click again and select
Highlight URLs again to remove the check. The Highlight URLs menu item is
available when a DWF file contains at least one URL.

NOTE

When viewing a DWF file contained in an HTML document that is being displayed in a scrollable frame, only the URLs directly under the Highlight URLs right-click menu box flash. The problem only exists in frames that are scrollable. By setting Scrolling to No in the frame definition code, the problem disappears.

INSIDER **T**IP

A keyboard accelerator exists for WHIP! URL highlighting. Holding down the Shift key acts as a shortcut for highlighting URLs. Releasing the Shift key is a shortcut for de-highlighting.

Using SaveAs

If you right-click and select SaveAs, you can save the DWF file to your local hard drive. You may choose to save the DWF file in any one of three formats: DWF, DWG, or Windows Bitmap (BMP). If you select DWG, WHIP! copies the DWG file used to generate the DWF, provided that the DWG file is found and available. The SaveAs menu item becomes available after the streaming of the DWF file completes.

NOTE

When looking for a DWG file, WHIP! looks in the directory where the DWF file is stored. The DWF file and DWG file must all reside in the same directory for this feature to work. Should the file not exist in the same directory, an error message is generated that indicates that the DWG file is not available and the SaveAs fails.

Printing DWF Files from Your Browser

You can print a DWF file in two different ways: from the WHIP! menu and from the Browser menu. If you right-click over a window containing a DWF file and select Print, the currently visible view is sent to the printer using the standard system controls. When you use WHIP!'s Print menu item, only the DWF file prints. Using your browser's Print button results in the entire HTML file including the embedded DWF file to print. When printing using the browser menu item, you have the option to force the background color of the DWF file to white via the Print dialog box.

Publishing Your Drawings on the Web

Now that you have mastered viewing and accessing DWG or DWF files with AutoCAD 2000 and the Internet, the time has come for you to start creating some of these files yourself and publishing them on the Internet. So how do you do this in such a manner that protects your investment in the drawing file data? How can you create enough interest in your data that people come to your site? This section presents an informative discussion regarding the considerations and decisions involved in publishing CAD data on the Web.

Strategies for a Secure Web Site

Your site should be partitioned for different levels of access. For example, you should have one level assigned for general public access, another access level for prospective clients, and yet another for existing clients or subcontractors. You can configure your firewall software to limit general public access, while delivering greater levels of access to your customers and total access to your own employees. A comprehensive discussion of firewall software and security issues is provided by Netscape on its Web site.

DWG-DWF File Co-Location

Autodesk recognizes the need for you to be able to adequately protect the intellectual property contained in the DWG files of your creation. To facilitate this need, the DWF to DWG drag-and-drop functionality has a very simple yet sophisticated security mechanism. When a DWF file is created, the file name of the parent DWG is embedded into the DWF file header. Only the file name is embedded, and all path information is stripped out. When AutoCAD receives a notification of an Internet-based drop event, AutoCAD 2000 searches the directory location passed to it during the notification process for the parent DWG file. Should the DWG file be located in the same directory as the child DWF file, then AutoCAD proceeds with the appropriate `Open` or `Insert` function. Should the parent DWG file not be located in the same directory as the DWF, however, the operation will abort with a `file not found` error.

Hence, it is a simple matter for you to control which DWG files you make available for downloading by visitors to your Web site. This activity is controlled by either including or excluding the parent DWG file from the directory containing the child DWF. This system allows for maximum flexibility and controlled access. With your firewall software, you can place your most sensitive DWG files (and associated DWFs) in those directories with the highest degree of secured access.

Using Drag and Drop to Open or Insert DWG Files

A great productivity enhancement included with AutoCAD 2000 is the DWF drag-and-drop feature. Rather than having to execute the OPEN command and type in the Web address, AutoCAD 2000 enables you to drag the DWF and drop the parent DWG into your current AutoCAD session.

While viewing a DWF file, you can open or insert the original DWG file in AutoCAD by dragging the DWF image from your Web browser into AutoCAD.

For drag and drop to work, the DWG file used to create the DWF file must exist in the same directory as the DWF file at the time you drag and drop.

To open a DWG in AutoCAD using drag and drop, follow these steps:

1. Press and hold the Ctrl and Shift keys simultaneously.

2. Click on the DWF image and drag it into AutoCAD.

3. Release the mouse button and then release the Ctrl and Shift keys.

To insert a DWG into a current AutoCAD drawing session using drag and drop, do the following:

1. Press and hold down the Ctrl key.

2. Click on the DWF image and drag it into AutoCAD.

3. Release the mouse button and then release the Ctrl key.

Hyperlinks

Hyperlinking is part of the ActiveX specification that promotes a document-centric approach to consolidating information recorded using disparate applications. ActiveX hyperlinking specifies a model of interaction among programs and documents that conform to the hyperlink specifications. The underlying idea behind this paradigm is remarkably simple, and leverages the point-and-click style of navigation popularized by the Web.

Creating and Executing Hyperlinks

Hyperlink-aware applications allow users to embed references (hyperlinks) to documents created by other applications, creating a single, logically linked document. The user can navigate from one document or application to another without having to explicitly switch away from the work context. In addition to AutoCAD 2000, Microsoft Office applications and Microsoft Internet Explorer can participate in ActiveX hyperlinking. This implies that a user can attach hyperlinks to Microsoft Word and Microsoft Excel documents in an AutoCAD 2000 drawing, and save these references as part of that drawing. Executing a Microsoft Word hyperlink, for instance, will launch Word, position it exactly over the AutoCAD window, and open the document specified in the hyperlink. The user can navigate back to the original drawing by clicking on the Back button on the Word toolbar. In addition, arbitrary URLs can also be inserted as hyperlinks to entities or blocks. Following such a URL hyperlink will launch the default Web browser registered on the computer and display the specified page.

You can also specify a named location to jump to in the hyperlink destination. This could be a bookmark in a word processing application like Microsoft Word, or a named view in an AutoCAD 2000 drawing. Additionally, you can create absolute as well as relative hyperlinks in AutoCAD 2000 drawings. *Absolute* hyperlinks store the complete path to a file location, whereas *relative* hyperlinks store a partial path, relative to default directory or URL specified by the HYPERLINKBASE system variable.

CREATING AND ATTACHING A HYPERLINK

1. From within AutoCAD in a saved drawing, select one or more graphical objects in your drawing to which to attach the hyperlink.

2. Click on the Insert Hyperlink toolbar button (see Figure 25.16), or pull down the Insert menu and select Hyperlink.

3. In the edit box labeled Link to File or URL, enter the path or URL of the file that the hyperlink will identify. An example is shown in Figure 24.17. You can also use the Browse button to launch a dialog box to help you navigate to the hyperlink target.

4. Optionally, you can specify a named location in the file that the hyperlink will point to—this can be a named view in an AutoCAD drawing.

5. Enter a brief description of the hyperlink, if desired.

6. Click the OK button.

7. Leave AutoCAD open for the following exercise.

Figure 25.16

The Hyperlink icon in AutoCAD 2000.

Figure 25.17

Editing a hyperlink.

By default, AutoCAD 2000 provides visual feedback to the user by changing the cursor shape when the crosshairs are positioned over a graphical entity that has an attached hyperlink. In addition to this cursor feedback, a tooltip with the description of the hyperlink is also displayed, as shown in Figure 25.18.

Figure 25.18

AutoCAD 2000 drawing window displaying the hyperlink cursor and an associated tooltip.

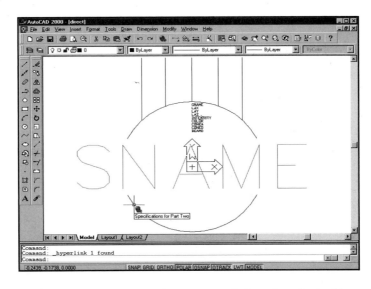

This default cursor feedback can be adjusted via the Hyperlink settings in the User Preferences tab of the Options dialog box (see Figure 25.19).

Figure 25.19

The User Preferences tab of the Options dialog box.

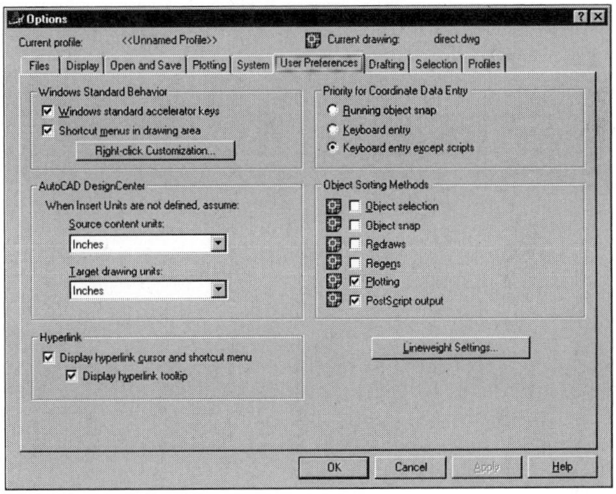

To execute a hyperlink associated with some entity in an AutoCAD 2000 drawing, follow the steps outlined below.

EXECUTING A HYPERLINK

1. From the previous exercise with the saved hyperlink, select a graphical entity with an attached hyperlink.

2. Right-click anywhere in the drawing area to display the context menu (see Figure 25.20).

3. Select Hyperlink, then select Open in the submenu. (The Open entry in the submenu is usually followed by the hyperlink description.)

4. Leave AutoCAD open for a following exercise.

Figure 25.20

The Hyperlink submenu in the right-click context menu.

The Web Toolbar

If an AutoCAD 2000 drawing is the destination of a hyperlink jump that originated in a document created in some other application, such as Microsoft Word, then you can just as easily navigate back to the Word document from the DWG file. The Web toolbar is a new addition to the Internet-related features in AutoCAD 2000 that allows you to follow hyperlinks along a chain of documents that include DWG files. See Figure 25.21.

Figure 25.21

The toolbar menu and the Web toolbar in AutoCAD 2000.

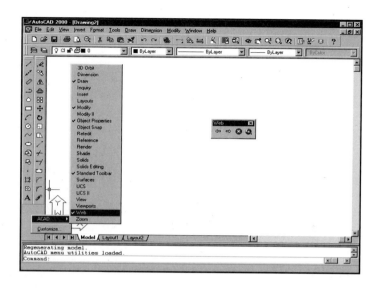

ePlot

AutoCAD 2000 formalizes the notion of an *electronic plot* by integrating the ability to create DWF files in the new plotting mechanism. Creating a DWF file is now no different from plotting a DWG. AutoCAD 2000 ships with two preconfigured ePlot plotter configuration (PC3) files. The DWF Classic.pc3 configuration creates DWF files that resemble the AutoCAD Release 14 DWFs, and the output drawing has a black background. The DWF ePlot.pc3 configuration file generates DWF with a white background and a paper boundary.

CREATING A DWF FILE

1. From within AutoCAD, choose the File pull-down menu, and select Plot.

2. In the Plot dialog box, click to activate the Plot Device tab.

3. Locate the Name drop-down box in the Plotter configuration section, and select an ePlot plotter from the list (see Figure 25.22).

4. Review the file name for the DWF ePlot in the File Name edit box and rename as desired.

5. In the Location field, enter a local or network folder, or a URL to which to plot the file.

6. Click OK. The DWF is now created and placed in the directory as directed.

7. Leave AutoCAD open for the following exercise.

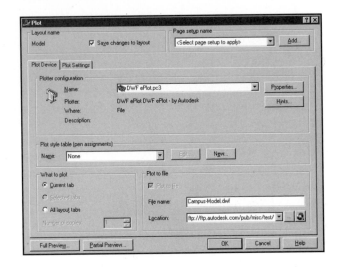

Figure 25.22

The Plot dialog box, with the Plot Device tab selected.

Creating an Effective CAD-Oriented Web Site

A great Web site is like a well-designed building: You always know where you are and where to go. The entrance into the Web site is the home page. It welcomes visitors, makes them want to stay, and guides them to what they seek. Done well, the home page guides visitors where the publisher wants them to go. This section covers how to embed CAD data into an HTML and delivers some insights as to how to build a Web site.

Creating Web Pages Containing CAD Data

Because DWF and DWG are not considered standard *MIME (Multipurpose Internet Mail Extension)* types, adding CAD data to an HTML file requires a bit of effort. This section outlines the structure and methodology of properly embedding DWF files. If you use the Autodesk View DwgX plug-in, the same structure also applies to embedding a DWG file.

Adding DWF Files to HTML Pages

After you have created a DWF file, you can add it to a Web page by adding special tags into the HTML document. There are two ways in which you can associate DWF files with HTML files: embedding and referencing. When *embedding* a DWF file into a HTML page, `<object>` and `<embed>` tags are used. *Referencing* is done through a traditional HREF tag.

NOTE

> To publish your Web pages to the Internet, you must have an Internet connection. If you already have an Internet connection, ask your Internet Service Provider or Webmaster how to put your files on the Internet server.

Object and Embed Tags

When embedding a DWF file into an HTML file the following two tags are used: `<object>` and `<tag>`. The `<object>` tag is used for Microsoft Internet Explorer. The `<embed>` tag is for Netscape Navigator. Netscape Navigator ignores the Microsoft Internet Explorer references, and vice versa. These tags are specific to their respective browsers, although the `<embed>` tag is nested within the `<object>` tag. In the sample HTML provided, some of the parts are specific to DWF—that is, *hardcoded*—whereas others are under your control.

As you will see in the exercise that follows, the parts of the `<object>` tag for Microsoft Internet Explorer include the following:

- **classid.** The `classid` value is specific to WHIP!. Do not change this value. The value specified is used to distinguish WHIP! from other controls for ActiveX.

- **codebase.** The URL specified in `codebase` is hardcoded to identify where users of Microsoft Internet Explorer get updates of the WHIP! ActiveX control. The current version of the control is 4.0-94, which is expressed as 4,0,42,94. Do not change this value except for intranet-only scenarios. In the case of intranet usage of Internet Explorer, the file whip.cab can be downloaded to the local site. For these situations only, the `codebase` portion of the `<object>` tag should be changed to reference the local copy rather than the whip.cab file on the Autodesk FTP site.

- **id.** The `id` portion enables you to give each DWF reference a unique ID that can be referenced by Java and JScript. This can be changed as desired. This is not to be confused with the `classid`.

- **width.** The horizontal size of the DWF file object is measured in pixels. You can modify the value of this field at your discretion.

- **height.** The vertical size of the DWF file object is measured in pixels (300). You can modify the value of this field at your discretion.

- **param name.** This parameter identifies the type of parameter you are specifying for the `<object>` tag.

- **Filename.** This parameter is required. You must specify the DWF filename in the value portion.

- **View.** This parameter is optional. The value portion is where you specify an initial view (in logical coordinates) for your DWF file. The initial view is specified by four values: left, right, bottom, and top.

- **NamedView.** This is also an optional parameter. It specifies a valid named view for the DWF file in the value portion.

- **UserInterface.** The UserInterface parameter is optional. The value portion is where you specify whether the WHIP! right-click menu and cursor are on or off.

The parts of the <embed> tag for Netscape Navigator include the following:

- **name.** This optional value gives each DWF reference a unique name that can be referenced by Java and JavaScript. Unlike the name="Filename" item on the Microsoft Internet Explorer <object> tag, this value can be changed as desired.

- **src.** This required value is used to specify the actual name of the DWF file being embedded.

- **pluginspage.** This parameter specifies a URL where users who do not have the WHIP! plug-in can go to download the plug-in. Do not change this value except for intranet-only scenarios.

- **width.** The horizontal size of the DWF file object is measured in pixels. You can modify the value of this field at your discretion.

- **height.** The vertical size of the DWF file object is measured in pixels. You can modify the value of this field at your discretion.

- **view.** This portion is optional and specifies an initial view (in logical coordinates) for your DWF file. The initial view is specified by four values: left, right, bottom, and top.

- **namedview.** namedview is also an optional field. It is used to specify an initial view for your DWF file.

NOTE

> The initial view is specified by using the name of the named view. If the specified named view has not been defined in the DWF file, the option is ignored. Either a namedview or a view (not both) may be used to specify an initial view. The specified initial view overrides the initial view that is stored inside the DWF file. The parameters are case-insensitive.

The following exercise explains how to embed a DWF file into an HTML document by adding special tags using an ASCII text editor. In this exercise, you will be using an HTML template to simplify the process for adding a DWF to an HTML page. The exercise will show you how to use this template for DWF embedding.

EMBEDDING A DWF FILE INTO AN HTML DOCUMENT

1. Open the file DWFTAGS.htm from the CD accompanying this book, or start your text editor and create a DWF HTML template by copying the following code as it appears. The template uses dummy names and values as placeholders. In this exercise, you will replace the placeholder text with actual file names and values.

NOTE

> You should save the DWF HTML template code into a separate file (I named my template dwftags.htm) before proceeding to step 2. This file is also on the CD.

```
<object
 id="dwfname"
 classid="clsid:B2BE75F3-9197-11CF-ABF4-08000996E931"
codebase="ftp://ftp.autodesk.com/pub/whip/english/
➥whip.cab#version=4,0,42,94"
 width=600
 height=400>
<param name="Filename"  value="dwfname.dwf">
<param name="View"      value="10000+30000+20000+40000">
<param name="NamedView" value="viewname">
<param name="UserInterface" value="on">
<embed name="dwfname"    src="dwfname.dwf"
 pluginspage="http://www.autodesk.com/whip.htm"
 width=600
 height=400
 view="10000+30000+20000+40000"
 namedview="viewname"
 userinterface="on">
</object>
```

2. In your text editor, open the sample HTML document filter.htm, provided with this book's CD-ROM.

3. Insert the DWF HTML template (created in step 1) into the HTML document at the point ① specified in Figure 25.23.

Figure 25.23

① *shows where the DWF file will appear in the document.*

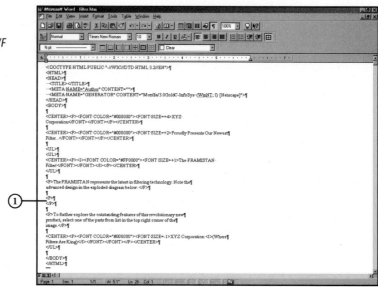

This is the location following the page description title that you want the DWF file to appear in the document.

4. Modify the merged text as follows:

NOTE

This step shows you how easy it is to change the DWF file reference and image size using the HTML template.

- Change the width of the DWF object by replacing the width= value of **600** with a value of **400**. (Do this for both the <object> and <embed> tags.)

- Change the height of the DWF object by replacing the height= value of **400** with a value of **300**. (Do this for both the <object> and <embed> tags.)

- Globally replace dwfname with **filter**.

- Replace viewname with **initial**.

- Replace the value **10000** with **860000000**.

- Replace the value **30000** with **1270000000**.

- Replace the value **20000** with **530000000**.

- Replace the value **40000** with **800000000**.

5. Save the file in HTML format.

6. Load and view the file in your browser.

Your completed file should appear as shown in Figure 25.24.

Figure 25.24

The HTML page as it appears after successful completion of the exercise.

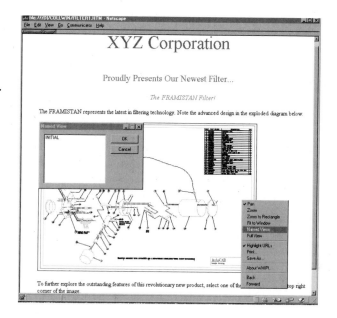

Referencing with HREF Tag

Referencing a file using the method of associating non-HTML files (for example DWF or JPG files) with an HTML file. Using an HREF tag causes the DWF file to appear as a link in the HTML page. When the link is selected, the DWF file occupies the entire window available to the HTML file. The other parts of the HTML file are not visible, so the DWF file does not appear to be "embedded" as part of the current HTML file.

The format used in an HREF tag is as follows:

```
<A HREF=http://myserver/myfile.dwf>myfile.dwf</A>
```

URL Format Information

The general format of a *Uniform Resource Locator (URL)* is as follows:

```
http://www.company.com/path/file.suffix#option=value
```

The suffix is typically html, htm, or dwf. For the purposes of DWF, the HREF tag option portion can be any of the following:

- target
- namedview
- view

Each of these options is explained in the following sections.

target Option

The target option indicates that the current link is to be loaded into a specified frame window. In a CAD Web site, you may want to embed DWF files into HTML pages using frames. Frames can separate active HTML pages containing DWF files from static pages such as a navigational bar. A *frame* is a window into a specific URL. The frame window name specified by a target must begin with an alpha-numeric character, for example, target=mywindow.

Working with frames can be tricky, but DWF files support certain "magic" window frame names to simplify programming a CAD-based HTML page. Magic window frame names are used by HTML targets inside of a frame to initiate specific behavior. Some magic window frame names have special properties. These magic window frame names begin with an underscore and are summarized in Table 25.1.

Table 25.1
DWF Magic Window Frame Name Options and Descriptions

Name	Description
target="_blank"	The link loads in a new blank window.
target="_self"	The link loads into the same window the link is in. This link is only useful for overriding a globally assigned target, which is different from the current window.

Name	Description
target="_parent"	The link loads in the immediate frameset parent of the current document. It defaults to "_self" if the document has no parent.
target="_top"	The link loads in a full window and exits the frame. This option is useful for leaving your site or exiting a deep frame nesting.

NOTE

> Any targeted window name beginning with an underscore (_) that is not one of the preceding options will be ignored.

namedview Option

The namedview option specifies a particular named view of a DWF file reference by using an existing named view already inside the DWF file. If a named view does not exist in the DWF file, the namedview option is ignored.

view Option

The view option specifies a particular view of a DWF file reference by using DWF file coordinates.

You can specify a #option=value item by itself—that is, without the preceding URL information—and have that option apply to the current instance. URLs of this type are always preceded by the # symbol.

NOTE

> Microsoft Internet Explorer does not support the view, namedview, and user interface HREF tag options.

Adding DWF Files as a MIME Type

To get your Internet server to recognize DWF files that WHIP! has invoked, you need to ask your Webmaster to add a new MIME type to your Internet server. The server software MIME environment needs to have the new data type `drawing/x-dwf` with the extension as `dwf` added. MIME types enable files to be opened by "helper" applications on Web browser clients, such as Microsoft Internet Explorer. Users who have not added the MIME type but try to view DWF files from their own servers experience the Torn icon. If you experience the Torn picture icon, you must also add the MIME type and then clear your browser cache to achieve correct results.

If you are using the Netscape FastTrack Server, follow these steps to add the new MIME type:

1. Search your drive(s) for the file mime.types.

2. Open each instance of the file with Notepad or another ASCII text editor.

3. Add the text **type=drawing/x-dwf exts=dwf** to the file (at the bottom of the file is okay).

4. Save the file and repeat for each instance of the mime.types file just to be safe.

5. Fully apply the changes by using your server software. Refer to your system administrator before proceeding to changing any files or rebooting of the server.

If you are using Microsoft's Internet Information Server (IIS), you can find instructions for adding MIME types at

```
http://support.microsoft.com/support/kb/articles/q142/5/58.asp
```

Currently, MIME types for Internet Information Server must be added manually to the Registry. MIME types can be edited graphically in IIS version 4.0 with the aid of the Microsoft Management Console (MMC). IIS installs the most common MIME types by default, but MIME types for new applications such as WHIP! are not among those added by default.

MIME entries can be added to the following registry location:

```
HKEY_LOCAL_MACHINE\SYSTEM\CurrentControlSet\Services\
InetInfo\Parameters\MimeMap
```

To add an entry, open the MimeMap key and choose Edit Value or Add Value. The MIME information needs to be placed in the Value Name box. You should set the data type for the entry to **REG_SZ** and leave the string field blank. The following is an example of a MIME entry:

```
drawing/x-dwf,dwf,,1:REG_SZ:
```

The unused field is represented by an extra comma between dwf and the letter 1 (lowercase L). The extra comma must be included for the MIME type to work correctly.

Elements of a CAD-Oriented Web Site

Some basic elements comprise a good CAD Web site. These elements, which are explained further in the following sections, are common to most compelling sites and include the following:

- Company background
- Portfolio
- Feedback

Company Information

Including background information about your company helps paint a picture of a successful firm with which to do business. Focus on presenting company information in a "lightweight" format—that is, don't get too heavy on the surface because you don't want to bore visitors to your site with dry corporate data. You can always place the detailed company information in secondary pages linked to the main page. Visitors who are interested in getting more data can "double-click down" to the more detailed pages.

Portfolio

Use your Web site to market your company by posting a portfolio of your work. Use the AutoCAD 2000 Internet tools and the exercises included in this chapter to create HTML pages containing DWF files representing your best work. Be sure to include customer testimonials, awards, press releases, published articles, and related marketing materials. You want visitors to download or print this type of prestigious information. Your site could attract audiences that you may never have anticipated, so blow your own horn and strut your stuff, but be sure to have compelling, valuable, CAD-based content to complement your marketing.

Feedback Mechanisms

Providing a method for eliciting feedback from visitors to your Web site is critical. This method can be as simple as including "mailto" options or as sophisticated as a registration site and chat room. You want people to ask questions about your services or products, so have the infrastructure in place to rapidly provide a brief recognition of any email sent. If you can budget the resources, a method for delivering answers in a timely fashion goes a long way toward building great customer relationships.

Use a registration form to elicit profile information of visitors to your site. You might consider offering some type of "freebie" to encourage registration. Building a profile of the visitors to your site provides invaluable insights into the needs of your customer base.

Marketing Your Work

Your Web site is your company's presence on the World Wide Web. There are major advantages to having your own site, if you know how to attract the right audience. A fundamental rule is to publish something of value for your audience. You want your site to compel prospective clients to visit and explore. Including information that is free, educational, and useful to your audience always works well. Having links to other CAD related sites of interest (such as `http://www.autodesk.com`) also increases the value of your site. In your site, provide promotional cues leading to areas where an exchange of value can take place, such as a sale of a product or service. An architectural firm might feature home designs, or a lighting manufacturer might include DWG data for insertion into drawings. For a design firm, having a CAD-oriented Web site opens countless possibilities for expanding your market.

You can take the following steps to ensure that your site can be found easily by those you want to attract:

- Register your site with all the popular search sites. Some sites will automate this process for you from one location on the Net.

- Print the URL of your site on your business cards, brochures, and advertisements just as you would your phone number and email address.

Another good reason to have a Web site is to provide your employees with remote access to company information, and through it, to the Internet for business reasons. Remote access is especially valuable for field personnel in construction, manufacturing, and sales.

Now that you've envisioned your Web site, how do you create it and where do you put it? Fortunately, you have many options to match your enthusiasm, need, and budget. The next section examines some of these options.

Building a Web Site

An entry-level Webmaster might consider using one of the online services offered by CompuServe or America Online. These vendors have simple facilities for creating and maintaining basic Web sites for a monthly fee. However, these vendors offer a very limited amount of space on their servers, which could make it difficult for you to build the type of CAD Web site you want.

What if you want to create a more sophisticated site than America Online or CompuServe provides, but don't want to spend a lot on a professional Web designer? Many excellent Web site authoring packages that automate HTML code generation are available. These modern Windows-based tools support drag-and-drop HTML page construction and are highly visual in nature. Despite many packages having automated page creation features, you still have to embed DWF files into your CAD-oriented HTML pages. Check out Netscape Communicator or Microsoft's FrontPage as basic examples of this functionality.

Perhaps this all sounds easy and wonderful, but you're too busy drafting to spend any time building a CAD-based Web site. What can you do? Perhaps you should consider hiring a professional Web design firm to create your site. If you can afford it, this strategy has numerous benefits. The cost can vary from several thousand to hundreds of thousands of dollars. An experienced Web site design firm can really help you showcase your designs and get your message across to your audience.

Self-Hosting Your Web Site Versus Using an ISP

The effort you invest in creating your own site can grow with your requirements and budget. You do not need to wait because the sophistication of your site can grow along with your needs. After you've created your site, where do you put it? The simplest method may be for you to start by renting a partition on a server with an Internet connection, and expand as Web presence requirement grows. You also have the option of setting up your own server or maintaining your home page with a service provider. Many Internet Service Providers offer this option, as do major online proprietary services. If you want your own server, turnkey systems are available from Sun Microsystems, DEC, and others that include the hardware and software you need. Keep in mind that you will still have to arrange for your server to be "plugged in" to the network, and the cost for this can vary widely depending on the speed of your connection. Visitors to your site generally will not tolerate slow response time—even if your content is very compelling.

As a Web publisher or intranet manager, you want to have your site linked to the Net via a T1 connection. A T1 connection can be either shared with others (*fractional* T1) or dedicated solely to your server. Your connection decision should be based on balancing the cost against the traffic you anticipate on your site. If you expect thousands of visitors, or *hits*, per day or during peak times, you may need a dedicated T1 or faster. If you can't afford a T1, you should consider hosting your site with a service provider that has a link to the Internet backbone. Satellite services are also available for Internet and intranet publishers.

Utilizing "Push" Technologies

So now that you have a site on the Web, how do you keep your clients, contractors, or other visitors apprised of changes to the drawing information displayed on your HTML pages or drawing files required for a specific project? Keeping subcontractors in sync or customers informed of changes to your Web site can be a difficult task. A simple solution to this situation can be handled through site registration and offering an email service notifying clients of any changes to the site. In addition, more sophisticated solutions involve utilizing software that implements Internet "push" technology. In essence, a *push* application sends updated information (such as revised DWG files) to subscribers that have set a filter requesting that they receive changes to these files.

For example, suppose you are a general contractor involved in coordinating numerous subcontractors on a large airport construction project. Changes to the base DWG file occur on a nearly daily basis, and you must get these updates out to the field each day. By using a push server (such as Marimba's Castanet Transmitter), you can "push" updated drawings on a daily (or hourly) basis to each subcontractor. This new Internet technology is becoming very commonplace. Both Netscape's Communicator NetCaster feature and the forthcoming Active Desktop of Microsoft's Internet Explorer 4.0 have embraced push functionality.

INSIDER TIP

Push technology can be a great asset to your Web site. It is believed that all industries that depend on staying in sync with distributed information must utilize this technology.

Using Other Web Tools

For those who are serious about using the Internet and AutoCAD, this section discusses the additional plug-ins and development tools that you can add to control Internet data in AutoCAD 2000 and at your Web site. The Web changes so rapidly that you need to be aware of those areas that undergo changes on a regular basis. Therefore, you can use this section as a guide and expect updates to have occurred since this book was written.

Java

Java is the programming language of the Web and is highly platform-independent and similar in structure to the C/C++ languages, but without the dependencies on pointers. You can integrate Java routines into your existing AutoCAD programming environment.

Using Java and JavaScript with DWF Files in HTML Pages

To Java-enable HTML pages containing DWF files, you have to add two tags—`<script>` and `<form>`—to the HTML file. As mentioned earlier in this chapter, the `<embed>` tag has a `name="drawingname"` reference parameter. This reference is very important for Java development because Java functions reference the `<embed>` tag's name parameter. These references are contained in the `<script>` portion of your HTML file.

If you want to set control buttons to manipulate the DWF file, you must use the `<form>` tag. Again, Java references the `<embed>` tag's `name=` parameter when calling a function to activate the navigational control button.

With the `<embed>` tag `name=` reference properly used, you can use the `<script>` and `<form>` tags to implement a great deal of interactivity to your Web pages. DWF files and WHIP! can be manipulated with Java. You can use Java to extract named views from DWF files. With Java it is also possible to embed links to the named views into an HTML page. With some elementary programming skill, you can build an interactive navigational front end to your CAD-based Web site.

Important Formats and Plug-Ins

No CAD-oriented Internet environment is complete without a number of plug-ins or controls. The following sections discuss some of the plug-ins that are useful when working with CAD data on the Web.

VRML2

VRML2, or *Virtual Reality Modeling Language Revision 2*, is a recent update to the Internet's three-dimensional graphics communications protocols. VRML is used to present a three-dimensional navigational view of a Web site. You can consider a VRML "room" the 3D evolutionary equivalent of a 2D HTML-based Web page. In a year or two, VRML may become the de facto interface standard for navigating the Internet.

Perhaps some analogies of basic behavior will help you understand the similarities between HTML and VRML a bit more. VRML expands the two-dimensional interface of HTML into three dimensions. Like HTML, VRML supports hypertext links (targets or anchors). Selecting a link embedded into an HTML page can send you to another Web site located elsewhere on the Internet. With VRML, selecting a 3D object (such as a door) can transport you to another VRML room located somewhere else on the Internet. Also like HTML, VRML supports *inlines* (objects embedded into the page that are not native to the page itself). With an HTML page, the DWF file does not have to reside in the same location as the text for the HTML page itself. The same paradigm exists for VRML; in essence, any object containing a hyperlink (for example, the door) can exist in a location (directory, server, Web site, and so on) separate from the VRML file.

INSIDER TIP

If you want to experiment with VRML2 browsing, I suggest obtaining a copy of CosmoPlayer from Silicon Graphics (`http://webspace.sgi.com/cosmoplayer/download.html`). CosmoPlayer is the premier VRML 2.0 browser tool, compliant with the VRML 2.0 specification, and supports interpolators, script nodes, sensors, and 3D sound. SGI & Netscape have entered into a partnership to integrate Live3D with CosmoPlayer. If you want to explore the 3D world of the Net, you should get CosmoPlayer.

PDF

If you are going to create an engineering document Web site, you may have a need to create portable document format (PDF) files. PDF encapsulates a business document into universal, platform-independent file format. Adobe Acrobat and Adobe PageMaker are PDF creation tools that enable you, according to Adobe marketing materials, "to create and share business documents on a cross-platform basis while they maintain their original look and feel."

NOTE

According to Adobe Systems, "Acrobat software is the fastest way to publish any document online." That very well may be, but putting the hype aside for a moment, I do find that viewing PDF files is useful and may be required at certain Web sites. The free Adobe Acrobat Reader enables you to view, navigate, and print PDF files across all major computing platforms.

You can download the Acrobat Reader from the Adobe Systems Web site at `http://www.adobe.com/prodindex/acrobat/readstep.html`. For more information on Acrobat, contact Adobe at `http://www.adobe.com/prodindex/acrobat/main.html`.

Marimba Castanet

Castanet automatically distributes and maintains software applications and content within a company or across the Internet. The Castanet Transmitter (server) and Castanet Tuner (client) work together to keep software and content always up-to-date. Create a "channel" and place it on a Castanet Transmitter. Castanet automatically distributes, installs, maintains, and updates the channel, all via the Internet. Castanet can support any type of channel: internal corporate applications, multimedia consumer channels, and more.

Hyperwire

The Kinetix/Discreet division of Autodesk has a product called Hyperwire that enables you to create dynamic, interactive, 3D content and harness the power of Java without writing a single line of code. This product is a boon for those who want to create cool interactive Web sites, but don't want to get bogged down with writing

Java code. Kinetix claims that "Hyperwire is a powerful 3D authoring tool that integrates seamlessly with 3D Studio MAX and other VRML applications." Hyperwire can be used to manipulate DWF files and WHIP!. Check out the AutoCAD Internet Publishing Kit for a great example of Hyperwire controlling WHIP! and displaying DWF files.

NOTE

> I consider Hyperwire another product in the realm of visual development tools (such as Symantec's Visual Cafe or Microsoft's Visual Basic) that have become so popular of late.

For more information, visit the Kinetix Web site at `http://www.ktx.com/hyperwire/hwhome.html-ssi`.

QuickTime

QuickTime is the multiplatform, industry-standard multimedia architecture used by software tool vendors and content creators to create and deliver synchronized graphics, sound, video, text, and music. QuickTime is an excellent choice for "author once, playback anywhere" multimedia. Numerous development tools exist for creating QuickTime files. To find out more about QuickTime and associated development tools, point your browser to `http://quicktime.apple.com`.

Shockwave

Shockwave is a family of multimedia authoring tools and players, designed to give you a wide range of interactive experiences on the Web. The Shockwave player is used by many Web authors for presenting interactive multimedia display and content. One drawback to Shockwave is that it is a proprietary Macromedia format supported only by their products (such as Director). Creating Shockwave files requires that you use a Macromedia application. For more information, check out `http://www.macromedia.com/shockwave/intro.html`.

Summary

In this chapter, you have learned how to use a Web-enabled AutoCAD 2000 to view, access, and publish CAD to the Web. You now know how to use the Internet utilities to open, insert, or save DWG files to the Internet. In addition, you have also learned about attaching URLs to objects in your DWG files and how to link one file to another. This chapter has also discussed the ins and outs of publishing CAD data on the Web with AutoCAD 2000.

Hopefully, your appetite for building a Web site has been whetted. Chapter 26, "Project Collaboration over the Internet," studies a live site and provides an in-depth analysis of what it takes to manage an effective CAD Web site. In addition, it describes Internet-oriented enhancements to xrefs in AutoCAD 2000, which provide truly remarkable opportunities for collaborative design.

Happy surfing!

26

PROJECT COLLABORATION OVER THE INTERNET

Project design is a collaborative process. From concept to final construction or manufacturing, a varying range of disciplines are involved in bringing an idea to reality. Each member of the design team has specific processes to follow and standards to apply. Effective management of the project design process requires timely communication and rapid distribution of design standards.

This chapter discusses how the World Wide Web benefits the design process by facilitating communication and delivering a collaborative environment. The chapter also covers some important Internet collaboration tools for the design and engineering space. Finally, this chapter examines a design firm that has embraced Internet technologies. You will study the business reasons that led this firm to become a leader in its field in the use of the Web. The firm's CAD Web site is examined here, with discussion of the problems and issues encountered, how they were overcome, and what the Web has meant for the firm's business. The discussion wraps up with a tour of the site itself. Specifically, this chapter covers the following topics:

- Coordination and the iterative design process

- Collaborative Internet technologies

- Internet-related enhancements to xrefs in AutoCAD 2000

- Case study background: Architekton

- Site implementation

- Going live online

- Taking the Architekton tour

Coordination and the Iterative Design Process

Constant communication between disparate (and possibly distant) parties such as consulting engineering firms, subcontractors, and suppliers is essential to a successful venture. In most cases, many firms, individuals, and sources are involved with the project. During the project design phase, a development team establishes the basic product design. A review and reiterative approval loop, perhaps involving external agencies, follows. Finally, ownership passes to engineering, which may contract with consulting engineering firms. At each step in the process design, changes will occur. Coordinating and communicating changes to the design is critical to keeping a project on schedule and costs under control.

Throughout the project life cycle, distribution of design and structural, construction, or manufacturing standards becomes an issue. By facilitating collaboration through rapid communication of design intent, you eliminate much of the reiteration involved. Coordinating engineering document flow and revision has always been a headache, even for companies with deep pockets. The Web, in conjunction with the proper graphical Internet client technologies, brings powerful tools for managing, viewing, accessing, and publishing CAD data for clients and agencies alike. Web servers provide central drawing management control and distribution mechanisms.

Real-Life Coordination Problems

Have you ever experienced a scenario similar to the following?

A general contractor contracts with your engineering firm to supply a set of drawings for a specific aspect of a building project. Numerous other portions of the project (including HVAC, electrical, structural, and lighting) are subcontracted to other consulting engineering firms.

You submit completed plans to the general contracting firm, invoice your client, and begin work on another project. Without your knowledge, the structural engineer alters the main load-bearing supports to meet new safety standards. After a few days, a call from the general contractor alerts you to the structural change. He is falling behind schedule and needs updated drawings immediately for your portion of the project. You put your current project on hold and address the issues arising from the structural changes made to the previous building project. A new cycle of engineering work begins while the deadline approaches for your existing project.

In a nearly perfect world, you would submit revised plans and return your focus to the "back-burnered" project. But this is real life, and Murphy's Law seems to always take precedence. Due to the structural modifications, the HVAC ducting has been rerouted, and you have to update your drawings again. By the time you resubmit the revised drawings, the number of hours you have spent on the project has nearly tripled. Not only that, but your current project is past deadline and the client has had to slip his schedule.

Do you know what this situation sounds like to me? Very expensive! Just try getting another job from the client who had to slip his schedule.

Using the Internet to Facilitate Coordination

How could such a problem be avoided? With better and more timely communication between the disparate parties, all the project delays could have been avoided. Even when you use the telephone, faxes, and email, the communications cycle is still imperfect. Real-time collaboration is the solution. The Internet (or a private intranet/extranet) with the visual benefits of the Web supports the collaborative design process in ways not addressed by any other technology.

With the Web, changes to CAD data can be communicated immediately on a global basis. The use of Web technologies as a foundation for design collaboration creates a "follow the sun" engineering environment. Properly implemented, a Web site devoted to a CAD project delivers worldwide access to relevant drawing data, immediately communicating design changes to all affected parties.

Staying on Top of Projects

Examine how the previous scenario plays out when you use Web technologies as a central point of communication. The following case is hypothetical, but based on real technologies and experiences.

Day 1, 8:30 AM. A week before the project deadline for engineering drawings, the general contractor and structural engineer simultaneously receive high-level information on their desktops about new structural safety regulations. Servers utilizing Push technologies such as Marimba Castanet, BackWeb, or the Point Cast Network deliver information in real time, based on the client's profile settings. The profile acts as a filter, enabling them to select the kind of information and discussion topics that interest them.

Day 1, 8:45 AM. Detailed data retrieved from the Web by using a search engine like Digital's Alta Vista, or Infoseek, indicates that the new earthquake safety regulations will affect the building project.

Day 1, 9:15 AM. The structural engineer fires off an email to a regulatory agency representative, asking about the new rules' impact on the current design.

Day 1, 10:00 AM. The engineer receives a confirmation by email that the safety standards apply to his project.

Day 1, 10:30 AM. Realizing that major structural design changes are necessary, the engineer points his Web browser to the project Web site, and fills out an online Engineering Change Order (ECO) request form.

Day 1, 10:45 AM. Having received a completed ECO request form, the general contractor's project management system automatically generates a notification of a pending ECO.

Day 1, 11:00 AM. The notice, indicating a potential change to the central drawing database, is sent via email or a Push server to involved or interested parties.

Day 1, 11:30 AM. A threaded or multiple party discussion of the design impact begins, using Web browser tools and groupware, such as IBM Lotus Notes or Novell GroupWise. Electronic whiteboard software, such as Netscape's CoolTalk and Autodesk View, is used in a collaborative redlining session. The whiteboard session enables the consulting engineers to visualize that potential structural changes will impact the HVAC design.

Day 1, 1:00 PM. The participating engineers agree to implement changes to the structural plans, and approve the ECO. The structural revisions are scheduled for delivery to the project Web server by the beginning of Day 2.

Day 1, 1:30 PM. Having current information, the consultants and contractors email their internal resources, shifting focus to their next scheduled project.

Day 2, 9:00 AM. The design revisions are uploaded to the project's central drawing database server, and are reviewed and approved by the project coordinator. New DWF files of the structural drawings are generated and posted, along with the associated DWG, to the Web server. Notification of the new postings, including the appropriate URLs, is emailed or pushed to the project participants.

Day 2, 10:00 AM. The consulting engineers download the revised drawings and continue their work. The project work stays on schedule and finishes on time.

In the preceding situation, the Web played a crucial role in the design process. Internet technologies were used to facilitate design team collaboration and keep the project on track. From a business perspective, the return on investment for using the World Wide Web as a CAD design collaboration tool is easily justified.

Collaborative Internet Technologies

The Web facilitates collaboration in ways never before possible. As a graphical interface to the Internet, the World Wide Web has spurred development of new tools designed to increase business communications and enable people separated by distance to work more closely together. This section discusses some important Internet-based tools and technologies that will help you expand your business into the virtual cyber realm.

Redlining Tools

Now, having viewed DWF and perhaps DWG files with your browser and plug-ins, you want to make some changes to the drawing file.

With redlining tools, you can mark up a drawing without changing the base file. Redlining data typically is saved to a specific layer or a separate file. The following section highlights a number of different redlining utilities and plug-ins you might want to investigate.

The Autodesk View DwgX Plug-In

Version 2.0 of the Autodesk View DwgX[M] plug-in component is free of charge, but requires that a runtime version of Autodesk View Release 2.0 (or Release 2.01) be installed on the computer. Autodesk View DwgX[M] plug-in supports layer control, paper space views, and xrefs.

The combination of Autodesk View (the desktop application) and the Autodesk View DwgX plug-in creates a powerful redlining tandem. The Netscape plug-in supports DWG and DXF, reading files into your browser for manipulation. Redlining is performed with Autodesk View, but the plug-in enables you to see the redlining information.

Redlining an AutoCAD DWG with Autodesk View 2.0 and the View plug-in combination aids in the collaborative design effort.

SoftSource Vdraft Internet Tools

SoftSource offers two Netscape plug-ins: one for viewing DWG and DXF files, and another that adds support for HTML links and *Simple Vector Format (SVF)* files, a proprietary format. The SoftSource plug-ins are free for noncommercial purposes, and cost $50 for commercial use. Both versions include navigational controls (zoom, pan, layer visibility) and vector graphics.

Whiteboarding

Internet-based whiteboard applications enable multiple sites or users to collaborate on projects in real time. Using one of these applications is just like using the whiteboard at work. "Markers" are used to call out areas of interest or write notes on the board. Most whiteboard applications support simultaneous telecommunications access and mark up of documents. You are able to talk on the phone with your colleagues while visually communicating with them. Whiteboard applications facilitate communication through engineering document collaboration, and "virtual" meetings.

To date, none of the whiteboard applications reads native engineering document formats such as DWG or DWF. At this point, the technology is limited to using screen captures of drawings, which, surprisingly, works quite well. Nevertheless, with the rapid changes occurring in Internet applications, this too will change. Before long, DWF or DWG redlining tools will probably be integrated into whiteboard applications. Following are some of the more popular applications to consider:

- Microsoft NetMeeting

- Netscape Communicator

- PictureTel GroupBoard/GroupShare

Microsoft NetMeeting

NetMeeting is an Internet whiteboard and conferencing tool that enables users to work together by sharing applications, exchanging information between shared applications through a shared clipboard, transferring files, collaborating on a shared whiteboard, and communicating with a text-based chat feature. NetMeeting supports Internet *telephony* (phone communications), application sharing, and data conferencing. The whiteboard program is a drawing program that enables the display and sharing of graphic information with other people during a conference session. The data-conferencing feature enables two or more users to work together and collaborate in real time over the Web, using application-sharing whiteboard and chat functionality. The Internet phone feature delivers point-to-point audio conferencing over the Web so that voice calls can be placed to associates around the world. With the application-sharing feature, your colleagues will be able to see the drawing information on your machine. With NetMeeting, you can "share" your local copy of AutoCAD 2000 with conference participants. The chat tool is a text-based medium for communicating with conference participants.

Netscape Communicator

The latest iteration of Netscape's Web browser—Communicator—includes Collabra group discussion software, and Netscape Conference real-time collaboration software. Also included in Netscape Communicator is support for *extranets*, which extend corporate intranets beyond the firewall. With Netscape Communicator, it is possible to communicate and share information over the Internet with partners, suppliers, and customers.

Netscape Conference brings tight integration of collaboration tools including whiteboard, chat, and file transfer into the Messenger (email) and Navigator (browser) components. With Conference, "virtual" conferencing sessions increase communication. As shown in Figure 26.1, participants can sketch or redline on a collaborative whiteboard, browse documents, and share data anywhere in the world. Also, as with other similar collaborative tools, meeting participants can converse by telephone, using the Internet instead of paying long distance connection charges.

Figure 26.1

Communicator's whiteboard includes sophisticated markup tools.

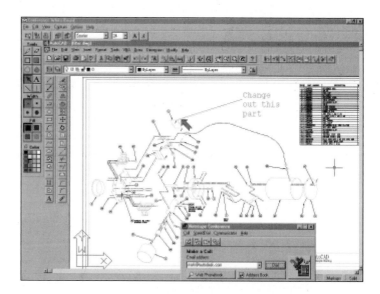

Netscape Collabra is a tool that facilitates the creation and management of threaded discussions. Like the AutoCAD Forum on CompuServe, a Collabra discussion forum is an electronic "room" where people can discuss key issues, solicit input, and communicate decisions. Collabra's discussion-group management features enable you to specify whether to ignore or watch specified topics, and to conduct advanced searches for information across forums.

PictureTel GroupBoard/GroupShare

GroupBoard supports multiple-site video conferencing, and an electronic whiteboard and flipchart. The whiteboard component of GroupBoard enables collaborative viewing, annotation, highlighting, and editing of files and presentations. More than just a simple whiteboard application for the Internet, the product supports the

TWAIN interface, allowing for scanned paper documents to be imported for collaborative mark-up and revision. Additional features include the capability to import many graphics and presentation formats, and then create and save multiple "pages" functions as an electronic flipchart.

GroupBoard brings easy-to-use information-exchange tools to the Internet-based collaborative experience. The tools contained in this product add a familiar element to virtual meetings. Colleagues scattered over great distances can interact more naturally. The result is greater collaboration, improved decision-making, and increased group productivity.

A superset of GroupBoard is the GroupShare product. GroupShare offers full application sharing, not just screen sharing. As with Microsoft's NetMeeting, only one PC needs to be running a particular application, such as AutoCAD 2000; another meeting participant can work with AutoCAD as if it were local. Users swap control of AutoCAD with the click of a mouse. A shared Clipboard enables participants to cut and paste images back and forth. Meeting participants can record notes in GroupShare's Message window. For this technology to work, each member of the conference must have a local copy of GroupBoard and GroupShare installed on his or her local machine.

Email

The life blood of all Internet collaboration and communication is electronic mail. Whether you use AOL or a more sophisticated Internet-based system, email has the distinct advantage of immediacy, compared to overnight package delivery or standard postal services. Typically more exact than telecommunications, the written word provides an opportunity to clearly articulate one's thoughts. Many industry analysts consider email the "killer" application of the Internet.

With today's improved email technologies, one can embed a multiplicity of data types in a document. Electronic mail has evolved from an ASCII format into a rich communications medium. With Netscape's email tool, it is possible to send colleagues HTML pages that contain DWF files. Embedding HTML in email is part of the Internet technological evolution.

Internet Xrefs

One of the most useful feature enhancements in AutoCAD 2000 is the ability to attach URLs as external references (xrefs) in a drawing. Although conceptually simple, this extension provides an extremely powerful mechanism to keep drawings accurate and up-to-date. Drawings that are updated frequently by contractors, for instance, can be stored on an FTP server on the Internet. Master drawings can then reference these drawings externally by specifying URLs to the FTP site. As with other Internet features, the familiar user interface to attach a conventional xref has been extended to accept URLs, as shown in Figure 26.2.

Figure 26.2

The Internet-enabled Select Reference File dialog box.

After a URL is specified as an xref, the corresponding file is downloaded from the remote server and displayed in the Path field of the External Reference dialog box (see Figure 26.3).

Figure 26.3

The External Reference dialog box displays URLs for remote xrefs.

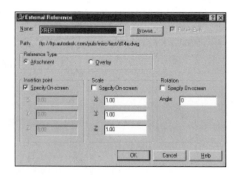

There really is no difference in user experience with Internet xrefs—they present the same paradigm as local xrefs. When the Xref manager is invoked (see Figure 26.4), it displays the URL corresponding to the Internet xref as well as the temporary file to which the xref was downloaded. Note that the actual URL is saved as the xref in the master drawing. When the master drawing is opened in a subsequent session, for instance, the xref is resolved dynamically at that instant, and the latest version of the remote xref is downloaded. This automatically keeps the master drawing up-to-date with the most recent versions of all Internet xrefs.

Figure 26.4

The Xref Manager dialog box displays the URL as well as the location of its temporary local copy.

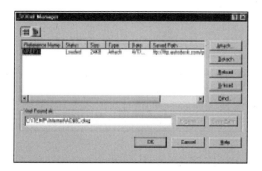

Note

Obviously, using this feature in AutoCAD 2000 is best done when a high throughput Internet link is available on both the client and server systems. Downloading a 1MB file can produce unacceptable performance on anything less than partial T1 connection.

Case Study Background: Architekton

Among design firms that have adopted Internet technologies for enhancing collaboration, one company stands out: Architekton. This company has fully embraced the Web, deriving immense business benefits from the Internet. What follows in this section is a case study of Architekton—how Architekton came to use the Web, the benefits it has brought the company's clients, how it has helped the company's business grow, and the tools Architekton has used. Whether you are very interested in using the Web or already have set up a corporate site on the Internet, this in-depth study should provide information that helps you to better understand how you can increase design project collaboration by using the Internet.

Company Information

Founded by four architects in 1989, Architekton's practice has expanded in a relatively short time. It is rare for a design firm to rapidly build a portfolio of successful endeavors, especially by tackling a wide variety of projects ranging from civic and public works to fuel-delivery facilities. How did Architekton accomplish this feat? By implementing cutting-edge technologies to address business needs, cultivating a reputation for superior service, and delivering high-quality designs for projects that require highly integrated, technical systems.

Company Philosophy

Architekton views design and service as inextricable components of each project. From Architekton's viewpoint, the marketplace demands both speed and personalized attention. One aspect of the firm's personality is its willingness to go beyond the boundaries of architectural practice. Diversity is the foundation of the Architekton philosophy. To quote the Architekton home page, that philosophy is "to engage all areas of architectural production to respond to clients' needs, and provide superior service by maintaining a leading role in the integration of technology and practice."

Architekton's organizational structure enables lateral, rather than top-down, project management. Many individuals in the firm become involved as they are consulted for their areas of expertise. Architekton believes that this management style is effective, and has repeatedly proven its value in numerous projects. It is rare to find such an organizational structure in an architectural office; yet, this environment has been instrumental in meeting the needs of multidisciplinary projects.

Technical expertise is a key element of the company's success; there are no technophobes at Architekton. The company is among the most technically advanced practices in the West. Use of CAD and Internet technology facilitates collaboration at every stage of the design process. Advanced technologies such as 3D modeling are used to accelerate the design process and to enhance communication.

Basic Business Case

Architekton, because it views the Internet as a revolutionary way to communicate with clients, has developed interactive tools with which consultants and clients can share information.

Why did an architectural design firm get into the business of using Internet technology? By offering World Wide Web-based Internet solutions to their clients, Architekton improved its own workflow processes. Architekton developed a method for communicating current engineering standards for their client base. By building interactive Web sites for their clients, the firm was able to simplify distribution of standards and changes. These standards are delivered to any consultant with a connection to the Internet in any geographic region.

Architekton principal Joseph Salvatore, AIA, is a chief proponent of Internet use for their clients. "One of our clients has a major presence in the Southwest with numerous convenience stores and gas stations," said Mr. Salvatore. Architekton had been working with this client for some time, developing prototype drawings, prototype buildings, working with existing building types, and placing them on specific sites.

Before becoming a client, this company came to Architekton seeking a solution to a problem distributing documents to consulting engineers throughout the West. According to Mr. Salvatore, "The problem they were having is that the consultants they use were not always using the most current engineering documents. Consultant A would have documents dated one day, while consultant B would have different documents from the previous day."

In this case, drawings were always changing because of new equipment, new technology, or new materials. With a large number of consultants spread throughout the country, keeping up with changes is extremely difficult. Prior to acceptance of the Internet as a business solution, engineering document distribution was tedious and inaccurate. The typical distribution scenario consisted of FedEx packages, bulletin boards, sending floppy disks through the mail, and telephone follow-up.

Giving an example of the severe nature of the problem their clients faced, Mr. Salvatore states, "It's been to the point where our client's engineers go out to their site and they're looking at the buildings. Their superiors come out and look at the site and say, 'What happened to the changes we made? Why weren't these incorporated?' That creates a lot of problems for our clients."

Before the engineering industry became automated through the use of computers, project schedules were significantly longer. Such protracted schedules were the norm due to limited communications technologies. It took a greater period of time for engineering data to circulate to members of the design team.

Automation and modern communications technologies compress the design cycle. Adopters of technological innovations benefit from advances in automation by having the ability to rapidly respond to changes in client criteria.

Building the Support Infrastructure

Laying the infrastructural groundwork for a Web site is not a simple task. Researching the various Internet products and platforms alone can consume vast quantities of time. Adding to this effort is the continuously changing Internet product landscape. Every few months great upheavals take place in Web technology. It seems that advances in feature sets or technologies are so rapid that we can never keep up.

The facilities Architekton uses for its Internet Media services are based on an exhaustive research effort. The firm evaluated both UNIX and Windows NT as networking platforms, ultimately deciding on Windows NT. Scott Harden, Architekton's Director of Internet Media Solutions at the time of implementation, states, "The decision to use NT was based on the direction the industry appears to be performing future development on." In many respects, the choice of NT over UNIX was a difficult one. UNIX, a tested and proven operating environment for Internet server technology, offers strong reliability. The deciding factor for Architekton's selection of NT was simplified networking. "However, NT offered a simplified networking solution to my limited knowledge in networking," said Mr. Harden.

Windows NT was the platform of choice for sites that were integrating back-end databases to front-end Web sites. "With the amount of information we were trying to distribute, the utilization of databases is only a short time away," Mr. Harden concluded.

Implementation

This section examines processes and decision points Architekton went through before attaining a satisfactory implementation. First, you will study the machinations Architekton went through as it built its own internal site. Next, you will look at the process Architekton used to go online. Finally, the section explains what Architekton did after the system was up, what changes the firm made, and why.

Site Planning

Architekton's process for Web-enabling (setting up a Web site) an established client entails a series of steps before the site gets published on the Internet. According to Mr. Harden, the first and most important step is much like architecture, designing how the information that the site will offer will be presented to the visitor.

Scott Harden explains the firm's first attempt at using the Internet for document distribution: "My process began as solving a document distribution problem between ourselves and our client. The original solution was to utilize the FTP (file transfer protocol) space allocated to us by our local ISP (Internet service provider) as a virtual file directory between offices. This solution, however, was marginal due to the fact that additional communication was essential (via phone or email) to ascertain the exact files required and at what time they would be placed on the FTP site."

The initial use of FTP and a hosted environment actually created another layer of complexity in the current problem. Staying synchronous with the client proved more difficult than relying on existing methods of document acquisition and distribution. Architekton then considered expanding its FTP-based Internet solution to the Web. "In search of a more efficient and autonomous solution," Mr. Harden states, "I explored the use of the Web as a medium for distributing project documentation between ourselves and clients. The Web offered us a method by which we could not only give access to the files available on the FTP site, but also offer visual previews of the information prior to download."

Content Creation

The site framework was developed next. "This is the interface through which the users will interact with the site," Mr. Harden explains. After the interface is completed, the process of uploading the working content into the framework takes place. With Architecture/Engineering-related sites, the information being incorporated into the site is usually drawings, specifications, and equipment information. "The amount of effort involved in this step is relative to the amount of information that is to be contained on the site," according to Mr. Harden.

With Architekton's Internet-based business model, one person or one source controls the documents that are uploaded to the project Web site. All the building types and drawings are uploaded by Architekton to the hosted site. Architekton is responsible for making all the drawing corrections as they occur, and for updating the site. With a project-oriented Web site, consultants all over the country immediately have access to the latest and most current drawings, eliminating the mistakes that can occur when consultants and drawings are out of synch.

Publishing

As Architekton developed their first client site, they published the following four main sections:

- Construction Drawings
- Construction Specifications
- Equipment Documentation
- Contact List

Each section was created with links to the actual files as well as previews of the data. "With the limitations of the Web (images/file size), we were restricted to low-quality images representing the actual drawing sheets," said Mr. Harden. The use of raster images to preview the contents of engineering drawings has a number of serious drawbacks. To be useful, the raster (GIF or JPG) imagery would have to be fairly large. The use of large images increases the size of the HTML page, which results in painfully slow load times. No wonder they call it the 'World Wide Wait'!' Also, the visual fidelity of the drawing is seriously compromised with a bitmapped (raster) image.

Autodesk has addressed the market need for a compact, yet accurate, method of publishing CAD data to the Web by developing the Drawing Web Format (DWF) file specification. These files are best created in AutoCAD 2000 by using the new Plot device mechanism ePlot. DWF files can then be embedded in HTML pages and viewed with the WHIP! browser tool. WHIP! is based on the same technology used to accelerate AutoCAD 2000 display operations. "When Autodesk offered the beta WHIP! plug-in, I tested its value in displaying drawings, and it eventually became an integral part of the site," claims Scott Harden. "The dynamic ability to preview drawings solved the last major hurdle in creating an efficient method to review and distribute construction data between consultants and clients," he adds.

With the completion of the first phase of the project, Architekton's client was amazed at how simple the process of distributing engineering information had become. During the implementation, Architekton had also been marketing the Web site to some of their corporate clients. Based on favorable responses from other customers, Architekton decided to offer Internet Media as a service.

Going Live Online

When a site has been fully developed internally and tested off the Web, it is ready to be published online. Architekton offers both site hosting and site development services. One of the services Architekton continues to offer is an ongoing mainte- nance contract for any modifications or upgrades.

Site Host Issues

The question faced by every company wanting to establish a presence on the Web is whether to build and maintain a site of its own, or outsource it. Many models will work—the problem is choosing the right one. You can start out with an ISP-hosted page, build it into a site, and then move it internally as your confidence and expertise increase. Perhaps your company is big enough to already have a site on the Web, but you want to add CAD collaboration functionality to it. Other firms have started out by self-hosting a Web site, and then, recognizing that their own value lies in providing content, gradually turn it over to a third party for maintenance. Or you might find that using a service from an outside vendor provides greater returns on your investment.

The value of a service such as that of Architekton lies in the firm's experience. Architekton offers not only experience in the building industry, but also technological experience in the Internet. "We have developed solutions that are based on solving problems for architects and engineers and have applied them to working relationships between ourselves and our clients," notes Scott Harden. The services offered by Architekton can help smaller companies succeed in a competitive environment that is based on rapidly changing technology. These systems are tools to help firms expand their business from a focus on regional markets to one of competing on global projects.

Client Educational Issues

One of the biggest issues that companies such as Architekton face is the client's lack of computer or Internet knowledge. The rapid changes in Internet technology pose additional barriers to client education. Training clients to use these new systems can be a formidable task. According to Mr. Harden, "Several firms that had minimal computer knowledge and resources had to be trained on the Internet and the Web." Be sure to budget adequately for training your CAD operators. Given the investment your firm makes when it embraces Internet technologies, maintaining operator productivity is essential to success.

In response to use of the Internet for design collaboration, Architekton has added another client service. Mr. Harden notes, "One of the services we have added, in addition to the Internet Media products, is Change Management Consulting. This way, we offer the ability for implementing the new communication system, and the qualified training to help clients fully utilize the potential."

Maintenance

Maintaining an active Web site presents new issues for you to address. Internet technology changes so rapidly that it is difficult to keep systems current. If you are an experienced Web surfer, you will notice that many sites regularly change their visual appearance and content. Consider dedicating some time each quarter to maintaining your site.

Staying Fresh

Keeping content fresh and compelling is essential if you want your Web site to draw new customers and encourage people to return. To keep a site from going stale, you must make a commitment to updating a site on an ongoing basis. A CAD-oriented Web site's focused approach makes it easier to refreshen than some other sites. Target the following areas for regular refreshing:

- **Change the Look and Feel.** Change the background, layout, and fonts to keep your Web pages looking new. Try to set aside some time every few months to complete this update. The beauty of HTML is that you don't need to change the underlying structure of the page to accomplish this task. A simple search-and-replace operation on the image files and font types embedded in the HTML content can bring about a whole new look. Consider changing the location of graphics and repositioning navigational aids. Even the most rudimentary HTML editing software can greatly simplify the task of moving images. Keep the site style consistent!

- **Add Information about New Projects or Services.** Don't wait for a regularly scheduled update to include information about a new client service or add to your Project Portfolio! Get information out to your clients as rapidly as possible. You may find that creating internal project documents in HTML form makes it easier to move them quickly to the Web.

- **Add New Links.** When you come across an interesting site that might have value for your clients, add a link from your site to that page. You no doubt can work out a reciprocal arrangement with the site to which you are linking.

Adopting and Integrating New Technologies

New design collaborative environments are becoming available for the Web daily. You need to develop a process for adding the most valuable of these tools to your site. If you have been through an update or upgrade of your AutoCAD system, you probably already have one in place! All you have to do is modify it appropriately to address the unique aspects of Web software. At a minimum, your process should include the following steps:

- **Research.** Many suppliers of Internet technologies are firms that do not have established reputations. In today's rapidly changing world, that shouldn't be a deterrent. With new companies springing up everywhere, spend some time studying the vendor's background and product offerings. The Web is a researcher's dream. Use it to gather applicable information about both the vendor and technology.

- **Evaluation.** Install the software or hardware locally, and put it through a rigorous testing cycle. Evaluate the tool for functionality, stability, and usability. Many of the new collaboration tools are released in beta form on the Web and might not be very stable. Be prepared for crashes and anomalous behavior. When a product is in full release, it should have gained the stability you expect of a production drafting tool. If not, move on to another supplier; there are many to choose from.

- **Integration.** Adding a new feature to your site requires careful integration; you must update affected pages and notify clients that it's available. Whether you are adding something simple, such as a registration form, or something with the complexity of push technology, the integration must minimize disruption of your current services. Remember to update all pages that will be affected. There is nothing worse than a site full of broken links or pages that don't function properly. Alert site visitors and clients to your new feature by updating your home page. Consider sending email notices to clients as well. Your implementation will go relatively smoothly if you carefully integrate the product into your existing site.

Taking the Architekton Tour

This section examines Architekton's use of Internet technologies in a real-life situation. A complete exercise follows, in which you navigate to the Architekton Web site, study the layout, browse portfolios and personnel resumes, view drawings, and engage in collaborative design.

NOTE

> By its very nature, the Web is dynamic, and content on the Internet is in a constant state of flux. The sites identified by URLs listed in the discussion that follows may have been updated by the time you read this monograph. For the most part, however, you will be able to navigate the sites by following the appropriate links.

Navigating the Architekton Site

Before you visit this Web site, ensure that you have all the tools necessary to effectively view the site. The Architekton site is optimized for Netscape Navigator or Microsoft Internet Explorer. If you don't have either browser, you should download one of them immediately. Navigator is available for download at `http://www.netscape.com`. You also need two plug-ins: Autodesk's WHIP! (`http://www.autodesk.com/whip`) and Adobe's Acrobat Reader, which is available from the Adobe Web site at `http://www.adobe.com`.

Type the URL for the Architekton Web site, `http://www.architekton.com`, in the address field of your browser, and press Enter. Add a bookmark to this site because you may return periodically to this page.

Depending on the speed of your connection, the page should load relatively quickly. This is an important point to consider. When a visitor first comes to your site, you want your home page to load quickly. Keeping the size of home pages small not only helps bring customers into the site, but also overcomes bandwidth limitations and connection speeds. Cool, animated GIFs and AVI movies are eye-catching additions to a Web site, but consume tremendous amounts of bandwidth.

Studying the Site Layout

The structure of Architekton's site provides insight into the effective presentation of CAD-related services and technologies to the architectural and engineering marketplace. The sequence of pages, links, and content flows logically. It is important to keep site navigation simple and structured. No single page overwhelms you with information, and links to related materials are presented at each level.

Navigational aids and supporting hyperlink text are always present to simplify moving about the site. As you can see in the images of Architekton's Web site in this chapter, it is structured in a straightforward fashion, which makes it simple to use. You never seem to find yourself so many pages deep that you become disoriented.

Home Page

Amazingly enough, Architekton doesn't present an information-laden home page. Rather, this site starts off in a very understated manner. The folks who put together this site figure that you came there on purpose, and didn't just "surf on in." The home page alerts you to any special plug-ins or tools necessary for visiting the site.

To continue to the contents page, select the version of the site you wish to peruse by clicking on the corresponding link on Architekton's Home Page (see Figure 26.5). The remainder of this discussion assumes that the reader selected the Version #1 link to explore the site.

Figure 26.5

Architekton home page.

Contents Page

The Contents page briefly informs you of Architekton's services and directs you to select an area of expertise to obtain additional information (see Figure 26.6). Topics you can select from include the firm's areas of expertise, a firm profile, events, and awards.

A vertical row of colored images is presented on the left side of the screen. Next to each image is a highlighted hyperlink text. As the cursor passes over each image, its shape changes to visually indicate the presence of a link. This page might take a while to load, even on a T1 line.

Figure 26.6

Architekton Web site
Contents page.

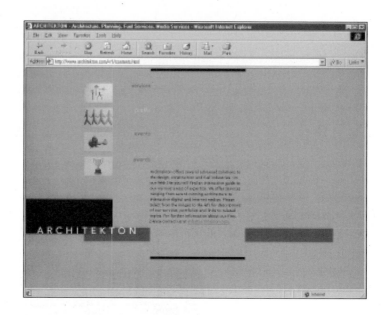

Browsing the Informational Material

Now that you understand the site layout, you will study the messages and informational content the site provides, starting with Architekton's profile information.
Select the firm profile image with a single click (see Figure 26.7).

Figure 26.7

Architekton Company
Profile page.

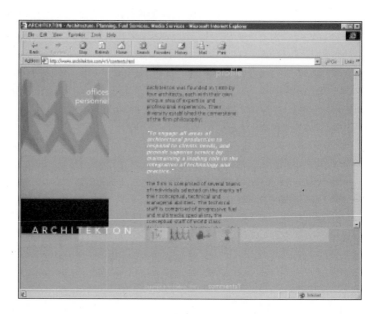

Firm Profile

The Profile page provides some data related to the company and its strengths. The content presented here is limited, at best. Hyperlinks are located at the left and at the bottom (as images) of each page. Next, click the Offices link (see Figure 26.8).

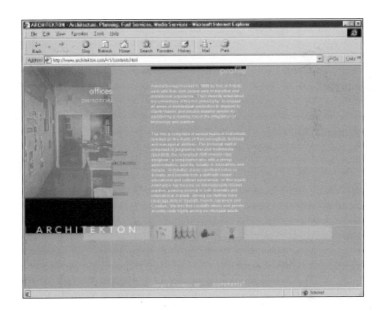

Take a look at what one of the links on the Offices page has to say. To select Architekton's main office, which is located in Tempe, Arizona, click on the Tempe link.

Here you find more detailed information about the client services that Architekton offers from its headquarters. To help you navigate, the service images are at the bottom of the page, with links to other office locations in the left quadrant.

The Personnel page, containing names of the company executives, is also accessible from the Profile page. You can easily send email to anybody listed on this page by clicking on the corresponding name, which will launch the default mail program on your computer.

All design and engineering firms should consider implementing a visual system for the personnel portfolio. Doing so shows dedication to the Internet as a serious business platform, and helps to build prestige while giving visitors a sense of the firm's stability.

Services (On the Main Contents Page)

After the Services page has loaded, it is almost disappointing (see Figure 26.9). There seems to be a dearth of information about the company's architectural strengths. Rather, the content seems more of a vision statement. Follow the Design link by clicking on it to arrive at the page shown in Figure 26.10.

Figure 26.9

Architekton Services page.

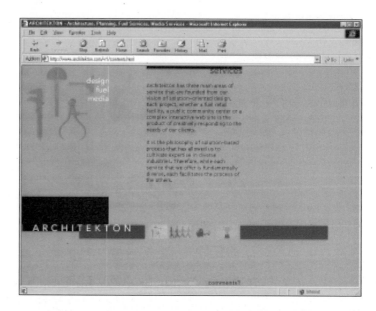

Figure 26.10

Architekton Design Services Page.

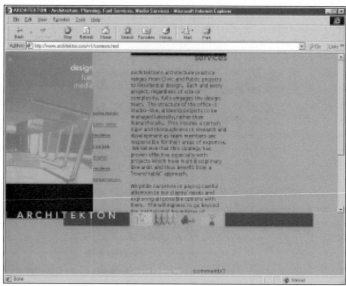

Several projects are displayed in a list on the left side of the page. Select the first link.

You see a definitive description of the project, the Tempe Police Substation. Note that many of the important structural details have been omitted (for security reasons, and to protect the intellectual property of the design firm). Remember that in public sites, you don't want to publish anything that compromises earnings capacity or contractual agreements. Architekton recognizes that the function of a portfolio section is to sell the firm, not to enlighten their competition.

Fuel Services

Next, you will investigate the Fuel Services area of Architekton's Web site. Select the link labeled Fuel (see Figure 26.11). As mentioned earlier, Architekton is a leading provider of architectural and client services to the petroleum industry. The Fuel Services page contains an in-depth discussion of their expertise in the areas of technical systems, rendering, and permitting.

Figure 26.11

Architekton Fuel Services page.

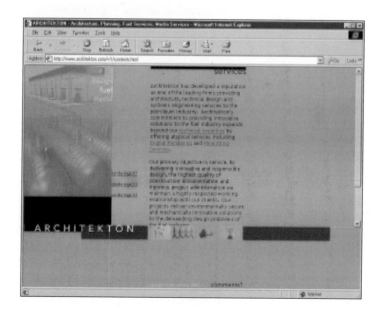

Media

The next stop on your site tour is the Internet Media page. To display the page, select the Media link (see Figure 26.12). This page contains detailed information about the firm's Web services, and numerous links. The wealth of information probably is due to the degree of experience Architekton has in this discipline. A small list of links to other interesting pages like Digital Video and Interactive CD-ROM can be found here.

Figure 26.12

Architekton Media Services page.

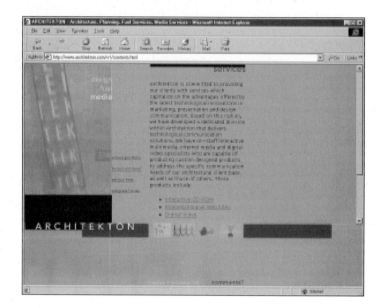

Viewing Drawing Data

Now that you have browsed through an external CAD-based Web site, it is time to thoroughly evaluate what an intranet-based CAD project Web site should look like. On the Media page, select the link cdrom portfolio. This takes you to the Architekton Office Brochure CD-ROM online. Examine the page and see how well-organized information can be not only visually appealing but also easy to absorb (see Figure 26.13).

Architekton uses this site to show prospective clients the type of high-quality Internet services they provide. As you tour this demonstration intranet, remember that Architekton generates revenue from their expertise in this area and can develop a site for your firm.

Figure 26.13

The CD-ROM Portfolio page.

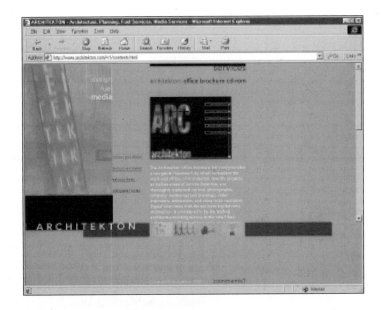

The design and navigation of this site is different from that of the other Architekton pages. The different look and feel serves to separate the technological demonstration area from the actual site content.

To move deeper into the demo site, from the home page (`http://www. architekton.com/internet/demo/home.html`), which is shown in Figure 26.14, select the services hotlink. The navigational system includes a vertical index frame to the left of the page, a horizontal frame with tabs across the top, and a central document window frame. The following indices are listed in the vertical navigation frame and covered in this section (see Figure 26.15):

■ Updates

■ Drawings

■ Specs

■ Equipment

■ Contacts

■ EDI

Figure 26.14

*Architekton Internet Demo
Start page.*

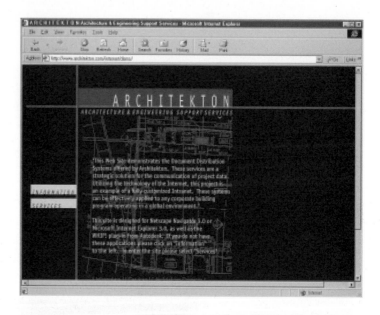

Figure 26.15

*Architekton Internet demo
Services page.*

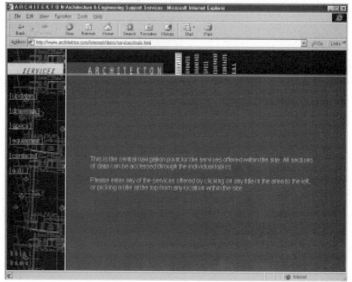

Updates

As noted earlier in this chapter, keeping track of the latest changes to current projects is always a difficult task. With a properly managed intranet, an update section can always supply the most current engineering documentation to those in the field. Architekton has chosen to make the update mechanism the most highly visible aspect of this intranet example. The Updates tab is the first navigational entry in the site. Select the Updates tab at the top of the screen to arrive at the page shown in Figure 26.16.

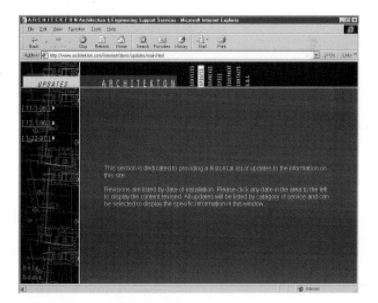

Figure 26.16

Internet demo Updates page.

The newly loaded page replaces the vertical categorical selections on the left frame with a date-oriented index. Select the first date entry (11-1-96); the vertical index frame exposes links to categories that contain updated documents (see Figure 26.17). To obtain additional information, select the drawings, specs, or equipment link.

Figure 26.17

A specific page in the Updates section.

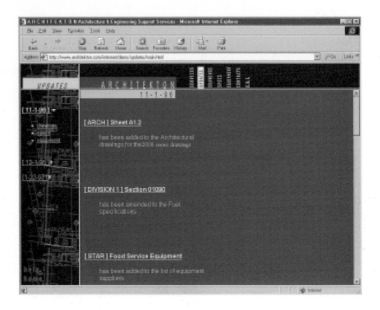

Drawings

For users of engineering documentation, one of the Internet's greatest benefits is that it facilitates creation of a repository for globally retrievable CAD data. With a centralized database of AutoCAD drawings, managing project drawings can be simplified. The embedding of DWF files derived from project .DWG files in HTML pages enables the user to view the drawing before opening it for editing.

Select the Drawings tab located at the top of the horizontal frame. The main HTML frame presents the visitor with sample information describing the nuances of previewing and accessing drawing data from the site. The vertical index frame reflects drawings of various building types, as you can see in Figure 26.18.

From a usability standpoint, this is an excellent system for navigating a company's large volume of architectural production drawings. This style might not work as well for mechanical assemblies or manufacturing drawings.

Figure 26.18

Figure 26.18

*Architekton Internet demo
Drawings page.*

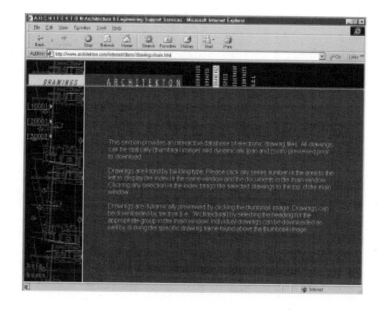

Specs

Construction specification is another aspect of engineering document distribution
that benefits from the Web. As noted earlier, concurrent dissemination of construction specifications was an arduous, tedious task until the World Wide Web became
CAD-enabled.

Click on the Specs tab, located in the top horizontal frame. This will take you to the
page shown in Figure 26.19. The index bar lists construction specification document
indexes for two service areas: fuel and building. A live site might have many different
entries here, depending on the business model. Click on the building link in the
vertical index frame to view the construction specifications for building projects.

By selecting the building link, you bring into the vertical frame an index that refers
to sections of the construction document displayed in the document window.
Clicking on the index reference causes the desired section of the construction
specification document to be displayed in the central frame. The specification text
can be scrolled with the vertical bar on the far right of the document window.

Figure 26.19

*Architekton Internet demo
Specs page.*

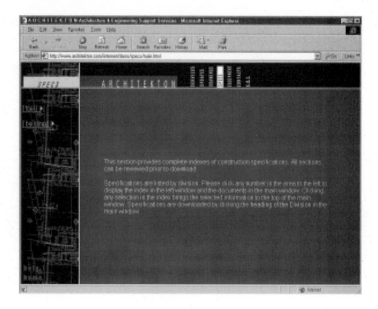

Whether on an intranet or an external Web site, links to document sections are common. Many long documents are difficult to navigate, however, without excessive use of the Back button. In the case of Architekton's sample CAD site, frames containing the link references simplify navigation. The process of building frame links is automated by most HTML software packages, including Communicator and Front Page. Use of the frame index technique is heartily recommended for posting complex or lengthy documents.

Equipment

For many design disciplines, tracking and managing equipment-related information is troublesome. Suppliers continually update their product lines, regularly introducing models and making others obsolete. New vendors also emerge, forcing changes to current documents and standards. As the Architekton sample site demonstrates, a complete CAD intranet should maintain current information about all equipment (and suppliers) used in their construction or engineering documents.

Select the Equipment tab from the horizontal top frame to display the site's equipment standards section. You will navigate to the page shown in Figure 26.20. Click on the building link, and then on the star link to invoke the Adobe Acrobat Reader plug-in. The Acrobat Reader enables you to view manufacturer-specific product information about the equipment used by the various building projects.

Figure 26.20

*Architekton Internet demo
Equipment page.*

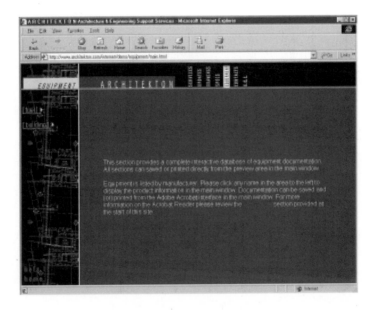

Figure 26.20

*Architekton Internet demo
Equipment page.*

Using Acrobat to view equipment documents is helpful because they contain both text and graphics. Other solutions (such as Hummingbird's Common Ground) exist, but the PDF format from Adobe is well established.

Contacts

A nice touch in the CAD intranet example developed by Architekton is a Contacts page. A current contact database, centrally available to all members with access to the intranet, is a great productivity tool. Maintaining contact information is always time consuming and often a redundant operation (because many individuals keep separate databases). Select the Contacts tab located in the upper horizontal frame to activate this page (see Figure 26.21).

The Contacts sample page index lists consultants and corporate contact options. Selecting the corporate contacts link reveals Architekton as a selection option. Click on Architekton to expose a list of contact information in the document window frame. The vertical index frame enables you to jump from contact to contact.

Figure 26.21

*Architekton Internet demo
Contacts page.*

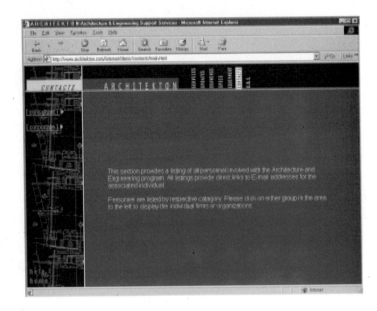

EDI

Production of quality construction drawings is what CAD is all about. As you have seen throughout this chapter, maintaining and distributing a set of standards for creating production drawings can be a difficult process. In concert with their clients and consultants, Architekton establishes a complete and exact set of standards for drawing data.

Select the EDI tab from the horizontal navigation frame. The vertical navigation frame displays a lengthy index of entries tied to the online EDI document (see Figure 26.22).

Scroll through the index frame, using the vertical bar located just to the right of the index links. Select the Sheet Order link. The main document jumps to the Sheet Order section, which displays information, related to this topic. You might want to pick other topics to further study this document.

Providing this degree of detail in an online format helps to ensure a high-quality drawing. As changes to the EDI standard occur, push technology makes updating the page and informing site users of those changes a simple matter.

Figure 26.22

*Architekton Internet demo
EDI page.*

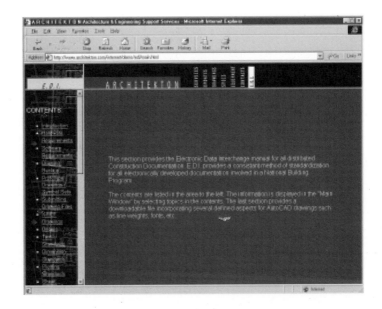

Summary

In this chapter, benefits of the Web for the design process were detailed. Hopefully, you have gained an understanding of how the Internet facilitates communication and delivers a collaborative environment. Although brief, this look at some important Internet collaboration tools for the design and engineering space should raise your interest. The ability to embed and resolve URL xrefs in AutoCAD 2000 drawings extends the concept of collaborative design by making it possible to refer to resources on the Internet.

The case study of Architekton showed how a design firm that has embraced Internet technologies experienced success and growth. The business reasons that led to their becoming a leader in the field through use of the Web tools were described. I believe that if Web tools are implemented correctly, your firm can benefit from use of the Internet as well.

By studying the firm's CAD Web site, you learned of issues you will confront and saw a solid structure for a site of your own. The sample CAD Internet site tour covered Web navigation and features. In conclusion, here is an important message: The Web is now CAD-friendly, AutoCAD 2000 is Web-oriented, and it is time for your design firm to become Internet-enabled!

27

INTRODUCTION TO 3D

Up to this point in this book you have been learning about drawing 2D representations of real-world 3D objects. This method of designing and drafting is limited because a 2D drawing must be visualized as a 3D real-world object. Drawing 3D objects as 3D objects largely eliminates the need to mentally visualize because the 3D information is included in the design drawing. Drawing and designing in 3D offers other advantages as well. For example, the viewpoint can be changed to help define the form of the object. In addition, shaded and rendered presentations—and even animations—are possible (see Figure 27.1). And manufacturing and other information, such as Finite Element Analysis (FEA) data, can be extracted.

Figure 27.1

A 3D solid model that has been shaded using AutoCAD's SHADE *command.*

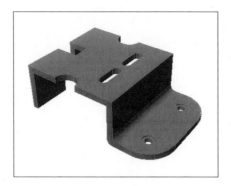

The 3D capabilities of AutoCAD can be a valuable addition to your design skills. This chapter introduces you to the following topics:

- Understanding 3D coordinate systems

- Defining a User Coordinate System (UCS) in 3D space

- Using viewports

- Interactive viewing in 3D

- Shading a model

Understanding 3D Coordinate Systems

Working in 3D is theoretically no more difficult than working in 2D. In practice, however, the presence of the third dimension greatly complicates your task. In 3D, you can work on an infinite number of drawing planes—not just the X-Y plane of 2D drawings.

Figure 27.2 shows the three axes that define AutoCAD's 3D world. The three axes shown in Figure 27.2 can be aligned with any number of working planes conforming to the geometry of the 3D model.

Figure 27.3 shows a simple 3D model with five of the many possible coordinates systems that you might define for use while working on the model. Each coordinate system is called a *User Coordinate System* or *UCS*. Of course, many other User Coordinate Systems are possible with just this one model. It is the flexibility of the UCS that makes constructing and working with 3D models possible.

Figure 27.2

Working in 3D means working with an additional axis, the Z axis.

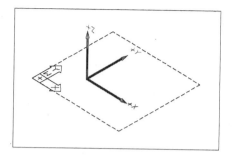

Figure 27.3

You can define an unlimited number of User Coordinate Systems in a 3D drawing.

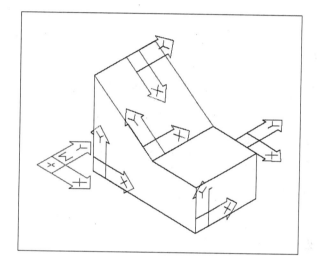

NOTE

Figure 27.3 is for illustration purposes only. There is no way of having more than one UCS icon appear at a time on your image.

Understanding how to position and manipulate 3D coordinate systems is the key to creating 3D models in AutoCAD. And the key to understanding 3D coordinates is an understanding of AutoCAD's User Coordinate System.

Defining a User Coordinate System in 3D Space

The UCS command provides the means of changing the location of the 0,0,0 origin point of a coordinate system, as well as the orientation of the XY plane and Z axis. Any plane or point in 3D space can be referenced, saved, and recalled, and you can define as many user coordinate systems as you require. Coordinate input and display are relative to the current UCS. In AutoCAD 2000, if multiple viewports are active, you can assign a different UCS to each.

NOTE

Prior to AutoCAD 2000, if multiple viewports were active, they all shared the same UCS. In AutoCAD 2000, to facilitate editing objects in different views, you can define a different UCS for each view. Each time you make a viewport current, you can begin drawing using the same UCS you used the last time that viewport was current.

Usually, it is easier to align the coordinate system with existing geometry than to determine the exact placement of a 3D point.

Defining a New UCS

You can define a user coordinate system in one of the following ways:

- Specify a new origin, new XY plane, or new Z axis
- Align the new UCS with an existing object
- Align the new UCS with the current viewing direction
- Align the new UCS with the face of a solid object
- Rotate the current UCS around any of its axes
- Select a preset UCS provided by AutoCAD

NOTE

The ability to align a UCS with the face of a solid is a new feature of AutoCAD 2000. Although you can align a UCS with a solid face using several other options of the UCS command, the new "face" option is usually much faster.

In the following exercise, you will use UCS command options that you might not be familiar with from work in 2D drawings to define user coordinate systems on 3D objects.

SPECIFYING A NEW UCS BY USING THE Z AXIS, 3POINT, OBJECT, VIEW, FACE, AND PRESET OPTIONS

1. Open the Chap-27.DWG drawing file on the accompanying CD-ROM. Your drawing should resemble Figure 27.4. If not, use the VIEW command to set the view VIEW1 current. Note the position of the World Coordinate System icon to the lower-left of the model. Although it's not necessary, you may want to set a running Endpoint osnap.

Figure 27.4

The Chap-27.DWG's 3D object with pick points for new UCSs.

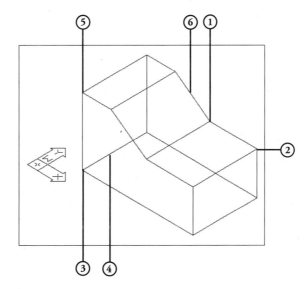

In the following step, you use the ZAxis option to define a new User Coordinate System. The ZAxis option specifies a new UCS origin and a point that lies on the positive Z axis.

2. Start the UCS command by typing **UCS** and pressing Enter. Specify the New option.

3. Choose the ZAxis option by typing **ZA** and pressing Enter. Specify the new origin point by snapping to the Endpoint at ① in Figure 27.4. Specify a point on the positive portion of the new Z axis by picking at ②. The UCS should appear as it does in the upper-left viewport of Figure 27.5.

    In the following step, you establish a new UCS using the 3point option. The 3point option allows you to specify the new UCS origin and the direction of its positive X and Y axes.

4. Press Enter to restart the **UCS** command, and specify the New option.

5. Choose the 3point option and specify the new origin by picking the Endpoint at ③ in Figure 27.4. Specify a point on the positive portion of the new X axis by using a Midpoint snap and picking at ④. Specify a point on the positive-Y portion of the XY plane by picking the Endpoint at ⑤. The new UCS should be placed as shown in the upper-right viewport of Figure 27.5.

    In the next step, you use the Object option of the **UCS** command to establish a new UCS. The Object option defines the UCS with the same extrusion (positive Z) direction as the selected object. The origin and orientation of the new XY plane depend upon the object chosen and are somewhat arbitrary.

6. Restart the **UCS** command and choose New. Type **OB** and press Enter to select the Object option.

7. At the prompt to `Select object to align UCS`, pick near ⑥ in Figure 27.4. The new UCS should conform to that shown in the lower-left viewport of Figure 27.5.

Figure 27.5

Four possible UCSs for the Chap-27.DWG model.

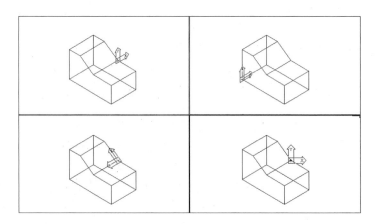

In the following step, you set a new UCS using the View option. The View option establishes a new UCS with the XY plane perpendicular to the viewing direction (parallel to the display screen). The origin is unchanged.

8. Start the UCS command and choose New. Select the View option. The UCS aligns the XY plane with the display screen without changing the UCS origin, as shown in the lower-right viewport of Figure 27.5.

INSIDER TIP

The View UCS is useful when you want to add text to a non-orthographic view. The text is automatically placed parallel to the plane of the display screen.

In the next step, you establish a preset UCS using the Orthographic option of the UCS command. An orthographic preset UCS includes one of the six standard orthographic UCSs provided with AutoCAD.

9. Start the UCS command and choose the Orthographic option by typing **G** and pressing Enter. Options for the six standard orthographic UCS orientations appear. Choose the Front option by typing **F** and pressing Enter. The UCS switches to the standard Front orientation, as shown in the upper-left viewport of Figure 27.6. Note that the Front UCS shares the World coordinate system's origin.

In the next step, you use the X,Y,Z rotation option to establish a new XY plane. The X,Y,Z option rotates the current UCS about a specified axis.

10. Start the UCS command, select New, then type **Y** to indicate that you want to rotate the current UCS about the Y axis. When you're prompted to specify the rotation about the Y axis, press Enter to accept the default of 90. The new UCS retains the same origin, but the XY plane is rotated about the Y axis 90 degrees as shown in the upper-right viewport of Figure 27.6. (See "Right Hand Rule" later in this chapter for rules governing rotations about a 3D axis.)

INSIDER TIP

When establishing a new UCS by rotating the current UCS about the X, Y, or Z axis, you can either specify a rotation angle or accept the default angle. This default angle can be changed using the UCSAXISANG system variable. Changing the angle to one you frequently use can save an input step when using the X, Y, or Z axis rotation options of the UCS command.

The Face option can be used to quickly align a new UCS with the face of a 3D solid. This option is shown in the next step.

11. Start the UCS command, choose New, then type **F**. At the prompt to Select face of solid object, pick near ① in the lower-left viewport of Figure 27.6. Type **Y** and press Enter to flip the UCS 180 degrees about the Y axis. Then type **X** and press Enter to flip the UCS 180 about the X axis. Then press Enter to accept the UCS as shown in the lower-left viewport of Figure 27.6.

NOTE

When you use the Face option, the X axis is aligned with the nearest edge of the first face found. The Xflip and Yflip options allow you to reorient the positive directions of each axis.

In the next step, you use the Move option of the UCS command. Just as the X,Y,Z option changes the XY plane without changing the origin, the Move option changes the origin without changing the XY plane orientation.

12. Start the UCS command and choose the Move option. When prompted for the new origin point, snap to the Endpoint at ② in the lower-right viewport of Figure 27.6. The XY plane orientation may differ from that shown in the lower-right image in Figure 27.6.

13. If you plan to continue with the next exercise now, leave this drawing open. Otherwise close the drawing without saving changes.

Figure 27.6

Moving the UCS around in a 3D model.

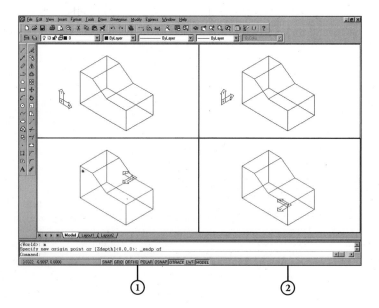

Right-Hand Rule

In the previous exercise, you established a new UCS by rotating the current UCS about one of its axes. The convention for defining the positive direction of rotation about an axis is summed up in the so-called "Right-Hand Rule." To determine the positive rotation direction about an axis, point your right thumb in the positive direction of the axis and then curl your fingers in a fist around the axis. The "curl" of your fingers indicates the positive rotation direction of the axis. This sense of the direction of rotation about an axis is used consistently throughout AutoCAD's 3D commands involving axes—such as the REVSURF command in surface modeling and the REVOLVE command used with solids. The positive rotation direction about the three axes is shown in Figure 27.7.

Figure 27.7

The direction of positive rotation about the X, Y, and Z axes.

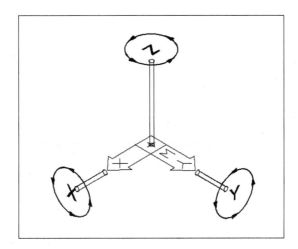

Using the UCS Manager

NEW
for R2000

Although the UCS command allows you maximum flexibility in setting, naming, restoring, and deleting a UCS, the UCSMAN (UCS Manager) command displays a multi-tabbed dialog box that presents a convenient, graphical method of restoring a saved UCS, establishing an orthographic UCS, and specifying UCS icon and UCS settings for viewports.

In the following exercise, you use the Orthographic UCSs tab of the UCS dialog box to establish and position a preset orthographic UCS.

SPECIFYING AND PLACING A PRESET UCS WITH THE UCS MANAGER

1. Continue in or open Chap-27.DWG from the accompanying CD-ROM. If necessary, restore a WCS by using the World option of the UCS command. (Start the UCS command and press Enter.) Your drawing should resemble Figure 27.4 from the previous exercise.

2. From the Tools menu, choose Orthographic UCS, then Preset. AutoCAD displays the UCS dialog box with the Orthographic UCSs tab current (as shown in Figure 27.8).

Figure 27.8

The UCS Manager's UCS dialog box with the Orthographic UCSs tab displayed.

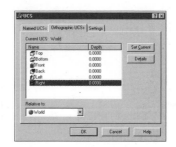

3. Choose the Right orthographic UCS. Select Set Current and click OK. AutoCAD establishes a standard right orthographic UCS. Note that this UCS shares the 0,0,0 origin of the WCS.

   In the next step, you change the origin of the current UCS using the Depth feature of the UCS dialog box. This allows you to move the origin along the current Z axis.

4. Press Enter to redisplay the UCS dialog box. With the Right orthographic UCS chosen, right-click and choose Depth to display the Orthographic UCS Depth dialog box, shown in Figure 27.9.

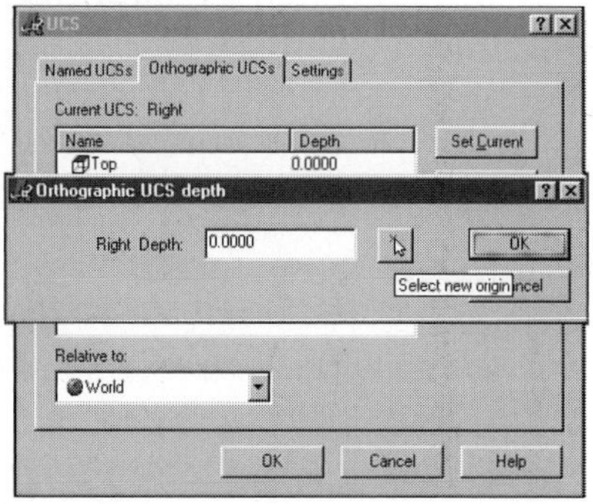

Figure 27.9

The Orthographic UCS Depth dialog box of the UCS dialog box.

5. Click the Select New Origin button and, in the drawing, use an Endpoint osnap to pick at ① in the upper-left viewport of Figure 27.10. In the Orthorgraphic UCS Depth dialog box, click OK, then click OK in the UCS dialog box. AutoCAD moves the origin of the UCS along its Z axis to equal the Z axis value of the point at ①.

    Now that you have established a new, non-preset UCS, in the next step, you name and save it.

Figure 27.10

Moving the UCS around your model.

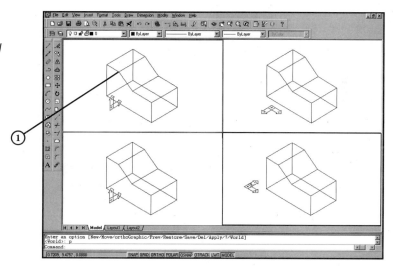

6. Start the UCS command by typing **UCS** and pressing Enter. Choose the Save option. When you're prompted for a name to save the current UCS to, type **MIDWAY** and press Enter. The UCS is saved with the name MIDWAY.

NOTE

You can restore named UCSs by using the Restore option of the UCS command or from the Named UCSs tab of the UCS dialog box. To access the UCS dialog box, open the Tools menu and choose Named UCS.

After you have named and saved a non-preset UCS as you did in steps 5 and 6, you can establish a new UCS relative to the named UCS, as shown in the next step.

7. From the Tools menu, choose Orthographic UCS, then Preset. On the UCS dialog box's Orthographic UCSs tab, choose (highlight) the Left preset orthographic UCS. Under Relative To:, choose Midway from the drop-down list. Choose Set Current and click OK. The new UCS is changed to a "back" orientation relative to the previously named Midway UCS, as shown in the upper-right viewport of Figure 27.10.

NOTE

In the previous step, you could have also simultaneously changed the depth of the new UCS by using The Depth feature of the UCS dialog box, as you did previously in steps 4 and 5.

AutoCAD keeps track of the last 10 coordinate systems created in both model and paper space. Repeating the Previous option of the UCS command steps back through the list. In the following step, you use the Previous option of the UCS command to return to the previous UCS.

8. Start the UCS command and select the Previous option. AutoCAD restores the most recent UCS (see the lower-left viewport in Figure 27.10).

In the last step of this exercise, you re-establish the World Coordinate System for the model.

9. Start the UCS command and accept the default World option by pressing Enter. AutoCAD restores the WCS as shown in the lower-right viewport of Figure 27.10.

10. Quit AutoCAD or close the drawing without saving.

INSIDER **T**IP

When you're working in the Orthographic UCSs tab of the UCS dialog box, be sure that the desired UCS is displayed in the Relative To: list before you change to any of the six preset UCSs. Orienting a new UCS relative to the World Coordinate System versus a UCS you have named can produce very different results.

UCSs and Viewports

The ability to have multiple viewports is helpful when you're working in 3D. Multiple viewports provide different views of your model and facilitate editing and visualizing your work. In addition to offering a different view, in AutoCAD 2000, each viewport can be assigned a different UCS. In addition, the UCS in one viewport can be transferred, or "copied," to any number of other viewports.

The UCS icon is normally visible in the lower-left corner of the viewport. It can, however, either be turned off or set to display at the origin of the current coordinate system on a per viewport basis. You can also configure the UCS to automatically change to the associated UCS whenever an orthographic view is restored in a viewport. Lastly, you can set each viewport to generate a plan view whenever you change coordinate systems. Two of these viewport features are demonstrated in the following exercise.

SETTING DIFFERENT COORDINATE SYSTEMS IN VIEWPORTS

1. Open Chap-27a.DWG from the accompanying CD-ROM. This drawing shows a solid model of a bracket. Make sure that the upper-left viewport is active. Your drawing will resemble Figure 27.11. The UCS in each viewport is controlled by the UCSVP system variable. When UCSVP is set to 1 in a viewport, the last used UCS in that viewport is saved and is restored when the viewport is once again made current. If UCSVP is set to 0 in a viewport, the UCS for that viewport always reflects the UCS in the current viewport.

Figure 27.11

The multi-view solid model drawing of the bracket.

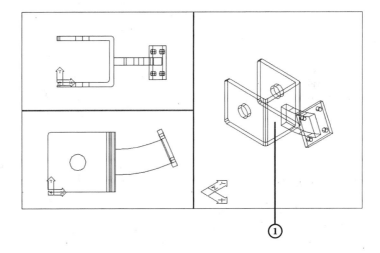

The three viewports of this drawing show a top view, a front view, and an isometric view. The UCSVP system variable in all three viewports is set to 1, allowing each viewport to have a separate UCS. In the next step, you set the UCSVP system variable for the right isometric viewport to 0.

2. Pick in the bottom-left viewport to set it current. Note that the UCSs in all three viewports remain unchanged. Now pick in the right isometric viewport to set it current. Type **UCSVP** and press Enter. When prompted, set the UCSVP variable to 0.

3. Now pick in the upper-left viewport to make it current. Note that the UCS in the isometric viewport changes to match the current viewport.

4. Pick in the lower-left viewport and note that the UCS in the isometric viewport again changes to match the current viewport. Note that as you alternately pick in the upper- and lower-left viewports, the UCS in the orthographic viewport changes to reflect the UCS of the current viewport.

In the next two steps, you establish a new UCS in the orthographic view and then transfer the UCS to the top view's viewport.

5. Pick in the isometric viewport to make it current. Start the UCS command and choose the New option. Select the Face option, and when you're prompted to `Select face of solid object:`, pick on the face at ① in Figure 27.11 and press Enter. A new UCS is established on the side face of the bracket.

6. Start the UCS command again and choose Apply. When you're prompted to `Pick viewport to apply current UCS...:`, pick in the upper-left viewport and press Enter. The UCS icon will turn to a broken pencil to show that UCS plane is perpendicular to the display.

7. With the top-left viewport still current, type **PLAN** and press Enter to start the PLAN command. Press Enter to accept the default current UCS. The upper-left viewport now shows a plan view of the new UCS.

8. Once again, alternately pick in the top-left and bottom-left viewports and note that the UCS in the isometric view changes to reflect the UCS in the current viewport. Your drawing should now resemble Figure 27.12.

Figure 27.12

Transferring a UCS from one viewport to another.

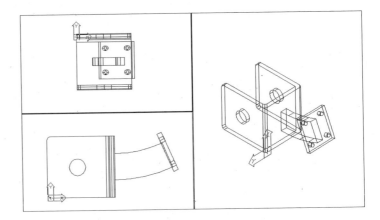

NOTE

Because you used the Face option of the UCS command, the orientation of the X and Y axes you obtained in step 5 may differ from that shown in Figure 27.12. As explained earlier in this chapter, using the Face and Object options of the UCS command yields X and Y axes orientations that depend upon the geometry of the object or solid face. If axis orientation is important for your editing work, you can reorient the X and Y axes using the Next, Xflip, and Yflip options of the Face option or the Z axis rotation option of the UCS command when the basic XY plane is established.

Being able to maintain separate UCSs on a per-viewport basis and being able to transfer a UCS from one viewport to other viewports are effective tools to help you quickly navigate to various planes and orientations in your model. In the next step, you turn the UCS icon off in the active viewport.

9. Pick in the isometric viewport to make it active. From the View menu, choose Display and then UCS Icon. Select ON to remove the check mark. The UCS icon in the active viewport is turned off.

10. Close this drawing without saving the changes you have made.

The ability to easily establish new coordinate systems as well as the ability to move, orient, name, recall, and associate UCSs with individual views are among the most important tools you have for working in 3D. The following list summarizes the many AutoCAD system variables that create or control User Coordinate Systems.

- **UCSAXISANG*** Stores the default angle when rotating the UCS around one of its axes using the X, Y, or Z option of the UCS command.

- **UCSBASE*** Stores the name of the UCS that defines the origin and orientation of orthographic UCS settings.

- **UCSFOLLOW** Generates a plan view whenever you change from one UCS to another (also controlled from the UCS Manager dialog box).

- **UCSICON** Displays the user coordinate system icon for the current viewport (also controlled from the UCS Manager dialog box).

- **UCSNAME** Stores the name of the current coordinate system for the current space.

- **UCSORG** Stores the origin point of the current coordinate system for the current space.

- **UCSORTHO*** Determines whether the related orthographic UCS setting is automatically restored when an orthographic view is restored (also controlled from the View dialog box).

- **UCSVIEW*** Determines whether the current UCS is saved with a named view.

- **UCSVP*** Determines whether the UCS in active viewports remains fixed or changes to reflect the UCS of the currently active viewport (also controlled from the UCS Manager dialog box).

- **UCSXDIR** Stores the X direction of the current UCS for the current space.

- **UCSYDIR** Stores the Y direction of the current UCS for the current space.

- **VIEWUCS*** Determines whether the current UCS is saved with a named view.

* = new AutoCAD 2000 functionality.

Using Viewports

Another important feature to help with your work in 3D is AutoCAD's ability to simultaneously display more than one model space viewport. In model space, AutoCAD usually displays a single viewport filling the entire drawing area. You can, however, divide the drawing area into several viewports. In model space, these viewports are "tiled" or fit together as adjacent rectangles much like tiles on a floor. Unlike the viewports of paper space discussed in Chapter 19, "Paper Space Layouts," model space viewports cover the entire screen and do not behave as editable objects. Figure 27.13 shows a 3D drawing with three viewports defined.

Multiple viewports are especially useful when you're working in 3D because you can set up a top (or plan) view in one viewport, set up a front (or elevation) view in another viewport, and have yet a third viewport show an isometric view of your model. You can see the effects of changes in one view reflected in the other views. And as you learned in an earlier section of this chapter, you can also set the User Coordinate System (UCS) in one viewport so that it is always the same as the UCS in the active or current viewport. Each viewport is largely independent of other viewports, giving you a great amount of flexibility in viewing and editing your model. In each viewport, for example, you can independently:

- Pan and zoom

- Set grid and snap distances

- Control the visibility and placement of the UCS icon
- Set coordinate systems and restore named views

Figure 27.13

A 3D drawing displayed in three viewports.

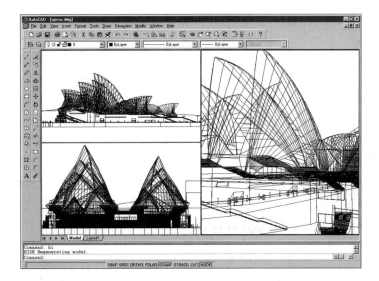

Most of the operations controlling tiled viewports can be carried out from the two tabs of the Viewports dialog box. To display this dialog box, shown in Figure 27.14, select the Display Viewports Dialog icon on the Standard toolbar and choose Viewports from the View, or enter **vports** at the command prompt.

Figure 27.14

The Viewports dialog box controls most viewport operations.

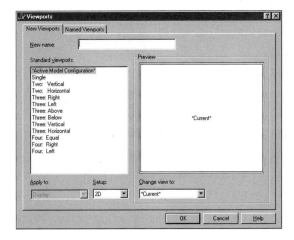

The functionality of the New Viewports tab of the Viewports dialog box is summarized here:

- **New Name:** If you want to save the viewports configuration you are creating, enter a name here. A list of named viewport configurations is displayed on the Named Viewports tab.

- **Standard Viewports:** The standard viewport configurations are listed here by name.

- **Preview:** Displays a preview of the viewport configuration you select under Standard Viewports. The default views assigned to individual viewports in each configuration are displayed.

- **Apply To:** Allows you to assign the configuration to either the display or the current viewport. Assigning to the display assigns the configuration to the entire display area. Assigning to the current viewport applies the configuration to the current viewport only.

- **Setup:** You can choose either a 2D or 3D setup. When you select 2D, the new viewport configuration is initially created with the current view in all of the viewports. When you select 3D, a set of standard orthogonal 3D views is applied to the viewports in the configuration.

- **Change View To:** Replaces the selected viewport configuration with the viewport configuration you select from the list. You can choose a named viewport configuration, or if you have selected 3D setup, you can select from the list of standard viewport configurations. Use the Preview area to view the viewport configuration choices.

In the following exercise, you learn about setting up multiple viewports configurations for work in 3D.

CONFIGURING VIEWPORTS FOR WORK IN 3D

1. Open LOCK.DWG from the accompanying CD. This drawing represents a model of a sliding glass door locking mechanism. Your drawing should resemble Figure 27.15.

Figure 27.15

*The initial single viewport
view of LOCK.DWG.*

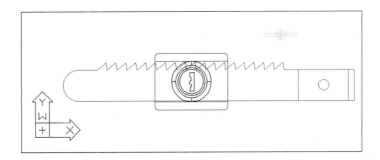

As mention earlier in this chapter, the **UCSORTHO** system variable determines whether the related orthographic UCS setting is restored automatically when a preset orthographic view is established in a viewport. In the next step, you ensure that this system variable is turned on.

2. Type **View**, or from the Standard toolbar, choose the Named View icon. In the View dialog box, choose the Orthographic & Isometric Views tab and, if necessary, select Restore Orthographic UCS with View option to place a mark in the check box. Click OK to close the dialog box.

NOTE

You can also display the View dialog box by opening the View menu and choosing Named Views. You can also set the UCSORTHO system variable by typing UCSORTHO at the command prompt.

In the next three steps, you establish and name a standard 3D three-viewport configuration.

3. From the Standard toolbar, choose Display Viewports Dialog. If necessary, select the New Viewports tab in the Viewports dialog box. In the New Name input box, type **INITIAL-3**.

4. In the Standard Viewports: selection box, select Three Right. Note that the Three Right viewport configuration is shown in the Preview window. The word Current indicates that the current screen view of your model will appear in each viewport.

5. To establish more meaningful views for 3D work in the three viewports, under Setup:, select 3D. Note that the viewports in the Preview window now have the standard Top, Front, and SE Isometric views assigned. Make sure Display is showing in the Apply To: selection box and click OK to exit the dialog box. Your drawing should now resemble Figure 27.16.

Figure 27.16

You can easily establish standard Top, Front, and Isometric views.

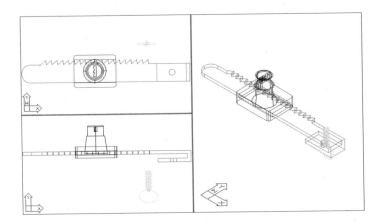

In the next step, you establish a Right view in the lower-left viewport.

6. Press Enter to redisplay the Viewports dialog box. In the Preview window, pick in the lower-left viewport to set it current. Under Change View To:, scroll to find the `Right` view and select it. The viewport should display `Right`. Click OK to close the dialog box. Your display should have a right view in the lower-left viewport.

   During the next step, note that the locking screw's position is dynamically updated in all three viewports as you drag it to a new position.

7. Set the upper-left viewport to current. Start the `MOVE` command, select the green locking screw, and press Enter. Drag the locking screw downward until it is approximately even with the screw hole at the right end of the main locking bar. Leave it in this new position.

8. To further divide a viewport, pick in the right isometric viewport to set it current. Redisplay the Viewports dialog box. In the Standard Viewports selection box, choose Two: Horizontal. Note the names of the proposed views in the Preview window. Select the top or upper viewport in the Preview window. Under Change View To:, select SW Isometric and note that the top viewport reflects the change. Under Apply To:, make sure Current Viewport is selected. Then close the dialog box. Your drawing should now resemble Figure 27.17.

   In the next step, you name the current viewport configuration, then you return to a single viewport configuration. In the final step, you restore a named viewport configuration.

9. Restate the Viewports dialog box and in the Edit box, type **4-SE-SW** in the New Name input box. Click OK to close the dialog box. Select the upper-left viewport to set it current. Then redisplay the Viewports dialog box. In the Standard viewports window, select Single. Make sure that Display is selected under Apply To: and close the dialog box. The previous "current" viewport is now the single viewport (as shown in Figure 27.15).

10. Redisplay the Viewports dialog box and select the Named Viewports tab. Under Named Viewports:, select 4-SE-SW. The configuration is shown in the Preview window. Click OK to close the dialog box and restore the 4-SE-SW configuration (as shown in Figure 27.17).

11. Close this drawing without saving changes.

Figure 27.17

You can quickly restore a named viewport configuration.

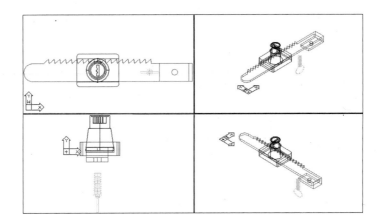

User-definable coordinate systems (UCSs) and the ability to quickly establish, name, and recall multiple viewport configurations represent two of the most useful tools in 3D modeling. Just as establishing a new UCS allows you to move the drawing's origin and XY plane to a position and orientation best suited for work on various parts or aspects of the model, multiple viewports allow you to see the model from the most advantageous viewpoint.

Interactive Viewing in 3D

NEW
for R2000   Whereas multiple viewports provide useful static views of a 3D model, the 3D ORBIT command allows you to view 3D models interactively. When the 3D ORBIT command is active, you manipulate the view with the screen pointing device (the mouse), and you can view the model from any point in 3D space.

The 3D orbit view overlays an "arcball" on the current view of the model. The arcball consists of a circle divided into four quadrants by smaller circles, as shown in Figure 27.18. The center of the arcball represents the target, which remains stationary. As you manipulate the view, the camera, or viewpoint, moves around the target depending upon where you place the pointing device. You click and drag the cursor to rotate the view.

Figure 27.18

The arcball symbol surrounds a 3D model.

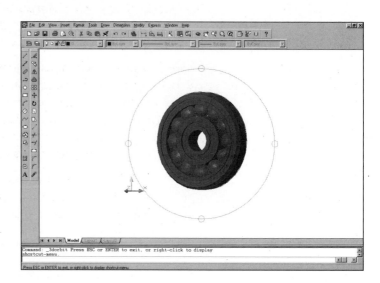

Different cursor icon symbols appear depending upon the position of the cursor with respect to the arcball. Four basic movements are possible. The following list shows the cursor icons and their associated movements:

 When the cursor is moved inside the arcball, a small sphere encircled by two arrowed lines appears. You can manipulate the view freely in all directions when this icon is active.

 When the cursor is moved outside the arcball, a circular arrow surrounding a sphere is displayed. When this cursor is active, clicking and dragging in a vertical motion causes the view to move around an axis that extends through the center of the arcball and perpendicular to the screen. If you move the cursor inside the arcball, it changes to the sphere encircled by two ellipses, and the view moves freely.

When you move the cursor over one of the small circles on either side of the arcball, a horizontal ellipse encircling a sphere appears. Clicking and dragging when this icon is active rotates the view around the vertical or Y axis that extends through the center of the arcball. This axis is represented by the vertical line in the cursor icon.

When you move the cursor over one of the circles at the top or bottom of the arcball, a vertical ellipse encircling a sphere appears. Clicking and dragging when this icon is active rotates the view around the horizontal or X axis that extends through the center of the arcball. This axis is represented by the horizontal line in the cursor icon.

With these four modes of movement, you can view the model from any position. Using any but the free movement mode that's available when the cursor is inside the arcball constrains motion to one axis. You practice manipulating 3D Orbit views in the following exercise.

VIEWING A MODEL WITH 3D ORBIT

1. Open BEARING.DWG from the accompanying CD-ROM. This model shows a ball bearing assembly from a side view (see Figure 27.19).

Figure 27.19

2D side view of a ball bearing assembly.

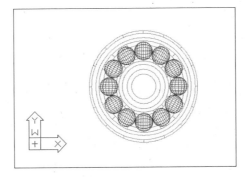

In the following steps, note the shape and orientation of the 3D Orbit UCS icon as you manipulate the view of the model.

2. From the View menu, choose **3D ORBIT** to start the **3D Orbit** command. Move the screen cursor to a position outside the large arcball circle and note the circular arrow icon. Remaining outside the arcball circle, click and drag the cursor in up and down motions. Observe that the model view rotates about an axis extending through the center of the arcball and perpendicular to the plane of the screen. Releasing the left mouse button "fixes" the view in a new orientation.

3. Right-click to display the 3D Orbit shortcut menu. Select Reset View to restore the original view of the model.

4. Move the screen cursor over either of the small circles at the left or right edge of the arcball circle. Note the horizontal elliptical arrow icon. Click and drag the cursor in horizontal motions. Observe the view rotating about an axis extending vertically through the arcball. Note that dragging the cursor outside the arcball has no effect on the axis of rotation or the icon shape. Releasing the left mouse button "fixes" the view in a new orientation.

5. The current display is wireframe. Now we will change to another type. Right-click to display the 3D Orbit shortcut menu. Choose Shading Modes and select one of the five remaining shade modes.

6. Repeat the previous step four times, choosing one of the other remaining shade modes each time.

7. With the model in a shade mode other than wireframe, move the screen cursor over either of the small circles at the top or bottom edge of the arcball. Note the vertical elliptical arrow icon. Click and drag the cursor in a series of vertical, up and down, motions. Observe the view rotating about an axis extending horizontally through the center of the arcball. Note that the model remains shaded as the view changes. Releasing the left mouse button "fixes" the view in a new orientation.

8. Right-click to display the 3D Orbit shortcut menu. Select Reset View to restore the original view of the model. Now move the icon anywhere inside the arcball. Note the double elliptical icon with both a horizontal and vertical arrow. Click and drag the cursor in a series of horizontal, vertical, and diagonal motions. Observe the view rotating freely. Releasing the left mouse button "fixes" the view in a new orientation.

9. Right-click to display the 3D Orbit shortcut menu and choose Reset View.

10. Close BEARING.DWG without saving changes.

The **3D ORBIT** command not only allows you to establish a shaded, static view of a model from virtually any vantage point, it allows you to view the model dynamically as you change the view. Shaded or hidden line removal modes persist even while the viewpoint is being dynamically and interactively modified. This capability allows you to gain new insights into the geometric relationships among the various aspects of even a simple model.

You should be aware of several features and limitations of the 3D ORBIT command:

■ Depending upon the complexity of the model and the efficiency of your particular CPU/graphics hardware, the components of the model may be reduced and displayed as simple 3D boxes during real-time manipulation of the view. These "bounding box" surrogates accurately represent the volumetric extents of the original elements. After dynamic motion input is stopped, the model reverts to its original geometric forms. Figure 27.20 shows this effect with BEARING.DWG.

Figure 27.20

Bounding boxes may substitute for more complex shapes in slower systems.

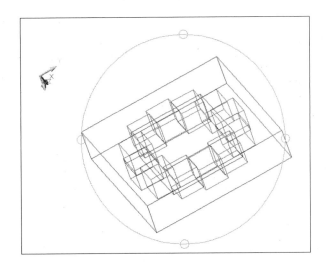

■ If you choose only individual elements of the model before entering the 3D ORBIT command, only those selected elements will participate in the dynamic viewing and any subsequent presentations. Choosing only a few key elements may allow a smoother, more accurate dynamic presentation.

■ As described in the following section, placing your model in a perspective presentation is helpful for establishing spatial relationships.

■ You cannot enter commands at the command line while 3D Orbit is active. However, commands such as ZOOM and PAN are available from the 3D Orbit right-click shortcut menu.

■ Keep in mind that 3D Orbit alters only the view of the model; the model remains stationary during dynamic viewing.

■ If the view of the model becomes ambiguous, the Reset View option available on the 3D Orbit right-click shortcut menu will restore the view in effect when 3D Orbit was last entered.

In addition to the modes of view manipulation and shading options demonstrated in the previous exercise, the right-click shortcut menu of the 3D ORBIT command presents several other features and options. You can pan and zoom, turn two additional viewing aids on and off, establish standard preset views, adjust camera distance and swivel the camera, and set either a parallel or perspective view. A means of establishing clipping planes is also available. Several of these features are demonstrated in the following exercise. The clipping planes feature will be demonstrated in a later exercise.

ADDITIONAL 3D ORBIT VIEWING OPTIONS

1. Open CANISTER.DWG from this book's accompanying CD-ROM. This drawing represents a model of a battery canister. The initial view is shown in Figure 27.21.

Figure 27.21

Isometric view of a battery canister.

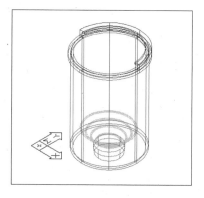

2. From the View menu, choose 3D Orbit. Note that the 3D Orbit arcball and UCS icon are displayed.

3. Right-click to display the 3D Orbit shortcut menu. Choose Visual Aids and select Grid. Note the 3D Orbit Grid display.

4. Repeat step 3 and select the Compass visual aid. While manipulating the view as you did in the preceding exercise, note the appearance of the grid and compass visual aids.

5. Use the right-click shortcut menu to turn off both the grid and compass visual aids.

6. Manipulate the view to resemble that shown in the right viewport of Figure 27.22.

7. Right-click to display the 3D Orbit shortcut menu. Choose Projection and select Perspective. Your view should more closely resemble the model in the left viewport of Figure 27.22.

Figure 27.22

A perspective view (on the left) versus a parallel view (on the right).

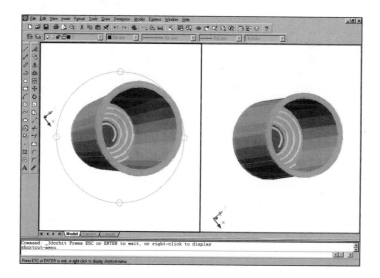

8. From the 3D Orbit shortcut menu, choose Preset views and select Front. Then leave this drawing open. You will continue from this view in the next exercise.

Adjusting Clipping Planes in 3D Orbit View

You can establish clipping planes in 3D Orbit view. When you use clipping planes, objects or portions of objects that move beyond a clipping plane become invisible in the view. Adjustments to clipping planes are made interactively in the Adjust Clipping Planes window shown in Figure 27.23. To display this window, right-click to open the 3D Orbit shortcut menu, choose More, then select Adjust Clipping Planes.

Figure 27.23

You adjust clipping planes in the Adjust Clipping Planes window.

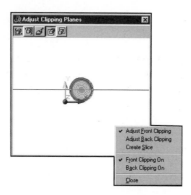

The Adjust Clipping Planes window shows two clipping planes, front and back. These planes are represented by two horizontal lines, which initially may be superimposed upon each other. To choose the clipping plane you want to adjust and to turn clipping planes on and off, you use buttons on the toolbar in the Adjust Clipping Planes window or the options available from the right-click shortcut menu shown in Figure 27.23. The following options are available:

- **Front Clipping On.** Toggles the front clipping plane on and off. When the front clipping planes is on, the results of moving this plane are shown interactively in the main 3D Orbit display.

- **Back Clipping On.** Toggles the back clipping plane on and off. When the back clipping plane is on, the results of moving this plane are shown interactively in the main 3D Orbit display.

- **Adjust Front Clipping.** Adjusts the front clipping plane. The line nearest the bottom of the window shows the front plane. If Front Clipping On is active, you see the results of moving the plane up or down in the main 3D Orbit display.

- **Adjust Back Clipping.** Adjusts the back clipping plane. The line nearest the top of the window shows the back plane. If Back Clipping On is active, you see the results of moving the plane up or down in the main 3D Orbit display.

- **Create Slice.** When this feature is active, the front and back clipping planes move together at their current separation distance, creating a "slice" of the objects contained between the two planes. If both Front Clipping On and Back Clipping On are active, the slice is displayed in the main 3D Orbit display.

NOTE

Except when using the Create Slice option, you can adjust only one clipping plane at a time. If the Create Slice button is clicked, you adjust both planes simultaneously. On the toolbar, the button for the plane you are adjusting appears to be pressed.

INSIDER TIP

Although you can establish clipping planes from any 3D Orbit view, standard orthogonal views such as front and side usually yield the most effective results.

The uses of front and back clipping planes and slices are demonstrated in the following exercise.

ESTABLISHING CLIPPING PLANES

1. Continue from the previous exercise with a front view of the model in CANISTER.DWG. From the 3D Orbit shortcut menu, choose More, and select Adjust Clipping Planes. Note that the view is rotated 90 degrees in the Adjust Clipping Planes window.

2. Right-click in the Adjust Clipping Planes window and make sure a check appears beside the Adjust Front Clipping and Front Clipping On options. Click in the Adjust Clipping Planes window to close the shortcut menu.

3. In the Adjust Clipping Planes window, the bottom line represents the position of the front clipping plane, and the top line represents the position of the back clipping plane. These two lines are initially superimposed and pass through the middle of the model.

4. Click and drag the special clipping plane icon downward and observe the view of the model in the main 3D Orbit display. As the clipping plane approaches the "front" of the model, more of the model becomes visible because less of the model is "clipped." In this model, this effect is most evident in the spring element.

5. With the front clipping plane line near the "front" of the model, select the Back Clipping On option from the right-click shortcut menu. (You can also activate the Back Clipping On/Off button on the Adjust Clipping Planes window toolbar.) The model is displayed as a slice, with only those portions falling between the current front and back clipping plane lines visible in the main display.

6. Activate the Create Slice button or select Create Slice from the shortcut menu. Click and drag the icon to vary the position of the slice. Note that the front and back planes appear closer together when Create Slice is active. Figure 27.24 shows a typical front view slice of the model.

Figure 27.24

A slice view through the middle of the canister model.

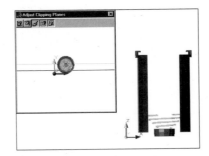

7. Close the Adjust Clipping Planes window by selecting Close from the shortcut menu. Manipulate the current view to observe the slice from different views. Restore the previous view by selecting Reset View from the shortcut menu.

8. From the 3D Orbit shortcut menu, choose More and select Back Clipping On to turn the back plane off. Notice that the display now shows all portions of the model behind the front clipping plane.

Leave this drawing open. You will continue from this view in the next exercise.

With clipping planes and the use of 3D Orbit's shading modes, you can establish new and informative views of your model. These clipped views remain when you exit 3D Orbit.

NOTE

Clipped views are especially helpful when combined with shaded views in 3D Orbit. They may not be as effective, however, when you exit 3D Orbit and return to standard 3D and 2D views. The 3D Orbit shortcut menu offers you a quick way to disable the front and back clipping planes before you exit the 3D ORBIT command.

Using Continuous Orbit

While 3D Orbit is active, you can choose to establish a continuous motion of the view around your model. Such continuous motion studies can yield information about the structure and geometric relationships in the model that are less apparent in static views. Continuous orbit is demonstrated in the following exercise.

ESTABLISHING A CONTINUOUS ORBIT

1. Continue from the previous exercise with a front shaded view of the model in CANISTER.DWG. From the shortcut menu, choose Shading Modes and select Flat Shaded.

2. From the shortcut menu, choose More and select Continuous Orbit. Note that the cursor changes to a small sphere encircled by two lines.

3. To start the continuous orbit motion, click and drag in the direction you want the continuous orbit to move and release the pick button. Observe that the model continues to move in the direction of the motion of the pointing device.

4. To change the direction of the continuous orbit motion, click and drag in a new direction and release the pick button.

5. To stop the motion at any point without leaving 3D Orbit, left-click while keeping the pointing device stationary.

6. To start a new continuous orbit motion, click, drag, and release again.

7. To change the projection type while in continuous orbit, right-click to display the shortcut menu and choose Projection. Then toggle the projection mode.

8. To stop the motion at any point and exit 3D Orbit, press the Esc key.

9. You are finished with this model. Close the drawing without saving changes.

While continuous orbit is active, you can modify the model view by right-clicking to display the shortcut menu and choosing Projection, Shading Modes, Visual Aids, Reset View, or Preset Views. You can also turn the front and back clipping planes on and off. You cannot, however, adjust the clipping planes while continuous orbit is active. Choosing Pan, Zoom, Orbit, or Adjust Clipping Planes from the shortcut menu will end continuous orbit.

NOTE

> The speed with which you drag the pointing device to establish continuous orbit determines the speed of the orbit motion. If your model is complex or your CPU/hardware is less efficient, you may want to make your orbit motions slower to yield smoother, less jerky results.

Continuous orbits are frequently more realistic with the projection mode set to perspective.

Shading a Model

AutoCAD 2000's SHADEMODE command replaces the older SHADE command and provides you with the same hidden line removal and enhanced shading options that are available inside the 3D ORBIT command. As with the 3D Orbit shade modes, the shading provided by SHADEMODE uses a fixed light source coming from behind and over your left shoulder. The various SHADEMODE command options are shown in Figure 27.25. Those options are described here:

- **2D Wireframe.** Displays the model objects using lines and curves to represent boundaries. This is AutoCAD's default display mode for 2D and 3D objects.

- **3D Wireframe.** Same as 2D Wireframe, but also displays a shaded 3D User Coordinate System icon.

- **Hidden.** Same as 3D Wireframe, but hides lines representing back faces. Similar to the results obtained with the HIDE command.

- **Flat Shaded.** Shades the objects between polygon faces. Objects appear flatter and less smooth than Gouraud shaded objects.

- **Gouraud Shaded.** Shades the objects and smoothes the edges between faces. Yields a smoother, more realistic appearance.

- **Flat Shaded, Edges On.** Combines the flat shaded and wireframe options. Objects appear flat shaded with wireframe showing.

- **Gouraud Shaded, Edges On.** Combines the Gouraud shaded and wireframe options. Objects appear Gouraud shaded with wireframe showing.

The options offered by the SHADEMODE command are available from the View menu. Choose Shade and select one of the six shading modes. You can also return your display to standard 2D wireframe mode from this menu. SHADEMODE is also available from the command line.

Figure 27.25

Shading and hidden line removal options available with SHADEMODE.

3D Wireframe   Hidden   Flat Shaded

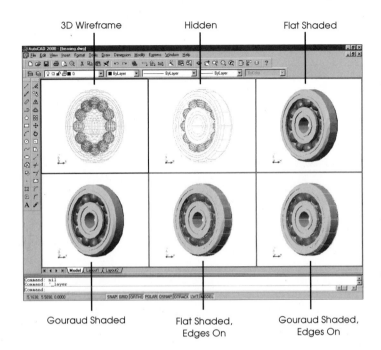

Gouraud Shaded   Flat Shaded,   Gouraud Shaded,
                    Edges On   Edges On

The behavior of shaded models in AutoCAD 2000 differs in important ways from that of previous releases of AutoCAD. In general, it is now much easier to work with shaded models. The AutoCAD 2000 shaded model improvements include the following:

- **3D Grid.** When any of the shade modes (including 3D Wireframe) are active, a distinctive "3D" grid is displayed if the grid feature is enabled. The grid features major (heavier) grid lines, with ten horizontal and vertical lines drawn between the major lines. The number of major lines corresponds to the value set using the grid spacing option of the GRID command and stored in the GRIDUNIT System Variable. The 3D grid is displayed coincidently with the current X-Y plane and "tracks" UCS changes. The 3D grid is shown in Figure 27.26

- **3D UCS Icon.** When any of the shade modes are active, a distinctive 3D USC icon is displayed whenever the UCS icon is enabled, as shown in Figure 27.26. This icon is a shaded with the X, Y, and Z axes labeled. The X axis is red, the Y axis is green and the Z axis is blue.

■ **3D Compass.** When any of the shade modes are active, a Compass feature can be activated. This feature superimposes on the model a 3D sphere composed of three lines representing the X, Y, and Z axes. The apparent center of the sphere coincides with the center of the viewport. The display of the 3D compass, shown in Figure 27.26, is controlled by the COMPASS system variable.

Figure 27.26

The 3D Icon, Compass, and Grid features are available in 3D shade modes.

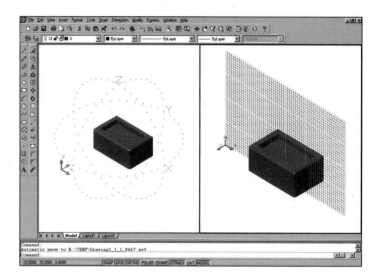

■ **Regeneration.** Regenerating the drawing does not affect shading.

■ **Editing.** You can edit shaded models by selecting them in the normal manner. If a shaded object is selected, the wireframe and grips appear on top of the shading.

■ **Saving.** You can save a drawing in which objects are shaded, and when you open it again, the objects are still shaded.

NOTE

If you exit 3D Orbit with a shade mode active, the only means of changing to a different shade mode or of returning to standard 2D wireframe mode is through the SHADEMODE command or the Shade options of the View menu.

Summary

Understanding the orientation of AutoCAD's 3D axes is the first step toward working comfortably in 3D space. The UCS command sets the orientation of the user coordinate system in three-dimensional space. Understanding and using multiple viewports allows you to easily orient yourself in 3D space, and provides an easy means for switching views of your model. AutoCAD 2000's 3D ORBIT command lets you move around and view a shaded model in real-time. Together these 3D tools make working in 3D space more efficient.

28

DRAWING IN 3D IN AUTOCAD

As you work with 3D models inside AutoCAD, you will soon find that there are two skills that will enable you to quickly become as comfortable working in 3D as you are working in 2D. One of these skills is the capability to move around inside the 3D model. The tools needed to develop this capability are discussed in Chapter 27, "Introduction to 3D." In that chapter you learned the tools and AutoCAD commands needed to establish user coordinate systems, various viewpoints from which to view your 3D geometry, and the usefulness of working with more than one viewport.

In this chapter you will learn about using AutoCAD commands already familiar to you from your work with 2D drawings in a different way as you apply these commands to 3D work. Familiar commands such as LINE *and* PLINE *can be used in 3D work as well—you just use them a little differently. Likewise, edit commands such as* ROTATE, MIRROR *and* ARRAY *have 3D counterparts in* 3DROTATE, MIRROR3D, *and* 3DARRAY. *You will also see that tools such as point filters and object snaps are even more important and necessary as you work with 3D space.*

Lastly, you will also learn how to create a special AutoCAD object called a Region that acts like a 2D object in some ways and like a 3D object in others.

The following topics are discussed and demonstrated in this chapter:

- Working with lines, polylines, and 3D polylines

- Using object snaps and point filters

- Using 3D editing commands

- Using EXTEND and TRIM in 3D

- Creating regions

Working with Lines, Polylines, and 3D Polylines

A standard line in AutoCAD is usually drawn in two dimensions and exists on the World Coordinate System or the current UCS. Each endpoint of this line is defined by a set of coordinates: X, Y, and Z. If you have spent most of your time drawing in 2D, then you have probably always left the Z value set to 0. By adjusting the Z value of either endpoint of the line, it becomes a line using all three dimensions.

The fact that the line is now in three dimensions, however, becomes apparent only by observing it from a different viewpoint. For example, a line may appear to be two-dimensional when viewed from the top, but appear three-dimensional when viewed from other angles (see Figure 28.1).

Figure 28.1

Three views of the same line, showing the importance of correctly viewing a 3D model.

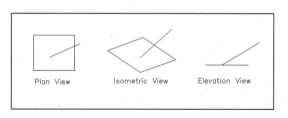

Plan View   Isometric View   Elevation View

The following exercise shows you how to draw a wireframe version of a box in 3D by using the LINE command. In the last chapter, you created a similar object, but you changed the UCS frequently. In this exercise, you will create the object without changing the UCS, which is a significantly faster.

USING THE LINE COMMAND TO DRAW A WIREFRAME BOX

1. Load AutoCAD if it is not already loaded and start a new drawing.

2. Select the LINE command from the Draw toolbar.

3. Type the following coordinates at the command prompt, then be sure to enter C to close the shape:

   ```
   0,0
   5,0
   5,5
   0,5
   C
   ```

   Press Enter to close the line command.

4. From the View menu, choose 3D Views, SW Isometric to switch to an isometric view of the drawing.

5. Select the COPY command from the Modify toolbar. At the Select Objects prompt, select the four lines and press Enter. Specify a displacement by typing **0,0,5** and press Enter twice. The four lines are copied "up" five units on the Z axis. Perform a ZOOM Extents to view the entire drawing. Figure 28.2 shows the drawing at this point.

Figure 28.2

The "top" and "bottom" of the 3D box from an SW isometric viewpoint

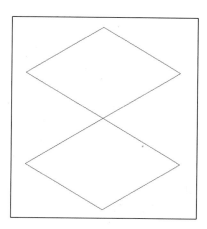

6. Start the LINE command again. Type the following coordinates:

   ```
   0,0,0
   0,0,5
   ```

   Press Enter to end the command.

7. Repeat step 6 three more times using these coordinate pairs for the From and To points:

   0,5,0 & 5,10,0
   5,5,0 & 10,10,0

   Your drawing should now resemble Figure 28.3

8. Save this drawing as 15SEBOX.DWG.

Figure 28.3

The completed wireframe box in an SW isometric view.

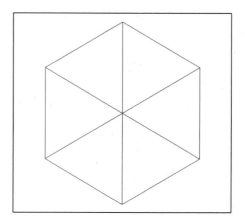

NOTE

During the last exercise, you created what is called a wireframe model of a box. A *wireframe* model does not have any 3D surfaces. It represents only the edges of the object you have drawn. These edges, however, can have surfaces applied between them later.

You can also give a line or polyline a thickness (similar to an extrusion) by changing the properties of the line with the PROPERTIES or CHANGE command.

As you can see from the previous exercise, drawing with a line in three dimensions with the LINE command is relatively easy; you just type in the coordinates. But it is also very tedious and potentially inaccurate. As you will see later in this chapter, the use of drawing aids can dramatically increase your 3D drafting speed and accuracy.

A standard polyline is not quite as flexible as a regular line in 3D work. When you create a standard polyline, the vertices must lie on the same two-dimensional plane. If you start a polyline at three units above the coordinate system, for example, all the vertices of the polyline would be at that height, regardless of where you select the points in the drawing. This makes polylines very useful for creating outlines or other planar construction elements that can later be surfaced with a variety of commands in AutoCAD.

NOTE

Surfacing is the process of creating continuous surfaces between boundary edges, such as lines. These surfaces can then be used to hide objects such as lines that exist behind them.

Because of the planar limitation of a polyline, AutoCAD also includes a 3D polyline object. This polyline differs from a standard polyline because you can place each vertex of the polyline at a different point in 3D space. Several of the polyline editing commands, however, are not available with the 3D polyline. For example, although you can still use PEDIT to create a spline curve from a 3D polyline, you cannot create a fit curve by using PEDIT. Figure 28.4 shows you a 3D polyline that has been changed into a spline curve by using PEDIT. As mentioned earlier, lines and polylines are frequently used in 3D work as construction elements upon which more complex surfaces are created. The actual choice as to which type of line you should use to create the construction elements will depend on your requirements and specific drawing conditions.

Figure 28.4

A 3D polyline changed into a splined curve. The curves are smoothly translated in both 2D and 3D space.

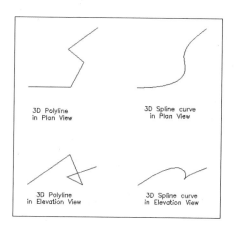

Now that you have an idea of how lines and polylines can be used to create three-dimensional drawings in AutoCAD, it is time to look at how those lines and polylines can be created more quickly and accurately using snaps and point filters.

Using Object Snaps and Point Filters

Drawing a line in three dimensions is relatively easy if you type in the coordinates for the end points of the line, rather than picking those points with a mouse. However, typing in points is not overly intuitive and can become tedious very quickly. To get around this, you need to make use of AutoCAD's drawing aids—in particular, object snaps and point filters.

Object Snaps

As you already know, an object snap is used to accurately input a point based upon an existing piece of geometry. Using object snap modes makes it easy to draw a line from the endpoint of one line to the endpoint of another. When you consider this concept from a three-dimensional perspective, object snaps become almost critical to the drawing process.

For example, if you draw a box in 3D by just entering the endpoints of the wireframe, you can draw only so much of the box in a 2D Plan view. To create the rest of the box, you must switch to a three-dimensional view, such as a SW Isometric view, to see the model in its three-dimensional form. You must make this switch because any lines that extend along the Z axis appear as dots in a Plan view. Only from a 3D view, such as an Isometric view, are you able to truly see the model. Because this is an Isometric view, however, what you see in the view might not be apparent. Figures 28.5 and 28.6 illustrate this problem.

Figure 28.5

A drawing that looks like a 3D box when viewed from a SW isometric viewpoint.

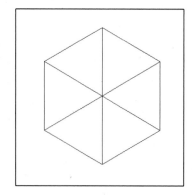

Figure 28.6

The same box view in Plan. This never was really drawn in three dimensions.

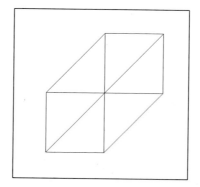

As you can see from Figures 28.5 and 28.6, it is very easy to draw lines that *appear* to be three-dimensional but that really exist only in the flat plane of the current UCS, instead of in three-dimensional space. This is where object snaps come in handy. By snapping to geometry that exists in three-dimensional space, you ensure that you will not run into this problem.

USING OBJECT SNAP MODES TO DRAW A 3D BOX

1. Start AutoCAD if it is not loaded and begin a new drawing.

2. Select the LINE command from the Draw toolbar.

3. Create a line with the following coordinates:

    0,0
    5,0
    5,5
    0,5
    C

    Press Enter to end the command.

4. Repeat from the View menu, select 3D Views, then select SW Isometric to switch to a 3D isometric view.

5. Copy the four lines "up" 3 units on the Z axis using the COPY command. Specify a displacement of **0,0,3** and press Enter twice to complete the copy. Perform a ZOOM Extents. Figure 28.7 shows the drawing at this point.

Figure 28.7

The box with completed "top" and "bottom."

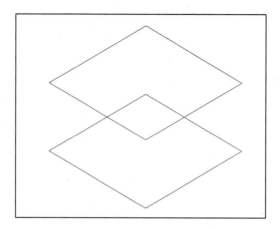

Now that you have built the "bottom" and the "top" of the box, it is time to use Object Snap modes to create the lines in between.

6. From the Tools menu, select Drafting Settings to display the Drafting Settings dialog box. Select the Object Snap tab to make it current as shown in Figure 28.8.

Figure 28.8

The Object Snap tab of the Drafting Settings dialog box.

7. Click the Clear All button if necessary to remove any checks from snap modes, then place a check next to the Endpoint osnap mode only. This enables Endpoint snapping. Click OK to exit the dialog box.

8. Select the LINE command from the Draw toolbar.

9. Draw a vertical line from the endpoint of each corner on the lower portion of the box to the corresponding upper portion, as shown in Figure 28.9.

10. End this drawing without saving.

Figure 28.9

*Constructing the vertical
lines of the box using
Endpoint osnaps.*

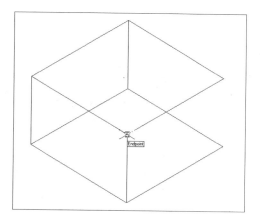

As you can see from this exercise, the use of Object Snap modes almost immediately gives you an immediate performance gain. It becomes quite easy to "snap" to a point in 3D.

But even object snaps can be troublesome from certain 3D viewpoints. Consider the box example again. Depending upon the dimensions of the sides of the box, when you view the box from an isometric view, you can have overlapping endpoints, as shown in Figure 28.10. To get around this problem, you can change the view of the 3D model so that the endpoints do not overlap visually.

Figure 28.10

*A view of a wireframe box
showing how endpoints
can overlap in certain
views.*

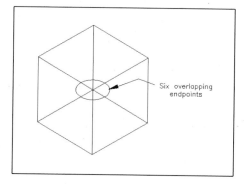

Six overlapping
endpoints

INSIDER TIP

3D views of wireframe models are notoriously ambiguous. When working in three dimensions, it is always a good idea to check your model from different views to make sure you have drawn it correctly. What looks correct in one view actually might be incorrect, but the view hides the problem. Because of this, even experienced AutoCAD users will occasionally unintentionally draw something incorrectly in three dimensions.

Point Filters

Point filters are a handy method of drawing three-dimensional lines without having to enter all three coordinates. A point filter, such as .XY (pronounced "point XY") filter for example, is used to isolate one or more of the three coordinates of a point selected, or *picked* with the mouse. For example, when you use the .XY filter, AutoCAD accepts only the X and Y coordinate values from the point you select. You then type, or pick, a .Z point filter to supply the Z coordinate. Because of the way they work, point filters—and especially the .XY filter—are extremely useful in 3D work.

Up to this stage, you have drawn lines in three dimensions by relying upon existing geometry or by typing in all three coordinates. By using Point filters, however, you can create 3D lines even more quickly and easily.

CONSTRUCTING THE VERTICAL LINES OF A BOX WITH A .XY FILTER

1. Start a new drawing in AutoCAD.

2. From the Tools menu, choose Drafting Settings and in the Drafting Settings dialog box's Snap and Grid tab, turn on both your grid and snap, with both set to 1 unit. Set a running Endpoint osnap as you did in step 7 of the previous exercise.

3. From the View menu, choose 3D Views, SW Isometric.

4. Choose the RECTANGLE command from the Draw toolbar and draw a rectangle by dragging the mouse. The size of the rectangle should resemble that shown in Figure 28.11.

Figure 28.11

The "base" of the box prior to using point filters to construct the vertical elements.

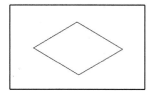

5. Choose the LINE command.

6. Select a corner of the box to set the start point of the line.

7. At the To Point: prompt, type in .XY and press Enter. AutoCAD then prompts with OF, meaning .XY "of" what point.

8. At the OF prompt, select the same point that you picked in step 6. AutoCAD then prompts you for a Z value.

9. Type a value of **3**. Figure 28.12 shows the box at this point.

Figure 28.12

The box with one vertical line segment drawn using a .XY filter.

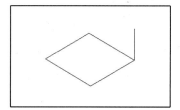

10. Repeat steps 5 through 9 for the remaining three corners, or use the COPY command to copy the vertical line to each corner.

11. Use the LINE command with the Endpoint osnap mode to complete the top of the box.

12. End this drawing without saving.

Point filters are always relative to the current UCS; therefore, make sure that you are aware of your current UCS orientation before using them, or you may get results you did not expect. Refer to Chapter 27, "Introduction to 3D," for a description of the UCS command.

Now that you have explored some of the basic commands used to draw lines and polylines in 3D, it is time to look at how AutoCAD handles editing in three dimensions.

3D AutoCAD Editing Commands

Like the line and polyline commands, most AutoCAD editing commands can be also utilized to work in three dimensions. In addition to the standard editing commands, AutoCAD also provides you with several 3D-specific editing commands intended for use in 3D. We will first look at the basic 2D editing commands to see how they are utilized in three dimensions.

Using MOVE, COPY, SCALE, and ROTATE in 3D

The basic 2D editing commands in AutoCAD include MOVE, COPY, SCALE, and ROTATE. Depending upon your view of the 3D model, each of these commands can be easily used in 3D as well. For example, consider the MOVE command. If you are working in an isometric view, you can use the MOVE command in combination with object snap modes to move and place objects in three-dimensional space. This works well when you have existing geometry to use—that is, when you have a 3D point to move from and to.

Suppose, however, you have drawn the outline of a table top and want to move it into the correct position in three-dimensional space and have no existing geometry to work with. In this situation, you have two options. First, you can combine the MOVE command with a .XY point filter to correctly move the tabletop. A second method involves using a shortcut in the MOVE command. When you select the MOVE command in AutoCAD, you are first prompted to select the object(s) you want to move. Then AutoCAD prompts you for the base point from which the move occurs. But rather than a base point, you can specify a displacement. If, for example, you type in a displacement of **0,0,10** and press Enter twice, the selected objects move 0 units in the X and Y axes but 10 units along the Z axis. The COPY command offers the same option at its Specify base point: prompt. Rather than specifying a base point, you can enter a three-dimensional displacement vector, press Enter twice and the copy will appear at the displaced distance. In some instances, even when reference geometry is present in the model, it is more convenient to specify displacements when moving or copying objects.

In the following exercise, you use the displacement option of the COPY and MOVE commands with 3D objects.

WORKING WITH MOVE IN 3D

1. Load the file SEBOX3.DWG from the accompanying CD-ROM. The model consists of a box within a box, as shown in Figure 28.13.

2. Choose Move from the Modify toolbar.

3. Select an edge of the smaller box and press Enter.

4. When prompted for the base point or displacement, type **0,0,1.5** and press Enter twice. The smaller box is displaced 1.5 units in the current Z direction, as shown in Figure 28.14.

Figure 28.13

A 3D model showing a box within a box.

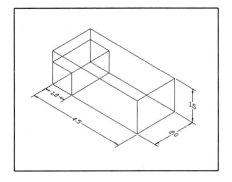

Figure 28.14

The 3D model after a move and copy displacement.

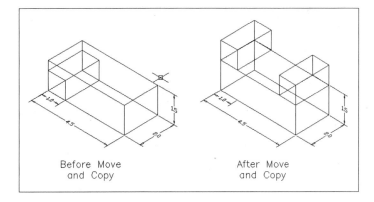

In the next steps you displace a copy of the box you just moved 3.5 units along the X axis.

5. Choose Copy from the Modify toolbar.

6. When prompted to select objects, type **P** for previous and press Enter.

7. When prompted for the base point or displacement, type **3.5,0,0** and press Enter a second time. A copy of the box is placed at the specified displacement (refer to Figure 28.14).

8. Close this drawing without saving.

As you can see from this exercise, using the MOVE and COPY commands with the displacement option is a fast and easy way to specify displacements of objects in 3D space. There are situations in which the displacement method is not practical and in these situations using Object Snaps, perhaps with point filters, and existing geometry reference points is the most efficient method.

Both the SCALE and ROTATE commands can also be used in three dimensions and work essentially as they do in a "flat" 2D model. Keep in mind that, when editing 3D models, it is essential that you move away from plan views and utilize isometric views so that the 3D geometry can be fully seen.

In addition to the standard 2D editing commands, AutoCAD provides several editing commands specifically intended for use in 3D modeling. These include MIRROR3D, 3DROTATE, ALIGN, and 3DARRAY. We will examine these specialized 3D editing commands in the following sections.

The MIRROR3D Command

The MIRROR3D command is a modified version of the standard MIRROR command. In the standard 2D command, the mirror line always lies in the XY plane of the current UCS. In the 3D version, provision is made to specify any plane in 3D space.

After selecting the objects you want to mirror, the following prompt appears:

```
Specify first point of mirror plane (3 points) or
[Object/Last/Zaxis/View/XY/YZ/ZX/3points] <3points>:
```

There are several methods of specifying the 3D mirroring plane:

■ **Object.** Use the plane of a current planar object as the mirroring plane. Qualifying objects include a circle, arc, or 2D polyline.

■ **Last.** Use the last specified mirroring plane.

- **Zaxis.** Define the plane with a point on the plane and a point normal to the plane.

- **View.** Use the current viewing plane as the mirroring plane.

- **XY/YZ/ZX.** Use one of the standard planes through a specified point.

- **3points.** Define the plane by specifying three points on the mirroring plane.

Often, two or more of these methods may work. The 3points method is the default and can usually be used when sufficient geometry is available.

WORKING WITH THE MIRROR3D Feature

1. Load the file 3DMIRROR.DWG from the accompanying CD. This drawing is shown in the Figure 28.15.

Figure 28.15

A 3D model for use with the MIRROR3D *command.*

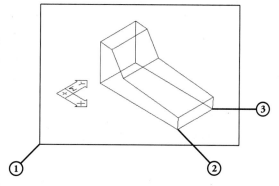

2. From the Modify menu, choose 3D Operations, Mirror 3D.

3. Select anywhere on the model and press Enter. You are prompted with the Mirror 3D options.

   Use the default 3points option to define the mirroring plane. Because 3points is the default method, you can immediately identify the first point.

4. Use an Endpoint osnap to pick at ①, ②, and ③ in Figure 28.15.

5. When prompted to delete the old objects, press Enter to accept the default: No. Figure 28.16 shows the mirrored result.

Figure 28.16

Figure 28.16

The model after using the
MIRROR3D *command.*

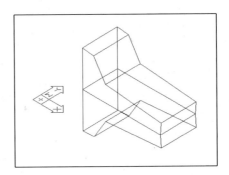

6. Type **U** and press Enter to undo the last command.

7. Next use the XY plane option to identify the mirroring plane.

8, Repeat steps 2 and 3 and specify the XY option.

9, When prompted for the point on the XY plane, use an Endpoint osnap and pick at ① in Figure 28.15. Press Enter to accept the default (No) when asked if you wish to delete source objects. Figure 28.16 again shows the same mirrored result.

10. If you are not continuing with the next exercise, close this drawing without saving.

As you can see from this exercise, the MIRROR3D command enables you to mirror one or more objects around any planar axis in 3D space, as long as you have three points on that plane to select.

The 3DROTATE Command

The 3DROTATE command is very much like the MIRROR3D command. It, too, differs from its 2D counterpart by enabling you to rotate an object around an axis, not just the current Z axis.

After selecting the objects you want to mirror, the following prompt appears:

```
Specify first point on axis or define axis by
[Object/Last/View/Xaxis/Yaxis/Zaxis/2points]:
```

You have various methods of specifying the 3D axis of rotation:

■   **Object.** Align the axis of rotation with an existing object. Qualifying objects include a line, circle, arc, or 2D polyline.

■   **Last.** Use the last specified axis of rotation.

- **View.** Align the axis of rotation with the current viewing direction.

- **X/Y/Z axis.** Align axis of rotation with one of the standard axes that passes through the selected point.

- **2Points.** Define the axis of rotation by specifying two points.

The 3D rotation routine is accessed from the Modify menu by choosing 3D Operations, 3DRotate, or by typing in **3DROTATE** at the command prompt. In the following exercise, you use the X/Y/Z axis method of specifying an axis of rotation for the **3DROTATE** command.

USING THE **3DROTATE** COMMAND

1. Either continue from the last exercise or open the drawing 3DROTATE.DWG. This drawing, shown in Figure 28.16, is from the preceding exercise.

2. From the Modify menu, choose 3D Operations, 3DRotate .

3. When prompted, select both halves of the mirrored model and press Enter.

4. From the options, type **Y** and press Enter to select the X axis around which to perform the rotation.

5. When prompted for a point on the Y axis, use an Endpoint osnap to pick ① in Figure 28.16.

6. When prompted for the rotation angle, type **90** and press Enter. The model is rotated 90 degrees about an axis parallel with the current Y axis and passing through the specified point as shown in Figure 28.17.

7. Close this drawing without saving.

Figure 28.17

The model after using the **3DROTATE** *command.*

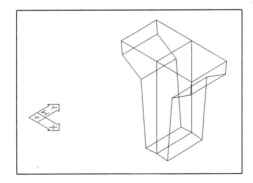

In the previous exercise you could have performed the same rotation of the model by first changing the UCS and then using the standard 2D ROTATE command. This would have involved aligning the new UCS so that its Z axis aligned with the desired axis. Although this would not have been a difficult UCS re-alignment, leaving the UCS intact and using an option of the 3DROTATE command is quicker and simpler. There are also circumstances when using the 3DROTATE command options provide the only convenient means of identifying the rotation axis.

The ALIGN Command

The ALIGN command is used to cause one object to line up, or *align*, with another object based on the source and destination points specified on the two objects. The two objects need not necessarily line-up exactly; the ALIGN command will either make the best alignment possible with the point you supply or, alternately, it will scale the object being aligned to the object to which it is being aligned. The ALIGN command is a very powerful 3D tool and one that is probably under used. The command is accessed from the Modify menu, 3D Operations, Align, or by typing ALIGN at the command prompt. The command prompts for the object(s) you want to align. You then pick source points on the selected object(s) and respective destination points on the destination object. The use of object snaps is essential. These points are then lined up and the object is moved and rotated as necessary to make it align with the destination object. In the following exercise, you use the ALIGN command to align one 3D object with another 3D object.

USING THE ALIGN COMMAND

1. Open the file ALIGN.DWG from the accompanying CD-ROM. The model consists of a 3D wedge and box. See Figure 28.18.

   Because the ALIGN command is difficult, if not impossible, to use effectively without object snaps, you first set a running Endpoint osnap.

Figure 28.18

*The first source and
destination points.*

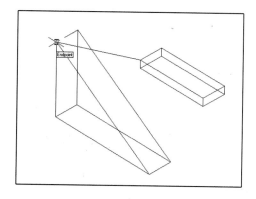

2. From the Tools menu, choose Drafting Settings and on the Object Snap tab of the dialog box, ensure that a check appears beside Object Snap On and the Endpoint mode. Click OK to close the dialog box.

3. From the Modify menu, choose 3D Operation, Align.

4. When prompted to select an object, select the box.

5. You are then prompted for the first source point and first destination point. These points are shown in Figure 28.18.

6. Create the second source and destination points, as shown in Figure 28.19.

Figure 28.19

*The second source and
destination points.*

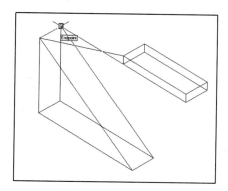

7. Create the third source and destination points, as shown in Figure 28.20.

Figure 28.20

The third source and destination points.

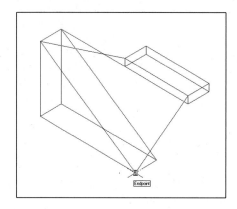

8. After selecting the third destination point, the box is aligned, as shown in Figure 28.21. You can exit this drawing without saving changes.

Figure 28.21

The newly aligned box.

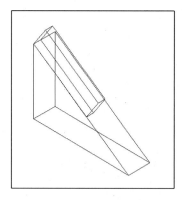

The first destination point determines the final *position* of the first source point of the selected object. The other source-destination points determine the *alignment*. In the preceding exercise, for example, if you were to switch the first and third pair of points, the box would be positioned at the bottom of the wedge rather than at the top.

If you supply only two sets of points to the ALIGN command, you can cause the source object to be scaled to "fit" the destination object with the two sets of points acting as a "reference" for the scaling operation. This may not always lead to the alignment you want but a subsequent ALIGN, MOVE, or 3DROTATE command may achieve the proper alignment.

The 3DARRAY Command

The last 3D editing command to discuss is the 3DARRAY command. Like the other 3D editing commands, this command is located on the Modify pull-down menu, or can be typed at the command prompt as **3DARRAY**. This command is a modified version of the standard ARRAY command but can create objects quickly in the third dimension. This is accomplished in the rectangular array by adding levels to the rows and columns.

USING THE 3DARRAY COMMAND

1. Load the file 3DARRAY.DWG from the accompanying CD-ROM. The file contains a three-element cell, as shown in Figure 28.22.

Figure 28.22

The basic cell used for the
3DARRAY *command.*

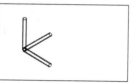

2. From the Modify menu, choose 3D Operation, 3DArray.

3. Select the three cylinders and press Enter.

4. Select **R** (for rectangular) as the type of array you want to create.

5. Set the number of rows, columns, and levels each to 4.

6. Specify the distances between rows, levels, and columns each as 1. When you complete this step, AutoCAD begins arraying the objects. Depending on the speed of your machine, this may take several seconds. You may need to perform a ZOOM/ Extents to view the entire array. Figure 28.23 shows the array after performing a HIDE command.

7. You can close this drawing without saving changes.

Figure 28.23

*The completed 64-unit
3Darray.*

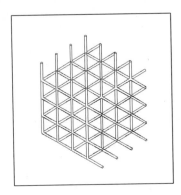

The 3DARRAY command also supports a polar option. As with the other specialized 3D editing commands, the ability to specify an axis or plane in space provides the command's unique 3D functionality.

The special 3D editing commands, MIRROR3D, 3DROTATE, and 3DARRAY, combined with the ALIGN command, allow you to easily edit objects in 3D space. Two other editing commands—TRIM and EXTEND—also have functionality that make them useful in 3D work.

EXTEND, TRIM, and Other Editing Commands in 3D

AutoCAD's TRIM and EXTEND commands both have a Projection option that allow you some degree of flexibility when using these commands in 3D space. As shown in Figure 28.24, for example, the EXTEND command can extend a line lying on one 3D plane to another line lying on a different plane. In this case, the boundary line can be "projected" onto the plane of the line being extended. Alternately, you can cause the extension of one line to be taken to a plane perpendicular to the current viewing plane. Using the Project mode you can have TRIM and EXTEND behave in the following ways:

- Using no projection causes TRIM and EXTEND to trim or extend to objects that actually intersect in 3D space.

- Using the UCS mode of Project causes objects to be projected onto the current XY plane.

- Using the View mode of Project causes the objects to be projected onto a plane perpendicular to the current viewing plane.

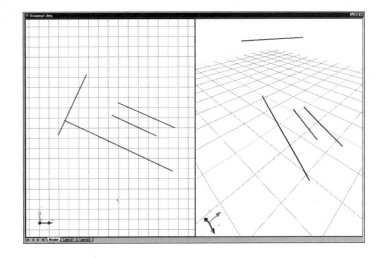

Figure 28.24

You can extend a line to another line on a different 3D plane.

The following exercise demonstrates the UCS and View modes of the Project option of the EXTEND command.

USING THE PROJECT MODE OF THE EXTEND COMMAND

1. Open the file PROJMODE.DWG from the accompanying CD-ROM. The file contains three polylines with thicknesses applied. The longest line is drawn at a higher elevation, as shown in Figure 28.25.

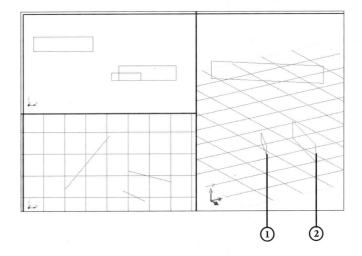

Figure 28.25

The views of the boundary line and the extension lines.

2. Click in the large, right viewport, if necessary, to make it active.

3. From the Modify menu, choose Extend. Note that the current setting for the Projection mode is reported on the command line.

4. When prompted to select boundary edges, select the longest line near the top of the viewport and press Enter.

5. At the prompt to select objects to extend, type **P** and press Enter. At the next prompt, ensure that the Projection mode is set to UCS and press Enter.

6. When prompted again for objects to extend, select the shorter line at ① in Figure 28.25. Note that the line is extended to the USC projection of the boundary line down onto the current XY plane.

7. When prompted again for objects to extend, type **P** and change the Projection mode to View by typing **V** and press Enter.

8. When prompted for objects to extend, choose the now shorter line at ② and press Enter to end the command. Note that the line is projected to appear to end at the current view of the boundary line. Your drawing should resemble Figure 28.26.

9. Close the drawing without saving changes.

Figure 28.26

The views of the boundary line and the extension lines.

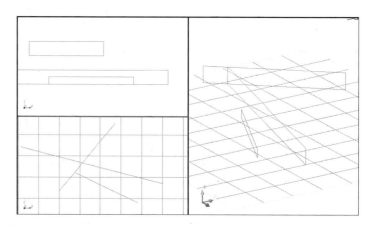

When working with the TRIM and EXTEND commands in 3D space, you may want to have the Project option of these commands set to UCS to insure accuracy no matter what viewpoint you are using to view the 3D geometry.

Before looking at actual 3D objects such as objects constructed with surfaces and objects composed of solids in the following two chapters, we should examine a special 2D object that behaves like a 3D object.

Working with Regions

Regions are special AutoCAD objects. In many ways, regions act like 2D planar objects; in other ways, regions exhibit many of the properties of 3D objects. Like 3D surfaces, for example, regions can hide objects "behind" them and can have materials applied to then for rendering purposes. Like 2D objects, regions have no third dimension, or Z axis information. In many ways, regions can be considered infinitely thin solids.

Technically, regions are enclosed 2D areas. You create regions from closed shapes. *Closed shapes* consist of a curve or a sequence of curves that define an area on a single plane with a non-self-intersecting boundary. *Closed curves* can be combinations of lines, polylines, circles, ellipses, elliptical arcs, splines, 3D faces, or solids. The objects that compose a closed curve must either be closed themselves or form a closed area by sharing endpoints with other objects.

As you can see, a large number of AutoCAD objects can join together to form a closed curve from which a region can be created. The only restrictions are that the object must be *co-planar*, or exist on the same plane, and sequential elements must share endpoints. Assuming that the arcs and lines shown in Figure 28.27 are co-planar, the set of curves on the left could not be converted into a region, whereas the curves on the right could.

Figure 28.27

Sets of overlapping and end-to-end curves. Only end-to-end curves can be used to create a region.

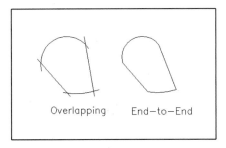

Overlapping   End—to—End

To convert a set of qualifying curves into a region, you use the REGION command. In the following exercise you create a region from a set of straight polyline "curves" using the RECTANG command.

CREATING REGIONS WITH THE REGION COMMAND

1. Open the file REGION27.DWG from the accompanying CD-ROM. This drawing is composed of only a circle and a polyline drawn at an elevation of –1.0 units

2. From the Draw menu, choose Rectangle. When prompted for the first corner of the rectangle, type **4,2**. At the Specify other corner prompt, type **@3.5,5.5**. Your drawing should now resemble Figure 28.28.

Figure 28.28

A closed polyline curve drawn over a circle and line.

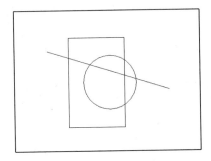

3. From the Draw menu, choose Region. At the Select objects prompt, select the rectangle you just created and press Enter. AutoCAD reports 1 Region created at the command line. The polyline used to create the rectangle has now been converted to a region.

4. Type **HIDE** and press Enter to invoke the HIDE command. Note that the newly created region acts as a planar surface hiding the circle and line objects behind it as shown in Figure 28.29.

Figure 28.29

A region created with the REGION *command. Regions hide objects behind them.*

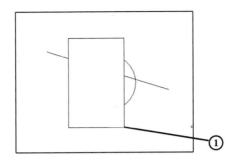

In the following step, you rotate the Region in 3D space.

5. From the Modify menu, choose 3D Operation, then Rotate 3D. When prompted to select objects, select the region and press Enter.

6. At the next prompt, type **Y** to indicate you want to rotate the region about its Y axis.

7. When prompted to specify a point on the Y axis, use an Endpoint osnap and pick at ① in Figure 28.29. To specify an angle of rotation, type **90** and press Enter.

8. From the View menu, choose 3D Views, then SE Isometric. Your drawing should resemble Figure 28.30.

Figure 28.30

Regions can be moved and positioned in 3D space.

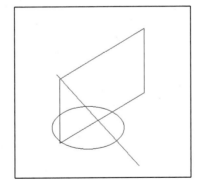

9. Again type **HIDE** to invoke the HIDE command. Note that the region is rotated in 3D space and hides objects behind it as shown in Figure 28.31.

10. You can close this drawing without saving changes.

Figure 28.31

Regions behave like solids and hide objects behind them.

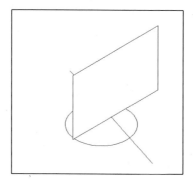

As you can see from the preceding exercise, regions have many of the properties of 3D surfaces; they hide objects behind them and they can be easily moved in 3D space. One of the most interesting and useful properties of regions is their ability to undergo Boolean operations—a trait they share with AutoCAD solids. Boolean operations will be discussed and demonstrated later in Chapter 30, "Solid Modeling."

Summary

In this chapter, you learned some of the basic principles of drawing in three dimensions. Starting with simple, basic lines and polylines, you learned the importance of using object snaps and point filters to insure accuracy in 3D space. You learned that many of the editing operations you use in 2D, such as MOVE and ROTATE, have equivalent 3D commands. Finally, you learned about a special 3D object called a region.

In the next chapter, you will learn how to create 3D surfaces by using the AutoCAD surfacing commands.

29

SURFACING IN 3D

In the previous two chapters, you learned how to create simple 3D objects in AutoCAD. By creating and manipulating these 3D primitives, you can create a wide variety of more complex objects such as chairs, tables, and so on. There are, however, many instances in which you need more flexibility in modeling complex objects such as irregularly curved surfaces.

Fortunately, AutoCAD provides a set of surfacing commands with which you can create the outlines of these types of objects in profile using lines or polylines and then create surfaces between these lines. This chapter takes a look at the various methods and techniques AutoCAD provides for creating both simple and complex 3D surfaces. This chapter covers the following topics:

■ *Basic surfacing techniques*

■ *Working with advanced surfacing commands*

■ *3D meshes*

■ *Editing mesh surfaces*

Basic Surfacing Techniques

In the previous chapter the techniques used to create 3D lines and polylines were discussed. Objects modeled with such lines are called *wireframe* models. To create a true 3D object, however, surfaces must be applied across or around the edges of the wire frame. Such surfaces can then be used to hide lines and other surfaces that lie "behind" other surfaces in any particular view. Surfaces can also have hatch patterns and even materials applied to them to yield more realistic-looking objects.

In some cases, you need to create the wireframe "skeleton" of an object before you create the surfaces, using the wireframe as a starting point from which to apply the surfaces. This method employs two relatively simply 3D objects: 3D faces and polyfaces.

NOTE

> All the surfacing commands discussed in this chapter are available from the pull-down menus. Most are also available on the Surfaces toolbar. To access the toolbar, right-click on any toolbar in AutoCAD to display the Toolbars menu. Scroll down the list and select Surfaces. When working with the exercises in this chapter, reference to the menu commands is usually made. You can also use the corresponding tools from the Surface toolbar. The basic commands are also available by typing them at the command prompt.

Using 3D Faces and Polyface Meshes

A 3D *face* is a surface defined by either three or four sides, forming either a rectangular or a triangular surface. In most instances, a triangular, three-sided face is preferable because a 3D face is a planar element. A rectangular 3D face can be either planar or non-planar. Figure 29.1 show a triangular and a rectangular 3D face with the upper-right corner of the rectangular face lying at a different elevation than the other three corners. Four-sided faces can be more difficult to visualize.

You construct 3D faces with the 3DFACE command, accessed by selecting Draw, Surfaces, 3D Face. Specifying the corner points creates the face. The 3DFACE command enables you to continue creating 3D faces by selecting more points.

Figure 29.1

A three-sided (left) and a four-sided 3D face. Three-sided faces must be planar, whereas four-sided faces may have vertices at different elevations.

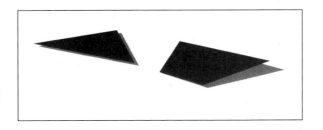

NOTE

3D faces can be difficult to visualize. To see if the 3D faces you created are correct, use the HIDE and SHADEMODE commands to check your drawing. Also check the drawing from different viewpoints to ensure that the faces are drawn correctly.

When creating your 3D face, always work your way around the perimeter of the face. This is especially important if you decide to create a four-sided face. If you select points in an X-wise fashion, a bow-tie effect will result, as shown in Figure 29.2.

Figure 29.2

Always specify the corners of a 3D face in a clockwise or counter-clockwise sequence.

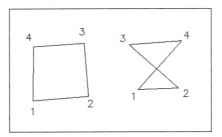

Although you can construct a surfaced box with the AI_BOX command, there are instances in which you may need to place 3D faces on a *wireframe* as shown in the following exercise.

USING THE 3DFACE COMMAND TO SURFACE A BOX

1. Load the drawing file 29EX01.DWG from the accompanying CD-ROM. The file contains a wireframe box, as shown in Figure 29.3. This "box" consists of 12 individual polylines arranged in such a way as to represent a three-dimensional box.

Figure 29.3

A wireframe "box" that you surface with the 3DFACE *command.*

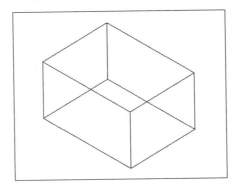

2. At the command prompt, type **HIDE** and press Enter. Because there are no surfaces in this collection of polylines, the HIDE command has no visual effect.

3. From the Tools menu, select Drafting Settings and in the Drafting Settings dialog box's Object Snap tab, ensure that the Object Snap On and Endpoint object snap options are checked. Click OK to close the dialog box.

4. From the Draw menu, choose Surfaces, 3D Face.

5. Select the seven corners of the box shown in ① through ⑦ in Figure 29.4. Be sure to select the corners in numerical sequence.

Figure 29.4

Choose the corners in sequence to apply 3D faces.

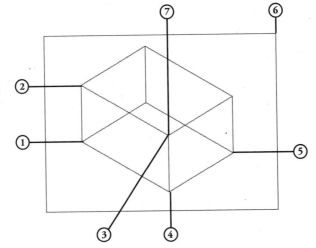

6. When you have selected the corner at ⑦, press Enter twice to end the **3DFACE** command.

7. Type **HIDE** and press Enter. Figure 29.5 shows you the resulting box.

Figure 29.5

The box with faces applied to two sides.

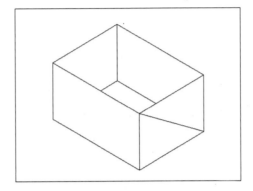

8. Leave this drawing open for use in the next exercise.

In the previous exercise, you constructed only two of the six required 3D faces to completely cover the frame of the box. The other four sides could be applied in a similar manner. The second face actually consists of two three-sided faces with the diagonal line appearing between corners 5 and 7 representing the shared edge. Because of the manner in which the **3DFACE** command works, four-sided faces are usually drawn this way because AutoCAD attempts to construct three-sided faces where possible.

AutoCAD provides two means to hide face edges. You can hide an edge during the construction of a face by typing an **i** just prior to specifying the first point that will create the edge. You can also make a 3D face edge invisible after it is formed by using the **EDGE** command.

The following exercise shows how to use the **EDGE** command to hide a face edge after it has been drawn.

USING THE EDGE COMMAND

1. Continue in 29EX01.DWG from the preceding exercise

2. From the Draw menu, select Surfaces, Edge.

3. When prompted, select the diagonal edge appearing between corners ⑤ and ⑦ in Figure 29.4. Notice that AutoCAD switches you to a Midpoint Object Snap mode automatically.

4. Press Return and the edge is hidden.

   After an edge is hidden, you can no longer select it. To unhide an edge, you can use the Display option of the EDGE command.

5. Press Enter to restart the EDGE command

6. Select an edge of the face containing the hidden edge. Select between ④ and ⑤, for example.

7. Type D (for display) and press Enter. You are then prompted with the Display options.

8. When prompted for the Display options, type A (for all) and press Enter. All the edges of the face become visible and highlighted.

9. Select the edge you want to make visible and press Enter. The visibility of the edge is restored.

10. Quit this drawing without saving changes.

Note

> The AutoCAD system variable SPLFRAME can be used to control the display of the invisible edges of 3D faces. If you are having trouble using the EDGE command to change the visibility of an edge, change SPLFRAME to 1 to display all edges. Then you can more easily use the EDGE command to make edges visible or invisible.

3D faces are limited as surfacing tools, principally because they are limited to three or four sides and do not serve well for the creation of curved objects. Applying 3D faces to define a large surface would be tedious work and likely yield less than satisfactory results. To get around this limitation, you can make use of the AutoCAD PFACE, or polyface, command, which enables you to create larger faces composed of many more individual faces by defining multiple faces which specify how the surface is created between points. Such a large non-planar surface is termed a *polyface mesh*. Here again, to construct a large polyface mesh manually would be tremendously tedious and time-consuming. The PFACE command is therefore usually used by other applications. The application "communicates" with the PFACE command through an application programming interface, such as AutoLISP, to automatically construct the mesh.

Working with Advanced Surfacing Commands

AutoCAD provides five true Surfacing commands. These commands make use of existing geometry—usually polylines—to create surfaces. These surfacing tools include the following commands:

- Edgesurf
- Rulesurf
- Tabsurf
- Revsurf
- 3D Mesh

EDGESURF

The EDGESURF command is used to create a 3D surface between four connected lines or polylines. Figure 29.6 shows you an example of the result of using EDGESURF.

Figure 29.6

Four splined curves before (left) and after applying the EDGESURF command.

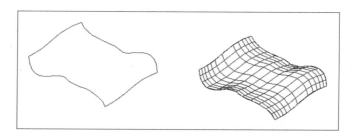

The EDGESURF command can be accessed by choosing the Draw menu, Surfaces, Edge Surface or by typing **EDGESURF** at the command prompt.

The resolution of the 3D surface generated by EDGESURF, as well as by the other surfacing commands, is controlled by two system variables: SURFTAB1 and SURFTAB2. These two variables represent the number of mesh faces in the M and N directions respectively. The letters M and N are used to reduce the confusion with the standard X and Y axes. The M direction, however, is generally considered to coincide with the

X axis direction and the N direction with the Y axis direction The default value of both SURFTAB1 and SURFTAB2 is 6. By increasing these values, you get more accurate surfaces because more individual faces are generated between the bounding edges. Figure 29.7 shows you the difference between a surface with both variables set to 6 and the same surface with both variables set to 24.

Figure 29.7

Two surfaces created with the EDGESURF *command. The surface on the left was created with* SURFTAB *settings of 6; the surface on the right with* SURFTAB *values set to 24.*

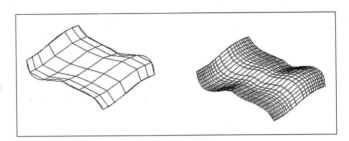

INSIDER **T**IP

The SURFTAB variables do not always have to be set to the same values. For example, if you have a set of four lines that you want to surface, but in one direction the lines are more complex than in the other direction. You might want to increase the SURFTAB value in the more complex direction only. This results in a more accurate mesh, without creating an overly complex mesh.

The following exercise shows you how to use EDGESURF to create the canopy of an airplane.

USING EDGESURF TO CREATE THE CANOPY

1. Load the file 29Canopy.DWG from the accompanying CD-ROM. The file contains the outline of an airplane canopy, as shown in Figure 29.8.

2. At the command prompt, type **SURFTAB1**. Set the value to **24**.

3. Repeat step 2, setting Surftab2 to a value to **24**.

4. From the Draw menu, select Surfaces, Edge Surface.

Figure 29.8

*The outline drawing of an
airplane canopy ready for
the* EDGESURF *command.*

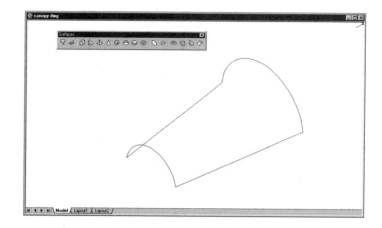

5. Select the four lines in the drawing. The surface is then created, as shown in Figure 29.9. Because the SURFTAB variables are set the same, the order of selection is not important.

6. Close this drawing without saving changes.

Figure 29.9

*The canopy with surface
applied.*

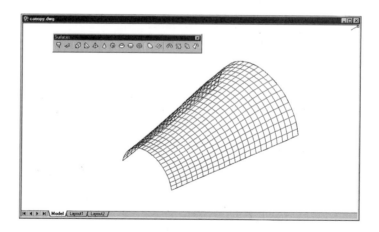

In this exercise, you set Surftab1 and Surftab2 to relatively high values. This resulted in a smoother surface at the expense of longer regeneration times and a larger drawing. If you change Surftab1 and Surftab2 to either higher or lower values, you must erase or undo the previous mesh and perform the surfacing operation again. Also note that the surface is generated on the current layer. As you work with EDGESURF, remember that the command neither removes your edges from the drawing nor gets attached to the mesh.

The **RULESURF** Command

The RULESURF command creates a ruled surface. Unlike the EDGESURF command, RULESURF requires only two defining edges instead of four. Because RULESURF works only between two lines, it makes use of just the SURFTAB1 system variable to establish the surface mesh density. Figure 29.10 shows examples of typical surfaces created with the RULESURF command. The defining edges can be points, lines, splines, circles, arcs, or polylines. If one of the edge objects is closed—a circle, for example—then the other object must also be closed.

Figure 29.10

Typical surface meshes created with the RULESURF *command.*

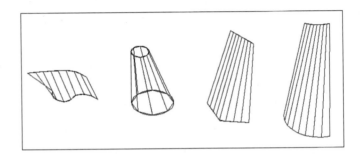

If you generate a surface between two open boundary edges, you must be careful about the points you use to select the boundaries. RULESURF starts generating the mesh at each boundary by dividing the boundary curve into a number of segments equal to the current setting of Surftab1, starting from the endpoint nearest the pick point. If you use pick points on opposite sides of the two boundary curves, the resulting curve will be self-intersecting as shown in Figure 29.11.

Figure 29.11

With open boundary edges, selecting objects at opposite ends creates a self-intersecting polygon mesh.

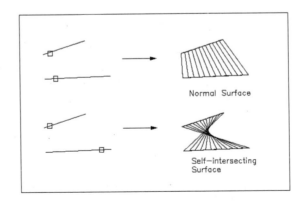

The following exercise shows you how to use RULESURF to surface the contours of a site.

USING RULESURF IN A MAPPING APPLICATION

1. Load the file 29Edge.DWG from the accompanying CD-ROM. The file contains four contours, as shown in Figure 29.12.

Figure 29.12

Four contour lines that you surface with RULESURF.

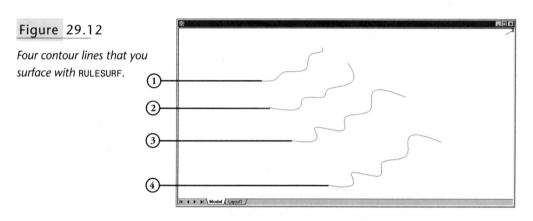

2. From the Draw menu, select Surfaces, Ruled Surface.

3. Select the top two lines in order ① then ② of Figure 29.12. The ruled surface is generated, as shown in Figure 29.13.

Figure 29.13

The first surface generated between the first two contour lines.

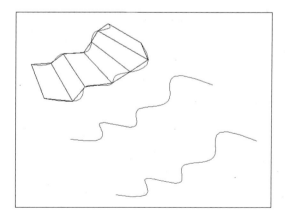

4. The smoothness of this curve is inadequate. Type **SURFTAB1** and set the value to **24**

5. Use the **ERASE** command to erase the surface. Repeat step 3 with the new `Surftab1` setting. The surface should now resemble Figure 29.14.

Figure 29.14

The first surface generated between the first two contour lines at higher density.

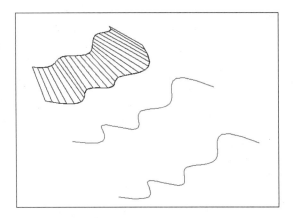

6. Select the new surface and use the **PROPERTIES** command to change its layer from 0 to Surface. Note that the Surface layer is currently frozen. Click OK in the frozen layer warning dialog box. The surface disappears when transferred to the frozen layer.

7. Repeat step 3 selecting at ② and ③ of Figure 29.12. **RULESURF** generates a second surface.

8. Use the same procedure as in step 6 to transfer the second surface to the Surface layer.

9. Use **RULESURF** and the boundaries at ③ and ④ to generate the third surface.

10. Transfer the third surface to Surface layer and thaw Surface layer. Your drawing should resemble Figure 29.15.

11. Close this drawing without saving changes.

This exercise demonstrates that the amount of detail necessary in a **RULESURF** mesh often depends upon the boundary object(s). With curved boundaries, `Surftab1` may need to be set to a higher value to cause the surface to follow the boundary edge more closely. With sequential boundaries such as in the preceding exercise, it is a good idea to create the surfaces on a separate layer then transfer them to a frozen layer. This allows the boundary edges to be more available for selecting.

Figure 29.15

The completed contour surfaces.

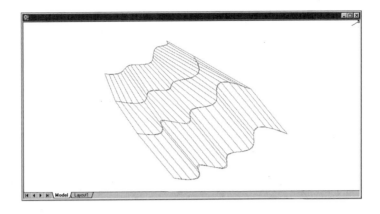

The TABSURF Command

The TABSURF command creates a *tabulated* surface, or a surface that is extruded along a linear path. TABSURF is accessed by choosing Draw, Surfaces, Tabulated Surface or by typing **TABSURF** at the command prompt.

To create a surface with TABSURF, you must have two elements: an outline, or curve, to be extruded and a direction vector indicating the direction and distance the curve is to be extended. Figure 29.16 shows several examples of tabulated surfaces.

Figure 29.16

Typical surfaces constructed with RULESURF.

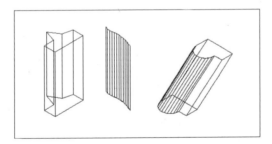

The path curve can consist of a line, arc, circle, ellipse, or a 2D or 3D polyline. TABSURF draws the surface starting at the point on the path curve closest to the selection point.

If the direction vector is a polyline, TABSURF considers only the first and last vertices of the line in determining the length and direction of the vector. In other words, TABSURF will extrude only a straight line. The end of the vector line chosen determines the direction of the extrusion. As with RULESURF, only Surftab1 has meaning with TABSURF.

The following exercise shows you how to use the TABSURF command to create a stair railing.

USING TABSURF TO CREATE A STAIR RAILING

1. Load the file 29Tab.DWG from the accompanying CD. This drawing is shown in Figure 29.17.

Figure 29.17

The path curve and direction vector for use in constructing a stair railing.

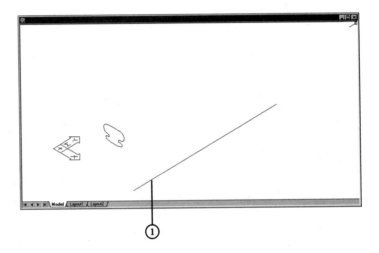

2. From the Draw menu, select Surfaces, Tabulated Surface.

3. Select the outline of the handrail.

4. Select the vertical line near ① in Figure 29.17. The curve is extruded, as shown in Figure 29.18.

5. Close this drawing without saving changes.

The REVSURF Command

REVSURF is perhaps the most useful of the 3D surfacing commands. REVSURF generates a 3D mesh object in the form of a surface of revolution by taking an outline—the path curve—and revolving it about an axis of revolution. As shown in Figure 29.19, the path curve is revolved around the axis of revolution to create the surface. The REVSURF command is accessed by selecting the Draw menu, Surfaces, Revolved Surface, or by typing **REVSURF** at the command prompt.

Figure 29.18

The completed railing.

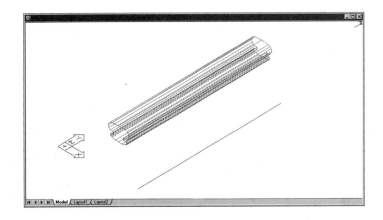

Figure 29.19

REVSURF *revolves an outline around an axis.*

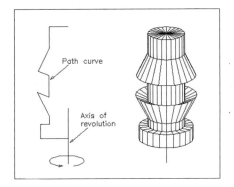

The *path curve* is the outline that will be revolved. It must be a single object: a line, arc, circle, ellipse, elliptical arc, polyline, polygon, spline, or donut.

The *axis of revolution* is the axis about which the path curve is revolved. The axis can be a line or an open 2D or 3D polyline. If a polyline is selected, the axis is assumed to be a line running through the first and last vertices.

REVSURF is made even more powerful by the fact that it can revolve the path curve through an included angle that can range from 0 to a full 360 degrees. The default angle is a full circle that results in the generation of a closed surface of revolution such as that shown in Figure 29.19. If you specify an angle less than 360 degrees, then the surface is generated in a counterclockwise direction. If you specify a negative angle less than 360 degrees, then the surface is generated in a clockwise direction.

You can also specify the *start angle*, which is the angular offset from the path curve at which the surface of revolution begins. The default value, 0, indicates that the surface of revolution will begin at the location of the path curve.

Determining the Positive Direction of Rotation

To have a start angle other than 0 degrees or an included angle other than a full circle, you must be able to determine the positive direction of rotation. REVSURF follows these conventions: A negative value dictates an angular distance in the clockwise direction, and a positive value dictates an angular distance in a counter-clockwise direction. You can determine the direction of rotation by applying the so-called "right-hand rule."

According to the *right-hand rule*, if you point your right thumb in the positive direction of the axis about which you are rotating and wrap your fingers of your right hand around the axis, the curl of your fingers indicates the direction of positive rotation. But how do you determine the positive direction of the axis?

The *positive direction* along the axis of rotation runs from the endpoint of the object nearest the pickpoint used to select the object to the other endpoint. For example, in Figure 29.20, if you select the line at point ①, then the positive direction of the axis runs from ① to ②. If you select the line near ②, then the positive direction of the axis runs from ② to ①.

Figure 29.20

Where you select the axis of revolution determines the positive direction of revolution.

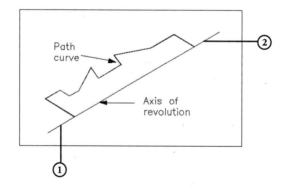

Unlike the surfaces generated by TABSURF and RULESURF, but similar to the surfaces generated by EDGESURF, REVSURF generates a two-dimensional mesh and, therefore, both Surftab1 and Surftab2 influence the density of the resulting mesh. Again, keep both Surftab values as low as is consistent with a mesh that meets your needs.

I NSIDER TIP

The original objects used to define the profile (path curve) and the axis are left untouched by REVSURF; they are not incorporated into the resulting mesh. They are often difficult to distinguish, however, because the mesh can obscure them. It is, therefore, a good habit to generate the surface mesh on a separate layer. This will allow you to freeze or turn off the two layers and isolate the path curve and axis object should you want to use them again. This tip applies equally to the TABSURF, EDGESURF, and RULESURF commands.

The following exercise shows you how to use REVSURF to create a rivet.

USING REVSURF TO CREATE A RIVET

1. Load the file 29Rev.DWG from the accompanying CD-ROM. The file contains an outline of the piston and its axis of rotation as shown in Figure 29.21.

Figure 29.21

The outline of a piston and the axis of rotation line.

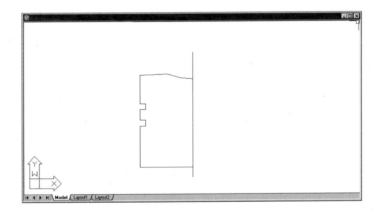

2. At the command prompt, type **Surftab1**. Set the value to 24. Type **Surftab2**. Set its value to **24**.

3. Change the current layer to Mesh.

4. From the Draw menu, select Surfaces, Revolved Surface.

5. When prompted for the object to revolve, pick the piston outline.

6. When prompted to select the object that defines the axis of revolution, pick the vertical line next to the outline.

7. Press Enter to accept the default start angle of 0 degrees.

8.   When prompted for the included angle, press Enter to accept the default of 360 degrees. REVSURF creates the revolved surface. Your drawing should now resemble Figure 29.22.

Figure 29.22

The revolved piston surface.

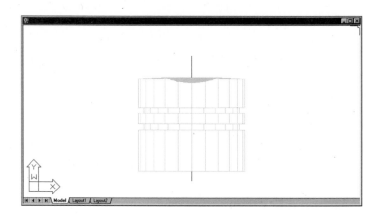

9.   From the Modify menu, select 3D Operation, Rotate 3D.

10. Type **All** then press Enter to select all objects for rotation. Press Enter again.

11. Type **X** then press Enter to specify the X axis as the axis of rotation.

12. When prompted for a point on the X axis, use a Midpoint osnap to pick the midpoint of the line representing the axis of rotation.

13. When prompted for the rotation angle, type **90**.

14. The piston, its outline, and the axis line are rotated 90 degrees around the X axis.

15. From the View menu, select 3D Views, SE Isometric. AutoCAD switches to an isometric view. Notice that the original piston outline and the axis line are visible.

16. From the View menu, select Shade, Flat Shaded. Your model should now resemble Figure 29.23.

17. Close this drawing without saving changes.

REVSURF offers more options and parameters than the other commands presented in this chapter. Although it is a somewhat complicated surfacing command, it is one of the most flexible and useful 3D tools available.

Figure 29.23

The revolved piston surface in a shaded rendering.

Considering 3D Meshes

Like the other 3D surfacing commands discussed in this chapter, the 3DMESH command creates a mesh of contiguous 3D faces. An *MxN* matrix, where *M* is generally associated with the X axis and *N* with the Y axis, defines the size of the mesh. To construct even a relatively simple mesh of this type requires a large amount of input and, if done manually, is quite tedious and error prone. The 3DMESH command, therefore, is intended primarily as the avenue of input for external programs. In this respect, 3DMESH is similar to the PFACE command discussed earlier in this chapter. Programs written in programming languages such as AutoLISP are adept in supplying the required vertex information required by the 3DMESH command.

Editing Mesh Surfaces

After a surface has been created using one of the commands described in this chapter, there are two methods for editing that surface in addition to the standard editing commands, such as MOVE, ROTATE, and SCALE. Those two methods are grip editing and the PEDIT command.

Grip editing works on a surface just as it does any other AutoCAD object. The one difference is that surfaces generally have more grips you can easily manipulate. However, all modes of Grip editing, including Move, Scale, Rotate, Mirror, and Stretch, will work with surfaces. Figure 29.24 shows the grip's density of a typical 3D surface.

Figure 29.24

A typical 3D mesh surface with (right) and without grips displayed.

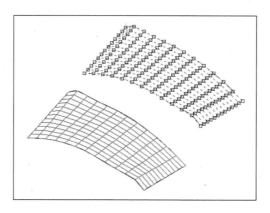

The PEDIT command provides the second method of editing any 3D mesh object. Much like you can edit a polyline with PEDIT, you can manipulate a mesh surface in certain ways. PEDIT can be used to perform the following functions on a 3D mesh surface:

- **Vertex editing.** This includes adding, moving, and deleting vertices from the mesh.

- **Smooth surfaces.** This is generally used with 3D meshes or other surfaces that are not already smoothed. This is very similar to the PEDIT SPLINE command for polylines, but it works in three dimensions instead of two.

- **Desmooth surfaces.** This removes any smoothing from surfaces that have been smoothed with the PEDIT SMOOTH command.

- **MOPEN, NOPEN, MCLOSE, and NCLOSE.** Basically, surfaces are created as polylines with 3D faces between them. These commands either open or close the polylines in the M or N directions. For example, if you create a surface that forms a dome, using MCLOSE and NCLOSE closes all the polylines in the M direction and forms a floor. An example of closing a 3D mesh in the M and N directions is shown in Figure 29.25.

Editing a 3D mesh surface is not easy. If you need to change a surface in AutoCAD, it is frequently more efficient to change the construction edges defining the surface rather than using grips or the PEDIT command to perform the editing.

Figure 29.25

Closing a 3D mesh in the M and N directions with the PEDIT *command.*

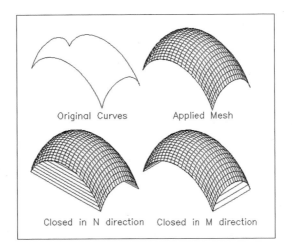

Original Curves   Applied Mesh

Closed in N direction   Closed in M direction

Summary

In this chapter, you learned how to create 3D surfaces based on existing geometry in your model by using a variety of 3D surfacing commands. Adjusting the SURFTAB1 and SURFTAB2 system variables controls the resolution of these surfaces. You also discovered how you can edit surfaces by using PEDIT. The 3DMESH and PFACE commands are used primarily by outside programs that provide the high amount of input required by these commands.

In the next chapter, you explore how to use AutoCAD's solid modeling commands to create many types of 3D solid objects that would be difficult, if not impossible, to create by using the surfacing commands covered in this chapter.

30

SOLID MODELING

Solid modeling is a relatively new method of modeling that has been around for only a few years and is now becoming very popular. Solid modeling consists of creating primitives and combining and manipulating those primitives into more complex objects. It is called solid modeling because you can attach material information to the model so that you can find information such as an object's center of gravity, how much it weighs, and so on.

This chapter focuses on how the ACIS solid modeler in AutoCAD 2000 works as an integrated modeling tool. Specifically, this chapter explores the following concepts:

- *The ACIS solid modeler*
- *Creating primitives*
- *Working with* EXTRUDE *and* REVOLVE
- *Working with 3D Boolean Commands*
- *Using* FILLET *and* CHAMFER
- *Controlling surface resolution*

- Advanced solid modeling commands
- Editing Solids

The ACIS Solid Modeler

The solid modeling commands in AutoCAD 2000 are supplied by the ACIS 4.0 solid modeler. This modeler takes advantage of the AutoCAD 2000 load-on-demand architecture, so the modeler program tools are loaded only when you access the commands. As a result, when you access any one of the various solid commands for the first time in a modeling session, there might be a slight delay as the set of modeler functions load.

The solid modeling commands are located on their own toolbar, called the *Solids toolbar*, as shown in the Figure 30.1.

Figure 30.1

The Solids toolbar.

NOTE

You can also access the solid modeling commands by selecting Solids from the Draw pull-down menu or by typing in the individual commands at the command prompt.

Creating Primitives

AutoCAD 2000 supports six different primitives:

- Box
- Sphere
- Cylinder
- Cone
- Wedge
- Torus

These rather simple solid geometric forms are termed *primitives* because they can be used in various combinations to produce hundreds of other, more complex solid geometric shapes. Primitives themselves are easy to construct.

Creating a solid box, for example, is as simple as selecting the BOX command from the Solids toolbar, specifying, in turn, the two points that define the opposite corners of the box, and the height. The resulting solid box appears similar to a 3D box created with surfaces. The display of solid objects, however, is quite different in some cases. Consider, for example, a surface and a solid sphere. The surface sphere looks quite different than the solid version, as shown in the Figure 30.2.

Figure 30.2

A surface sphere compared with a solid sphere.

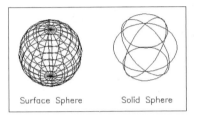

The displays differ because the solid modeler works with *boundaries*, whereas the surface modeler works only with faces joined together to form surfaces. When you hide the solid sphere or render it, it is converted to a surface-like model for that purpose only. Figure 30.3 shows the spheres represented in Figure 30.2 after using the HIDE command.

Figure 30.3

A surface sphere and a solid sphere after using the HIDE command.

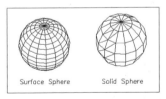

NOTE

The lines used to visually display AutoCAD's solids are called *isolines*. Usually, four isolines per solid object adequately represent the shape and form of a solid; therefore, the default value for isolines is 4. The system variable ISOLINES controls the number of isolines used to show solids. For more complex solids, or in views containing a large number of solid objects, you may wish to increase the number of isolines. A value of 8 or 16 is usually sufficient. Values significantly higher than 16 may slow down operations such as regens. If you alter the number of isolines, you must perform a regen to have the display change for solids already drawn.

The following exercise shows you how to use solid primitives to create a simple chair model.

USING THE SOLID PRIMITIVES TO CREATE A SIMPLE CHAIR

1. Open the drawing 30ex01.DWG found on the accompanying CD-ROM.

2. At the command prompt, type **BOX**, or select Box from the Solids toolbar.

3. Specify the corners at 0,0 and 1,1. Specify a height of 24.

4. Copy this box 18 units along the X axis.

5. Copy both existing boxes 18 units along the Y axis. Figure 30.4 shows you the drawing at this point.

Figure 30.4

The chair after creating the four legs.

Next you create the seat of the chair.

6. Create another box with corners at –0.5,–0.5 and 19.5,19.5 and a height of 1.

7. Choose Move from the Modify toolbar. Select the box and move the box 24 units along the Z axis by typing in 0,0,24 then pressing Enter twice.

8. Now create three boxes to form the backrest of the chair. You will create these boxes "on the ground," and then move them into position on top of the chair.

9. From the View pull-down menu, choose 3D Viewpoint, SW Isometric.

10. Create a box with corners at 18,0 and 19,1 and a height of 18. This box should appear "inside" the lower-right leg.

11. Choose Move from the Modify toolbar. Type **L** (for last) at the Select Objects prompt and press Enter. Specify a displacement of 0,0,25 and press Enter twice to move this box 25 units along the Z axis. Perform a Zoom/Extents to show the objects you have modeled so far.

12. Choose Copy from the Modify toolbar and make a copy of the box. Place it over the upper-right leg of the chair by specifying a displacement of 0,18.

13. Make a second copy of the box by selecting the previous selection. Place this copy between the two other backrest supports by specifying a displacement of 0,9.

14. Draw the back's top cross bar using the other options of the **BOX** command. Specify the first corner at 18,0,43. Now type **L** to indicate you want to next specify a length. Enter a value of 1. At the width prompt, type **19**. Specify a height of 1.

     Figure 30.5 shows you the drawing at this point.

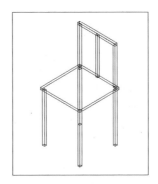

Figure 30.5

The chair after creating the seat and backrest.

Now you can add a little decoration to the chair.

15. At the command prompt, type **PLAN** and press Enter twice. This switches you back to a Plan view. Perform a Zoom/0.8X to generate a slightly zoomed-out view.

16. Choose Sphere from the Solids toolbar.

17. Create a sphere with its center at 18.5,0.5, and a radius of 0.5.

18. Choose Copy from the Modify toolbar and copy the sphere to the other side of the back of the chair. Copy the sphere using 0,18 as the displacement and press Enter twice.

19. From the View pull-down menu, choose 3D Viewpoint, SW Isometric. Figure 30.6 shows you the final chair model.

20. Save the drawing.

Figure 30.6

The completed chair
model in isometric view.

As you can see from this exercise, modeling with primitives is not that different from modeling with surface primitives. As always, when working with 3D models, you need to change your view direction frequently in order to keep the spatial relationships of the model's components in view.

Working with EXTRUDE and REVOLVE

As mentioned before, solid primitives, such as Box, Sphere, Cone, and so on, are frequently used in combinations to produce new solid shapes. In addition to primitives, AutoCAD provides two powerful commands that produce non-primitive, often complex, shapes from closed 2D curves: EXTRUDE and REVOLVE.

The EXTRUDE command is useful for objects that contain fillets, chamfers (discussed later in this chapter), and other details that might otherwise be difficult to reproduce except in a profile. The REVOLVE command creates a solid by revolving a two-dimensional object (profile) about an axis. 2D objects capable of being revolved include closed polylines, polygons, circles, ellipses, closed splines, donuts, and regions.

Using the EXTRUDE Command

With the EXTRUDE command you can extrude, or give thickness to, certain 2D objects. You can extrude along a path or you can specify a height and taper angle. Objects must be "closed" to qualify for extrusion. Such objects can include planar 3D faces, closed polylines, polygons, circles, ellipses, closed splines, donuts, and regions. 2D objects such as these are termed *profiles*.

A common usage of the EXTRUDE command is the creation of 3D walls. The following exercise shows you how to create a wall by using the EXTRUDE command.

USING THE EXTRUDE COMMAND TO CREATE A WALL

1. Load the file 30EX02.dwg from the accompanying CD-ROM. The file contains the outline of a wall, as shown in Figure 30.7.

Figure 30.7

The outline of a wall with openings ready to be extruded.

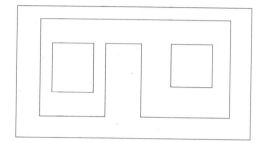

2. From the Solids toolbar, choose EXTRUDE, or type **EXTRUDE** at the command prompt.

3. Select the three polylines in the view (the wall and two window openings).

4. When prompted for an EXTRUDE height, type **0.5**.

5. Accept the default taper angle of 0 by pressing Enter. The objects are extruded.

6. From the View pull-down menu, choose 3D Viewpoint, SW Isometric.

7. At the command prompt, type **HIDE**. The wall parts after the extrusion process are shown in Figure 30.8.

8. Save the file as 30ex02a.dwg on your hard drive for use in a later exercise.

Figure 30.8

The wall parts after extrusion. The windows are extruded as separate objects.

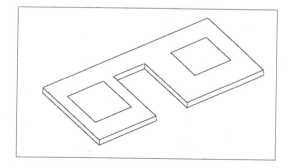

As you can see, using the EXTRUDE command to extrude a profile in the object's Z axis is simple and straightforward. If you extrude a closed polyline that is itself enclosed within the boundary of another extruded closed polyline, as in the preceding exercise, you end up with multiple objects. This would be a common situation when extruding walls with window openings. The windows can be subtracted using the SUBTRACT command. You will do this in an exercise in the later section "Working with 3D Boolean Operations."

In addition to extruding straight up or down, with or without a taper, you can extrude a closed 2D object along a path. The following exercise shows you how to create a pipe by using the [Path] option. This exercise shows you some of the flexibility of the EXTRUDE command and how it can be useful for modeling many different objects.

EXTRUDING ALONG A PATH

1. Load the file 30ex03.dwg from the accompanying CD-ROM. The file contains a circle and polyline path, as shown in Figure 30.9.

Figure 30.9

A circle and the polyline path along which it is extruded.

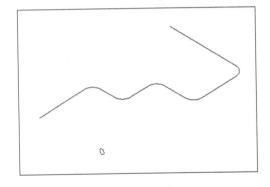

2. From the Solids toolbar, choose EXTRUDE, or type **EXTRUDE** at the command prompt.

3. Select the circle as the object to extrude.

4. When prompted, type **P** for Path.

5. Select the polyline. The object is then extruded along the path. Note that the path is moved by AutoCAD to match the center of the shape.

6. Type **HIDE** at the command prompt. The circle extrudes along the path, as shown in Figure 30.10.

Figure 30.10

The circle after being extruded alone the polyline path.

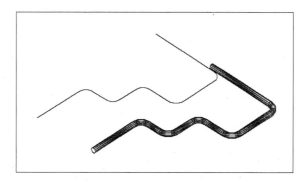

As you can see from this exercise, extruding along a path is relatively easy. Just make sure that the shape you want to extrude is perpendicular to the path, as it was in this exercise. If not, you will not be able to extrude the object.

INSIDER TIP

Extruding along a path works well with polylines and splines as long as they are not closed. When a closed polyline or spline is used as a path, the extrusion may not always work.

Using the REVOLVE Command

The REVOLVE command produces solid objects from 2D profiles much like the EXTRUDE command. With REVOLVE, however, an axis of revolution is specified. 3D objects produced with the REVOLVE command therefore have a radial axis of symmetry. You can revolve any number of degrees about the axis of revolution, although full 360-degree revolutions are most common. In the following exercise, you use two different amounts of rotation to produce two models of a piston.

USING REVOLVE TO PRODUCE A PISTON

1. Load the file 30ex04.dwg from the accompanying CD-ROM. The file contains two identical profiles of a piston. The axis of revolution is indicated with both profiles, as shown in Figure 30.11.

2. Choose REVOLVE from the Solids toolbar or type **REVOLVE** at the command prompt.

3. Select the left piston outline and press Enter.

4. When prompted, type **0** for Object.

Figure 30.11

Two profiles of pistons ready to revolve.

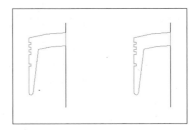

5. Select the vertical line associated with the profile. This line will serve as the axis of revolution.

6. Press Enter to accept a full 360 degrees of revolution.

7. Restart the REVOLVE command by pressing Enter. Repeat steps 3–5 with the right piston profile.

8. When prompted to specify the angle of revolution, Enter 230.

9. From the Views pull-down menu, choose Named Views, and set the SW Isometric view current.

10. Type **HIDE** at the command prompt. Figure 30.12 shows you the resulting solid objects.

11. Save the file as 31ex04a.dwg for use in a later exercise.

Figure 30.12

Pistons' profiles fully and partially revolved about an axis.

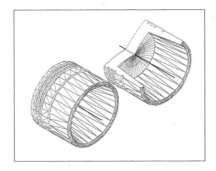

As you can see, the REVOLVE command can be a flexible 3D design tool. Similar to EXTRUDE, REVOLVE is useful for objects that contain fillets or other details that would otherwise be difficult to reproduce in a common profile.

INSIDER TIP

If you create a profile using lines or arcs that meet a polyline, use the PEDIT Join option to convert them to a single closed polyline object before you use REVOLVE.

Working with 3D Boolean Operations

Much of the power of Solid modeling comes from the ability to use Boolean operations as modeling tools. In Chapter 28, "Drawing in 3D AutoCAD," you were introduced to Boolean operations while working with regions. These same Boolean commands work at the 3D level to enable you to quickly and easily create complex objects from simple primitives.

There are three Boolean types that you can create: Union, Intersect, and Subtract. Figure 30.13 shows two primitives and the object that results when you apply each of the three Boolean operations to the primitives.

Figure 30.13

Examples of each of the three Boolean operations.

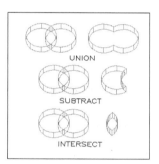

The following exercise shows you how to use a Boolean Subtract operation to create holes in a wall that you built earlier in this chapter.

USING SUBTRACT TO CREATE HOLES IN A WALL

1. Load the file 30ex02a.dwg from the earlier exercise. If you did not complete the exercise, load the file from the CD-ROM.

2. At the command prompt type **Subtract**, or from the Modify pull-down menu, choose Solids Editing and Subtract.

3. Select the large wall object as the object to subtract from and press Enter. Then select the two boxes representing the windows as the objects to subtract and press Enter.

4. To show the result of the subtraction, type **HIDE** and press Enter. The wall with window openings is shown in Figure 30.14.

Figure 30.14

*The wall after subtracting
the window openings.*

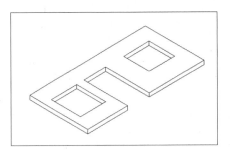

As you can see from the last exercise, Boolean operations are easy to carry out. In some instances, performing a Boolean intersect or subtract operation is virtually the only way to obtain the solid object you want. The following exercise shows you a more complex example of another subtract operation.

CREATING A GROOVE WITH SUBTRACT

1. Load the file 30ex05.dwg from the accompanying CD-ROM. The file contains a box and a pipe, as shown in Figure 30.15.

Figure 30.15

*A solid box and the pipe
that will form a groove
when subtracted.*

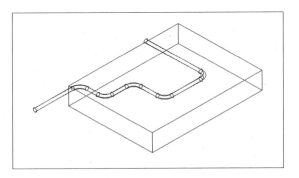

2. From the pull-down menu, select Modify, Solids Editing, Subtract.

3. Select the box as the object to subtract from and press Enter.

4. Select the pipe as the object to subtract and press Enter. The subtraction is created.

5. Hide the drawing to achieve the result shown in Figure 30.16.

Figure 30.16

The box with the pipe subtracted to create a groove.

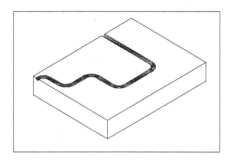

Figure 30.16

The box with the pipe subtracted to create a groove.

Imagine trying to create the 3D model in the last exercise without the Boolean subtract operation. This would be difficult if not impossible to do using simple surfaces.

Using the FILLET and CHAMFER Commands

Although true solids editing capabilities are introduced for the first time in AutoCAD 2000, AutoCAD has allowed adding fillets and chamfers to solids since Release 13 using the standard "2D" FILLET and CHAMFER commands. To fillet or chamfer the edges of an AutoCAD solid you simply execute the FILLET and CHAMFER commands, respectively.

The following exercise shows you how to use the FILLET and CHAMFER commands to edit the edges of a solid model of a phone handset.

USING THE FILLET AND CHAMFER COMMANDS

1. Load the file 30ex06.dwg from the accompanying CD-ROM. The model consists of three unioned boxes, as shown in Figure 30.17.

Figure 30.17

A set of three solid boxes representing a basic telephone handset design.

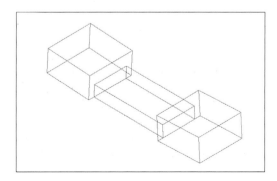

You will first use the FILLET command to round the edges and refine the receiver end of the model.

2. Choose Fillet from the Modify toolbar or simply type **FILLET** and press Enter.

3. At the prompt to select first object, select the vertical edge of the receiver portion, as shown at ① in Figure 30.18.

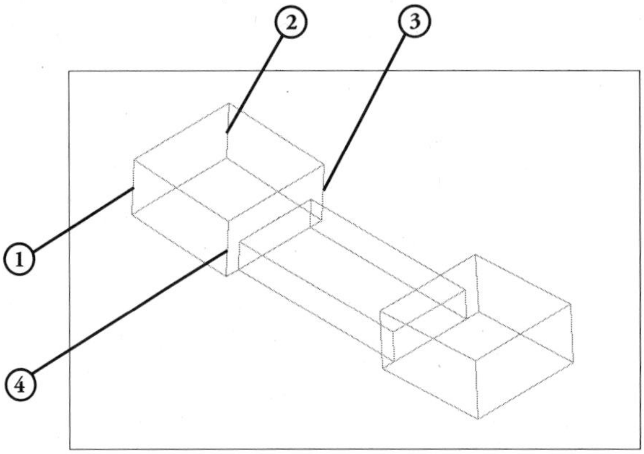

Figure 30.18

Preparing to fillet four vertical edges.

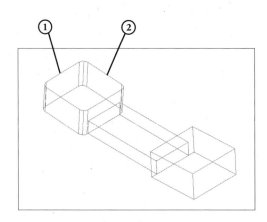

4. Specify a fillet radius of 0.20 and press Enter.

5. At the Select an Edge or Chain prompt, select the other three vertical edges shown at ② through ④ of Figure 30.18, then press Enter. AutoCAD fillets the four edges as seen in Figure 30.19.

    In the following steps, you use the Chain option of the FILLET command.

6. Choose FILLET again by pressing either the spacebar or Enter.

7. Select the upper edge of the receiver portion, as shown at ① in Figure 30.19.

Figure 30.19

Preparing to fillet a chain of edges.

8. Accept the default radius of 0.2 by pressing Enter.

9. At the Select an Edge or Chain prompt, type **C** for Chain and select any of the eight edges making up the top surface of the receiver, keeping in mind that the newly filleted corners now constitute edges. ② of Figure 30.19 is a valid choice. Note that selecting any edge selects all connected edges in the chain. Press Enter to complete the fillet operation. At this point, your model should resemble Figure 30.20.

Figure 30.20

A total of eight edges are filleted at one time using the Chain option.

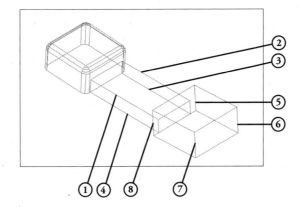

10. Repeat the **FILLET** command and pick the edge shown at ① in Figure 30.20 when prompted for first object.

11. Enter a new radius of 0.15

12. Select the edges shown at ② through ⑧ in Figure 30.20. Press Enter to carry out the fillet operation. Your model should now resemble Figure 30.21.

Figure 30.21

Preparing to chamfer the handle and transmitter portions.

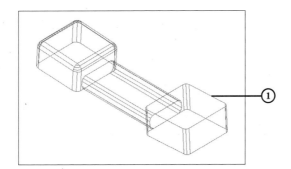

In the following steps you use the CHAMFER command to mold the top edges of the transmitter portion of the model.

13. From the Modify menu, choose Chamfer.

14. When prompted for first line, pick ① in Figure 30.21. If necessary, type **N** and press Enter until the top surface of the transmitter portion is highlighted, then press Enter to OK the selection.

15. When prompted, specify a base surface distance of 0.10 and specify the other surface distance of 0.10 At the next prompt, type **L** for the Loop option and pick ① again to select an edge loop.

16. Press Enter to chamfer the top surface. Issue the HIDE command by typing **HI** and pressing Enter. Your model should resemble Figure 30.22.

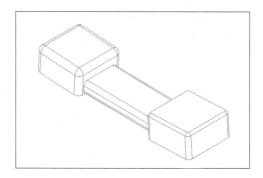

Figure 30.22

The finished model with filleted and chamfered edges and hidden lines removed.

As you can see from the exercise, adding a third dimension presents many more edges that can be filleted and chamfered. In this exercise you also took advantage of the Chain option of the FILLET command and the Loop option of the CHAMFER command. These options provide you with the ability to quickly fillet or chamfer and edge that has a continuous string of chamfered or filleted component edges.

Controlling Surface Resolution

As mentioned earlier in this chapter, AutoCAD displays solid objects onscreen as boundary representations of the objects (see Figure 30.23). Solid objects are converted to surfaces only when you hide, shade, render, plot, or export the solid geometry.

Figure 30.23

Figure 30.23

Solids are represented onscreen by lines and curves denoting boundaries.

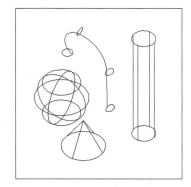

The process of converting a boundary representation into a surface representation is called *tessellation*. Tessellation places a series of contiguous three- and four-sided tiles on the solid's boundaries, resulting in a surface mesh that can be shaded, rendered, and used in a hide operation. Figure 30.24 shows the same solids as in the previous figure with tessellated surfaces applied.

Figure 30.24

Low resolution tessellation of solid objects.

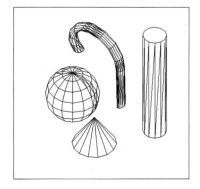

The density of the surface mesh applied during tessellation is controlled by the system variable FACETRES (for facet resolution). The default value for FACETRES is 0.5 but can be set anywhere from 0.01 to 10. Higher values result in finer meshes generated from the solid objects, but higher resolution meshes also take much longer to hide, render, or export to other programs. Figure 30.24 has FACETRES set to a value of 0.5. Compare Figure 30.24 with Figure 30.25, in which FACETRES is set to a value of 2.0.

Figure 30.25

Figure 30.25

Increasing the value of FACETRES *increases the resolution of the surface representation of solids.*

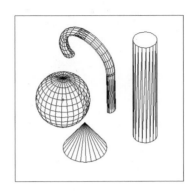

Advanced Solid Modeling Commands

AutoCAD also provides you with three advanced solid modeling commands that can be quite useful:

- SLICE
- SECTION
- INTERFERENCE

The following sections define these advanced commands and take you through exercises designed to show you how you can use each to help build your solid models.

The SLICE Command

The SLICE command is used to divide solid objects on either side of a plane. If, for example, you create a complex model and want to cut it in half, the SLICE command will accomplish the task.

There are five methods you can use to define the slicing, or cutting, plane:

- **3 points.** Defines the slicing plane using three points. If the desired plane is not parallel with the current XY, YZ, or ZX plane, the 3-point method is usually the best choice.

- **Object.** Aligns the cutting plane with a circle, ellipse, circular or elliptical arc, 2D spline, or a 2D polyline. The object need not be separated from the volume of the solid.

- **View.** Aligns the cutting plane with the current viewport's viewing plane. Specifying a point defines the location of the cutting plane along the Z axis of the view plane.

- **Z axis.** Defines the cutting plane by specifying a point on the plane and another point on the Z axis (normal) of the plane.

- **XY, YZ, and ZX.** Aligns the cutting plane with the XY, YZ, or ZX plane of the current UCS. Specifying a point defines the location of the cutting plane.

Note that the 3-point method defines the plane immediately; no further point is required. The other four methods first align the plane; you must supply an additional point to place the plane relative to the model.

After the slice has been carried out, AutoCAD prompts for a point on the desired side of the plane. You must specify a point to determine which side of the sliced solids your drawing retains. This point cannot lie on the cutting plane. You can also choose to keep both sides. This option retains both sides of the sliced solids. Slicing a single solid into two pieces creates two solids from the pieces on either side of the plane.

Often, you can use more than one method to accomplish the same slice. The method you choose will often depend upon the geometry available to you.

INSIDER **T**IP

Don't hesitate to use the 3-point method merely because a convenient third-point is not available. Often you can use a relative coordinate designation (such as @0,0,1) after specifying the second point to identify a point co-planar with the first two.

All you have to do to make slice work is create the 3D ACIS model you want to slice and then determine a slicing plane. The following exercise illustrates this to you.

USING SLICE TO CUT A COMPLEX MODEL IN HALF

1. Load the file 30EX07.dwg. This is a model of a piston similar to the one you created earlier in the chapter. Note that the line used to define the axis of revolution in forming the piston from its profile is also visible. The piston is sitting on a plane coincident with the XY plane (see Figure 30.26).

Figure 30.26

Increasing the value of
FACETRES *increases the resolution of the surface representation of solids.*

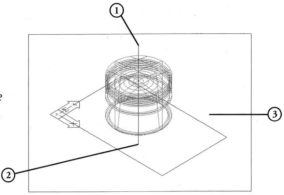

2. Choose SLICE from the Draw, Solids, Slice menu.

3. When prompted, select the piston and press Enter.

4. Type **ZX** and press Enter to indicate that you want to define the slicing plane parallel with the current ZX plane.

5. When prompted to specify a point on the ZX plane, snap to either the endpoint of the line defining the axis of revolution (①) or (②) in Figure 30.26).

6. When prompted to specify a point on the desired side of the plane, pick a point in the northeast corner of the ground plane rectangle near (③) and click. AutoCAD completes the slice.

7. Choose Hide from the View menu to see a result similar to the one shown in Figure 30.27.

Figure 30.27

The hidden line display of the sliced piston.

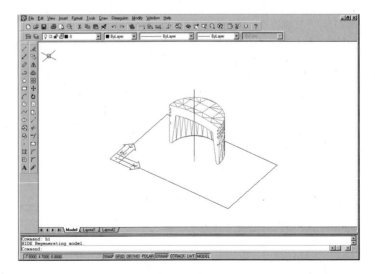

8. Before closing this model, you may want to practice using other methods of specifying a slicing plane. Note that once a slice has been completed, you can use the Undo option of the SLICE command to restore the solid to its original state.

9. Close the drawing with or without saving.

This exercise gives you practice in visualizing and specifying "invisible" slicing planes. With practice, you will be able to slice solids quickly and precisely.

The SECTION Command

The SECTION command works almost exactly the same as the SLICE command, with only one major difference. Rather than slicing the object, the SECTION command generates a region that is representative of a section of the selected ACIS solid object on the chosen plane. Suppose you model this great 3D part and want to draw a section of it for manufacturing purposes. The SECTION command can automatically generate most of the 2D drawing from your 3D model, with very little effort.

The following exercise shows you how to create a section of a solid object.

CREATING A SECTION OF A SOLID OBJECT

1. Load the file 30ex06a.dwg. This is a completed telephone handset similar to the one you built earlier in this chapter. The model will resemble Figure 30.28

Figure 30.28

The three points you use to specify the exercise's section plane.

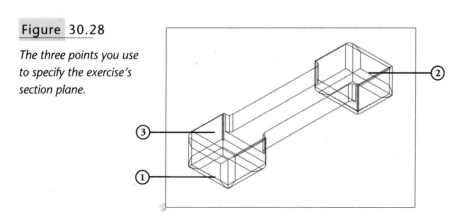

2. Select SECTION from the Solids toolbar, or type **SECTION** at the command prompt.

3. Select the handset and press Enter.

4. Press Enter again to define the section plane by three points.

5. When prompted for the first point, choose Midpoint and select the middle point of the end of the receiver at ① in Figure 30.27.

6. Select the next two points by using Midpoint, as shown at ② and ③.

7. Choose Move from the Modify toolbar.

8. When prompted to select objects, type **L** for last and press Enter.

9. Move the section so it is outside of the 3D object. Figure 30.29 shows you the resulting 3D object and section.

Figure 30.29

After creating a section of the model, use Move to relocate the section line.

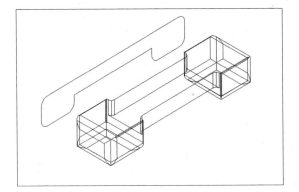

As this exercise shows, the way the SLICE and SECTION commands are used is very similar. The difference between the two is revealed in their results. The SLICE command enables you to cut a model into pieces. When you use the SECTION command, however, the result is a region. This region can be converted to a series of lines by exploding it, if you need to further edit the section. You can also use it to develop new solids by extruding it, or you could also hatch this region for further use.

The INTERFERE Command

The last advanced command that is addressed here is the INTERFERE command. This command is used to determine whether two solids overlap, or *interfere*, with each other. If they do, you can generate a new solid that is the volume of the area where the two solids interfere. This enables you to quickly calculate how much volume is interfering between the two solids. The INTERFERE uses a Boolean intersect operation to generate any interference information.

Editing Solids

Just as with all other AutoCAD objects, after you create solid objects you may want to edit them. Prior to AutoCAD 2000, editing solids inside AutoCAD was, at best, moderately difficult and often impossible. If, for example, in Release 13 or 14 you needed to decrease the diameter of a circular bore into a solid, you needed to first fill in the current bore and then re-bore by subtracting another cylinder with the smaller diameter. This was hardly solid editing, but rather re-doing your work.

In AutoCAD 2000, however, AutoCAD introduces a solid editing facility that enables you to easily edit, or modify, the size and geometry of AutoCAD solids. Through the new SOLIDEDIT command, you can move, rotate, taper, resize, or even remove features of a solid. Blends created with the FILLET command, for example, can be removed.

Through SOLIDEDIT you can also copy a face or edge from of a solid as a BODY or REGION in the case of faces, or as a LINE, ARC, CIRCLE, ELLIPSE, or SPLINE object in the case of edges (see Figure 30.30). You cannot, however, copy a feature, such as a hole, in a solid to make a second hole. This is technically not a valid edit operation.

Figure 30.30

An overview of the SOLIDEDIT *operations.*

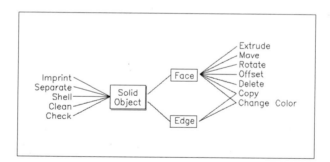

SOLIDEDIT Operations

The following operations are performed by the SOLIDEDIT command. Two solid editing operations, Color and Copy, are common to both faces and edges. The Imprint, Shell, Separate, and Clean operations are performed on entire 3D solid bodies.

- **Extrude.** Extrudes selected planar faces of a 3D solid object to a specified height or along a path. You can select multiple faces at one time.

- **Move.** Moves selected faces on a 3D solid object to a specified height or distance. You can select multiple faces at one time.

- **Rotate.** Rotates one or more faces, or a collection of features, on a solid about a specified axis.

- **Offset.** Offsets faces equally by a specified distance or through a specified point. A positive value increases the size or volume of the solid; a negative value decreases the size or volume of the solid.

- **Taper.** Tapers faces with an angle. The rotation of the taper angle is determined by the selection sequence of the base point and the second point along the selected vector.

- **Delete.** Deletes or removes faces, including fillets and chamfers.

- **Copy.** With faces: Copies faces as a region or a body. If you specify two points, AutoCAD uses the first point as a base point and places a single copy relative to the base point. If you specify a single point (usually entered as a coordinate) and then press Enter, AutoCAD uses the coordinate as the new location. With edges: Copies 3D edges. Every 3D solid edge is copied as a line, arc, ellipse, or spline.

- **Color.** With faces: Changes the color of faces. With edges: Changes the color of edges.

- **Imprint.** Imprints an object on the selected solid. The object to be imprinted must intersect one or more faces on the selected solid in order for imprinting to be successful. Imprinting is limited to the following objects: arcs, circles, lines, 2D and 3D polylines, ellipses, splines, regions, bodies, and 3D solids.

- **Separate.** Separates 3D solid objects with disjointed volumes into independent 3D solid objects.

- **Shell.** Creates a hollow, thin wall with a specified thickness. You can specify a constant wall thickness for all the faces. You can also exclude faces from the shell by selecting them. A 3D solid can have only one shell. AutoCAD creates new faces by offsetting existing ones outside their original positions. Specifying a positive value creates a shell from the outside of the perimeter; specifying a negative value creates a shell from the inside.

- **Clean.** Removes shared edges or vertices having the same surface or curve definition on either side of the edge or vertex. Removes all redundant edges and vertices, imprinted as well as unused geometry.

- **Check.** Validates the 3D solid object as a valid ACIS solid, independent of the SOLIDCHECK system variable setting.

Picking Edges and Faces with SOLIDEDIT

The SOLIDEDIT is the only AutoCAD command that requests that you select faces on 3D solid objects to perform some of its operations. Selecting individual faces while in the SOLIDEDIT command, however, can be tricky. If you pick an edge at a [Select faces:] prompt, the two faces that share the picked edge will be highlighted and you must remove the unwanted face from the selection set.

To alleviate this inconvenience, an additional method of selecting, called *boundary sets*, is automatically available during SOLIDEDIT operations involving faces. With boundary set selection, you can pick on a face inside the edges that define the face. Whereas elsewhere in AutoCAD picking on "empty space" will, at best, establish one corner of a selection window (if system variable PICKAUTO is set to its default value of 1), in editing operations involving 3D solid faces, you can successfully pick within the boundary of a face.

In the following exercises, the boundary set pick method will be demonstrated as some of the options of the SOLIDEDIT command are examined.

Note

Even with the convenience of the boundary set selection method, if there is any ambiguity due to the view, picking on the two faces will select the "closest" one visually. Picking again will select the second, more "distant" face. You must then remove the "top" face from the boundary selection set.

In the following exercise, you will explore some of the capabilities of the new SOLIDEDIT command. This command allows you to perform common editing operations on AutoCAD solids that were not possible in previous releases of AutoCAD. You begin by moving the "front" face of a solid inward 20 units by performing a negative extrusion.

USING BOUNDARY SELECTION TO EDIT 3D FACES

1. Open the drawing chap30.dwg. The layer EXTRUDE should be current. Your screen should resemble Figure 30.31.

2. From the Modify menu, choose Solids Editing and then Extrude Faces. When prompted to select faces, select the front face. Use a single pick boundary selection by picking at ① in Figure 30.31. Notice that using a boundary selection allows you to select the face by picking inside the face boundary.

Figure 30.31

Using boundary sets to select faces.

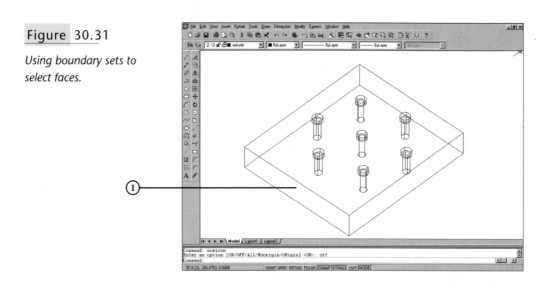

3. Press Enter to close the selection set. At the prompt to specify the height of the extrusion, type **-20**. When prompted to specify the angle of the taper for extrusion, press Enter to accept the default value of 0. The front face is extruded in a negative direction by 20 units with a zero taper angle. Press Enter twice to exit the SOLIDEDIT command.

   Next you will extrude the top of the block and all of the countersink holes upward by 20 units. Because "auto-windowing" is disabled during solid face editing to allow boundary set selection, you must manually start a crossing window.

4. From the Modify menu, choose Solids Editing, Extrude Faces. When prompted to select faces, start a crossing window by typing **C** and pressing Enter. Specify a crossing window that includes all faces and all countersink holes (see Figure 30.32).

Figure 30.32

Choosing faces with a crossing window.

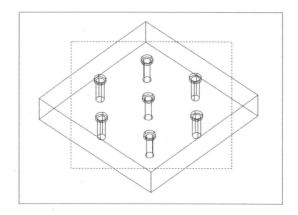

This step selects all the faces of the model. Because you want to extrude only the seven countersink holes and the top face, in the next step you remove the side and bottom faces.

5. While still being prompted to select faces, choose the Remove option by typing **R** and pressing Enter. When prompted to remove faces, pick the edges at ①, ②, ③, and ④ (see Figure 30.33). Press Enter to end face selection. Notice that the first edge that you select removes two faces: the side face and the bottom face.

6. When prompted to specify the height of extrusion, type **20**, then press Enter to accept the default zero angle for taper of extrusion. The top face and the seven countersink holes are extruded by 20 units. Press Enter twice to exit the **SOLIDEDIT** command.

Figure 30.33

Removing faces by selecting common edges.

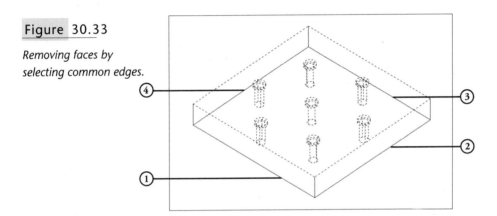

In the next steps, you will rotate the array of countersink holes to align them better with the sides of the block.

7. Using the **VIEW** command, restore the view Rotate. From the Modify menu, choose Solids Editing, then Rotate Faces. When prompted to select faces, initiate a crossing window by typing **C** and pressing Enter. Specify a window enclosing all of the countersink holes.

In the next step, you will take advantage of boundary set selection to remove faces from the current set.

8. While still being prompted to select faces, choose the Remove option. When prompted to remove faces, pick on the sides, top, and bottom faces by picking at ①, ②, ③, ④, ⑤, and ⑥ in Figure 30.34. Note that selecting at ① chooses the top face because it is "closest" in this view; picking at ② then removes the bottom face. Press Enter to end selection.

Figure 30.34

*Using boundary set
selection to remove faces.*

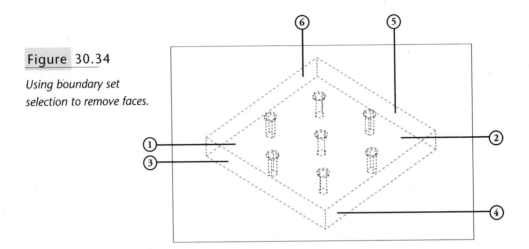

In the next step, you specify the axis of rotation by picking the center of the array and then specifying a vector.

9. Respond to the prompt to specify an axis point by choosing a Center osnap then picking at the bottom of the center of the central hole. Specify the second point on the rotation axis by typing the relative coordinate **@0,0,1** and pressing Enter. Specify a rotation angle by typing **-15** and pressing Enter. The array of holes rotates 15 degrees clockwise.

    In the next steps, you use the Offset option of SOLIDEDIT to edit the diameter of the central countersink hole.

10. Choose Offset from the Face Edit choices by typing **0**. Select faces by typing **C** and pressing Enter, then specifying a crossing window enclosing only the center counter-sink hole. Remove the top and bottom faces of the box as you did in step 8 and press Enter to end selecting.

11. Specify the offset distance by typing **-1.5**. Notice that supplying a negative offset distance decreases the volume of the solid by increasing the diameter of the counter-sink hole. End the command by pressing Enter twice. The model should now resemble Figure 30.35.

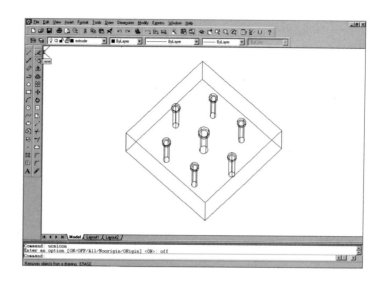

Distinguishing Between Extrude and Offset

Although similar in their effects, the Offset and Extrude options of the SOLIDEDIT command can yield quite different results. In Figure 30.36, the faces highlighted on the center solid are extruded and offset by the same amount in the left and right solids. The solid on the left underwent an extrusion; the solid on the right was offset.

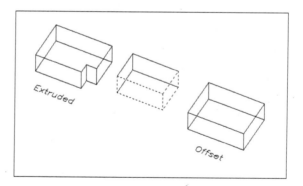

In the following exercise you will investigate the Move, Delete, and Taper options of the SOLIDEDIT command.

USING THE MOVE, DELETE, AND TAPER OPTIONS OF SOLIDEDIT

1. If necessary, open chap30.dwg. Thaw the layer DELETE and set it current. Freeze the layer EXTRUDE. Use the VIEW command to set the view EXTRUDE current. The drawing should resemble Figure 30.37.

Figure 30.37

Using the Move and Delete options of SOLIDEDIT.

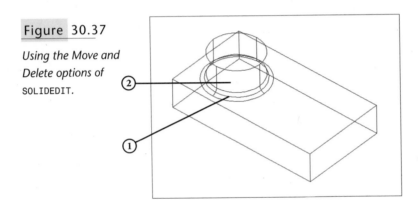

2. To move the filleted structure on top of the block, from the Modify menu, choose Solids Editing, Move Faces. Pick the filleted face at ① and the cylinder at ② in Figure 30.37. Press Enter to end selection. Specify a displacement by typing **25,10** and press Enter twice.

3. Specify the Delete option by typing **D**. Select the filleted face again and press Enter to end selection and remove the face.

4. To taper the cylinder, choose the Taper option. Pick the cylinder face using a boundary set selection method and press Enter.

5. Use a Center osnap and pick the lower or upper center of the cylinder. Specify another point along the axis of tapering by typing **@0,0,1**. When prompted for the taper angle, type **6**. Your drawing should now resemble Figure 30.38.

Figure 30.38

Using the Taper option of SOLIDEDIT.

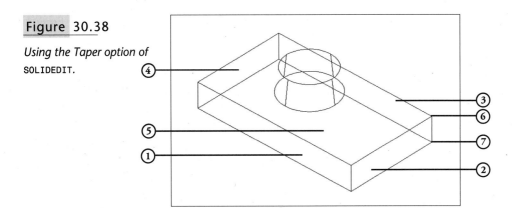

In the next steps, you will taper the four side faces in the drawing.

6. Choose the Taper option again. Referring to Figure 30.38, pick the four side faces of the model by picking at ① and ②, then twice at ③ to select the top and then back face; then pick at ④.To remove the top and bottom faces, choose the Remove option and pick at ⑤ twice. Press Enter to end face selection.

7. Specify the taper base point by using an Endpoint osnap and picking at ⑥. Specify another point along the taper axis by using an Endpoint osnap and picking at ⑦.

8. Specify the taper angle by typing **-12**. This completes your work on this layer. Your drawing should now resemble Figure 30.39.

9. Note that the rotation of the taper angle is determined by the selection sequence of the base point and the second point along the taper axis. Tapering the selected face with a positive angle tapers the face in, and tapering the face with a negative angle tapers the face out. If the pick sequence of ⑥ and ⑦ in step 7 had been reversed, for example, the specified tapering angle of –12 degrees would have resulted in an "inward" taper.

Figure 30.39

Finished model with faces moved, deleted, and tapered.

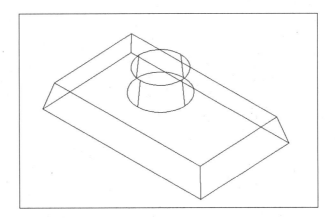

Understanding the Imprint and Shell Options

The Imprint and Shell options of SOLIDEDIT, although technically not editing, provide ways to alter a solid object. You can, for example, create new faces or solids by imprinting arcs, lines, circles, etc., onto existing faces. Once imprinted, you can use the imprinted face as the basis for extrusions. With the shell option, you can "hollow out" a solid forming a thin wall of specified thickness.

In the following exercise, you use the Imprint and Shell options of the SOLIDEDIT command to further develop object in CHAP30.dwg.

USING THE IMPRINT AND SHELL OPTIONS OF SOLIDEDIT

1. In chap30.dwg, thaw and set the IMPRINT layer current and freeze the DELETE and EXTRUDE layers. Use the VIEW command to set the view IMPRINT current. Lastly, use the UCS command to restore the IMPRINT UCS. Your drawing should resemble Figure 30.40.

Figure 30.40

Preparing to add imprinted figures.

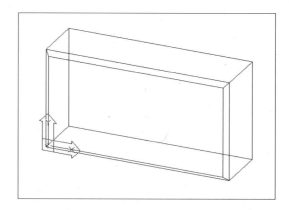

In the next steps you draw a rectangle on the face of the box.

2. Start the RECTANG command by typing **RECTANG** and pressing Enter. Type **F** to choose the Fillet option and specify a fillet radius of 5 units. When prompted for the first corner of the rectangle, type **8,40**. Enter a coordinate of **46,10** for the opposite corner.

3. To imprint the rectangle on the face, from the Modify menu, choose Solids Editing, Imprint. Pick anywhere on the solid. When prompted to select an object to imprint, select the rectangle. Press Enter to retain the source object. Press Enter again to end the select objects prompt. Your drawing should resemble Figure 30.41.

Figure 30.41

Imprinted figures on a solid face.

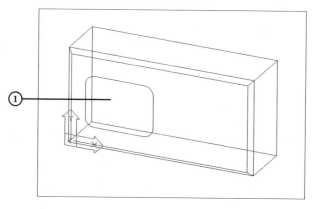

After objects are imprinted on a solid, they can form the basis for both positive and negative embossments.

4. Continuing from the previous step, press Enter to display the parent solid edit command line prompts. Choose the Face option by typing **F**, then choose the Extrude option.

5. Select the rectangular imprint by picking at ① within the boundary of the rectangle and pressing Enter (refer to Figure 30.41). Press Enter again to end selection of faces. Specify a height of extrusion of **2.5** and press Enter to accept the default of 0 degree angle of extrusion. Press Enter twice to end the SOLIDEDIT command. Your drawing should resemble Figure 30.42

Figure 30.42

Adding an embossed surface with Imprint.

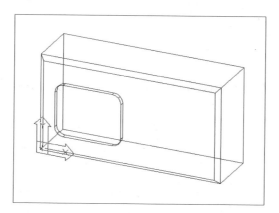

In the following steps, you use the Shell option to "hollow out" the solid.

6. From the main menu, choose Modify, Solids Edits, Shell. Because you do not want to remove any faces, pick anywhere on the solid and press Enter.

7. Enter a shell offset distance of **2** then press Enter twice to end the SOLIDEDIT command.

    In the next steps, you use the SLICE command to examine the effects of the previous shell operation.

8. Type **UCS** and press Enter twice to change the UCS to World UCS. From the main menu, choose Draw, Solids, Slice, and then pick anywhere on the solid and press Enter.

9. Enter the following three coordinates to define a slicing plane. After typing each coordinate, press Enter: **48,70,0**, then **48,140,0**, then **48,100,1**. When prompted to specify a point on the desired side of the slicing plane, pick near ① in Figure 30.43.

10. Use the HIDE command (type **HI** and press Enter) to remove hidden lines from the view. Your drawing should resemble Figure 30.43. Note that the original rectangle used to generate the imprint remains at ②.

Figure 30.43

The result of using the Shell option.

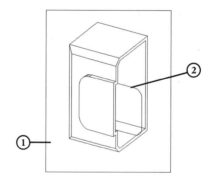

Summary

Solid modeling is a powerful method of creating complex models by combining and editing solid primitives and extruded 2D shapes. To make these models, you can use the Boolean operations of Union, Subtract, and Intersect as well as the EXTRUDE, SLICE, REVOLVE, and SECTION solids commands. The new AutoCAD 2000 SOLIDEDIT command allows you to copy and modify solid edges and faces after they are created. You can also imprint shapes onto solid objects and create shells from parent solids.

Chapter 31, "Rendering in 3D," takes 3D modeling a step further and adds rendering to the visual model "package."

31

RENDERING IN 3D

Up to this point, you have explored several different methods of modeling in three dimensions in AutoCAD. To produce a "picture" of the model, you will probably want to render it. Rendering is a process in which you attach materials to the surfaces of your 3D objects, create lights to illuminate the objects, establish a viewpoint from which to view the model, and then transform the scene into a realistic rendering—or picture.

This process is generally straightforward, but it can require a bit of trial and error as well as an understanding of artistic and photographic principals to produce good results. This chapter focuses on the basics of rendering and the rendering tools found in AutoCAD 2000. It is beyond the scope of this chapter to cover all aspects of rendering, so the reader is encouraged to investigate many of AutoCAD's more advanced rendering capabilities on their own. The topics of this chapter will introduce the basic rendering process, including how to set up and create simple renderings inside AutoCAD. In particular, this chapter addresses the following topics:

- Types of rendering supported by AutoCAD
- Creating a view
- Creating and assigning materials
- Creating lights
- Rendering the model
- Generating output

Types of Rendering Supported by AutoCAD

AutoCAD 2000 incorporates a full-featured rendering engine that is capable of producing rendering ranging from simple shaded models to full photo-realistic renderings. Generally, three types, or levels, of rendering are offered by the rendering facility inside AutoCAD 2000:

- Render
- Photo Real
- Photo Raytrace

These three different types of rendering produce increasingly more realistic outputs, of which Photo Raytrace is the most realistic. You pay a price for realism, however: Increased realism requires increased rendering times.

The line of demarcation between shading and rendering is somewhat arbitrary. The shading modes available with the SHADEMODE command (discussed in Chapter 27, "Introduction to 3D") could be considered simple rendering because the surfaces of a model are depicted as they appear with a single light source. AutoCAD's RENDER command, however, takes up where simple shading leaves off, providing the ability to apply materials to surfaces, to supply various types of lighting, and to cast realistic shadows. The three levels of rendering offered with the RENDER command are summarized here:

- **RENDER.** Basic Render is the next logical step beyond the Gouraud shading mode offered by the SHADEMODE and 3DORBIT commands. Render mode has the added advantage of allowing you to assign materials to surfaces. You can assign materials such as brick, chrome, and wood to objects in the model on a per layer, per color, or per object basis. In addition, you can add any of three types of light sources to the scene. In the basic Render mode, however, light sources are not capable of casting shadows. Other enhancements, such as backgrounds and plants, are also supported. Figure 31.1 shows a typical rendering using the Render mode.

Figure 31.1

Typical rendering using the Render mode of the RENDER *command. Note the absence of shadows.*

- **PHOTO REAL.** The Photo Real mode shares all the features of Render mode, but adds the ability to cast shadows and to use bitmaps for materials (see Figure 31.2).

Figure 31.2

Typical rendering using the Photo Real mode of the RENDER *command. Shadows and materials are present.*

- **PHOTO RAYTRACE.** The Photo Raytrace provides the most realistic renderings. It adds the ability to generate reflections, refraction effects, and true detailed shadows. Figure 31.3 shows a rendering using the Photo Raytrace mode.

Figure 31.3

Typical rendering using the Photo Raytrace mode of the RENDER *command. Note the presence of shadows and reflections.*

The Rendering Process

Rendering takes place after you have constructed a 3D model. Hopefully, the preceding chapters have given you the knowledge you need to build models you want to render.

Now it is time to look at how to set up your scenes for rendering. In general, you can follow this simple process to render your scenes:

1. Create a view of the scene. Most of the views in AutoCAD are orthogonal, such as an SW isometric. For true realism, you must create a Perspective view by using DVIEW.

2. After setting up the perspective, create and assign the materials in the scene. A material is a set of surface attributes that describe how that surface looks at render time. You must define these attributes and assign them to the appropriate surfaces.

3. After you apply your materials, create lights for the scene. Without lights, you do not have any illumination or shadows in the scene. Correct placement of lights adds to the realism.

4. After you have set up the scene, you begin to create test renderings of it. Here you make sure the materials, lights, and geometry are correct. Most of the time, you will create your test renders with the Photo Real method. You might end up creating dozens of test renders before achieving the look you want.

5. Set up the final Photo Raytrace rendering and save the rendering to a bitmap file for printing or use outside of AutoCAD.

These are the basic steps necessary to create a rendering. Now it is time to take a closer look at each step, starting with creating a view.

Creating a View

Establishing a compelling view of the model is one of the most important steps toward creating an effective rendering. No matter how much effort and time you devote to selecting and applying materials and establishing realistic lighting, a rendering of the model from an uninteresting point-of-view will detract from your efforts. Put another way, an interesting or even dramatic view of the model can make the difference between an average-looking rendering and a memorable one.

During the construction of the model, you can effectively use the 3DORBIT command to view and study the various parts of the model. 3DORBIT's ability to dynamically change the viewpoint in real-time is useful because it gives you a sense of the model's spatial relationships. For the final rendering, however, you generally will want more control of the viewpoint. Such flexibility and control are offered by the DVIEW command. Like 3DORBIT, DVIEW allows you to view the model from a perspective projection, which is almost always preferable because it is the way we view objects in the real world. In addition, DVIEW allows you to easily set and fine-tune such factors as the camera to subject distance and the field-of-view.

To use DVIEW to establish a perspective view of your model, you must know two things:

■ **Camera point.** The location in the model from which you want to be looking.

■ **Target point.** The location in the model that you want to look at.

As soon as you establish these points, you can adjust the perspective until you are happy with it. If you have any experience with 35mm photography, many of the terms, such as "focal length," that are used to adjust viewing angle of the camera will be familiar to you.

NOTE

AutoCAD 2000's new CAMERA command prompts you for a camera point and a target point. These points only establish a vector along which the camera and target lie; you have little control over the exact placement of the actual camera position. You cannot adjust the focal length or the camera to target distance directly from within the CAMERA command. The DVIEW command gives you more control.

After you set up the view by using DVIEW, you use the VIEW command to save the view so you do not have to re-create it later.

The following exercise shows you how to set up a view using the DVIEW command. You will then save the view with the VIEW command.

SETTING UP A VIEW WITH DVIEW

1. Load the file 31ex01.dwg from the accompanying CD-ROM. The file contains a model of a 12-story office building, as shown in Figure 31.4. For reference, the roof of this building has an elevation of approximately 154 feet above ground.

Figure 31.4

A model of a 12-story office building shown in an isometric, Gouraud shaded view.

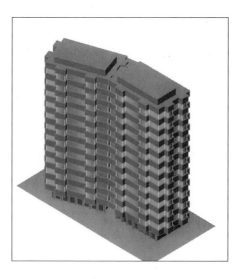

2. From the View menu, select Shade, then 2D Wireframe. Open the View menu and choose Named Views. In the View dialog box, right-click on view AAA and choose Set Current from the shortcut menu. Click OK to exit the dialog box. The model should now resemble Figure 31.5.

Figure 31.5

A model of a 12-story office building shown in plan view.

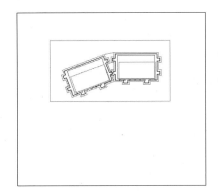

In the next three steps, you draw the "sight-line," which will establish the viewpoint for the rendering. You place a line from the intended camera point to the target point.

3. From the Draw menu, choose Line. When you're prompted to specify the start point, type **.XY** and press Enter to indicate that you will specify the X and Y coordinates on-screen. Pick a point near ① in Figure 31.6. (This point should be near 163', −174'.)

4. When prompted for the Z value, type **8'5"**. This establishes the camera position for the view.

5. When prompted for the next point, again type **.XY** and pick a point near ②. (This should be near 24', 33'.) When prompted for the Z value, type **83'**. Then press Enter to end the **LINE** command. The completed line-of-sight will resemble that in Figure 31.6. This line starts 8'5" off the ground and aims at a point a little more than halfway up the building.

Figure 31.6

The first step in establishing a view is drawing the line-of-sight from camera to target.

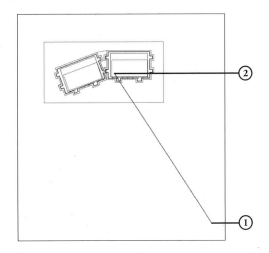

In the next steps, you use the Points options of the DVIEW command to establish a view along the line-of-sight.

6. To start the DVIEW command, at the Command line, type **dview** and press Enter. When you're prompted to select objects, pick only the line-of-sight line, and press Enter. Note that all the model's objects except the line you drew in steps 3–5 temporarily disappear.

7. Type **PO** and press Enter to select the Points option of the DVIEW command.

8. When you're prompted for the target point, use an Endpoint osnap and pick at ② in Figure 31.6 to specify the target end of the line. When you're prompted for the camera point, again use an Endpoint osnap to pick at ①. Although all the model's objects seem to have disappeared, DVIEW has established a view looking down the line-of-sight from camera to target point.

9. Type **D** and press Enter to choose the Distance option of the DVIEW command. Press Enter to accept the default distance—the distance of the line-of-sight.

10. At the next prompt, type **Z** and press Enter to select the Zoom option. Specify a lens length of **33** mm and press Enter. Then press Enter again to end the DVIEW command. The resulting view of the model should resemble Figure 31.7.

Figure 31.7

The view resulting from looking "down" the line-of-sight.

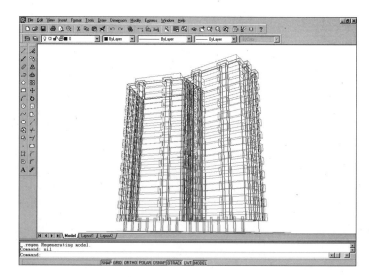

11. To generate a better view of the building, open the View menu, choose Shade, then choose Hidden. Figure 31.8 show a hidden line view.

12. Use the VIEW command to save this view under the name **Camera1**.

13. Save this drawing as **31ex01a.dwg** on your hard drive. You will use it in a later exercise.

Figure 31.8

A view of the model with hidden lines removed.

The advantage to using the line-of-sight method with the DVIEW command is that you have complete control of the resulting viewpoint. Fine-tuning of distance, field of view, and target point and direction make establishing the exact view that you have in mind a straightforward matter of adjusting the line-of-sight line and then using the DVIEW command and the method in the preceding exercise to generate the view.

NOTE

If you're setting up a view using the line-of-sight method, be careful when adjusting the camera-target distance. If the objects represent a ground plane, increasing the distance using the Distance option of the DVIEW command may place the camera point below this plane. This will result in a rendering in which all the model's geometry is hidden.

Creating and Assigning Materials

After you establish a view of the model, you can begin assigning materials to the model's surfaces. A material is a set of graphic attributes assigned to a surface. These attributes include such qualities as color, smoothness, reflectivity, texture, and transparency. When the model is rendered, the rendering engine takes into account those attributes and colors of the image accordingly.

Materials are handled through the Materials and Materials Library dialog boxes in AutoCAD 2000's built-in rendering engine. The Material dialog box is used to assign, create, or modify materials and their associated set of attributes. The Materials Library is used to store a group of pre-defined materials or materials you create.

You use the Materials Library to choose materials you want to import into your model for assignment to surfaces or for use as the basis for creating a modified or new material. You access the Materials Library by choosing Materials Library from the Render toolbar, or by selecting View > Render > Materials Library, or by typing **MATLIB** at the command prompt. Figure 31.9 shows the Materials Library dialog box.

Figure 31.9

The Materials Library dialog box.

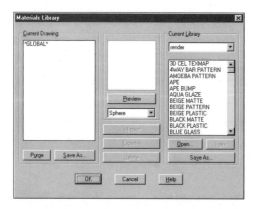

The Materials Library dialog box is divided into three main sections:

- **Current Drawing list.** This lists all the materials currently loaded for use or that are assigned in the current drawing.

  - *Purge.* Deletes all unassigned materials from the Current Drawing list.

  - *Save As.* Allows you to save the current drawing list to a material library (MLI) file.

■ **Preview window.** This is a small window that gives you a preview of what a material would look like if you applied it to a sphere or cube object.

■ *<-Import.* Adds materials selected in the Current Library list to the Current Drawing list.

■ *Export->.* Adds materials selected in the Current Drawing list to the Current Library list.

■ *Delete.* Deletes materials selected in the Current Drawing list or the Current Library list.

■ **Current Library list.** A list of all the materials contained in the current library. All material libraries for AutoCAD have an .MLI extension. By default, AutoCAD ships with one library file—the Render.MLI library.

■ *Open.* Displays a standard file selection dialog box listing MLI files.

■ *Save.* Saves the changes to the current MLI file in the current folder.

■ *Save As.* Displays a standard file selection dialog box where you can specify the name of the materials library (MLI) file in which AutoCAD saves the Current Library list.

INSIDER TIP

The small preview window in the Materials Library is a 256-color display. This means the final rendering will invariably look better than this simple preview window. Keep this in mind when selecting materials. If you are not sure how a material will look, use AutoCAD 2000's Multiple Drawing Environment to create a new drawing with a simple object in it. Use this second drawing to test how a material will appear in the larger model.

You use the Materials dialog box (shown in Figure 31.10) to manage the materials selected for use in your model. You access the Materials dialog box by choosing Materials from the Render toolbar, or by selecting View, Render, Materials, or by typing **RMAT** at the command prompt.

Figure 31.10

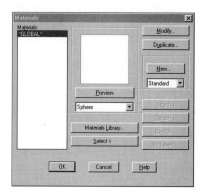

The Materials dialog box.

The Materials dialog box is divided into the following functions:

■ **Materials.** Lists the available materials. The default for objects with no other material attached is GLOBAL.

■ **Preview.** Displays a selected material on either a sphere or a cube.

■ **Materials Library.** Displays the Materials Library dialog box, from which you can select a material.

■ **Select <** Closes the dialog box temporarily so you can select an object with the pointing device and display the attached material. After you select the object, the Materials dialog box is redisplayed with the method of attachment specified at the bottom of the dialog box.

■ **Modify.** Displays one of four dialog boxes, depending on which material type is selected in the list under the New button: Standard, Marble, Granite, or Wood. Use the dialog box to edit an existing material.

■ **Duplicate.** Duplicates a material and displays one of four dialog boxes, depending on which material type is selected in the list under the New button: Standard, Marble, Granite, or Wood. Use the dialog box to name the new material and define attributes.

■ **New.** Displays one of four dialog boxes, depending on which material type is selected in the list under the New button.

■ **Attach <.** Closes the dialog box temporarily so you can select an object and attach the current material to it.

■ **Detach <.** Closes the dialog box temporarily so you can select an object and detach the material from it.

- **By ACI.** Displays the Attach by AutoCAD Color Index dialog box, from which you can select an ACI to attach a material to.

- **By Layer.** Displays the Attach by Layer dialog box, in which you can select a layer to attach a material to.

The following exercise shows you how to load a few materials from the Materials library and assign them to objects in a scene.

ASSIGNING MATERIALS FROM THE MATERIALS LIBRARY TO A MODEL

1.   Load the file 32ex01A.dwg, which you worked on in the last exercise. If you did not complete the last exercise, you can load the file from the accompanying CD-ROM. Display the Render toolbar by right-clicking on any displayed toolbar and selecting Render from the shortcut toolbar list.

2.   From the Render toolbar, choose Materials, or type **RMAT** at the command prompt. AutoCAD displays the Materials dialog box shown in Figure 31.10.

3.   Click the Materials Library button to launch the Materials Library dialog box (refer to Figure 31.9).

4.   Select the material named Blue Glass on the right.

5.   Click the Import button. This places Blue Glass material on the list of materials available for use in the current drawing.

6.   Repeat steps 4 and 5 for the Dark Brown Matte material.

7.   Click OK to return to the Materials dialog box. The materials you just imported now appear in the Materials list. The Materials dialog box should now look like Figure 31.11.

Figure 31.11

The Materials dialog box after you've selected materials for use in the model.

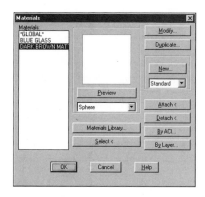

8. Select the Blue Glass material in the list.

9. Select By Layer and in the Attach by Layer dialog box, select the glass layer from the Select Layer list. Click Attach to attach Blue Glass material to objects on the glass layer.

10. Repeat steps 8 and 9 to attach Dark Brown Matte material to concrete layer. The Attach by Layer dialog box should resemble Figure 31.12. Click OK to exit the Attach by Layer dialog box. Click OK again to exit the Materials dialog box.

Figure 31.12

The Attach by Layer dialog box shows current layer/ material attachments.

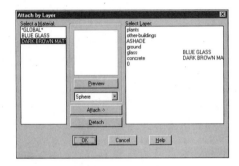

11. Choose Render from the Render toolbar to display the Render dialog box. Under Rendering Type, select Photo Raytrace. Under Rendering Options, make sure the Smooth Shade, Apply Materials, and Shadows options are all selected. The settings for this rendering are shown in Figure 31.13.

Figure 31.13

The Render dialog box settings.

12. Click Render, and the scene is rendered, as shown in Figure 31.14. Depending on your equipment, the rendering process may take a minute or two.

13. Save the file as 32ex01b.dwg for use later.

Figure 31.14

The rendered model with materials applied.

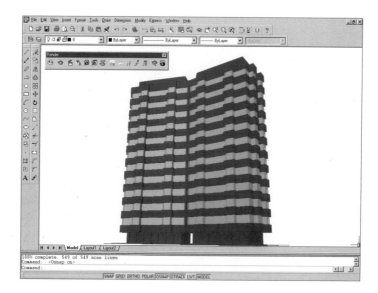

This exercise shows that even with simple "off-the-shelf" materials and no lighting effects, effective renderings are possible. The key to such renderings is the viewpoint. In this example, a perspective viewpoint from near the ground looking upward at the building yields a life-like view—one you might see if you were standing in front of the building.

In this exercise, you assigned materials on a "by-layer" basis. You can also assign materials on a "by-color" or "by-object" basis. The advantage to assigning materials by-layer is a more orderly material assignment process. Just as using layers in 2D drafting help you organize a drawing, placing objects in your model on layers that share a rendered material makes assigning materials much more orderly and easy. Because the "by-layer" method offers a distinct advantage, you should adopt a layer-conscious scheme as you construct a model.

Materials can be roughly divided into two categories: basic materials and mapped materials. Mapped materials make use of a bitmap, or image, to represent the color or some other attribute of a material. A brick material, for example, may have a bitmap of the brick pattern superimposed along with the other material attributes.

Basic materials achieve their appearance without the use of bitmaps. Defining mapped materials may require more effort, but mapped materials can yield more realistic results with materials that exhibit prominent textures or patterns.

Basic Materials

A basic material is a simple material that does not use any sort of bitmap. Generally, these are materials that have no prominent surface textures or significant surface patterns. Examples of such materials include metals, paints, plastics, and glass.

Looking at the Modify Standard Material dialog box shown in Figure 31.15, you see the attributes you can modify. Each is briefly described in the following list:

- **Color/Pattern.** This is the general color of the material. It is defined in either the RGB (Red, Green, Blue) color system or the HSV (Hue, Saturation, Value) color system. The color can also be derived from the ACI Color value of the object to which it is assigned. The Value slider is used to control the overall intensity of the color.

- **Ambient.** This is the color of the material when it has a shadow cast on it. Generally speaking, this is simply a darker version of the color/pattern color.

- **Reflection.** This attribute determines the amount of reflection the material has. The Value slider determines the strength of that reflection. In general, most reflections are subtle and have a value of .20 or less. The Lock check box can be used to lock all the colors together, and the Mirror check box can be used to turn the material into a mirror, based on the color. For example, a true mirror material would have Lock turned on, have Mirror turned on, and have a white Color/Pattern value.

- **Roughness.** This attribute adds roughness to the material. The adjustment you make here controls the value of the roughness. The higher the value, the rougher the material appears.

- **Transparency.** This attribute is used to determine the amount of light that passes through an object. For example, glass is highly transparent, whereas concrete is not. The amount of transparency is controlled with the Value slider.

■ **Refraction.** Refraction is the bending of light as it passes through an object. For example, if you look at a pencil in a glass of water, from the side the pencil appears bent or broken. You can set the Value slider to determine the amount of refraction.

■ **Bump Map.** This is the only attribute that makes reference to a bitmap. A bump map is used to make the surface of the object appear to have more detail or texture, such as mortar joints, without having to model the joints themselves. This detail and appearance of texture comes from a bitmap such as one created from a photograph of a set of bricks.

Figure 31.15

From the Modify Standard Material dialog box, you can assign attributes to a new material.

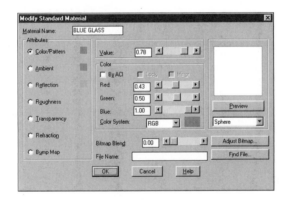

By setting one or more of these attributes, you can create just about any material you want. In the following exercise, you create a new glass material for use in the model in 31ex01b.dwg from the preceding exercise. Because the new material is a modification of an existing material, most of the material attributes will remain unchanged. Other attributes will be changed slightly to yield a more appropriate material.

CREATING A SIMPLE MATERIAL

1. Continue in or open 31ex01b.DWG from the preceding exercise. If necessary, display the Render toolbar. From the Render toolbar, choose Materials, or type **RMAT** at the command prompt.

2. From the Materials list, select the Blue Glass material.

3. Select Duplicate. AutoCAD displays the New Standard Materials dialog box.

4. In the Material Name input box, type **Dark Blue Glass**.

5. Make sure the Color/Pattern radio button is active. Verify that the ACI check box is turned off. Then in the Color section of the dialog box, select the Color swatch. This opens the Color dialog box shown in Figure 31.16.

Figure 31.16

From the Color dialog box, you can assign colors to materials.

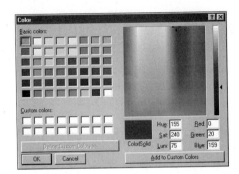

6. Set the Red, Green, and Blue values to **0**, **20**, and **160** respectively, which creates a dark blue.

7. Click OK to return to the New Standard Material dialog box. With Color/Pattern still selected, set the Value slider to **0.15**.

8. Click the Ambient radio button and select the Lock check box to place a check in it.

9. Click the Reflection radio button and set the Value slider to **0.10**.

10. With the Reflection attribute still selected, select the color swatch in the Color section to display the Color dialog box (as you did in step 4). Set the Red, Green, and Blue values to **0**, **7**, and **77** respectively. Click OK to close the Color dialog box. The New Standard Material dialog box should now resemble Figure 31.17.

Figure 31.17

The New Standard Material dialog box after you define the new Dark Blue Glass material.

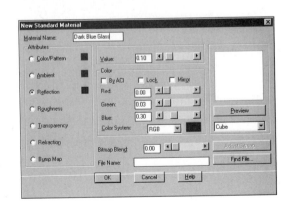

11. Click OK to return to the Materials dialog box. The Dark Blue Glass material now appears in the Material list.

12. With Dark Blue Glass selected in the Materials list, select the By Layer button.

13. From the Select Layer list, choose the glass layer, then select the Attach button to assign Dark Blue Glass to all objects on the glass layer.

14. Click OK to close the Attach by Layer dialog box, and click OK again to close the Materials dialog box.

15. From the Render toolbar, choose Render to display the Render dialog box. Verify that the settings duplicate those shown in Figure 31.13.

16. Click the Render button, and AutoCAD renders the model. The model should now resemble Figure 31.18.

17. Leave this drawing open. You will use it in the next exercise.

Figure 31.18

The office building model with the new Dark Blue Glass material applied to the Glass layer.

As you can see from this exercise, creating a new basic material is not difficult. As in this exercise, you can frequently use a currently defined material and modify one or more attributes to create the new material. The existing material serves as a template for the new material.

After you have created a new material, you may want to save it for use in other models. The following exercise demonstrates how to add a newly created material to the material library.

SAVING A NEW MATERIAL

1. Continue in 31ex01b.DWG from the preceding exercise. From the Render toolbar, choose Materials, or type **RMAT** at the command prompt.

2. Click the Materials Library button.

3. In the Materials Library dialog box, select Dark Blue Glass in the Materials list.

4. Click the Export button to add the selected material to the Current Library.

5. In the Current Library list box, scroll down to find Dark Blue Glass added to the list.

6. Click OK. In the Library Notification dialog box, select Save Changes to save the modification. Then click OK to close the Materials dialog box.

7. You can save and close this drawing.

Mapped Materials

A mapped material varies from a basic material because one or more of the attributes is replaced with a bitmap image. For example, by replacing the color/pattern attribute with a photograph image of a wood pattern, you can make the surface of an object appear to have that wood pattern.

In AutoCAD, working with mapped materials is slightly more complicated because you also need to supply mapping coordinates. Mapping coordinates tell the rendering engine where and how to place the map on the surface of the object. Without correct mapping coordinates, the texture may not appear at the desired orientation or will not be on the same scale as the rest of the scene.

When you look at the Modify Standard Material dialog box in Figure 31.19, you will see the bitmap controls below and to the right of the color controls. If you choose the Find File button, you can navigate to any directory on your system and select a bitmap file for use in the material. You can use any bitmap file format supported by AutoCAD. These include the BMP, JPG, PNG, TIF, TGA, PCX, and GIF formats.

NOTE

> To use a particular bitmap in your scene, that bitmap should reside in either the same directory as the drawing or one of the directories listed under Texture Maps Search Paths in the AutoCAD options. Otherwise, AutoCAD may not be able to find the file.

Figure 31.19

The Modify Standard Material dialog box. The bitmap controls appear near the bottom-right.

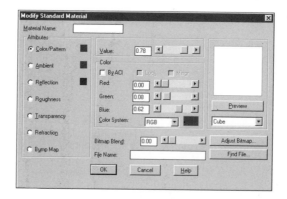

After you select the bitmap, you can click the Adjust Bitmap button to crop and trim the bitmap as needed. Figure 31.20 shows you the dialog box that appears when you click this button.

Figure 31.20

The Adjust Material Bitmap Placement dialog box.

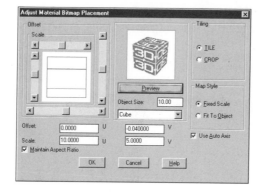

Although in many instances, you will not need to adjust the bitmap, in some circumstances, you will have to adjust the bitmap to obtain the effect you want. If, for example you need to create a "decal" map—such as the label on a bottle of wine—you can set the tiling to crop instead of tile, and only one copy of the image will appear on the object. Figure 31.21 shows you the difference between a tiled material and a cropped material. You will learn more about mapping materials to objects later in this chapter.

Figure 31.21

A tiled material (left) and a cropped material (right).

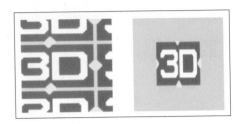

The following exercise shows you how to create a wood grain material with a bitmap.

USING A BITMAP TO CREATE A WOOD GRAIN

1. Start a new drawing.

2. Open the Materials dialog box by choosing Materials from the Render toolbar or by typing **RMAT** at the command prompt.

3. Choose New to create a new material.

4. Name the material by typing **Wood2** in the Material Name input box.

5. With the Color/Pattern radio button selected, choose Find File in the lower-right corner. AutoCAD displays the Bitmap File dialog box. Make sure that the Files of Type input box is set to display *.tga files.

6. Navigate to the Textures directory in your AutoCAD 2000 installation.

7. Choose Teak.tga and click Open to open the file. At this point, you are returned to the New Standard Material dialog box.

8. Set the Value slider to **1.00** and choose Preview to view the teak bitmap. Figure 31.22 shows the dialog box at this point.

Figure 31.22

The New Standard Material dialog box displaying the new Wood2 material.

9. Click the Bump Map radio button.

10. Click OK to accept the new material and return to the Materials dialog box. The new Wood2 material now appears in the Materials list.

11. To save the new material and add it to the materials library, first click the Materials Library button.

12. In the Materials Library dialog box, select Wood2 from the Current Drawing list. Then select the Export button to add the material to the current library. Save the changes to the library by clicking the Save button.

13. Click OK twice to close the Materials Library dialog box and the Materials dialog box. Close the drawing without saving.

This exercise demonstrates that creating a mapped material is easy as long as you have the bitmap file and know its location. You can also supply your own bitmaps for use in defining new materials. Several libraries of third-party bitmaps suitable for use in making new materials are available. You can also create bitmap files by scanning photographs of materials such as metals, woods, and construction materials, to mention just a few. You can use bitmap files of various types, including BMP, PNG, JPG, TGA, TIF, GIF, and PCX file types.

Applying Mapping Coordinates

As was mentioned earlier, when you use materials that are composed wholly or in part of bitmap images, you usually have to apply mapping coordinates to the object. To do so, use the Mapping icon on the Render toolbar or type **SETUV** at the command prompt. You are then prompted to select the objects to which you want to apply the mapping coordinates. Select the appropriate objects, and the Mapping dialog box shown in Figure 31.23 appears.

Figure 31.23

In the Mapping dialog box, you select the type of mapping to apply to an object.

AutoCAD supports four types of mapping: planar, spherical, cylindrical, and solid. The first three generally refer to how the bitmap is wrapped around the object to which the mapping is applied. Figure 31.24 shows the various mapping types.

Figure 31.24

The four mapping types in AutoCAD: planar, cylindrical, spherical, and solid.

The last mapping type is called a solid mapping type. This type of mapping is intended for use with procedural materials such as Wood, Marble, and Granite. These materials are generated based on mathematical formulas and do not make use of bitmaps. The solid mapping coordinates are used when you have a procedural material assigned to an object with highly varying geometry, such as a box with a sphere subtracted out of it. The curved inner portion of the subtracted area stretches the bitmap due to the Mapping coordinates, but a solid procedural material always appears correct.

After you select the type of mapping you want to use, you can select the Adjust Coordinates button to fine-tune the mapping. Which specific dialog box appears depends upon whether you choose a planar, cylindrical, spherical, or solid mapped object. As an example of the scope of adjustments available for mapping and adjusting coordinates, Figure 31.25 shows the Adjust Planar Coordinates dialog box.

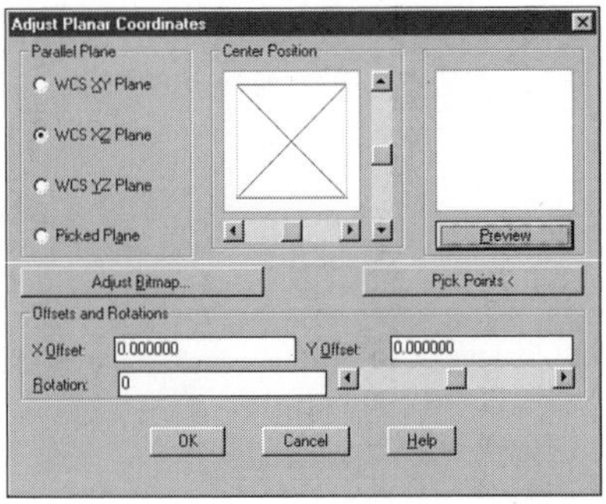

Figure 31.25

The Adjust Planar Coordinates dialog box for adjusting mapping settings on planar objects.

In the dialog box, you can select the World Coordinate System plane along which the mapping coordinates are aligned. You can also pick your own 3D plane by picking three points on that plane, much like you can define your own User Coordinate System (UCS).

In the Center Position section of the dialog box, you will actually see a wireframe representation of the selected object. A light blue outline, called the Mapping icon, appears around this box as well.

The blue outline represents the mapping coordinates and indicates the size of one copy of the bitmap on the surface of the object. By adjusting the slider to the right and bottom of the preview, you can control the position of the bitmap on the surface of the object. At the bottom of the dialog box, you can control the offset and rotation of the Mapping icon. If you want to control the scale of the bitmap, click the Adjust Bitmap button.

The combinations of geometric shapes and mapping planes make adjusting bitmapped materials a somewhat complex operation due principally to the number of choices available. The procedures are relatively straightforward, however, and by adjusting the offset, rotation, scale, and coordinates of bitmapped materials, you can exert a great deal of control over how materials based on bitmaps will appear in the rendered model.

Creating Lights

After you select and perhaps create and then apply materials to the objects in your model, the next logical step is to add sources of light. Lighting is one of the most important aspects of creating an effective rendering. Without realistic lighting, the surfaces and materials of an otherwise realistic model will appear "flat" looking. Lighting also provides the means for adding realistic shadows to your model.

You create lights by selecting the Lights button from the Render toolbar or by typing **LIGHT** at the command prompt. Either method displays the Lights dialog box, shown in Figure 31.26.

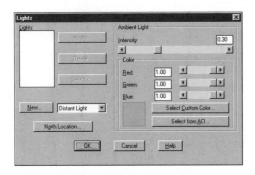

In the Lights dialog box, you will see a list of all the current lights in the scene, as well as the Ambient Light controls, the Light Creation controls, and the North Location button.

The ambient light is the overall brightness of the scene. By adjusting the ambient light, you can set the overall brightness of the scene. Higher ambient values are good for outside light, whereas lower values are good for interior or night scenes. Strive to avoid extreme settings of ambient light. Usually, values between 30 and 70 yield suitable amounts of ambient light. You can also adjust the ambient light color to provide basic color tinting to the scene. Keep ambient light color variations very subtle for the most realistic effects. Ambient light exhibits no source and, therefore, is not capable of casting shadows.

The North Location button allows you to set the north direction in your models. By default, north coincides with the positive Y direction. You may want to alter the north direction in architectural models.

Types of Lights

AutoCAD supports three types of lights:

- **Point Light.** This type of light is similar to a single light bulb. Light is radiated from a single point in all directions. You can specify no attenuation or attenuation that is inverse linear or inverse square.

- **Spotlight.** This type of light is similar to the light emitted from a flashlight. The spotlight has a source and a target location. Light from a spotlight is cast in a cone fashion and you can define the angle of the cone. You can specify no attenuation or attenuation that is inverse linear or inverse square.

- **Distant.** A distant light emits parallel light beams in one direction. Distant light sources cannot exhibit any attenuation; the light intensity remains constant regardless of its distance.

Typically, point lights are used for general illumination in the scene, spotlights are used to add special highlighting in a relatively small area, and distant lights are used to simulate sunlight.

Creating a Light

As you can see in the Lights dialog box shown in Figure 31.26, you create a light simply by choosing the type of light from the drop-down list next to the New button and clicking the New button. Each of the three light types has its own dialog box for specifying the attributes of the light. The dialog box for a spotlight is shown in Figure 31.27.

Figure 31.27

The New Spotlight dialog box, where you create and set the attributes of a spotlight.

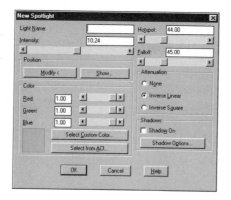

Every light that you create in an AutoCAD model must have a name. You enter the name in the Light Name input box. Choose a name that is descriptive, such as Spot1 or Point-main.

With point lights and spotlights, you need to position the light in the model. Point lights require only the location of the light source. However, because spotlights are directional, you must specify the position of both the source and the target. You specify these locations by choosing the Modify button in the Position section of the dialog box. In the case of spotlights, you are then prompted to pick the target of the light followed by the location of the light. AutoCAD temporarily hides the dialog box to allow you to pick these points in the model. Using point filters (as described in Chapter 28, "Drawing in 3D AutoCAD") makes specifying light locations easier. With distant lights, you need to specify the source direction as well as its height above the horizon.

After you position a light, you are returned to the New Light dialog box, where you set the remaining parameters associated with the light, which are explained here:

■ **Intensity.** Sets the intensity or brightness of the light. Entering 0 turns off a light. The maximum point light intensity depends on the attenuation setting and the extents of the drawing. With no attenuation, maximum intensity is 1. If attenuation is inverse linear, maximum intensity is the value of twice the extents distance. If attenuation is inverse square, maximum intensity is twice the square of the extents distance.

■ **Color.** You can assign a different color to each light in the scene. For example, florescent lighting often has a slight blue cast, while typical incandescent lighting tends to be slightly yellow. For special effects such as sunrise or sunset, you may want to give a distant light a slightly red color. Keep these color assignments minimal for the best results.

■ **Attenuation.** In real life, light fades or grows weaker as the distance between source and objects increases. In AutoCAD, lights remain the same strength over a distance unless you specify an attenuation factor. There are two types of attenuation: inverse linear and inverse square. Inverse square drops off much faster than inverse linear does. For point lights and spotlights, inverse linear is the default attenuation factor and generally yields the most effective results. Direct lights exhibit no attenuation.

■ **Shadows.** All lights in AutoCAD are capable of casting shadows. The type of shadow depends on the current render type (Photo Real or Photo Raytrace) and the settings in the Shadow Options dialog box. The shadow casting capability of any light can be turned on or off with the Shadow On check box in the Shadows section of the new Lights dialog box.

In addition to these basic controls common to all light types, the New Spotlight dialog box allows you to adjust the angle of the cone and its falloff rate and the New Distant Light dialog box provides settings for sun position.

The following exercise shows you how to create a spotlight for use in a model.

CREATING A SPOTLIGHT

1. Load the file 31ex02.dwg from the accompanying CD-ROM. The drawing presents a model of a telephone handset unit, as shown in Figure 31.28.

Figure 31.28

*Model of a telephone
handset before rendering.*

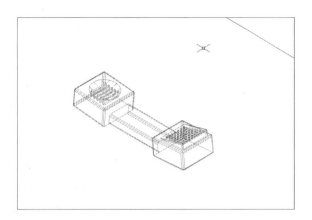

2. From the View menu, choose 3D Views, Plan View, World UCS. This switches you to a Plan view. From this view, you will add a spotlight.

3. Select Lights from the Render toolbar or type **LIGHT** at the command prompt.

4. In the Lights dialog box, choose Spotlight from the drop-down list and click the New button.

5. In the New Spotlight dialog box, type the name **Spot1** in the Light Name input box.

6. In the Position section, click the Modify button. AutoCAD hides the dialog box and displays the drawing.

7. At the `Enter light target` prompt, type in the coordinates **8.5,7.0**. At the `Enter light location` prompt, type **.xy** to indicate that next you will provide the X-Y location of the light location.

8. At the `of` prompt, type in the coordinates **-2,14**. At the `(need Z)` prompt, type **25**. This places the light location 25 units above the model. AutoCAD returns to the New Spotlight dialog box.

9. Configure the remaining settings in the New Spotlight dialog box, as shown in Figure 31.29.

Figure 31.29

Settings of the New Spotlight dialog box for the model's new spotlight.

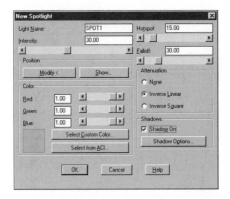

10. In the Shadow section of the New Spotlight dialog box, select Shadow Options, and in the Shadow Options dialog box, check the Shadow Volume/Ray Traced Shadows check box. Click OK to close the Shadow Options dialog box. Then click OK to close the New Spotlight dialog box.

11. In the Lights dialog box, set the Ambient Light Intensity to **0.5**. Click OK to accept the settings and close the dialog box.

12. From the View menu, choose Named Views. In the View dialog box, select View1 and then Set Current. Click OK to close the dialog box and restore the opening view.

13. From the Render toolbar, choose Render or enter **Render** at the command prompt.

14. Configure the settings in the Render dialog box like those shown in Figure 31.30.

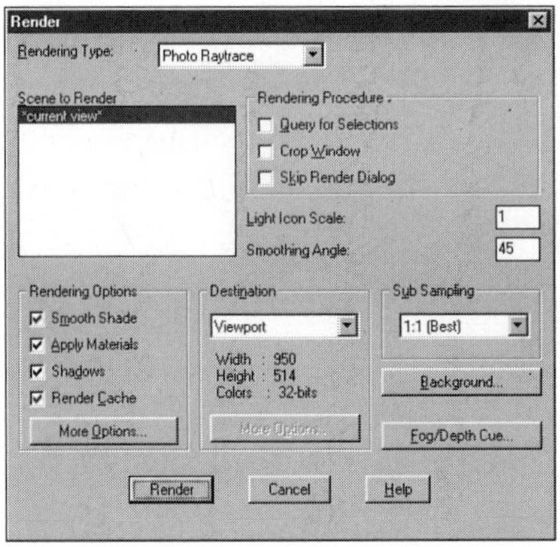

Figure 31.30

Settings of the Render dialog box prior to rendering the model.

15. In the Render dialog box, choose Render. After a few moments, the rendered model appears. The rendering should resemble Figure 31.31.

16. You may want to render this model again after adjusting the Hotspot and Falloff angles as well as the intensities of the spotlight and ambient light. You can then close this drawing without saving.

Figure 31.31

The rendered model is illuminated with the new spotlight.

As you learned in this exercise, creating lights for a model is not difficult. Proper lighting of a model, however, is an art form in itself. Good results can be produced quickly, but great results take time and a lot of testing and adjusting of the lights in the scene.

When testing different light types, positions, and intensities, you can speed up your test renderings in several ways. First, you need not render the complete model or view. Often, rendering a smaller portion of the view will give you the information you need to decide if further adjustments are needed. Referring to the Render dialog box shown in Figure 31.32, in the Rendering Procedure section, the Crop Window option allows you to window a portion of the model for rendering. In a similar way, the Query for Selections option allows you to select portions on the model for rendering on an object-by-object basis. Using one or both of these options can greatly speed the rendering of portions of the model as you make lighting adjustments.

If you need to render the entire model view while making adjustments, you can make "course" renderings using the Sub Sampling options found in the Render dialog box. Sub-sampling reduces rendering time and image quality without losing lighting effects such as shadows by rendering a fraction of all of the pixels. A sub-sampling ratio of 1:1 renders all pixels and takes the most time. A sub-sampling of 3:1, however, renders only every third pixel, greatly reducing rendering times. Shadows also increase rendering times. Turning off the Shadow option in the Rendering Options section of the Render dialog box is yet another way to make successive test renderings more attractive.

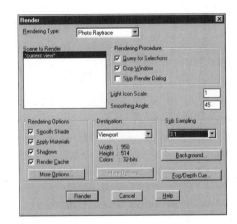

Figure 31.32

The Render dialog box offers methods for speeding up test renderings.

Creating Sunlight

Sunlight—in both exterior and interior views of your model—can be the most important light you use. You can manually set a Distant light to simulate sunlight from any direction to yield any effect you want. You can also use AutoCAD's built-in Sun Angle Calculator to calculate the exact position of the sun for any point on earth on any day of the year at any time of day. Being able to place the sun so precisely is often important in renderings of exterior architectural models where the exact position and extent of shadows cast by buildings or other structures may be important. In the following exercise, you learn how to create precise sun shadows using the Sun Angle Calculator.

USING THE SUNLIGHT SYSTEM TO CREATE A DISTANT LIGHT

1. Load the file 31ex03.dwg from the accompanying CD-ROM. This drawing contains a model of an apartment building with an adjoining urban park.

2. Choose Lights from the Render toolbar. In the Light Type drop-down list, set the light type to Distant and click the New button.

3. In the New Distant Light dialog box, create a new Distant light. Name this light Sun. Set its intensity to **1.00**.

4. In the Shadows section, select Shadow On. Select Shadow Options and, in the Shadow Options dialog box, select the Shadow Volume/Ray Traced Shadows. Click OK to close the Shadow Options dialog box.

5. In the New Distant Light dialog box, select Sun Angle Calculator. AutoCAD displays the Sun Angle Calculator dialog box shown in Figure 31.33.

Figure 31.33

The Sun Angle Calculator dialog box, where you set the geographical location and date/time.

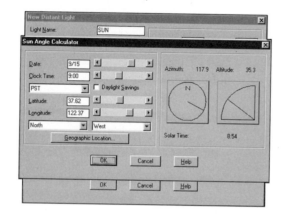

6. Select Geographic Location to display the Geographic Location dialog box. Select San Francisco from the City list box and click OK to close the dialog box.

7. In the Sun Angle Calculator dialog box, set the Date and Clock Time as shown in Figure 31.33, then click OK to return to the New Distant Light dialog box. Click OK to close this dialog box.

8. In the Lights dialog box, check that the Ambient Light intensity is set to 0.90. Click OK to close this dialog box.

9. Select Render from the Render toolbar or type **Render** at the command prompt.

10. In the Render dialog box, set the Rendering Type to Photo Raytrace. In the Rendering Options section, make sure the Shadows option is checked.

11. Click the Render button to begin rendering the model. After a few moments, your rendered model should resemble Figure 31.34. Close this drawing without saving.

Figure 31.34

The rendered building model showing the cast shadows on a specific date and time.

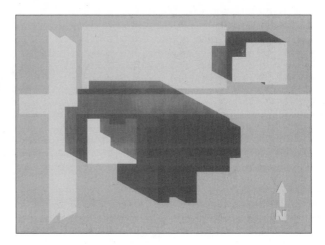

> **NOTE**
>
> The Sun Angle Calculator takes its north as the current AutoCAD north direction. By default, this is the positive Y axis direction of the current coordinate direction. You can change the north direction in the North Direction dialog box, which is accessible from the Lights dialog box.

This exercise demonstrates that the Sun Angle Calculator can be effectively used to place a distant light that's capable of producing accurate object shadows. Of course, a distant light can also be used more conventionally as a directional light source.

Generating an Output

The Default Rendering method in AutoCAD renders the output to the current viewport. This is the method used in the exercises in this chapter. To print the image or use it in other programs, however, you must be able to save the rendered image to a file. You accomplish this by choosing File from the Destination drop-down list in the Render dialog box. After you select File, click the More Options button to define the file type.

AutoCAD allows you to render the image out to one of five different file types: TARGA, TIF, Postscript, BMP, and PCX file formats. Below the File Type drop-down list, you can select the resolution to which you want to render. Higher resolutions, of course, take longer to render.

NOTE

There are other advanced features of the Rendering system in AutoCAD to explore. These include fog, backgrounds, vegetation, and several others. This chapter is intended to give you an introduction to the principals of rendering and the basic capabilities of the rendering feature in AutoCAD 2000. Rendering is as much an art as a science, and you use this chapter's information to serve as a basis for individual exploration of rendering inside AutoCAD.

Summary

After you have constructed a 3D model using the principals discussed in the 3D chapters of this book, you can use AutoCAD to render the model. Rendering consists of applying materials to the objects in the model and setting lights to illuminate the model. One of the most important steps in carrying out an interesting and informative rendering is establishing an effective viewpoint. After you carry out these basic preparation steps, rendering is often a matter of trial and error and fine-tuning.

P ART

VIII

ADVANCED TOPICS

32

VISUAL LISP

Understanding AutoLISP and Visual LISP

AutoLISP is a subset of the popular LISP programming language developed in the late fifties. LISP, which is an acronym for LISt Processing, is one of the few programming languages from that era still in active use today. Developed principally for use in Artificial Intelligence (AI) applications, LISP is still popular in the AI community. AutoLISP was first introduced into AutoCAD as its principle programming language with Release 2.18 in January 1986. It was chosen as the initial AutoCAD programming language for two important reasons: LISP structurally relies upon lists to contain its data types and most of CAD relies upon lists of coordinates or data that can be easily expressed in list form. Just as important, LISP, and AutoLISP by extension, is uniquely suited for the relatively unstructured design environment of CAD projects, which typically involve repeatedly applying different solution to the design process.

In the years since 1986, AutoLISP has become widely popular and well accepted as an easy-to-learn, easy-to-use customization language for use in AutoCAD. More than 1.25 million AutoCAD customers currently use AutoLISP either directly or through third-party applications integrated with AutoCAD. However, despite its popularity and adoption by the communities of AutoCAD users and developers, AutoLISP began to show some serious limitations as AutoCAD, and the machines on which it is run, improved in functionality and speed.

Beginning with AutoCAD Release 14, a new implementation of "AutoLISP," termed Visual LISP, was introduced. Visual LISP can be best described as a complete development environment for creating applications and customizing AutoCAD using the LISP programming language. Visual LISP is also an extension and an enhancement to the "old" AutoLISP found in Release 14 and before. Visual LISP provides greater functionality, improved productivity and performance, increased security, and a new Integrated Development Environment (IDE). It is important to realize that if you are already familiar with AutoLISP, the transition to Visual LISP is virtually seamless. Although there are new functions in Visual LISP, the "old" AutoLISP has been essentially retained, and your investment in learning AutoLISP can be easily transported into Visual LISP.

Much of the increased functionality and improved productivity of Visual LISP is centered upon the fact that it is an Object ARX application, and it has a completely new LISP interpreter. It greatly expands AutoCAD's ActiveX support by including additional ActiveX objects and events. Although much of the advanced aspects of Visual LISP are outside the scope of this chapter, Visual LISP does also include several new elements that aid in the writing and debugging of AutoLISP/Visual LISP code and that serve all AutoLISP users—both novice and expert.

NOTE

The term 'AutoLISP' should be taken to mean the AutoLISP programming language. 'Visual LISP' is a development environment, within which programs written in AutoLISP (the language) are developed, debugged, and optionally compiled into Object ARX applications. 'Visual LISP' provides its own AutoLISP evaluator that, in effect, replaces the pre-AutoCAD 2000 AutoLISP evaluator. In this chapter, as with the AutoCAD community in general, the term 'AutoLISP' is still valid and refers to the programming language used by Visual LISP.

Understanding the Visual LISP Interface

Among its many features, Visual LISP offers an integrated set of tools and facilities specifically intended to make the writing of AutoLISP code easier. Most of these new features are visually oriented and represented as integral components of the Visual LISP interface. These features include

- Color-coded source display

- Source syntax checker

- Autoformat and Smart Indent

- Parentheses matching

- Direct LISP function evaluation

- Source-level debugging features

The interface itself consists of an application window and several component windows. Like any Windows application, Visual LISP offers toolbars, menus, and an online Help system. The various windows can be moved, re-sized, and minimized. The default Visual LISP application is shown in Figure 32.1

Figure 32.1

The Visual LISP interface.

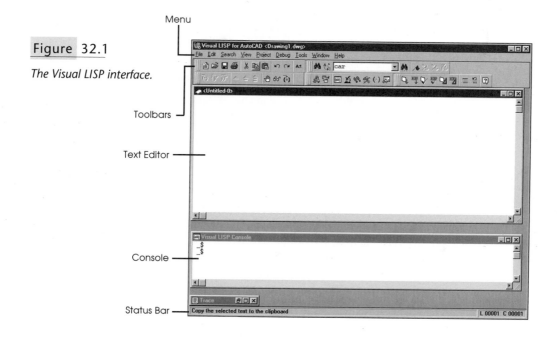

NOTE

> Although Visual LISP has the appearance of a typical Windows application with a set of windows, toolbars, and a menu bar, it cannot run independently of AutoCAD 2000. To work in Visual LISP, AutoCAD must be running.

In the following exercise, you start and explore some of the interface elements of Visual LISP.

STARTING VISUAL LISP

1. Start AutoCAD 2000. From the Tools menu, select AutoLISP, and then Visual LISP Editor. The Visual LISP window opens as shown in Figure 32.1. You can also start Visual LISP by typing **vlide** and pressing Enter at the command prompt.

2. If your Visual LISP does not display the Text Editor window, open it: From the File menu, select New File. You can also start a new file in the Text Editor window by pressing Ctrl+N or by selecting the New tool from the Standard toolbar.

3. With Visual LISP open, use standard Windows methods to move and resize the Text Editor or Console windows. The window elements within the Visual LISP interface behave as normal windows.

4. From the Visual LISP menu bar, choose View to display the contents of the View menu. This menu lists the various Visual LISP interface windows.

5. From the View menu, choose Trace Stack to display the Trace Stack window. This is one of several Visual LISP windows used in debugging Visual LISP code. Close this window by selecting the "X" button in the upper right corner.

6. If you are not continuing with the next exercise, close Visual LISP: From the File menu, choose Exit or select the Close button in the upper-right corner of the Visual LISP application window.

As you can see from the preceding exercise, the Visual LISP application window has many of the features and characteristics of a standard Windows application. Sub-windows might be opened, moved, sized, and closed. In addition, the five Visual LISP toolbars can be displayed or hidden and placed in either a docked or a floated location. To control some of these features, you can use the Toolbars option of the View menu. The features of the individual Visual LISP interface elements enable you a large degree of flexibility in configuring the appearance of the Visual LISP interface.

NOTE

> To appreciate and utilize many of the features of the Visual LISP programming environment, you need to be familiar with the AutoLISP programming language. Most of the discussion found in this chapter assumes such knowledge. To learn more about AutoLISP, see Chapter 22, "Introduction to AutoLISP Programming."

Exploring the Console Window

The Visual LISP Console window (shown in Figure 32.2) enables you to enter and run AutoLISP expressions and to see the results immediately. In many ways, it serves as a "scratch pad" for testing or verifying AutoLISP code. In this respect, it serves much as the AutoCAD command window where you can also enter AutoLISP code. However, the Console window offers many advantages over typing AutoLISP input at AutoCAD's command prompt. The following is a summary of some of the important features of the Console window:

- Enter multiple AutoLISP expressions on multiple lines. Press Ctrl+Enter to continue typing without forcing an evaluation.

- Evaluate multiple expressions simultaneously.

- Return to previously entered expressions using the Tab key. The Console window retains a history of all entered expressions. You can "scroll" backward using the Tab key, scroll forward with Shift+Tab.

- Perform an associative search through the input history. For example, typing (foreach followed by the Tab key, finds and retrieves the last expression in the history that began with (foreach. Reverse the direction of the search with Ctrl+Tab.

- Pressing Esc clears any text at the current Console prompt.

- Save a log record of all Console activity to a log file.

- Toggle to AutoCAD mode via a right-click menu to transfer Console input to AutoCAD's command prompt.

- Display the value of an AutoLISP variable by merely typing the variable and pressing Enter.

- Cut and Paste text from the Console to the Text Editor window.

■ Automatic color-coding assigns a separate color to AutoLISP data types
(functions have the color blue, parentheses are red, strings are magenta,
and so on). Matching parentheses are highlighted as they are entered.

Figure 32.2

*The Visual LISP Console
window.*

Furthermore, the Console window is where Visual LISP displays messages, including
diagnostic messages, from the code that is entered in Text Editor. Together, these
and several other features make working with AutoLISP code in the Visual LISP
Console window both easier and less error-prone. Combined with the Visual
LISP Text Editor window, the Console provides a powerful development tool for
developing both simple and complex AutoLISP code. In the following exercise,
some of the features of the Console window are demonstrated.

NOTE

In this and many of the following exercises, you enter AutoLISP expressions into either the
Visual LISP Console or the Text Editor windows. In these exercises, this data is shown in
bold-faced type.

In the following exercise, you start and explore some of the interface elements of
Visual LISP

EXPLORING THE CONSOLE WINDOW

1. Continue from the previous exercise or start Visual LISP. Make the Console window
current by clicking anywhere in it or by choosing the Window menu, and then
selecting Visual LISP Console.

2. As you type the following code into the Console window, note the color-coding for
each type of element. Enter only the text shown; do not yet type matching right
parentheses:

```
$(setq xyz (* (+ (/ 6 2.5
```

Notice that AutoLISP functions are blue, integers are green, variables are black, real numbers are teal, and parentheses are red.

3. As you complete the previous expression by typing the required closing, or right, parenthesis notice that as each right parenthesis is typed, its matching opening, or left, parenthesis is momentarily highlighted with a cursor bar. After typing the four closing parentheses, do not press the Enter key. The completed expression is:

```
$(setq xyz (* (+ (/ 6 2.5))))
```

4. Continue typing on the same line and enter the following AutoLISP expression. Again, note the highlighting of parentheses as you enter the matching closing parenthesis. (Do not press Enter yet.)

```
_$(strcat "@" (rtos xyz) "<" (rtos 45 2 2))
```

5. Press Enter. Notice that the results of evaluating both expressions are returned. Also, notice that Visual LISP assigns the color green to string elements. The Console should now display the following:

```
2.4
"@2.4000<45.00"
_$
```

6. Cycle back through the Console input history buffer by pressing the Tab key twice. Cycle forward by pressing the Shift+Tab keys twice.

7. If you are continuing with the next exercise, leave Visual LISP open.

The preceding exercise demonstrates some of the features that enable the Console window to be used as a powerful adjunct to writing and testing your AutoLISP code.

Exploring Text Editor

The Visual LISP Text Editor is the central and most important component of the Visual LISP environment. Although the Visual LISP Console window serves well for entering short AutoLISP expressions, you should use Visual LISP's Text Editor for extended AutoLISP code that you want to save to a file for later use. If you have written AutoLISP code in the past, you have undoubtedly used some form of text editor, even if it was only Microsoft Notepad. Notepad (and other generic text editors) offers the basic text editing functions and the capability to save text to a file, but it lacks any tools intended for use in a programming context.

Visual LISP's built-in Text Editor is designed to meet a programmer's needs, and it has a number of features and tools specifically intended to support and enhance AutoLISP programming. These features include the following:

- **Color-coding**—As you enter text into Text Editor, it is automatically color-coded, based upon its specific AutoLISP functionality. For example, all internally defined AutoLISP functions are coded in blue, parentheses are red, string elements appear in magenta, *and so on*. This automatic color-coding enables you to quickly identify various programming elements, and it serves as an effective debugging aid.

- **Parenthesis matching**—AutoLISP is notorious for its parentheses and unmatched parentheses are one of the leading causes of errors in a program. With parentheses matching, you can track parenthesis pairs as you enter code and easily find any given parenthesis's match in completed code.

- **Formatting**—As you enter AutoLISP code, Text Editor is "intelligent" enough to automatically apply appropriate indentation, making your code easier to read. After code has been entered (or imported), you can apply formatting using any of several formatting styles.

- **Syntax checking**—You can check all or any portion of typed code for syntax errors. The specific error and the offending expression are printed in a separate window.

- **Expression checking**—You can test portions of entered code without leaving the editor.

- **File searching**—You can search for a word or expression in several files with a single command.

- **Immediate help**—You can highlight any function and press Ctrl+F1, or the Help button on the Tools toolbar, to display the help page for that function.

- **Advanced debugging**—There is a number of advanced debugging features, such as breakpoint insertion, variable watching, stack tracing, animation, and AutoCAD entity viewing.

All these features are intended to increase the efficiency with which programming code can be entered and debugged. Tools, such as parenthesis checking and auto formatting, can be used and appreciated by even the novice AutoLISP programmer working with relatively simple coding, whereas the more advanced debugging tools enable the detection and correction of errors in complicated Visual LISP projects. Together, the features designed into the Visual LISP Text Editor make the writing of

AutoLISP code and the development of Visual LISP projects easier.

In the following exercise, you will explore some of the features that make the Visual LISP Text Editor such a useful tool in AutoLISP programming.

NOTE

> As with all the AutoLISP code used in this chapter's exercises, the code in the following exercise serves no practical purpose other than to demonstrate Visual LISP functionality. Knowledge of AutoLISP is assumed.

EXPLORING THE VISUAL LISP TEXT EDITOR

1. With AutoCAD running, start Visual LISP by typing **VLIDE** and pressing Enter at the command prompt. Depending upon how you last exited Visual LISP, there might be a file opened in Text Editor.

2. Open a new Visual LISP file by performing one of the following: From the File menu, choose New File or select New file from the Standard toolbar. Your current AutoCAD/Visual LISP interface should resemble Figure 32.3.

Figure 32.3

The Visual LISP interface with a new file opened.

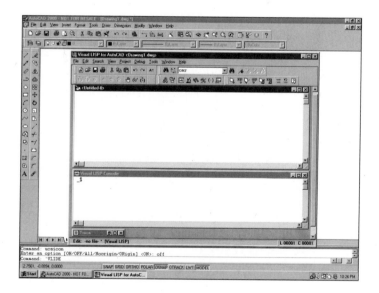

3. As you type the following code into Text Editor, notice the automatic color-coding. Notice that when you type a right parenthesis, the matching left parenthesis is momentarily identified by a bar cursor. Also, notice that if you press Enter at the end of the first line, the second line is automatically indented because this line follows a (defun…) expression. Carefully enter the following code as shown, disregarding the syntax error:

```
(defun foo2 (a b)
       (sqrt a b)
       (print b))
```

4. The code for the foo2 function contains a syntax error. To see how the Visual LISP syntax checker works, select Check Text from Text Editor's Tools menu or press Ctrl+Alt+C. The (sqrt ...) function contains too many arguments. Visual LISP displays the error message, as shown in Figure 32.4, identifying both the error and the offending expression.

Figure 32.4

The Syntax Checker displays the error and the offending expression.

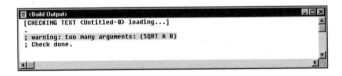

5. Correct the error by removing one argument from the (sqrt ...) function call. Notice that Text Editor behaves as a standard text editor when editing entered text. Correct the code to appear as follows (note the change to the last line):

```
(defun foo2 (a b)
       (sqrt a)
       (print (+ a b))
```

6. Attempt to load this function into memory. With the Text Editor window active, from the Editor's Tools menu, choose Load Text or press Ctrl+Alt+E. A load error is reported in the Console window as shown in Figure 32.5. A "malformed list" error means the file is missing a closing parenthesis.

Figure 32.5

Loading errors are printed in the Console window.

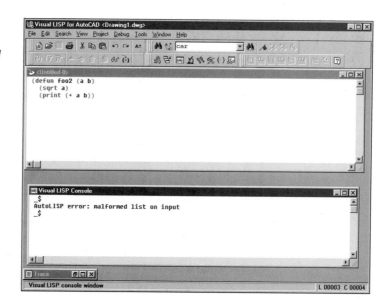

NOTE

Although the missing parenthesis is easy to find in this exercise, the tools and technique used here make parentheses checking and function definitions easier and faster in more deeply nested expressions.

7. To find the missing closing parenthesis, begin checking opening parentheses. With Text Editor active, place the cursor immediately in front of the parenthesis at (`print` ... and double-click. Visual LISP highlights the opening and closing parentheses (if any) and all expressions in between. In this case, the entire (`print` ... expression and its nested expression are properly formed, as seen in Figure 32.6.

Figure 32.6

Checking for matching parentheses.

8. Check the entire function for balanced parentheses. Place the Text Editor cursor immediately in front of the first opening parenthesis for the entire function, `(defun foo2...` and double-click. Because no matching parenthesis is found, the entire function requires a final closing parenthesis.

9. Use Visual LISP's formatting tool to supply the missing parenthesis: From Text Editor's Tools menu, choose Format code or press Ctrl+Alt+F. Visual LISP displays the dialog box shown in Figure 32.7. Choose Yes to have Visual LISP automatically place the missing parenthesis. Choose Yes if Visual LISP informs you that one closing parenthesis was added to your code.

Figure 32.7

Formatting adds missing parentheses.

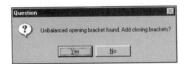

After formatting, the code appears as shown in Figure 32.8. The Visual LISP formatting tool corrected and formatted the code in one step.

Figure 32.8

The corrected and formatted code.

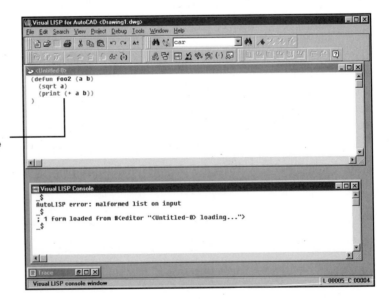

Corrected and formatted code

10. Attempt to reload the `(foo2)` function. With the Text Editor window active, choose Load Text from the Tools menu or press Ctrl+Alt+E. The message in the Console window indicates that the function was loaded successfully as shown in Figure 32.8.

11. Test the (foo2) function by typing the following in the Console window followed by Enter:

    (foo2 16 3)

    The function returns and prints the evaluation of its two arguments, the number 19.

12. Check the current value of the (foo2) function's two variables, a and b. At the Console window's _$ prompt, type the two variable names, separated by at least one space, and then press Enter. Visual LISP reports that both variables have lost their local (foo2) values and now have a value of nil as shown in Figure 32.9.

Figure 32.9

Checking the value of a variable in Visual LISP.

13. If you are continuing to the next exercise, keep Visual LISP open.

In the preceding exercise, you gained skills using some of Visual LISP's programming tools. You saw how the Text Editor functions as a "LISP aware" editor and how it interacts with the Console window. Although not shown in this exercise, both the Text Editor and Console windows have useful right-click menus that enable you to bypass the pull-down menus in initiating many of the functions you use frequently while working in these two windows. Keep in mind that Text Editor, in addition to supporting a large number of LISP-specific functions, possesses virtually all the standard file editor features, such as cut and paste, text find, multiple file open and save, undo, and so on. Most of your Visual LISP development and debugging activities use Text Editor and the tools discussed in this section. In the next section, you will investigate some of the more sophisticated abilities available to you in Visual LISP.

Understanding the Advanced Programming Tools

As some of the preceding exercises have shown, programming tools, such as color-coding, parenthesis and syntax checking, and auto formatting, are helpful in writing and debugging AutoLISP code. Chances are that these tools are the ones you use most often because they address the vast majority of LISP programming concerns.

However, Visual LISP offers a set of more advanced programming tools. These include

■ **Break loop mode**—You can halt program execution at user-specified points to inspect and modify the value of programming objects, such as AutoLISP variables, expressions, and functions.

■ **Animation**—You can watch as Visual LISP steps through your program code and evaluates each expression. Each expression is highlighted as it is evaluated.

■ **Inspect**—You can obtain detailed information about an AutoLISP object in a separate Inspect dialog box. Nested objects (such as association lists) can be expanded or recursively examined down to an atomic (*for example,* symbol, number) level.

■ **Watch window**—You can watch the value of user-identified variables during program execution.

■ **Trace facility**—This mimics the standard AutoLISP trace function that enables the printing of calls and returned values of traced functions in a devoted Trace window.

■ **Trace stack**—You can view the contents of AutoLISP's call stack. Visual LISP records the history of called functions as they are executed.

Although an explanation of the functionality and the ramifications of these advanced tools is beyond the scope of this chapter, the remaining chapter exercises offer an introduction and brief demonstration of the power and flexibility of several of these advanced features.

Working with Advanced Programming Tools

The following exercise demonstrates several of Visual LISP's advanced tools. The Watch window facility, the Break Point tool, and the animation and formatting tools can be used to develop and debug written code. The animation feature not only steps through code, highlighting each expression as it is encountered, it also serves to slow execution down so that various program features, such as programming loops, can be observed. It is often helpful to use the animation feature in conjunction with a Watch window so that you can observe the value of selected variables as they change during program execution. The auto-formatting feature is not only a timesaving tool for use while entering AutoLISP code; it also serves to visually present program code in a form in which program flow is more immediately apparent.

NOTE

The program used in the following example serves no practical purpose other than to demonstrate some of the advanced Visual LISP programming features. Knowledge of AutoLISP is assumed.

EXPLORING ADVANCED VISUAL LISP PROGRAMMING AIDS

1. In AutoCAD, open the CHAP-32N.DWG file from the accompanying CD. (This drawing currently contains a small donut in the lower left corner of the opening view.) If necessary, start Visual LISP by typing **VLIDE** and pressing Enter at the command prompt. Depending upon how you last exited Visual LISP, there might be a file opened in Text Editor.

2. From the Visual LISP File menu, choose Open File. In the Open file to edit/view dialog box, navigate to this book's CD, and then select and open the GIZMO2.LSP file from the `chapter 32` directory. Your Text Editor window should now resemble Figure 32.10.

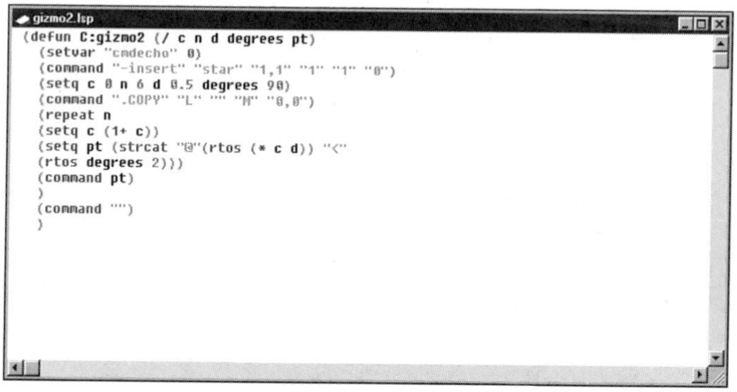

Figure 32.10

Loading GIZMO2.LSP into Text Editor.

```
gizmo2.lsp
(defun C:gizmo2 (/ c n d degrees pt)
  (setvar "cmdecho" 0)
  (command "-insert" "star" "1,1" "1" "1" "0")
  (setq c 0 n 6 d 0.5 degrees 90)
  (command ".COPY" "L" "" "M" "0,0")
  (repeat n
    (setq c (1+ c))
    (setq pt (strcat "@"(rtos (* c d)) "<"
    (rtos degrees 2)))
    (command pt))
    )
  (command "")
  )
```

GIZMO2.LSP defines a function that inserts a block and then makes six copies, 0.5 units apart, along the Y-axis. The program, as written, requires no user input. Note the color-coding assigned to the various elements of GIZMO2.LSP. Also, notice that other than the indenting after the first line of code there is little useful formatting in the code.

3. First, use the Visual LISP formatting feature to format the code into a more readable form. With the Text Editor window active, from the Tools menu, choose Format code in Editor. The code now resembles that in Figure 32.11.

Figure 32.11

GIZMO2.LSP re-formatted into a form that is more readable.

```
gizmo2.lsp
(defun C:gizmo2 (/ c n d degrees pt)
  (setvar "cmdecho" 0)
  (command "-insert" "star" "1,1" "1" "1" "0")
  (setq c 0
        n 6
        d 0.5
        degrees 90
  )
  (command ".COPY" "L" "" "M" "0,0")
  (repeat n
    (setq c (1+ c))
    (setq pt (strcat "@"
                     (rtos (* c d))
                     "<"
                     (rtos degrees 2)
             )
    )
    (command pt)
  )
  (command "")
)
```

Re-formatting the code makes the intent of the `C:Gizmo2` function clearer. For example, the repeat loop and entire (`strcat...`) function are more evident and their purpose within the overall function is easier to discern.

NOTE

Both the color-coding and formatting features are customizable. This chapter uses the Visual LISP default settings for both features. Consult the Visual LISP documentation or Online Help for details about customizing these features.

4. Next, load the `C:Gizmo2` function into memory. From Text Editor's Tools menu, choose Load Text. The result of the loading attempt is reported in the Console window (refer to Figure 32.12).

Figure 32.12

The result of loading program code is shown in the Console window.

```
Visual LISP Console
_$
; 1 form loaded from #<editor "I:/Program Files/ACAD2000/TUTORIAL/VisualLISP/gizmo2.1
_$ |
```

5. From the Debug menu, choose Animate. This activates the animate feature.

NOTE

You can control the speed of the animation. From the Tools menu, choose Environment Options, and then General Options. Choose the Diagnostic tab in the General Options dialog box. In the Animation delay text box, enter the delay, in milliseconds, for each animation step. A delay of 500 milliseconds is usually long enough to enable the progress of the evaluation to be seen clearly.

6. Establish a Break Point. Place the Text Editor cursor at the end of the (setq...) expression, as shown in Figure 32.13, and press F9. This causes the program to stop at this point, and it enables you to check the value of variable c on each iteration of the repeat loop.

Figure 32.13

Establishing a Break Point.

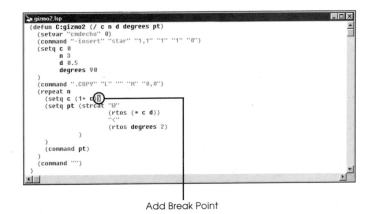

Add Break Point

7. Next, set a Watch window to observe the value of the program's variable c. On the same line in which you set the Break Point, highlight the variable c in the (setq c ...) expression. Then from the Debug menu, choose Add Watch. Visual LISP displays the Watch window displaying the current value (nil) of variable c. Add the program's variable pt by adding it to the Watch window using the Add Watch tool, as shown in Figure 32.14, and by typing **pt** in the Add Watch dialog box. The Watch window now resembles Figure 32.15.

Figure 32.14

Adding program variables to the Watch window.

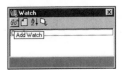

Figure 32.15

Watching two of the variables in GIZMO2.LSP.

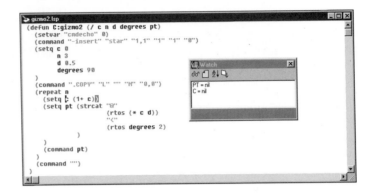

```
gizmo2.lsp
(defun C:gizmo2 (/ c n d degrees pt)
  (setvar "cmdecho" 0)
  (command "-insert" "star" "1,1" "1" "1" "0")
  (setq c 0
        n 3
        d 0.5
        degrees 90
  )
  (command ".COPY" "L" "" "M" "0,0")
  (repeat n
    (setq c (1+ c))
    (setq pt (strcat "@"
                     (rtos (* c d))
                     "<"
                     (rtos degrees 2)
             )
    )
    (command pt)
  )
  (command "")
)
```

```
Watch
PT = nil
C = nil
```

8. If necessary, move the Visual LISP application window until the small donut in the lower left of the drawing view is visible.

9. Click in the Console window to make it active. Run the C:gizmo function by typing the following at the _$ prompt in the Console window followed by pressing Enter:

    (C:gizmo2)

10. Watch the C:gizmo2 program run. Notice that the program executes one expression at a time as the Animate feature highlights and pauses each expression. As line three is executed, AutoCAD inserts a block in the drawing. In the next line of code, the variable c is set to the value zero. This is shown in the Watch window.

11. Observe the value of variable c when the program halts at the Break Point. Notice that the value of variable pt is still nil. In the next step, watch the values of both c and pt as they increment on each successive pass through the repeat loop.

12. Step past the Break Point by pressing Ctrl+F8. Observe each expression in the repeat loop as it is evaluated and returns to the Break Point. Press Ctrl+F8 to step past the Break Point on each pass.

13. Observe that after six passes through the repeat loop the program concludes and the original block insertion has been copied six times. Also, notice that because the variables, c and pt, are local to this function their values are now nil again.

14. If you are continuing to the next exercise, leave Visual LISP and the CHAP-32N.dwg file open. Use the ERASE command to erase the Star blocks inserted in this exercise.

In the preceding exercise, you used some of the more advanced programming tools available in Visual LISP. Break Points can be useful in helping to find the specific point in a program at which an error occurs. The Watch function records the value of variables—even local variables—as the program executes and enables these variables to be inspected in the context of the program. The animation function not only "forces" a series of mini-break points, but also enables you to watch the program progress visually.

Working with AutoCAD's Database

Visual LISP provides tools for viewing objects (entities) in the AutoCAD database. You can select an entity and inspect its raw data. AutoLISP provides the same capability through its (entget function. With the Inspect tools in Visual LISP, you can quickly display the data of one or more objects. You can also view the various AutoCAD Symbol Tables, such as the tables for Layers, Linetypes, Styles, User Coordinate Systems, and so on. Block and Extended Data tables are also accessible through the Inspect tool.

In the following exercise, you use Visual LISP's Inspect feature to view AutoCAD object data.

 N O T E

> It is not the intent of this chapter to discuss drawing database structure or manipulation. The following exercise is intended only to demonstrate how AutoCAD object data can be accessed from within Visual LISP.

USING VISUAL LISP TO VIEW OBJECT DATA

1. Continue from the preceding exercise or start AutoCAD and open the CHAP-32N.DWG file from the accompanying CD. This drawing contains a small donut in the lower left corner of the drawing limits. If necessary, start Visual LISP by typing **VLIDE** and pressing Enter at the command prompt. Depending upon how you last exited Visual LISP, there might be a file opened in Text Editor.

2. Switch to AutoCAD by clicking anywhere in the AutoCAD window or by choosing Activate AutoCAD from the Visual LISP Window menu.

3. Use the Alt+Tab key combination to return to Visual LISP.

4. From the View pull-down menu, choose Browse Drawing Database, and then Browse Selection. Visual LISP displays the Inspect:PICKSET window, as shown in Figure 32.16.

Figure 32.16

*Displaying the Entity name
of a selected drawing
object.*

5. Double-click on the Entity name to display additional data. Right-click on the Entity name again to display a context menu. From the context menu, choose Inspect Raw Data. Visual LISP displays the expanded association list for the donut object, as shown in Figure 32.17.

Figure 32.17

*Displaying the association
list for a selected drawing
object.*

6. Close the last three Inspect dialog boxes that appeared in Steps 5 & 6.

7. From the View menu, choose Browse Drawing Database, and then Browse Tables. Visual LISP displays the Drawing Tables dialog box, as shown in Figure 32.18.

Figure 32.18

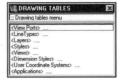

*Displaying AutoCAD
tables.*

8. Double-click on the <Layers> entry to display the Layers data tables. Double-click on the <star> layer entry. Visual LISP displays the AutoCAD Table Entry dialog box, as shown in Figure 32.19.

Figure 32.19

Layer table data.

9. Now double-click on the {raw-data} entry to display the expanded raw data for the star layer. Visual LISP displays the Inspect: List dialog box containing the association list for the star layer data, as shown in Figure 32.20.

Figure 32.20

*Displaying a layer
association list.*

10. This completes this chapter's exercises.

Summary

Visual LISP is an integrated programming environment within which AutoLISP programs are developed and debugged. It includes a full-featured, AutoLISP-aware text editor and a palette of tools intended to make the writing of AutoLISP programs easier and faster. This chapter gave you a brief tour of some of these facilities and tools. Several of the important features of Visual LISP fall beyond the intent of this chapter, which was to provide you with an introductory glimpse into some of the power, flexibility, and functionality of Visual LISP. You should now feel comfortable experimenting within the Visual LISP Development Environment.

CHAPTER 33

ADVANCED CUSTOMIZATION

AutoCAD stands as the most popular Computer Aided Design (CAD) software in the world today. Worldwide, there are nearly 2 million AutoCAD users in some 80 countries employing AutoCAD to generate high-quality engineering and architectural drawings on both desktop PCs as well as engineering workstations. This extensive user base has made AutoCAD the defacto CAD leader in computer-generated drawings and models. One of the primary reasons that AutoCAD has gained this leadership position is its so-called "open architecture," or its capability to be programmed and customized by its users. For example, AutoCAD users can easily change the appearance of the software's interface to suit their personal preferences. You can modify existing toolbars or add new ones. You can modify the way AutoCAD commands work and even develop an entire menu system to control specialized or sophisticated tasks.

As important as AutoCAD's open architecture is the ease with which most customization can be carried out. Even relatively unsophisticated computer users can quickly learn to perform AutoCAD customization tasks that will lead to significant increases in productivity. This chapter specifically addresses the customization of AutoCAD menus and toolbars—two areas of customization that are easy to learn and yet can yield meaningful increases in your ability to work faster and smarter with AutoCAD.

This chapter includes the following topics:

■ Understanding AutoCAD menu file types

■ Understanding and using AutoCAD menu file sections

■ Understanding and creating menu macros

■ Using AutoLISP expressions in menu macros

■ Creating custom toolbars

Understanding AutoCAD Menu File Types

The menus used by AutoCAD are defined by various menu files. The files that you are concerned with in customization work are in standard text-file format that you can easily modify. You can also define new menus. If you create or edit a menu, you assign items to the menu. You associate menu macros to these items that perform specific AutoCAD functions. A menu macro can be as simple as a sequence of standard AutoCAD commands or as complex as a combination of commands and AutoLISP or DIESEL code or a combination of all three. Menu macros can be thought of as "command strings." If the user picks a menu item, the associated macro is executed. Later in this chapter, you learn how to construct menu macros. The menu files also describe the appearance and position of menu items in relation to the overall AutoCAD user interface.

There are several types of menu files, each distinguished by its file extension. These types include MNU, MNS, MNC, MNR, and MNL files. The base AutoCAD menu, for example, is called ACAD.MNU. For this base file there is also an associated ACAD.MNS, ACAD.MNC, ACAD.MNR, and ACAD.MNL file. The function and format of the various menu file types are described in Table 33.1.

Table 33.1

Menu File Types

Menu Type	Description
.MNU	This is a Template menu file in standard ASCII text format.
.MNS	This is a menu source file, in standard (ASCII) text format, which is generated by AutoCAD from the MNU file.
.MNC	This is a binary format file compiled from the MNS file. This file is actually loaded.
.MNR	This is a binary file containing the bitmaps used by the menu.
.MNL	This is a menu support file in standard ASCII text format containing the AutoLISP code required by the menu.

If you start AutoCAD, the last menu used is automatically loaded. The name of this menu is stored in the system registry. You can manually load a different menu using AutoCAD's MENU, or MENULOAD, command. Whether loaded automatically or manually, AutoCAD finds and loads the specified menu using the following search sequence:

1. AutoCAD looks for a MNS source file of the specified name, following the AutoCAD Library Search Path.

   ■ If an MNS file is found, AutoCAD looks for the compiled (MNC) version of the same file in the same directory. If AutoCAD finds a MNC file with the same or later date and time as the MNS file, it loads this MNC file. Otherwise, AutoCAD compiles the MNS file, generating a new MNC file, and then loads this file.

   ■ If an MNS file is not found, AutoCAD looks for a compiled (MNC) menu file of the specified name in *library search path*. If AutoCAD finds this MNC file, it loads it.

   ■ If AutoCAD finds neither a MNS or MNC file, it searches the library search path for a menu template (MNU) file of the specified name. If found, the MNU file is used to generate a MNS source file. This MNS file then generates a compiled MNC file, and AutoCAD loads this MNC file.

   ■ If AutoCAD finds no menu files of the specified name, it generates an error message prompting for another menu name.

2. After finding (or compiling) and loading the MNC file, AutoCAD searches the library search path for a menu LISP (MNL) file. If AutoCAD finds this file, it evaluates the LISP code and loads it into memory.

3. Any time AutoCAD compiles an MNC file, it also generates a new resource (MNR) file, containing the bitmap (toolbar icons) definitions used by the associated menu.

NOTE

The library search path consists of the *support files search path* specified under support files search path on the Files tab of the OPTIONS command's dialog box and the following locations: the current directory (typically, the "Start In" setting on your shortcut icon), the directory that contains the current drawing file, and the directory that contains the AutoCAD program files. Some of these search locations might overlap.

As you can see in Table 33.1 and in the menu loading procedure, the compiled MNC version of any given menu that is loaded. Also, note that the MNC file is compiled from the MNS, not the MNU, file. In fact, the MNU template file is essentially useless in a Windows environment, and as you will see when we discuss custom toolbars later in this chapter, the MNU file can be dangerous. It is therefore recommended that you move the MNU file (for example, ACAD.MNU) out of the library search path so that AutoCAD never reads it when menu files are loaded or reloaded. *Perform all your menu customization using a MNS file.*

INSIDER **T**IP

There are several ways that you can keep the MNU file from interfering with the MNS and MNC files. You might leave the MNU file in its original location and rename it to ACAD-TEMPLATE.MNU, for example. Alternatively, you could create a new directory named \Safe, and move the ACAD.MNU file there. The second method has the advantage of providing a directory to store other AutoCAD files that you want to protect—such as the original ACAD.PGP or ACAD.LIN files. Never delete the original MNU file. *In an emergency, it can be used to rebuild the MNS file, although you will lose all of your AutoCAD generated menu customization.*

Understanding AutoCAD Menu File Sections

All AutoCAD menu files are made up of one or more major *sections*. Each section is associated with a specific area of the AutoCAD menu interface, such as the main menu, pull-down menu, the toolbars, and so on. Each menu section contains menu entries, providing instructions for the appearance and action associated with the menu entry. Each menu section is identified by a section *label* having the form ***section_name*. The various section labels and their associated menu areas are listed in Table 33.2.

Table 33.2

Menu Section Labels

Section Label	Menu Area
***Menugroup	Menu file group name
***Buttons*n*	Pointing-device button menu
***Aux*n*	System pointing device menu
***Pop*n*	Pull-down/Shortcut menu areas
***Toolbars	Toolbar definitions
***Image	Image tile menu area
***Screen	Screen menu area
***Tablet*n*	Tablet menu area
***Helpstrings	Text displayed in the status bar if a pull-down or shortcut menu item is highlighted or if the cursor is rested on a toolbar item
***Accelerators	Accelerator key definitions

Within a given menu section, there can be one or more *alias* sections in the form **alias. Note that section labels have the three asterisk prefix, ***, whereas alias labels have a two asterisk, **, prefix. For the purposes of the customization done in this chapter, you can ignore the *alias* labels.

You can include comments within a menu file for documentation or notes by placing the comments on a line that begins with two slashes, //. These lines are invisible to the AutoCAD menu interpreter. Such notes are often useful if viewing the file in a text editor. There are several useful and informative comment lines found in the ACAD.MNU file, for example.

The various sections of an AutoCAD menu differ in their functionality and appearance. A description of the ***BUTTONS, ***AUX and ***POP sections appears later in this chapter. Several of the menu types are shown in Figure 33.1. We will limit our menu file customization to the ***POP section in this chapter. Later, we use the interface features of AutoCAD 2000 to customize toolbars. Macros for ***POP sections are considered later.

Figure 33.1

AutoCAD menu types.

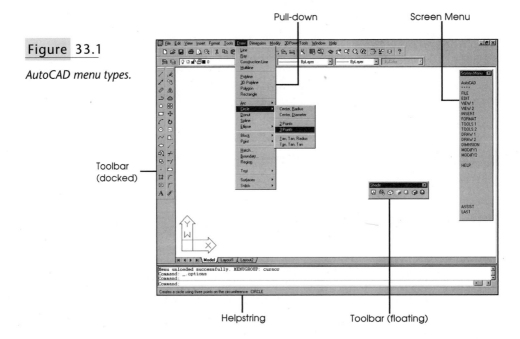

Using the ***Buttons and ***Aux Sections

The ***Buttons and ***Aux sections appear near the top of the standard ACAD.MNU and ACAD.MNS files, and they are used to customize your system-pointing device. These two sections are functionally identical, and the section that your system uses depends upon the type of pointing device you use. The standard Windows system mouse uses the ***Aux section and any other input device (a digitizer puck, for example) uses the ***Buttons section. In this chapter, we confine our discussion to the ***Aux (mouse button) section.

All input devices have a pick button, used to specify points and to select objects on the screen. On a normally configured, standard Windows mouse, this is the left button. On most digitizing pucks, this is normally labeled button 1. This pick button is not customizable and no accommodation for its function is found in AutoCAD menus. The remaining button(s) can have commands, functions, or macros assigned to them.

The ***AUX*n* sections of the menu file define the actions (commands or macros) associated with the buttons on your mouse. Each line, in any given section (***AUX1 or ***AUX2, for example), represents a mouse button. You can access each button menu with the key/button combination shown in the Table 33.3.

Table 33.3

Buttons and Associated Menu Sections

Key/Button Combination	Menu Section
Simple click	***AUX1 and ***BUTTONS1
Shift+click	***AUX2 and ***BUTTONS2
Ctrl+click	***AUX3 and ***BUTTONS3
Ctrl+Shift+click	***AUX4 and ***BUTTONS4

NOTE

The first line after the menu section label ***AUX1 or ***BUTTONS1 is used only if the SHORTCUTMENU system variable is set to 0. If SHORTCUTMENU is set to a value other than 0, the built-in menu is used. Similarly, the second line after the ***AUX1 or ***BUTTONS1 label is used only when the MBUTTONPAN system variable is set to 0.

Consider a typical ***AUX1 section. (The items in brackets do not appear in the actual menu.) Refer to Table 33.4 for a listing of menu macrocodes.

```
***AUX1
;                       [button no.2 Enter]
^C^C                    [button no.3 Cancel]
^B                      [button n0.4 Toggles Snap]
^O                      [button no.5 Toggles Ortho]
^G                      [button no.6 Toggles Grid]
^D                      [button no.7 Toggles Coords]
^E                      [button no.8 Cycles to next isometric plane]
^T                      [button no.9 Toggles Tablet]
```

Remember that the pick button cannot be assigned and is therefore not included in the menu. The first line after the ***AUX1 section label (;) therefore represents the next button after the pick button—usually button two or the right button. On a two-button mouse, therefore, only the first line of this listing has any meaning. The second line (^c^c) after the section label applies to button three on a three-button mouse, with the remaining lines having no meaning. Later, you see that the semicolon (;) and the ^c^c codes represent an Enter and a Cancel command, respectively.

Now consider a typical ***AUX2 section.

```
***AUX2
$P0=SNAP $p0=*       [button no.2]
$P0=SNAP $p0=*       [button no.3]
```

Referring to Table 33.3, the ***AUX2 section defines the actions taken when a combination of Shift and a button is pressed. In this AUX2 listing, there is a defined action for Shift+button2 and Shift+button3. Again, with a two-button mouse, the second code line has no meaning. Each line in this example is the same, and the code causes the POP0 cursor menu to be loaded and displayed using the following menu code format:

```
$Pn=name $p0=*
```

In the previous code, $ is the special character code for loading a menu area; P*n* specifies the ***Pop menu section with *n* being the name of the section; and =* forces a display of the named section. You learn more about ***POP menu sections later in this chapter. This section and this code display the ***POP0 cursor menu if you Shift+right+click the mouse.

The ***AUX and ***BUTTONS sections of the ACAD.MNU provide several opportunities for the customization of the functions performed by your input device. If you use a 10- or 12-button digitizer puck, you can program up to 27 or 33 button functions, respectively. Moreover, even with the standard two-button mouse, the right button can be programmed to perform three different tasks.

Using the ***POP Section

The ***POP menu section contains the definitions for the pull-down and shortcut menus. This section is perhaps the most frequently customized section. These menus are displayed in a "pop-up," or cascading, fashion as shown in Figures 33.2 and 33.3. Pull-downs have the advantage of being easy to read and use, although not permanently using screen space.

Figure 33.2

A typical pull-down menu.

Shortcut menus are usually displayed while commands are in progress, and they often duplicate the various command options that are available and displayed at the command line. Shortcut menus are displayed at or near the crosshairs or the cursor in the screen area. A typical shortcut menu (for the PEDIT command) is shown in Figure 33.3.

Figure 33.3

A typical shortcut menu with a cascaded menu area.

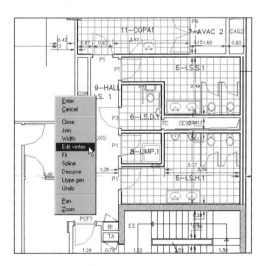

Pull-down menus are defined in the ***POP1 through ***POP499 menu sections. Shortcut menus are defined in the ***POP0 and ***POP500 through ***POP999 sections. AutoCAD constructs the menu bar across the top of the screen from the ***POP1 through ***POP16 menu sections. If no ***POP1 through ***POP16 definitions are found, AutoCAD constructs a menu bar containing a default File and Edit menu.

The following example shows a typical pull-down menu. The specific syntax and menu code for pull-down menus is discussed later in this chapter. The actual appearance of the menu is shown in Figure 33.4.

```
***POP14
**MYTOOLS
M_Tools      [&MyTools]
M_Cursor     [&CursorFlip]'cursorflip;
M_BreakF     [Break-F]^C^Cbreak;\f;\
             [--]
M_Bubble
[Bubble]^C^CCircle;\1;Text;M;@;0.5;0;Line;nea;\\;donut;0;.125;@;;
             [--]
M_View       [View1]^C^C -view;R;Perspective-1;
M_View       [View1]^C^C -view;R;Perspective-2;
```

Figure 33.4

*A new customized
pull-down menu.*

In this example, the first functional line (M_Cursor) calls an AutoLISP routine, whereas the other lines contain menu macros. Menu macros are discussed in the following section.

Creating Menu Macros

Now that you have a basic understanding of the ***Aux, ***Buttons, and ***Pop sections of an AutoCAD menu, it is time to learn how to build new menu items and place them into a menu. To do this you need to know the special codes used in menu macros. If you want to include command parameters in a menu item, you need to know the sequence in which the command expects its parameters. Every character in a menu macro is significant, even blank spaces. We will devote our attention to the ***Pop menu section; however, with little or no revision, most menu macros work equally well in other menu sections.

Note

> If command input comes from a menu item, the settings of the PICKADD and PICKAUTO system variables are assumed to be 1 and 0, respectively. This preserves compatibility with previous releases of AutoCAD and makes customization easier because you are not required to check the settings of these variables.

A menu macro is a kind of shorthand, or coded, method of representing the keystrokes that you would type at the Command prompt. Often the macro merely contains what you would actually type. There is, however, a group of codes used to represent certain keyboard entries. These special characters are listed in Table 33.4.

Table 33.4

Special Characters Used in Menu Macros

Character	Description
;	Issues ENTER.
^M	Issues ENTER.
^I	Issues TAB.
SPACEBAR	Enters a space; a blank space between command items in a menu entry is equivalent to pressing the spacebar.
\	Pauses for user input.
.	A period can be used immediately before a native AutoCAD command to override any redefinition of that command, which might be in effect.
_	An underscore character; translates the AutoCAD commands and keywords that are immediately beneath.
+	Continues menu macro to the next line if it is the last character on a line.
=*	Displays the current top-level image, pull-down, or shortcut menu.
*^C^C	Prefix for a repeating item.
$	Loads a menu section or introduces a condition DIESEL macro expression ($M=).

continues

Table 33.4, continued

Special Characters Used in Menu Macros

Character	Description
^B	Toggles Snap on or off (Ctrl+B).
^C	Cancels command or prompt (ESC).
^D	Toggles Coords on or off (Ctrl+D).
^E	Sets the next isometric plane (Ctrl+E).
^G	Toggles Grid on or off (Ctrl+G).
^H	Issues backspace.
^O	Toggles Ortho on or off (Ctrl+O).
^P	Toggles MENUECHO on or off.
^Q	Echoes all prompts, status listings, and input to the printer (Ctrl+Q).
^T	Toggles Tablet on or off (Ctrl+T).
^V	Changes current view port (Ctrl+V).
^Z	Null character that suppresses the automatic addition of SPACEBAR at the end of a menu item.

Several of the special characters in Table 33.4 are rarely used, whereas others are used frequently. You should refer to Table 33.4 frequently until you become familiar with the more common codes.

The general form of functional menu entry items is consistent in most menu sections. The general format is as follows:

    Name_tag [label]menu_macro

The following line is an example taken from the Draw pull-down menu:

    ID_Line   [&Line]^C^C_line

At least one space should separate the Name_tag element from the label element. There can be no space between the label and the menu_macro. The label must be enclosed within a set of brackets. In the example, the first item, ID_Line, is the nametag for the entry. The label, [&Line], displays the word Line on the pull-down. The ampersand character, &, appears immediately before the alphanumeric character in the label that appears underscored onscreen indicating that that character is the Alt+character hotkey for the entry. The menu macro in this example consists of the code `^C^C_line`, which issues a cancel followed by AutoCAD's LINE command. If the Line item is selected from the standard Draw pull-down menu, this menu macro is executed.

> **N**OTE
>
> *Name_tag* elements are used as "aliases" or shorthand methods of referring to the associated menu macro from other portions of the menu, most notably from the Accelerator key definitions. As such, they are beyond the scope of this chapter, although they are included in the chapter's examples.

Building Menu Macros

In this section, you will actually construct several menu macros and place them in a separate pull-down that you incorporate into your current main menu.

> **N**OTE
>
> For the purposes of gaining practice in constructing menu macros, we assume that your current menu is defined in the file ACAD.MNS. You should review the various menu file types discussed earlier in this chapter—and the distinction between the ACAD.MNU and ACAD.MNS should be especially kept in mind. If your current menu is other than ACAD.MNS, substitute your menu's name in the examples that follow or load ACAD.MNS using the MENU command.

As you work with the following menu macros, you are modifying the base menu. It is important that you make a backup copy of this menu so that you can restore a known, working menu if necessary. There are several methods of doing this. The following steps outline one method.

1. Open Windows Explorer and navigate to the directory containing the ACAD.MNS file. This is usually found in the \Support folder of your AutoCAD 2000 installation.

2. Select the file ACAD.MNS to highlight it.

3. Right+click the highlighted file to display the Explorer shortcut menu and select Copy. (Or with the file highlighted, press Ctrl+C.)

4. Press Ctrl+V. This places a copy of the highlighted file in the same directory.

5. Press Ctrl+End to navigate to the end of the directory and verify that a file titled Copy of ACAD.MNS exists. This is your backup menu file that you can rename to ACAD.MNS if necessary.

Now that you have a safe copy of the ACAD.MNS file, you can proceed to make your own pull-down menu. Recall that the pull-down menus are called ***POP*n* menus, where *n* is a number from 0 through 499. As it comes out of the box, AutoCAD has 11 menu bar pull-down menus—***POP1 through ***POP11. In the following exercise, you add a ***POP12 pull down named MyMenu. This pull-down contains several types of menu macros, which you will add in the following exercises. (The new ***POP12 menu initially appears to the right of the Help pull-down. You can later move it to appear between the current Modify and Window pull-downs.)

ADDING A NEW PULL-DOWN — PART 1

1. Load ACAD.MNS into Notepad. AutoCAD should already be open.

2. Scroll down the file to the section that begins with ***POP500. Directly before the ***POP500 entries, start a new ***POP16 section by adding the following lines:

```
***POP16
**MYMENU
ID_Mymenu        [&MyMenu]
ID_Break_f       [&Break-F]^C^C_.Break;\f;\
```

3. Check your typing closely. The number of spaces between the *name_tag* and the label elements is not important. Format these elements so that they are easy to read. Use the menu text that appears in the following ***POP500 section as a guide.

4. Save the changes that you have made to the file and minimize Microsoft Notepad.

5. From AutoCAD's Tools menu, choose Customize Menus to display the Menu Customization dialog box. Ensure the Menu Groups tab is active, as shown in Figure 33.5.

Figure 33.5

*The Menu Customization
dialog box.*

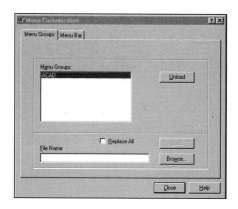

6. In the Menu Customization dialog box, choose Browse. In the Select Menu File dialog box, ensure that the Files of type box is set to show `*.MNC` and `*.MNC` file types (refer to Figure 33.6).

7. In the Select Menu File dialog box, find and select the `ACAD.MNS` file as shown in Figure 33.6. Choose Open.

Figure 33.6

*The Select Menu File
dialog box.*

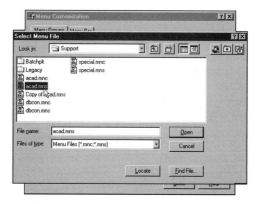

8. In the Menu Customization dialog box, ensure that the `ACAD.MNS` file is shown in the File name box, and then choose Load. AutoCAD uses the MNS file to generate a new MNC file and loads it.

9. The new MyMenu pull-down menu label should appear to the right of the Help pull-down.

10. Select the MyMenu pull-down. The menu should resemble Figure 33.7.

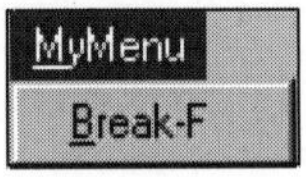

Figure 33.7

*The new MyMenu
pull-down menu.*

Using the Break-F Menu Macro

AutoCAD's native BREAK command has often been the subject of menu macro customization. In the BREAK command, if you select the object using your pointing device, AutoCAD both selects the object and treats the selection point as the first break point. At the next prompt, you can continue by specifying the second point or override the first point by typing an **f**. In many cases, this default mechanism of having the object-pick-point become the first specified break point is inconvenient. The following menu macro automatically enters the overriding **f**.

```
[&Break-F]^C^C_.Break;\f;\
```

Refer to Table 33.4 and the following list for an explanation of this macro.

`[&Break-F]`	This is the label for the macro as it appears on the menu. The **&B** signifies the character that appears underlined and is the Alt+Character shortcut for the macro.
`^C^C`	The double `^c` duplicates two cancel commands (Esc) to ensure that any ongoing commands are canceled.
`_Break;`	This supplies the BREAK command. The semicolon issues an Enter. The leading underscore character permits foreign language translation.(The initial uppercase character is optional).
`\`	This halts the macro to enable user input, *that is,* selecting the object to be broken.
`f;`	This supplies an **f** to override the default "specify second break point" prompt. The semicolon issues an Enter. AutoCAD issues a "specify a first break point" prompt.
`\`	This halts the macro to enable user input of second break point. If this point is successfully supplied, the command is completed.

INSIDER TIP

As noted in Table 33.4, a semicolon, ;, and a space both act as keyboard Enters in a macro. Using a semicolon is preferred because it is visually less ambiguous than a space. This is especially true when a space is used as the last element in a macro or when two spaces are used successively. If you use a semicolon, there is no question as to whether an Enter is intended.

NOTE

An explicit Enter is not required after the use of the \ character; after the user completes input in the normal fashion, AutoCAD issues an Enter.

This menu-macro is named Break-F to impart some sense of its function and to distinguish it from the standard BREAK command.

Break-F is a typical menu macro. It uses only standard AutoCAD command input and represents nothing more than a means to automatically supply the equivalent of conventional keyboard input. In constructing a menu macro, such as Break-F, it is useful to run the command sequence "manually," noting the exact keyboard input you supply in response to each issued AutoCAD prompt. It is often helpful to write out the prompt and keyboard response sequence before attempting to duplicate the procedure in macrocode. It is easy to forget, for example, that in the place of every keyboard Enter, you must use either a semicolon or a space in the macro, or that the backslash character is used to represent either screen picks or typed responses to prompts.

INSIDE TIP

Reviewing the command and response sequence for macros that you want to construct is often easier if you carry out the procedure and if you want to use AutoCAD's Text window to visually review the sequence as it took place at the command prompt. Remember that the F2 key displays this text screen.

Like many menu macros, the Break-F macro is quite simple. It gains its effectiveness in the time and effort it saves. In the next section, you see how AutoLISP can be utilized in another simple but effective menu macro.

Using AutoLISP Expressions in Menu Macros

You can use AutoLISP expressions and variables to create menu macros ranging from extremely complex to very simple. One of the principle advantages of AutoLISP programming is the capability to "branch" into two or more programming directions depending upon user input or the state of the drawing environment. This can lead to rather complex macros that possess "intelligence" and the capability to make "decisions." Shorter, less complex AutoLISP macros can also exhibit this decision-making capability as well. Often, these less complex macros utilize the state of AutoCAD's system variable settings to perform useful tasks that would be more cumbersome and time-consuming to perform from the keyboard or through a series of toolbar or menu picks.

The system variable CURSORSIZE records the current size of the screen cursor, or crosshairs, as a percentage of the screen size. Valid settings range from 1 to 100 percent. If the variable is set to 100, the crosshairs are full-screen and the ends of the crosshairs are never visible. If the variable is less than 100, the ends of the crosshairs might be visible when the cursor is moved to one edge of the screen. Some users prefer a small CURSORSIZE in certain situations (such as when working with 3D objects or with views other than plan view), whereas they prefer a full CURSORSIZE if working in plan views or editing 2D objects.

In the following menu macro, AutoLISP functions are used to obtain the value of the CURSORSIZE system variable. If the current value is 100, an AutoLISP function is used to set it to a value of 5. If it has a current value other than 100, it is set to 100. By utilizing this macro, it is easy to flip the size of the cursor back and forth between its smallest and largest sizes. The macro is as follows:

```
^C^C(setvar "cursorsize" (if (= 100 (getvar "cursorsize")) 5 100))
```

It is important to realize that this macro is a combination of menu macrocode (as outlined in Table 33.4) and AutoLISP code. The ^C^C is standard menu macrocode, although the remainder of the macro is expressed in AutoLISP code. The two are compatible and work together effectively.

NOTE

Refer to Chapter 22, "Introduction to AutoLISP Programming," for an explanation of AutoLISP expressions.

In the following exercise, you will add the Cursorsize menu macro to your MyMenu pull-down.

ADDING A NEW PULL-DOWN — PART 2

1. Load **ACAD.MNS** into Microsoft Notepad and scroll to the *****POP16** menu section that you began in the preceding exercise.

2. Immediately below the **Break-F** macro, which you added previously, add the following line.

   ```
   ID_CursorF    [&Cursor Flip]^C^C(setvar "cursorsize" (if (= 100
   ➥(getvar "cursorsize")) 5 100))
   ```

3. Check your typing, and then save the file.

4. Repeat Steps 5–10 of the preceding exercise to load the new **ACAD.MNS**. Select the MyMenu pull-down. Your menu should resemble Figure 33.8.

5. Test the Cursor Flip macro to verify that the CURSORSIZE changes back and forth between the two sizes.

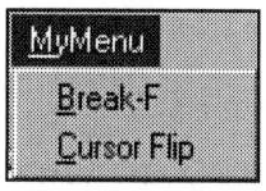

Figure 33.8

*The new MyMenu
pull-down menu.*

Of course, other menu macros can be devised to perform tasks that require repetitive user input. The special menu macrocode ^c^c* serves as a prefix for macros that repeat themselves until either canceled at the keyboard or canceled by choosing another menu item. The following macro is a typical example:

```
[&Repeat_Circ]*^C^CCircle;
```

In this example, the circle command is automatically repeated until canceled by the user.

Menu macros can become complex if they are designed to perform a successive series of AutoCAD commands and to require user input as well. For example, a user might find that he or she needs to perform the following series of operations frequently:

1. Draw a circle of fixed radius.

2. Pause for alphanumeric user input (text) centered within the circle.

3. Start a line from a user-specified point on the circumference of the circle.

4. End the line at a user-specified point.

5. Attach a solid donut (dot) of fixed size at the end of the line.

Performing this task manually takes as many as 32 separate input steps. The following macro accomplishes the tasks with as few as six input steps:

```
^C^CCircle;\1;Text;M;@;0.5;0;Line;nea;\\;donut;0;.125;@;;
```

Although this "Bubble" macro is complicated, it is composed of a series of simpler steps utilizing basic AutoCAD commands translated into macrocode. Figure 33.9 diagrams the entire macro.

Figure 33.9

The diagrammed Bubble macro.

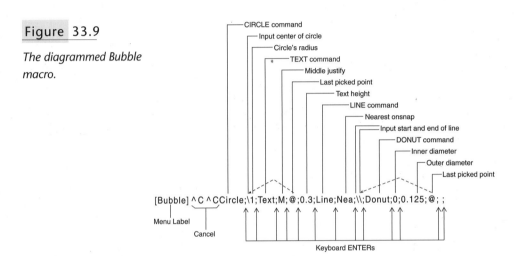

Menu macros are intended to save both the user's time and effort. Frequently the macros that increase efficiency the most are simple in concept and in the amount of macrocode required. As you have seen in the macro exercises, placing macros into a menu is a relatively simple process. The time and effort that you spend developing and implementing the macros, which apply to your particular work requirements, is quickly repaid, enabling you to work faster and smarter.

Creating Custom Toolbars

Creating new toolbars is an effective way to customize your AutoCAD interface and increase your efficiency. You might want to create a new toolbar that groups the tools you use most frequently. This not only saves time in selecting tools but also saves space in the drawing area because you do not need to keep several toolbars open. After it is created, new toolbars behave as standard toolbars and can be hidden or displayed in either a docked or a floating position on the screen.

Toolbars that you create can have two general types of tools: existing icons, representing existing tools from other toolbars, and icons that you create, representing new macros that you define. Both types of tools can be placed on the same toolbar. In this respect, custom toolbars are similar to new or modified pull-down menus that you might add to AutoCAD's basic menu bar. Toolbars, however, have the added advantage of being able to be placed anywhere in the drawing area or even hidden from view.

Creating a New Toolbar

In the following exercise, you create a toolbar composed of tools that are copied from existing toolbars. You will create this new toolbar and add it to the existing ACAD.MNS file. You can remove the toolbar from the menu later. Before beginning this exercise, make sure that the Draw toolbar is displayed.

WARNING

> Until you become adept at creating new toolbars, there is a possibility of losing some tool icons from current toolbars. For safety, make a backup copy of your current ACAD.MNS file before starting the following exercise.

CREATING A NEW TOOLBAR

1. From the View menu, choose Toolbars. This displays the Toolbars dialog box, as shown in Figure 33.10. You can also display this dialog box by right+clicking on any displayed tool and choosing Customize or by typing Toolbar and pressing Enter.

Figure 33.10

The Toolbars dialog box.

2. In the Toolbars dialog box, select the New button. AutoCAD displays the New Toolbar dialog box, as shown in Figure 33.11.

Figure 33.11

The New Toolbar dialog box.

3. In the Toolbar Name: input box type **Mytools** and select OK. Note that the name of the new toolbar appears in the Toolbars box of the Toolbars dialog box. Also, note that a new, blank toolbar appears onscreen. (The new toolbar usually appears to be floating over the Object Properties toolbar and might be difficult to see initially.) Drag the toolbar to an empty area of the screen (see Figure 33.12).

4. In the Toolbars dialog box, select Customize. AutoCAD displays the Customize Toolbars dialog box, as shown in Figure 33.12.

Figure 33.12

The Customize Toolbars dialog box.

5. In the Customize Toolbars dialog box, select the down arrow (under categories) to display the Tools categories. Select the Dimensioning category to display the dimensioning tools.

6. Note that by selecting (clicking on) a dimensioning tool icon, the description of the tool's function and the AutoCAD command it executes appears in the Description box, as shown in Figure 33.13.

Figure 33.13

Identifying icon functions.

7. Select and drag the Linear Dimension tool icon onto the new Mytools toolbar. Note that while dragging a tool icon, a small tool symbol and a plus sign (+) appear at the cursor. Drop the dimension tool icon onto the new toolbar. The Mytools toolbar resembles the toolbar shown in Figure 33.14.

Figure 33.14

The Mytools toolbar.

8. Repeat Step 7, choosing two or three other dimensioning tool icons.

NOTE

You can also drag buttons from one toolbar to another while the Customize Toolbars dialog box is displayed. To copy buttons, rather than move them, buttons across toolbars, hold down Ctrl while you drag.

9. On the Draw toolbar, with the Ctrl key pressed, click and drag the Multiline Text tool icon and place it at the right end of your new Mytools toolbar. The toolbar should now resemble Figure 33.15.

Figure 33.15

Figure 33.15

Additions to the Mytools toolbar.

10. If you are continuing on to the next exercise immediately, leave the current dialog boxes open. If not, use the Close buttons to close the Customize Toolbars and Toolbars dialog boxes.

You can make several new toolbars, each containing a group of tools that you use frequently, to perform related tasks. The Mytools toolbar you created in the last exercise, for example, might be used while dimensioning architectural floor plans.

Adding a Customized Tool to a Toolbar

You can also add new tools composed of customized menu macros or AutoLISP routines to a new or existing toolbar. In the following exercise, you use a menu macro to create a new tool. You also design an associated icon and add the tool and the icon to the Mytools toolbar created in the previous exercise. Make sure the Mytools toolbar is displayed before beginning this exercise.

ADDING A CUSTOMIZED TOOL TO A TOOLBAR

1. If you are continuing from the preceding exercise, skip to Step 2. Otherwise, open the Toolbars dialog box by right+clicking on the Mytools toolbar and then choosing Customize. Choose Customize to display the Customize Toolbars dialog box. (Refer to Figures 33.12 and 33.13.)

2. In the Customize Toolbars dialog box, select the Custom category from the Categories list box.

3. Referring to the arrow shown in Figure 33.16, click and drag a blank tool button to the right end of the Mytools toolbar.

Figure 33.16

Adding a blank tool button to a toolbar.

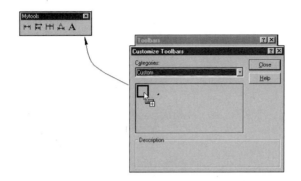

4. On the Mytools toolbar, right+click the blank tool button to display the Button Properties dialog box, as shown in Figure 33.17.

Figure 33.17

The Button Properties dialog box.

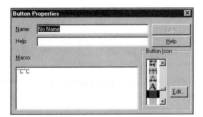

5. In the Name input box of the Button Properties dialog box, type the name **My-Break**, and in the Help input box, type **Break with auto first-point prompt**.

6. In the Macro input box of the Button Properties dialog box, type the following macro immediately following the ^C^C (refer to Figure 33.18).

   _Break;\f

7. In the next steps, you will define an icon for the My-Break tool. In the Button Icon area of the Button Properties dialog box, scroll to and select the icon for the BREAK command, as shown in Figure 33.19.

Figure 33.18

Naming and defining a new tool.

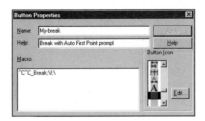

Figure 33.19

Choosing the BREAK command icon.

8. In the Button Icon area of the Button Properties dialog box, choose Edit. AutoCAD displays the Button Editor dialog box with the BREAK command icon, as shown in Figure 33.20.

9. In the Button Editor dialog box, choose Grid. AutoCAD displays a grid across the icon image as shown in Figure 33.20.

Figure 33.20

Loading an existing icon for editing.

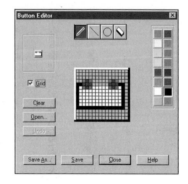

10. Using the tools, palette, and preview window on the Button Editor dialog box and referring to Figure 33.21, draw a letter **F** in the icon editor.

11. If you are satisfied with your design, choose Save As in the Button Editor dialog box and save the icon to the name MYTOOL1.BMP in the \Support directory. Note that the new icon design appears in the Button Icon area of the Button Properties dialog box.

Drawing tools

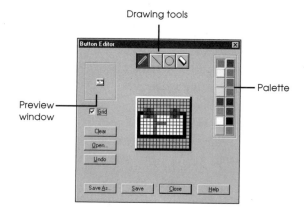

Figure 33.21

The modified BREAK command icon.

Preview
window

Palette

12. To save all your changes in the Buttons Properties dialog box, choose Apply. Note that the new icon design appears in the My-Break tool on the Mytools toolbar, as shown in Figure 33.22. Close the Button Properties dialog box by clicking on the X in the upper right corner.

13. Close the Customize Toolbars and Toolbars dialog boxes.

Figure 33.22

The completed My-Break tool.

INSIDER TIP

If you use the Edit function of the Button Properties dialog box to design your own button icon and then use the Save As button to assign a name to the icon's BMP file, AutoCAD assigns the resulting bitmap file a random number (for example, ICON9169.BMP) in the MNS file. You can replace the random bitmap filename with the name you used by manually editing the icon's name in the toolbar definition of the MNS file. In the MNS file, search for the toolbar name and manually edit the BMP filename.

Of course, you can add other tools to you Mytools toolbar. Often toolbars are more convenient to use than items placed on pull-down menus. You might therefore want to transfer customized menu macros, such as those you wrote earlier in this chapter, onto new or existing toolbars. The menu macrocode utilized in both menu pull-down items and individual tools on toolbars is exactly the same.

Summary

AutoCAD offers a myriad of ways to customize both its commands and its command interface. Such customization offers the advantages of saving time and increasing your drawing efficiency. In this chapter, you have gained the basic understanding of AutoCAD menus and the special language used to build timesaving menu macros. You also learned how to construct new toolbars containing standard as well as customized AutoCAD functions. You now have the tools to build simple menu macros or to use in investigating menu customization further.

34

AutoCAD 2000
Migration Assistance

Each new release of AutoCAD presents veteran users with the sometimes-arduous task of learning the new release's tools and key concepts. Although learning the new tools and key concepts can be challenging, it is certainly rewarding. By learning AutoCAD's new tools and key concepts, you can increase your productivity, often dramatically.

However, there's more to upgrading to the next release of AutoCAD than just learning new tools and key concepts. Compounding the task of learning the new release's features is the challenge of upgrading existing files. Converting existing drawings to the current version, checking old AutoLISP routines to ensure that they work properly, and installing custom menus and toolbars from previous releases into AutoCAD 2000 all present challenges to veteran users. Before the new release of AutoCAD can be used productively, you must ensure that your existing drawings and your current tools will continue to function properly, thereby ensuring proven project workflow methods and processes are minimally affected.

To ease the task of updating existing files to the newest release, AutoCAD 2000 provides a new application called AutoCAD 2000 Migration Assistance. Through this application, you can access tools that automate the process of upgrading existing files, including drawings, AutoLISP routines, and custom menus and toolbars, to AutoCAD 2000. Additionally, the application includes tools that make the network installation of AutoCAD 2000 easier and utilities that automate certain repetitive tasks.

This chapter discusses the following subjects:

- Converting multiple drawings to AutoCAD 2000 simultaneously

- Checking existing AutoLISP routines for compatibility with AutoCAD 2000

- Porting existing custom menus and PGP files to AutoCAD 2000

- Converting color-dependent, plot style drawings to a named plot style format

- Using tools to ease the task of deploying AutoCAD 2000 over a network

- Executing a series of commands on multiple drawings automatically

Understanding AutoCAD 2000 Migration Assistance

The AutoCAD 2000 Migration Assistance application consists of nine major features. These features are individual applications designed to perform specific functions, and they represent the tools you need to complete the common tasks you encounter when migrating to a new release of AutoCAD. By using these features, you automate the process of upgrading to AutoCAD 2000 and ease the challenge of maintaining productivity on your current projects.

The features provided by AutoCAD 2000 Migration Assistance are briefly described as follows:

- **Batch Drawing Converter**—This feature enables you to convert drawings to and from Release 12, Release 13, Release 14, and Release 2000 formats.

- **AutoLISP Compatibility Analyzer**—This feature helps you identify changes you must make to your AutoLISP files so that they function properly in Release 2000.

- **Menu and Toolbar Porter**—This feature enables you to import your existing custom menus and toolbars from Release 12, Release 13, and Release 14 versions to Release 2000.

- **Command Alias (PGP) Porter**—This feature enables you to quickly copy existing PGP file command aliases from Release 12, Release 13, and Release 14 versions to Release 2000.

- **Color to Named tools**—This feature enables you to convert color-dependent, plot style drawings to named plot style drawings.

- **Network Deployment tool**—This feature automates the process of installing and configuring multiple customized AutoCAD configurations across your network.

- **Serial Number Harvester**—This feature automatically generates a report listing the total number of AutoCAD seats across your entire network and includes their release versions and serial numbers.

- **ScriptPro utility**—This feature enables you to easily create AutoCAD script files, which when executed, automatically perform a series of repetitive commands on a list of selected drawings.

- **Compatibility Information**—This feature provides detailed information about migrating to AutoCAD 2000.

The AutoCAD 2000 Migration Assistance application runs independent of AutoCAD. You launch the application from the Windows taskbar by choosing Start, Programs, AutoCAD 2000 Migration Assistance, AutoCAD 2000 Migration Assistance, which opens the application's opening window, as shown in Figure 34.1. From the opening window, you can launch the previously described tools and utilities by choosing the desired feature from the list. Additionally, you can launch the AutoCAD Learning Assistant, which is a multimedia-training tool that requires an accompanying CD. After you are finished using its tools and utilities, you close the AutoCAD 2000 Migration Assistance window by choosing Exit.

Figure 34.1

The AutoCAD 2000 Migration Assistance opening window.

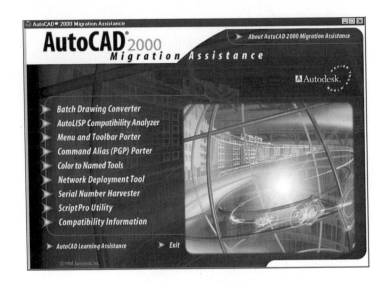

NOTE

Although the AutoCAD 2000 Migration Assistance application runs independent of AutoCAD, some of its features require that AutoCAD 2000 be loaded on your computer and functioning properly.

When you install AutoCAD 2000, the AutoCAD 2000 Migration Assistance application is not automatically installed. During the AutoCAD 2000 installation process, you must select the proper option when prompted to install the AutoCAD 2000 Migration Assistance application. However, if you choose not to install the application when installing AutoCAD 2000, you can install the AutoCAD 2000 Migration Assistance application later.

The following sections describe in detail the various features of the AutoCAD 2000 Migration Assistance application, and provide exercises that walk you through using its tools and utilities.

Understanding the Batch Drawing Converter

The Batch Drawing Converter enables you to convert AutoCAD drawings from one release version to another. You can use it to migrate R12, R13, and R14 version files into R2000. You can convert an AutoCAD drawing from its current release version to R12, R13, R14, or R2000.

The Batch Drawing Converter is simple to use. By launching the Converter, you can compile a list of drawings that you want to convert. You can identify CFG, PCP, and PC2 files that contain pen-width information, and you can convert the pen widths to AutoCAD 2000 lineweights. You can also identify R2000 drawings that contain Page Setups, and then apply those page setups to drawings that you are converting to the R2000 format. The Batch Drawing Converter is a powerful tool that makes converting drawings from one release format to another easy.

The following exercise explains how to use the Batch Drawing Converter to migrate R14 drawings into the R2000 format.

MIGRATING DRAWINGS FROM R14 TO R2000

1. Copy the following files from the accompanying CD to a new folder on your system, and then name the new folder R2000.

   - **X2DWG01.DWG**—The Page Setups from this R2000 drawing are applied to the newly converted drawings.

   - **X2DWG01A.DWG**—An R14 drawing file that is converted to R2000 format.

   - **X2DWG01B.DWG**—An R14 drawing file that is converted to R2000 format.

   - **X2DWG01C.DWG**—An R14 drawing file that is converted to R2000 format.

   - **X2DWG01A.PC2**—The Plot Configuration (PC2) file that contains the pen widths for R14 drawing files, and that is used to define the R2000 drawing's lineweights.

   After copying the files to the new folder, right-click on each file, choose Properties, and then clear the Read-only attribute.

2. Launch the AutoCAD 2000 Migration Assistance application from the Windows taskbar by choosing Start, Programs, AutoCAD 2000 Migration Assistance, AutoCAD 2000 Migration Assistance. The application's main window opens.

3. Choose the Batch Drawing Converter option. The AutoCAD Batch Convert dialog box appears.

4. From the Convert To pull-down list, choose AutoCAD 2000 DWG.

NOTE

Use the Convert To pull-down list to identify the format into which you want to convert the listed drawings. You can convert listed drawings into R12, R13, R14, or R2000 format.

Next, you will add the R14 version drawing files to the dialog box, thereby creating a list of drawings to convert to R2000.

5. Choose the Add button. The Select Drawing dialog box appears.

6. Browse to the R2000 folder into which you copied the drawing files in Step 1, and then select the following R14 version drawings, as shown in Figure 34.2:

    ■ **X2DWG01A.DWG**

    ■ **X2DWG01B.DWG**

    ■ **X2DWG01C.DWG**

Figure 34.2

The R14 files to be converted are selected.

7. With the drawings selected, choose Open. The R14 drawing files are added to the Batch Drawing Converter.

    Next, you will identify the R14 PC2 file that contains the pen widths the application will convert to R2000 lineweights.

8. From the AutoCAD Batch Convert dialog box, select the Convert Pen Width Settings to Lineweights option in the AutoCAD 2000 Options area. The Configuration File Browse button activates.

9. Choose the Browse button. The Open dialog box appears.

10. From the R2000 folder, choose the X2DWG01A.PC2 file (as shown in Figure 34.3) and then choose Open. The R14 PC2 file displays in the Configuration File text box.

Figure 34.3

Figure 34.3

The pen width settings from the selected R14 PC2 file are converted to R2000 lineweights.

Next, you will identify the R2000 Page Setups to apply to the R14 drawings during their conversion to R2000 format.

11. From the AutoCAD Batch Convert dialog box, select the Include Page Setups option in the AutoCAD 2000 Options area. The Page Setups button activates.

12. Choose the Page Setups button. The Page Setups dialog box appears.

13. Choose the Browse button. The Select File dialog box appears.

14. From the R2000 folder, choose the X2DWG01.DWG file (as shown in Figure 34.4) and then choose Open. The page setups available to the selected R2000 drawing file display in the Page Setups list.

Figure 34.4

The R2000 file is selected, and its Page Setups are copied into the converted drawings.

15. In the Page Setups area, select the A-Size page setup (as shown in Figure 34.5) and then choose OK.

Figure 34.5

*The A-Size Sheet is
selected in the Page
Setups area.*

I N S I D E R   T I P

You can select multiple page setups from the list of Page Setups, and copy all selected page setups into the drawings being converted to the R2000 format.

N O T E

The Batch Drawing Converter enables you to replace the existing page setups in R2000 drawings with new page setups by converting the exiting R2000 drawings into new R2000 drawings.

W A R N I N G

If you use the Batch Drawing Converter to replace page setups in existing R2000 drawings with new page setups in converted drawings, the process removes all existing page setups before installing any new page setups.

Next, you will save the list of drawings.

16. Choose the Save List button. The Save Batch Control List dialog box appears.

   You can save the list of drawing files as a Batch Convert List (BCL) file. This file can be recalled and drawings can be added or removed from the list. Additionally, you can also append existing BCL files to the current list of drawings.

17. In the R2000 folder, name the BCL file R14 to R2000, as shown in Figure 34.6, and then choose Save. The list of drawings is saved as a BCL file.

Figure 34.6

The list of drawings is
saved as a BCL file.

18. Be sure the Create Backup (.BAK) Files option is selected. This instructs the application to create backup copies of the existing drawings.

WARNING

The AutoCAD 2000 Migration Assistance application overwrites existing drawings with newly converted drawings.

INSIDER TIP

It's good practice to save a copy of the existing drawings in another folder before converting them to a new format, thereby ensuring the original version of the drawings are not permanently lost.

The listed drawings are now ready for conversion, as shown in Figure 34.7.

Figure 34.7

The list of R14 drawings
is ready for conversion
to R2000.

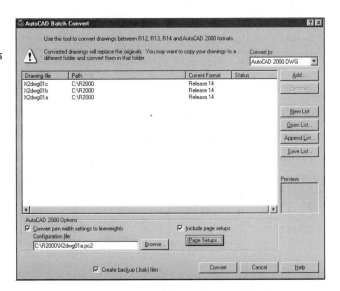

19. Choose the Convert button. The R14 drawings are converted to R2000, as shown in Figure 34.8.

Figure 34.8

The R14 drawings are successfully converted to R2000 format.

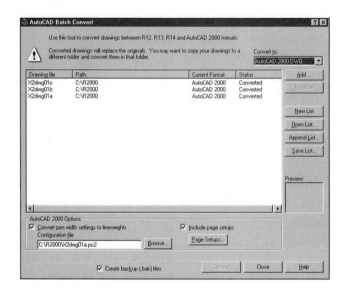

INSIDER TIP

Unlike working inside AutoCAD with the overhead of loading the drawing and displaying it, the Batch Converter works independently of AutoCAD. Therefore, it is extremely fast and sometimes one can misconceive that nothing happened. Rest assured, your drawings are now converted as requested.

20. You can close the AutoCAD Batch Convert dialog box, and you can close the AutoCAD 2000 Migration Assistance application.

To see the results of the conversion process, you can open one of the newly converted drawings in AutoCAD 2000. After you open the drawing (by opening the Page Setup dialog box for Layout1), notice that the A-Size Sheet page setup appears in the Page Setup Name pull-down list, as shown in Figure 34.9. You can also verify that the R14 PC2 file's pen widths were converted to lineweights by opening the Layer Manager and reviewing the drawing's layer settings, as shown in Figure 34.10.

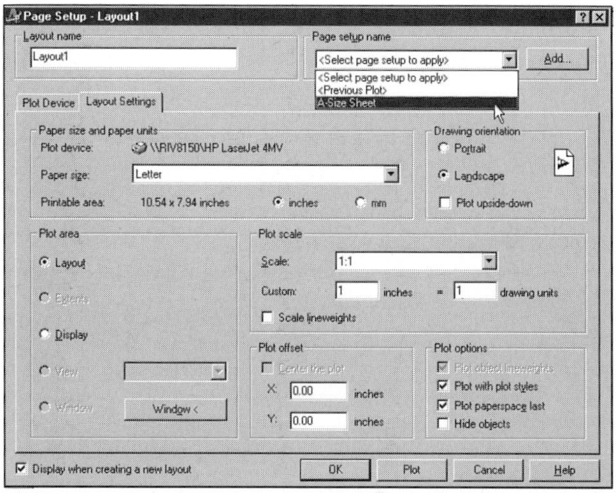

Figure 34.9

The A-Size page setup appears in the Page Setup dialog box for Layout1.

Figure 34.10

The Layer Manager's Lineweight column shows that the R14 PC2 file's pen widths were converted to lineweights.

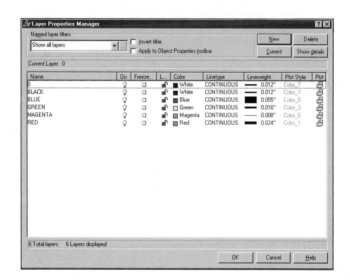

The Batch Drawing Converter is useful for converting AutoCAD drawings from one format to another. You can identify a list of drawings and convert them from and to R12, R13, R14, or R2000 formats. You can associate a CFG, PCP, or PC2 file with the drawings that are being converted into R2000 format, and thereby convert the configuration file's pen widths to R2000 lineweights. You can also select an existing R2000 drawing, and indicate which of its page setups to insert into the new drawings during the conversion process. You can also save the list of files to convert as a BCL file, and later recall the file, and then add or remove drawings from the list or append another BCL file's list of drawings. By using the Batch Drawing Converter, you can easily convert multiple drawings from one drawing format to another.

Next, you will review a new tool that checks for compatibility problems with old AutoLISP routines, thereby ensuring that they will work properly in AutoCAD 2000.

Understanding the AutoLISP Compatibility Analyzer (LCA)

The LCA enables you to check existing AutoLISP files to ensure that they work with AutoCAD 2000 drawings. Because of the many changes and enhancements made to AutoCAD 2000, numerous commands and variables were removed, replaced, or enhanced with additional properties. Consequently, before executing an AutoLISP routine that worked fine in previous versions of AutoCAD, you should use the LCA to confirm the routine performs as intended in AutoCAD 2000.

The LCA provides a dialog driven interface that enables you to identify the AutoLISP file(s) you want to check. After the file is identified, the LCA opens the AutoLISP routine and then steps through the code, line-by-line, checking each line of code for compatibility issues. If an issue is discovered, the LCA displays an explanation of the issue and enables you to make modifications. After you have finished checking the AutoLISP routine and have made any necessary modifications, the LCA saves the routine, and it is now ready to run properly in AutoCAD 2000.

INSIDER TIP

The LCA also analyzes Menu LISP files.

The following exercise steps you through the process of checking an AutoLISP routine with the LCA, by using a routine that functioned properly in version R14. The routine is provided on the accompanying CD, and although the routine contains a compatibility issue, it does not require any AutoLISP programming skill to perform the exercise and ensure that the routine functions properly in R2000.

ANALYZING AUTOLISP ROUTINES FOR R2000 COMPATIBILITY ISSUES

1. Copy the ICL.LSP AutoLISP routine from the accompanying CD to the R2000 folder created in the exercise in the Batch Drawing Converter section. If the folder does not exist, create a new folder and name it R2000.

    After copying the file to the new folder, right-click on the file, choose Properties, and then clear the Read-only attribute.

2. Launch the AutoCAD 2000 Migration Assistance application from the Windows taskbar, by choosing Start, Programs, AutoCAD 2000 Migration Assistance, AutoCAD 2000 Migration Assistance. The application's window opens.

3. Choose the AutoLISP Compatibility Analyzer option. The AutoLISP Compatibility Analyzer window opens.

    Next, you will open the ICL.LSP AutoLISP routine.

4. Choose the Open File button. The Select AutoLISP Files to Analyze dialog box appears.

5. Browse to the R2000 folder (into which you copied the AutoLISP file in Step 1), select the ICL.LSP file (as shown in Figure 34.11), and then choose Open. The AutoLISP routine's source code displays.

Figure 34.11

The ICL.LSP *AutoLISP routine is selected for analysis.*

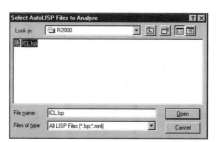

> **NOTE**
>
> You can select multiple AutoLISP files to analyze from the Select AutoLISP Files to Analyze dialog box. If you select multiple AutoLISP files, the LCA loads and then checks each AutoLISP file one at a time.

> ## INSIDER TIP
>
> To automatically analyze entire groups of AutoLISP files, choose the Open Folder button to display the Browse for Folder dialog box. From this dialog box, all AutoLISP routines in the selected folder, including any sub-folders, are loaded and analyzed one at a time.

Next, you will analyze the `ICL.LSP` AutoLISP routine for R2000 compatibility issues.

6. Choose the Find button. The LCA checks each line of code and identifies a compatibility issue, as shown in Figure 34.12.

Figure 34.12

The LCA identifies an R2000 compatibility issue in the `ICL.LSP` *AutoLISP routine.*

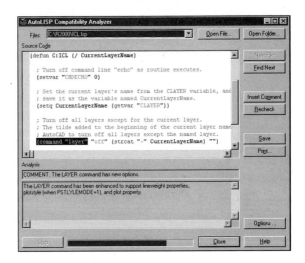

Notice that the LCA highlights the portion of code that represents a compatibility issue, provides a comment about the issue, and describes the impact that the issue has regarding R2000 compatibility.

In this particular case, the issue is a comment noting that the LAYER command has several new options that might also be used. Because this particular AutoLISP routine does not need to use the LAYER command's new options, there is no need to modify the routine's source code. However, you should insert a comment into the routine noting that the LAYER command has new options.

7. Choose the Insert Comment button. The LCA inserts a single line of text directly above the source code containing the compatibility issue, as shown in Figure 34.13.

Figure 34.13

By choosing the Insert Comment button, the LCA automatically inserts a comment above the source code containing the compatibility issue that was identified in the ICL.LSP *AutoLISP routine.*

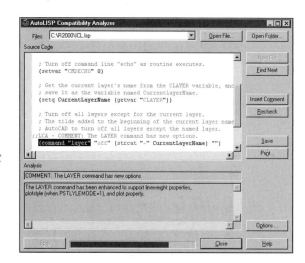

Next, you will continue analyzing the AutoLISP routine for compatibility issues.

8. Choose the Find Next button. The LCA continues analyzing the source code for compatibility issues, and then it indicates that it has completed its analysis, as shown in Figure 34.14.

Figure 34.14

The LCA successfully completes analyzing the ICL.LSP *AutoLISP routine for R2000 compatibility issues.*

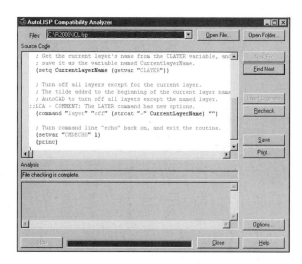

Next, you will save the `ICL.LSP` AutoLISP routine.

9. Choose the Save button. The LCA saves the AutoLISP routine and includes the comment you inserted.

10. You can close the AutoLISP Compatibility Analyzer window, and you can close the AutoCAD 2000 Migration Assistance application.

The LCA provides several features that are useful for analyzing AutoLISP routines for R2000 compatibility issues. In addition to the features demonstrated in the previous exercise, the AutoLISP Compatibility Analyzer window contains three other buttons that provide three additional features, described as follows:

■ The Recheck button restarts the R2000 compatibility analysis process at the beginning of the AutoLISP routine's source code.

■ The Print button enables you to print the AutoLISP routine's source code.

■ The Options button displays the Options dialog box, which lists the rules that the LCA uses for identifying R2000 compatibility issues, as shown in Figure 34.15.

Figure 34.15

The LCA successfully completes the analysis of the `ICL.LSP` AutoLISP routine for R2000 compatibility issues.

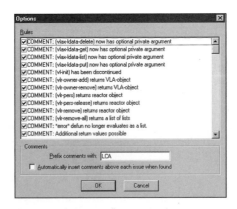

Exploring the LCA's Options

The Options dialog box enables you to select the rules that the LCA uses when checking for R2000 compatibility issues. By default, all rules are selected. In addition to selecting the rules, you can also indicate the prefix to append to comments that are inserted into the source code. You can also automatically insert comments above each compatibility issue when found, by selecting the option shown in the Comments area.

NOTE

The rules used by the LCA when checking for R2000 compatibility issues consist of three types:

- **COMMENT**—This rule typically identifies new properties that are added to R2000 commands, functions, and system variables, and which do not necessarily affect the routine's performance.

- **ERROR**—This rule typically identifies commands, functions, and system variables that have been either renamed or removed in AutoCAD 2000, and which definitely affect the routine's performance.

- **WARNING**—This rule typically identifies commands, functions, and system variables that are either renamed or removed, or whose properties were modified in AutoCAD 2000, and which might affect the routine's performance.

The LCA provides an easy interface to use for selecting and then analyzing AutoLISP routines for R2000 compatibility issues. The application checks each selected routine for compatibility issues by comparing it to a predefined set of rules and indicates where potential compatibility issues exist. By using the LCA, you can quickly search through an AutoLISP routine's source code, identify and correct compatibility issues, and resave the updated AutoLISP routine, which can then be successfully used in AutoCAD 2000.

Next, you will review a new tool that enables you to import existing custom menus and toolbars from previous AutoCAD versions to Release 2000.

Understanding the Menu and Toolbar Porter

The Menu and Toolbar Porter enables you to import your existing custom menus and toolbars from Release 12, Release 13, and Release 14 versions to Release 2000. Using this Porter, you can add, replace, remove, or rearrange menu items and toolbars in a menu file. By using the Menu and Toolbar Porter, you can quickly and easily modify a menu file and transfer selected menu items and toolbars between two different AutoCAD menu files.

The Menu and Toolbar Porter consists of a window with two tabs. One tab is for working with menus, and the other tab is for working with toolbars. By selecting the desired tab, you can modify either menu commands or toolbars and transfer data between two different AutoCAD menu files.

Each tab enables you to identify a source menu file and a target menu file. The source menu file contains the items you want to transfer to the target menu file. The source menu file is opened in read-only mode, whereas the target menu is opened in read-write mode, thereby enabling you to modify the target menu file and save your changes.

In the next section, you will learn about modifying AutoCAD's pull-down menus.

Exploring the Menus Tab

The Menus tab enables you to work with AutoCAD's pull-down, or POP, menus. Through the Menus tab, you can select a source menu file that contains menu items you want to transfer to another menu file, and you can identify the target menu file that you want to modify. Additionally, you can use this tab to modify the target menu by removing and rearranging its menu items. Finally, after you finish modifying the target menu, you can save your modifications to the original menu file, or you can save them as a new menu file.

NOTE

If the target menu file is the ACAD.MNU file, then the Save button will not activate. This is to deter you from overwriting the ACAD.MNU file, and thereby, you avoid encountering problems with the ACAD.MNU file in the event your modifications adversely affect the menu and cause it to not function properly.

INSIDER **T**IP

Its good practice to avoid altering the ACAD.MNU file; instead, you should create, rename, and then load your own custom menu files.

In the following exercise, you will work with two different menu files, and then modify one of the files using the Menu and Toolbar Porter.

MODIFYING MENU FILES

1. Copy the ACADR14.MNU and ACADR2000.MNU files from the accompanying CD to the R2000 folder created in the exercise in the Batch Drawing Converter section of this chapter. If the folder does not exist, create a new folder and name it R2000.

   After copying the files to the new folder, right-click on each file, choose Properties, and then clear the Read-only attribute.

2. Launch the AutoCAD 2000 Migration Assistance application from the Windows taskbar by choosing Start, Programs, AutoCAD 2000 Migration Assistance, AutoCAD 2000 Migration Assistance. The application's window opens.

3. Choose the Menu and Toolbar Porter option. The Menu and Toolbar Porter window opens.

   Next, you will open the two menu files.

4. Choose the Open Source File button. The Open dialog box appears.

5. Browse to the R2000 folder into which you copied the two menu files in Step 1, then select the ACADR2000.MNU file (as shown in Figure 34.16), and then choose Open. The file's menu items display in the Source list box.

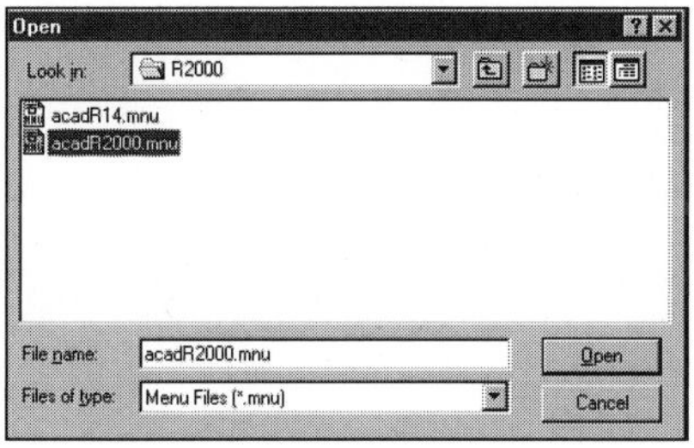

Figure 34.16

The Source menu file is selected.

6. Choose the Open Target File button. The Open dialog box appears.

7. Browse to the R2000 folder into which you copied the two menu files in Step 1, then select the ACADR14.MNU file (as shown in Figure 34.17), and then choose Open. The file's menu items display in the Target list box.

Figure 34.17

The Target menu file is selected.

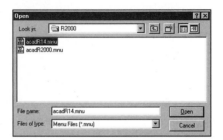

Next, you will add a menu item to the ACADR14.MNU file.

8. In the Source list box, choose the plus (expand) sign next to the Window menu item. The commands within the Window menu appear.

9. Choose the Window menu item in the Source list box. The Window item is highlighted.

10. In the Target list box, choose the ACADR14.MNU filename. The menu filename is highlighted and the Add button activates.

11. Choose the Add button. The Window menu item is added to the Target menu file.

12. In the Target list box, choose the plus (expand) sign next to the Window menu item. The commands within the Window menu appear, as shown in Figure 34.18.

NOTE

Notice in the Target menu file that the Window menu item and all its commands are copied to the Target menu file. Anytime you add or replace a menu item, all its commands and sub-menus are included.

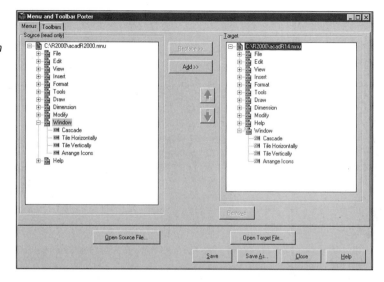

Figure 34.18

The Window menu item in the Source menu file is added to the Target menu file.

Next, you will replace a menu item to the ACADR14.MNU file.

13. In the Source list box, choose the Modify menu item. The Modify item is highlighted.

14. In the Target list box, choose the Modify menu item. The Modify menu item is highlighted and the Replace button activates.

15. Choose the Replace button. The Modify menu item from the Source menu file replaces the Modify menu item in the Target menu file.

    It's not easy to see, but the Modify menu in the Target menu file has a small icon next to it indicating that it is modified, as shown in Figure 34.19.

Figure 34.19

The Modify menu item in the Target menu file has a small icon next to it indicating the menu item is modified.

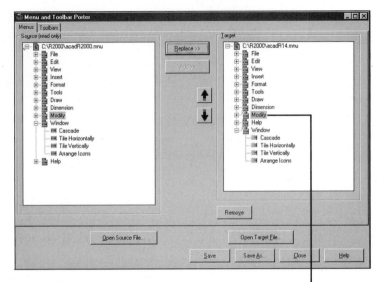

Icon indicating modified file.

Next, you will add commands within a menu item to the ACADR14.MNU file.

16. In the Source list box, choose the plus (expand) sign next to the Help menu item. The commands within the Help menu appear.

17. In the Source list box, under the Help menu item, choose the Support Assistance command. The Support Assistance command is highlighted.

18. In the Target list box, choose the plus (expand) sign next to the Help menu item. The commands within the Help menu appear.

19. In the Target list box, choose the Help menu item. The Help menu is highlighted and the Add button activates.

20. Choose the Add button. The Support Assistance command is added to the Target menu file, as shown in Figure 34.20.

Figure 34.20

The Support Assistance command is added to the Help menu in the Target menu file.

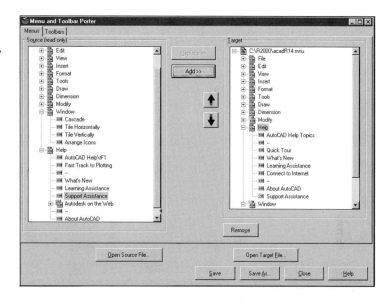

Note

It is important to understand the conditions that cause either the Replace or the Add button to activate. If the selected item in the Source menu file is at the same hierarchy level as the item selected in the Target menu file, the Replace button activates. For example, when a command level item is selected in the source drawing and then a command level item is selected in the Target drawing, the Replace button activates enabling you to replace the Target file's command with the Source file's command. In contrast, when a command level item is selected in the source drawing and then a menu level item is selected in the Target drawing, the Add button activates enabling you to add the Source file's command to the Target file's menu.

Next, you will move the Help menu within the Target menu file.

21. In the Target list box, choose the Help menu item. The Help menu is highlighted and the Up and Down arrow buttons activate.

22. Choose the Down arrow button, clicking only once. The Help menu item is moved below the Window menu item, as shown in Figure 34.21.

Figure 34.21

The Help menu item in the
Target file is moved below
the Window menu item.

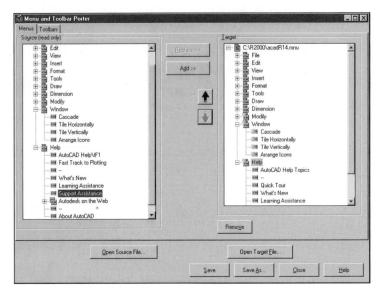

23. You can close the Menu and Toolbar Porter dialog box without saving your changes, and you can close the AutoCAD 2000 Migration Assistance application.

The Menu and Toolbar Porter's Menu tab enables you to add and replace menu items and commands from one menu file to another. From the Menu tab, you can also modify the position of menu items and commands, and you can remove menu items and commands from the Target menu file. By using the Menu tab, you can easily modify and update AutoCAD's menu files.

In the next section, you will learn about modifying AutoCAD's pull-down menus.

Exploring the Toolbars Tab

The Toolbars tab functions in the same fashion as the Menus tab, except that it enables you to work with AutoCAD menu file's Toolbars. Through the Toolbars tab, you can select a source menu file that contains toolbars that you want to transfer to another menu file, and you can identify the target menu file that you want to modify. Additionally, you can use this tab to modify the target menu by removing undesired toolbars. Finally, after you finish modifying the target menu, you can save your modifications to the original menu file, or save them as a new menu file.

The only significant difference between the Toolbars tab and the Menus tab is that the Toolbars tab does not have a Replace button. Therefore, you cannot replace a toolbar in the Target menu file with a toolbar from the Source menu file. In addition, there are no Up and Down arrow buttons. Consequently, you cannot move a toolbar in the Target menu above or below another toolbar. This is because of the non-stacking nature of the toolbar system.

A useful feature of the Toolbars tab is that it displays icons next to toolbars in the Source menu that do not exist in the Target menu. For example, in Figure 34.22, only a few toolbars in the Source list box have icons next to them. Notice that the toolbars in the Source list box with no icons, already appear in the Target menu. Therefore, there's no need to copy the toolbars to the Target menu file. As noted previously, this also means you cannot use the Menu and Toolbar Porter to replace toolbars in the Target menu file with toolbars from the Source menu file.

Figure 34.22

Icons appear next to the toolbars in the Source menu list that can be added to the Target menu file.

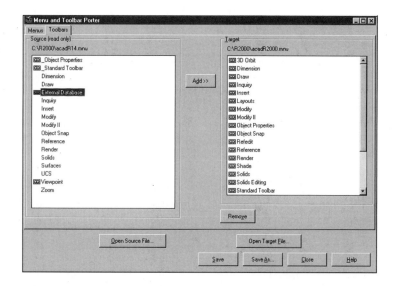

The Menu and Toolbar Porter enable you to add and replace menu commands and to add toolbars from one menu file to another. You can also remove menus and commands, and remove toolbars from menu files, as well as rearrange the order of menus and commands in the Target menu file. Through the Menu and Toolbar Porter, you can easily manipulate AutoCAD menu files.

Next, you will learn how to quickly copy PGP file command aliases from previous AutoCAD releases to Release 2000.

Understanding the Command Alias (PGP) Porter

The Command Alias (PGP) Porter enables you to import your existing `ACAD.PGP` file command aliases from Release 12, Release 13, and Release 14 versions to Release 2000. Using this Porter, you can add, replace, and remove command aliases in a PGP file. By using the Command Alias (PGP) Porter, you can quickly and easily modify a PGP file and transfer selected command aliases between two different AutoCAD PGP files.

The Command Alias (PGP) Porter consists of a dialog box with two tabs. One tab is for working with AutoCAD command aliases, and the other tab is for working with external command aliases. By selecting the desired tab, you can modify either AutoCAD command aliases or external command aliases, and then transfer data between two different AutoCAD PGP files.

Each tab enables you to identify a source PGP file and a target PGP file. The source PGP file contains the aliases you want to transfer to the target PGP file. The source PGP file is opened in read-only mode, whereas the target PGP is opened in read-write mode, thereby enabling you to modify the target PGP file and to save your changes.

In the next section, you will learn about modifying AutoCAD's command aliases.

Exploring the AutoCAD Alias Tab

The AutoCAD Alias tab enables you to work with AutoCAD's command-line aliases. Through the AutoCAD Alias tab, you can select a source PGP file that contains command aliases you want to transfer to another PGP file, and you can identify the target PGP file that you want to modify. Additionally, you can use this tab to modify the target PGP file by removing its command aliases. Finally, after you finish modifying the target PGP file, you can save your modifications to the original PGP file, or you can save them as a new PGP file.

In the following exercise, you will work with two different PGP files and modify one of the files using the Command Alias (PGP) Porter.

MODIFYING PGP FILES

1. Copy the ACADR14.PGP and ACADR2000.PGP files from the accompanying CD to the R2000 folder created in the exercise in the Batch Drawing Converter section. If the folder does not exist, then create a new folder and name it R2000.

    After copying the files to the new folder, right-click on each file, choose Properties, and then clear the Read-only attribute.

2. Launch the AutoCAD 2000 Migration Assistance application from the Windows taskbar by choosing Start, Programs, AutoCAD 2000 Migration Assistance, AutoCAD 2000 Migration Assistance. The application's window opens.

3. Choose the Command Alias (PGP) Porter option. The Command Alias (PGP) Porter window opens.

    Next, you will open the two PGP files.

4. Choose the Open Source File button. The Open dialog box appears.

5. Browse to the R2000 folder into which you copied the two PGP files in Step 1, select the ACADR14.PGP file (as shown in Figure 34.23), and then choose Open. The file's AutoCAD command aliases appear in the Source list box.

Figure 34.23

The Source PGP file is selected.

6. Choose the Open Target File button. The Open dialog box appears.

7. Browse to the R2000 folder into which you copied the two PGP files in Step 1, select the ACADR2000.PGP file (as shown in Figure 34.24), and then choose Open. The file's AutoCAD command aliases appear in the Target list box.

Figure 34.24

The Target PGP file is selected.

Next, you will add a command alias to the ACADR2000.PGP file.

8. In the Source list box, choose the AT command alias. The command alias is high-lighted and the Add button activates.

9. Choose the Add button. The AT command alias is added to the Target PGP file, as shown in Figure 34.25.

Figure 34.25

The AT command alias in the Source PGP file is added to the Target PGP file.

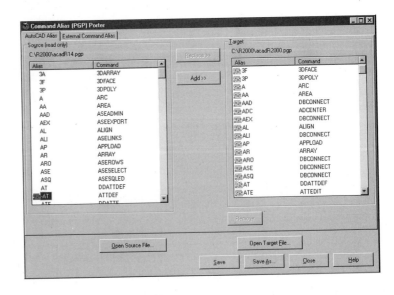

NOTE

Because duplicate entries cannot exist in the PGP file, a small icon is displayed in the source file to the left of the entries that are not in the target file and are, therefore, available to add.

Next, you will replace a command alias in the `ACADR2000.PGP` file.

10. In the Source list box, choose the ALI command alias. The ALI command alias is highlighted.

11. In the Target list box, choose the ALI command alias. The ALI command alias is highlighted and the Replace button activates.

12. Choose the Replace button. The ALI command alias from the Source PGP file replaces the ALI command alias in the Target PGP file.

    It's not easy to see, but the ALI command alias in the Target PGP file has a small icon next to it, indicating it is modified, as shown in Figure 34.26.

Figure 34.26

The ALI command alias in the Target PGP file has a small icon next to it, indicating the ALI command alias is modified.

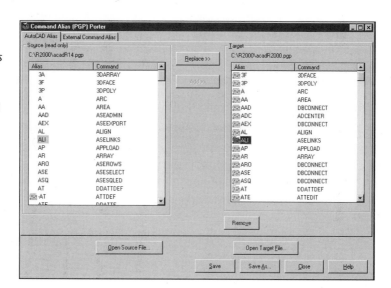

13. You can close the Command Alias (PGP) Porter dialog box without saving your changes, and you can close the AutoCAD 2000 Migration Assistance application.

The Command Alias (PGP) Porter's AutoCAD Alias tab enables you to add and replace command aliases from one PGP file to another. From the AutoCAD Alias tab, you can also remove command aliases from the Target PGP file. By using the AutoCAD Alias tab, you can easily modify and update AutoCAD's PGP files.

In the next section, you will learn about modifying AutoCAD's external command aliases.

Exploring the External Command Alias Tab

The External Command Alias tab functions in the same fashion as the AutoCAD Alias tab, except that it enables you to work with external command aliases. Through the External Command Alias tab, you can select a source PGP file that contains external command aliases you want to transfer to another PGP file and you can identify the target PGP file that you want to modify. Additionally, you can use this tab to modify the target PGP, by removing undesired external command aliases. Finally, after you finish modifying the target PGP file, you can save your modifications to the original PGP file, or save them as a new PGP file.

A useful feature of the External Command Alias tab is that it displays icons next to external command aliases in the Source PGP file that do not exist in the Target PGP file. For example, in Figure 34.27, only one external command alias in the Source list box has an icon next to it. Notice that the external command aliases in the Source list box with no icons already appear in the Target PGP file. Therefore, there is no need to copy the external command aliases to the Target PGP file.

Figure 34.27

Icons appear next to the external command aliases in the Source PGP file list that can be added to a Target PGP file.

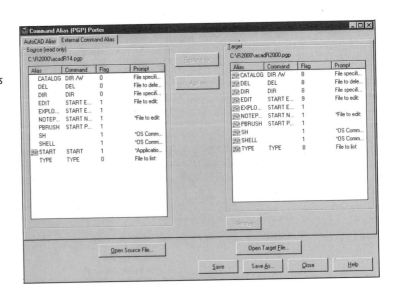

The Command Alias (PGP) Porter enables you to add and replace AutoCAD command aliases, and to add and replace external command aliases from one PGP file to another. You can also remove AutoCAD command aliases, and remove external command aliases from PGP files in the Target PGP file. Through the Command Alias (PGP) Porter, you can easily manipulate AutoCAD PGP files.

Next, you will learn how to convert color-dependent plot style drawings to named plot style drawings.

Understanding the Color to Named Tools

The Color to Named Tools feature enables you to convert a drawing and its plot style table from the color-dependent plot style format to the named plot style format.

Although the Color to Named Tools feature is listed as one of the tools of the AutoCAD 2000 Migration Assistance application, it's actually a feature that is executed from within AutoCAD 2000. If you select the Color to Named Tools option from the AutoCAD 2000 Migration Assistance application, the application simply opens a window that instructs you to access the feature from AutoCAD 2000. Consequently, there's no need to launch the AutoCAD 2000 Migration Assistance application to access the Color to Named Tools feature.

The Color to Named Tools feature consists of two commands. The first command is CONVERTCTB, and it enables you to convert a color-dependent plot style table (CTB) to a named plot style table (STB). The second command is CONVERTPSTYLES, and it enables you to convert a drawing that uses color-dependent styles into a drawing that uses named plot styles. Both commands are launched from AutoCAD's command line. By using these two commands, you can convert any drawing and its plot style table from a color-dependent plot style format to a named plot style format.

NOTE

AutoCAD 2000 drawings are designed to use either color-dependent plot styles or named plot styles but not both. More importantly, R2000 drawings are not designed to switch between the two format types. When you create a drawing, the plot-style table format assigned to the drawing is intended to be permanent.

However, because there might be occasions when you need to convert a drawing that uses the color-dependent plot style format into a drawing that uses the named plot style format, AutoCAD provides the Color to Named Tools feature.

For more information about plot style tables, refer to the section titled, "Defining Plot Styles," in Chapter 20, "Productive Plotting."

WARNING

Although you can use the CONVERTCTB and CONVERTPSTYLES commands to convert a drawing from a color-dependent plot style format to a named plot style format, you cannot convert a drawing from a named plot style format to a color-dependent plot style format. Therefore, if you convert a drawing from a color-dependent plot style format to a named plot style format, the conversion is permanent.

Furthermore, most drawings use CTB-type plotting, a leftover from the R14 days. This method of plotting is actually effective as well. You should investigate your specific named plot style needs before converting a drawing.

The following exercise takes you through the process of converting a drawing and its plot style table from a color-dependent plot style format to a named plot style format.

USING THE COLOR TO NAMED TOOLS FEATURE

1. Copy the X2DWG02.DWG drawing file from the accompanying CD to the R2000 folder created in the exercise in the Batch Drawing Converter section. If the folder does not exist, then create a new folder and name it R2000.

   After copying the file to the new folder, right-click on the file, choose Properties, and then clear the Read-only attribute.

2. Copy the X2DWG02.CTB file from the accompanying CD to the Plot Styles folder, which is accessed from AutoCAD's File menu by choosing Plot Style Manager.

   After copying the file, right-click the CTB file, choose Properties, and then clear the Read-only attribute.

   The first step in converting a drawing to the named plot style format is to convert its plot style table. By converting the plot style table first, you can then attach the converted table to the drawing when the drawing is converted to the named plot style format.

3. Type **CONVERTCTB** at the AutoCAD command line, and then press Enter. The Open dialog box appears and lists the CTB files in AutoCAD's Plot Styles folder.

4. Choose the X2DWG02.CTB (as shown in Figure 34.28) and then choose Open. The Save As dialog box appears.

Figure 34.28

The X2DWG02.CTB color-dependent plot style table file is selected for conversion to a named plot style table file.

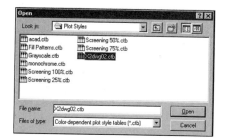

At this point, AutoCAD has automatically converted the color-dependent plot style table to a named plot style table. The only remaining step to complete the conversion of the plot style table is to assign the new plot style table a name, and then save the file.

For the STB filename, AutoCAD automatically chooses the same name as the CTB file. Although you can assign a different plot style table name, for this exercise, you will use the default name provided by AutoCAD, as shown in Figure 34.29.

Figure 34.29

AutoCAD automatically creates the new named plot style table and assigns it the same name as the color-dependent plot style table.

5. Choose Save. AutoCAD displays a message noting that the new plot style table was successfully created.

6. Choose OK to close the dialog box.

7. When AutoCAD converts the color-dependent plot style table to a named plot style table, the plot style names in the CTB file are changed from Color_1, Color_2, and so on, to Style_1, Style_2, and so on, in the STB file.

NOTE

The plot styles in a color-dependent plot style table are automatically named after the AutoCAD's 255 predefined colors. When AutoCAD converts the CTB file to a named plot style table, all the CTB file's plot style names that have the exact same settings are saved as a single plot style. Each unique plot style is given a new name. Therefore, although a CTB file automatically has 255 pre-named plot styles, after conversion, the STB file has only enough plot styles to properly represent the number of different plot styles that existed in the CTB file.

For more information about plot styles, refer to the section titled, "Choosing the Plot Style Table Type," in Chapter 20.

The next step is to convert the drawing from a color-dependent plot style format to a named plot style format.

8. Open the X2DWG02.DWG drawing file you copied to the R2000 folder. AutoCAD displays the drawing.

9. Type **CONVERTPSTYLES** at the AutoCAD command line and then press Enter. AutoCAD displays a warning noting that the command converts a drawing from color-dependent plot style format to a named plot style format.

10. Choose OK to close the message box. The Select File dialog box appears.

11. Choose the X2DWG02.STB (as shown in Figure 34.30), and then choose Open. AutoCAD converts the drawing from color-dependent plot style format to a named plot style format.

Figure 34.30

AutoCAD prompts you for the named plot style table to which to assign to the converted drawing.

WARNING

AutoCAD converts the original drawing from a color-dependent plot style format to a named plot style format. Therefore, you must create a copy of the original drawing before conversion if you want to maintain a color-dependent plot style version of the drawing.

12. If you open the Properties Layer Manager and view the drawing's plot style names, you'll notice that the plot style names changed from `Color_1`, `Color_2`, and so on, as shown in Figure 34.31, to `Style_1`, `Style_2`, and so on, as shown in Figure 34.32.

Figure 34.31

The Layer Properties Manager displays the names of the color-dependent plot styles before converting the drawing.

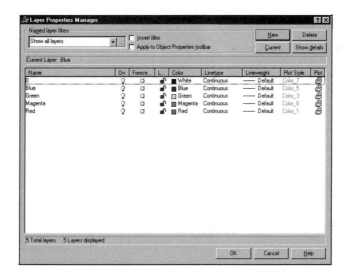

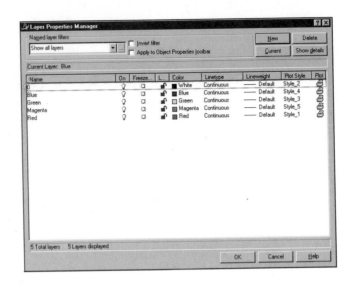

The Layer Manager displays the names of the named plot styles after converting the drawing.

13. You can close the drawing without saving your changes.

The process of converting a drawing from a color-dependent plot style format to a named plot style format is straightforward. If you intend to convert a drawing that uses color-dependent styles, you must first use the CONVERTCTB command to convert the drawing's plot style table, and then use the CONVERTPSTYLES command to convert the drawing. By executing these two commands from AutoCAD's command line, you can easily convert a drawing from the color-dependent plot style format to a named plot style format.

Next, you will review the automated process of installing and configuring multiple customized AutoCAD configurations.

Understanding the Network Deployment Tool

The Network Deployment tool automates the process of installing and configuring multiple customized AutoCAD configurations across your network. By using this feature, you can ease the process of upgrading existing AutoCAD installations to AutoCAD 2000.

The Network Deployment tool describes the steps necessary to install and then use PictureTaker, a third party application included with AutoCAD 2000. PictureTaker is designed to enable you to upgrade and modify applications and configuration files across your network. The 30-day trial version of PictureTaker Enterprise Edition ships with AutoCAD.

PictureTaker is designed for use by your system administrator, and it requires high-end, user privileges to upgrade applications across your network. Because of the intended target audience of this application (system administrators), it is not discussed in detail in this chapter. See Chapter 36, "Installing 2000 in the Business Environment," for more specific information about installing AutoCAD 2000 across a network.

Next, you will review a tool that enables you to generate a list of AutoCAD seats that exist across your entire network.

Understanding the Serial Number Harvester

The Serial Number Harvester is a tool that searches your system for installed AutoCAD seats, and then it automatically generates a report listing the total number of AutoCAD seats found, including their release versions and serial numbers. This tool can search your local system, or it can search across your network. It searches for all installations of AutoCAD, and it categorizes found installations by release version. By using the Serial Number Harvester, you can easily determine the number of AutoCAD installations on your local system, or across your network.

You access the Serial Number Harvester from the AutoCAD 2000 Migration Assistance application, by choosing the Serial Number Harvester option. After it is selected, the application launches and opens the Serial Number Harvester window.

To perform a search of installed AutoCAD seats, you first indicate if you want the Serial Number Harvester to search for installations of AutoCAD on local drives, across the network, or both. Then, choose the Find button to start the application searching for installed seats of AutoCAD.

After the Serial Number Harvester completes its search, it displays the search results, as shown in Figure 34.33. For the purposes of this discussion, I searched my local system for AutoCAD installations. Notice in Figure 34.33 that the Serial Number Harvester found two versions of AutoCAD on my system. The information provided includes the path where AutoCAD is installed and the computer's name on which AutoCAD is installed, and it lists each found seat's serial number and version number. By using the Serial Number Harvester, I easily located and identified the two AutoCAD versions installed on my system.

Figure 34.33

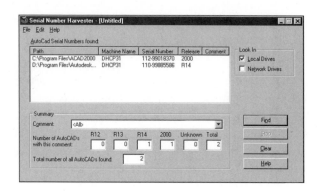

The Serial Number Harvester displays the results of its search for installed seats of AutoCAD.

The Serial Number Harvester enables you to add comments to listed AutoCAD installations. For example, I can select the R14 AutoCAD installation from the list and add the comment, "AutoCAD Map R3." Then, the list of results can be saved and recalled later for review.

The Serial Number Harvester provides a simple way to locate and identify all versions of AutoCAD that exist on your system, or across your network. Using this tool, you can generate lists of installed seats of AutoCAD, add comments, and then save the list for later reference. By using the Serial Number Harvester, you can easily generate a list of all your installed seats of AutoCAD.

Next, you will learn about creating AutoCAD script files using the new ScriptPro utility.

Understanding the ScriptPro Utility

The ScriptPro utility is a new tool that makes the process of creating AutoCAD script files easy. You can create script files, define a list of drawings on which to run the script file, and save the script files and drawing list as a ScriptPro project. By using ScriptPro, you can more easily develop scripts and define lists of drawings on which to run the scripts.

In this section, you learn about AutoCAD scripts, and how to use the new ScriptPro utility to develop and run scripts on multiple drawings.

Understanding AutoCAD Script Files

An AutoCAD script is a file that automatically executes a series of AutoCAD commands on the current drawing. For example, you can create a script that automatically inserts a block and defines its insertion point, rotation, and scale. The script can also populate any attributes attached to the block, which is a useful feature when inserting title blocks into drawings. By using scripts, you can automatically execute a series of commands within AutoCAD.

An AutoCAD script is a file that contains a series of AutoCAD commands listed in the order you want the commands to execute. The list of commands is created in an ASCII text file, which is saved with a .SCR extension. By using an ASCII text editor, you can create a script file that you run from within AutoCAD, and one that executes AutoCAD commands in the order listed.

N OTE

> AutoCAD script files can be created using any ASCII text editor, such as Microsoft Notepad or Microsoft Word.

Using Batch Processing with Scripts

The usefulness of scripts goes beyond executing a series of AutoCAD commands on a single drawing. You can expand the usefulness of scripts by using batch processing, which enables you to identify a list of drawings on which to execute the script. For example, suppose you have a large number of drawings into which you need to insert a standard title block. By creating a single script file that lists the commands needed to insert the title block and then creating a batch file that identifies the drawings on which to apply the script, you can use the script to automatically insert the title block into all the identified drawings. By combining a script file with batch processing, you can automatically execute a series of AutoCAD commands on a list of drawings.

The only problem with using batch processing to execute a script on a series of drawings is that most AutoCAD users don't know how to create batch files. To solve this problem, Autodesk created the ScriptPro utility, which enables you to easily identify a script file and to define a list of drawings on which to apply the script. By using the ScriptPro utility, you do not need to know how to create a batch file to execute a script on multiple drawings.

In the following sections, you will learn how to use the ScriptPro utility to create a script file and to define lists of drawings on which to apply the script.

Using the ScriptPro Utility

The ScriptPro utility makes the process of creating a script file easy. Additionally, ScriptPro enables you to identify a group of drawings on which to apply the script. By using ScriptPro, you can easily create and edit AutoCAD scripts, and then apply the script to multiple drawings.

When you use ScriptPro to assign a script to a list of drawings, you are actually creating a ScriptPro Project. The ScriptPro Project identifies the script and the drawings to which the script is assigned, and it can be saved as a ScriptPro Project file. After it is saved, the Project file can be recalled, modified if desired, and then executed. By saving the script and its associated list of drawings as a ScriptPro Project, you can easily recall the Project for later use.

The following exercise takes you through the process of using the ScriptPro utility to create an AutoCAD script, to assign the script to a list of drawings, and then to save the information as a ScriptPro Project.

USING THE SCRIPTPRO UTILITY

1. Copy the following files from the accompanying CD to the R2000 folder created in the exercise in the Batch Drawing Converter section. If the folder does not exist, then create a new folder and name it R2000.

   - **X2DWG03.DWG**—This file is an R2000 drawing defined as a title blockand containing an attribute.

   - **X2DWG03A.DWG**—This file is a blank R2000 drawing file, into which you insert the X2DWG03.DWG block.

   - **X2DWG03B.DWG**—This file is a blank R2000 drawing file, into which you insert the X2DWG03.DWG block.

   - **X2DWG03C.DWG**—This file is a blank R2000 drawing file, into which you insert the X2DWG03.DWG block.

   - **SCRIPT ONE.SCR**—This file is an empty AutoCAD script file.

   After copying the files to the new folder, right-click on each file, choose Properties, and then clear the Read-only attribute.

2. Launch the AutoCAD 2000 Migration Assistance application from the Windows taskbar by choosing Start, Programs, AutoCAD 2000 Migration Assistance, AutoCAD 2000 Migration Assistance. The application's window opens.

3. Choose the ScriptPro utility option. The ScriptPro window opens.

   Next, you will go through the process of editing a script file that inserts the X2DWG03.DWG title block and assigning a value to the block's attribute.

4. From the Script File area, choose the Browse button. The Open dialog box appears.

5. Browse to the R2000 folder, choose the Script One file (as shown in Figure 34.34), and then choose Open. ScriptPro selects the SCRIPT ONE.SCR file.

Figure 34.34

The SCRIPT ONE.SCR *file is selected.*

WARNING

It might take the ScriptPro utility several moments to open the SCRIPT ONE.SCR file.

Next, you will edit the SCRIPT ONE.SCR file.

6. From the Script File area, choose the Edit button. ScriptPro starts the text editor application associated with script files and loads the script file.

NOTE

In the book's example, ScriptPro launched Microsoft Notepad to edit the script file.

Next, you will add AutoCAD commands that insert the title block into a drawing and then save the drawing.

7.   In the text editor, type the following commands:

```
;Begin script
;Start the INSERT command
insert
;Insert the block
X2dwg03.dwg
;Indicate insertion point
0,0
;Indicate X and Y scale factors
1
1
;Indicate rotation
0
;Indicate attribute value
My Drawing
;Save the drawing
Save

;End script
```

Notice that the script file contains commands, command responses, and comments. When creating a script, it is important both that you know the responses a command requires and that you respond appropriately. In addition, AutoCAD ignores any text string that begins with a semicolon as it executes the script, enabling you to add useful comments to your script. Finally, notice that a blank line follows the Save command. This represents a hard-carriage return, which simulates pressing the Enter key after typing the command.

WARNING

It is necessary to end each command with a hard-carriage return, which is accomplished by pressing the Enter key. This includes ending the last command in the script with a hard-carriage return.

NOTE

A hard-carriage return and a space perform the same function, which is to simulate pressing the Enter key after typing a command. Consequently, you can substitute a space for a hard-carriage return. To make the code readable, use spaces between responses passed to commands, such as PEDIT, and use carriage returns between commands.

8. In the text editor's File menu, choose Save. The script file should appear as shown in Figure 34.35.

Figure 34.35

The AutoCAD commands and command responses are entered in SCRIPT ONE.SCR *file.*

9. In the text editor's File menu, choose Exit. The text editor closes.

    Next, you will select the drawings to which you will apply the SCRIPT ONE.SCR file.

10. From ScriptPro's Drawings menu, choose Add. The ScriptPro Add/Remove files in drawing list dialog box appears.

11. In the Name list box, choose the X2DWG03A.DWG, X2DWG03B.DWG, and X2DWG03C.DWG drawings, and then choose the Add button. The selected drawings are displayed in the Files to Apply Script to list, as shown in Figure 34.36.

Figure 34.36

The drawings are selected to which to apply the script file.

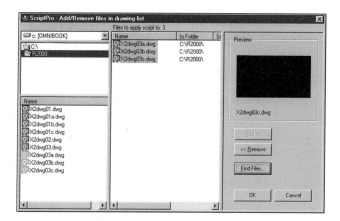

12. Choose OK. The selected drawing files are displayed in the ScriptPro drawing list, as shown in Figure 34.37.

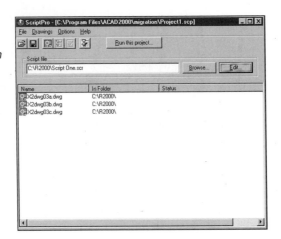

Next, you will save the settings as a ScriptPro Project.

13. From ScriptPro's File menu, choose Save Project. The Save As dialog box appears.

14. Browse to the R2000 folder, type **Project One** in the File name text box (as shown in Figure 34.38), and then choose Save. ScriptPro saves the Project file.

Next, you will run the ScriptPro Project.

15. Choose the Run This Project button. ScriptPro runs the Project and launches AutoCAD 2000, opening each drawing in the list and applying the commands in the SCRIPT ONE.SCR file.

When finished executing the script, AutoCAD displays the Project Completed message box indicating the project run is complete. Additionally, the Project Completed message box asks if you want to view the log file, which contains detailed information about the project run.

You can run a ScriptPro Project from AutoCAD by entering **SCRIPTPRO** at the command prompt.

16. Choose No to close the Project Completed message box. The ScriptPro dialog box displays the status of each drawing, which indicates that the drawings are done, as shown in Figure 34.39.

Figure 34.39

The ScriptPro utility indicates all drawings are done.

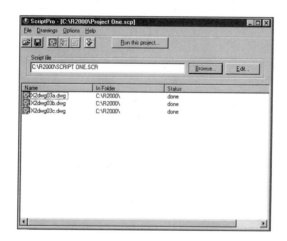

17. Exit the ScriptPro utility.

The ScriptPro utility automates the process of editing a script file and then applying the script file to a list of drawings. ScriptPro enables you to browse for script files and then to edit the selected script file. ScriptPro also enables you to browse for drawings and then to add those drawings to the list to which ScriptPro applies the selected script. By using ScriptPro, you can easily define and then run a series of commands on a list of pre-selected drawings.

Using ScriptPro's Advanced Features

The ScriptPro utility contains advanced features that make running scripts easier. For example, you can use keywords to indicate drawing names, and you can use Calls to launch script files from within a script. ScriptPro also includes special save commands for saving drawings as DXF files, or as previous versions of AutoCAD. By using ScriptPro's advanced features, you can create powerful scripts.

The following exercise takes you through the process of using the ScriptPro utility's advanced features.

Note

The following exercise uses the X2DWG03.DWG drawing file and the SCRIPT ONE.SCR file from the previous exercise.

Using Advanced Features of the ScriptPro Utility

1. Copy the following files from the accompanying CD to the R2000 folder used in the previous exercise.

    ■   **X2DWG04A.DWG**—This is a blank R2000 drawing file, into which you insert the X2DWG03.DWG block.

    ■   **X2DWG04B.DWG**—This is a blank R2000 drawing file, into which you insert the X2DWG03.DWG block.

    ■   **X2DWG04C.DWG**—This is a blank R2000 drawing file, into which you insert the X2DWG03.DWG block.

    ■   **SCRIPT TWO.SCR**—This is an empty AutoCAD script file.

    After copying the files to the new folder, right-click on each file, choose Properties, and then clear the Read-only attribute.

2. Launch the AutoCAD 2000 Migration Assistance application from the Windows taskbar by choosing Start, Programs, AutoCAD 2000 Migration Assistance, AutoCAD 2000 Migration Assistance. The application's window opens.

3. Choose the ScriptPro utility option. The ScriptPro window opens.

4. From the Script File area, choose the Browse button. The Open dialog box appears.

5. Browse to the R2000 folder, choose the Script Two file (as shown in Figure 34.40), and then choose Open. ScriptPro selects the SCRIPT TWO.SCR file.

Figure 34.40

The Script Two file is selected.

Next, you will edit the `SCRIPT TWO.SCR` file.

6. From the Script File area, choose the Edit button. ScriptPro starts the text editor application associated with script files and loads the script file.

Next, you will use the ScriptPro CALL command to run the `SCRIPT ONE.SCR` file from within the `SCRIPT TWO.SCR` file.

7. In the text editor, type the following commands:

```
;Begin script
;Call the Script One file
CALL "SCRIPT ONE.SCR"
```

The ScriptPro CALL command instructs AutoCAD to open the `SCRIPT ONE.SCR` file and execute its commands. After completion, AutoCAD returns to the `SCRIPT TWO.SCR` file and continues executing the remaining commands. Notice that the `SCRIPT ONE.SCR` filename is enclosed in quotes. This enables ScriptPro to work with files that use the long-filename format, which can include spaces in the filename.

Next, you will use two special ScriptPro command features to save the edited drawing. The first is a ScriptPro save command, and the second is a ScriptPro keyword command.

8. In the text editor, type the following commands:

```
;Save drawing as DXF file
SCR-DXFOUT-2000 "<acet:cFolderName><acet:cBaseName>.dxf"
;End script
```

The text string `SCR-DXFOUT-2000 "<acet:cFolderName><acet:cBaseName>.dxf"` contains three ScriptPro commands. The first is `SCR-DXFOUT-2000`, and is a special ScriptPro save command that instructs AutoCAD to save the drawing as an R2000 format DXF file. The second is the keyword `<acet:cFolderName>`, and it indicates the folder name in which the current drawing resides. The third is the keyword `<acet:cBaseName>`, and it indicates the name of the current drawing, excluding path and filename extension. Notice that by combining the two keywords with the .DXF file extension and then enclosing the string in quotes, you instruct AutoCAD to save the DXF file to the current drawing's folder, using the current drawing's name with .DXF appended.

For a detailed list of ScriptPro save commands, refer to Table 34.1. For a detailed list of ScriptPro keywords, refer to Table 34.2.

9. From the text editor's File menu, choose Save. The script file should appear as shown in Figure 34.41.

Figure 34.41

The ScriptPro commands and their command responses are entered in the SCRIPT TWO.SCR file.

10. From the text editor's File menu, choose Exit. The text editor closes.

Next, you will select the drawings to which you apply the SCRIPT TWO.SCR file.

11. From ScriptPro's Drawings menu, choose Add. The ScriptPro Add/Remove files in drawing list dialog box appears.

12. In the Name list box, choose the X2DWG04A.DWG, X2DWG04B.DWG, and X2DWG04C.DWG drawings, and then choose the Add button. The selected drawings are displayed in the Files to Apply Script to list, as shown in Figure 34.42.

Figure 34.42

The drawings are selected to which to apply the script file.

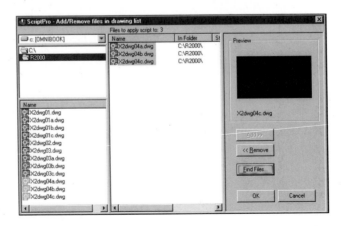

13. Choose OK. The selected drawing files are displayed in the ScriptPro drawing list, as shown in Figure 34.43.

Figure 34.43

ScriptPro is ready to run and to apply the SCRIPT TWO.SCR *file to the listed drawings.*

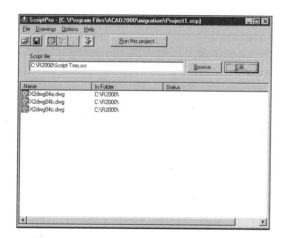

Next, you will save the settings as a ScriptPro Project.

14. From ScriptPro's File menu, choose Save Project. The Save As dialog box appears.

15. Browse to the R2000 folder, type **Project Two** in the File name text box (as shown in Figure 34.44), and then choose Save. ScriptPro saves the Project file.

Figure 34.44

The settings are saved as a ScriptPro Project.

Next, you will run the ScriptPro Project.

16. Choose the Run This Project button. ScriptPro runs the Project and launches AutoCAD 2000, opening each drawing in the list and applying the commands in the SCRIPT TWO.SCR file.

When finished executing the script, AutoCAD displays the Project Completed message box indicating the project run is complete. Additionally, the Project Completed message box asks if you want to view the log file, which contains detailed information about the project run.

17. Choose No to close the Project Completed message box. The ScriptPro window displays the status of each drawing, which indicates all drawings are done (see Figure 34.45).

Figure 34.45

The ScriptPro utility indicates all drawings are done.

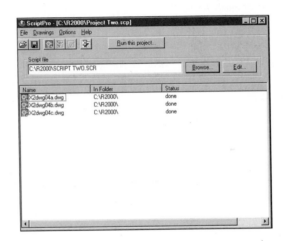

18. Exit the ScriptPro utility.

The ScriptPro utility's command features enable you to expand the capabilities of scripts. You can use ScriptPro calls to run other scripts from within the current script file. You can use ScriptPro save commands to save the current drawing as a DXF file, or as another version of AutoCAD. You can also use ScriptPro's keywords to identify the current drawing's name, or the folder that contains the current drawing. By using ScriptPro's advanced features, you can develop powerful AutoCAD scripts.

Table 34.1   ScriptPro Save Commands

Save Command	Description
SCR-DXFOUT-2000	Saves the current drawing in AutoCAD 2000 DXF format
SCR-DXFOUT-R14	Saves the current drawing in AutoCAD R14 DXF format
SCR-DXFOUT-R13	Saves the current drawing in AutoCAD R13 DXF format
SCR-DXFOUT-R12	Saves the current drawing in AutoCAD R12 DXF format

Save Command	Description
SCR-SAVEAS-2000	Saves the current drawing in AutoCAD 2000 DWG format
SCR-SAVEAS-R14	Saves the current drawing in AutoCAD R14 DWG format
SCR-SAVEAS-R13	Saves the current drawing in AutoCAD R13 DWG format

Table 34.2   ScriptPro Keywords

Keyword	Description
<acet:cFolderName>	Specifies the folder name in which the current drawing resides.
<acet:cBaseName>	Specifies the current drawing's base filename, excluding its path and extension.
<acet:cExtension>	Specifies the extension for the current drawing file (DWG, DWT, or DXF).
<acet:cFileName>	Specifies the base name of the current drawing, including its extension.
<acet:cFullFileName>	Specifies the full filename of the current drawing, including its path and extension.

Understanding the Compatibility Information Feature

The Compatibility Information feature provides access to the Migrating to AutoCAD 2000 CAD Managers Guide, which contains a wealth of information. The Guide includes information that explains how to install and configure AutoCAD 2000. Additionally, the Guide explains how to manage a networked AutoCAD environment, and it explains how to transfer your current AutoCAD setup to AutoCAD 2000. By reviewing the Guide, you can seek important information about installing, deploying, configuring, and managing AutoCAD over a network.

The Guide consists of HTML files that are displayed on your system's browser. After you access the Guide by selecting the Compatibility Information feature, your browser launches, and then displays the opening page of the Guide. From within the browser, you can either scroll through the various topics included in the Guide or select bookmarks (hyperlinks) that instantly take you to the various topics in the Guide.

The Guide includes 15 major topics, briefly described as follows:

- **Assessing Your Current Installation**—This topic explains how to check that all your hardware and network protocols meet the minimumspecifications for AutoCAD 2000.

- **Installation, Configuration, and Registration**—This topic explains methods for network deployment and licensing for AutoCAD 2000.

- **Environment Changes**—This topic highlights command and environment changes that are likely to affect script and custom utility migrations to AutoCAD 2000.

- **Customization Migration**—This topic describes tools to help you migrate your custom menus, scripts, PGP files, and AutoLISP code to AutoCAD 2000.

- **Converting Drawing Files**—This topic provides reasons for converting drawings from earlier AutoCAD release formats to the AutoCAD 2000 format, and it describes methods and tools to assist in the conversion.

- **Plotting Enhancements**—This topic explains the new plotting, and related features, in AutoCAD 2000.

- **Working in a Mixed Release Environment**—This topic explains how to use AutoCAD 2000 to edit drawings while maintaining maximum compatibility with previous AutoCAD release drawing formats.

- **Migration Resources**—This topic provides tables that list resources, which can help you to migrate to AutoCAD 2000.

- **New, Retired, and Changed Commands**—This topic provides tables that describe new, removed, and enhanced AutoCAD commands.

- **New, Retired, and Changed System Variables**—This topic provides tables that describe new, obsolete, and expanded AutoCAD system variables.

- **AutoLISP and the Multiple Design Environment**—This topic explains the AutoCAD 2000 Visual LISP environment and how to use Visual LISP with AutoCAD's new multiple documents feature.

- **Changes to AutoLISP**—This topic describes the new, changed, and retired AutoLISP commands.

- **AutoCAD Release 14 Custom Files Directory**—This topic lists the files migrated to AutoCAD 2000 when you select the Migration checkbox during a single-user installation.

- **New Group Codes for Objects and Other Changes**—This topic provides a table that lists new AutoCAD 2000 group codes, which point to new properties or data.

- **Migration Tools and Wizards**—This topic provides a listing of the tools and wizards available to assist you with migrating to AutoCAD 2000.

Summary

In this chapter, you learned about numerous tools and features provided by AutoCAD 2000 Migration Assistance. These tools automate the process of migrating from previous releases of AutoCAD to AutoCAD 2000. You worked through exercises that showed you how to simultaneously convert multiple drawings to AutoCAD 2000 and how to check existing AutoLISP routines for compatibility with AutoCAD 2000. You reviewed tools that enable you to port existing custom menus and PGP files to AutoCAD 2000 and that enable you to convert color-dependent plot style drawings to named plot style format. You learned about tools that ease the task of deploying AutoCAD 2000 over a network and that simplify the process of creating an AutoCAD script file, which can automatically execute a series of commands on multiple drawings. In this chapter, you learned how to use the tools and features of the AutoCAD 2000 Migration Assistance application to ease the process of migrating your drawings and your custom files and applications to AutoCAD 2000.

35

CUSTOMIZING WITH **DIESEL**

*DIESEL is an acronym for **D**irect **I**nterpretively **E**valuated **S**tring* *E**xpression **L**anguage. Like AutoLISP, DIESEL is an AutoCAD Applica-* *tion Programming Interface, or API. Unlike AutoLISP, which derives* *from and is a dialect of the larger, well-known LISP language, DIESEL* *is unique to AutoCAD. Although DIESEL resembles AutoLISP in several* *important ways, it is not dependent upon AutoLISP for its operation. On* *the one hand, knowledge of AutoLISP certainly makes learning and* *using DIESEL easier. Similarly, having a working knowledge of DIESEL* *helps anyone wanting to learn AutoLISP.*

In addition to the catalog of frequently used DIESEL functions that *appears at the end of this chapter, the following topics are covered:*

■ *Understanding the mechanics of DIESEL*

■ *Learning DIESEL functions*

■ *Writing DIESEL expressions*

■ *Debugging DIESEL expressions*

■ *Using the MODEMACRO system variable*

■ *Using AutoLISP with DIESEL*

Introducing DIESEL

Although the DIESEL language is not as fast, robust, or flexible as AutoLISP, it does have several distinct capabilities not available with AutoLISP. First, you can configure the MODEMACRO system variable using a DIESEL expression. The content of the MODEMACRO system variable is displayed in a left-aligned pane in the status bar at the bottom of the AutoCAD window, as shown in Figure 35.1. Although the MODEMACRO system variable has no initial value by default, it can be made to display useful information using DIESEL. Historically, this is the primary use of DIESEL, and it is the usage discussed in this chapter.

Although beyond the scope of this chapter, DIESEL can also be used in pull-down menu labels. A DIESEL expression incorporated in this manner is evaluated dynamically each time the pull-down is activated, enableing label items to change appearance according to the conditions tested for by the underlying DIESEL expression.

Lastly, DIESEL expressions can also be placed in menu macros. If such a macro is executed, the DIESEL expression itself is evaluated. This enables you to add a degree of intelligence to menu macros without resorting to the use of AutoLISP.

NOTE

Like AutoLISP, DIESEL code is enclosed in parentheses; nesting is not only allowed but is frequently utilized. Any written DIESEL code that is intended to be evaluated and to have its output employed for some useful purpose is referred to as a DIESEL expression.

Figure 35.1

A customized status line added with the MODEMACRO system variable.

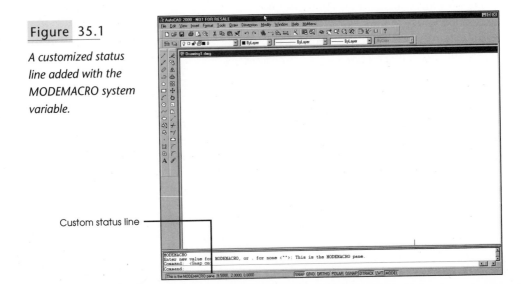

Custom status line

Understanding the Mechanics of DIESEL

Before beginning to work with DIESEL, you need to understand some of the basic characteristics of this specialized AutoCAD programming language. If you are familiar with AutoLISP, you should find DIESEL similar in most respects—especially, in DIESEL's use of parentheses and in its basic syntax. If, on the other hand, you have little or no experience with AutoLISP, learning the basics of DIESEL serves as a good foundation for learning AutoLISP later. Neither of the two languages pre-supposes knowledge of the other.

NOTE

For information about AutoLISP, refer to Chapter 22, "Introduction to AutoLISP Programming."

DIESEL is a macro-string evaluation language. It consists of a relatively small group of some twenty-eight functions that manipulate and process data in *string* form. A string is a data type that is common to most programming languages. Generally, strings are anything enclosed within a pair of double quotation marks. DIESEL expressions always generate string output.

As previously mentioned, both AutoLISP and DIESEL expressions are delimited by parentheses, and the first element following the open, or left, parenthesis is the name of the function. Generally, the function names in DIESEL are the same as their counterparts in AutoLISP. As in AutoLISP, DIESEL function names are not case-sensitive, but the rest of the data in a DIESEL expression is. The general form of a DIESEL expression is as follows:

```
$(function,argument1,argument2,…)
```

The following features are distinctive to DIESEL:

- A dollar sign ($) immediately precedes each opening (left) parenthesis.

- Each element (function or argument) within a parenthesis pair is considered a member of a list and, except for the final element, is followed by a comma.

- Two commas appearing consecutively, with nothing between them, represent a *null*, or empty, string.

- Each element in a DIESEL expression is delimited by a comma. Therefore, spaces that appear between two consecutive commas are interpreted literally, and they will appear in the result.

Here is a typical DIESEL function call:

```
$(getvar,snapunit)
```

In this example, the DIESEL function `getvar` returns the value of the AutoCAD system variable SNAPUNIT. The string that is returned contains the X and Y value of the current snap increment.

NOTE

> You cannot use DIESEL expressions, such as the preceding one, directly at the command prompt. Later in this chapter, an AutoLISP function is presented that enables you to enter DIESEL expressions at a command line prompt.

The following DIESEL expression uses the DIESEL function for addition:

```
$(+,2,5)
```

In this example, the sum of the integers, 2 and 5, would be returned as a string.

The following expression demonstrates the nesting of DIESEL expressions:

```
$(rtos,$(getvar,ltscale),2,4)
```

In this example, the current value of the LTSCALE system variable is first evaluated using the `getvar` function. This value, a real number, is then used as an argument for the `rtos` (real-to-string) function, which is formatted in decimal units to four places.

Learning DIESEL Functions

It is beyond the scope of this chapter to present all DIESEL functions with their required arguments and examples of their implementation. However, this can be easily accomplished anytime you have AutoCAD running, as shown in the following exercise.

ACCESSING DIESEL FUNCTION DEFINITIONS

1. In AutoCAD, with no command in progress, press F1.

2. In the Help Topics: AutoCAD Help dialog box, double-click Customization Guide, as seen in Figure 35.2.

Figure 35.2

Select the Customization Guide from the Help menu.

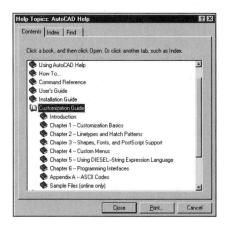

3. Double-click on Chapter 5, and in the contents list, double-click on the Catalog of DIESEL String Functions topic, as shown in Figure 35.3.

Figure 35.3

Select the Catalog of DIESEL String Functions from the Help Topics dialog box.

4. In the list of DIESEL string functions, select the function about which you want to learn, see Figure 35.4.

Figure 35.4

The catalog listing of DIESEL string functions available from Help.

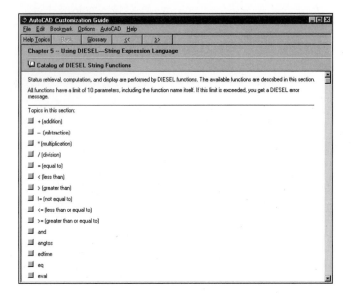

Practicing DIESEL Expressions

As mentioned earlier, you cannot enter DIESEL expressions directly on the command line as you can AutoLISP expressions. However, there is a "work-around" for this pesky limitation. The AutoLISP function, menucmd, enables the direct input and interpretation of DIESEL expressions. The following user-defined, AutoLISP function adds the DIESEL command to AutoCAD. After it is loaded, this new DIESEL command lets you enter DIESEL expressions on the command line. The expressions are evaluated and the result is displayed. This enables you to quickly test DIESEL expressions.

```
(Defun C:DIESEL (/ dsl)
  (while (/= "" (setq dsl (getstring T "\nDiesel>: ")))
    (print (menucmd (strcat "M=" dsl)))
  )
(princ)
)
```

NOTE

This C:DIESEL AutoLISP function appears on the accompanying CD as the file DIESEL.LSP. You might want to copy this file from the CD to a directory in your current AutoCAD library path, for example, the \SUPPORT directory under your AutoCAD installation.

In the following exercise, you first load the C:DIESEL function, and then use it to test several DIESEL functions.

TESTING DIESEL FUNCTIONS WITH C:DIESEL

1. In AutoCAD 2000's Tools menu, select AutoLISP, Load to display the Load/Unload Applications dialog box, as shown in Figure 35.5.

Figure 35.5

The Load/Unload
Applications dialog box.

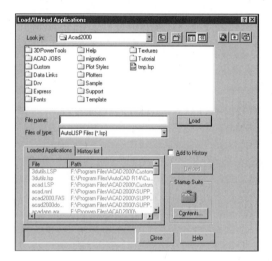

2. Using the file management facilities in the upper portion of the dialog box, navigate to the file DIESEL.LSP on the accompanying CD. (If you have copied this file to your AutoCAD directory structure, navigate there.)

3. With the DIESEL.LSP file appearing in the File name: input box, select the Load button as indicated in Figure 35.6. The statement "DIESEL.LSP loaded successfully." is displayed on the command line. Choose Close to close the dialog box.

Figure 35.6

Loading the DIESEL.LSP
file.

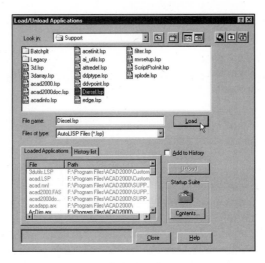

4. At the command prompt, type **DIESEL** and press Enter. The DIESEL>: prompt appears.

5. Enter **$(getvar, DWGNAME)**. DIESEL returns:

   ```
   "Drawing1.dwg"
   DIESEL>:
   ```

   If your current drawing name is different, that name will be returned.

6. Press Enter. The standard, AutoCAD command prompt returns.

7. Type **CIRCLE** (or **C**) and press Enter. Answer the following prompts as shown:

   ```
   Specify center point for circle or [3P/2P/Ttr (tan tan radius)]:
   ```

   Type **2.0,4.5** and press Enter.

   ```
   Specify radius of circle or [Diameter]:
   ```

   Type **1** and press Enter.

8. At the command prompt, again type **DIESEL** and press Enter. The DIESEL>: prompt appears.

9. Enter **$(getvar, CIRCLERAD)**. DIESEL returns:

   ```
   "1"
   DIESEL>:
   ```

10. Enter **$(getvar, LASTPOINT)**. DIESEL returns:

    ```
    "2,4.5,0"
    DIESEL>:
    ```

    (The "2,4.5,0" represents the value of the last point chosen.)

11. Enter **$(index, 1,$(getvar, LASTPOINT))**. DIESEL returns:

    ```
    "4.5"
    DIESEL>:
    ```

    (The "**4.5**" represents the value of the second element of the LASTPOINT system variable.)

12. Press Enter. The standard, AutoCAD command prompt returns.

After it is loaded into memory, the C:DIESEL AutoLISP function can be called by typing **DIESEL** at the command prompt. Pressing Enter at any DIESEL>: prompt causes the standard AutoCAD command prompt to return.

NOTE

> Notice that all the data returned by the C:DIESEL function in the preceding exercise is in the form of strings—they are surrounded by double quotation marks. Even the expressions that would be expected to output integer, or real number, data print their output as strings. Although a result of the way that the AutoLISP routine is written, it mimics the string data type produced by DIESEL.

The C:DIESEL function is a convenient and helpful aid to use while learning and testing DIESEL expressions. In most cases, the output of C:DIESEL reports typing or syntax errors as well as valid output. This capability is a helpful learning tool. For example, the following C:DIESEL input generates a corresponding error output:

```
DIESEL>: $(+ 3,5,2)
" $(+ 3)?? "
```

The error message points to the problem: The comma following the function (+, in this example) is absent, and the error message states that the function $(+ 3) is unknown. Correcting the expression to the following results in a valid output:

```
DIESEL>: $(+,3,5,2)
"10"
```

The C:DIESEL function also demonstrates that AutoLISP and DIESEL can co-exist. Keep in mind, however, that C:DIESEL is merely a handy learning and development aid; it performs no otherwise useful work.

Debugging DIESEL Expressions

As with AutoLISP expressions, DIESEL expressions can quickly become quite complex, with expressions nested within other expressions. Typographical and syntactical errors become frequent and are difficult to locate visually. A missing comma can quickly bring expression evaluation to a halt. Fortunately, a step-by-step method of tracing DIESEL expressions is built-in, helping to isolate such errors. AutoCAD's *undocumented* MACROTRACE system variable enables you to trace even the most complex DIESEL expression, pinpointing any errors. If you activate the MACROTRACE system variable (set it to a value of 1), the evaluation of all DIESEL expressions is *traced,* with each DIESEL expression (including any nested expressions) displayed as it is evaluated. The following exercise demonstrates how the MACROTRACE system variable works.

NOTE

The following exercise assumes that you have previously loaded the AutoLISP function C:DIESEL. This function is contained on the accompanying CD as the file DIESEL.LSP. (Refer to the preceding exercise for loading instructions.) If C:DIESEL is loaded, you can proceed to the following exercise.

TRACING DIESEL EXPRESSIONS

1. At the command prompt, type **MACROTRACE** and press enter. Answer the following prompt as shown:

    ```
    Enter new value for MACROTRACE <0>:
    ```

    Type **1** and press Enter.

2. At the command prompt, type **DIESEL** and press Enter. The following prompt appears:

    ```
    DIESEL>:
    ```

3. Carefully type the following DIESEL expression:

    ```
    $(if,$(=,$(+, 4,3),$(-, 10,3)),The Answer is Ten!)
    ```

4. Press Enter.

5. The following expression trace appears:

```
Eval: $(IF, $(=,$(+, 4,3),$(-, 10,3)), The Answer is Ten!)
Eval: $(=, $(+, 4,3), $(-, 10,3))
Eval: $(+,  4, 3)
===>  7
Eval: $(-,  10, 3)
===>  7
===>  1
===>  The Answer is Ten!
```

6. Enter the following DIESEL expression (the syntax error is intentional):

    $(*,10,$(+ 2,3))

7. The following expression trace appears:

```
Eval: $(*, 10, $(+ 2,3))
Eval: $(+ 2, 3)
Err:   $(+ 2)??
Err:   $(*,??)
```

8. Enter the following DIESEL expression:

    $(=,3,3)

9. The following expression trace appears:

```
Eval: $(=,  3, 3)
===>  1
"1"
```

10. Enter the following DIESEL expression:

    $(=,3,5)

11. The following expression trace appears:

```
Eval: $(=,  3, 5)
===>  0
"0"
```

12. At the DIESEL>: prompt, press Enter to return to a standard AutoCAD command prompt.

13. Type **MACROTRACE** and press Enter. Answer the following prompt as shown:

    ```
    Enter new value for MACROTRACE <1>:
    ```

    Type **0** and then press Enter.

14. The following expression trace appears:

    ```
    $(if,$(=,$(+, 4,3),$(-, 10,3)),The Answer is Ten!)
    ```

In Step 3 of the preceding exercise, you entered a complex DIESEL expression, nested two levels deep. This expression can be translated into non-code language as follows: "If the sum of the integers 4 and 3 is equal to the difference of the integers 10 and 3, return the string "The Answer is Ten!"." By following each successive line of the trace, you can see MACROTRACE's evaluation of each of the nested expressions. The addition expression is first evaluated and its value is then "printed." Next, the subtraction expression that is evaluated is its value printed. The entire IF expression is next evaluated and its value, 1, is printed. Finally, the "then" clause of the IF expression is printed, or returned. In this case, the string The Answer is Ten! is returned because the value of the IF expression is not nil, or True.

It is important to note that DIESEL expressions that evaluate as True (or non-nil) return the string 1, whereas nil (or False) expressions return the string 0. This is an important distinction from AutoLISP (and most other programming languages), which in evaluating True/False expressions returns the value T (for True) and nil for False. This is also demonstrated in Steps 8 through 11 of the preceding exercise. This difference becomes advantageous if DIESEL is employed to use various system variables as test predicates because system variables often are either "on" or "off"—or 1 or 0— respectively.

In Step 6 of the preceding exercise, the entered expression contains an syntactical error in that the $(+ function is not immediately followed by a comma. This is shown in the trace, which reports an error when $(+ 2 is encountered.

There are four error messages generated by MACROTRACE to help pinpoint the source, or nature, of the error. These messages are listed in the following table.

Error Message	Description
$?	Syntax error
$?(func,??)	Incorrect argument to a function
$(++)	Output string too long
$(func)??	Function unknown

As previously mentioned, the MACROTRACE system variable is undocumented but available in AutoCAD 2000. In combination with the C:DIESEL AutoLISP function, it is a valuable learning and error-tracing tool.

Creating Custom Status Lines with DIESEL

DIESEL was first introduced in AutoCAD Release 12. Its primary purpose was to provide a means of customizing AutoCAD's status line. The status line in AutoCAD is the bar appearing at the bottom of the AutoCAD application window. Without any customization, the status line appears as shown in Figure 35.7.

The status line is a valuable resource, providing the user with rapid access to frequently used functions, such as Grid and Snap settings. The status line also contains the coordinate read-out panel, which can be set to give a continuous display of the screen cursor's current position or the relative coordinates from a picked point. An additional, user-defined panel can be added immediately to the left of the coordinate readout panel. This customized, or expanded, status line can be configured to display a wide variety of useful information. The content of any customized status line is controlled by the MODEMACRO system variable.

Using the MODEMACRO System Variable

The MODEMACRO system variable displays a string of text, usually written in DIESEL or in a combination of DIESEL and AutoLISP languages on the status line. Unlike most other AutoCAD system variables that report (or "hold") data, such as the current drawing name or the on/off status of the ORTHO mode, MODEMACRO can be made to contain virtually any string of alpha-numeric characters you devise.

At startup, the value of the MODEMACRO system variable is set to the null string. In other words, it contains nothing. In this condition, the coordinate read-out panel appears at the extreme left of AutoCAD's status line as shown in Figure 35.7. To create a customized panel, give the MODEMACRO system variable a string value. It can be set to any string (such as text) value, the length of which is limited only by the size of the AutoCAD window. In practice, a long string assigned to MODEMACRO can force the standard AutoCAD panels completely off the display.

To set the MODEMACRO system variable, enter **MODEMACRO** at the command prompt or use the SETVAR command in conjunction with an AutoLISP expression. In the following exercise, you will see how the MODEMACRO system variable works by entering a static status line text display.

ASSIGNING A STATIC VALUE TO MODEMACRO

1. At the command prompt, enter **MODEMACRO**. Answer the following prompt as shown:

   Enter new value for MODEMACRO, or . for none <"">:

   Type **Dave's Macro Boutique** and press Enter (see Figure 35.8).

2. Press Enter to display the MODEMACRO prompt again. Answer the prompt by typing a period and pressing Enter. Note that the previous macro's status line setting is removed.

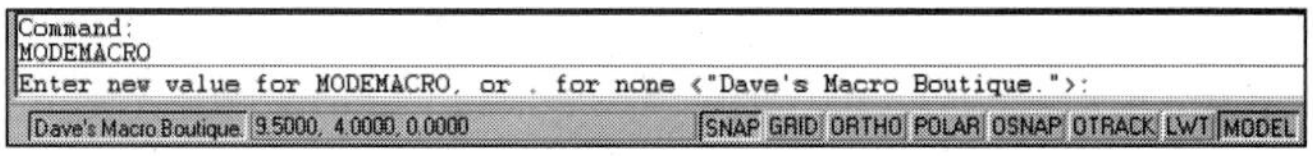

Figure 35.8

Displaying a static status line.

As you can see from the preceding exercise, assigning a value to MODEMACRO is not difficult. If you type a string at the MODEMACRO prompt, that string remains displayed on the status line for the remainder of your AutoCAD session or until you change it. However, it is not saved anywhere; you must type the message every time AutoCAD is started. The message Dave's Macro Boutique is uninformative, static, and conveys little with respect to the opened, active drawing. Fortunately, MODEMACRO can interactively display information that is more useful. Any of the many AutoCAD system variables, for example, can be displayed using DIESEL expressions. In the following exercise, you will use DIESEL to display the current drawing's name and prefix.

ASSIGNING A DYNAMIC VALUE TO MODEMACRO

1. At the command prompt, enter **MODEMACRO**. Answer the following prompt as shown:

   Enter new value for MODEMACRO, or . for none <"">:

   Type **$(getvar, dwgprefix)** and press Enter (see Figure 35.9).

Figure 35.9

*Displaying a static status
line with DIESEL.*

2. Press Enter to repeat the MODEMACRO command. Answer the prompt as shown:

   Enter new value for MODEMACRO, or . for none <"">:

   Type **$(getvar, dwgprefix)>>>$(getvar,dwgname)** and press Enter (see Figure 35.10).

Figure 35.10

*Adding more information
to the macro.*

NOTE

> Although the text of the MODEMACRO is displayed on multiple lines in the following step, you should type the text continuously at the MODEMACRO prompt.

3. Press Enter to re-start the MODEMACRO command. Type the following at the prompt:

   Enter new value for MODEMACRO, or . for none <"">:

   Type **$(getvar, dwgprefix)>>$(getvar,dwgname)>>Elapsed timer: $(rtos, $(*,24,$(getvar,TDUSRTIMER)),2,2) Hrs.** and press Enter (see Figure 35.11).

Figure 35.11

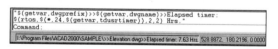

*Combining text and
DIESEL expressions in the
macro.*

In the preceding exercise, you added more information to the status line by expanding the MODEMACRO text string. In Step 1 (Figure 35.9), a simple DIESEL expression obtains the value of the DWGPREFIX system variable:

```
$(getvar,dwgprefix)
```

AutoCAD prints the current drawing name at the top of the drawing window, but the addition of the prefix adds useful information.

In Step 2 (Figure 35.10), the value of system variable DWGNAME is added. Two > characters are used to visually separate the two items.

```
$(getvar,dwgprefix)>>$(getvar,dwgname)
```

Any text typed at the MODEMACRO prompt—including typed spaces—is interpreted literally, and it appears along with evaluated DIESEL expressions. Typed text characters can be placed before, between, or following DIESEL expressions.

In Step 3 (Figure 35.11), additional text and a nested DIESEL expression are added:

```
$(getvar, dwgprefix)>>$(getvar,dwgname)>>Elapsed timer: $(rtos,
$(*,24,$(getvar,TDUSRTIMER)),2,2) Hrs.
```

The nested DIESEL expression uses the DIESEL function rtos, which prints a real number in a specified format and precision. The rtos function has the following general form:

```
$(rtos, value [,mode, precision])
```

The value argument to the rtos function in the preceding exercise is itself a nested expression that multiplies the value of the TDUSRTIMER system variable by 24 and that expresses the result in decimal mode (mode 2) to a precision of 2 decimal places. The TDUSRTIMER variable records the time of the user-elapsed timer expressed in days. Additional formatting is provided by the addition of the text phrases Elapsed timer: and Hrs..

The MODEMACRO string entered in the preceding exercise is typical of the information that you can format to appear on the status line. Virtually all data known to AutoCAD through its system variables can be displayed. In addition, DIESEL offers at least one function, EDTIME, which greatly facilitates the display of the current time as maintained by your computer. A listing of the most commonly used DIESEL functions can be found later in this chapter

Using AutoLISP with DIESEL

If you typed the DIESEL expressions found in the preceding exercise, you probably discovered that entering DIESEL and text manually at the MODEMACRO prompt is a tedious and error-prone process. In addition, you need to manually enter any customized status line macro display every time you start AutoCAD. Using AutoLISP to format, record, and load your MODEMACRO strings makes this procedure easier, faster, and error-free.

You can assign a value to the MODEMACRO system variable using the AutoLISP function `setvar`. The following user-defined AutoLISP function takes the DIESEL/ text input in Step 3 of the preceding exercise and automatically sets the value of MODEMACRO.

LISTING 35.1   CODE LISTING FOR MODE1 AUTOLISP FUNCTION

```
(defun C:mode1 ()
  (setvar "MODEMACRO"
    (strcat
      "$(getvar, dwgprefix)>>"
      "$(getvar,dwgname)>>"
      "Elapsed timer: $(rtos,
      $(*,24,$(getvar,TDUSRTIMER)),2,2) Hrs."
    )
  )
)
```

NOTE

> The MODEMACRO input code for this function is visually broken down into two relatively short strings and one longer string for clarity. See Chapter 22 for more about AutoLISP. The code for this macro is contained on the accompanying CD as the file MODE1.LSP.

Type this code into any text editor, such as Microsoft Notepad, and save it as MODE1.LSP in your AutoCAD installation's \Support directory. In the following exercise, you load and run this function.

LOADING AND RUNNING AN AUTOLISP MODEMACRO

1. At the command prompt, press Enter and observe the following:

   ```
   Command: (load "mode1")
   C:MODE1
   Command: mode1 Enter
   ```

2. Observe the status line. It should appear similar to Figure 35.11.

3. To return to the standard AutoCAD status line, answer the following prompts as shown:

   ```
   Command:
   ```

   Type **MODEMACRO** and press Enter.

   ```
   Enter new value for MODEMACRO, or . for none
   ➥<"$(getvar,dwgprefix)>>$(getvar,dwgname)>>Elapsed timer: $(rt...">:
   ```

   Type a period (.) and press Enter.

As an alternative, you can place the AutoLISP code for the preceding MODE1.LSP AutoLISP function in a file named ACAD.LSP. This causes the mode1 function to be evaluated and loaded into memory every time AutoCAD is started. Then, to display the mode1 status line, you need only type **mode1** and press enter at the command prompt. (See Chapter 22 for more information about the ACAD.LSP file.)

Using a Status Line for 3D Work

You can devise status line macros to display all types of information that is known internally to AutoCAD through its system variables. The following AutoLISP function, C:macro3D, is an example of a status line macro intended to display information helpful to those working in a 3D environment.

Listing 35.2 Code Listing for macro3D AutoLISP Function

```
(defun C:macro3D ()
 (setvar "modemacro"
  (strcat
   "<$(if,$(=,1,$(getvar,Highlight)) ,HI,hi)>"
```

```
     " USC= $(if,$(eq,"",$(getvar,ucsname)),none,$(getvar,ucsname))"
     " Elev= $(getvar,Elevation)"
     " Thick= $(getvar,Thickness) "
   )
  )
 )
```

Again, in this code listing, the macro is broken up into four separate strings to make reading and possible editing easier. The strings are "glued" back together function-ally with the AutoLISP `strcat` function. The DIESEL IF,= and eq functions are used in this macro to test the values of the HIGHLIGHT and UCSNAME system variables. A catalog of frequently used DIESEL functions appears at the end of this chapter.

NOTE

> The AutoLISP code for C:macro3d appears on the accompanying CD as the file MACRO3D.LSP.

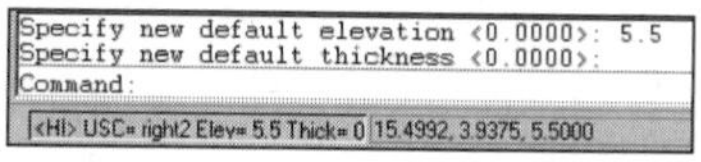

Figure 35.12

A custom status line for 3D work.

As with the C:mode1 listing, the code for C:macro3D can be placed in a file named ACAD.LSP and loaded automatically when AutoCAD starts. To display the macro3D status line, type **macro3D** at the command prompt.

You can use the mode1 and macro3D listings as models, or templates, for other status line macros.

Catalog of Frequently Used DIESEL Functions

Like the functions in AutoLISP—to which they bear a strong resemblance—the various DIESEL functions can be used to perform a variety of useful work, including mathematical and logical operations, the retrieval of AutoCAD system variable values, and the printing of data to the status line. DIESEL functions are not as numerous as those available in AutoLISP and they are limited to a maximum of ten parameters, including the name of the function. The +, or addition, function can accept only nine arguments, for example. Unlike AutoLISP, you cannot define new DIESEL functions. Despite these, and certain other limitations, the catalog of DIESEL functions is more than adequate for working with and composing customized status line macros.

Keep in mind that DIESEL is a string-processing language, and it expects strings as input and returns strings to its environment.

The following is a list of the more commonly used DIESEL functions and examples of their use.

Addition, +

```
$(+,num1,num2[,...num9])
```

This function calculates and returns the sum of up to nine numbers. The numbers can be integers or real numbers.

```
$(+,5.5,10,2)              →"17.5"
```

Subtraction, -

```
$(-,num1,num2[,...num9])
```

This function calculates and returns the result of subtracting num2 through num9 from num1.

```
$(-, 12,9)                 →"3"
$(-,12,9,2)                →"1"
```

Multiplication, *

```
$(*, num1,num2[,...num9])
```

This function calculates and returns the result of multiplying num1, num2, ...num9.

```
$(*,2,5)                   →"10"
$(*,2,5,3.0)               →"30.0"
```

Division, /

```
$(/,num1[,num2...num9])
```

This function calculates and returns the result of dividing num1 by num2..num9.

```
$(/, 14,7)                 →"2"
$(/,150,5,2.0)             →"15"
$(/,7,2)                   →"3.5"
```

Equal to, =
`$(=,num1,num2)`

This function compares two numbers and determines whether they are equal. If they are, the condition is True and the function returns 1. If the two numbers are not equal, the condition is False and the function returns 0 (zero).

`$(=,4,4)`	→"1"
`$(=,4,4.0)`	→"1"
`$(=,4,8)`	→"0"
`$(=,6,$(*,2,3))`	→"1"

Not Equal to, !=
`$(!=,num1,num2)`

This function compares two numbers and determines whether they are not equal. If they are, the condition is True and the function returns 1. If the two numbers are equal, the condition is False and the function returns 0.

`$(!=,4,4)`	→"0"
`$(!=,4,4.0)`	→"0"
`$(!=,4,8)`	→"1"
`$(!=,6,$(*,2,3))`	→"0"

Greater than, >
`$(>,num1,num2)`

This function checks to see if num1 is greater than num2. The function returns 1 if the condition is True, and if it is False, 0.

`$(>,12,8)`	→"1"
`$(>,8,12)`	→"0"

Less than, <
`$(<,num1,num2)`

This function checks to see if num1 is less than num2. The function returns 1 if the condition is True, and if it is False, 0.

`$(<,8,12)`	→"1"
`$(<,12,8)`	→"0"

Greater than or equal to, >=
`$(>=,num1,num2)`

This function checks to see if num1 is greater than or equal to num2. The function returns 1 if the condition is True, and if it is False, 0.

`$(>=,7,7)`	→"1"
`$(>=,4,3)`	→"1"
`$(>=,4,2)`	→"0"

Less than or equal to, <=
`$(<=,num1,num2)`

This function checks to see if num1 is less than or equal to num2. The function returns 1 if the condition is True, and if it is False, 0.

```
$(<=,7,7)              →"1"
$(<=,4,3)              →"0"
$(<=,4,2)              →"1"
```

and
`$(and,int1 [,int2,...int9])`

This function returns the bit-wise logical and of integers int1 through int9.

```
$(and,5,7)             →"5"
$(and,4,7,15)          →"4"
$(and,16,32)           →"0"
```

angtos
`$(angtos,angle [,mode,precision]`

This function returns the angle (expressed in radians) in the mode and precision specified. If no mode or precision is included, the angle is expressed in the current mode and the precision as specified by the UNITS command. The following list gives the modes available:

Mode	Format
01	Degrees
02	Degrees/minutes/seconds
03	Grads
04	Radians
05	Surveyor's units

```
$(angtos,0.79,0,3)     →"45.264"
$(angtos,0.79,1,2)     →"45d16'"
$(angtos,.79,3,4)      →"0.7900r"
$(angtos,.79,4,2)      '"N 44d44' E"
```

edtime
`$(edtime, time, format)`

This function edits the AutoCAD Julian date given in time (from $(getvar, date) for example) in the specified format. The form consists of format phrases as shown in the following list:

Format	Output	Format	Output
D	5	H	4
DD	05	HH	04
DDD	Sat	MM	53
DDDD	Saturday	SS	17
M	9	MSEC	506
MO	09	AM/PM	AM
MON	Sep	am/pm	am
MONTH	September	A/P	A
YY	98	a/p	a
YYYY	1998		

```
$(edtime,$(getvar,date),ddd mo yy      "11 Oct 99"
$(edtime,$(getvar,date),dddd dd mo yy","hh:mm)
                                    Monday 11 Oct 99,12:19
```

Notice, in the second example, the inclusion of the comma and colon characters. The comma must be enclosed in double quote to prevent it being evaluated as the standard DIESEL list separator.

eq

$(eq,string1,string2)

This function checks whether two string values are identical. If they are identical the function returns 1, otherwise it returns 0. In the next example, assume the current UCS is named "front-elev."

```
$(eq,$(getvar,ucsname),front-elev)      ➜"1"
```

fix

$(fix,real)

This function converts a real number into an integer, truncating the digits after the decimal.

```
$(fix,45.765)              ➜"45"
```

getvar

$(getvar,sysvar)

This function returns the value of an AutoCAD system variable. In the following examples, assume the current drawing is named "1-floor-plan", Snap is turned off, and a running Osnap of Endpoint, Midpoint, and Quadrant are set.

```
$(getvar,dwgname)          →"1-floor-plan"
$(getvar,snapmode)         →"0"
$(getvar,osmode)           '"19"
```

rtos

$(rtos,num [,mode,precision])

This function converts a number into a real number expressed in the specified mode and to the specified precision. If no mode or precision is specified, it returns the number in the current mode and the precision as set in UNITS command. The following modes are available:

Mode	Format
1	Scientific
2	Decimal
3	Engineering
4	Architectural
5	Fractional

```
$(rtos,40,2,2)             →"40.00"
$(rtos,40,4,1)             →"3'-4\""
$(rtos,2.75,5,3)           →"2 _"
```

if

$(if,condition,then[,else])

This function evaluates condition. If condition is other than zero, then is evaluated; otherwise, else is evaluated.

```
$(if,$(=,3,3),equal,not equal)       →"equal"
$(if,$(!=,4,4),,fails)               →"fails"
```

strlen
$(strlen,string)

This function returns the number of characters in a string.

```
$(strlen,abra kadabra)          →"12"
$(strlen,abrakadabra)           →"11"
```

Summary

In this chapter you have used DIESEL, the string expression language embedded inside AutoCAD, to compose a customized status line, thereby providing a more informative, dynamic user interface. The chapter's examples and exercises provide you with the basic principles of how DIESEL can be used to extract useful information and to display it in a convenient manner. Using these examples, you can build customized status line displays that can make your particular AutoCAD interface work more efficiently.

INSTALLING **2000** IN THE BUSINESS ENVIRONMENT

This chapter discusses the methods to install and configure AutoCAD 2000 on Microsoft Windows 95, 98, and NT operating systems on a network. Although considered network administrator territory, knowledge of the methods used to setup a network installation of AutoCAD 2000 can be helpful when network systems change and need adjustment.

The primary need for a network installation of AutoCAD is greater utilization of software resources. Instead of purchasing individual AutoCAD licenses for each user, you can assign each user a percentage of your total AutoCAD needs. By sharing the application licensing, you can often save up to 50 percent of your software costs. In addition to controlling expenses, sharing AutoCAD on a network can greatly increase the ease of installation and the maintenance of the application. Therefore, even if you do not need to share the program license, using a network installation can greatly decrease your support needs.

This chapter discusses the following subjects:

- Installing all network modules on a single server
- Networking communication protocols
- Using the Network Setup Wizard
- Licensing and activation
- Installing an AutoCAD image

Planning Your Network Installation

The process involved in setting up AutoCAD to run in a network environment can be intimidating, although it is not very complicated. Success is not guaranteed because of the varying network configurations and the process followed. The AutoCAD 2000 Installation Guide provides extensive documentation of the multiple methods possible in preparing a network installation of AutoCAD. We will provide a clear step-by-step process using a typical networking option.

Understanding Networking Configurations

The AutoCAD 2000 Network Installation package consists of three modules that enable you to select the optimum configuration for your network system. The various options associated with these modules are determined by factors specific to your network, including the number of users you have, the access speed your users require, and your server's performance capabilities. By selecting the network installation options most appropriate for your needs, you can provide your users with the optimum method of installation and usability for AutoCAD 2000.

The network installation contains three modules:

- **Autodesk License Manager (AdLM)**—This program controls the available licenses of various Autodesk products, including AutoCAD 2000. This ensures that AutoCAD can only be executed if an available license is not being used.

- **AutoCAD Run Tree**—A network-based drive in which AutoCAD 2000 is installed. All AutoCAD users connected to this network run AutoCAD from this remote drive.

- **Deployment Location**—A network drive on which a pre-configured AutoCAD setup is located. A network client user would execute the SETUP.EXE file located here to install AutoCAD to their local drive.

Each of these network modules can be located on the same server drive or on separate servers. Several issues, such as network performance, help to guide you to the best network installation option.

Installing All Modules on a Single Server

In most typical situations (where you require less than 100 AutoCAD seats), you can install the AdLM, an AutoCAD Run Tree, and the Deployment Location, all on a single server. The server only needs to provide enough storage space for the AutoCAD files (500MG/minute) and an adequate network connection.

For these smaller networks (using less than 100 license seats), installing the elements on a single server enables AutoCAD users to still experience high performance while at the same time, the AutoCAD system administration and maintenance are greatly simplified.

In large networks where you have more than 100 AutoCAD seats, the AdLM, an AutoCAD Run Tree, and the Deployment Location should probably be located on separate servers. For example, one could place the AdLM on the primary or DHCP server, the Run Tree on a File Server with a fast hard drive, and the Deployment Location on a system used for software installation storage. This maintains the optimum levels of performance, both at the time of installation and during times of AutoCAD usage.

Exploring Network Communication Protocols

The AdLM program uses either TCP/IP or IPX network protocols to manage Autodesk products, AutoCAD 2000. TCP/IP is the preferred format for the Windows NT environment, whereas IPX is preferred for Novell networks. The protocol you choose is largely based on your network type.

The AdLM automatically defaults to the network protocol TCP/IP. This protocol requires Windows NT 4.0 or higher on the server or workstation products.

For Novell networking systems, only versions 3.12 and 5.x are compatible with the IPX version of the AdLM. They also must be run from a system, or a remote console. If you choose to use Novell, you need to manually install the AdLM on the server after using the Network Setup Wizard.

NOTE

Please refer to the AutoCAD 2000 Installation Guide for more information on using AutoCAD 2000 with a Novell network installation.

Using the Network Setup Wizard

AutoCAD provides a Network Setup Wizard, which steps you through the process of setting up AutoCAD to run on your server or client workstations. The wizard enables you to choose from three basic installation types, all of which include loading the AdLM. By using the wizard, you can easily load the AdLM and select the installation options that best suit your needs.

NOTE

The network installation process requires access to the server on which you intend to install the AdLM and access to a client workstation.

The following exercise describes the process of installing the AdLM:

INSTALLING ADLM

1. Log on to the server computer station as Administrator. This station houses the AdLM.

   Insert the AutoCAD 2000 CD into the CD-ROM drive.

2. If an installation program begins, cancel it and exit.

3. From the Start menu, pick Run and type in the CD-ROM drive letter followed by **\netsetup\setup**. On a typical station, this would be **D:\netsetup\setup**. The Network Installation Selection dialog box is shown in Figure 36.1.

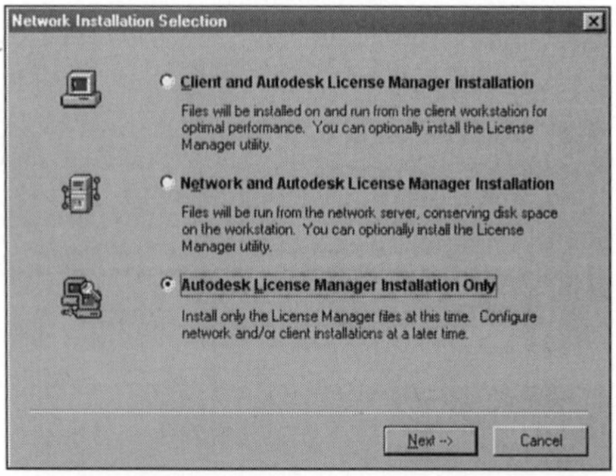

Figure 36.1

The Network Installation Selection dialog box lets you customize the entire installation process.

4. Select the Autodesk License Manager Installation Only option and click Next. The Autodesk License Manager Installation dialog box appears (see Figure 36.2).

Figure 36.2

This dialog box controls the portions of the AdLM to install, the directory name used, and the networking protocol to use.

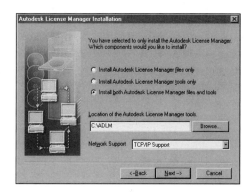

5. For the location of the files, use the text box and provide a drive and directory in which to store the AdLM files. Typically, the default suffices, but alternatives can be used.

NOTE

You cannot use a remote or non-local drive as a location for the AdLM files.

6. In the Network support list, choose TCP/IP Support and click Next. The Folder Name dialog box appears as shown in Figure 36.3.

Figure 36.3

The Folder Name dialog box controls Start menu placement.

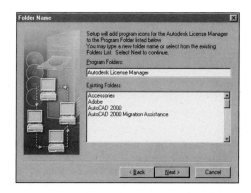

7. Select the desired folder location for the AdLM tools start menu shortcuts and click Next. The Setup Confirmation dialog box appears as shown in Figure 36.4.

Figure 36.4

The Setup Confirmation dialog box summarizes your setup parameters.

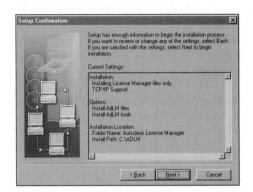

8. The AdLM installation is complete. You need to restart the server to start the service and register the AdLM product properly.

After the AdLM has been installed, the next step is to activate the AutoCAD 2000 licenses that the AdLM software uses. The next section provides an example for this process.

Activating Your Software Licenses

After installing the many files for the AdLM Manager, you need to configure the AdLM for your software licenses and quantities. The following exercise provides an example for the procedure.

CONFIGURING AdLM FOR YOUR SOFTWARE LICENSES

1. Log on to the AdLM server computer station as Administrator.

2. From the Start menu in Windows, select Programs, Autodesk License Manager, and then AdLM Admin. The AdLM license dialog box appears (see Figure 36.5).

Figure 36.5

The AdLM: TCP/IP Create Floating License dialog box enables you to install licenses for Autodesk network compatible software.

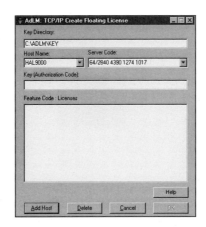

Review the AdLM dialog box. The Key Directory is where the AdLM was installed in the previous exercise. The Host Name is the machine name of the computer system where the AdLM software is installed. Moreover, the Server Code is a value generated using the Server's TCP/IP address and an internal software algorithm.

NOTE

The Server Code is based on the IP address on the server. If this address is changed, you are required to retrieve a new Authorization Code from Autodesk for the network applications to find a network lock.

3. After obtaining your Authorization Code from Autodesk, enter the sequence into the Key (Authorization Code) text box (see Figure 36.6).

Figure 36.6

The Authorization Code for creating 10 licenses of AutoCAD 2000 on an AdLM Installation.

4. After successful input of the code, the OK button is enabled. Click the OK button to complete the Key creation (see Figure 36.7).

Figure 36.7

Once you successfully install a license for AutoCAD 2000, you are shown an AdLM dialog box notifying the feature (150 is AutoCAD 2000) and the quantity of the licenses now available.

5. After verifying the appropriate licenses, click the OK button to close the message box and the AdLM License dialog box automatically closes. You can once again start the AdLM License dialog box to review the new settings (see Figure 36.8).

Figure 36.8

The AdLM License dialog box now shows 10 licenses for feature 150 (AutoCAD 2000) and the key box is now cleared.

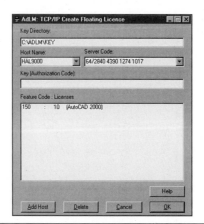

NOTE

As you need to add or subtract licenses from the AdLM installation, simply obtain a new Key Authentication Code and enter it into the AdLM License dialog box. If you are changing an existing serial number, it will simply reflect the new license count when complete. If you are adding another product, such as Mechanical Desktop, you find another entry with another product code and license count.

After completing the AdLM installation and creating a license quantity to use AutoCAD on the network, the next step is to install a setup image on the server. This image is what users on the network use to install AutoCAD 2000 on their workstation's C: drive.

The next section shows the procedure to install the setup image from a client station to a server on the network.

Creating the Client Image

Now that we have completed the AdLM installation and activation, the next step is to install the client deployment location. You will have better success installing these files if done from a client station on the network rather than from the AdLM server. The following steps outline this process.

NOTE

It is best to install the image using a client station rather than the server itself. This helps you verify network paths and sharing.

INSTALLING THE CLIENT DEPLOYMENT LOCATION

1. From the client workstation, log on to a client computer station as Administrator.

2. Insert the AutoCAD 2000 CD into the CD-ROM drive.

   If an installation program begins, cancel it and exit.

3. From the Start menu, pick Run and type in the CD-ROM drive letter followed by **\netsetup\setup**. On a typical station, this would be **D:\netsetup\setup**. The Network setup dialog box appears (see Figure 36.9).

Figure 36.9

The Network Installation Selection dialog box with three options.

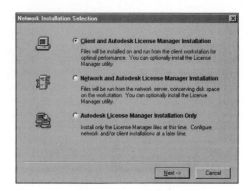

4. Select the Client and Autodesk License Manager Installation option and click Next. The Autodesk License Manager Installation dialog box appears (see Figure 36.10).

Figure 36.10

The available Autodesk License Manager Installation options.

5. In the Installation Options area, select to Install Autodesk License Manager files later and click Next. The Installation Directories dialog box appears (see Figure 36.11).

NOTE

Earlier we installed the AdLM onto the server computer so it is unnecessary to install it again. By selecting to 'Install Autodesk License Manager files later,' we are simply skipping that process because it is already completed.

Figure 36.11

The Installation Folders dialog box enables network placement for the AutoCAD setup image.

6. In the Client Deployment Location text box enter the network server and share name in which to store the files.

NOTE

In this example, we are using a server and share name plus directory structures to locate the files. The key to remember is that this path is what is used to install the files, so the client workstations need a location to which they have access. You also do not want a location that changes after you install.

NOTE

If you move these files after installation, it will disable the setup program's capability to find the image files.

7. Verify that the Client installations will be run in Silent mode option is checked and click Next. The Client Installation Location dialog box appears (see Figure 36.12).

NOTE

This control enables the administrator to predetermine what AutoCAD 2000 modules are installed so that all clients' setups are identical. It is recommended to enable this option.

Figure 36.12

The Client Installation Location dialog box controls where AutoCAD is installed on the client station's hard drive.

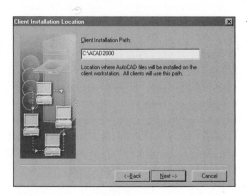

8. In the Client Installation Path text box enter in **C:\ACAD2000** and click Next. The Client Setup Type dialog box appears (see Figure 36.13).

NOTE

A typical non-network, single installation defaults to C:\Program Files\Acad2000, and that can be used here as well; but quick access to the AutoCAD directory structure can be helpful. Using a long file path makes access much more difficult in a shell or DOS command prompt window. It is recommended to use just C:\ACAD2000, which requires that the client workstation's C: drive has sufficient disk space.

Figure 36.13

The Client Setup Type dialog box determines what installation type is installed to the client stations.

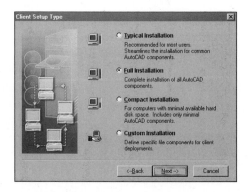

9. Select the Full Installation option and click Next. The Serial Number dialog box appears (see Figure 36.14).

NOTE

> If you select the Typical or Compact installation, a number of files, such as Express Tools, Samples, and portions of Help, are not installed. If you select this option, some users might need secondary access to the Installation CD to install these files. It is recommended for network systems to use the Full Installation option.

Figure 36.14

The Serial Number dialog box requires your valid master serial number and CD key.

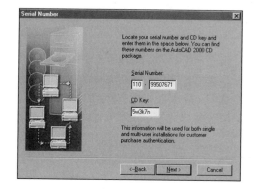

10. Enter your primary, or master, serial number into the text boxes provided on this dialog box and click Next. The Personal Information dialog box appears (see Figure 36.15).

NOTE

> Enter the CD Key provided in the AutoCAD 2000 packaging. This can be found on the back of the Installation Book and materials pack.

Figure 36.15

The Personal Information dialog box provides a location to enter your name, company, and reseller data. This information can later be accessed through the Help, About menu option within AutoCAD.

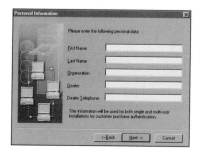

11. Enter all applicable personal, organization, and dealer information into the text boxes provided and click Next. The Setup Configuration dialog box appears (see Figure 36.16).

NOTE

Be aware that all installations will provide this information, so in large installations it is recommended to provide phone information to the IT (Information Technology) department instead of the actual software dealer. It can become expensive and unproductive to have your network users calling the software dealer, and it should be controlled.

Figure 36.16

The Setup Configuration dialog box enables you to review settings before proceeding with the image installation.

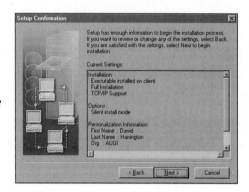

12.   Verify all setup parameters and click Next to complete the installation.

Now that the setup files have been successfully installed to the server, each client workstation only has to execute the SETUP.EXE file stored in the \ACAD2000 directory on the server to install their own local copy of AutoCAD 2000. The following section shows how quick and easy this process is.

Installing an AutoCAD Image

If the AutoCAD image is completely stored on the server, you can then install AutoCAD 2000 on the client workstations so that it can be used. The process to do this cannot get any easier: a single click does all the work. The example of this activity follows.

INSTALLING AUTOCAD 2000 ON CLIENT WORKSTATIONS

1. From the client workstation, log on to the server computer station as Administrator.

2. Browse the network to the server and share name where the AutoCAD 2000 image was stored. In our preceding example, this was `\\hal9000\software\autodesk\acad2000`.

3. In this directory, you'll find a `SETUP.EXE` file; click it to begin the installation.

   As this installation proceeds, information as to what is happening is listed for your perusal (see Figure 36.17). There is nothing more for you to do now. Just sit back and enjoy the beauty of silent installations.

Figure 36.17

The Installing AutoCAD dialog box provides basic information on the installation process.

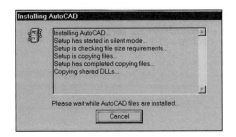

> **N**OTE
>
> After it is finished, the dialog box closes automatically. It does not force a restart of the system so you will need to do this manually.

When the system comes back up after restart, AutoCAD 2000 is now ready to configure and use.

4. Repeat this process on all stations that share the network installation.

Summary

This chapter showed what issues need preplanning before implementing a network installation. You saw how the typical Windows NT network would be used to install the AdLM using TCP/IP protocols. Then, you learned how to do a typical image setup based on a server share with a full installation option. Finally, you experienced the ease of actually installing AutoCAD onto a station using the shared client deployment location. Now you and your company can truly benefit from sharing AutoCAD resources and saving on licensing fees.

37

ADVANCED PLOTTING

AutoCAD provides two useful features that enhance your plotting ability. The first is AutoCAD's ePlot feature, which enables you to create plots that display over the Internet. The other is AutoCAD 2000's Batch Plot Utility, which enables you to identify a group of drawings and then plot them all automatically, using a single command. By using these two features, you can enhance your productivity either by sharing drawings over the Internet, with clients and colleagues, or by automatically plotting dozens, or even hundreds of drawings with a single button click.

This chapter discusses the following subjects:

■ *Using the ePlot feature to create DWF files*

■ *Creating a DWF Plot Configuration file*

■ *Creating Batch Plot (BP3) files*

■ *Editing Batch Plot files*

■ *Automatically plotting multiple drawings using a Batch Plot file*

This chapter is divided into two major sections. The first discusses the AutoCAD's ePlot feature. The second discusses the AutoCAD Batch Plot Utility.

Publishing Drawings on the Internet with ePlot

The Internet provides a way to do many different things. You can use the Internet to shop for products, such as this book, from any location in the world. You can view the activities and services of local, state, and federal governments. You can do online banking and investing. Through the Internet, you can use your PC to do many useful things, all from the convenience of your home or office.

AutoCAD 2000 extends the usefulness of the Internet by helping you to meet certain plotting demands. Through AutoCAD's ePlot feature, you can create electronic plots of drawings and publish them to your Web. Through the ePlot feature, you can distribute and share plots of your drawings over the Internet with anyone, anywhere in the world. By using ePlot, you can instantly transmit plots of your drawings to clients and colleagues throughout the world.

What makes the ePlot feature so powerful is its capability to enable others to not only view drawings through their Internet browser, but to also create hardcopy plots of the drawings using their own plotter. This means that if you must deliver a set of hardcopy plots to your colleagues, you can do so by using ePlot to publish your drawings on the Internet, and then instruct your colleagues to create hardcopy plots of your drawings at their location through their Internet browser. By using ePlot, you can quickly allow anyone, anywhere, to create hardcopy plots of your drawings from their Internet browser, using their own plotter.

NOTE

> For detailed information on publishing ePlot files to the Web and sharing them over the Internet, see Chapter 25, "Publishing on the Web."

In the following section, you learn about the relationship between the new ePlot feature and AutoCAD's DWF file format.

Using ePlot to Create DWF Files

If you create an electronic plot using ePlot, you are actually creating a DWF (Drawing Web Format) file. The DWF format was first introduced with AutoCAD Release 13, and it is a special file type that can be viewed through an Internet browser using Autodesk's Whip!® 4.0 plug-in.

NOTE

> The Autodesk WHIP!® 4.0 plug-in enables anyone to open, view, and plot DWF files without using AutoCAD. The plug-in also supports real-time panning and zooming, and it enables you to control the display of layers and to recall named views.
>
> You can review detailed information about the WHIP!® 4.0 plug-in's features in Chapter 25, in the section titled "Viewing DWF Files with WHIP!"
>
> The WHIP!® 4.0 plug-in is a free download from Autodesk's Web site at http://www.autodesk.com/whip/.

To create a DWF file using the new ePlot feature, you must first create a DWF plot configuration file, as demonstrated in the following section.

Creating a DWF Plot Configuration File

To create a DWF file using the new ePlot feature, you must use a plot configuration (PC3) file configured for the DWF file format. AutoCAD 2000 provides twoPC3 files that are already pre-configured for the DWF file format, and you can use these files to create DWF files. However, Autodesk enables you to set certain values in the PC3 file that affect the appearance of the final DWF file; you can set these values by configuring your own PC3 files. By creating your own PC3 files to use with the new ePlot feature, you control how your DWF files appear when shared over the Internet.

You configure PC3 files using the Add-A-Plotter Wizard, which is accessed from the new Autodesk Plotter Manager. The Add-A-Plotter Wizard steps you through the process of creating PC3 files. By using the Add-A-Plotter Wizard, you can easily create a PC3 file that is configured for the DWF file format.

NOTE

> For detailed information on the new Autodesk Plotter Manager, see Chapter 20, "Productive Plotting," in the section titled "The New Autodesk Plotter Manager."

In the following exercise, you use the Add-A-Plotter Wizard to create a PC3 file configured for the DWF file format.

CREATING A DWF PLOT CONFIGURATION FILE

1. From the File menu, select Plotter Manager.

   AutoCAD displays the Plotter Manager folder, as shown in Figure 37.1. This folder is where AutoCAD stores PC3 files and where you access the Add-A-Plotter Wizard.

Figure 37.1

The Autodesk Plotter Manager stores PC3 files in the same directory in which you access the Add-A-Plotter Wizard.

2. Double-click the Add-A-Plotter Wizard. The Wizard displays the Add Plotter — Introduction Page.

3. Select the Next button. The Wizard displays the Add Plotter — Begin page. You indicate the print device that you want to use on the Begin page.

4. Select the My Computer radio button, and then select the Next button. The Wizard displays the Add Plotter — Plotter Model page.

   You select the printer/plotter manufacturer and model type on the Plotter Model page.

5. From the Manufacturers list, select Autodesk ePlot (DWF).

6. From the Models list, select DWF ePlot (shown in Figure 37.2) and then select the Next button.

Figure 37.2

Select the Autodesk ePlot (DWF) plot device on the Plotter Model page.

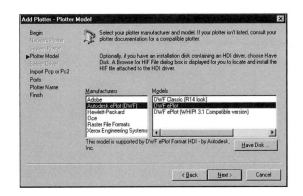

The Wizard displays the Add Plotter — Import PCP or PC2 page. This page enables you to import certain PCP and PC2 file information into the PC3 file.

NO T E

AutoCAD enables PC3 files to import certain PCP and PC2 information, such as pen optimization, plot-to-file configurations, paper size and orientation, resolution, device name, and plot destination.

7. Select the Next button. The Wizard displays the Add Plotter — Ports page. This page is where you indicate that you want to plot to a file.

8. Be sure the Plot to File radio button is selected, and then select the Next button. The Wizard displays the Add Plotter — Plotter Name page. This page is where you assign a descriptive name to the PC3 file. Because you are defining a PC3 file that creates a high-resolution DWF file, you should choose an appropriate name.

9. In the Plotter Name text box, type **Hi-Res ePlot** (as shown in Figure 37.3), and then select the Next button.

Figure 37.3

Assign a descriptive name to the PC3 file at the Plotter Name page.

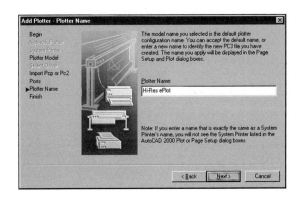

The Wizard displays the Add Plotter — Finish page. This page notes that the PC3 file is installed, and it enables you to edit the PC3 file settings. You will edit the PC3 file settings in the following exercise.

10. Select the Finish button.

The Hi-Res ePlot PC3 file is created and saved in the Plotter Manager folder, and is now available for use as a plotter configuration.

Creating PC3 files is easy with the new Add-A-Plotter Wizard. Next, you use the Plotter Configuration Editor to edit the Hi-Res ePlot PC3 file and modify several of its settings.

EDITING A DWF PLOT CONFIGURATION FILE

1. From the File menu, select Plotter Manager. AutoCAD displays the Plotter Manager folder.

   This exercise uses a PC3 file created in the previous exercise. Alternatively, you can copy the HI-RES EPLOT.PC3 file from the accompanying CD to the Plotter Manager folder. After copying the file, right-click the PC3 file, select Properties, and then clear the Read-only attribute.

2. Double-click the HI-RES EPLOT.PC3 file. The Plotter Configuration Editor appears.

3. From the General tab, type **Configured for high-resolution ePlots** in the Description box, as shown in Figure 37.4.

Figure 37.4

The PC3 file's description is set.

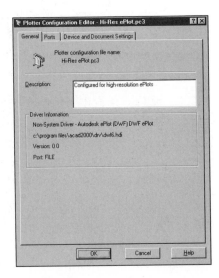

The Ports tab enables you to select a port to which to send your plot. The HI-RES EPLOT.PC3 file is currently set to Plot to File. This instructs AutoCAD to create a plot file of the drawing, as opposed to sending the file to an actual plotter.

4. Select the Device and Document Settings tab.

    The Device and Document Settings tab enables you to define many of the PC3 file's settings. These include the paper source and size, as well as custom property settings for the device.

5. In the tree view window, under the Graphics branch, select Custom Properties. The Access Custom Dialog area displays in the lower half of the dialog box, as shown in Figure 37.5.

Figure 37.5

The Access Custom Dialog area enables you to access DWF Properties dialog box.

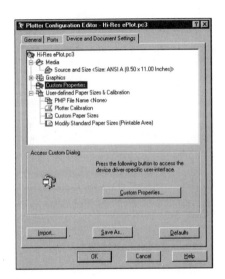

6. In the Access Custom Dialog area, select the Custom Properties button. The DWF Properties dialog box appears.

    The DWF Properties dialog box enables you to control several values for the DWF file, including the file's resolution. By setting the file's resolution higher, you increase the precision at which the DWF file displays in an Internet browser. This means as you zoom-in closer to small objects using your browser, those small objects display their true shape more accurately than they would at lower resolution settings. However, by setting the resolution higher, you also increase the DWF file's size, which makes for longer download times over the Internet. Autodesk suggests that a medium resolution setting is best for most DWF files.

7. In the DWF Properties dialog box, in the Resolution area, slide the Resolution button toward the right to the Extreme setting.

8. In the Format area, be sure the Compressed Binary (recommended) radio button is selected.

The Format area enables you to save the DWF file in one of three formats:

- Compressed Binary (recommended)—format plots DWF files as compressed binary files, and it creates the smallest file sizes. The compression does not result in any data loss, and it is the recommended file format for most DWF files.

- Uncompressed Binary—format plots DWF files as uncompressed binary files, and results in file sizes that are larger than compressed binary files.

- ASCII—format plots DWF files as uncompressed ASCII text files, and it typically produces the largest DWF file size.

9. From the Background color list, select the color White.

The Background color setting controls the background color of the DWF file as it is viewed in an Internet browser.

10. Be sure the Include Layer information option is selected.

This option specifies whether to include layer information in plotted DWF files. If this option is selected, any layers that are turned on and thawed when the ePlot is created become available for manipulation in the plotted DWF file. This means layer visibility can be controlled through the Internet browser. If this option is cleared, no layer information is available when the DWF file is viewed in an external Internet browser.

11. Be sure the Include Scale and measurement information option is selected.

This option specifies whether to include scale and measurement information in plotted DWF files.

12. Be sure the Include Paper boundaries option is selected.

This option specifies whether to include a paper boundary in plotted DWF files. The paper boundary is similar to what is displayed with drawings in a layout tab.

13. Be sure the Convert .DWG hyperlink extensions to .DWF option is selected, as shown in Figure 37.6.

This option specifies whether to convert all .DWG hyperlink extensions to .DWF in plotted DWF files. If your drawing contains hyperlinks to other drawings and you are creating ePlots (.DWF files) of the linked drawings to share over the Internet, and then you should select this option.

Figure 37.6

The DWF Properties dialog box enables you to control the appearance of plotted DWF files.

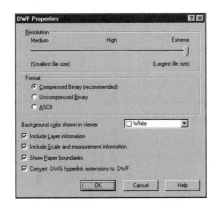

14. Select the OK button. The modifications are saved and the DWF Properties dialog box is closed.

15. Select the OK button. The Plotter Configuration Editor modifies the HI-RES EPLOT.PC3 file and saves the changes.

16. You can close the Plotter Manager folder.

The Plotter Configuration Editor makes modifying PC3 files easy. This is especially useful if you want to create several nearly identical PC3 files, whose settings vary slightly. For example, by creating a single PC3 file using the Autodesk Plotter Manager and then copying the PC3 file, you can use the Plotter Configuration Editor to quickly make minor changes to the PC3 file copy. This saves time by duplicating all the settings from the original PC3 file, and it enables you to change the one or two settings necessary to customize the file.

By using the Autodesk Plotter Manager and the Plotter Configuration Editor, you can easily create and edit PC3 files that are configured for DWF files. After a PC3 file is configured for DWF files, you can use it with AutoCAD's new ePlot feature to create electronic plot files that you can publish on your Web and share over the Internet.

Understanding the AutoCAD Batch Plot Utility

AutoCAD is designed to enable you to plot one drawing at a time. Although plotting only one drawing at a time probably satisfies most of your needs, there probably are occasions in which you want to plot multiple drawings by executing a single command. To meet the demands of plotting multiple drawings from a single command, AutoCAD provides a specially designed application called the AutoCAD Batch Plot Utility. By using the Utility, you can plot an entire set of drawings by issuing a single command.

This section provides an overview of the AutoCAD Batch Plot Utility and explains how to use its features.

Reviewing the AutoCAD Batch Plot Utility

The AutoCAD Batch Plot Utility is a Visual Basic application that runs independent of AutoCAD. By using the Utility, you can create a list of drawings to plot, and then plot all the drawings by a picking a single button. After you pick the button, the Utility takes control of AutoCAD 2000 and loads each drawing in utility's list into AutoCAD, and then sends the drawing to the plotter engine using AutoCAD's Plot command. By using the AutoCAD Batch Plot Utility, you can plot an entire set of AutoCAD drawings repeatedly without having to manually load and plot each drawing from AutoCAD.

The AutoCAD Batch Plot Utility is designed to enable you to easily create a list of drawings to plot. As you add a drawing to the list, you can select which layers to plot for the drawing and associate a different layout and PC3 file to use when plotting the drawing. After you finish creating the list of drawings, you can save the list as a BP3 file that can be recalled later. By creating a BP3 file, you can plot entire sets of drawings by simply loading the list into the AutoCAD Batch Plot Utility and clicking a single button.

NOTE

It is important that you do not interfere with the Utility after it takes control of AutoCAD. Doing so could cause the Utility to stop functioning.

The following section explains how to use the AutoCAD Batch Plot Utility to create a list of drawings to plot and then to save the list as a BP3 file.

Creating a Batch Plot File

The process of creating a BP3 file is straightforward. From the Utility, create a list by selecting the drawings you want to plot. Then set any plot parameters you desire, such as assigning the Page Setup and the Plot Device to use for plotting each drawing. Next, save the list and its plot parameters as a BP3 file. The saved BP3 file can be recalled at anytime to plot all the drawings in the file's list. By using the AutoCAD Batch Plot Utility, you can easily create a BP3 file and use it to plot an entire set of drawings.

In the following exercise, you will use the AutoCAD Batch Plot Utility to create and then save a BP3 file.

CREATING AND SAVING A BP3 FILE

1. From the Windows Taskbar, select Start>Programs>AutoCAD 2000>Batch Plot Utility. The Batch Plot Utility launches, which, in turn, launches AutoCAD 2000.

   This exercise uses three AutoCAD drawings that you must copy from the accompanying CD to a folder on your PC. You must copy the drawings named 37DWG01.DWG, 37DWG02.DWG, and 37DWG03.DWG to a folder that you select. After copying the drawings, right-click the drawings, select Properties, and then clear the Read-only attribute.

2. From the AutoCAD Batch Plot Utility, select the Add Drawing button. The Add Drawing File dialog box appears.

3. From the Add Drawing File dialog box, browse to the folder into which you copied the three drawings, select all three drawings, and select Open. The three drawing file names appear in the Batch Plot Utility list, as shown in Figure 37.7.

Figure 37.7

Three drawings are added to the Batch Plot Utility list.

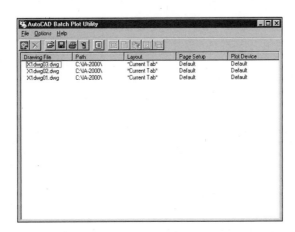

Next, you will indicate the layout to plot for the **37DWG01.DWG** drawing.

4. From the list of drawings displayed in the Batch Plot Utility window, select **37DWG01.DWG**, and then select the Layouts button. The Layouts dialog box appears.

INSIDER **T**IP

> You can also display the Layouts dialog box by choosing the selected drawing's current layout value, which is displayed in the drawing list under the Layout column.

5. From the Layouts dialog box, select the Show all layouts button. All the layouts in the **37DWG01.DWG** drawing are displayed in the box.

6. From the list of layouts, select layout Three as shown in Figure 37.8, and then select OK. The Batch Plot Utility displays updates and indicates that layout Three will be plotted for drawing **37DWG01.DWG**.

Figure 37.8

The 37DWG01.DWG *drawing's layout Three is used when the drawing is plotted.*

INSIDER **T**IP

> You can select multiple layouts to plot by holding down the Ctrl key as you click on the layout names.

Next, you will indicate the page setup to use for plotting the 37DWG01.DWG drawing.

7. With the **37DWG01.DWG** drawing still selected, select the Page Setups button. The Page Setups dialog box appears.

8. From the list of page setups, select Drawing One, as shown in Figure 37.9, and then select OK. The Batch Plot Utility display updates and indicates that page setup Drawing One will be used to plot drawing **37DWG01.DWG**.

Figure 37.9

The 37DWG01.DWG
*drawing's page setup
Drawing One will be used
to plot the drawing.*

NOTE

For more information about page setups, see the section "Creating Page Setups"
in Chapter 20.

Next, you will indicate the plot device to use for the 37DWG02.DWG drawing.

9. From the list of drawings displayed in the Batch Plot Utility, select 37DWG02.DWG, and
    then select the Plot Devices button. The Plot Devices dialog box appears.

10. From the list of plot devices, select the plot device named DWF ePlot PC3, as shown
    in Figure 37.10, and then select OK. The Batch Plot Utility display updates, indicating
    that plot device DWF ePlot PC3 will be used to plot drawing 37DWG02.DWG, as shown
    in Figure 37.11.

Figure 37.10

*The DWF ePlot PC3 plot
device is selected to use for
plotting the* 37DWG02.DWG
drawing.

NOTE

> The list of plot devices displayed in the Plot Devices dialog box depends on the plot devices that are configured for your system.

Figure 37.11

The AutoCAD Batch Plot Utility drawing list, with its plotting parameters, is ready to be saved.

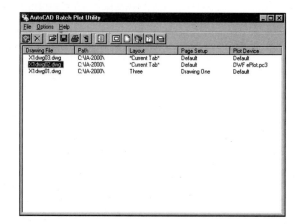

Next, you will save the current list of drawings and their settings as a BP3 file.

11. From the AutoCAD Batch Plot Utility, select the Save List button. The Save Batch Plot List File dialog box appears.

12. From the Save Batch Plot List File dialog box, browse to the folder into which you copied the three drawings, save the BP3 file as LIST ONE (as shown in Figure 37.12), and then select Save. The Batch Plot Utility creates the BP3 file.

Figure 37.12

The Batch Plot file is saved as LIST ONE.BP3.

13. You can quit the AutoCAD Batch Plot Utility by choosing Exit from the File menu. If prompted to quit the batch plot, select OK. If you are prompted to save changes to the drawing, select No.

The AutoCAD Batch Plot Utility enables you to easily create a list of drawings to plot. Additionally, you can set plotting parameters to use for plotting each drawing in the list, and thereby control which layout to plot and which page setup and plot device to use. By using the AutoCAD Batch Plot Utility, you can easily create a list of drawings to plot and control specific plotting parameters to use for each drawing.

The following section explains how to use the AutoCAD Batch Plot Utility to edit an existing BP3 file.

Editing a BP3 File

The process of editing a BP3 file is simple. After you launch the AutoCAD Batch Plot Utility, select the BP3 file you want to edit. Modify the plot parameters you want to change, and then save the updated BP3 file. After it is saved, the BP3 file can then be used to plot all the drawings in the file's list using the new parameters. By using the AutoCAD Batch Plot Utility, you can easily edit an existing BP3 file, setting new plot parameters to use for plotting the drawings in the list.

In the following exercise, you will use the AutoCAD Batch Plot Utility to edit an existing BP3 file.

EDITING AN EXISTING BP3 FILE

1. From the Windows Taskbar, select Start>Programs>AutoCAD 2000>Batch Plot Utility. The Batch Plot Utility launches, which, in turn, launches AutoCAD 2000.

   This exercise uses the LIST ONE.BP3 file created in the previous exercise.

2. From the AutoCAD Batch Plot Utility dialog box, select the Open List button. The Open Batch Plot List File dialog box appears.

3. Browse to the folder in which the LIST ONE.BP3 file was saved in the previous exercise, select the file (as shown in Figure 37.13), and then select Open. The LIST ONE.BP3 file is opened, and its settings displayed in the AutoCAD Batch Plot Utility.

Figure 37.13

The LIST ONE.BP3 *file is opened for editing using the Open Batch Plot List File dialog box.*

Next, you will modify the list of drawings by removing two of the drawings from the list.

4. While holding down the Ctrl key, select the **37DWG01.DWG** and **37DWG02.DWG** drawing file names from the list of drawings displayed in the AutoCAD Batch Plot Utility dialog box, and then select the Remove button. The utility prompts you to verify that you want to remove the selected files.

5. Select Yes. The utility removes the selected drawing file names from the list of drawings, leaving only the **37DWG03.DWG** drawing.

Next, you will modify the layout to use for plotting the 37DWG03.DWG drawing.

6. Select the **37DWG03.DWG** drawing file name, and then select Layouts button. The Layouts dialog box appears.

7. Select the Plot selected layouts radio button, select the Model Tab layout (as shown in Figure 37.14), and then select OK. The utility changes the layout to plot to the Model Tab.

Figure 37.14

The layout to plot is changed in the Model Tab.

Next, you will modify the plot settings to use for plotting the 37DWG03.DWG drawing.

8. With the **37DWG03.DWG** drawing file name still selected, select the Plot Settings button. The Plot Settings dialog box appears.

The Plot Settings dialog box contains two tabs: The Plot Settings tab and the Layers tab. The Plot Settings tab enables you to set the area to plot, the plot scale to use, and the file name and location to use when plotting drawings to a file. The Layers tab enables you to turn off and on layers, thereby controlling which layers to plot.

9. From the Plot Settings tab, select the Extents radio button in the Plot area, as shown in Figure 37.15. The area to plot is set to the drawing extents.

Figure 37.15

The drawing Extents option is selected as the area to plot.

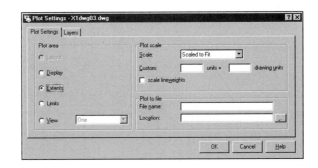

WARNING

Notice in Figure 37.15 that you can select a named view as the area to plot. At the time of this writing, this feature did not work properly.

INSIDER **T**IP

Although it might be useful at times to define the area to plot using the Plot Settings dialog box, it is not the best way to plot the area you desire. To ensure that the area you desire is plotted, you should open each drawing before using the AutoCAD Batch Plot Utility, zoom to the view you want to plot, and then save the drawing. Then, as the Utility loads each drawing, it plots the last view displayed when you saved the drawing file.

10. From the Plot Settings tab, select 1:1 from the Scale drop-down list in the Plot scale area, as shown in Figure 37.16. The plot scale is set to 1:1.

Figure 37.16

The drawing's plot scale is set to 1:1.

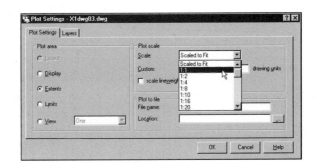

11. From the Plot Settings tab, select the ellipsis button next to the Location text box in the Plot to file area. The Plot-To-File Filename dialog box appears.

12. In the Plot-To-File Filename dialog box, enter **Drawing Three** in the File name text box, as shown in Figure 37.17, and then select Save. The file name and location are set, as shown in Figure 37.18.

Figure 37.17

The plotted drawing's file name is set to Drawing Three.

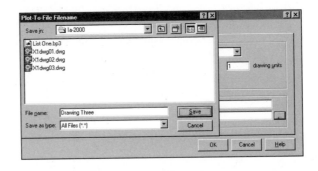

Figure 37.18

If the plotted drawing is saved to a file, its file name and location are as shown in the Plot to file area.

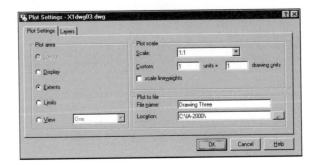

Next, you will modify the layers to plot.

13. Select the Layers tab. The **37DWG03.DWG** drawing file's layers are then displayed.

14. From the Layers tab, hold the Ctrl key down, and select the layer names Red and Blue, select the Off button (as shown in Figure 37.19), and then select OK. The Plot Settings dialog box is closed, and its settings are assigned to the **37DWG03.DWG**.

Figure 37.19

The layers named Red and Blue are turned off, and therefore do not plot.

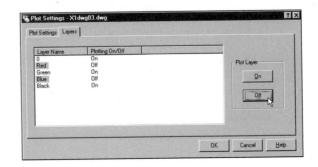

Next, you will indicate the drawing's plot device.

15. From the AutoCAD Batch Plot Utility, with the 37DWG03.DWG drawing name still highlighted, select the Plot Devices button. The Plot Devices dialog box appears.

16. From the list of plot devices, select the plot device named DWF EPLOT.PC3, (as shown in Figure 37.20), and then select OK. The Batch Plot Utility display updates and indicates plot device DWF EPLOT.PC3 will be used to plot drawing 37DWG03.DWG.

Figure 37.20

The DWF EPLOT.PC3 *plot device is selected to use for plotting the* 37DWG03.DWG *drawing.*

Next, you will save the modified list as a new BP3 file.

17. From the AutoCAD Batch Plot Utility, select the Save List button. The Save Batch Plot List File dialog box appears.

18. In the File name text box, enter **List Two** (as shown in Figure 37.21), and then select Save. The Batch Plot Utility creates the new BP3 file.

Figure 37.21

The edited BP3 file is saved as a new file.

19. You can quit the AutoCAD Batch Plot Utility by choosing Exit from the File menu. If prompted to quit the batch plot, select OK. If you are prompted to save changes to the drawing, select No.

The AutoCAD Batch Plot Utility enables you to quickly edit an existing BP3 file. You can modify plotting parameters to use for plotting each drawing in the list, and can add drawings to, or remove drawings from the list. Additionally, as demonstrated in the previous exercise, the AutoCAD Batch Plot Utility enables you to control a drawings plot area, plot scale, and which layers of the drawing to plot. By using the AutoCAD Batch Plot Utility, you can easily edit an existing BP3 file, and thereby modify its list of drawings, and the plotting parameters to use for each drawing.

The following section explains how to use the AutoCAD Batch Plot Utility to plot drawings from an existing BP3 file.

Plotting Drawings Using a BP3 File

The ultimate purpose for creating a BP3 file is to recall a list of drawings and then to plot the drawings by picking a single button. After you launch the AutoCAD Batch Plot Utility, you can load an existing BP3 file, which contains a list of drawings and their plotting parameters. Then, plot the drawings listed in the BP3 file by simply clicking the Plot button. By saving a list of drawings in a BP3 file, you can quickly load the file into the AutoCAD Batch Plot Utility and then plot all the drawings.

In the following exercise, you will use the AutoCAD Batch Plot Utility to plot an existing BP3 file.

PLOTTING AN EXISTING BP3 FILE

1. From the Windows Taskbar, select Start>Programs>AutoCAD 2000>Batch Plot Utility. The Batch Plot Utility launches, which, in turn, launches AutoCAD 2000.

    This exercise uses the LIST TWO.BP3 file created in the previous exercise.

2. From the AutoCAD Batch Plot Utility dialog box, select the Open List button. The Open Batch Plot List File dialog box appears.

3. Browse to the folder where the LIST TWO.BP3 file was saved in the previous exercise, select the file (as shown in Figure 37.22), and then select Open. The LIST TWO.BP3 file is opened, and its settings are displayed in the AutoCAD Batch Plot Utility.

Figure 37.22

The LIST TWO.BP3
*file is opened using the
Open Batch Plot List
File dialog box.*

The AutoCAD Batch Plot Utility provides two useful features of which you can take advantage when preparing to plot the drawings listed in a BP3 file. The first feature is the Logging feature, and the second feature is the Plot Test feature. By using these two features, you can track and record important information about the plotting process and you can ensure that AutoCAD can find all the files necessary to successfully plot the drawings.

Next, you will use the logging feature.

4. From the AutoCAD Batch Plot Utility dialog box, select the Logging button. The Logging dialog box appears.

    The Logging feature enables you to create two different types of logs. One log is a plot journal log, which records who plotted each drawing and when. The other log is an error log, which records any errors encountered during plotting.

    Next, you will enable the Journal Logging feature.

5. From the Logging dialog box, in the Plot Journal area, be sure the Enable Journal Logging option is selected.

6. From the Logging dialog box, select the Browse button (located next to the File name text box) in the Plot Journal area. The Journal Filename dialog box appears.

7. Browse to the folder where the LIST TWO.BP3 file was opened, enter **Journal Log** (as shown in Figure 37.23), and then select Save. The JOURNAL LOG.LOG file is ready to be created.

Figure 37.23

The JOURNAL LOG.LOG *file is created.*

8. From the Logging dialog box, select the Append radio button in the Plot Journal area. The Plot Journal Log data is appended to the designated file every time there is an entry, instead of overwriting the previous file.

NOTE

The Header and Comments text boxes enable you to include text that is inserted at the beginning of each log entry. You can leave these boxes blank.

Next, you will enable the Error logging feature.

9. From the Logging dialog box, in the Error Log area, be sure the Enable Error Logging option is selected.

10. From the Logging dialog box, select the Browse button (Located next to the File name text box) in the Error Log area. The Error Log Filename dialog box appears.

11. Browse to the folder where the LIST TWO.BP3 file was opened, enter **Error Log** (as shown in Figure 37.24) in the Error Log area, and then select Save. The ERROR LOG.LOG file is ready to be created.

Figure 37.24

The ERROR LOG.LOG *file is created.*

12. From the Logging dialog box, select the Append radio button in the Error Log area. The Error Log data is appended to the designated file every time there is an entry, instead of overwriting the previous file. The ERROR LOG.LOG file is ready to be created, as shown in Figure 37.25.

Figure 37.25

The log files are enabled in the Logging dialog box.

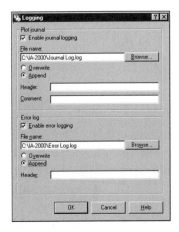

13. From the Logging dialog box, select OK. The two log files are created and saved.

Next, you will use the Plot Test feature.

14. From the AutoCAD Batch Plot Utility dialog box, select the Plot Test button. The Plot Test Results dialog box displays (as shown in Figure 37.26) and lists any errors.

The Plot Test feature causes the Utility to load the drawings in the list into AutoCAD 2000 and check for missing xrefs, fonts, or shape files. The Plot Test feature only loads the drawings; it does not plot them.

In this particular example, because there are no xrefs or shapes in the drawing and because the font file was found, the plot test was successful. However, if you look at Figure 37.26, you will notice one error is listed. This error does not indicate that there is a problem if the BP3 file is used to plot the drawing. It simply notes that the optional xref log file could not be located.

Figure 37.26

The Plot Test Results dialog box displays any errors encountered trying to load the drawings into AutoCAD 2000.

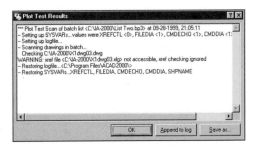

15. From the Plot Test Results dialog box, select the Append to log button, and then select OK. The Plot Test Results dialog box data is appended to the JOURNAL LOG.LOG file.

Next, you will plot the drawing listed in the BP3 file.

16. From the AutoCAD Batch Plot Utility dialog box, select the Plot button. The utility loads the 37DWG03.DWG drawing into AutoCAD 2000 and creates a plot file. Additionally, the plotting information is generated and appended to the JOURNAL LOG.LOG file.

NOTE

If the plot is created successfully, a small check mark appears to the left of the drawing's file name, as shown in Figure 37.27. However, if an error were encountered during the plot process, an X mark would appear instead.

Figure 37.27

The small check mark shown to the left of the drawing's file name indicates that the plot was generated successfully.

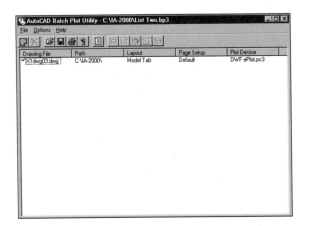

17. You can quit the AutoCAD Batch Plot Utility by choosing Exit from the File menu. If prompted to quit the batch plot, select OK. If you are prompted to save changes to the BP3 file, or the drawing file, select No.

INSIDER **T**IP

You should customize the Batch Plot Utility icon that you use to start the program so that it starts in a directory where paths to the xrefs and fonts be found.

By using AutoCAD's Batch Plot Utility, you can create and save predefined lists of drawings in BP3 files, and you can automatically plot large sets of drawings without needing to attend the plot process. You can plot many drawings overnight, or over the weekend, and retrieve the finished plots the following morning.

Summary

In this chapter, you learned about using AutoCAD's ePlot feature to publish drawings on the Internet. You also learned how to configure a DWF plot device and about creating a DWF plot file using the new ePlot feature. Additionally, you reviewed the AutoCAD Batch Plot Utility, and learned how to create and edit BP3 files. Finally, you learned about using BP3 files to plot multiple drawings by picking a single button, how to enable Journal Logs and Error Logs, and to use them to track the Batch Plot Utility's plotting progress.

In this chapter, you learned about two useful features: AutoCAD's ePlot feature, and the AutoCAD Batch Plot Utility. By using these two features, you can enhance your ability to quickly create and share plots with colleagues and clients, ultimately increasing your productivity.

REFERENCE MATERIALS

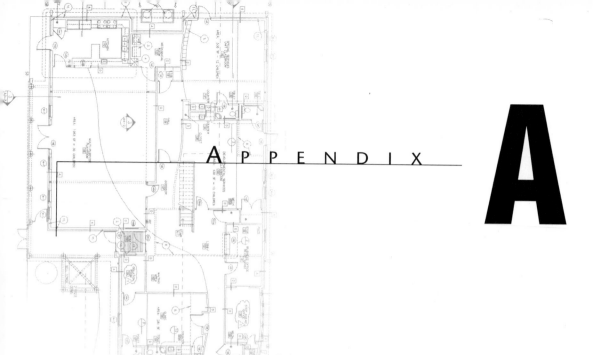

BEFORE THE DRAWING BEGINS: PLANNING AND ORGANIZING PROJECTS

AutoCAD is designed to save time by drawing efficiently. However, drawing efficiently with AutoCAD is only one element in saving time on your projects. By analyzing the overall process required to complete a project, you can identify elements of your project that are not necessarily drawing-based, but that have a lot to do with saving time. Then, through proper planning and organization methods, you can maximize efficiency and complete your project on time.

In this appendix, you learn about techniques that show how to use both AutoCAD and the Microsoft Windows environment to help you work more efficiently. Among the topics discussed are the following:

■ *Key organization factors*

■ *Initial drawing setup*

■ *AutoCAD project organization features*

■ *Creating title blocks and template files*

Getting Started: Key Factors to Organize First

The ultimate goal of project organization is to save time by working efficiently. In general, there is one simple rule to keep in mind that will help you work efficiently and save time:

Reduce repetition: Don't repeat what you have already done.

Before you can reduce repetition, you must first identify the organizational elements of your project. The following sections discuss various organizational elements that you should consider prior to beginning your project. These preliminary organizational elements include determining the following:

- How many drawings are needed to complete the project?

- How much detail is required on each drawing?

- What is an efficient method of workflow management?

- How many different ways will you display the drawing?

- What project elements can be used more than once?

Determining How Many Drawings Are Necessary

When you start drawing a project, one of your earliest tasks is to determine just how many and what type of drawings you will need. Two important issues should be considered when establishing the number of drawings to create.

First and foremost, you should address the computing power versus drawing size factor. Computing power consists of storage space, both long-term (such as with a hard disk, tape, and network server) and short-term (such as how much RAM you have), coupled with the speed of your graphics card and CPU. Autodesk and other experts toss about many factors relating to how much memory and hard disk you need to handle each megabyte of drawing. Unfortunately, no hard-and-fast rule exists. If you use xrefs, extended entity data, attributes, and 3D solids, and if you will need to open multiple drawings sessions in AutoCAD at once, then your needs vary substantially from someone who stores 2D vector information in a drawing without any bells and whistles. Therefore, you must ascertain your ideal drawing size through experience and simple trial and error.

INSIDER TIP

A good set of guidelines when estimating the ideal, or maximum, drawing size for your system is to use 32 times your drawing size in memory and 64 times your drawing size in free disk space.

When you have a good feel for how large your drawings can be before the performance of your system hinders your work, you can determine how you want to organize your drawing data into individual drawings. The following examples discuss various options for organizing a project into drawings with AutoCAD:

■ Your model exists in one drawing, and you can view the model through various Layout pages (with paper space viewports). Keep in mind that a model can be 3D or 2D. The model can then be viewed and annotated differently in each Layout page.

■ Each of your drawings comprises a very detailed portion of a much larger product. You can then assemble the various portions into a single model using external references (xrefs). The xrefs help you organize your drawings by listing the location of and relationship between each drawing.

■ You can develop a new drawing by cutting and pasting elements from existing drawings. You can use AutoCAD 2000's new Multiple Document Environment (MDE) and open multiple drawings in a single session of AutoCAD, making copying elements between drawings very simple.

■ Your drawings are only a small portion of your project documentation, and the drawings are linked to text documents, images, and other files using Object Linking and Embedding (OLE).

You will learn more about the use of xrefs in Chapter 14, "Working with Drawings and External References Productively," the use of paper space in Chapter 19, "Paper Space Layouts," and about OLE in Chapter 23, "Effective Applications for OLE Objects in AutoCAD 2000."

It is important that you consider a variety of approaches when creating your drawings and that you develop a tried-and-true method that delivers exactly what you need a majority of the time. After you develop your approach to building your drawings, you can begin to predict how many drawings you will need, what their contents will be, and how they will relate to each other. This will be critical to estimating how long a given project will take to complete.

Developing Drawing and Task Lists

After you have developed your approach to build your drawings, you should then develop a list of your project's drawings, and then a task list that goes with each drawing. This list of drawings and their associated task lists should be flexible and expandable. Spreadsheet applications such as Microsoft Excel are excellent tools for creating task lists.

A convenient way to associate a task list with a drawing is to link a spreadsheet into the drawing's paper space layout. By linking the task list in the drawing, you create a drawing-specific storehouse for your task list that is visible in each drawing. You also can plot this task list with your drawing so that you can easily measure your progress when you create progress prints of your project. Finally, you can update this task list as you work in each drawing. By using a linked spreadsheet, you can quickly add and edit tasks in your list while working in the drawing.

You will learn some simple steps for creating a linked spreadsheet task list in an exercise later in this appendix. Figure A.1 shows a sample task list, and Figure A.2 shows the placement of the spreadsheet task list within a drawing.

Figure A.1

A sample task list for a series of drawings.

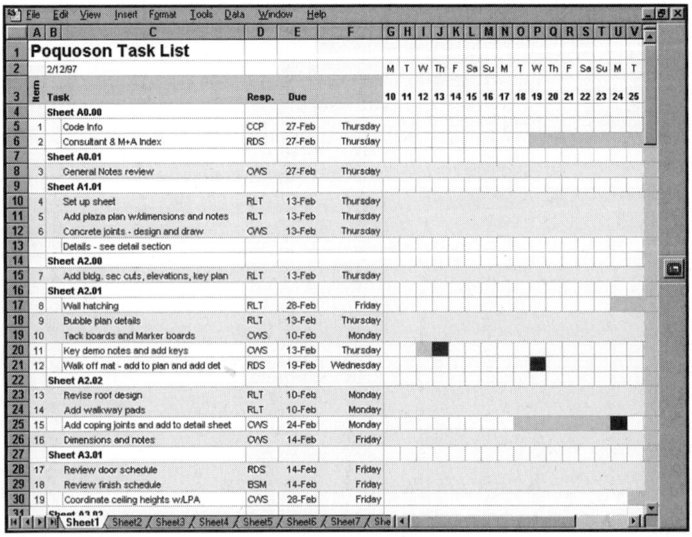

You can insert the task list OLE object on a unique layer and then use the layer plot option to control its plotting visibility. Alternatively, you could use the thaw/freeze or on/ off layer controls as well to control visibility.

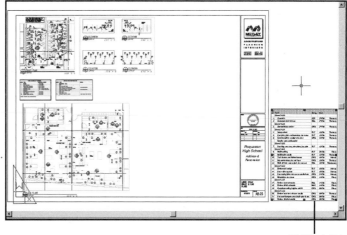

OLE Task List

Determining How Much Detail Is Required

Another important factor in the organization of your project is determining how much detail is required for the drawing. Because AutoCAD is so accurate, you can easily fall into the trap of creating minuscule details that might not have anything to do with the actual production of your project from your drawings. It is important that you implement only what the final user of your drawing(s) will need in order to accomplish the specific job. In addition, you should keep in mind that the person actually creating your project might have better, more effective methods of building the product in the field than you do on the drawing. The following list of questions will be discussed in this section to help you determine the extent of the detail in each drawing and in your project as a whole:

- What should be documented?

- When should it be implemented?

- How should it be approached?

- Who should explain it?

- Where should it be presented?

The answers to these questions might seem obvious to you at first glance, but after you take a look at how they affect your project's organization, you may realize the questions aren't as simple as they may seem.

Answering the Questions

In answering the first question, "What should be explained?," you should not be concerned with only the parts of your project that you will draw. You also should consider how to organize your drawings in a way that describes your project in the most efficient and effective manner. For example, you might need to define a continuous chamfer that surrounds a faceplate, as well as the location of the holes in the faceplate and the specific location of tooling on the faceplate. To adequately describe these conditions, you would need two sections—one horizontal and one vertical through the faceplate—as well as a front view of the faceplate. Two isometric views can accomplish the same thing with one fewer drawing required.

The second question, "When should it be explained?," might mean that you won't need to draw some details of your project at all because you will get back a set of shop drawings from a vendor that determines how the detailing will be done. Answering this second question also might determine the order of the drawings within a set of project drawings.

It might seem obvious to you that the third question, "How should it be explained?," concerns the type of drawing (such as isometric, or plan and section drawings) that you need. However, you also should think about using photographs, annotation, and shaded 3D models as part of the explanation.

The fourth question, "Who should explain it?," might mean that you have a vendor finishing your work for you in the form of shop drawings, but also involves finding a person within the project team to work on the design. A conceptual designer, for example, might not have the CAD skills that are needed to complete a detailed 3D model. Therefore, you might have to alter your preferred choice of drawing technique based upon who is doing the design and who is doing the drawing.

After you have completed the first four questions, you are prepared to ask the fifth and final question, "Where should it be explained?," which ultimately determines the organization of your drawings. For example, you must determine whether you have so many details that they must be displayed on their own detail sheets, or whether these details will fit as blow-ups on the same sheets that display your working model. You also must establish a systematized approach to the order of your drawings that works for every project. Furthermore, you should address whether you can readily insert new drawings into the drawing sequence if you discover that one is needed well into your project. Two key concepts that can help you manage this portion of your effort are:

■ Developing an efficient numbering system used within the drawings

■ Developing a file naming/folder naming system that corresponds with the drawing numbering system

Developing an Efficient Numbering System

You need a way to name or number your drawings that works the same way every time and allows flexibility in the order of your drawings and the number of each type of drawing. A perfect example of a system that works in this way is a library catalogue system, better known as the Dewey Decimal System. If you organize your drawings into categories, and then sequence the drawings within a category, this type of system might work for you. For example, in the AEC industry, drawings have categories, such as Cover Sheet and General Information Sheets, Floor Plans, Elevations, and Sections. Each category might contain a sequence of drawings, such as the First Floor Plan and the Second Floor Plan. Following this format, you could define a drawing numbering system that meets the goals of predictability, flexibility, and expandability. The following list details a numbering system you could implement:

0.00, 0.01, 0.02, and so on—Cover Sheets and General Information

1.00, 1.01, 1.02, and so on—Floor Plans

2.00, 2.01, 2.02, and so on—Elevations

3.00, 3.01, 3.02, and so on—Sections

...and so forth.

NOTE

Note that a new floor plan drawing can be added to the end of the Floor Plans category at any time without adversely affecting the drawing numbers in the categories that follow, such as the Elevations category. The limitation with the numbering system as shown is that a maximum of nine drawing categories, and a maximum of 99 drawings in each category, can be created. If you need more, simply add more numbers to your filenames, as in 01.000.

Developing a File and Folder Naming System

You can carry the numbering system shown in the previous section a bit further and use it to name the drawing files while also adding project numbers and a drawing description. If you design your drawing-numbering and file-naming conventions with some forethought, the filenames will sort themselves in the Open or Save File dialog boxes in the desired order, so you will know what a drawing contains without opening the drawing. The only limitations in Windows 95/98 and Windows NT is that the filename can't contain more than 255 characters, and it can't contain any of the following characters: \ / : * ? " < > |. Of course, if you make your filenames 255 characters long, you can't have the files in a folder, and you will spend a lot of time typing the filenames, and many file dialog boxes won't display the entire name within them. Therefore, a responsible file-naming system might include a project or work-order number, a drawing number, and a predictable maximum number of characters for a description. The following example illustrates the format of a filename using this system:

```
<project number>-<drawing number>-<revision number><drawing owner>-
➥<sheet title>.dwg

9701-1.00-01cws-OVERALL BUILDING PLAN.dwg
```

Note that Windows 95/98 and Windows NT also "remember" the uppercased letters separately from lowercased letters. Using upper- and lowercased letters can help with the legibility of the drawing filename. Also note that the final extension for the filename is always .dwg, because AutoCAD must see the .dwg file extension to load the file. Even if you can see only the first 15 characters of this filename, you would know that the file belongs to project number 9701, that it's a plan of some type, that it's revision number 1, and that someone with the initials "cws" originated the drawing. This file-naming convention also first sorts the drawing files by project number, then by drawing number, then by revision, and then by author. Figure A.3 shows an example of what the results might be.

Figure A.3

Using filenames with logical naming will save you time and help organize your project.

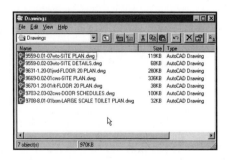

NOTE

> If you create new drawings on a regular basis, an involved filename might become counterproductive. In other words, the amount of information that you include in your file name is partly based upon the shelf life of your drawings.

If you organize your drawings into folders that have some logical hierarchy to them, the filenames also can become simpler. For instance, the previous example could have a folder structure similar to the one shown in Figure A.4.

Figure A.4

The judicious use of folders can simplify file-naming needs.

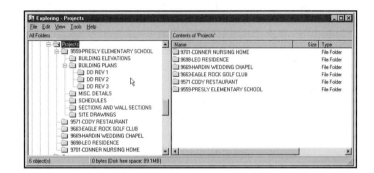

Using the folders in Figure A.4, the filename used previously could become 9701-1.00cws-OVERALL.dwg.

It's always a good idea to keep the project number or work order number as part of the drawing filename so that drawings that might be accidentally misplaced can be tied to their project with relative ease. You also must consider how many versions of any one portion of the filename you might have. For example, the project number 9701 enables you to have 99 projects in the year 1997. If you think you will have more than 99 projects, you should use a number with five digits, as in 97001. Likewise, 1.00 means that only 99 floors can exist in the building (1.01 through 1.99), and using 01 for a revision marker means that up to 99 revisions can exist. Additionally, with the advent of the year 2000, it may be useful to include the full year numeric value for project numbers, such as 1997001. Otherwise, you may have difficulty displaying drawings in proper numeric order if you continue with a numbering system that only displays the last two digits of the year—a unique example of the Y2K problem.

Make sure that you don't limit yourself to having to change your file-naming scheme in a year or two. Take the time to study the types and number of events that you need to record in your filename by looking over past projects that you or other members of your company have completed. Don't hesitate to run your ideas by others to see if they can spot any shortcomings.

Determining How Your Drawings Relate

This topic can become very complex, because not only can AutoCAD drawings be linked to other documents, and other documents be linked to your drawings, but complex relationships can also exist between the drawings themselves. You can organize your thoughts about the interrelationships between your drawings and other drawings or documents by asking a few simple questions:

- What information must be shared between drawings?
- What other documents will be included in the drawings?
- What other documents will the drawings be included within?

At this point, it's usually a good idea to create a mock-up set of drawings using a standard form. If you have a number of drawings and documents that make up your project and your sheets are standard and uniformly sized, then a mock-up is easy to do and beneficial. If your projects are small in terms of document count or widely varied in document format and size, you may not find a mock-up on a form to be that helpful.

You can create this mock-up as a basis for your drawing set in AutoCAD, or you can draw a free-hand mock-up using preprinted sheets and a pencil. Creating electronic mock-ups of your project will be helpful in the long run because the effort will contribute to the creation of the final documents.

However you choose to create a mock-up, it should organize key information. In the section, "Determining Which Elements Can Be Used More Than Once," Figure A.8 shows an example of a mock-up form that contains places that provide the information to answer the three questions just reviewed. This shared information is placed in the drawing window on the form by using callouts (or *bubbles*) that reference another drawing. Additionally, such useful information as drawing number, drawing name, date, project name, and author is included on the form.

If you want to create your mock-ups electronically, you can place the mock-up right on the drawing to aid in its creation. This can be set up ahead of time by using a form in place of a title block in a template drawing. (This process will be briefly discussed later in this appendix.) After the mock-up has served its purpose, you can substitute a real title block for the mock-up form. If you keep your mock-ups separate from your drawings, then it's a good idea to create your mock-up as an 8 1/2 × 11-inch sheet so that you can plot "mini" sets of your entire project until you complete the production drawing set.

Using Object Linking and Embedding (OLE)

When you insert a document within your AutoCAD drawing, you can use Object Linking and Embedding (OLE). By using OLE, you can either link the inserted object to the original document, or embed it as a duplicate of the original document. If you link the inserted object to the original document, every time the drawing is opened, AutoCAD automatically locates the original document, and then updates the inserted object based on the latest version of the original document. By linking the inserted object to the original document, you ensure that the latest version of the original document is always displayed in your drawing, which is a very useful feature if the original document is being edited on a regular basis. Figure A.5 shows an example of a document being inserted as a linked object in an AutoCAD drawing.

Figure A.5

Linking an object to the original document when inserting it into an AutoCAD drawing using OLE.

Bitmap images are easy to include in your drawings

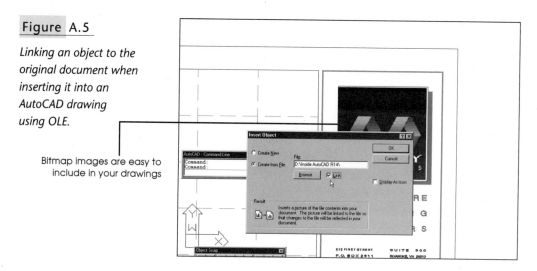

Embedding an object, on the other hand, inserts a duplicate of the original document, but does not link the inserted object to the original document. Consequently, any edits made to the original document are not reflected when the drawing is reopened. This feature is useful if you want to insert a copy of the original document, without fear of the copy being overwritten by an updated version.

The following example illustrates how to create a task list and insert it into a drawing using OLE.

> **NOTE**
>
> This exercise uses a spreadsheet to create a task list because a spreadsheet makes insertion and numbering of tasks relatively simple. If you don't have a spreadsheet product, you can use WordPad (which comes with Windows 95/98 and Windows NT 4.0) to accomplish the same goal.

USING OLE TO EMBED TASK LISTS IN YOUR DRAWINGS

1. First, use a spreadsheet application to create a task list with a few items listed. If you have a current project for which you need a task list, that would be a good place to start—otherwise, just make one up. The task list can be any width and length, but Windows products limit the size of the embedded object to approximate a printed 8 1/2 × 11-inch page size. Consequently, if you create a large spreadsheet, only a portion of it will appear.

2. After you create and save the task list, highlight the tasks by clicking and dragging your cursor over them, then open the application's Edit pull-down menu and choose Copy. The highlighted items are copied to the clipboard.

3. Launch AutoCAD. The Startup dialog box appears (unless it is disabled).

4. Click the Use a Template button (the third button from the left in the upper-left corner of the dialog box). The Select a Template list appears.

5. From the Select a Template list, choose Ansi d-named plot styles.dwt, then click OK. AutoCAD switches to layout view, then inserts the template.

6. From the Edit pull-down menu, choose Paste Special.

7. From the Paste Special dialog box, click Paste Link. Only your spreadsheet application is listed in the dialog box.

8. Click OK. AutoCAD inserts your task list OLE object into the drawing.

9. Move your cursor into the center of the OLE object and select the object. The object's grips are enabled and the cursor becomes a four-headed arrow.

10. Click and drag the task list object to the right of the drawing area.

11. With the object still selected, move the cursor over one of the corners. The cursor will turn into a diagonal two-headed arrow.

12. Click and drag the corner to resize the object.

The result should appear similar to Figure A.2, shown earlier in this appendix. Using this technique, you can insert any variety of objects into your drawing from the Windows clipboard.

For a more complete review of using OLE, refer to Chapter 23.

Developing Efficient Workflow Management

If more than one person will work on a drawing, you must determine how each person will know which drawing is the current drawing. This aspect of project delivery is known as *workflow management*. Consider a scenario, for example, in which outside consultants or contractors work on your drawings, and you want to make changes to those drawings. How will you know if the drawing you have contains the most recent information? If you do not address this concern, you might edit an outdated drawing.

Another problem you may encounter is one in which two people need to work on the same drawing at the same time. By applying workflow management to your project, you can avoid conflicts and limit mistakes.

Proper Network File Control

Your organization of the project and its documents and your management of file access are key to avoiding disaster with multiple document users or authors. If you work on a network that provides multiple access to a drawing, then your network software must support file locking. Most contemporary network products enable you to open files in Read Only mode and won't let you overwrite the file on which someone else is working. Proper network file control means that the first person to open a drawing is the only editor that can actually save changes to the drawing. All subsequent users can open the drawing only in Read Only mode. If someone absolutely must record changes to a drawing that is currently open by someone else, he must save his changes as a new drawing. Recording these changes on a unique layer name and saving the changes as a new drawing enables the changes to be merged with the original drawing later.

> **NOTE**
>
> AutoCAD 2000 introduces a new feature called *in-place reference editing*, which allows users to edit blocks and xrefs, and save changes back to the original object or drawing file. This feature is discussed in detail in Chapter 14, "Working with Drawings and External References Productively."

Using Redlines

Users also can record redlines on a unique layer that can be merged with a drawing. *Redlines* list comments, questions, and editing instructions for a drawing that are acted upon by someone else later. Figure A.6 shows an example of redlines.

Figure A.6

Inserting redline revision instructions does not require sophisticated AutoCAD commands.

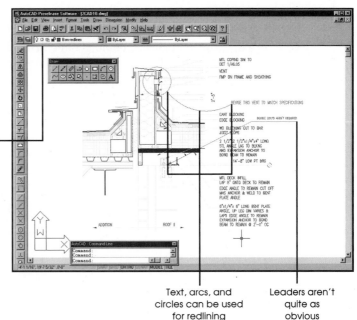

Create redline layers

Text, arcs, and circles can be used for redlining

Leaders aren't quite as obvious

> **INSIDER TIP**
>
> Because redlines can be created using basic AutoCAD commands, you could create your own toolbar that contains basic redlining commands such as text, lines, arcs, circles, and leaders. In this way, individuals who are not sophisticated AutoCAD users can still contribute to your drawings electronically, saving time and paper.

An alternative to creating a new redline layer in the current drawing is to xref the drawing into a new drawing, and create the redlines in the new drawing. In either event, you should name the drawing file and the layers used for redlines based upon a standard. For example, the filename, or the layer name, could include the redliner's initials, a date, and the term *redlines* in its name. This simplifies the identification of the redlines.

Determining Which Elements Can Be Used More than Once

As mentioned earlier, you can use xrefs to create more than one drawing from the same drawing. Although the use of xrefs can help ensure that numerous drawings contain exactly the same information and reduce total project drawing storage needs, xrefs also can help you avoid creating drawing elements more than once.

If you use a drawing template, as demonstrated in the previous exercise, you might not want to include a drawing border in the template drawing. Instead, you could devise a project border sheet that contains the project name, issue date, project number, project address, your firm's logo, address, and other information, and insert it into drawings as an xref. Therefore, each new project drawing would include the border as an xref, and changes to the border would need to be made only once in the original xref.

NOTE

> Using this method, you should design the xref so that it contains only the information common to all project drawings. For example, elements like issue date and sheet revision data would stay unique to the drawing file and not appear in the xref file.

Using an element more than once can mean more than creating an exact duplicate of objects. You might want to use different guides in all your project drawings, such as the format of text, a key plan with different portions hatched in each drawing, or a sheet grid that doesn't plot. For example, you can create a block that contains only attributes that fill in your title block. The drawing author, checker, sheet number, sheet name, and date can be filled in separately for each drawing, but such elements as the text style, height, and layer will always be the same. (You will learn more about blocks in Chapter 13, "Creating and Using Blocks.") Suppose your projects usually involve a large number of drawings. By combining the use of block attributes inside blocks and xref drawings, you can increase efficiency by creating a template drawing that contains the border as an xref, the sheet-specific text as attributes, and a sheet grid on a non-plottable layer. Figure A.7 shows an example of a template drawing that incorporates a number of unifying features.

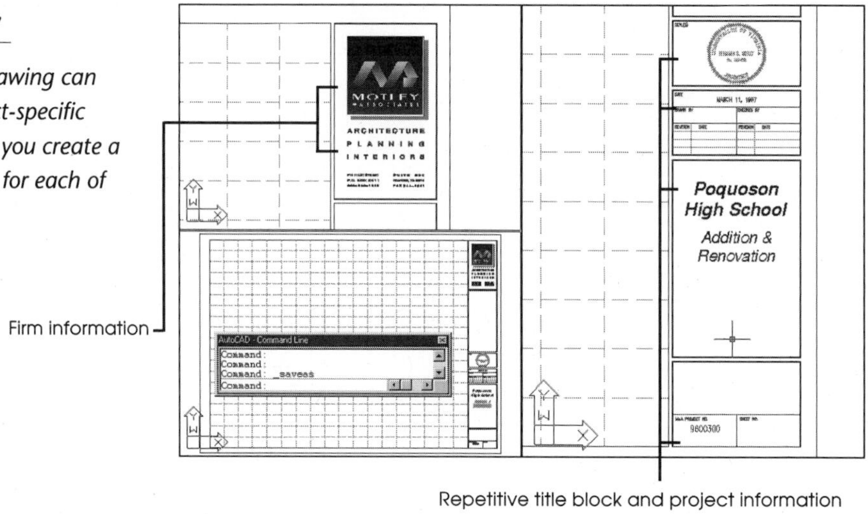

Figure A.7

A template drawing can contain project-specific information if you create a new template for each of your projects.

Firm information

Repetitive title block and project information

An important factor to consider is that, at the start of a project, you must map out as many multiple-use opportunities as you can, including organizing portions of drawings that you can reuse from earlier projects or from standard drawings that you have developed over numerous projects. Using the mock-up set discussed earlier, you should also map out the use of viewports to display the necessary views of your model. Figure A.8 shows an example of a mock-up of a portion of an architectural project.

Determining How a Drawing Will Be Displayed

The final, and possibly most complex, issue to consider when laying out a project, is the number of ways that a drawing will be displayed. As discussed in Chapter 25, "Publishing on the Web," AutoCAD 2000 enables you to publish your drawings on the Internet. In addition, you might need to plot the drawing on a number of different sheet sizes, or you might need to create both drawings and renderings of the drawings for the project. Finally, as is the case for many drawings in this book, you might need to publish your drawings in a shop manual or a technical publication. As you can imagine, large drawings with a significant amount of detail don't publish very well on computer screens (if they did, the AutoCAD ZOOM command wouldn't exist).

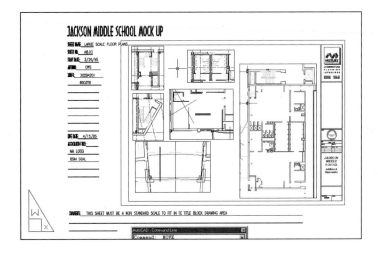

If you create documents that will be displayed on the Internet, published in a technical publication, and plotted on a sheet of paper, something will have to give. You might need to create completely different drawings for each type of media due to one single factor: Your text and symbols won't work for each and every possible publishing method. Although a perfect solution doesn't exist for these broad publishing requirements, planning for the project's needs from the start can save a lot of time and headaches. If your publication must vary from project to project, it might be a good idea to obtain a drawing from a previous project that is similar to the one you will use for the current project. Using this drawing, you could try to publish it under all the conditions that you must meet. This process will help you uncover any problems that you might encounter.

Setting Up Your Drawing

After you have pondered each of the issues discussed so far, it is time to set up your drawings. You must follow a sequential set of steps to determine how you can accomplish this task. If you use the following steps, you will avoid revising text sizes, drawing configurations, and a number of other complications later in a project:

- Determining paper size
- Determining drawing scale
- Developing title blocks
- Determining units and angles

Determining Paper Size

The first and foremost determination you must make is the final plot size of your drawings. If you plot your drawings to paper, the paper sizes that your plotter handles define your options for the drawing size. Using a mock-up process—whether a formal one, such as the process discussed earlier, or simply figuring out how much paper area is required for an appropriate scale of your drawings—is the first step. Paper comes in an extensive set of sizes, and each industry generally settles upon a set of standard sizes. One important factor to consider about paper is whether you can create a modular approach to your paper sizes. Figure A.9 shows a progression of paper sizes that will expand or contract between sheet sizes while maintaining the same aspect ratio between sheets. Maintaining the same aspect ratio means that you can enlarge or minimize your drawings without concern for whether the drawing will fit the same way on the larger or smaller sheet.

Figure A.9

Using paper sizes that are modular is an important consideration.

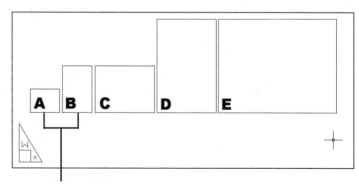

Each paper size is one-half the size of the next larger size

Obtaining modular sheet sizes might not be an easy task. If you are in the AEC industry, for example, nothing about standard AEC sheet sizes is modular. The AEC industry is hopelessly antiquated in this area and is making no rapid movement toward changing the system. Although they have a modular set, no copier or standard envelope will use a 9×12-inch paper size. Table A.1 lists standard paper sizes that are available.

Table A.1

Standard Paper

Paper Size	Standard	MM	In
Eight Crown	IMP	1461×1060	57 1/2 × 41 3/4
Antiquarian	IMP	1346×533	53 × 21
Quad Demy	IMP	1118×826	44 × 32 1/2
Double Princess	IMP	1118×711	44 × 28
Quad Crown	IMP	1016×762	40 × 30
Double Elephant	IMP	1016×686	40 × 27
B0	ISO	1000×1414	39.37 × 55.67
Arch-E	USA	$914 \times 1,219$	36 × 48
Double Demy	IMP	889×572	35 × 22 1/2
E	ANSI	864×1118	34 × 44
A0	ISO	841×1189	33.11 × 46.81
Imperial	IMP	762×559	30 × 22
Princess	IMP	711×546	28 × 21 12
B1	ISO	707×1000	27.83 × 39.37
Arch-D	USA	610×914	24 × 36
A1	ISO	594×841	23.39 × 33.11
Demy	IMP	584×470	23 × 18 1/2
D	ANSI	559×864	22 × 34
B2	ISO	500×707	19.68 × 27.83

continues

Table A.1, continued

Standard Paper

Paper Size	Standard	MM	In
Arch-C	USA	457 × 610	18 × 24
C	ANSI	432 × 559	17 × 22
A2	ISO	420 × 594	16.54 × 23.39
B3	ISO	353 × 500	13.90 × 19.68
Brief	IMP	333 × 470	13 1/8 × 18 1/2
Foolscap Folio	IMP	333 × 210	13 1/8 × 8 1/4
Arch-B	USA	305 × 457	12 × 18
A3	ISO	297 × 420	11.69 × 16.54
B	ANSI	279 × 432	11 × 17
Demy quarto	IMP	273 × 216	10 3/4 × 8 1/2
B4	ISO	250 × 353	9.84 × 13.90
Crown quarto	IMP	241 × 184	9 1/2 × 7 1/4
Royal octavo	IMP	241 × 152	9 1/2 × 6
Arch-A	USA	229 × 305	9 × 12
Demy octavo	IMP	222 × 137	8 3/4 × 5 3/8
A	ANSI	216 × 279	8.5 × 11
Legal	USA	216 × 356	8.5 × 14
A4	ISO	210 × 297	8.27 × 11.69
Foolscap quarto	IMP	206 × 165	8 1/8 × 6 1/2
Crown Octavo	IMP	181 × 121	7 1/8 × 4 1/4
B5	ISO	176 × 250	6.93 × 9.84
A5	ISO	148 × 210	5.83 × 8.27
	USA	140 × 216	5.5 × 8.5
	USA	127 × 178	5 × 7

Paper Size	Standard	MM	In
A6	ISO	105 × 148	4.13 × 5.83
	USA	102 × 127	4 × 5
	USA	76 × 102	3 × 5
A7	ISO	74 × 105	2.91 × 4.13
A8	ISO	52 × 74	2.05 × 2.91
A9	ISO	37 × 52	1.46 × 2.05
A10	ISO	26 × 37	1.02 × 1.46

Determining Drawing Scale

After the paper sizes have been established, the next step is to determine the appropriate scale for your drawings. The scale of a drawing is a deceptively simple concept, and it involves more than simply figuring out what size your drawing must be to fit on the paper. The real issue about drawing scale is that the information contained on the drawing must be legible, yet the drawing scale must be standard in your industry and the sheet size must be as convenient to handle as possible. Your drawing must place the model, notes, dimensions, hatching, and symbols in their most favorable and legible light. If you have to cram a drawing full of symbols and text, the line work that represents the object of your drawing may become difficult to discern. Creating the drawing at the appropriate scale allows for space between text, dimensions, and symbols both within and around your drawing.

Of course, if you always create drawings at full-scale, then the only option you are faced with is the selection of the sheet size for your paper. Using the full-scale might require you to cut up your drawing into sections rather than display the entire model on one sheet of paper. You might think that a drawing spanning more than one sheet seems inconvenient, but legibility is more important in this case.

Using Paper Space Viewports to Scale a Model

When plotting, you can set the scale of your model in two ways. You can either provide a scale factor at plot time and plot from model space, or you can pre-scale your model through paper space viewports. But because both result in a drawing that is plotted at the appropriate scale, which one is the best choice?

At one time, users avoided paper space because zooming and panning caused a regen every time, which made working in paper space very time consuming. However, since Release 14, panning and zooming in paper space no longer causes a regen. Consequently, the chief argument against using paper space viewports to scale models is gone. And a major advantage to using paper space viewports is that you get instant feedback from your drawing as to what drawing scale fits on your sheet because you immediately see what your plotted sheet will look like in your layout. Therefore, scaling views of your model in paper space viewports is the better choice.

To use a paper space viewport for plotting to scale, you must zoom in on your model at a predetermined scale factor. The following steps summarize the entire process of determining and setting the proper zoom-scale factor:

1. First, you must calculate the required scale factor. If your drawings use a decimal scale, this is a relatively simple feat. For example, a drawing created at 1:10 uses a scale factor of .10. The AEC industry uses non-decimal scale factors, however, and the calculation requires a few more steps. A 1/8-inch = 1 foot scale drawing requires a scale factor of 1/96. To convert AEC scales, simply multiply your drawing scale (in this case, 1/8) by 1/12 (12.0/0.125). Therefore, the scale factor for a 1/4-inch = 1 foot drawing is 1/48, and a 3-inch = 1 foot drawing is 1/4.

2. Next, click inside the paper space viewport to make it the focus.

3. Then, perform a Zoom Extents to see all your model.

4. Next, perform a Zoom Center and select a point on the model that you want to be in the middle of the viewport.

5. Finally, when you are prompted for magnification or height, type your scale factor, followed by **XP**, as shown in Figure A.10.

The area of the drawing you selected is centered in the viewport at the desired scale, as shown in Figure A.11.

Using this technique, you can set up numerous plot scales of your drawing for any specific needs that you might have. Note also that any text, symbols, or other elements placed in model space will be scaled as well. If you want to display the same model at different scales, you must create symbols, dimensions, and text on different layers and at appropriate sizes for each scale, or draw them all in paper space. The great thing about drawing symbols, text, or other elements in paper space is that you can create them at their actual size without having to convert for scale.

This means, for example, that text that is 1/8-inch high is the same height in all drawings, no matter what scale is used to plot the model. Be mindful, however, that if the objects in model space move at all, the relative position of the annotation objects in paper space and the model will be changed and may no longer align properly.

Figure A.10

Type the scale factor when prompted, followed by **XP**.

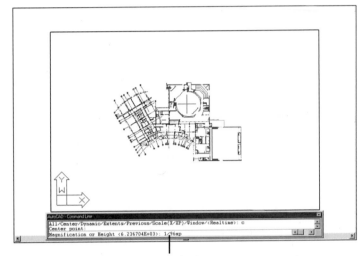

The scale factor

Figure A.11

The model is displayed in the paper space viewport at the correct scale.

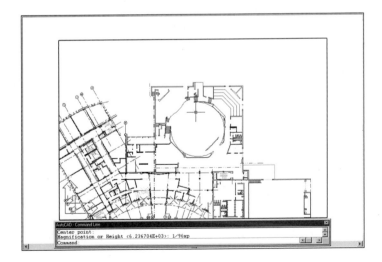

Developing Title Blocks

Almost any drawing, whether a work order, a maintenance drawing, or a sophisticated manufacturing document, should have a title block. A title block provides informational—and often legally required—verification of what the drawing represents in terms of the object of the drawing, the time of day the drawing was created, and the origin of the drawing. If you only publish your drawings electronically, then the title block might differ considerably from one that eventually will be used for plotting or printing. For now, it is assumed that a paper plot is the ultimate goal of an AutoCAD drawing. The following list serves as a guide for the elements your title block should include:

- The name, address, and phone numbers of the firm originating the drawing

- The names, addresses, and phone numbers of any consultants working on the drawing

- The date on which the drawing was originally created and approved for use

- A revision history, including who performed the revision, what the revision was, and when the revision occurred

- A drawing title

- A project name or work order title

- A location for seals, stamps, and/or approval signatures

- A drawing number

- A project or work order number

- The author of the drawing and the name of individual(s) who checked the drawing, if required

- The name of the AutoCAD drawing file

- The date that the drawing was printed or plotted

- A copyright notice, if required

- Additional general information, such as a project address, plant name, and owner's name

- Line work that organizes the title block information and its relationship to the drawing

The design of title blocks is often the source of great debate within a company. No perfect title block design exists, and your needs might include items not listed in the preceding guide. Generally, the more information (either critical or organizational in nature) that you can place in the lower-right corner of the sheet, the easier it will be for others to quickly find the desired drawing. The title block should provide the information legibly for all size plots, but not dominate the sheet. You also might need to develop a title block for multiple sheet sizes. Most likely, you will not be able to use the same title block for an 8 1/2 × 11-inch sheet as you can for a 34 × 44-inch sheet. You will need to experiment with different designs until you have a set of title blocks that works for all content possibilities and sizes.

Additionally, the title block can contain a grid design that promotes the modular development of your drawings. For example, if you typically develop details that can be printed on 8 1/2 × 11-inch paper, then you could develop a drawing module that enables you to piece together a number of small modular drawings into a larger drawing. In this case, you should be concerned with the drawing area within the title block for the module size rather than the sheet of paper size. This is because you will transfer the drawing area from one sheet to the next. Figure A.12 shows one example of a modular approach to the drawing area.

Figure A.12

Using a modular grid for drawing development enables you to use modular drawings more effectively.

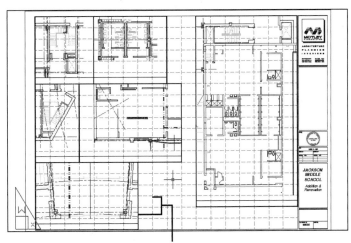

Align viewports with modular divisions
of the drawing area to save time

Determining Units and Angles

The discipline and country in which you work determines whether you'll use fractional inches, feet and fractional inches, decimal feet, decimal inches, meters, or centimeters in the creation of drawings. Additionally, you must determine how accurately to display the dimensions. AutoCAD does not understand any specific system of the division of distance—the program simply draws using units. As a result, you must tell AutoCAD how you want those units displayed. You change the display of units and angles in AutoCAD from the Drawing Units dialog box, which is accessed by choosing Units from the Format pull-down menu. The Drawing Units dialog box is shown in Figure A.13.

Figure A.13

The Drawing Units dialog box is used to set AutoCAD units and angles.

You should set up the default units that you will typically use in your template drawings. By doing so, all new drawings that use the template will automatically use the default units and angles settings. You should also note that you could select the precision of the display of your units and angles.

INSIDER TIP

Don't confuse the precision setting for units and angles with the precision setting for dimensions. You set the dimension precision independently when you define dimensioning defaults. Chapter 17, "Productive Dimensioning," discusses dimensioning in greater detail.

When selecting the units' and angles' precision, your primary concern should be how much precision you need to see when you create your AutoCAD drawings. High-precision settings often cause AutoCAD to display the drawing coordinates using scientific notation, such as 1.07E+10, which usually isn't much help. On the other hand, if you're trying to track down a drafting error, high-precision settings can tell you that a line has been drawn at an angle of 179.91846 degrees rather than 180 degrees. The simple process of trial and error can help you determine the best settings for your needs.

Converting Between Units

If you need to convert your drawings from feet and inches to metric units, the units in which you create your drawing will not automatically convert. This is because you are drawing in units, not in real-world sizes. For example, when you create a drawing in feet and inches, one unit is an inch. When you convert to a metric drawing, you must change units to decimal units and convert the drawing to a metric drawing by scaling the drawing by the proper conversion factor. As a result of this component of AutoCAD's units architecture, you must determine what the drawing should represent before you start creating lines, circles, and arcs. You can instruct AutoCAD to dimension objects by scaling them between different units of measure (accomplished by setting a linear scale factor for dimensioning), but the model will not be drawn true to size in the converted units. For more information, refer to Chapter 6, "Accuracy in Creating Drawings with AutoCAD 2000."

Using AutoCAD Features that Help in Project Delivery

In this book, you learn how to use many AutoCAD features that help you work on a project more effectively. When you set up your projects, you must keep the capability of certain AutoCAD features or commands in mind as you develop your approach to a project, or to project standards.

Although this appendix discusses the use of these commands, its focus is on how these commands relate to project setup. To understand how to use these commands to their fullest, you should read this book's more detailed discussions in the appropriate chapters. For now, concentrate on the concepts that are being presented instead of concerning yourself with the detailed use of a command or concept.

When you learn how to use these commands in other chapters, think about how they relate to project delivery. After you have learned to use these commands, you can return to this appendix to review their use in terms of project delivery.

Drawing Layers

One of the most powerful features offered by AutoCAD—and a feature that makes project delivery more efficient—is the use of drawing layers. *Layers* allow you to organize different objects in your drawing. Layers also can minimize the number of drawings needed for a project by reducing replication of objects. By using layers effectively, you increase efficiency and reduce errors.

Drawing layers are created using AutoCAD's LAYER command, and are used to set up drawing data in hierarchical groups that can be turned on or off, or locked from editing. In this way, you can, for example, create text that defines how a shop manufactures a part on one layer, and text that helps a salesman explain the product on a different layer. By turning layers off and on, you can plot two drawings that serve different purposes from the same drawing.

You also can use AutoCAD's capability to *freeze* layers (a condition in which the layer information isn't displayed or loaded into memory) to save drawing load-time, as well as display various objects of the same model. You can freeze layers of drawings that are xref'd into the current drawing, or you can freeze layers within individual paper space viewports. This means that one AEC drawing or viewport could contain a floor plan, and another drawing or viewport could contain a reflected ceiling plan, while allowing you to use the same model for both drawings. In addition, you can develop non-printing layers for information that you don't want plotted, but will use with the drawing.

Using AutoCAD's DEFPOINTS Layer and Non-Plotting Feature

AutoCAD has a special layer called *DEFPOINTS* that never plots. Objects on the DEFPOINTS layer appear onscreen, but fail to plot. You can therefore draw information for reference purposes, such as floor plan areas, thread counts, or volumes and weights, on the DEFPOINTS layer. The DEFPOINTS layer automatically is added to your drawing when you create an associative dimension, or you can add it manually by creating a new layer named DEFPOINTS.

You can also create non-plotting layers. To do so, simply create a new layer, then choose the Printer icon in the Layer Properties Manager to turn printing off. The layer remains visible onscreen, but will not plot.

Note

> Non-plotting layers other than DEFPOINTS are new to AutoCAD 2000 and therefore are not supported in previous releases. Research as to future data use should be done.

Non-plotting layers, as well as the DEFPOINTS layer, help you avoid re-plotting drawings because you won't have to remember to freeze or turn off layers that you don't want to plot.

Other Uses for Layers

As discussed earlier in this appendix, you can use layers for redlining purposes. Additionally, you can store project data and design information on layers that are needed by other software. Many third-party applications require that certain data be stored on layers with specific names. For example, point data from a site survey must be on a specific layer so a third-party application can locate the data, and use it to generate site contours. You must take these types of specialized layers into account if you use third-party products when you develop your prototype drawings.

Furthermore, you can organize different objects in your model by placing them on different layers. By using different layers, you can quickly apply a new color, linetype, or lineweight for all objects on a layer. This method is useful for controlling the display of hidden lines, for example. By turning off hidden lines onscreen, you remove clutter, and make viewing the model easier. Then, you can turn hidden lines back on for plotting purposes.

Meeting Industry Standards

Finally, your industry might have organizations that have developed layering standards for use in electronic drawings. If your drawings are required to meet certain industry standards, you must set up your layers accordingly. Other industries, such as the AEC industry, might have guidelines only for layer names and use, but these guidelines will help you in developing your own layering standards. The point is that some research is required before you define your use of layers in your projects. After you have developed layering standards, you can easily store them in template drawings. You can also create custom menu pull-downs and create, set, and reset layers from a quick menu.

Layers in AutoCAD are created and managed in the Layer Properties Manager shown in Figure A.14. You will learn more about layer creation and management in Chapter 4, "Organizing a Drawing with Layers."

The Layer Properties Manager dialog box manages layers in AutoCAD.

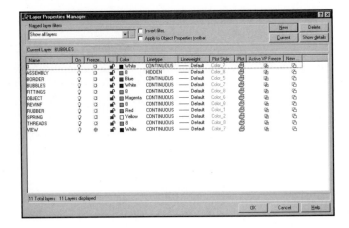

Defining Linetypes

Linetypes represent different things for different industries. AutoCAD comes with a variety of pre-defined linetypes, and also enables you to define a wide variety of your own linetypes. You can define linetypes that contain symbols within the linetype, or that have varying spacing between line components. Linetypes also can be defined as an industry drafting standard. If so, you should create a set of linetypes that meet your industry's requirements, and include them in the linetype file. You can also load linetypes into your template drawing so that they are readily available. It is not absolutely necessary to pre-load linetypes, however, because they are relatively easy to retrieve from the AutoCAD linetype file. You will learn more about creating and loading linetypes in Chapter 5, "Using Linetypes and Lineweights Effectively." Figure A.15 shows some examples of the types of lines that you can create and use in AutoCAD.

Figure A.15

A variety of linetypes can be created within AutoCAD.

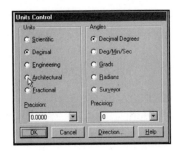

Defining Lineweights

NEW for R2000 New to AutoCAD 2000 is a feature called *lineweights*, which allows you to control the width of a line. Lineweights may be displayed onscreen and plotted on paper. By using lineweights, you can more easily identify different objects in your drawing. As with linetypes, discussed previously, varying lineweights can be used to differentiate objects that are hidden or lie beneath other objects. You will learn more about assigning lineweights in Chapter 5. Figure A.16 shows the new Lineweight Settings dialog box.

Figure A.16

The new Lineweight Settings dialog box.

Selecting Text Styles

AutoCAD enables you to use any font that comes with Windows (.ttf), as well as text fonts (.shx) that are supplied with AutoCAD. You must select the font or fonts that work best with your drawing size and plotter or printer. It is equally important that the fonts you use are legible for a wide variety of reproduction sizes. For example, many drawings are placed on microfilm as a matter of storage. To ensure that the lettering is visible on the microfilm, you should use text styles that are a minimum of 1/8 inch in plotted height.

After you have experimented with a variety of plotted output and text styles, you will want to select a few styles to serve for general text, sheet title block information, drawing titles, and emphasized text. Everyone has distinct taste in text appearance, so AutoCAD supports a host of variations in the appearance of text. Therefore, it might be best for you to find examples of text that you and your firm find acceptable, and then find text settings and fonts in AutoCAD that best approximate your desired results.

Text can have different angles, line spacing, heights, weights, effects (upside down, backward, and/or vertical), and width factors. Figure A.17 shows examples of what can be accomplished with a single text font in AutoCAD. You will learn more about the use of text in Chapter 15, "Text Annotation."

Figure A.17

The variety of text style effects in AutoCAD creates many opportunities for expression.

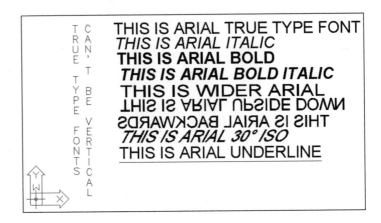

Saving Views

AutoCAD enables you to save views of your drawings to which you can return time and time again. The reuse of views can result in considerable time savings if you have a predictable set of views upon which all users can rely. For example, everyone will need a view of the entire drawing, including its title block. You could save this view as a view named Overall by using the AutoCAD VIEW command. Views can be saved in either paper space or model space. You might want to save standard views that are 1/4 portions of the drawing and call them UL, UR, LL, and LR for upper-left, upper-right, lower-left, and lower-right. Saving these views in a template drawing ensures that they are available in all your drawings.

Paper Space Versus Model Space Viewports

AutoCAD uses paper space layouts for real-world paper sizes and model space for real-world model sizes. The proper use of these two spaces means that you never need to be concerned about scaling a drawing up or down for a plot. In pre-paper space days, users had to remember the scale of each drawing so that when the drawings were plotted, the users could enter the correct scale factor in response to plot setup questions presented by AutoCAD.

Proper use of paper space layouts takes some getting used to because you view your model through ports from paper space to model space. You create your model and work on it in model space, which allows you to view the model as close to full-screen as possible. Figure A.18 shows how a model appears within a paper space viewport that does not fill the screen.

Figure A.18

A paper space viewport does not necessarily provide a full-screen view of your model.

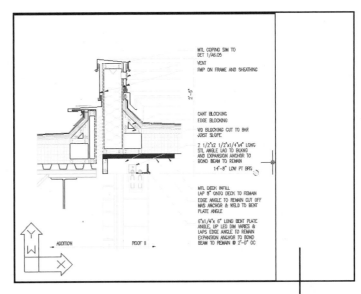

MTL COPING SIM TO
DET 1/A6.05
VENT
PMP ON FRAME AND SHEATHING

CANT BLOCKING
EDGE BLOCKING
WD BLOCKING CUT TO BAR
JOIST SLOPE
2 1/2"x2 1/2"x1/4"x4" LONG
STL ANGLE LAG TO BLKNG
AND EXPANSION ANCHOR TO
BOND BEAM TO REMAIN
14'-8" LOW PT BRG

MTL DECK INFILL
LAP 8" ONTO DECK TO REMAIN
EDGE ANGLE TO REMAIN CUT OFF
MAS ANCHOR & WELD TO BENT
PLATE ANGLE

6"x1/4"x 6" LONG BENT PLATE
ANGLE, UP LEG DIM VARIES &
LAPS EDGE ANGLE TO REMAIN
EXPANSION ANCHOR TO BOND
BEAM TO REMAIN @ 2'-0" OC

ADDITION   ROOF II

This area of the screen
beyond the viewport
cannot be used for
modular space drawing

I N S I D E R   T I P

You might want to consider creating a viewport that is as big as the drawing area within your title block to store with your template drawing. This viewport can provide a good starting place for any drawing and can be resized, copied, or turned off as the drawing develops.

Unless your drawings are very predictable, you won't be able to create multiple viewports that will work every time. However, using the overall viewport saves some time when you create a drawing. You will learn more about the use of paper space in Chapter 19, "Paper Space Layouts."

Setting Dimension Styles

Each discipline or industry has its own standards and preferences for dimensioning. AutoCAD enables you to store dimensioning standards as dimension styles. You can set the color of individual portions of a dimension, the text style the dimension uses, the arrow style, the way the dimension extension lines work, and the format of the dimension annotation. Each dimension feature, however, must be scaled appropriately for the scale that you use for the drawing. You can set dimensions to be scaled based upon paper space viewport scaling, and AutoCAD will adjust the dimension features for you.

You should set up a generic dimension style for each type of dimension that you use (such as radial, leader, and linear) and save them in your template drawing. Figure A.19 shows the Dimension Style Manager dialog box that grants access to custom dimension styles and sets the dimension scale factor.

Figure A.19

Using the Dimension Style Manager dialog box enables you to set up custom dimension styles.

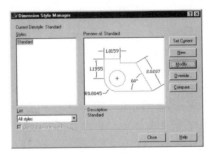

Note that you must set up your text style standards in your drawing before you set the dimension text style. You also can create custom blocks for use as arrows. Dimensions are made up from a complex set of options, and it will take some time and study on your part to tailor them for your needs and tastes. You will learn more about using dimension styles and the DDIM command in Chapter 17, "Productive Dimensioning," and Chapter 18, "Advanced Dimensioning."

Using Xrefs

This appendix has already briefly discussed a variety of situations in which xrefs can be helpful in the delivery of a project. You should be aware of a few things when using xrefs. First, if you intend to share your drawings with consultants or clients, you must make them aware of your folder structure. Although organizing your drawings and xrefs with folders is good practice, if those with whom you share your drawings aren't aware of your structure, AutoCAD may not find xrefs attached to an opened drawing. This problem can be avoided by locating all drawings, including xrefs, in the same folder so that AutoCAD can find all pertinent files, but it is better practice to use a proper folder structure and pass along this structure to those with whom you share your drawings.

A second issue arises when problems are found in an xref drawing. In many situations, you will notice that something must be fixed in a drawing while you're working on an entirely different aspect of the drawing. For example, you could be dimensioning walls in a floor plan that is xref'd into the current drawing when you discover that a wall is drawn incorrectly. In previous releases, this presented quite a problem because the methods used to correct the problem required opening multiple sessions of AutoCAD, and working in two drawings simultaneously—the current drawing and the xref.

With AutoCAD 2000, the difficulty of updating xrefs is dramatically minimized. As noted previously, AutoCAD 2000 has a new feature called *In-Place Reference Editing*. This new feature allows users to edit blocks and xrefs, and save changes back to the original object or drawing file. More importantly, it allows you to do this from within the current drawing that contains the questioned xref.

A third point to keep in mind is that if you need to use only part of an xref'd drawing, you can insert and clip the xref so that the desired portion of the drawing remains. You still have the advantages of current updates to the xref'd portion of the drawing, but you won't have the entire xref attached to the current drawing. If you don't anticipate changes to the xref'd drawing, you can attach the xref to make it a permanent part of the drawing. In this case, the xref'd drawing becomes an AutoCAD block that you can explode, modify, and clip as you desire. This appendix discusses blocks in a later section, and points out the differences between using blocks and xrefs. You will learn more about xrefs in Chapter 14.

INSIDER **T**IP

AutoCAD 2000 introduces a new and powerful feature: *viewport clipping*. This new feature allows you to create non-rectangular viewports in paper space.

Creating Multiline Styles

AutoCAD enables you to draw *multiple lines*, which is a set of lines offset from a center line path, by using the Multiline Styles dialog box shown in Figure A.20. If you draw streets with curbs, multiple data lines, cavity walls, or other multiple-line objects, you might find it helpful to create standard multiline styles, and save them, ready for use in your projects.

Although multilines are very convenient, their usefulness is somewhat limited. Multiline components must be edited via the MLEDIT command, which has editing limitations. For example, it is difficult to insert a door or window into a wall created by a multiline, because you can't easily break the wall. Also, if you grip-edit a multiline, you can edit only the outer boundary of the multiline.

Despite their editing limitations, you may find multilines a useful feature in certain situations. Because multilines behave as a single object, you can save considerable time in drawing creation and edits if you plan for their use. For example, if you must change a room configuration, editing a single multiline changes all wall lines instantly.

INSIDER TIP

In general, any time that you have basic objects that are made up of multiple lines, you can make good use of multilines. If, however, multiple variations exist in the width, composition, and interruptions of the multilines, then you should carefully consider their use. Also, multilines cannot be converted into 3D lines, nor can their intersecting lines have a radius applied.

Figure A.20

Creating custom multilines can ease tedious line creation.

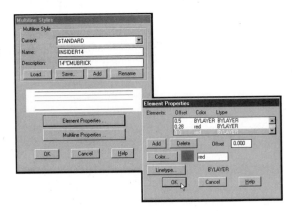

Using Blocks

Blocks are primary components that contribute to huge time savings in project delivery, because they can be used in many ways. The importance of blocks cannot be overstated. Blocks can be used for symbols, components, details, standard text notation, and many other situations. The use of blocks also saves drawing disk space if multiple instances of their use exist because one definition of the block is saved in the drawing, and that definition is copied throughout the drawing without repeating all the block's components for each insertion. You should build a library of blocks that are used for repeating objects in your projects and keep them readily available for use. Or, you could purchase block libraries from third-party vendors.

Blocks can be created on layer 0 so that they inherit the characteristics of the layer in which they are inserted, or they can contain multiple layer, color, linetype, and lineweight definitions so that they maintain their appearance regardless of the layer on which they are inserted. Blocks also can be used with the ARRAY, MINSERT, DIVIDE, and MEASURE commands so that multiple copies can be created easily for such things as stair treads, elevations of fences and grilles, and flooring patterns. As with multilines, the use of blocks requires careful planning and repetitive standards for layer names, linetypes, block names, and component design. A sophisticated use of blocks also enables the assembly of projects from a kit of parts. For example, many national companies use a kit of parts for the assembly of their new branch offices throughout the country. You will learn more about blocks in Chapter 13, "Creating and Using Blocks."

The use of xrefs has also been discussed in this appendix. As a general rule of thumb, you should address two prime considerations when deciding whether to use xrefs or blocks. First, if the need for continual updating isn't required, then blocks are more convenient to use than xrefs. Second, and more important, if you want to freeze your drawings in time so that the electronic copy on disk matches the last version plotted, you should not use xrefs because xrefs are updated each time you open the drawing.

DesignCenter

AutoCAD 2000 introduces a powerful new feature called *AutoCAD DesignCenter (ADC)*. One of its capabilities enables you to easily locate and insert blocks, using a new Find feature. Figure A.21 displays a sample window of the DesignCenter. By entering a block's name or description, ADC will search all drawing files in the specified folders for blocks matching the description. Then, icons of the blocks are displayed, along with detailed descriptions. ADC also allows you to drag and drop blocks into a drawing, and if the block has drawing units associated with it, AutoCAD automatically scales the block based on the current drawing's units.

ADC also allows you to drag and drop symbol table items. This feature allows you to quickly copy symbol table items from existing drawings, and gives you the ability to restore the current drawing's original settings. You can quickly insert layers, dimension styles, text styles, and linetype styles from other drawings.

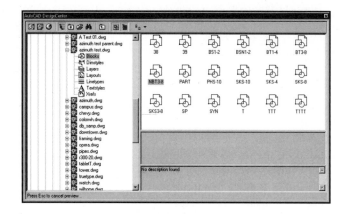

Summary

In this appendix, you learned about the components of an effective project-delivery system. You also learned how to use AutoCAD features to help you in the management of project delivery. You learned the factors needed to get organized before creating a drawing, as well as how to use OLE to create a task list that is embedded in each drawing. You learned how to use a mock-up process to view your entire project as a whole for planning purposes based upon priorities, how much detail is necessary, how your drawings relate to other drawings and documents, and how to account for the people who work on the drawings.

Other sections discussed the use of repetitive elements and considerations for the number of different ways drawings can be displayed or published. You then reviewed the basic factors used in the initial drawing setup, such as paper, scale, units, angles, and precision. Finally, you learned about commands and new AutoCAD 2000 features that can save time in project delivery.

B

THE EXPRESS TOOLS

AutoCAD 2000 ships with a large group of tools collectively called Express Tools. For the most part, these tools consist of AutoLISP routines and executable AutoCAD Runtime Extension (ARX) and VBA functions written by the Express Tools Team of programmers at Autodesk. Many are the result of requests for extended or new command features from AutoCAD users. The Express Tools are fully supported by Autodesk and you can communicate with the Express Tools Team indirectly by visiting the AutoCAD Express Tools newsgroup news:// adesknews.autodesk.com/autodesk.expresstools.

Express Tools Team members regularly monitor this newsgroup, which provides a rare means of quickly communicating with Autodesk programmers to answer Express Tools questions or to make suggestions for future tools.

Installing the Express Tools

The AutoCAD Express Tools are automatically installed when AutoCAD is installed with either the Full option or with the Custom option with Express Tools selected. If you installed AutoCAD using the Typical option, the Express Tools were probably not installed. You can install them subsequent to an initial install procedure by rerunning the AutoCAD installation, choosing Add, and selecting Express Tools. The function and supporting files for Express Tools are, by default, placed in a folder named Express directly under the main AutoCAD2000 folder.

To enable the Express Tools after installing them, use the EXPRESSTOOLS command. This command places the Express directory on AutoCAD's search path, then loads and places the Express menu on the menu bar. You can use this command to make the Express Tools available in the current profile. After the EXPRESSTOOLS command is used, the AutoCAD Express Tools functions load whenever AutoCAD is launched.

Displaying the Express Tools Toolbars

Many of the Express Tools are also available on four toolbars grouped by category. To display one or more of these toolbars, use the TOOLBAR command (View, Toolbars) to display the Toolbars dialog box. In this dialog box, find the Menu Group list and select Express. A list of toolbars is displayed with check boxes. Select the box next to the toolbar you want to display, then click Close. You can hide toolbars by again using the TOOLBAR command and un-checking the toolbars you want to hide.

Express Tools At-A-Glance

Table B.1 lists all the Express Tools that ship with AutoCAD 2000. The table lists the tool name, command-line name, and a brief description of its function. There are approximately 54 tools presented on the Express menu, grouped by general function such as Layer Tools, Dimension Tools, and so on. The table lists tools as they appear on the Express menu. There are a number of command-line and operating system level-only tools not included in the following table. The Help item on the Express menu provides complete information on all the Express tools.

An asterisk next to a name of an Express routine indicates that there is a tutorial for that routine in the second part of this appendix.

Table B.1

Express Tools Reference Table

Express Routine Name	Command Name	Description
Layer Tools		
*LAYER MANAGER	LMAN	Manages layer settings. Saves and restores layer configurations as "layer states" that can be modified, recalled, or renamed within an AutoCAD session. Layer states are saved within the drawing file but can also be exported to or imported from external <*filename*>.LAY files.
LAYER MATCH	LAYMCH	Changes the layer(s) of selected object(s) to match the layer of a selected object.
CHANGE TO CURRENT LAYER	LAYCUR	Changes the layer of one or more selected objects to the current layer.
*LAYER ISOLATE	LAYISO	Isolates the layer of one or more selected objects by turning all other layers off.
LAYER FREEZE	LAYFRZ	Freezes layer of selected object(s).
*LAYER OFF	LAYOFF	Turns off layer of selected object(s).
LAYER LOCK	LAYLCK	Locks layer of selected object.
LAYER UNLOCK	LAYULK	Unlocks layer of selected object.
LAYER MERGE	LAYMRG	Moves all objects from source layer to target layer. Deletes source layer.

continues

Table B.1, continued

Express Tools Reference Table

Express Routine Name	Command Name	Description
Layer Tools		
LAYER DELETE	LAYDEL	Deletes all objects on the selected layer and purges the layer from the drawing.
TURN ALL LAYERS ON	LAYON	Turns on all layers.
THAW ALL LAYERS	LAYTHW	Thaws all layers.
Block Tools		
LIST BLOCK ENTITIES	BLOCK?	Lists the entities in a block definition.
COPY NESTED OBJECTS	NCOPY	Copies objects nested in an xref or block.
TRIM TO BLOCK ENTITIES	BTRIM	Trims objects using block or xref objects as cutting edge.
EXTEND TO BLOCK ENTITIES	BEXTEND	Extends objects using block or xref objects as a boundary edge.
GLOBAL ATTRIBUTE EDIT	GATTE	Globally changes attribute values for all duplicate blocks.
EXPLODE ATTRIBUTES TO TEXT	BURST	Explodes blocks, converting attribute values to text objects.
Text Tools		
REMOTE TEXT	RTEXT	Allows you to embed text from an ASCII text file. The source of the text is maintained in an external file. You can also display the value of a DIESEL expression.

Express Routine Name	Command Name	Description
Text Tools		
*FIT TEXT BETWEEN POINTS	TEXTFIT	Shrinks or stretches text by picking new start and end points.
*TEXT MASK	TEXTMASK	Creates an invisible rectangular frame around text objects masking underlying objects.
UNMASK TEXT	TEXTUNMASK	Undoes TEXTMASK.
EXPLODE TEXT	TXTEXP	Explodes text into polyline entities.
CONVERT TEXT TO MTEXT	TXT2MTXT	Converts text or dtext objects to Mtext objects.
*ARC ALIGNED TEXT	ARCTEXT	Places a type of text entity along an arc.
Dimension Tools		
ATTACH LEADER TO ANNOTATION	QLATTACH	Attaches leader lines to Mtext, Tolerances, or Block reference objects.
DETACH LEADER	QLDETACHSET	Detaches leader lines from Mtext, Tolerances, or Block reference objects.
GLOBAL ATTACH LEADER TO ANNOTATION	QLATTACHSET	Globally attaches leader lines to Mtext, Tolerance, or Block reference objects.
DIMSTYLE EXPORT	DIMEX	Exports named dimension styles and settings to external file.
DIMSTYLE IMPORT	DIMIN	Imports named dimension styles and settings from external file.

continues

Table B.1, continued

Express Tools Reference Table

Express Routine Name	Command Name	Description
	Selection Tools	
GET SELECTION SET	GETSEL	Creates a temporary selection set.
EXCLUSIONARY SELECTION SETS	SSTOOLS	Creates exclusionary selection sets.
	Modify Tools	
*MULTIPLE ENTITY STRETCH	MSTRETCH	Allows multiple crossing windows and/or crossing polygons to define objects for stretch operation.
*MOVE COPY ROTATE	MOCORO	Moves, copies, rotates, and scales object(s) with a single command.
COOKIE CUTTER TRIM	ETRIM	Trims objects at cutting edge defined by polyline, line circle, arc, ellipse, text, Mtext, or attribute definition.
EXTENDED CLIP	CLIPIT	Allows curved clipping; isolates specified portions of blocks, xrefs, images, or Wipeouts.
POLYLINE JOIN	PLJOIN	Joins two or more polylines whose ends do not exactly meet.
MULTIPLE PEDIT	MPEDIT	Edits multiple polylines.
	Draw Tools	
SUPERHATCH	SUPERHATCH	Allows you to use an image, block, xref, or Wipeout object as a hatch pattern.
WIPEOUT	WIPEOUT	Covers area defined by a polyline with current background color.
*REVISION CLOUD	REVCLOUD	Creates a freehand polyline of sequential arcs to form a revision cloud.

Express Routine Name	Command Name	Description
Miscellaneous Tools		
PACK 'N GO	PACK	Copies all files associated with a drawing (fonts, xrefs, and so on) to a specified location.
FULLSCREEN	FULLSCREEN	Resizes the drawing screen to a maximum area. Hides the title bar and menu bar in AutoCAD window. FULLSCREEN command toggles screen between normal and full size.
MAKE LINETYPE	MKLTYPE	Creates a linetype based on selected objects.
MAKE SHAPE	MKSHAPE	Creates a shape definition based on selected objects.
PATH SUBSTITUTION	REDIR	Redefines hard-coded paths in xrefs, images, shapes, styles, and rtext.
COUNT BLOCKS	BCOUNT	Counts, itemizes, and displays the number of insertions of each block in the selected objects or the entire drawing (formerly COUNT).
POLYLINE JOIN	PLJOIN	Joins two or more polylines whose ends do not exactly meet.
SHOW URLs	SHOWURLS	Shows and edits URLs embedded in a drawing.
ATTACH XDATA	XDATA	Attaches extended entity data (xdata) to a selected entity.
LIST ENTITY DATA	XDLIST	Lists extended entity data (xdata) associated with an object.

Express Tools Tutorials

The following tutorials demonstrate a representative sampling of the Express Tools. Not all the options or features of these tools are included in these short exercises, but you should get a feeling for what these tools are capable of doing. Please refer to the Express Help facility found on the Express pull-down menu for the options available with each of these and the other Express tools.

LAYER MANAGER

1. Open the drawing APP-1.DWG from this book's CD-ROM.

2. Start Layer Manager in one of the following ways:

    ■ Click on the Layer Manager tool from the Express Layer Tools toolbar.

    ■ Choose the Express pull-down menu, then Layers, Layer Manager.

    ■ Type **lman** and press Enter at the command prompt.

3. The Layer Manager dialog box appears. If necessary, place the screen pointer in the title bar of the dialog box, click and drag the box to the position shown in Figure B.1. Notice in the bottom-left corner that the current layer state is titled PLAN-ONLY.

Figure B.1

The Layer Manager dialog box.

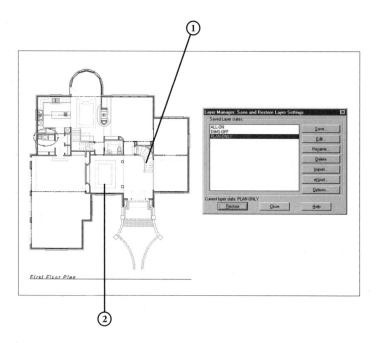

4. With the Layer Manager dialog box still displayed, highlight the ALL-ON layer state, then click Restore.

    Note that the ALL-ON layer state makes all layers visible.

5. Highlight the layer state DIMS-OFF and click Restore. Note that the Dimension layers are turned off.

6. Close the Layer Manager dialog box.

7. Using AutoCAD's Layer Control drop-down list on the Object Properties toolbar, turn off the layer BRTITLES.

8. Select Layer Manager to display the Layer Manager dialog box again. Create and save the current layer state by clicking the Save button. Save the current layer state as **NO-NOTES**. Then Select and Restore the layer state DIMS-OFF.

9. Restore the layer state NO-NOTES and note that the layer BRTITLES is not displayed.

10. Delete the layer state NO-NOTES by clicking the Delete button and clicking Yes in the Warning dialog box.

11. Finally, restore the layer state PLAN-ONLY and close the Layer Manager dialog box.

12. Leave this drawing open if you plan to continue in the next exercise.

NOTE

Layer states may be saved to and restored from an external file as well. The file extension for these saved layer states is .lay.

LAYER TOOLS

1. If necessary, open the drawing APP-1.DWG from this book's CD-ROM.

2. Select the Isolate Layer Express feature in one of the following ways:

    ■ Click on the Isolate Object's Layer tool from the Express Layer Tools toolbar.

    ■ Choose the Express pull-down menu, then Layers, Layer Isolate.

    ■ Enter **layiso** and press Enter at the command prompt.

3. At the Select object(s) on the layer(s) to be ISOLATED: prompt, pick the stairway at ① in Figure B.1 and press Enter.

4. Note that all layers except the layer you picked are turned off. Undo the last operation by typing **u** and pressing Enter.

5. Select the Turn Object's Layer Off Express feature in one of the following ways:

    - Click on the Turn Object's Layer Off tool from the Express Layer Tools toolbar.

    - Choose the Express pull-down menu, then Layers, Layer Off.

    - Type **layoff** and press Enter at the command prompt.

6. At the `Options/Undo/<Pick an object on the layer to be turned OFF>:` prompt, select the object at ② in Figure B.1. Note that the layer of the object picked, ARHEADER, is turned off.

7. With the prompt in the preceding step still active, type **u** and press Enter to turn the ARHEADER layer back on. Exit the command by pressing Enter.

    Leave this drawing open if you plan to continue to the next exercise.

REVISION CLOUD

1. If necessary, open the drawing APP-1.DWG from this book's CD-ROM. Restore the view REVISE.

2. Select the Revision Cloud Express feature in one of the following ways:

    - Click on the Revision tool from the Express Standard toolbar.

    - Choose the Express pull-down menu, then Draw, Revision Cloud.

    - Type **revcloud** and press Enter at the command prompt.

3. At the `Specify cloud starting point or [eXit/Options] <eXit>:` prompt, type **O** to open the Revcloud Options dialog box. In the Arc Chord Length edit box, change the value to **12.0**. Then click OK to close the dialog box.

N OTE

You could click the Pick button to select a distance on screen for the arc chord distance.

4. At the `Specify cloud starting point or [eXit/Options] <eXit>:` prompt, pick a point near ① in Figure B.2 and guide the cursor in a counterclockwise direction to surround the objects following the path shown in Figure B.2. AutoCAD draws the revision cloud along the path automatically as you outline the revision, and closes the cloud when you get within an arc length distance from the starting point.

5. Close this drawing without saving changes.

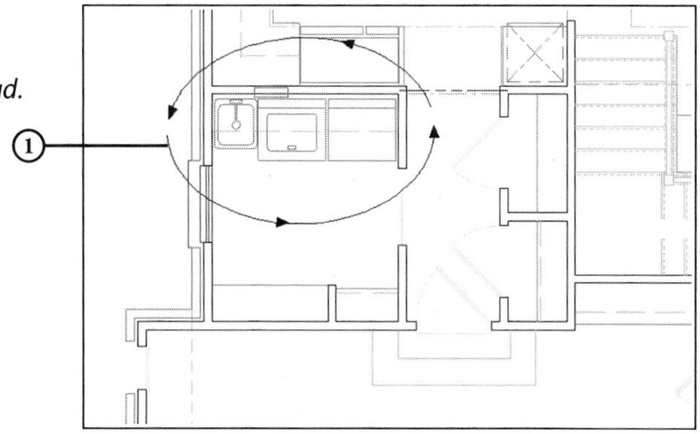

Figure B.2

Placing a Revision Cloud.

MULTIPLE ENTITY STRETCH

1. Open APP-2.DWG from the book's CD-ROM. Check that Layer1 is Thawed, On, and Current and that Layer2 is turned off.

2. Start the Multiple Entity Stretch Express feature in one of the following ways:

   ■ Click on the Multiple Entity Stretch tool on the Express Standard toolbar.

   ■ Select the Express pull-down menu, then Modify, Multiple Entity Stretch.

   ■ Type **mstretch** and press Enter at the command prompt.

   The following prompts appear:

   ```
   Crossing Polygon or Crossing first point
   Specify an option [CP/C] <Crossing first point>:
   ```

3. Form the two crossing boxes at the ends of boxes 1 and 3 as shown in Figure B.3. Then press Enter.

Figure B.3

Using Multiple Stretch.

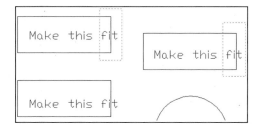

4. Respond to the following prompts as follows:

```
Done defining windows for stretch...
Specify an option [Remove objects] <Base point>:
```

Pick anywhere in the drawing area. The following prompt appears:

```
Second base point: @0.75,0
```

The Express routine stretches the two areas defined by the rectangles. Note that in the previous step you could have entered the stretch distance using direct distance entry, or you could have stretched the boxes dynamically with a click and drag motion.

Your drawing should now resemble Figure B.4.

5. Leave this drawing open if you plan to continue with the next Express tutorial; otherwise, close the drawing without saving changes.

Figure B.4

After using Multiple Stretch.

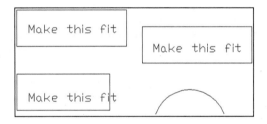

FIT TEXT BETWEEN POINTS AND ARC TEXT

1. Continue from the previous Express tutorial or open drawing APP-2.DWG from the book's CD-ROM. Check that Layer1 is Thawed, On, and Current and that Layer2 is turned off.

2. Start the Text Fit Express feature in one of the following ways:

   - Click on the Text Fit icon on the Express Text Tools toolbar.

   - Choose the Express pull-down menu, then Text, Text Fit.

   - Type **textfit** and press Enter at the command prompt.

   The following prompt appears:

   ```
   Select Text to stretch or shrink:
   ```

3. Pick the text in box 2. The following prompt appears:

   ```
   Specify end point or [Start point]:
   ```

4. Position the cursor to the right and pick near ① in Figure B.5.

   The Express routine fits the text as shown in Figure B.5.

Figure B.5

Fit between text points.

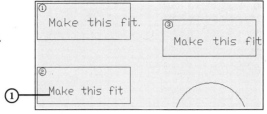

5.   Start the Express Arctext feature in one of the following ways:

■   Click on the Text Along Arc icon on the Express Text Tools toolbar.

■   Choose the Express pull-down menu, then Text, Arc Aligned Text.

■   Type **arctext** and press Enter at the command prompt.

The following prompt appears:

```
Select an Arc or an ArcAlignedText:
```

6.   Pick the arc. The ArcAligned Text Workshop dialog box appears as shown in Figure B.6.

Figure B.6

The ArcAlignedText Workshop dialog box.

7.   In the ArcAlignedText Workshop dialog box, enter the following values:

Text height: **0.2**

Offset from arc: **0.2**

Leave all other values at their default settings. In the Text edit box, enter the following text:

Fit this text along an arc.

Then click the OK button.

The Express routine fits the text along the arc as shown in Figure B.7.

8.   If you want to continue in these tutorials, leave this drawing open. Otherwise, quit AutoCAD without saving changes.

Figure B.7

Text along an arc.

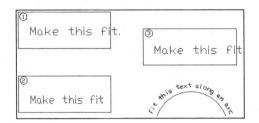

TEXT MASK

1. Continue from the previous Express tutorial or open drawing APP-2.DWG from the book's CD-ROM. Check that Layer2 is Thawed, On, and Current and that Layer1 is turned off. Your drawing should resemble Figure B.8.

Figure B.8

The Text Mask exercise drawing.

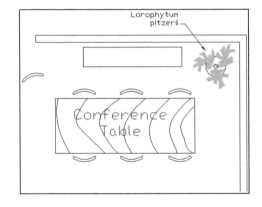

2. Start the Text Mask tool by using any of the three following methods:

    ■ Click on the Text Mask tool on the Express Text Tools toolbar.

    ■ Choose the Express pull-down menu, then Text, Text Mask.

    ■ Type **TEXTMASK** and press Enter at the command prompt.

    When the following prompt appears, type **O** to enter the Offset control. Change the default value of 0.35 to **0.45** and exit by pressing Enter.

    ```
    Current settings: Offset factor = 0.3500, Mask type = Wipeout
    Select text objects to mask or [Masktype/Offset]:
    ```

3. At the `Select text objects to mask or [Masktype/Offset]:` prompt, pick the Conference Table text items and press Enter. AutoCAD creates the text mask as shown in Figure B.9.

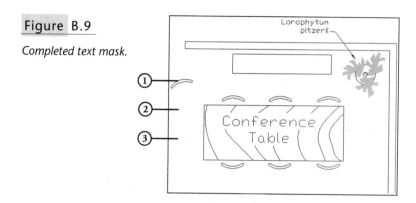

Figure B.9

Completed text mask.

4. If you plan to continue in these tutorials, leave this drawing open. Otherwise, quit AutoCAD without saving changes.

MOVE COPY ROTATE

1. Continue from the previous Express tutorial or open drawing APP-2.DWG from the book's CD-ROM. Check that Layer2 is Thawed, On, and Current and that Layer1 is turned off. Your drawing should resemble Figure B.9, resulting from the previous tutorial.

2. Start the Move Copy Rotate Express feature by using any of the three following methods:

   ■ Click on the Move Copy Rotate tool on the Express Standard toolbar.

   ■ Choose the Express pull-down menu, then Modify, Move Copy Rotate.

   ■ Type **mocoro** and press Enter at the command prompt.

3. At the `Select Objects:` prompt, pick the chair at ① in Figure B.9 and press Enter.

4. At the `Base point:` prompt, pick near ②. The following options prompt appears:
   `[Move/Copy/Rotate/Scale/Base/Undo]<eXit>:`

5. Choose the Move option by typing **m** and pressing Enter. At the `Second point of displacement:` prompt, move the cursor and pick near ③. The options prompt returns.

6. Choose the Rotate option by typing **r** and pressing Enter. At the `Rotation angle:` prompt, move the cursor to orient the chair as shown in Figure B.10 and pick. The options prompt returns.

Figure B.10

Move Copy Rotate tool.

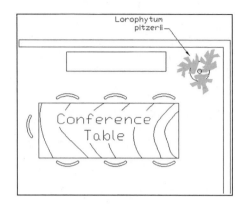

7. End the Move Copy Rotate feature by pressing Enter.

8. This completes the tutorials for the Express Package. Quit AutoCAD without saving changes to the drawing.

"ANTI" SELECTION SETS

1. Open drawing APP-3 from the book's CD-ROM. Assume that you wish to erase all objects in this drawing *except* the lines.

2. Activate the exclusionary Fence selection method by typing **EXF** and pressing Enter.

3. At the `Specify first fence point:` prompt, start the fence line by picking at ① in Figure B.11.

Figure B.11

Designating "Anti-Selection Sets."

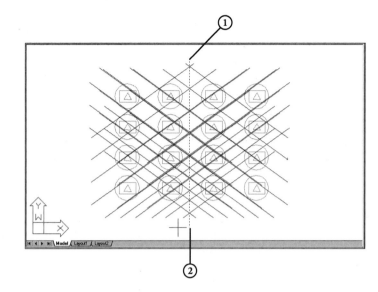

4. Extend the fence line downward through the drawing's lines and pick at ②.

5. Press Enter to end the fence selection method. Note that all the drawing's objects except those not touched by the fence line are now highlighted and gripped as shown in Figure B.12.

Figure B.12

All but selected objects are highlighted.

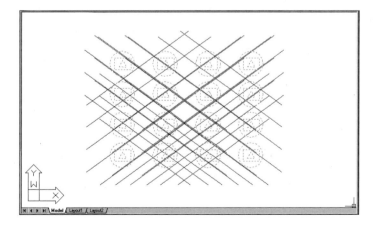

6. Start the ERASE command and erase the current selection set by typing **E** and pressing Enter. All objects in the current selection set are then erased.

NOTE

Any of the other selection methods (Window, Crossing, and so on) can be employed with the "anti" selection set method. Just precede the method with an "ex" prefix, such as EXF for fence, EXC for crossing, EXWP for Window Polygon, and so on.

Shapes are similar to blocks. Although blocks are generally more versatile, shapes are still used to insert standard symbols (such as arrows) into drawings. Shapes can also be used to create complex linetypes. The following exercise shows how to use the MKSHAPE Express tool to create a custom shape and the MKLTYPE Express tool to make a custom linetype.

CREATING CUSTOM SHAPES AND LINETYPES

1. Open drawing APP-4 from the book's CD-ROM. This drawing shows a symbol drawn with plines and an arc as shown in Figure B.13. To convert this symbol into a shape, we will use the MKSHAPE Express tool.

Figure B.13

A line-of-sight symbol.

2. Start the MKSHAPE Express tool by using either of the following methods:

    ■ From the Express menu, choose Tools, Make Shape.

    ■ Type **MKSHAPE** and press Enter at the command prompt.

3. When the Select Shape File dialog box appears, type the name **LOS** and press Save to exit the dialog box.

4. At the `Enter the name of the shape:` prompt, type **LOS** and press Enter.

5. Type in a resolution of **256**.

6. At the `Specify insertion base point:` prompt, specify the endpoint of the line at ① in Figure B.13. Select all objects and press Enter to end the command. The shape file will be automatically compiled and loaded into the current drawing. You will see messages at the command line reporting the status of the operation. When the operation is complete, erase the original objects.

7. Type **SHAPE** and press Enter to start the SHAPE command and insert the LOS shape at approximately the same position. Specify a height of **1.0** and a rotation angle of **0** degrees. Your drawing should once again resemble Figure B.13.

    Now that you have made a shape and inserted it into the drawing, the LOS symbol is ready to become the basis for a new custom linetype.

8. Start the MKLTYPE Express tool by using either of the following methods:

    ■ From the Express menu, choose Tools, Make Linetype.

    ■ Type **MKLTYPE** and press Enter at the command prompt.

9. Provide a .lin file name (such as **LOS**).

10. Enter a name for the linetype (such as **LOS**).

11. Enter a brief description of the linetype, such as **Line-of-sight**.

12. Pick the starting and endpoints by picking at ① and ② as shown in Figure B.13. You should use the Insert Osnap to select the shape object.

13. Select the shape. The new linetype will automatically load into the drawing and be ready to use.

14. Perform a ZOOM 0.5X to zoom out a bit.

15. Use the Linetype pull-down menu to set the LOS linetype current. Draw a few lines. Your lines should resemble that shown in Figure B.14.

Figure B.14

The new LOS linetype.

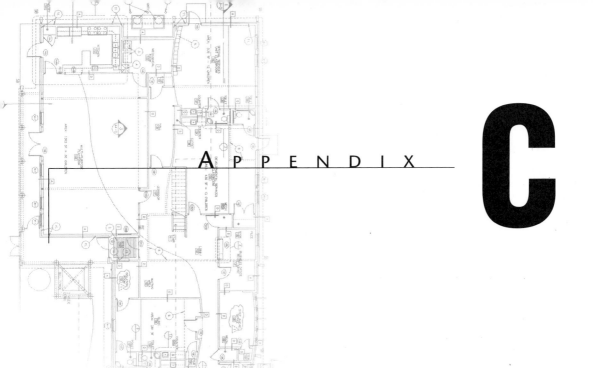

WHAT YOU'LL FIND ON THE CD-ROM

The accompanying CD-ROM is packed with all sorts of exercise files and products to help you work with this book and with AutoCAD 2000. The following sections contain detailed descriptions of the CD's contents.

For more information about the use of this CD, please review the ReadMe.txt file in the root directory. This file includes important disclaimer information as well as information about installation, system requirements, troubleshooting, and technical support.

System Requirements

This CD-ROM was configured for use on systems running Windows NT Workstation, Windows 95, or Windows 98 on an Intel, or Intel processor-compatible system. Your machine will need to meet the following system requirements in order for this CD to operate properly:

Processor: 486DX or higher processor (Pentium preferred)

Operating System: MS- Windows® 95/98/NT

Memory (RAM): 24MB minimum (32MB recommended)

Storage: Hard disk space for shareware and demo programs—97.5MB minimum

Video: TrueColor (24 bit), 2MB card minimum, TrueColor 8MB card recommended

Other: Mouse or compatible pointing device, CD-ROM drive, Web browser such as Netscape Navigator 4 or higher, or Microsoft Internet Explorer 4 or higher

Loading the CD Files

To load the files from the CD, insert the disc into your CD-ROM drive. If autoplay is enabled on your machine, the CD-ROM setup program starts automatically the first time you insert the disc. You may copy the files to your hard drive, or use them right off the disc.

NOTE: This CD-ROM uses long and mixed-case filenames, requiring the use of a protected mode CD-ROM driver.

Exercise Files

This CD contains all the files you'll need to complete the exercises in *Inside AutoCAD 2000 Limited Edition*. These files can be found in the root directory's Exercise Files folder. Please note, however, that you'll not find any folders for chapters 1, 2, 3, 26, 33, or 36; these chapters contain exercises for which you do not need to access any drawing or project files.

Autodesk White Papers

You can find various Autodesk White Papers in PDF format in the 3rdParty/ Autodesk/AutoCAD 2K White Papers directory. (You'll need a copy of Adobe Acrobat Reader to read these files. A copy of Acrobat Reader 4.0 has been included on the CD in the 3rdParty/Adobe/Acrobat directory.)

- Autodesk AutoCAD 2000 Preview (1features.pdf)

- Unleashing the Power of Plotting (2unleash.pdf)

- Fast Track to Plotting Your First Drawing (3fastrac.pdf)

- Instant Payback Using AutoCAD 2000 (4payback.pdf)

- Plotting with AutoCAD 2000 (5CAD_autodesk9905.pdf)

- AutoLISP Customization and MDI (6autolisp.pdf)

- ADS in AutoCAD 2000 (7ads.pdf)

Third-Party Programs

This CD also contains several third-party programs and demos from leading industry companies. These programs have been carefully selected to help you strengthen your professional skills in AutoCAD.

Note

Please note that some of the programs included on this CD-ROM are shareware-"try-before-you-buy"-software. Please support these independent vendors by purchasing or registering any shareware software that you use for more than 30 days. Check with the documentation provided with the software on where and how to register the product.

- AutoCAD 2000 Splash Screen Saver. Use this free screen saver to brighten your desktop. Directory: 3rdParty/Autodesk/ScreenSvr.

- AutoManager View 3.1 Demo from Cyco Software. Enables you to view CAD and other documents from three to ten times faster than you can view them in their native applications. Directory: 3rdParty/Cycosw.

- Adobe Acrobat Reader 4.0. Acrobat Reader will enable you to view the PDF documents included on this CD. You'll need a copy of Adobe Acrobat Reader to read these files. Directory: 3rdParty/Adobe/Acrobat.

- Web Browsers. Last but not least, this CD includes copies of Earthlink, Netscape Communicator 4.7, and Microsoft Internet Explorer 5. Directory: 3rdParty/WEB UTILITIES.

Technical Support/Customer Support Issues

Call 1-317-581-3833, from 10:00 a.m. to 3 p.m. US EST (CST from April through October of each year—unlike most of the United States, Indiana doesn't change to Daylight Savings Time each April).

You can also email our tech support team at userservices@macmillanusa.com, and you can access our tech support website at http://www.mcp.com/product_support/mail_support.cfm.

INDEX

Symbols

O

New Riders Professional Library

3D Studio MAX 3 Fundamentals
Michael Todd Peterson
0-7357-0049-4

3D Studio MAX 3 Effects Magic
New Riders Development
0-7357-0867-3

3D Studio MAX 3 Media Animation
John Chismar
0-7357-0050-8

3D Studio MAX 3 Professional Animation
Angela Jones, et al.
0-7357-0945-9

Adobe Photoshop 5.5 Fundamentals
with ImageReady 2
Gary Bouton
0-7357-0928-9

Bert Monroy: Photorealistic Techniques
with Photoshop & Illustrator
Bert Monroy
0-7357-0969-6

CG 101: A Computer Graphics Industry Reference
Terrence Masson
0-7357-0046-X

Click Here
Raymond Pirouz and Lynda Weinman
1-56205-792-8

<coloring web graphics.2>
Lynda Weinman and Bruce Heavin
1-56205-818-5

Creating Killer Web Sites, Second Edition
David Siegel
1-56830-433-1

<creative html design>
Lynda Weinman and William Weinman
1-56205-704-9

<designing web graphics.3>
Lynda Weinman
1-56205-949-1

Designing Web Usability
Jakob Nielsen
1-56205-810-X

[digital] Character Animation 2
Volume 1: Essential Techniques
George Maestri
1-56205-930-0

Essentials of Digital Photography
Akari Kasai and Russell Sparkman
1-56205-762-6

Fine Art Photoshop
Michael J. Nolan and Renee LeWinter
1-56205-829-0

Flash 4 Magic
David Emberton and J. Scott Hamlin
0-7357-0949-1

Flash Web Design
Hillman Curtis
0-7357-0896-7

HTML Artistry: More than Code
Ardith Ibañez and Natalie Zee
1-56830-454-4

HTML Web Magic
Raymond Pirouz
1-56830-475-7

Illustrator 8 Magic
Raymond Pirouz
1-56205-952-1

Inside 3D Studio MAX 3
Phil Miller, et al.
0-7357-0905-X

Inside 3D Studio MAX 3:
Modeling, Materials, and Rendering
Ted Boardman and Jeremy Hubbell
0-7357-0085-0

Inside AutoCAD 2000
David Pitzer and Bill Burchard
0-7357-0851-7

Inside LightWave 3D
Dan Ablan
1-56205-799-5

Inside Adobe Photoshop 5
Gary David Bouton and Barbara Bouton
1-56205-884-3

Inside Adobe Photoshop 5, Limited Edition
Gary David Bouton and Barbara Bouton
1-56205-951-3

Inside trueSpace 4
Frank Rivera
1-56205-957-2

Inside SoftImage 3D
Anthony Rossano
1-56205-885-1

Maya 2 Character Animation
Nathan Vogel, Sherri Sheridan, and Tim Coleman
0-7357-0866-5

Net Results: Web Marketing that Works
USWeb and Rick E. Bruner
1-56830-414-5

Photoshop 5 & 5.5 Artistry
Barry Haynes and Wendy Crumpler
0-7457-0994-7

Photoshop 5 Type Magic
Greg Simsic
1-56830-465-X

Photoshop 5 Web Magic
Michael Ninness
1-56205-913-0

Photoshop Channel Chops
David Biedney, Bert Monroy, and Nathan Moody
1-56205-723-5

<preparing web graphics>
Lynda Weinman
1-56205-686-7

Rhino NURBS 3D Modeling
Margaret Becker
0-7357-0925-4

Secrets of Successful Web Sites
David Siegel
1-56830-382-3

Web Concept & Design
Crystal Waters
1-56205-648-4

Web Design Templates Sourcebook
Lisa Schmeiser
1-56205-754-5